Leib Glantz – The Man Who Spoke To God

JERRY GLANTZ

published by

The Tel Aviv Institute for Jewish Liturgical Music

Visit the book's website at www.TheManWhoSpokeToGod.com

Cover and Compact Disks designed by Dan Gonzalez, Ampersand Design Group, Miami, Florida
www.AmpersandMiami.com

End page design, based on 1988 poster for Leib Glantz concert in Tel Aviv: Eliezer Weishoff, Weishoff Creations, Tel Aviv, Israel. www.weishoff.com

Portrait of Leib Glantz by Saul Raskin

Page Layout: Lee Lewis Walsh, Words Plus Design, Tecumseh, Michigan
www.wordsplusdesign.com

Proofreading: Martha Zubrow, Coral Springs, Florida.

Compact Disk musical editor & photography editor: Noam Brown, Bangkok, Thailand.

Translations and transcription of musical notes: Cantor Chaim Feifel, Zichron Yaakov, Israel.

Musical notes editor on "Finale" software: Cantor Evan Cohen, Jerusalem, Israel.

Printed in China

First Edition: January 2008

Library of Congress Cataloging in Publication Data

Glantz, Jerry
The Man Who Spoke To God

Summary: Leib Glantz — Cantor and composer; his writings, lectures and research; academic essays by writers, philosophers, cantors, conductors, composers and musicologists defining his historical importance as an icon of Jewish music. Including two compact disks with Leib Glantz singing thirty of his most important compositions.

ISBN: 978-0-615-19665-7

Includes essays, biography, historical documents,
discography, list of compositions, glossary of foreign terms, index
and two musical compact disks.

1. Music.   2. Jewish music.   3. Musicology.   4. Cantorial = Chazanut.
5. Cantor = Chazan (Hazzan).   6. Synagogue music.   7. Ashkenazic prayer modes.
8. Chasidism.   9. Chasidic music.   10. Zionism.   11. Israel.

For my precious children — Shani and Tomer,
who were born after their grandfather's untimely passing.
They never met him, but inherited his amazing talents.

Leib Glantz – The Man Who Spoke To God

Part 2: Analyses of Leib Glantz's Historical Significance as Cantor, Composer, Researcher, Pedagogue and Zionist Leader

Part 3: Writings and Lectures of Leib Glantz

Appendices

Introduction

A few years ago, on one of my journeys to Israel, I received a phone call from the Israeli Opera, asking me if I would be kind enough to take two world-famous opera singers to play golf at the ancient Roman port city of Caesarea.

The following morning I picked up the two gentlemen from their Tel Aviv hotel. Both were in their late thirties, perhaps early forties. The English baritone was a Church of England Christian, and the tenor from Finland was a Christian of Evangelical Lutheran denomination. They were very happy to get away from their rehearsals at the opera and spend a day playing golf under the bright Mediterranean sun.

After introducing ourselves, they preferred sitting together in the back seat of the car. As I switched on the ignition, the compact disk that was playing earlier resumed playing. It was a live recording of my father's "Midnight *Se'li'chot* Service." My first instinct was to reach over and turn the music off, but as I was about to do so, I noticed in the car's rear view mirror that my guests were looking towards each other with excitement in reaction to the singing voice. I thought to myself that it might be interesting to enable them to hear more and to observe their reactions. The drive lasted for an hour with not a word uttered. Periodically, I glanced at them through my rear view mirror. Every once and a while they would look at each other as if to express amazement.

We arrived at our destination just as the music came to an end. There was an extended silence. For some reason no one dared to break the spell. Finally, the Englishman, in his deep baritone voice, uttered: "What was *that?*" I replied that this was cantorial music, *Cha'za'nut* in Hebrew, the music chanted in Jewish synagogues to express the meanings and emotions of the prayers. The tenor from Finland corrected me with the authority and intonation of a phenomenal opera star: "No! No! No! ***That man was speaking to God!*** No one in the world sings like that! I sensed this heavenly singing in every bone of my body!" The baritone reinforced this, adding: "This was the most moving music I have ever heard! It was as though I was lifted into the heavens, experiencing sights and sounds of another world!"

Then and there I realized that my father's music was not only the divine music of the Jewish people. It was music of a universal nature. Two world class musicians, both of Christian faith, who knew not a word of Hebrew, the language of the prayers to which they were listening so attentively, were capable of "feeling" the passion inherent in this singing, almost to the point of "sensing" the meaning of the text. I concluded that if this was true, then this music needs to be exposed to every human being in the world, regardless of religion, race or nationality. This has become my mission.

Classical music has encompassed numerous religious works. It is sufficient to mention Beethoven's "*Missa Solemnis*" — the music of a Catholic Mass, or Verdi and Mozart's Requiems, which are masses for the repose of the souls of the dead. I wondered if people of different religions come to the classical music concert halls in order to experience *religious* ceremonies. Obviously not. These music lovers come to enjoy *beautiful music* — performed by symphony orchestras, singers and choirs. Therefore, it seems only natural that my father's music is destined to become accessible to all who are moved and enthralled by beautiful music.

On the way home from our golf outing, a memory surfaced from a very distant past. I was eighteen years old, walking with my father to the synagogue on a sunny Sabbath Tel Aviv morning. My father suddenly stopped and turned toward me as if to tell me something very important — something that he had never before dared to say:

> "My son! I know that I have created in my musical compositions and my singing something very unique. Unfortunately, in this current generation there are few who are truly capable of comprehending and appreciating my life's work. I assume that I 'appeared' in this world long before my time. I believe it might take forty years before my creative work is truly understood and appreciated… You, my son, will live to witness this."

He died less than a month later.

Forty-four years after his death, suffering a fatal stroke while appearing before a devoted audience on a Tel Aviv stage, these two opera singers had now mysteriously communicated a message from the heavens: the time had come to revive Leib Glantz's memory and establish his legacy!

Strangely, a few months later I received a phone call from Bangkok, Thailand, from a man with an impressive voice asking me if I was the son of "the great Leibele Glantz." He introduced himself as a twenty-three-year-old Dutchman, born in Amsterdam and living in Bangkok. He claimed to be a great admirer of my father's music:

> "The first time I heard your father's recording, it shattered my world. It was totally different from anything I had ever heard before. I felt that this man was actually ***talking to God*** with great passion! His voice commands its way to the heavens — to be heard and to be answered. I was stunned. I wondered if I could consider this music to be of the same category as the *Cha'za'nut* I was accustomed to. I sensed that it was different. It was pure, honest and real."

I wondered if this was a fulfillment of those predictions my father had made shortly before his death. I asked this young man to write to me, and to try to explain exactly what it was that intrigued a man born twenty years *after* my father's passing. His letter arrived just a few days later:

> "I feel that Glantz was determined to reveal God's greatness to the whole world. He penetrated into the soul of every word, letter and sound. He unveiled our prayers by displaying their true meaning both intellectually and emotionally. I can sense the love and devotion he felt towards every word he uttered. When I listen to him sing, I am amazingly drawn closer to God. Your father became my guide; without him I feel lost. He always confidently seems to know the right path."

As a teenager, I wrote a very similar letter to my father, who, in 1963, was abroad on a four-month concert tour in North America:

> "When I close my eyes and listen to the record of the *'Se'li'chot'* prayers... I feel drawn, as if by magic, into another world... as if suddenly there is no one around me — no walls, no house, no city. Just the two of us — alone! I imagine watching you and wondering how you succeed in summoning the angels and how you speak to them as equals! It seems as if God is listening, peeking down from the heavens and delightfully shuddering in reaction to the meaningful penetration of your voice. You seem to be able to understand and interpret the deepest meanings of each and every word, attaching it to the perfect melody, while remaining purely loyal to the ancient Jewish prayer modes, which seemingly exist in your blood."

Before sealing the envelope, I added a small note, begging him not to respond. Evidently he could not resist, and he mailed me a note with just these words:

> "My dear son: You asked that I refrain from responding to your precious words. However, I cannot but convey to you that a silent tear dropped from my eyes (*Ne'tof Nat'fa Ha'Dim'ah*)..."

Leib Glantz grew up in the Ukrainian city of Kiev, in a religious Chasidic family. His life was totally immersed in Orthodox Judaism. The synagogue was the center of his family's life, and the prayer services were their ultimate joy. As the son, grandson and great-grandson of famous cantors, Jewish music was the focal point of young Leibele's life. The *Nu'sach* — the ancient Jewish prayer modes, having been passed along from generation to generation, were genetically branded into his being. This was the characteristic background of most of the great cantors of the *Golden Age of Cha'za'nut* (cantorial art) — in the first half of the twentieth century.

Leib Glantz's life was full of paradoxes. Early in his life, he became active in a movement dedicated to the fulfillment of the Zionist dream of reestablishing a homeland for the Jewish people in the Promised Land of Zion. His political activism took place among the ranks of *secular* Labor Zionists, who were somewhat indifferent, if not in opposition, to religion and to the centrality of the synagogue in Jewish community life. Glantz was forced to divide his loyalties. This paradox continued to play an important role in his life until his very last day.

Another paradox was related to his musical career. From his father he received an education in Jewish literature and cantorial music. Fortunately, in addition to studying the Jewish holy books, his father encouraged him to acquire a secular education as well as a general musical education. This eventually led him to study piano and composition at the Kiev Conservatory under some of the most important musical educators of that era, and he qualified to become a composer and classical piano soloist. Upon arriving in the United States, at age twenty-eight, he found himself confronted with a dilemma: whether to become an opera star, as did some of his cantorial colleagues, or to devote his life to being a cantor and composer of Jewish music. Fortunately, he came to the conclusion that it was his destiny to become an important creative artist in the field of cantorial art and Jewish music.

Eventually the two tracks were on a collision course: in order for Glantz and his family to immigrate to the Jewish homeland, and to continue his sacred journey as a cantor and composer of Jewish music, he was required by the leaders of the religious political parties in Israel to disengage from his affiliation with the secular Labor Zionist political party, and to associate himself with one of the religious parties. The political system in Palestine (which continued in the newly independent State of Israel as of 1948) allocated control of all religious life to the "custody" of these religious political parties. This included control over the appointments of rabbis and cantors in all Israeli synagogues. This proved to be an impossible requirement. Leib Glantz was a man of principle. He could not betray his ideals and his lifelong ideological partners. It was therefore impossible for him to be appointed to a permanent position in any synagogue in Palestine (and later in Israel). Tragically, Glantz and his family patiently resided in New York and Los Angeles from 1926 until 1954, when he was invited by a group of synagogue officers who "defied the political decree," and engaged him as cantor of the *Tif'e'ret Zvi* synagogue in Tel Aviv.

In 1954, when he arrived in Israel with his family, finally able to fulfill his Zionist dream of set-tling in the homeland of the Jewish people, another conflict needed to be resolved. Being a Labor Zionist, he was urged to become active in Labor party politics and eventually be appoint-ed as a minister in the Israeli government, as were many of his closest friends. However, Glantz declined, convinced that it was his true destiny to continue on his life's mission of creating beautiful and meaningful music for his people.

I often wondered if Leib Glantz's religious cantorial track and his secular Zionist track truly represent a contradiction. After a great deal of research, trying to comprehend the trends of his life, I came to the conclusion that this was not the case. For Glantz — *Cha'za'nut* and Zionism were bound together! It is clearly evident in his music. Many of his great cantorial compositions were filled with oriental themes and with a flavor characteristic of the music of the early Jewish pioneer settlers (*Cha'lu'tzim*) in Palestine. In his mind, Zionism was part of being a Jew. Being a Jew entailed conducting a religious life. Religion was more than just per-forming the rituals and traditions. Religion was a philosophy — a state of mind. God, for my father, was tangible — a God Whom one was capable of addressing. Glantz considered him-self worthy of representing his people before God by creating authentic interpretations in the form of divine music. He sang with a passion — praising God's glory, demanding, begging and vying for mercy and forgiveness. He deeply believed in every word he uttered in prayer. At the same time, he devoted much of his life and energy to the Zionist cause. The return of the Jewish people to their historic homeland in Zion, as promised by God in the bible, was, for him, a prerequisite for the survival of the Jewish religion and of the Jewish people. Glantz believed that if the State of Israel were not formed, the Jewish people were doomed to assim-ilate and to disappear in the Diaspora, or even worse — to be annihilated by antisemitic pogroms and holocausts. In other words, a Jew must be a Zionist, and the place for a Jew to live was in Palestine (later to become Israel). If some were less observant, it was acceptable — as long as they resided in the historical homeland.

My father lived in Israel for the last ten years of his life. Many of his greatest compositions were written during this period, as he finally found himself in the ideal setting: he could com-pose and perform for an audience that was capable of appreciating the Hebrew nuances of his musical interpretations of the ancient prayer texts. In this period he also solidified his lifelong research into the origins of Jewish music, including the defining and clarifying of the proper *Nu'sach* prayer modes for each and every prayer service. He also founded an academic research institute, which included an academic school for cantors. At the same time he continued his political activism; he represented Israel as a delegate to two World Zionist Congresses, in addi-tion to the nine to which he was delegated on behalf of European and American Jewry before his arrival in Israel.

I began writing this book with the intention of telling my father's story. As word of the planned book spread around the world, I became virtually flooded with requests from cantors, composers, conductors, Zionists, and admirers, offering to write essays about him and his music. Of these, more than fifty essays were chosen — each analyzing Glantz from a different angle — the composer, the singer, the cantor, the teacher, the political activist, and above all, Glantz the person. These essays are more meaningful and more powerful than anything I could have written. As a result, this book has been transformed into a living testimony of Leib Glantz's tremendous impact on the art of cantorial and Jewish music. It is an endeavor to define Leib Glantz's historical importance within the culture of the Jewish people. Happily, more than four decades after his death, his life's work remains alive and vibrant.

Leib Glantz is considered by many the greatest cantor who ever lived. For a hundred years, cantors throughout the world have recognized his brilliance. In addition, Glantz was the people's cantor. Crowds filled the streets to hear him perform. His admirers thrilled to and wept with emotion at the sound of his voice. His music penetrated souls and inspired young people, many who themselves would later become famous cantors and musicians.

Long gone are the monumental days of the *Golden Age of Cha'za'nut* — a period of several decades during which some of the greatest cantors and composers of Jewish music flourished. Many claim that *Cha'za'nut* is dying. Some even declare it dead! Authentic Jewish music, a national cultural asset, is in danger of annihilation, as more and more foreign music contaminates its purity and character. Unfortunately, the concert hall has replaced the synagogue as its main venue. This book makes the case for how much is lost with the popularization and contamination of ritual.

I firmly believe that a new "*Golden Age*" is on the horizon, and in this modern renewal, Leib Glantz will become the model upon which a new generation of great young cantors and composers of Jewish music will build their foundations. I pray that this book will be the spark that will ignite the fire.

Acknowledgments

Five individuals traveled with my father on his amazing journey.

Sara Wachs played a very important role in Leib Glantz's life. She was not only his manager and agent in the United States, but his most loyal friend and undoubtedly his greatest admirer.

My mother, Miriam Lipton Glantz, was the most loving, supporting and loyal wife. She deserves unlimited credit for partnering with him and helping him fulfill his wonderful artistic potential.

Itzchak Raziel, the president of the *Tif'e'ret Zvi* synagogue in Tel Aviv, was the brave man who dared to engage Glantz as Chief Cantor, defying the limitations of the Israeli political scene, and thereafter proving to be a great friend and supporter.

Professor Yehuda Even-Shmuel Kaufman was my father's soul mate. Perhaps more than anyone else in the world, he sensed the enormity of the Glantz phenomenon.

The distinguished Israeli writer, Eliezer Steinman, was my father's intellectual partner. Together they enriched the culture of the Jewish people with literature, poetry, music and insight.

The following wonderful people were more than instrumental in creating this book. They breathed life into it.

Noam Brown, with his enthusiasm and adoration of my father's art, contributed immensely to the contents of this book. He interviewed cantors, investigated and discovered relevant photographs and historical material, provided assistance in compiling the music for the two compact disks that accompany the book, including the transliterations and translations of the compositions sung by Leib Glantz on these compact disks. He also assisted in compiling Leib Glantz's discography of recordings, the list of his compositions and the technical preparation of the photos included in this book.

Cantor Chaim Feifel studied *Cha'za'nut* with my father in Tel Aviv fifty years ago. The encouragement he offered me regarding the importance and value of writing the book, and the friendship that developed between us, are a treasure I will forever cherish. He devoted time and effort to translate and interpret many of my father's writings and lectures so that every word and every note would be clear, understandable and correct.

My dear brother, Dr. Kalman Glantz, provided wonderful insight and solid judgment regarding the choice of material and the use of language. His enthusiasm and experience were an important factor in bringing this "mission" to completion.

Cantor Evan Cohen excellently executed the task of editing and preparing the musical notes for publication.

I am very grateful to Professor Alan Berger who encouraged me to write this book and contributed much valuable guidance.

Akiva Zimmerman, my long-time friend, and one of the greatest admirers of Leib Glantz, was responsible for the naming of a street in Tel Aviv — "Leib Glantz Street" — and for the City of Tel Aviv's designation of the house in which Glantz lived and worked, on 56 Ben Gurion Boulevard, as a historical site. In this house Glantz composed some of his greatest compositions. Zimmerman, an authority on cantors and on the history of the Cantorate, continuously lectures on the legacy of Leib Glantz throughout the world.

Most of all, I would like to thank Katty Cohen, whose encouragement throughout this endeavor made it all possible.

I am gratefully indebted to many people who have given me their time, ideas, and trust. These wonderful reviewers, colleagues and friends have contributed immeasurably to this book's growth and improvement. Specifically I would like to thank Chaim Adler, Aaron Bensoussan, Louis Danto, Alan Dershowitz, Sid Dworkin, Sam Fordis, Ronen Geva, Talia Glantz, Shani Glantz, Tomer Glantz, Schlomo Goldhour, Raymond Goldstein, Erik Greenberg Anjou, Naftali Herstik, Elli Jaffe, Sholom Kalib, Amit Klein, Moshe Kraus, Joseph Levine, Avraham Lubin, Benjamin Maissner, Jacob Ben-Zion Mendelson, Solomon Mendelson, Benzion Miller, Benjamin Muller, Aharon Noff, Macy Nulman, Moshe Schulhof, Yaakov Schwartzman, Nava Semel, Barry Serota, Edwin Seroussi, Noam and Ella Sheriff, Mordechai Sobol, Udi Spielman, Victoria Sunshine, Arie Subar, Boaz Tarsi, Saul Wachs, Lee Lewis Walsh, Sam Weiss, Eliezer and Ella Weishoff, Elie Wiesel and Avshalom Zfira. Without their assistance and encouragement — this book would never have seen the light of day.

"Music was created not only for pleasing the ear.
It must have a meaning, express an activity,
a natural or supernatural force, a feeling.
Without meaning, it loses its reason for being."

Yaya Diallo
A drummer from Mali, Africa

Quoted from *Work Songs,* by Ted Gioia, Duke University Press, 2006.

Part One

Reflections on Leib Glantz

The transliteration of Hebrew and Yiddish terms in this book has been created to make it easier for readers who do not speak these languages. Hebrew and Yiddish words appear in italics, begin with capital letters, and an apostrophe separates every syllable. The Hebrew and Yiddish words and sentences are followed by the English translation (in parentheses). Several authors of essays have used a different transliteration system; however, an effort has been made to use the same transliteration system throughout the book.

1

Biography of Leib Glantz

Leib Glantz was born in 1898[1] in the city of Kiev in the Ukraine. His father, Kalman, was cantor of the Talner Chasidic synagogue in Kiev for thirty years. His paternal grandfather, Naftali, was one of the leaders of the Talner Chasidim in Soroki, Besarabia, where he officiated as chief cantor for twenty-five years.

Leib's mother, Golda, was the daughter of a cantor, Nachum, who officiated in Obochov, Kiev, and later as chief cantor of the Great Synagogue of Dimievka, a Kiev suburb. Glantz's brother, Yonah (Yonia), who emigrated to Canada and later to the United States, became a well-known cantor in Portland, Oregon. Leib's younger brother, Azriel, died of typhoid fever as a teenager in 1919. Leib had three sisters — Esther, Rachel (Feldman) and Leah (Hersonsky).

As a child, Glantz studied in a *Che'der*[2] and later in the *Ye'shi'va*[3] of Rabbi Shlomo Hacohen Aharonson.

> *Leibele, as he was fondly nicknamed, was eight years old when he first appeared as cantor in his grandfather Nachum's synagogue in Dimievka.*

Leibele, as he was fondly nicknamed, was eight years old when he first appeared as cantor in his grandfather Nachum's synagogue in Dimievka. He first sang *Maf'tir*, and the *Ga'ba'yim* (officers of the

---

1 Glantz's Hebrew calendar birth date: 23rd day of the Hebrew month of *Si'van*, in the year 5,658 (*Kaf Gim'el Si'van, Taf Reish Nun Chet*).

2 *Che'der* — in Hebrew: "room," a traditional elementary school or class teaching the basics of Judaism and the Hebrew language.

3 *Ye'shi'va* — An institute of learning where students study sacred texts, primarily the Talmud.

synagogue) were so impressed that they asked him to continue singing the complete Sabbath *Mu'saf* service. The following week Leibele was asked to perform the complete Sabbath service — *Ka'bba'lat Sha'bbat, Ma'a'riv, Shach'rit and Mu'saf*. Word of the child prodigy spread swiftly, and he was invited to chant in several cities in the region. Soon after, invitations to appear flowed in from throughout Europe. Glantz, accompanied by his father, traveled across the continent, appearing in every important synagogue and making unforgettable impressions.

In his early teens (1912-1913), as his voice was mutating, his father ordered him to refrain from singing in order to protect his vocal chords for the future. During this period, the young Glantz organized and conducted a large choir in his father's synagogue. This choir would sing complex choral compositions by Baruch Schorr, Solomon Sulzer, Louis Lewandowski, Avraham Berkovitz-Kalechnik, Joseph Goldstein, Nissan Belzer, David Nowakowsky and Eliezer Mordechai Gerovitsch.

Three people greatly influenced Glantz's style: his father, Cantor Kalman Glantz, who was known for his ecstatic Chasidic *D'vei'kut*, a form of devotion to God; Joseph Shtrumberg, an important cantor from Kiev; and Cantor Avraham Berkovitz-Kalechnik from Kishinev, Besarabia. At age thirteen, Leibele was sent by his father to Kishinev to study the secrets of musical *D'vei'kut* from Kalechnik.

In 1916, as the First World War was raging in Europe, the antisemitic pogroms in the Ukraine forced 18-year-old Glantz to move to Virtuzhen (today called Vertiujeni, part of The Republic of Moldava), in the Soroki region of Besarabia (today — Soroca, Moldava). There he lived at the home of his sister Rachel Feldman. On *Rosh Ha'Sha'na,* the Jewish New Year, he captured the hearts of his listeners in prayer at the local synagogue. Cantor Kalechnik, one of the most important cantors in Jewish liturgy, after hearing Glantz perform, exclaimed that he had not dreamed that in his own generation he would live to hear a cantor as great as Yerucham Ha'Katan!

> *The distinguished cantor Avraham Berkovitz-Kalechnik, after hearing the young Glantz, was quoted exclaiming that he had not dreamed that in his own generation he would live to hear a cantor as great as the famous Yerucham Ha'Katan!*

In 1917, the year of the Bolshevik Revolution, Glantz returned to Kiev and became active in the leadership of the *Tse'i'rei Zion* Zionist youth movement. He completed his secular education, earned his high school graduation certificate and was accepted to the University of Kiev. At the same time, Glantz studied piano at the music school of the Ukrainian pianist and composer, Nikolai Tutkovski (1857-1930), composer of the Russian opera *"Boyni Viatar."* Upon graduation, Glantz continued his musical education, studying composition at the Kiev Music Conservatory with Reinhold Gliere (1875-1956). Gliere was the composer of some of the most important Russian symphonies, operas and ballets. Influenced by these studies, Glantz began applying his classical music tools towards composing Jewish liturgical music as well as Hebrew and Yiddish art songs.

Glantz returned to Besarabia in 1920. The city of Kishinev was a very important center for both Zionist and cantorial activity. He joined a group of activists of *Tse'i'rei Zion* and *He'Cha'lutz* ("The Pioneer," a Zionist movement) that had come to Kishinev from the Ukraine, and formed the leadership of the local Zionist movements. In those days Glantz devoted himself mainly to Zionism. In spite of many offers, he refused to become a permanent synagogue cantor. He would officiate on the High Holidays, the three Festivals *(Pe'sach, Sha'vu'ot* and *Su'ccot),* but very rarely on Sabbath services. He often volunteered to sing at fundraising events for Jewish and Zionist causes. He taught music and conducted the choir of the *Tar'but*[4] Teachers Seminary for Women in Kishinev and that of the Yiddish Professional School of the *Bund.*[5]

Leib Glantz at age 7 with his father, Cantor Kalman Glantz, in Kiev, Ukraine, 1905

Glantz traveled numerous times as a delegate to congresses of the *He'Cha'lutz* movement and to World Zionist Congresses. He was appointed chief editor of the Labor Zionist newspaper *Ard Un Ar'beit* and wrote serious articles about Zionism and about issues of importance to the Jewish community. He also wrote extensively on the subject of Jewish music. The most important of these was a series of essays called "Jewish Motifs" that was published in *Un'zer Zeit,* a daily newspaper that was initiated by the *Tse'i'rei Zion* movement in Kishinev.

---

4 *Tar'but* — a Zionist network of Hebrew-language educational institutions founded in 1922.
5 *Bund* — an Ashkenazi Jewish socialist movement founded in Russia in 1897.

Leibele at age 8, with tuning fork, officiating as cantor on the prayer pulpit in the Talner Synagogue in Kiev, Ukraine, 1906.

In those years Glantz composed songs to the lyrics of the national poet Chaim Nachman Bialik: *Yam Ha'D'ma'ma,*[6] *Za'ri'ti La'Ru'ach An'cha'ti,*[7] and *A'cha'rei Mo'ti.*[8] He also presented a series of lectures on Hebrew Music throughout Romania on behalf of the Zionist Histadrut.

Glantz made plans to emigrate to Palestine in 1923; however, the sudden death of his father necessitated a change in plans as his family became desperately dependent on his financial support. The Zionist organizations in Besarabia also demanded his leadership, and eventually elected him as their delegate to the 1925 Zionist World Congress in Vienna.

This all came to an end in July 1926. Due to his intensive Zionist activism, and the Romanian regime's growing antagonism towards the Jews, Glantz decided that it was time to leave Eastern Europe for the United States.

Upon his arrival in New York, on August 17, 1926, Glantz was invited to appear in an important cantorial concert. His singing was received with great enthusiasm and he was offered the prestigious position of chief cantor at the famous *O'hev Sha'lom* synagogue in New York.

Sara Wachs, an impresario, was one of those greatly impressed by his appearance, and she offered to become his manager and agent. Eventually, she became one of Glantz's greatest admirers and a lifelong friend. By 1928 Glantz was engaged as a recording artist with RCA Victor, and appeared on their most prestigious "Red Label" record series. The first recordings

---

6 "*Yam Ha'D'ma'ma Po'let So'dot*" ("The Sea of Quiet Casts Its Secrets"), 1901.
7 "*Za'ri'ti La'Ru'ach An'cha'ti*" ("I Have Scattered My Sighs Into the Wind"), 1901.
8 "*A'cha'rei Mo'ti*" ("After My Death"), 1904.

began appearing in 1929 and included twelve of his original compositions: *Sheʾma Yisʾraʾel, Teʾfiʾlat Tal, Shoʾmer Yisʾraʾel, Av HaʾRaʾchaʾmim, Kol Aʾdoʾnai, Leʾchu Neʾraʾneʾna, Birʾkat Koʾhaʾnim, Ki KeʾShimʾcha, Ki Hiʾneh KaʾChoʾmer, Ein KeʾErʾkeʾcha, Dʾvoiʾreʾle* and *Aʾchaʾrei Moʾti.* These recordings established Glantz as one of the leading cantors of *"The Golden Age of Chaʾzaʾnut."*

Glantz energetically continued his Labor Zionist activity in America, writing articles in Yiddish in Zionist periodicals such as *"Far ʾn Falk"* and raising funds to support the Zionist movement in the Soviet Union and in Palestine. He established himself as one of the leaders of the Labor Zionist movement in the United States. At the fiftieth anniversary celebration of *HaʾPoʾel HaʾTzaʾir* ("The Young Laborer") Zionist movement, Glantz lectured on the importance of achieving the political goal of the Zionist movement — creating a homeland for the Jewish people in Palestine. Chaim Arlozoroff and Chaim Greenberg, the most important Zionist leaders of that era, were his counterparts on the podium. As an elected delegate from the United States to World Zionist Congresses, Glantz traveled to Zurich (1929), Basle (1931), Prague (1933), Lucerne (1935), Zurich (1937), Geneva (1939) and Basle (1946).[9] In total, Glantz was a delegate to eleven World Zionist Congresses.[10]

Glantzʾs first trip to Palestine took place in May 1930. The British, who had received a Mandate from the League of Nations to rule over the area, governed Palestine at the time. The British government, in the so-called "Balfour Declaration," stated their intention to create a homeland for the Jewish people in Palestine.[11]

Glantz was received in Palestine as a hero. The reaction to his concerts was inspiring. In his discussions with the leaders of the *Yeʾshuv* (as Israelʾs Jewish population called itself in the pre-independence era), Glantz was encouraged to contribute to the Zionist cause by remaining in the United States, where, through his leadership, he could raise political support and funds for the future independent Jewish state. Upon his return to New York, Glantz wrote a series of articles about his experiences in Palestine in the Yiddish paper *Der Tag*.

At the same time, he continued to enhance his musical education and his voice development under the guidance of Professor Aspinol, the vocal teacher of the great opera singers Enrico Caruso and Benjamino Gigli.

---

9 Glantz was elected as a delegate to the following World Zionist Congresses: 1921 & 1925 representing Besarabia; 1929, 1931, 1933, 1935, 1937, 1939 & 1946 representing the United States; 1956 & 1961 representing Israel.

10 The Zionist Organization was founded by Theodore Herzl at the First Zionist Congress in Basle in 1897. Its primary political goal was set forth in the "Basle Program": "Zionism seeks to establish a home for the Jewish people in Palestine." It was renamed the World Zionist Organization in 1960.

11 The "Balfour Declaration" of Nov. 2, 1917, was a statement issued by the British Foreign Secretary, Lord Arthur James Balfour, in a letter to Lionel Walter Rothschild, a leader of British Jewry, promising the establishment of a homeland for the Jewish people in Palestine that would "not disturb" the non-Jewish groups already residing there. The League of Nations mandate was created in the aftermath of World War I (1914-1918) after the collapse of the Ottoman Empire, which had controlled the area since the 16th century. The British mandate lasted from 1920 till May 1948, after which the Independence of the State of Israel was declared by David Ben Gurion, Israelʾs first Prime Minister.

Leib and Miriam Lipton Glantz on their honeymoon, June 1936.

In the following years, Glantz appeared in concert halls and synagogues throughout the United States, as well as in Canada, Mexico, South America, Western and Eastern Europe, South Africa, and Palestine.

In June 1936 Glantz married Miriam Lipton, whom he had met six years earlier. They had two children: Kalman, born in 1937, and Ezra (Jerry), born in 1945. Their three grandchildren are: Shani (1975), Tomer (1979) and Ari (1988).

Glantz was one of the founding members of the *Cantors Cultural Society* (founded in New York in 1930), and was elected as the Society's president. The Board of Directors included

Leib and Miriam Glantz with their son Kalman, 1937.

renowned cantors such as Mordechai Hershman, Adolf Katchko, Max Wohlberg, Zavel Kwartin, and David Roitman.

In 1941, Glantz and his family moved from New York to Los Angeles, California, where he served as chief cantor of Sinai Temple (1941-1946), and later as chief cantor at the *Sha'a'rei Te'fi'la* Synagogue (1949-1954).

The Besa Record Company issued an LP recording of Chasidic Spirituals named *Cha'si'dim Be'Ri'na,* featuring melodies composed by Glantz in different *Cha'si'dic* styles such as *Bratz'lav, Ba'al Shem Tov,* Israeli, Yemenite, *Cha'bad* and *Talner.* Another album featured Hebrew and Yiddish songs to words by Jewish poets such as Chaim Nachman Bialik, Shaul Tchernichovsky and Jacob Fichman. Other recordings were issued by the Reena Recording Company and the Asch Recording Company.[12]

In 1946, following the Second World War and the catastrophe of the Holocaust, Glantz embarked on an extensive concert tour throughout Europe, singing in numerous Jewish refugee camps. After attending the 1946 World Zionist Congress in Basle, he continued to Palestine for his second visit, followed by a third trip in 1947, appearing in concerts and prayer services in Tel Aviv, Haifa and Jerusalem. On his return journey to Los Angeles, he appeared in three concerts in London, and a gala concert at the Metropolitan Opera House in New York, commemorating the fiftieth anniversary of the *Chazonim Farband* (The Jewish Ministers Cantors Association of America), of which Leib Glantz was Honorary President. In 1948 he lectured before the delegates of the First Annual Conference of the Cantors Assembly of America on the subject: *"How the Jewish Nus'cha'ot* (prayer modes) *Were Created."*

When David Ben Gurion declared the independence of the State of Israel, in May 1948, Glantz was ecstatic. After years of political activism in the Labor Zionist movement, witnessing pogroms in Eastern Europe, antisemitism in America, and constant battles between Jews and Arabs in Palestine, Glantz believed he could finally realize his dream to live in Israel.

Unfortunately, several religious political parties controlled the religious life in Israel. The leaders of these parties recognized Glantz as one of the greatest cantors in the world, but were politically opposed to enabling him to assume a permanent position in any Israeli synagogue unless he became a member of a religious political party and agreed to relinquish his connections with the secular Labor Zionist *Ma'pai* party,[13] with whom he was closely affiliated

---

12 See Appendices for complete recording history and discography.

13 *Ma'pai* — *Mif'le'get Po'a'lei E'retz Yis'ra'el* (The Party of the Workers of the Land of Israel), later renamed the Israeli Labor Party. The party's leader was David Ben Gurion, Israel's first Prime Minister.

> *Glantz could not agree to turn his back on his lifelong friends and his political beliefs. He decided to wait for the opportunity to combine his loyalty and his political principles with his cantorial aspirations.*

Leib Glantz with his mother, Golda, and sister, Esther, in Winnipeg, Canada, 1936.

throughout his life. Glantz could not agree to turn his back on his lifelong friends and his political beliefs, and decided to wait for the opportunity to combine his loyalty and his political principles with his cantorial aspirations.

In 1949 Glantz traveled to Israel and introduced his newest composition "*Ha'loch Ve'Ka'ra'ta Be'Oz'nei Ye'ru'sha'la'yim,*"[14] a composition he dedicated to Israel's first Prime Minister David Ben Gurion. In August, 1952, he was invited to sing at the opening ceremony of the first *Zim'ri'ya* on Mount Herzl in Jerusalem, where 1,200 choir singers from all over the world performed before an audience of 40,000 Israelis.

Leib Glantz articulated his musical theories in a monumental lecture before the delegates of the Fifth Annual Convention of the Cantors Assembly of America in 1952.[15] His lecture, based on extensive research, created a serious debate at the convention. His original ideas were considered a new path toward the analysis and understanding of the concealed secrets of the ancient Jewish prayer modes. Glantz also lectured as a Professor of Cantorial and Jewish Music at the University for Jewish Studies in Los Angeles, California.

---

14 "Go and Proclaim So That Jerusalem Will Hear!"
15 "The Musical Basis of *Nu'sach Ha'Te'fi'la.*" (See this lecture in Part 3 of this book.)

The opportunity to emigrate to Israel arrived in 1954. The newly elected officers of the *Tif'er'et Zvi* synagogue in Tel Aviv, led by chairman Itzchak Raziel, invited Glantz to assume the position of chief cantor. Glantz departed for Israel, and his wife and two sons followed shortly thereafter. His first appearance at the Midnight *Se'li'chot* Service was a national event before a fully packed synagogue, with four thousand additional worshippers crowding the surrounding streets, listening to his voice through loudspeakers.

Glantz lived in Israel for the last ten years of his life. In Israel he enjoyed intimate interaction with a congregation that understood the language of the prayers and was accustomed to the style of Eastern European cantors. These worshippers were capable of appreciating Glantz's unique and inspiring interpretations of the prayer texts, his religious adherence to the ancient Jewish prayer modes, and his authentic musical innovations. He became immensely popular in Israel — a household name.

Some of Glantz's greatest compositions were composed during this period of his life in Tel Aviv, including *A'na Be'Cho'ach, Be'Tzeit Yis'ra'el, A'hav'ti, U'Ve'Nu'cho Yo'mar, Ha'loch Ve'Ka'ra'ta*, and *Mach'ni'sei Ra'cha'mim*. Five LP records[16] consisting of forty-eight of Glantz's compositions were produced in New York in 1958 by Sara Wachs. In total, Leib Glantz composed 216 compositions of *Cha'za'nut*, Chasidic *Ni'gu'nim*, Yiddish and Hebrew songs.

In 1956 and again in 1961 Glantz was elected as a delegate to the World Zionist Congresses in Jerusalem, this time proudly representing the State of Israel. In 1958, Glantz was honored to present an artistic program at the cornerstone ceremony for the new Israeli parliament building — the *Kne'sset*.

In 1963, Famous Records, a recording company in New York, produced Leib Glantz's "*Midnight Se'li'chot Service*" — two LP records compiled from the *Kol Yis'ra'el* radio broadcasts of the *Se'li'chot* services that were recorded live from the *Tif'e'ret Zvi* synagogue in Tel Aviv. The complete service was composed by Leib Glantz and is considered his most inspiring work. Many cantors and scholars consider Glantz's *Se'li'chot* service as the most important cantorial work ever published.[17]

> *Many cantors and scholars consider Glantz's* Se'li'chot *service as the most important cantorial work ever published.*

In 1961 Glantz gave a series of popular radio lectures on *Kol Yis'ra'el* national radio, on the subject of Jewish Music and the Prayer Modes.[18]

---

16 The five LP record albums: *Ri'nat Ha'Ko'desh, Tif'er'et Te'fi'la, Ha'llel Ve'Zim'ra, Cha'zon Ve'Shi'ra* and *Cha'si'dim Be'Ri'na*.

17 Israel Music issued a technically improved CD reproduction of this LP in 2001 (ICD-5095).

18 These six lectures, translated into English, appear in part three of this book.

Leib, with brother Cantor Yonah (Yonia) Glantz and Yonah's wife Sarah, in Portland, Oregon.

In addition to his cantorial career, Glantz appeared in leading tenor roles in several operas, including Alan Hovhaness' "*Shepherd of Israel,*"[19] Jacques Halévy's "*La Juive,*"[20] and Joseph Tal's "*Saul at Ein Dor.*"[21]

Glantz served as a director of ACUM (The Composers, Authors and Publishers Society of Israel), and as a judge on the prestigious "Yoel Engel Prize" for original Israeli musical achievements. He was a director of the Israeli Composers Association and served as editor of the periodical *"Bat Kol."*

In 1959, in collaboration with two of his avid admirers and friends, Professor Yehuda Even-Shmuel Kaufman and the famous Israeli writer Eliezer Steinman, Glantz founded the *Tel Aviv Institute for Jewish Liturgical Music,* and under its auspices, an academic level conservatory for

---

19 Alan Hovhaness (1911-2000) was an American-Armenian who in 1953 composed "Shepherd of Israel" (Psalm 80) for tenor cantor, soprano (or flute), trumpet and string quartet (or string orchestra).

20 Jacques Halévy (1799–1862), French operatic composer of the 1835 opera *"La Juive"* ("The Jewish Woman"). Born in Paris, the son of a cantor (Elie Halfon Halévy), who was the secretary of the Jewish community of Paris, as well as a writer and a teacher of Hebrew.

21 Joseph Tal (born 1910), Polish born Israeli composer of the opera *"Saul at Ein Dor."*

training cantors, the *Cantors Academy* (*Ha'A'ka'dèmia Le'Cha'za'nut*). With Glantz at its helm, many important scholars and musicians considered it a great honor to join the academic faculty. This school functioned until Glantz's death in 1964. More than 50 students passed the demanding admission requirements and received university level education in a variety of subjects, such as voice training, music, prayer modes, Hebrew language, Jewish and world history, and sacred scriptures.

Following Glantz's sudden passing on January 27, 1964,[22] while singing on stage at the *Beit Hamlin* concert hall in Tel Aviv, the *Tel Aviv Institute for Jewish Liturgical Music* was transformed into the publishing organ of Leib Glantz's musical compositions, his research and his literary work. This body published seven books[23] of Glantz's musical compositions and the 1965 Hebrew book *Zeharim — In Memory of Leib Glantz* (edited by Eliezer Steinman and prepared for print by David Vinitzky).

Leib Glantz's funeral was attended by thousands of admirers. Among them were his close friend, President of Israel, Zalman Shazar, Ministers of the Israeli Cabinet, Members of Parliament, judges, rabbis, cantors, musicians, and many members of the Israeli intelligentsia. He was buried at the *Kir'yat Sha'ul* cemetery in North Tel Aviv. His loving wife, Miriam, a psychiatric social worker and one of Israel's most important teachers and leaders of the social work profession, passed away in 1988, and was buried at his side.

---

22 The Hebrew date of Leib Glantz's passing was *Yod Gìmel* of the month *Sh'vat,* the year *Taf Shin Kaf Da'let* (5,724). He was 66 years old.

23 The series "Selected Works Rinat Hakodesh" includes: (1) Prayer Modes (*Nu'sa'chei Te'fi'la);* (2) Friday Evening Service; (3) Sabbath Morning Service; (4) Hallel and Three Festivals; (5) Selichot Service; (6) High Holidays; (7) Songs. [available to order via website: www.TheManWhoSpokeToGod.com].

2

Growing Up with Leibel in Kiev and Kishinev

DR. CHAIM BAR-DAYAN[1]

The first time I met Leibel, as we used to call him, was in 1908. My father brought my brother and me to the Makarovi Synagogue on Nijney Val Street, in the Podol district of lower Kiev. There was a special excitement in the synagogue on that Sabbath morning. Next to the cantor, Reb Abba, sat a young boy, a bit older than myself. He was tall, thin, with a gentle, pale face, and sharp shining eyes. He was wrapped in a *Ta'lit* (prayer shawl), and his head was covered by a beautiful *Yar'mul'ka* (skullcap). The ten year old kept his eyes concentrated on a large prayer book, attentively listening to the chanting of the morning *Shach'rit* prayers. During the reading of the *To'rah* he didn't move, totally ignoring the excitement surrounding him.

> *This was the first time in my life that I experienced singing that was more beautiful and more powerful than what I was used to listening to on our gramophone. It was a feeling that spread swiftly throughout the whole congregation. His tall and confident posture, his sweet, soft soprano, his trills and transitions charmed my soul.*

Then he confidently stood up and strode toward the *A'mud* (prayer lectern), opening his mouth in prayer as if he were old and experienced. This was the first time in my life that I experienced singing that was more beautiful and more powerful than what I was used to listening to on our gramophone. It was a feeling that spread swiftly throughout the whole congregation. His tall and confident posture, his sweet, soft soprano, his trills and transitions charmed my soul.

1 Dr. Chaim Bar-Dayan — researcher and Zionist activist. He was a lifelong friend of Leib Glantz.

Leib Glantz (center) in Kishinev, Bessarabia, in 1923, with fellow Zionist activists.

At the conclusion of the prayer service, the young cantor returned triumphantly to his seat next to his father. There was a commotion of well wishers, shaking his hand and blessing him with *Yi'shar Ko'ach* (well done — more power to you). I couldn't find the courage to come closer to him. However, I can't forget the wonderful thrill and excitement that engulfed me while walking home that day.

His appearance was the main topic of discussion in our town for weeks. The word had spread that he was discovered at age 4, and appeared as cantor before he was six. At eight his father, Kalman, the cantor of the Talner Chasidim in Kiev, took him to appear in Vienna, Berlin and Budapest, the great centers of cantorial in those days. Glantz had amazed his listeners.

Two years later, in 1910, I finally had the opportunity to actually meet Leibel. His father had forbidden him to sing while his voice was mutating, and I expressed my sorrow that I could not enjoy his singing once more. I learned from him that his father was teaching him *To'rah* and *Tal'mud,* demanding that he concentrate on the completion of his secular education as well. Furthermore, in addition to daily piano lessons, he would practice piano more than six hours a day.

We became very close friends. We used to frequent different synagogues and listen to prayers of different communities, both Ashkenazic and Sephardic. The one Leib preferred most was

Leib Glantz with Nachum and Ahuva (Luba) Tal (Tulchinsky), in Kiev, Ukraine in 1921. They were active in the Zionist youth movement *He'Cha'lutz*.

the *Ka'ra'ite* synagogue. He loved to hear the unique Hebrew pronunciation of the cantor, with its oriental flavor. We also used to go to listen to Russian Orthodox and Catholic services, especially enjoying the choral singing. On Sundays we would go to the Municipal Opera, the Sadovski Theatre, or the Russian Music Society's Chamber Orchestra. During summer we would enjoy going to the free outdoor symphony concerts and Ukrainian operettas. Musical life in Kiev at that period was flourishing, as rich as it was in Moscow or St. Petersburg. The relative closeness of Kiev to Western Europe enabled many guest artists from the West to perform in Kiev frequently.

By 1911, Glantz had become such an excellent piano player that he was accepted to the music conservatory of the famous Nikolai Tutkovski (1857-1930), then considered the best music school in Russia. He received piano instruction from the distinguished pianist Dombrovsky. Musical Theory and Harmony he learned with Nikolai Lisenko (1842-1911), the composer of six Ukrainian operas.

Between ourselves we always spoke Hebrew. I invited him to join the Hebrew youth movement *Ha'Zfi'ra* that I myself formed. Later he actually became our leader, frequently lecturing on issues of Jewish life in the Diaspora and in Palestine. He convinced us to join the Zionist youth movement *Tse'i'rei Zion* ("The Young Zionists"), and thanks to him we found ourselves compelled to read Zionist books such as *"Rome and Jerusalem"* by Moshe Hess, *"The Jewish State"* by Theodore Herzl, and *"Auto-Emancipation"* by Leon Pinsker. We learned to respond to the literature of our times, both Zionist and Socialist. Leibel was always the sharpest and most enthusiastic debater of every meeting.

Leib Glantz in his cantor's garb in Kishinev, Bessarabia (today part of Moldava), age 22, 1920.

Zeev Zeliken, a student at the Kiev Polytechnical Institute, was considered by all of us a man of great vision. His ideas had an enormous impact on Glantz's life. Zeliken professed that it was the duty of every Jewish young man and woman to commit to Jewish national goals, and to be ready to serve its national forces. He called for complete devotion to the popular Zionist movement by working towards educational, organizational and practical achievements, with the ultimate goal being the formation of a Jewish homeland in the biblical Zion (the Land of Israel).

These words of Zeliken revolutionized Glantz's life. He felt that his destiny was this Zionist path and he would have to relinquish his cantorial dream. Not knowing how his voice would emerge from the years of silence during his voice mutation, he came to the conclusion that in that time of disaster for the Jewish people, musicians and artists are less important than combatants for such a noble cause.

His parents, Kalman and Golda, witnessed this tremendous change in their son, and wisely did not try to oppose him. They believed that as he matured, and his voice emerged, he would come to his senses, and realize that he was destined to become the flag bearer of cantorial art.

Our ways parted for a while when my parents sent me away to study. Upon my return in 1913, I sensed a change in Leibel. Even though he was still studying piano and music with Dombrovsky at Tutkovski's school, his piano playing lacked the excitement and dedication of the past. In his final exams he did receive great compliments for playing a Mendelssohn concerto and a Beethoven sonata. He received the highest grades of his class. However, in his heart, he felt that he would not achieve greatness as a pianist, mainly because he began playing the piano too late in his life.

Leibel and I decided to make plans to emigrate to Palestine in order to study at the Hebrew High School in Tel Aviv, *Gym'na'si'a Herz'li'ya*. Leibel's father would hear nothing of it, and this caused deep resentment. However, he knew that there was nothing he could do to change his father's mind.

In 1916, at age eighteen, Leib was compelled to move to Besarabia. The antisemitic pogroms made it impossible to remain in Kiev. He felt comfortable in Besarabia, as his paternal grandfather, Naftali (known in the cantorial world as Reb Naftali Soroker), lived in Soroki. Leib's sister, Rachel Feldman, was married and lived in Soroki as well. The distinguished Cantor Avraham Berkovitz-Kalechnik lived in nearby Kishinev. His influence on Glantz's cantorial was immense.

By now Glantz was a mature young man, his voice mutation complete, and he resumed his liturgical singing in Kishinev, a city with a Jewish population very enthusiastic about cantorial.

In 1917, the year of the communist revolution, the composer Reinhold Gliere (1875-1956), head of the prestigious Kiev Conservatory of Music, offered to teach Glantz composition. Gliere was very close to Glantz and considered him a musical genius. He encouraged his young protégé to dedicate himself to musical composition. Glantz was also inclined to concentrate on conducting choirs, as he had done successfully in his father's Talner synagogue in Kiev. These years turned out to be the most important in his musical education. I was enrolled at the Kiev Conservatory as well, and as students in the Conservatory, Glantz and I were entitled to attend the famous concerts of the Russian Musical Society, and to participate in the meetings of the teachers and students of the

> *The renowned composer Reinhold Gliere, head of the prestigious Kiev Conservatory of Music, invited Glantz to study composition. Gliere was very close to Glantz and considered him a musical genius. He encouraged his young protégé to dedicate himself to musical composition.*

Conservatory with the world's greatest musicians of that period, such as Sergei Prokofiev, Alexander Glazonov, and many others.

Glantz left Kishinev for America in July 1926. I emigrated to Palestine. The next time we met was in Palestine in 1930.

3

Letter From a Son

Dear Father:

It is very difficult for me to write this letter to you. I know that you will not be expecting it. Yet, I feel a tremendous impulse to write to you. It is impossible to hold inside what I have to say. It is your genius in prayer that compels me, in an inexplicable way, to write this. I am sure that if you were now here in Israel, I wouldn't have the courage to write this letter to you.

I am writing to you as an eighteen-year-old son. I am far from being a great musical expert, and, as you well know, I am not a particularly great follower of *Cha'za'nut,* especially the boring and monotonous way it is performed in our time.

During your absence from Israel these past months, I had the opportunity to listen to all your recordings, as somewhat of a compensation for your being abroad during this year's High Holidays. Suddenly I realized how much I miss our holiday synagogue prayers, and our traditional holiday feasts. I want to try to describe my feelings and emotions.

When I close my eyes and listen to the record of the *"Se'li'chot"* prayers that you composed and sang (and I did so many times in the past two months), I feel drawn as if by magic into another world. I feel as if suddenly there is no one around me — no walls, no house, no city. Just

---

1 Written from Israel by Jerry (Ezra) Glantz to his father, Cantor Leib Glantz, then in New York, three months prior to Leib Glantz's untimely death. Translated from Hebrew.

the two of us — alone! I imagine watching you and wondering how you succeed in summoning the angels and how you speak to them as equals! It seems as if God is listening, peeking down from the heavens and delightfully shivering in reaction to the meaningful penetration of your voice.

> *I imagine watching you and wondering how you succeed in summoning the angels and how you speak to them as equals!*

You seem to be able to understand and interpret the deepest meanings of each and every word, attaching it to the perfect melody, while remaining purely loyal to the ancient Jewish prayer modes, which seemingly exist in your blood. It is amazing to witness how you combine your deep religious belief, your sweet voice, and your musical genius. But above all, it is your

Leib with wife Miriam and sons Kalman and Ezra (Jerry) Glantz, at Kalman's Bar Mitzva celebration in Los Angeles, October, 1950.

beautiful soul that combines all these wonderful attributes into a great artistic masterpiece, the kind that appears only once in a thousand years.

When I listen to you sing, tears run from my eyes — tears of identification and delight. You elevate my spirit high above this mundane and material world. I believe that the greatest achievement of any artist is to enable fellow human beings to identify and elevate their spirit to the highest of spheres. I wonder if we are really capable of grasping your greatness.

Believe me, it would have been easier to say all this to you if you were not my father. You might discount my words as just coming from your mischievous teenage son. Who knows me better than you do? Please ignore the disarray of my ideas and my obvious immaturity. I hope you understand that this letter does not stem only from a son's love for his father, but from a recognition by your son of your great artistic stature.

At last I am capable of understanding the admiration of your many followers, all of whom, I am sure, have experienced this wonderful elation and joy of listening to the heavenly music you create.

> *The Almighty endowed you with a powerful gift, and you have presented it to mankind with fervor, awe, and perfection.*

The Almighty endowed you with a powerful gift, and you have presented it to mankind with fervor, awe, and perfection.

You, my father, are the greatest of all — and so you will remain forever!

Your most loving son,

Ezra
Tel Aviv, October 19, 1963

4

Letter From Bangkok

AVINOAM BROWN[1]

Dear Ezra Glantz:

I would like to write to you, the son of Cantor Leib Glantz, about my feelings toward your father.

I was an avid collector of recordings of most of the classical *"Golden Age of Cha'za'nut"* cantors. In my collection I had two recordings of your father, but somehow never made an effort to listen to them. I probably expected him to be just one more cantor, whose sobbing the text was the main character of the prayer. When I did listen to one of his tracks — his famous *She'ma Yis'ra'el* composition — I must admit, it sounded strange and foreign in comparison to others.

I then played Glantz's *"Se'li'chot* Midnight Service." I was amazed to hear his voice pronouncing the words *Eich Nif'tach Peh Le'fa'ne'cha* ("How can we dare open our mouths before you, God?"). This just shattered my world. It was totally different from everything I had ever heard before. I felt that this man was actually talking to God with passion! His voice was commanding its way up to the heavens — to be heard and to be answered. I was stunned. I wondered if

> *Glantz's singing of the Se'li'chot prayers just shattered my world . . . I felt that this man was actually talking to God with passion! His voice was commanding its way up to the heavens.*

---

1 Avinoam (Noam) Brown (age 23) was born in Amsterdam, Holland, and resides in Bangkok, Thailand. This letter was written on February 22, 2006.

I could consider this in the same category as the *Cha'za'nut* I was accustomed to. I sensed that it was much greater. It was pure, honest and real.

I began collecting all the Leib Glantz's recordings that I could possibly find. It took me months to collect his records from all over the world; I found some as far away as Argentina. I discovered more and more of the treasures that he had left for us. I realized that there was no one of his stature before him, during his lifetime, and definitely not since he passed away. No one could match this rare combination of talents that make him so unique in the cantorial world.

As I studied Glantz's compositions and recordings, I discovered the diverse character of each and every composition. No composition was the same in sound or meaning. Every piece had its particular message. Each revealed something very refreshing, a different tone and a different mood. I loved the way he renewed all the old conservative musical styles of the liturgy with a mixture of singing and speaking, something I had never appreciated before. As I concentrated on Glantz's recordings, I became more and more intrigued — trying to understand why he would emphasize a word here and speak out a word there. It led me to a deeper understanding of the prayers.

> *No composition was the same in sound or meaning. Every piece had its particular message. Each revealed something very refreshing, a different tone and a different mood.*

Glantz's RCA recordings from the late 1920s and early 1930s enabled me to link old cantorial styles with Glantz's interpretations. Later, I explored his compositions from his Israeli period [1954-1964]. I found myself identifying deeply with Glantz's cries, demands and even "threats" towards God. In this world, burning with atrocities and suffering, Glantz seemed to be calling out that if only God would answer our prayers — life could be wonderful. In his composition *Shomer Yis'ra'el* (Guardian of Israel), he demands of God to answer our pleas. This is similar to the way I feel in my own personal life.

I feel that Glantz was determined to reveal God's greatness to the whole world. He penetrated into the soul of every word, letter and sound. He unveiled our prayers by displaying their true meaning in both intellectual and emotional ways. I often sensed the love and devotion he felt towards every word he uttered. When I listen to him sing, I am amazingly drawn closer to God. He is my guide, without him I feel lost. He always seems to confidently know the right path.

Listening to Glantz, I sense his straightforwardness and honesty. I wish to deal with people in my own surroundings in the same manner, as part of my pursuit of happiness and enlightenment.

Within his brilliant innovations, Glantz always remained loyal to the *Nu'sach* [Jewish prayer modes], building new creations on the basis of thousands of years of Jewish tradition. His *Tefi'lot* (prayer services) are full of life. They replace the dying cantorial routine that somehow, along the journey of time, has lost its vitality.

Glantz has raised me to the highest spiritual levels. He opens the gates of heaven and miraculously enables me to glimpse into the divine atmosphere. He enlightened me with an awareness of the deeper meanings of text and the holiness of the *Nu'sach*. I will forever be grateful to him for enriching my life with music — music that accompanies me every day in my personal journey through life.

Leib Glantz never succumbed to the musical taste of the masses. He was fearful of God, not of his audiences. He considered it his holy mission to provide his listeners with a unique musical and interpretive experience. Glantz was similar to the great painters of the end of the nineteenth century. They too were far ahead of their time, and very few of their contemporaries grasped the beauty and importance of their art. Glantz, as well, bravely created new musical

> *Leib Glantz never succumbed to the musical taste of the masses. He was fearful of God, not of his audiences.*

images that would express ancient virtues and feelings. He devoted his entire life to creating for us and for future generations spiritual and meaningful music.

At times, this world we live in makes no sense to me. Colors, sounds, feelings and words weigh down on me in distorted and twisted ways like a giant waterfall. I find it difficult to decipher their meanings. Then I listen to Leib Glantz, as he restructures sounds, words and feelings in such a way that, in a flash, everything makes sense, and I realize that my life is not in vain.

Sincerely,

Noam Brown

5

Leib Glantz at *Tif'e'ret Zvi* Synagogue

MEMORIES OF A TEN-YEAR-OLD

AHARON NOFF[1]

It was the summer of 1954. I was confused about the unusual commotion in *Tif'e'ret Zvi*, our Orthodox synagogue. The ancient external walls that were never painted because of lack of funds received a bright new coat of paint. The great synagogue dome was painted inside and out. Upstairs, in the women's gallery, special ramps were being built to enable the women to see the central pulpit. Steel fences surrounding the synagogue were erected in order to prevent the crowds standing outside from forcing their way in without tickets.

I was just ten years old. When I enquired what all this tumult was about, I was told that one of the greatest cantors in the world was about to arrive, and many important people from Israel and abroad would be coming to hear him. Therefore, the synagogue had to be made attractive and respectable.

> *The synagogue was bursting with people, and thousands gathered in the surrounding streets. Policemen on horseback were trying to control the crowd. Loudspeakers were set up in order to enable those unfortunate admirers lacking tickets to at least hear the proceedings.*

The grand gala opening was the Midnight *Se'li'chot* Service. The synagogue was bursting with people, and thousands gathered in the surrounding streets. Policemen on horseback were trying to control the crowd. Loudspeakers were set up in order to enable those unfortunate admirers lacking tickets to at least hear the proceedings.

---

1 Aharon Noff is a member of the Israeli "Yuval" cantorial concert choir.

Tif'e'ret Zvi **synagogue in Tel Aviv, Israel, where Glantz officiated as chief cantor from 1954 till 1963.**

The choir, dressed in their best suits, convened on the pulpit. Suddenly, there was a loud noise, as the *Sha'mash,* the synagogue beadle, demanded quiet, announcing the majestic entrance of the cantor. The silence inside the synagogue became deafening as the door to the cantor's chamber opened slowly. The first thing I could notice was the beautiful robe, adorned by a silver-lined *Ta'lit* (prayer shawl) and an impressive cantor's hat, made of pure silk.

This was the first time I encountered, with my very own eyes, the great cantor Leib Glantz. He impressed me as a warm, intelligent and very confident man. His awesome entrance as he walked very slowly toward the central pulpit, made an unforgettable impression on the congregation. As a little boy, I made my way close to the pulpit in order to get a close view of the cantor and the choir.

The *Se'li'chot* service lasted for more than two hours and left me with a feeling of emotional excitement. This was something that I had never experienced before. From his lips it seemed

> *From his lips it seemed as if flames of ecstacy were flowing and engulfing the whole congregation. His arms and body accompanied his praying as if he were sacrificing his heart and his soul.*

as if flames of ecstacy were flowing and engulfing the whole congregation. His arms and body accompanied his praying as if he were sacrificing his heart and his soul. The atmosphere in the synagogue was that of spiritual exaltation. This was the first time in my life that I heard a cantor accompanied by a choir. I knew then and there that the seeds of my love for *Cha'za'nut* were sown.

The respect for Leib Glantz was so great that he could impose norms of behavior during the services. He commanded total silence during his prayers. If he sensed commotion — he would pause and send glaring eyes toward the source of the disturbance, continuing only after peace was restored.

My favorite part of the services was when Glantz would improvise with "spoken voice," not really singing but speaking the words like an actor on the stage. I considered these moments the pinnacle of the service. This is where he defined his genius as a cantor, exposing his unique emotional sensitivity.

A year or two later, my brother and I would sneak into the synagogue in order to listen to Glantz and his choir during their rehearsals before the High Holidays. Suddenly, Glantz announced that he intended to incorporate a few solo melodies to be sung by children. We were offered the opportunity to audition, along with other children. My brother and I were selected, and for the next few years (until our voices began to mutate) we sang the children's solos in Leib Glantz's services. Obviously, this was a wonderful experience.

Later in life, I studied *Cha'za'nut* with Cantor Yitzchak Eshel, who was a great admirer of Glantz. He often sat with me and analyzed Glantz's compositions in great detail. To this day I sing in the *"Yu'val"* Cantors Choir in Israel, where we are exposed to many great compositions from the cantorial world. But deep in my heart I know that Leib Glantz was the cantor, the artist and the genius on a level high above any one else in the history of *Cha'za'nut*, and it is doubtful that anyone will ever soar to his great stature.

6

Astounded as a Six-Year-Old

Yaakov Schwartzman [1]

It has been almost fifty years since I last heard Leib Glantz singing at the *Tif'e'ret Zvi* synagogue in Tel Aviv. I was but six years old when my father first took me to hear Glantz. The impact of that experience lingers on in my mind to this very day. It seems as if it was just yesterday.

There was such a unique atmosphere in the synagogue during his prayers. The worshippers expressed great respect during the services. No one would dare to be distracted, not wanting to miss even one note.

Glantz himself was always dressed in an impressive black or white cantor's gown, creating a truly ceremonial sight.

As a child, I was so impressed by the way he swiftly activated his tuning fork [2] in order to set his voice to the proper musical key for each prayer. Then he would glance at the choir who were standing before him at the steps leading up to the *To'rah's* ark, signaling with a swift motion of his eyes for the conductor, Yehoshua Zohar, to commence singing.

I cannot forget the impression it made on me when Glantz and the choir sang *"A'na Be'Cho'ach"* ("By the great power of Thy right hand") on the Friday night *Ka'bba'lat Sha'bbat* service. The opening was a very quiet *pianissimo,* followed by a forceful, almost demanding,

---

1 Yaakov Schwartzman writes poetry and lives in Herzlia, Israel.
2 A tuning fork is a two-pronged steel device used by musicians, which vibrates when struck to give a note of specific pitch.

> *One always had the feeling that Glantz truly understood the inner meanings of the prayers, and through his musical interpretations passed these secret meanings on to us, the worshippers.*

Shav'a'tei'nu Ka'bel ("accept our prayer, hear our cry"), and then ending the mystical liturgical poem with almost a whispering of the words *Yo'de'a Ta'a'lu'mot* ("Thou knowest secret thoughts"). One always had the feeling that Glantz truly understood the inner meanings of the prayers, and through his musical interpretations passed these secret meanings on to us, the worshippers.

I was just a child but I was amazed by how much Glantz seemed truly to love the music he sang. It was evident by looking at his facial and body expressions and his demeanor. One could feel that he was actually "living" the music and the texts. Glantz mostly sang compositions that he himself composed.

When the prayer services were over, Glantz would sit down on a special marble chair on the prayer pulpit, and the members of the congregation would come over, one by one, to shake his hands and express their excited impressions and gratitude. I remember walking up to him and shaking his warm hand. He smiled at me and I was thrilled.

The Sabbath prayer services were open to everyone. However, on the High Holidays and Festivals one needed to purchase a ticket in advance. The synagogue was always overflowing with worshippers. The sad reality of today's synagogues in Tel Aviv is such that they barely draw a *Min'yan*[3] ...

Itzchak Raziel — Chairman of *Tif'e'ret Zvi* Synagogue in Tel Aviv, who was responsible for inviting Glantz to immigrate to Israel and officiate as chief cantor.

Another vivid memory is the *Bar Mitz'va* celebration of Leib Glantz's

---

3 *Min'yan* — The minimum number of ten adult Jews or, among the Orthodox, Jewish men, required for a communal religious service.

younger son, Ezra (Jerry) Glantz, in 1958. It was a custom in the Glantz family that when a son reached the age of thirteen, he would be called upon to officiate as a cantor, praying the *Shach'rit* and *Mu'saf* Sabbath services as well as the readings of the *To'rah* and *Haf'ta'ra*. Ezra amazed the thousands of worshippers, singing his father's compositions with great feeling and a beautiful voice. The young Glantz enjoyed the accompaniment of a better choir than his father, as his choir included a tenor named Leib Glantz...

I was struck with awe when I first heard Glantz's classical masterpiece, *Shema Yis'ra'el* ("Hear O Israel"), one of the most exciting cantorial compositions ever written. Many cantors try to emulate Leib Glantz's singing, but it is almost impossible to recreate the heavenly sounds that came from Glantz's unbelievable voice.

> *In my childish fantasies I sensed that Glantz was singing from the depths of his heart, as if he were a volcano, uttering flames of fire.*

In my childish fantasies I sensed that Glantz was singing from the depths of his heart, as if he were a volcano, uttering flames of fire.

A Voice That Encompassed The Synagogue With Beautiful Music

CANTOR UDI SPIELMAN[1]

I was but five or six years old when my father, Joseph Spielman, began taking me with him to the *Tif'e'ret Zvi* synagogue in north Tel Aviv to listen to the divine prayers of Cantor Leib Glantz.

I vividly remember the very first time I saw him singing from the prayer pulpit. The synagogue seemed so gigantic to me as I was just a child. Beautiful golden chandeliers surrounded Glantz. He was tall, handsome, and dressed in an impressive cantor's attire. I was amazed when his voice rang out and encompassed the synagogue with beautiful music.

Glantz attracted people from every facet of Israeli society — from the very orthodox to the extremely secular. Famous writers, poets, philosophers, painters, sculptors and musicians filled the wooden benches of the synagogue. When he held services, the synagogue would overflow with worshippers. Many had to be satisfied with crowding around the doors and windows. Some had to remain outside in the surrounding streets, listening excitedly for hours, trying not to miss a word or a tone.

These childhood experiences left upon me an enormous impression and eventually influenced me to become a cantor myself. Interestingly, I was very fortunate to study *Cha'za'nut* at the highly acclaimed Tel Aviv Cantorial Institute, where my two most important teachers were actually students of Leib Glantz — Cantor Naftali Herstik and Cantor Chaim Feifel. This institute proudly continues the legacy of the Tel Aviv Institute of Jewish Liturgical Music and its "Cantors Academy," founded in 1959 by no other than Cantor Leibele Glantz.

---

1 Cantor Udi Spielman, born in Tel Aviv, Israel, is cantor of the *Bnei Torah* synagogue in Boca Raton, Florida.

A Lion to Sing His Will

Rabbi Avraham Soltes[1]

Making music is an art instinctive to all men, yet in our rich civilization, it is a highly trained skill as well, with a vast body of communicable knowledge. As in all arts that spring from the soul, and then come under intellectual control, there are instinctive musicians through whom the divine creates as if without premeditation — like a fountain gushing water; and there are artists whose training and experience are apparent in their every phrase. As a wise interpreter of Judaism said in explaining the threefold repetition of "God" in the *A'vot* prayer — "the God of Abraham, the God of Isaac, and the God of Jacob" — there are those who know God only as an inheritance from their fathers and there are those who know Him from deep personal encounter. Happy is the man who is blessed with both the richness of Divine heritage and the excitement of his own vision.

Such a man was *Cha'zan* Leib Glantz. Nurtured in the bosom of Chasidic tradition, Glantz, from his childhood to his untimely passing, manifested this unique and inspired blend of instinctive yearning after the Divine, disciplined by a keen and incisive intellect.

When Leibele Glantz stood before the Ark at the age of eight, in the synagogue of his grandfather in Kiev, chanting the *Sha'bbat* Service, the enthralled congregation beheld "clouds of glory" trailing the growing boy, as the words of the prayer book were enkindled by his improvisations and burned with a vivid *Hit'la'ha'vut* (excitement). Word of the *wunder-kind* spread throughout the Ukraine; congregations of the Jewish "Pale," hungry for the Divine glow that sparkled from tread-worn words when they were issued from pure young lips still close to the

---

1 Rabbi Avraham Soltes — *"A Lion to Sing His Will..." — The Artistic Life of Leib Glantz,* Published by the National Jewish Music Council, National Jewish Welfare Board (1965).

> *The remarkable thing about Glantz's Cha'za'nut was that despite the sophistication of years of formal training, he retained the glow of a heavenly vision to the end of his days.*

"Light," invited him to lead them in Sabbath and holiday worship.

The remarkable thing about Glantz's *Cha'za'nut* was that despite the sophistication of years of formal training, he retained the glow of a heavenly vision to the end of his days. As Yariv Ezrachi wrote:

"Glantz's *Se'li'chot* service attained a degree of exaltation that made one forget everything but communion with the prayers and the *Pi'yut* (liturgical poems) in a state of uninterrupted inner emotion. For two hours, without pause and without revealing the slightest fatigue, Glantz chanted every word and sentence of the service, penetrating their innermost meaning. . . with the power of his religious devotion, his inspiration of soul and ecstasy. . ."[2]

Yet, Glantz's creativity was not the pure instinct of a beardless child or the groping improvisation of a gospel singer. As a youngster in Kiev, he studied theory, piano, harmony and counterpoint with the distinguished Russian composer of operas and pedagogue, Professor Nikolai Tutkovski. In the Kiev Conservatory he studied composition with Reinhold Gliere. At fourteen, he organized a High Holiday choir which performed, in the Chasidic synagogue of his father, the artful works of Schorr, Sulzer, Lewandowski, Nowakowski, Gerovitch and others. Never had Chasidic worship stirred to such complex musical treatment!

Leib Glantz singing at a wedding in Tel Aviv, 1955.

2 Yariv Ezrachi — Israeli music critic, in the Hebrew daily newspaper *Ha'Bo'ker.*

Must there be an inevitable conflict between man's heart and his mind? Is the only true piety born of *naiveté* and childlike faith? Or did not the God who formed our heart also shape our brain? Does not the wisdom that sensitive men have acquired through the centuries also reflect the Light of Creation? The lifetime goal of Glantz's striving was the utilization of man's accumulated musical experience as a fruitful soil, which might nourish flowers of unique creative beauty, whose contemplation would turn men's souls to the seeking after the *Ein Sof* (eternity).

> "Flower in the crannied wall. . .
> Little flower — but if I could understand
> What you are, root and all, and all and all,
> I should know what God and man is!"

Most men are fortunate if, through their activities, an occasional flower blossoms in beauty. There are those who are blessed with careers that continually produce living blooms. The life of Leib Glantz was a garden of three contiguous flowerbeds that enriched and cross-fertilized each other with virile and potent seeds. He was first, a performer of music — a *Cha'zan*, whose voice and technique touched the simple as it stirred the sophisticated:

> "It is essentially a lyric tenor, but can be most effective at dramatic moments as well. It is not only a sweet and resonant voice; one marvels at its rich colors, at its technique, at the contrasts at which Glantz is such a master — from the still, silent tones that penetrate into one's very heart to the ringing *fortissimo*; whether in quiet lament or pathetic complaint; in richly expressive tones that resemble the blasts of a trumpet or *Sho'far*; in sounds that recall flutes or violins; in charming trills that are completely unostentatious; in dramatic recitative, and in reading that is half singing and is seldom approached in quality by the actors in our theatres; in rare musical feeling and in all the descriptive, narrative power of a remarkable dramatist. With all these great resources at his command, Leib Glantz makes of the *Se'li'chot* and of every prayer an experience to which one never becomes accustomed, but which is new and overpowering each time."[3]

Five continents were blessed with such an experience: the villages of Ukraine and Besarabia that wondered at him as a child; the communities of America, that welcomed him when his father's early passing forced him to seek the means to support his family in 1926; New York and Los Angeles where he filled permanent posts; Canada, Mexico, South America, England, Europe, and South Africa which delighted in his guest appearances; and last and dearest, Israel — the *Tif'e'ret Zvi* synagogue in Tel-Aviv, to which he was called in 1954 as Chief Cantor.

Vast crowds flocked to hear him, often blocking off traffic on the surrounding streets. Whole families hung on the grills of the synagogue windows to catch an echo of his prayers. In the words of the eminent critic, Waldo Frank:

---

3 Idov Cohen — Israeli Member of Parliament, in the Hebrew daily newspaper *"Ha'Bo'ker."*

> *"How Leibel Glantz gushed forth the passion of Israel in roulades, trills, tonal filigrees and cadenzas! . . . The passion . . . was musical . . . Why did I keep thinking of the Metropolitan Opera or the* La Scala *in Milano? Glantz sang better — had a better theme."*

"I heard one cantor in a synagogue...whose voice is more magnificent than any opera tenor's. How Leibel Glantz gushed forth the passion of Israel in roulades, trills, tonal filigrees and cadenzas! But the passion, one felt, was musical... Why did I keep thinking of the Metropolitan Opera or the *La Scala* in Milano? Glantz sang better — had a better theme."[4]

Leading intellectuals were drawn to worship by his Chasidic fervor, even in Israel's non-religious circles. Poets like Nathan Alterman, composers like Paul Ben-Haim, painters like Reuven Rubin, writers like Sholom Asch and Zalman Shazar, ascerbic critics like Alexander Uria Boskovitz could be found among his congregation on holidays or Sabbath eve. Boskovitz wrote:

> "I must confess that in recent years I have seldom attended synagogue services; I felt that the low standard of religious music and particularly, the dubious taste with which it is performed, destroy the possibility of a true spiritual experience. But ever since I heard Leib Glantz's *Mu'saf* Service on *Rosh Ha'Sha'na* in the *Tif'e'ret Zvi* synagogue in Tel-Aviv, I have been converted."[5]

Such "conversion" was due to the scope of Glantz's development, which never blocked his innate vision, but lent it wings. He had taken advantage of the voice training that has enriched Western civilization over many centuries and used it to enhance the blessed instrument that God had bestowed upon him. Unlike so many of his colleagues and most of the musicians of the Orient [Middle East], who rely solely on an initial gift of nature or a single style, and become thereby endlessly repetitious, Glantz, like a master gardener, strengthened his natural gifts, pruned them of distractions, and absorbed the sunshine and rain of universal experience to bring out the infinite color and eternal vigor of Jewish prayer.

Glantz appeared in 1957 with the Kol Israel Orchestra under Shalom Ronly-Riklis, to perform the distinctive work of the Armenian composer, Alan Hovhaness' *Shepherd of Israel.* He sang the leading role in Josef Tal's concert-opera, *Saul at Ein-Dor,* in 1958. His voice has been recorded by RCA Victor and other companies over a range of liturgical, folk and art songs that preserve for future generations the magic of his singing.

---

4 Waldo Frank — *Bridgehead — The Drama of Israel,* Published by George Braziller, Inc., NY, 1957.
5 Alexander Uria Boskovitz — (1907-1964), composer and music critic, in *"Ha'A'retz"* Israeli Hebrew daily newspaper, Israel, 1957.

Yet, for Glantz, musical expression never became an end in itself; it was only an instrument by which he exalted the words he was singing; it was a crystal *Ki'ddush* cup that holds the wine high for all the congregation to see, turning it now this way and now that, bringing out its many facets of warmth, sparkle and fragrance:

> "Through his interpretation, the words achieve a clear, distinct and realistic meaning. He appeals to the intellect of his listener, as well as to his sentiments. Many of his 'sayings' seem therefore rather strange and unusual, but repeated listening makes them astonishingly refreshing and meaningful."[6]

To Glantz, singing was never an end in itself. For to be a true cantor one must also possess the skill of a composer and the instinct of a teacher:

> "He constructs, organizes and executes his intonations on a sound musical basis. The different prayers become closed units and acquire a continuous logical musical line of development and climax."[7]

In the field of Jewish musical composition, Glantz raised up a second flowerbed of distinctive fragrance. Drawing upon the deep folk sources that he imbibed with his mother's milk and his father's labors, he early sensed, instinctively, the interlacing of dissonant elements in contemporary cantorial art. He assiduously searched hundreds of compositions and subjected the melodies he heard the world-over to extensive theoretical analysis, in order to come closer to the authentic sources of the true *Nu'sach*, appropriate for the prayers of Israel.

He developed his theories and produced a wealth of compositions to express the devout insights of his research. Almost one hundred compositions have been recorded or published; hundreds more remain in manuscript. Of his work, *Cha'zan* Max Wohlberg has written,

> "In these records Glantz justified anew his fame as the *Cha'zan's Cha'zan* (the cantor's cantor), as the 'innovator par excellence,' as the most original artist in the cantorial field of our generation."[8]

His originality stemmed from his fluent musical instincts, disciplined by a recognition of the vigorous musical cadences of the Hebrew tongue and a philosophical grasp of the intangible

His originality stemmed from his fluent musical instincts, disciplined by a recognition of the vigorous musical cadences of the Hebrew tongue and a philosophical grasp of the intangible intent of profound prayers.

---

6 Binyamin Bar-Am — in the English Israeli daily newspaper *"Jerusalem Post."*
7 Ibid.
8 Cantor Max Wohlberg — published in "The Cantor's Voice" journal and in Hebrew in the Israeli daily newspaper *"Ha'A'retz"* in 1954.

intent of profound prayers. Often criticized for his departures from established cantorial patterns, one finds, on deeper consideration that he eschewed the tried techniques for amusing the congregation with a popular melody, empty of content. He sought out soul-deep, penetrating themes that express the still small voice of meditation and spread like fire throughout the body, till every bone sings out Divine praise. His quality was recognized and welcomed by the Israel Composers League and he served as the chairman of its liturgical division, and on the editorial board of *Bat Kol* — the Israel Music Journal. He served on the juries of Israeli musical prize awards, and was working at the time of his death on a comprehensive guide to the Ashkenazic liturgical modes.

The essence of his contributions as a composer was epitomized in the words of Dr. Chaim Harris in an article in *Bi'tza'ron:*

> "Glantz has succeeded in uncovering the well from which the original Chasidic music had sprung. Having contrived to eliminate the foreign elements that crept into it accidentally, he has created a music which in all its characteristics is the very incarnation of the Chasidic spirit. It is as if a spark of the holy spirit of the founders of this music has somehow found its way into his soul."[9]

The basic drive of Judaism in all generations is contained in the Deuteronomic phrase, repeated lovingly by the faithful twice daily: "And thou shall teach them diligently unto thy children." A skill, an insight hard-won from the recalcitrant clay of experience — we yearn to preserve it for mankind before our own mortality buries it again as dust in the cold earth. So, the excitement of the Parting of the Red Sea, the exaltation of the thunder and lightning at Mt. Sinai, the ecstasy of the confrontation at the Burning Bush are preserved for us in the pages of the Book of Books.

It is true that the essence of each experience is incommunicable, but *Shi'rat Ha'Yam,*[10] the *A'se'ret Ha'Dib'rot*[11] and *E'he'ye A'sher E'he'ye*[12] have provided sensitive heirs of Moses with sufficient stimulation to evoke a living echo that continues to grow in literature and commentary to this very day.

> "To see the world in a grain of sand,
> And Heaven in a wild flower,
> Hold Infinity in the palm of your hand,
> And Eternity in an hour. . ."[13]

9   Dr. Chaim Harris — "A Combination of Torah and Art," *Bitzaron* — Quarterly review of Hebrew letters, *Riv'on Le'Sif'rut, Ha'gut, U'Mech'kar,* June-July 1958.

10 *Shi'rat Ha'Yam* — The song of the parting and crossing of the Red Sea (Exodus 15).

11 *A'se'ret Ha'Dib'rot* — the Ten Commandments.

12 *E'he'ye A'sher E'he'ye* — "I am that I am" — God's revelation of his name to Moses (Exodus 3, 14).

13 William Blake — English poet (1757 – 1827).

To the understanding heart — *Dai Le'Cha'ki'ma Bir'mi'za*[14] — a hint is sufficient; but the intellectual portion of wisdom is surely susceptible of communication. A flower may on occasion bloom in the desert in splendid isolation; but given a soil enriched by water and minerals, the probability of success infinitely increases. Stimulated by the vivid example of such success in modern Israel's battle against the desert, Glantz undertook to do similar battle against the wilderness that had engulfed synagogue music in the Garden of the Lord, in the absence of an organized program for the training of its chief gardeners — the cantors. Strange thorns and thistles were flourishing in the sacred precincts; the beauty of Israel's musical Eden was being choked by spasmodic pandering to popular taste; each flower of true *Nu'sach* struggled alone and unaided against the storms and wind and drought.

> *Stimulated by the vivid example of such success in modern Israel's battle against the desert, Glantz undertook to do similar battle against the wilderness that had engulfed synagogue music in the Garden of the Lord.*

With the collaboration of philosopher Dr. Yehuda Even-Shmuel Kaufman and writer Eliezer Steinman, Glantz established the Institute for Jewish Liturgical Music and the *Cantors Academy* in Tel-Aviv on the second day of the Hebrew month of *Sh'vat* in the year 5720; therein he set forth a program of education for cantors that would bring them the many facets of skill and knowledge that are truly required for a Jewish cantor in our day. To this end Glantz brought the rich background that he himself had acquired through the perceptive insights of his genius and years of research and experience — a background now uniquely available in *E'retz Yis'ra'el* through the historic ingathering of scholars and communities in one concentrated country. The course of study included general musical background and skills, Jewish music in its varied forms, the interrelationship between Jewish and general culture, the background of Jewish prayer and thought, the customs of folk culture of Jewish communities the world over; it represented Glantz's lifetime dream of a program to restore *Cha'za'nut* to its true position of dignity as a lofty spiritual and intellectual calling.

It was a belief in the power of the intellect, an almost Maimonidean contrast to the emotional Chasidism into which he was born, which drove Glantz to his research on the history of Jewish music. For as Eliezer Steinman pointed out in his column "The Last Sabbath" (*"Ha'Sha'bat Ha'Ach'ro'na"*), Glantz loved intellectual exchange almost as much as he loved music:

---

14 *Dai Le'Cha'ki'ma Bir'mi'za* — "a word to the wise is enough…"

"Leib Glantz possessed a generous heart and sought the good of his fellow man. He was therefore a man of words — 'come, let us discuss it' — he would say. He loved to listen and to hold forth, to raise questions and to offer solutions, to accept an insight and to convince. He believed in the power of logic and possessed a passion for argument, saying: 'everything requires clarification.'"[15]

It was perhaps this combination of intellectual and emotional love for Judaism that drew him, at the climax of his career, to the land of his fathers. In his youth, unlike most musicians, he did not withdraw from the struggles of community life. As a speaker, writer and editor, he was active in the leadership of *He'Cha'lutz* and *Tse'i'rei Zion,* Zionist youth movements. He retained his active interest in Zionism, its fund-raising and cultural programs, serving as a delegate to no less than eleven World Zionist Congresses. He visited Palestine numerous times.

When he was established in popular acclaim and economic security, he still sought fulfillment for the deeper yearnings of his soul; he accepted the invitation extended by Congregation *Tif'e'ret Zvi* to serve as its cantor in Tel-Aviv, crowning his career with the service to Israel so universally hailed by both the learned and the man in the crowded street.

Rabbi Yehoshua Ben Levi said: "He who sings in this world will sing also in the next." On *Sha'bbat Shi'ra,* in the year 5724, it was decided in the Congregation on High that a new singer was needed for the Heavenly Hosts; as the Sabbath departed, Leib Glantz, a lion of the Lord, was drafted for eternal service in the celestial choir. "The music that he made below is now the music of the spheres;" but the echo of the *Shchi'na*, the Divine Presence,[16] that we heard in his voice and sensed in his labors will live on in our hearts and memories for blessing, as the Psalms of David still stir our souls and the remembrance of a beloved melody lingers long after the strings are silent.

> *On* **Sha'bbat Shi'ra,** *in the year 5724, it was decided in the Congregation on High that a new singer was needed for the Heavenly Hosts; as the Sabbath departed, Leib Glantz, a lion of the Lord, was drafted for eternal service in the Celestial Choir.* *"The music that he made below is now the music of the spheres..."*

---

15 Eliezer Steinman — Israeli writer, *"The Last Sabbath,"* in the Hebrew daily newspaper *"Da'var,"* 1964.
16 In classic Jewish thought, The *Shchi'na* refers to the dwelling or settling of God, the Divine Presence.

9

Roots and Partitions

ELIEZER STEINMAN[1]

My first encounter with Leib Glantz was at the World Zionist Congress in Lucern, Switzerland, in 1935. I was told that he was a cantor from America as well as a delegate on behalf of the Labour Zionists — a very unusual combination.

Twelve years later in Israel, I went to hear him sing at the *O'hel Shem* auditorium in Tel Aviv. I was so moved that I went to every one of his appearances during his short visit to Israel, whether concert or synagogue prayer. I drank up his melodies with thirst and with yearning. Every time I heard him sing I was overcome by longing for them, as if any moment they were about to come to an end and lost to me forever. I embraced his tones of beauty and magical force. He created a yearning to embrace all the Sabbaths of my childhood that resurfaced in my mind one after another.

I loved listening to Glantz in song and prayer. The sweetness of his voice, the charm of his posture on the pulpit, his shocking cry, his silent voice — all coming from the very roots of his soul. He could sing with utter restraint, with controlled rebellion, with pride and humility.

He conducted dialogues with the Almighty, complaining and demanding on behalf of the congregation. He combined courage and fear when opening his mouth before God. He pronounced words in a way that served as an interpretation of their meaning. He had the unique ability to *speak* words with barely an inkling of music.

---

1 Eliezer Steinman — Writer and a leading figure in Israeli literary circles, was originally an extremely secular and anti-religious Israeli. Amid his contacts with Menachem Mendel Schneerson, the Lubavicher Rebbe, he wrote a monumental multi-volume work on the history and philosophy of Chasidism — *"Be'er HaChasidut."* After completing his research for this book, Steinman changed his entire outlook, publicly retracting his earlier writings and becoming a believing and practicing Jew. He was a great friend and admirer of Glantz. This translated and abridged essay was specially written by Steinman for the book *"Zeharim— In Memory of Leib Glantz"* (1965), which he himself edited.

> *While singing, his hands would reach out towards the heavens, transforming the prayer pulpit on which he stood into a spectacular sight, creating a sacred forum for his music.*

While singing, his hands would reach out towards the heavens, transforming the prayer pulpit on which he stood into a spectacular sight, creating a sacred forum for his music.

I loved hearing Glantz. His singing aroused in me longings for past beginnings. Through his voice, generations of Jews expressed their great achievements as well as their gloomy disasters. Hope and disappointment merged into one. He would bring me back to my origins — to the place where I was born, to my earliest days.

Glantz's singing was like a fairy tale. No human voice ever shocked the pillars of my soul as did his voice. No crying melody ever planted in me such shudders as did his cry. No silent whisper ever appeased me within the chaos of the creation as did his whisper. His rebelliousness did not cause disharmony to my ears and his plea did not shame my soul. When he called out *"Eich Nif'tach Peh"* ("how dare we open our mouths before Thee"), I sensed his fear for daring to speak out. The logic of a wise musician guided him to sing *"Shma Tsa'aka'tei'nu"* ("Hear our cries") in his composition *"A'na Be'Cho'ach,"* whispering and causing a trembling of our souls.

No one was as loyal to the *Nu'sach* and adherent to the traditional texts (*"Ma'so'rá"*). Not one crease of the Jewish soul was hidden from his eyes.

He was closer than anyone to the roots of the ancient melodies of the Israelites. The Holy Temple for Glantz was not just a thing of the distant past — an ancient and abstract symbol. He visualized it, lived in it and brought it to life in his melodies. His visions of ancient life, as he brought them to us, were tangible and sensual.

To understand Leib Glantz's unique qualities we must appreciate that he was intertwined with opposites and contradictions. He was a musician who religiously feared God and at the same time was a human being who deeply loved his fellow mankind. His mind and heart immersed in the spheres of pure music.

From his youngest days he honestly believed that he could simultaneously be active as a cantor as well as a Labor Zionist activist. He was very active in public life, constantly lecturing and participating in meetings and congresses. Unfortunately, being a Labor Zionist, he personified the opposition to all the other movements that were competing for the support of the Jewish public at that time.

Glantz, a brave man, refused to stand back. His soul demanded that he be active for his people and his country and he devoted most of his life to the Zionist cause. However, as strange as it may sound, in the eyes of his fellow activists, he was considered somewhat of an "intruder,"

Leib Glantz conducted the funeral service for Moshe Hess,[2] in the presence of Israel's Prime Minister David Ben Gurion, future Prime Ministers Moshe Sharett, Golda Meir, Levi Eshkol, President Zalman Shazar, Foreign Minister Abba Eban, and many of Israel's leaders (Jerusalem, 1961).

someone of whom "professional" activists must beware. His energy could be utilized by the movement, but he must not be given "privileges" and influence. Furthermore, since he was an activist who was not seeking financial advantages and salaries, he was free to speak his ideas and beliefs with no constraints. This was the kind of colleague who was feared.

With the declaration of Israel's independence in 1948, Glantz considered the national and political realization as a life potion for his Jewish creative talents. In a letter he wrote in his youth, he declared:

> A new light shines over Zion. Hopefully it will be blended with a light for *all* of the human race. I would like to reflect these connections in my music.

He devised the concept that the Jewish *ear* would benefit from the exaltation of Judaism:

> The Jewish ear is more devoted than the Jewish eye. The Greek culture, for example, was first and foremost a culture of sight — painting, sculpture and mask. The eye is worldly and sensual. The ear is more spiritual and abstract; therefore, in Judaism we consistently emphasize sounds.

---

2 Moshe Hess (1812-1875) was a Jewish philosopher and one of the founders of Socialism; he was a friend of Karl Marx and Friedrich Engels. In 1862 he wrote "Rome and Jerusalem," calling for a Jewish state. The book influenced such proponents of Zionism as Theodore Herzl. He was originally buried in 1875 in the Jewish cemetery in Cologne, Germany, but in 1961 he was re-interred in the Kinneret cemetery in Israel.

The cover of the book "Zeharim — In Memory of Leib Glantz," edited by Eliezer Steinman and David Vinitzky (Published in Tel Aviv in 1965).

Glantz was a warrior in a holy war. He had to confront those who totally disregarded and denied the existence of *Cha'za'nut* and Jewish music either because of their illiteracy or because of their mental backwardness. He had to confront those who rejected the idea of rejuvenating the prayers of Israel — those defenders of the derelict and neglected *Nu'sach* of the Jewish melodies. He also had to defend against those who contaminated Jewish music by introducing foreign elements, transforming the Hebrew prayers into a mongrel experience. And Glantz fought bravely against "renovators" who stripped from their melodies every aspect of Jewishness.

Glantz considered the insult to cantorial as a personal insult to himself. He once stated:

Cantorial is perhaps the most difficult art in the world. It contains secrets of secrets of secrets, all demanding complex explanations. Unfortunately, there are no Jewish musical critics among us who understand cantorial. At the same time we have numerous Jewish critics who can criticize Mozart. These same critics have not a clue regarding *Cha'za'nut*. There is not one critic who can appreciate the enormous revolution that was created thanks to the great compositions of Pinchas Minkowsky, Baruch Schorr, Boruch Leib Rozowsky and David Nowakowsky. Unfortunately, *non-Jewish* critics write about Jewish cantorial with deeper understanding than their Jewish counterparts! Personally, I consider *Cha'za'nut* a mission. When I stand before the ark, I endulge in our historical past and envision the future.

Glantz's dream was to combine the past and the future, blending the old with the new.

The great sin of the last generations is that *Cha'za'nut* has become superficial. Its tears, even if they are moist, are void of vitality, of charm and of melody. As Glantz explained:

There is a place for crying in certain prayers. However, one must cry in such a way that it will not make others laugh . . . Cantorial does represent the great tragedies of our people, but it does not call for hysterical sobbing. On the other hand cantorial promises a new kind of joy. But just as it is not proper to sob without measure, so it is improper to exaggerate with outbursts of joy. Uninhibited joyfulness is apt to deteriorate into debauchery . . .

Art demands self-restraint, self-criticism, refined sensitivity, forbearance and in-depth understanding. According to Glantz, cantorial is equivalent to a *Mik've Te'ha'ra* (a ritual bath): "It is the whip that beats on our souls and the hand that pulls out the weeds from our souls."

In a letter from 1924, the 26 year old Glantz writes from Kishinev:

You should have seen and heard me in these High Holidays. A great force burst out from inside me. The congregation of worshippers was shocked and all joined in my prayers. My soul almost yearned to expire from life! Why can't I pray just once all the way to the end of my life? How does my heart not explode?

Have words such as these ever been uttered by a cantor?

Glantz once called me, saying: "Come with me to pray. Come with me to cry. Perhaps the heavens will break open from our crying out…?"

> *"A great force burst out from inside me. The congregation of worshippers was shocked and all joined in my prayers. My soul almost yearned to expire from life! Why can't I pray just once all the way to the end of my life? How does my heart not explode?"*

Glantz was grieved and depressed due to the degradation of the synagogue in Israel. Synagogues were managed by a generation of officers (*Ga'ba'yim*) who had not the faintest idea about what constitutes true *Cha'za'nut*. These were mostly people who gained their positions due to their economic status. A man like Glantz could not mix with these people nor pray according to their lowly standards.

Glantz once wrote to Cantor Israel Alter:

How can we direct *Cha'za'nut* to a path of true inspiration, to seek the new truth of cantorial, the noble yearnings for its solemn true essence, to its warm flames, to the sparks of sacred fire and leaps to the heavens? How can we extricate our beloved *Cha'za'nut* from the banality of the swamps in which it is drowning, in order to bring it to a respectable spiritual level, such as it was in the days of the great cantor-composers of the past . . . ? How can we insert into cantorial some of the ancient charm as well as some of the beauty of our new world? I have just listened to the classical composition "Pictures at an Exhibition" by Mussorgsky[3] and I was fascinated! What richness of imagination and renewal Maurice Ravel added to its spirit!

The perplexity and dismay were enormous. The true prince of Jewish melody actually found the gates of the synagogue slowly locking before him. Narrow-minded people constricted his functionality. The synagogue prayer pulpits were evidently destined for the mediocre. They were too narrow to contain the greatest, the unique, the true artist.

Being a member of a secular political party,[4] he was naturally ostracized by the opposing religious parties, as well as by ultra-secular people who "excommunicated" Jewish prayer in its totality. So the man who expressed in his song generations of sadness and suffering, marched alone within his own generation. Glantz was indeed alone but he was not bitter. He was enraged but not angry.

Glantz was a true friend. Always open hearted, even if he kept his anguish to himself. When he spoke openly, there was always an inner quietness.

Glantz cut down the failing branches of the old Jewish music, and at the same time strengthened its roots, removed sick plots and rejuvenated healthy ones, creating new grafts with amazing new experiments. Being a genius of music as well as a genius of improvisation, he would not agree to dip into the same melodic spring more than once. He continuously discovered and composed new ideas for every prayer and every melody.

> *Being a genius of music as well as a genius of improvisation — he would not agree to dip into the same melodic spring more than once. He continuously discovered and composed new ideas for every prayer and every melody.*

We who drank from Glantz's perennial spring loved him. However, we did not really know him. It was impossible to know him and to reach up to him, just as it is impossible to hug our arms around a giant tree with an enormous trunk, whose branches are reaching up to the skies above. Glantz kept rising up the ladder, higher and higher. Once in a while we could catch a glimpse of him, as if it was the first time again and again. Is it at all possible to recognize and appreciate such a great man who constantly climbed upward on a giant ladder with no limits?

I saw him — but it was as if I did not see him. The miraculous cannot truly be seen!

---

3 Modest Mussorgsky (1839-1881) — a Russian composer. He composed the piano suite *Pictures at an Exhibition* (1874), later orchestrated by French composer Maurice Ravel (1875-1937).
4 *Ma'pai — Mif'le'get Po'a'lei E'retz Yis'ra'el* (The Party of the Workers of the Land of Israel).

10

The Final Sabbath

ELIEZER STEINMAN[1]

A day will come when the collection of melodies created by Leib Glantz, will become a torch to shine in a superior place on the altar of the Songs of Israel. New generations will realize that Glantz was like a holiday within our people, and his name and memory will be enshrined forever.

Leib Glantz was the champion of Jewish music. There was no one of his stature as an interpreter of the logic of the prayers. He did this while remaining truly loyal to our ancient prayer modes — the Jewish *Nu'sach*. With his death, the Pulpit of Prayer has been orphaned and our Temple of Music deserted.

> *New generations will realize that Glantz was like a holiday within our people, and his name and memory will be enshrined forever.*

Glantz's cohabitant in the Hall of Fame of cantorial greatness was Pinchas Minkowsky, one of the greatest cantors of the past. In the twentieth century there is no one even close to the stature of these giants. Both were high priests of the cantorial temple. Both devoted their lives

---

1 Eliezer Steinman — This is an article published in *Da'var,* the Israeli daily newspaper, following Leib Glantz's death in 1964. The translated article is abridged. Steinman, a writer and leading figure in Israeli literary circles was an extremely secular and anti-religious Israeli. Amid contacts with Menachem Mendel Schneerson, the Lubavicher Rebbe, he wrote a monumental multi-volume work on the history and philosophy of Chasidism — *Be'er Ha'Cha'si'dut.* After completing his research, Steinman changed his entire outlook, publicly retracting his earlier writings and becoming a believing and practicing Jew. He was a great friend and admirer of Glantz and editor of the book *"Zeharim— In Memory of Leib Glantz"* (1965).

President of Israel, Zalman Shazar, writer and close friend Eliezer Steinman, and Leib Glantz at the opening of the Tel Aviv Institute for Jewish Liturgical Music and its Cantors Academy in Tel Aviv, 1959.

to refine and perfect the *Nu'sach,* to purify and raise it to the sacred echelon it deserved. Both were wise and scholarly. Both despised forgery, contamination by foreign elements, and unnecessary sobbing. Both were illustrious interpreters of the texts.

Of the two, I believe Leib Glantz surpassed Minkowsky with the force of his emotion, the depth of his achievements and the complexity of his compositions. Glantz was more daring in his attitude toward the Almighty. He bombarded and attacked, causing the hearts of his listeners to tremble. His chanting was an outpouring of his soul. He proudly stood on the prayer pulpit before God the Almighty, ready to accept God's decrees, but at the same time stubbornly demanding logical reasoning for God's deeds toward mankind. He could express fury and rage without a hint of frustration.

> *He proudly stood on the prayer pulpit before God the Almighty, ready to accept God's decrees, but at the same time stubbornly demanding logical reasoning for God's deeds toward mankind.*

Glantz was a phenomenal artist who knew how to engage his powerful voice in order to express his musical interpretations. Wisely, as no one else could, he shocked the chords of our hearts with silent sounds, gentle whispers and even whispers of whispers.

Minkowsky and Glantz passed away on the same date, exactly 40 years apart, both 65 years old. Significantly, they died on *Sha'bbat Shi'ra* (Sabbath of Song)!

Were Pinchas Minkowsky and Leib Glantz the last great cantors of our great Jewish nation?

11

A Poet at Heart

Prof. Yehuda Even-Shmuel Kaufman[1]

Leib Glantz was a poet at heart — a heart overflowing with song. He sang a psalm of love to Israel's prayers, its music, its festivals, its *To'rah* and its faith.

In a sense, his singing was but a manifestation of the poetry in his heart. He saw the world in terms of poetry, and people who could transcend themselves through song. The "People of Israel" represented for Glantz the "Song of God." The Israel renaissance in Zion was symbolized for him in the words: "O sing unto the Lord a new song!"

Can we comprehend the magnitude of Glantz's love for the Jewish people as they stand before God? Who can describe his admiration of Israel's festivals and of the light radiating from Israel's *To'rah* and customs?

> *Who among us who has heard Glantz's prayers can free himself of the impression that here stood a man whose whole soul was invested in every word he uttered?*

Who among us who has heard Glantz's prayers can free himself of the impression that here stood a man whose whole soul was invested in every word he uttered? In the same way as Rabbi Akiva's school dealt with the *Ha'la'cha*, finding an interpretation for every

---

1 From the introduction to the Leib Glantz book of music "*Ha'llel* and Three Festivals" *(Ha'llel Ve'Sha'losh Re'ga'lim)* from the series of selected works *"Ri'nat Ha'Ko'desh,"* ed. David Loeb, published by The Tel Aviv Institute of Jewish Liturgical Music in conjunction with the Israel Music Institute, Tel Aviv, Israel, 1968. Professor Yehuda Even-Shmuel Kaufman, a great scholar, philosopher and writer of numerous books, was a close friend of Leib Glantz. He was a co-founder of The Tel Aviv Institute for Jewish Liturgical Music and its Cantors Academy.

60

ornamentation on every letter in every measure, so this outstanding musician dealt with melody, the ornamentation in his case being converted to musical tones, each of which he invested with a new, rich quality.

His style was so different from the accepted melodies in the cantorial world, that some claimed that he was "not one of us!" However, in opposition to some ignorant cantors, musicians and musicologists, the Jewish masses proclaimed clearly: "Leib Glantz's style is our style!"

Many generations will be grateful to Glantz for having restored the Major modes to our liturgy, which had been dominated by the Minor mode as a result of the many tribulations endured in the Diaspora, to the point where even the *Ha'llel* service was sung in the Minor key. There is no doubt that this contribution by Glantz will be recognized as having refreshed the Jewish soul and paved the way to new creativity.

But even in Glantz's prayers, on Sabbaths and on holidays, the Minor mode does have its proper place. Whenever there were prayers of supplication, the pathos was heartrending. He who had fought a holy war against liturgical lachrymosity when it was out of place — how great he was when he wept, how precious to him every tear he shed and every tear shed by those who heard him!

In one of the legends about the destruction of the Temple it is related that God said to the prophet Jeremiah: "Go and call Abraham, Isaac, Jacob and Moses — for they know how to weep!" It may be said of Glantz that he knew how to weep and how to bring others to tears. After hearing the service as sung by Glantz, young and old would come out of the synagogue shaken to the depths of their being, shaken — but spiritually elevated.

> *It may be said of Glantz that he knew how to weep and how to bring others to tears. After hearing the service as sung by Glantz, young and old would come out of the synagogue shaken to the depths of their being. Shaken but spiritually elevated.*

Glantz lived in a generation that had devoted its life to the love of the people of Israel, to aspiration for the rebirth of the land of Israel, and faith in the renaissance of the life of the Jewish people in their country. It was a generation of dauntless people who renewed a great deal in the life of the nation — a generation that revived the Hebrew language as its national tongue, an achievement not accomplished by generations of Jewish scholars such as the Tannaites, the Ammoraites, the *Pay'ta'nim* and the poets.

Leib Glantz with his great friend and admirer, Professor Yehuda Even-Shmuel Kaufman, at the opening of the Tel Aviv Institute for Jewish Liturgical Music and its Cantors Academy in Tel Aviv, 1959.

It was this generation that Glantz addressed, calling its sons to come to the synagogue to pray with him. Young people rediscovered their own music — the music of God — finding that it throbs in their hearts as it throbbed in the hearts of their fathers before them. Even the elders felt that Glantz had become a bridge between themselves and their sons, spanning the gap between generations that came before, and the generations yet to come.

Swept from Celestial Heights to Abysmal Depths

DR. BARUCH BEN-YEHUDA[1]

I can hear his vibrant and dynamic voice. This was the voice that knew when to rejoice, when to cry out in pain, when to plead, when to demand, when to threaten, and when to bow to the inevitable. This was cantor Leib Glantz.

How marvelously he created that rare synthesis of the startlingly new and the truly traditional, escaping the routine and the banal and yet remaining completely faithful and true to Jewish tradition and to Jewish *Nu'sach*.

What treasures we find in his work! One is swept from celestial heights to abysmal depths, and begins to experience that strange transfiguration which is the essence of Jewish mysticism.

> *What treasures we find in his work! One is swept from celestial heights to abysmal depths, and begins to experience that strange transfiguration which is the essence of Jewish mysticism.*

This is the strength and power of a truly great composer: each of us finds what he needs and what he seeks, as he sings or plays or listens to the music. Worshippers will be inspired by the fiery soaring religiosity of Glantz's works, and music lovers will discover the provocative originality and rare wealth of expression.

---

1 From the introduction by Dr. Baruch Ben-Yehuda to the Leib Glantz book of music "Friday Evening Service" (*Te'fi'lot Leil Sha'bbat*) from the series of selected works *Ri'nat Ha'Ko'desh,* ed. David Loeb, published by The Tel Aviv Institute of Jewish Liturgical Music in conjunction with the Israel Music Institute. Tel Aviv, Israel, 1967.

The Greatest Innovative and Creative Cantor
of the Twentieth Century

CANTOR CHAIM FEIFEL[1]

It was like a dream. I had been given the opportunity to study with the greatest innovative and creative cantor of the twentieth century. Cantor Leib Glantz agreed to give me lessons in cantorial art in the winter of 1958.

My journey in search of Cantor Glantz began when I was a fourth year student at the Cantorial School of the Jewish Theological Seminary in New York. There I was exposed to Glantz's cantorial recitatives. Of all the wonderful cantors, Glantz attracted my heart and intellect more than any other. I felt a great urge to meet him and study his creative capacities. I believed that he was the only person who could enhance my knowledge of this great art. Therefore, after my graduation from the seminary, I traveled to Israel to seek him out.

Our first meeting took place at his home on Keren Kayemet Boulevard in Tel Aviv.[2] I felt somewhat intimidated being in his presence. His stature was impressive. I was too young to grasp the enormous extent of his creative powers, but I was immediately inspired by his personality. Glantz was very curious about my cantorial schooling, asking questions about the curriculum and the quality and character of the studies at the seminary. His interest most probably stemmed from his desire to create his own cantorial school in Israel, which was established a few years later.

---

1 Cantor Chaim Feifel is a graduate of the Cantorial School of the Jewish Theological Seminary in New York. Upon graduation he spent a year in Israel, studying at the Rubin Academy of Music and privately with Cantor Leib Glantz. He served as cantor of various congregations in the U.S. for twenty years and received a Masters degree in Rehabilitation Counseling. Following A'li'ya to Israel, the Feifel family was one of the pioneers of the Sinai city of Yamit. He is a highly respected teacher of Cha'za'nut at the Tel Aviv Cantorial Institute (TACI) and at the Cantorial School of the Hebrew Union College in Jerusalem.

2 Keren Kayemet Boulevard was changed to Ben Gurion Boulevard in 1973 following the death of David Ben Gurion, Israel's first Prime Minister, at age 87.

In order to appraise the quality of my voice he asked me to chant a recitative. Then he asked me to sight-read some music. At first he gave me something simple, followed by more complicated materials. I was thrilled when he decided to take me on as a student, and he offered to forego the tuition if I sang in his choir at the *Tif'e'ret Zvi* synagogue in Tel Aviv.

The lessons took place in his home. I felt as if I were on a journey to a different dimension — as if Glantz was revealing to me all the hidden secrets of *Cha'za'nut*. For him, a creative person needed to be, like the biblical story of Jacob's ladder, with feet firmly on the ground and mind and soul reaching up into the heavens. Glantz definitely had his feet on the ground, but he could soar to the heavens — creating exciting *Cha'za'nut* that was capable of raising the worshipper along with him to an ecstatic vision of God! In order to truly appreciate Leib Glantz, one has to understand that his music and prayers penetrate the heavens. His creative energies permeated my soul and changed my life and my attitude towards my profession. At the time, Glantz had taught me not only to become an authentic cantor, but also to become a teacher of *Cha'za'nut* without my being aware of it!

> *Glantz . . . could soar to the heavens — creating exciting* Cha'za'nut *that was capable of raising the worshipper along with him to an ecstatic vision of God!*

At the time it was difficult for me to grasp everything that he tried to teach me. Yet as the years passed, his spirit and his intentions became vividly clear to me. There was pure divinity in his voice. All one had to do was open one's soul in order to feel the divine spark in his music.

I have been asked numerous times what it was like to study with Leibele Glantz. He was an exceptional teacher. He always knew how to elevate me to a higher level, to spiritually charge my soul. With each session I absorbed some of his energy. He infused me with *his* truth; he encouraged me to be totally independent, to be brave in expressing my inner soul. Glantz lived his life exactly that way and I felt vibrantly alive during every moment of studying with him.

My teacher gave me the capacity to understand the mysteries of cantorial art. Many cantors emotionally express the beauty of our art, but, unfortunately, have little knowledge regarding the essence of their performance. Glantz succeeded in making me attuned to the depth of our traditional language.

Our first lessons were not easy. Glantz was looking to pinpoint my strengths and weaknesses — to become more familiar with what I actually knew. As our sessions continued, he wanted to teach me some of his own compositions, but after a while he realized that I didn't possess the voice range to do justice to them. We then agreed to work on material that I was more familiar with. Through that music, he taught me how to apply his own principles of *Cha'za'nut*. He seemed to appreciate the opportunity to work with material that other cantors had composed. It was amazing to witness the ease with which Glantz approached this materi-al — recitatives composed by cantors such as Israel Alter, Max Wohlberg and Adolph Katchko. He appreciated their musical intelligence and mastery of *Nu'sach*. He taught me how to use discrimination and to have the courage to challenge faults and mistakes of *Nu'sach* in the chants that I had previously been taught.

He always challenged me with difficult questions — forcing me to think. On one memorable occasion, I had used a typical "sobbing effect" while singing *Le'Dor Va'Dor*. He asked why I was crying. I replied that the musical motif seemed to justify it. He gave me a detailed expla-nation why the traditional motif was simply incorrect! There was really no justification to cry this text because the prayer expresses a very positive thought. He added that since the Jewish people have finally returned to *E'retz Yis'ra'el*, the land of their forefathers, there is no reason for excessive tear shedding. The truth is that *Le'Dor Va'Dor* is in fact a positive prayer — prais-ing the Lord. Glantz was of the opinion that *Cha'za'nut*, because of the tragic nature of Jewish history, had incorporated unnecessary qualities of self-pity, excessive sentimentality, tearful-ness, and schmaltziness. From that day on I ceased to employ unnecessary "sobbing effects" in my chants.

In one of our lessons I sang an abundance of *coloratura*[3] patterns. Glantz asked me what my reasoning was for this. The question caught me by surprise and I had no logical answer. He constantly reminded me that I must think about everything I do and become more aware of every aspect of the text. He then laid out what amounted to his theory of *coloratura*. He explained that in addition to using it for ornamentation, *coloratura* could be used to arouse the worshipper to pray. It could also be used to emphasize a very meaningful word. Often, the *coloratura* is sung on a single-syllable word in order to emphasize the word that follows. After this penetrating exposition I grasped his intention in the opening proclamation of his classic composition *She'ma Yis'ra'el*: The opening *coloratura* he used on the word *She'ma* was intended to arouse the worshipper and at the same time emphasize the word that followed — *Yis'ra'el*. Glantz had great admiration for certain words. *"Yis'ra'el"* was one of these words. We spent sev-eral wonderful sessions on how to employ different aspects of the *coloratura*.

Cantorial song is fundamentally an "*a cappella*" art — music without any instrumental accom-paniment. There-fore, we worked on creating varieties of contrast, on thematic balance and timing — elements that hold the chant together. We delved into spacing, phrasing, tempo changes, dynamics, and above all — the importance of the words themselves. In many cases,

---

3 *Coloratura* is the elaborate ornamentation of a vocal melody.

> *In many cases, the older generation of cantors often sang prayers in which the word served the music. Glantz emphasized, over and over again, that the music must serve the words.*

the older generation of cantors often sang prayers in which the word served the music. Glantz emphasized over and over again that the music must serve the words. He made me keenly aware of the deeper meanings of words and of the different ways to express them, in order to enlighten the spirit of the worshipper. Often we hear cantors who do not give any serious thought to the content of what they are singing. Glantz tried to teach me to use speech voice ("*Sprechstimme*") as a basic form in the prayer service. This, for him, was one of the essences of Davening.[4]

We also discussed the importance of improvisation and how it relates to Davening. He would tell me that improvisation is a wonderful way of expression, bringing the cantor into a here-and-now mood so that he becomes totally immersed in the prayer. Glantz was a master of improvisation. I especially love the opening of his composition *Mit'ra'tze Be'Ra'cha'mim*, in essence a tone poem in which he uses a "Davening" style, praying partly aloud and partly to oneself. An intense mood is created in which the listener can sense the depths of the worshipper's supplication, humbly begging God for forgiveness.

He systematically guided me to understand important concepts that helped me overcome difficulties in using the speech dynamic in chanting a prayer. He encouraged me to read and recite the words, in order to better understand the rhythms of the text. He would then ask me to sing the texts in the same rhythmic patterns as I originally read them. These were the exercises that really taught me the art of Davening.

It was not always easy to understand Glantz's unique way of manipulating the *Nu'sach*. I asked him why he frequently prayed in ways that were not what was considered traditional *Nu'sach*. Here was his colorful answer: "At the beach, the lifeguards usually set up ropes so that swimmers can be safe from drowning. The really good swimmers go beyond the ropes, into the vast ocean, in order to enjoy a great swim. It is there that they can be as creative as they want. Eventually they always return to the safe area. The safe area is the equivalent of the 'traditional' *Nu'sach*…"

Glantz was very bold with his innovations. There were worshippers who found it difficult to accept his unique style. The way he interpreted the prayer texts and his use of rhythm probably came across somewhat differently from what some people were accustomed to. They wanted to pray in a way that was familiar to them, that reminded them of their past in the Diaspora. These worshippers and lovers of *Cha'za'nut* probably did have their feet solidly on

---

4 Davening — an Anglicized Yiddish word: to recite Jewish liturgical prayers.

the ground, but were not capable of following Glantz to the upper realms of heaven. His fellow cantors, on the other hand, widely admired him. He was often referred to as the *Cha'zan* of the *Cha'za'nim* — the cantor of the cantors.

Cantors such as Israel Alter, Max Wohlberg and Adolf Katchko were able to successfully combine East European *Nu'sach* with Western *Nu'sach*. Glantz was on a different track. His dream was to create a legitimate and authentic Israeli *Nu'sach* that would combine Israeli art and folk elements with traditional *Nu'sach*. His composition *A'hav'ti* from the *Ha'llel* prayer service is a fine example. It starts in a creative poetic mood, in a minor key, and leads the listener to actively imagine that he is overhearing a personal conversation between the cantor and God: "I would love if the Lord would listen to my voice, to my supplications." Glantz preached adamantly that the *Ha'llel* prayers should be sung in the Major musical mode. Yet he himself used the Minor mode for most of *A'hav'ti*, because the somber text called for it. At the conclusion of the prayer, Glantz surprisingly creates a dramatic musical change, reverting back to the traditional East European *Nu'sach* in a very forceful manner. At first it does not seem to be in character with the composition's mood. However, when one analyzes the text, the transition becomes logically appropriate. He reverts back to Major when he arrives at the final optimistic words — *Et'ha'lech Lif'nei Ha'Shem Be'Ar'tzot Ha'Cha'im* ("I shall walk before the Lord in the lands of the living") — words that are a cause for rejoicing. Glantz knew exactly what he was doing: the text here definitely justifies this positive optimistic reversal.

> *Glantz's dream was to create a legitimate and authentic Israeli* Nu'sach *that would combine Israeli art and folk elements with traditional prayer modes.*

Glantz was well on his way in his quest to synthesize Israeli art songs with traditional *Nu'sach*. His untimely death at age sixty-six left his endeavor unfinished. As a Zionist leader, he frequently expressed joy that the Jewish people were able to return to Israel, their homeland. He strove to preserve the ancient Jewish musical traditions while finding a way to connect them with the new Israeli experience, so as to form a beautiful new musical language. Unfortunately, until this day there has been no one of his stature who could continue from the point where he left off.

Glantz's composition, *She'va Pe'a'mim A'ta* ("Seven Times 'Thou'") is the most dramatic demonstration of his deep understanding of *Nu'sach*. Glantz recites seven unrelated prayers that begin with the word *A'ta* (Thou), each of which is associated with a different *Nu'sach*, improvising appropriately on each one. This composition was originally improvised at the spur of the moment during a concert with several cantors at Carnegie Hall in New York in the

1940s. The composition is a classic lesson for anyone who wants to understand the different Jewish prayer modes.

Glantz was constantly engaged in serious research in an effort to uncover the historical origins of Jewish music in general, and specifically the prayer modes. He stubbornly sought to trace the origins parallel to Jewish history, as far back as the era of the Holy Temples of Jerusalem, an almost impossible task.

> *Glantz was constantly engaged in serious research in an effort to uncover the historical origins of Jewish music in general, and specifically the prayer modes. He stubbornly sought to trace the origins parallel to Jewish history, as far back as the era of the Holy Temples of Jerusalem.*

Eventually, I had to return to the United States to begin my career as a cantor. To this day I regret that I had to cease studying with Cantor Glantz after a short period of only eight months. Back in America, I realized how much I missed his instruction, his high-powered energy, and his intensity. Most of all, I missed the warm bonding that was established between us.

For the next twenty years, as I served as a cantor in America, Glantz's spirit never really left me. People would often mention that my Davening reminded them of Glantz. I believe that Leib Glantz saw in me one who potentially could continue to develop his path.

When my wife and I decided to live in Israel, I realized that I was really following in Glantz's footsteps. In Israel I have been teaching *Cha'za'nut* for the past twenty-three years. In the process of teaching, I came to realize that Glantz had an enormous impact on me. As a teacher I am filled with his energy. His spirit is very much alive in me, and I teach my students in the same spirit as he taught me. Each and every student of mine absorbs Glantz's spirit and principles. Some of these students are not even aware of the source of this unique energy. Nevertheless, my students carry his spirit, and in the future these students will transfer to their students the same spirit and principles. They will benefit indirectly from the man whom I consider the most creative cantor of the twentieth century. His soul is definitely bound with the spirit of the living. His contributions continue to live on in many ways. He has truly enriched my life and thanks to him I will continue to dedicate myself to the advancement of his intentions. My dream eventually turned into a reality.

14

My Great Teacher

CANTOR CHAIM ADLER[1]

In the early 1960s, my father, Rabbi Zvi Adler, recorded Cantor Leib Glantz's "Midnight *Se'li'chot* Service" from the radio. It was broadcast on *Kol Yis'ra'el*, the Israeli national radio station. He told me: "Listen to Glantz, and carefully follow the text along with the music." I was amazed to hear such exciting sounds. This was music I had never heard before. Today, I realize that I was experiencing the most profound expression of *Cha'za'nut*. This divine music rings in my heart and soul to this very day.

> *I was amazed to hear such exciting sounds.*
> *This was music I had never heard before.*
> *I realize that I was experiencing the most profound expression of* Cha'za'nut.
> *This divine music rings in my heart and soul to this very day.*

I was determined to become a distinguished cantor. Even though I was already officiating as a cantor, I enrolled at the Cantors Academy of the Tel Aviv Institute for Jewish Liturgical Music that was founded by Glantz. I had made up my mind that I wanted to follow Glantz's unique path and not the styles of other *Cha'za'nim*. Many of the students of the Cantors Academy actually evolved to become famous musicians.

Glantz constructed a curriculum that strove to develop cantors and musicians with inspiring personalities, capable of understanding the deeper meanings of the prayers. He wanted his students to become individuals who could master the ancient prayer modes (*Nu'sach*) as well as

---

1 Chaim Adler — Cantor of the City of Tel Aviv, Israel. He officiates at the Great Synagogue in Tel Aviv and at Congregation *Ahavath Torah* in Englewood, New Jersey. An ordained Rabbi who studied at the Hevron Yeshiva in Jerusalem, he was a student at Leib Glantz's Cantors Academy at the Tel Aviv Institute for Jewish Liturgical Music.

to become highly professional musicians.

Thanks to his prominence in society, as a musician, a scholar, and an intellectual, Glantz attracted the most qualified teachers and lecturers in the country. It was considered an honor to be a member of the faculty. Professor Yehuda Even-Shmuel Kaufman from the Hebrew University in Jerusalem lectured on *Jewish Philosophy*; Professor David Margalit of the Tel-Aviv University taught *Origins and Laws of Jewish Prayer*; Dr. Michael Pearlman instructed *Musical Cantillation of the To'rah*; Dr. Zvi Keren of Tel-Aviv University's Music School lectured on *Music*; Maestro Yehoshua Zohar taught *Choir Conducting*; and Rosa Damph coached *Voice Development*. Others famous teachers were the composer Paul Ben-Haim, Menashe Ravina, Dr. Haim Bar-Dayan, Aryeh Graff, and Dr. Herzl Shmueli.

Leib Glantz's penetrating and inspiring lectures were the highlight of our studies. He focused on the musical scales of the different prayer modes, explaining and demonstrating the complicated tones and intervals appropriate for each and every prayer service.

The students sensed that their mentor was a musical genius, offering insights into the complex secrets of Jewish music in particular and music in general. Indeed Glantz's research into the origins of Jewish music gave the world solid conclusions that withstand any criticism to this day.

I will always remember his very first lecture regarding the Pentatonic scale. He demonstrated the scale using only the black keys on the piano. These are the same tones used for the cantillation of the *To'rah*.[2] He then moved on to analyze the holy books of the Prophets and the *Me'gi'lot* (scrolls), leading us to an amazing encounter with Jewish music from the earliest periods of our history.

Once I asked him to explain to our class what was the correct *Nu'sach* for praying for rain, *Te'fi'lat Ge'shem*. His advice to me was to study the text of the prayer, after which he would test

---

2 Cantillation of the bible: (Hebrew: *Ta`a'mei Ha'Mik'ra)*; The primary purpose of the cantillation signs is to guide the chanting of the sacred texts during public worship.

my comprehension of the words. After having been satisfied with my interpretation, he encouraged me to try to compose my own music for the prayer. That was Glantz's secret — his striving to understand the true meaning of each and every word of the prayer texts. Music was his unique way of interpreting the words.

In Glantz's lectures at the Cantors Academy, he would explain the prevalent mistakes often made in *Nu'sach* and in interpretation. He analyzed the compositions of the great cantors and composers of former generations such as Nissi Belzer, Yerucham Hakatan, Pinchas Minkowsky, Avraham Rozovsky, and David Brod, to name a few. According to Glantz, these men were not only great cantors and composers; they were also individuals with great personalities and intelligence.

Every composition that Glantz created was unique. Each had its special nuances, modulations, intervals, musical architecture, and artistic subtlety. In *A'hav'ti* ("I love that the lord heareth my voice and my supplications") from the *Ha'llel* prayer service, he opens with a delicate *pianissimo* and follows with very confident demands of God. His version of the *Ha'llel* service was very different from anything that was written before. In his *Te'fi'lat Tal* (Prayer for Dew), the music almost enables one to smell the scents of springtime!

As students, we learned from Glantz that cantorial has two main purposes: to coach and lead the worshippers in prayer and to faithfully represent the worshippers before God Almighty. Every person that has ever witnessed his prayer services in the synagogue felt immersed in a passionate river of flames.

For Leib Glantz — every word in every prayer was meaningful and important. Glantz was the first to emphasize this, and he influenced many cantors, composers and singers to follow his path. We intimately describe this as "the Glantz thought process."

> *For Leib Glantz — every word in every prayer was important and meaningful. Glantz was the first to emphasize that, and he influenced many cantors, composers and singers to follow this path, intimately described as the "Glantz Thought Process."*

Leib Glantz treated each and every one of his students with love and warmth, as if they were his own sons. He considered each and every student a treasure. I was invited to his home numerous times to discuss *Cha'za'nut* — a memorable experience. He enjoyed passing on his precious knowledge to others.

Today, every lover of cantorial art recognizes Leib Glantz's greatness. Similar to many other great artists — he was far ahead of his time. In my heart, he will always live on as a heroic image, a great man whose path every cantor should follow.

15

In the Pantheon of the Greatest

CANTOR SAMUEL FORDIS[1]

I first became aware of *Cha'zan* Leib Glantz (endearingly called Leibele) in 1935 in Los Angeles, California. It was Sabbath and he Davened[2] at the Breed Street *Shul*, the largest Orthodox synagogue in the very densely populated Jewish community of Boyle Heights, Los Angeles. Many of the outstanding cantors in the United States were invited to officiate there.

I was a young teenager, and I was deeply moved by the impressive beauty of Glantz's lyric tenor. He had a unique musical style that was not only passionate, but also truly mesmerizing.

The next time I heard him was on a Sabbath in 1941. Glantz officiated as cantor of the only Conservative synagogue in Los Angeles — Sinai Temple. His organist was Lillian Klass, who accompanied him in his many public concerts.

In 1948, I joined his male quartet at the Orthodox *Sha'a'rei Te'fi'la* synagogue in the Western Fairfax area of Los Angeles. I sang in this choir till 1952. Glantz would officiate once a month, before an immensely appreciative congregation.

One of his choral compositions, "*U'Ve'nu'cho Yo'mar,*" was based on the Pentatonic scale. This was a markedly unique creation. I was fascinated by this work. I recall discussing it with him, asking him about the unusual roaming bass part and the unique vocal lines. We always held a common respect for each other's musical knowledge and enjoyed our discussions.

---

1 Cantor Samuel Fordis — cantor, composer, violinist and teacher of *Cha'za'nut.*
2 Davened — an originally exclusively Yiddish verb meaning "pray;" it is widely used by Ashkenazic Orthodox Jews. This has become the Anglicized "Davening."

Sinai Temple, Los Angeles, California, 1942. Leib Glantz officiated as chief cantor at Sinai Temple from 1941 till 1946.

I recall his lecturing on the musical theory of liturgical chant to young students at the University of Judaism in Los Angeles, an adjunct of the Jewish Theological Seminary of New York. One of the statements that he made remains in my consciousness to this day. He was asked by a student, "What constitutes the *Sha'bbat Nu'sach* scale or mode?" Glantz patiently explained that the appropriate musical mode was called "*A'ha'va Ra'bbah.*" He pointed out that if one sings the Chasidic melody "*Ha'va Na'gi'la,*" the "*A'ha'va Ra'bbah*" scale is exactly similar to that melody. He also pointed out that this scale is of relatively new vintage, most probably extracted from the Mongol invasion of Eastern Europe. He referred to this mode as the "love child" of the Jewish people.

Glantz's mesmerizing ability was demonstrated many times during my choral experience with him. In particular, I must speak of his overwhelming power of expression during one *Pe'ssach* holiday in the *Ha'llel* prayer service. He produced what I refer to as his liturgical *aria,* "*A'hav'ti,*" from Psalm 116. Here he improvised the most technically difficult and emotionally moving exposition that I have ever experienced. He sang continuously for eight solid minutes. The eight members of the choir were so moved by his singing that when, in the *coda* section of the prayer, we were supposed to sing the *finale,* not one of us could sing a note. Our throats and our lungs

> *The eight members of the choir were so moved by his singing that when, in the* coda *section of the prayer, we were supposed to sing the* finale, *not one of us could sing a note. Our throats and our lungs were so immobilized by his majestic interpretation that we were simply incapable of singing . . .*

were so immobilized by his majestic interpretation that we were simply incapable of singing. Ben Pollack, our conductor, in desperation, attempted to sing, but was incapable of making anything more than a squeak, and, unfortunately, this produced a small ripple of laughter from some of the congregants. Following the service, I apologized to Glantz for our inability to intone the *finale*, but he was kind to dismiss the error, seemingly understanding our plight . . .

In my youth, I studied *Cha'za'nut* with my father, who himself was a fine cantor. As an adult, I extended my Chazanic knowledge with the revered Morris Forster. Glantz was well aware of my desire to become a cantor. He invited me to appear at a *Sha'bbat* service at his synagogue. Following my service, his comment was that I had ability, feeling and a quality tenor voice. He advised me not to use hand movements when vocally expressing myself, something of which, at the time, I was completely unaware, and I was truly grateful.

I studied Glantz's style diligently during my years of serving in his choir and utilized many of his ideas. In January 1952, I began my 46-year career as a cantor in Los Angeles. I learned from Glantz how to express my emotions musically, how to employ different intonations to express various feelings, how to produce drama in the rendition of the prayers and how to create intervals that were different from the standard ones traditionally used in *Cha'za'nut*. This allowed me to create a unique individuality in my vocal expression.

I was cantor at Valley Beth Shalom Congregation for twenty years. I remember meeting a young man who had just emigrated from Israel to Los Angeles. After hearing me pray one Sabbath, he told me that he was an avid admirer of Leib Glantz, having prayed in his synagogue in Tel Aviv for a number of years. His comments on my Davening truly pleased me. He stated that of all the cantors he had heard in America, I was the only one who reminded him of the style of Leib Glantz.

In the scope of historical Chazanic achievement, my belief is that Glantz's contribution to the art of *Cha'za'nut* will be evaluated in the pantheon of the greatest! It was a privilege to have known him and to have had the opportunity to learn so much from him.

16

A Daring and Brave Innovator

Maestro Schlomo Goldhour[1]

I was blessed with the great honor of working with Cantor Leib Glantz. I was his first choir conductor upon his arrival in Israel in 1954.

In Yiddish, Leib means lion, and Glantz means shining. He fought like a lion for his strict principles, creating innovations and introducing them to the world of cantorial. Moreover, he proved to be an artist of the highest degree, shining and lighting up every service, making it a unique experience.

On the eve of his arrival in Israel, Glantz wrote to the officers of the *Tif'e'ret Zvi* synagogue, listing the choir conductors he would be interested in working with and his requirements as to the quality of the choir. The singers were required to be capable of reading musical notes and possess cultured voices. It was not at all difficult to comply with his wishes, as every singer in Israel considered it a privilege to be part of the choir of the great Leib Glantz. The list of candidates was long, and the very best were chosen. Some of these singers were members of the famous "*Kol Zion La'Go'la*" choir of the Israel Broadcasting Authority in Jerusalem.

> *Every singer in Israel considered it a privilege to be part of the choir of the great Leib Glantz.*

---

1 Maestro Schlomo Goldhour — a leading Israeli musician and choir leader who assembled and conducted Glantz's choir during his first year in Israel (1954-1955).

Many went on to become famous conductors and musicians highly respected in Israel and around the world.

My first encounter with Glantz upon his arrival in Israel took place in my parents' apartment in Jerusalem, where our first rehearsal took place. The word spread quickly from mouth to ear that Cantor Leibele Glantz would be arriving for a choir rehearsal, and the garden of our house was much too small to accommodate the hundreds of gathering admirers.

At this first choir rehearsal, Glantz praised the quality of the singing, but added: "What is missing in your singing is an authentic expression of emotion. You need to be capable of intellectually penetrating into the prayer's textual content."

Glantz's compositions were not easy to perform. They were courageous and demanding, filled with luster and musical inspiration. I studied these compositions very seriously, sitting next to Glantz at the piano for hours, patiently analyzing every piece, articulating every aspect, concentrating on every motif, and interpreting every musical phrase. A whole new world was opening before my eyes. I suddenly realized the banality of the cantorial that I was accustomed to, which possessed external beauty, but was actually very superficial.

> *A whole new world was opening before my eyes. I suddenly realized the banality of the cantorial that I was accustomed to, which possessed external beauty, but was actually very superficial.*

Glantz was a true guardian of the traditional prayer modes (*Nu'sach Ha'Te'fi'la*). He created a mode of his own, which we called "*Nu'sach* Glantz." It was brave and rich, loaded with new and meaningful interpretations to the words of the prayers. He was constantly innovating. His contribution to the art of cantorial was enormous. Glantz was a unique commentator, paving a modern path for cantorial.

Glantz's courageous spacing, his surprising modulations and his exciting motifs gained him recognition as a unique composer with a totally new method and an original style in the world of cantorial. The Midnight *Se'li'chot* Service composed by Glantz was completely original, different from the *Se'li'chot* service of any other cantor. The first reaction of traditional cantorial admirers was somewhat negative, describing it as "a daring and misunderstood reform." However, more and more of those who were capable of comprehending the poetic content of the *Se'li'chot* prayers appreciated the depth of these emotional expressions of the soul. Today, the Glantz *Se'li'chot* service is considered by all as the epitome of cantorial musical expression.

Working with Cantor Glantz revolutionized my musicality. I found myself on a new and original path, abundant with content and creativity. It was totally different from the musical education I had received in the conservatory. This music was unique, sublime, penetrating and most important — intellectual.

After working with Glantz, it was impossible for me to tolerate "classic" cantorial. Every other cantor, famous as he might have been, became dwarfed when compared with Glantz. What was missing in those cantors was the enthusiasm, the rich modulations, the complex transitions, the improvisational journeys that were so courageous, as he distanced himself from the traditional melodic tones of the prayer, then returned miraculously to the authentic prayer mode.

Fifty-two years later, when I hear a recording of Leib Glantz's voice, a shiver passes through me, reminding me of this truly great man to whom I owe so much. When Glantz was chanting in the synagogue, we knew we were witnessing not only the sounds of ancient cantorial, but also music of a new era of *Cha'za'nut*.

As a musician, Glantz created musical transitions of the most complex nature. He would insert into the prayers beautiful decorations while journeying through rich improvisational transitions, switching from one *Nu'sach* to another, from one musical scale to another. This daring journey was loaded with treacherous dangers. However, Glantz's musical maturity consistently proved undefeatable. When improvising, he always reached his music's intended destination exactly as he had intended from the very first notes.

During the prayer services, the singers of the choir needed to be concentrated and alert in order to provide Glantz with choral support and timely responses. He would never give me an indication as to which scale he would lead to. This created a constant tension among the choir members.

Glantz himself would rise to a level of exaltation that would make everyone in the synagogue concentrate on prayer. He succeeded in making every prayer a religious elation. He bridged the gap between universal music and Jewish religious music. For years he dedicated himself to research of the ancient Jewish prayer modes.

Many cantors have tried to imitate Leib Glantz, but it is doubtful if this can be achieved. This is due to his elaborate musical technique, his solid musical education, his vocal *coloratura*, and his courage to express his enthusiastic artistic vision. Leib Glantz was unique. He was one of a kind, and so was the music he created.

Many cantors have tried to imitate Leib Glantz, but it is doubtful if this can be achieved. This is due to his elaborate musical technique, his solid musical education, his vocal coloratura, and his courage to express his enthusiastic artistic vision. Leib Glantz was unique. He was one of a kind, and so was the music he created.

17

Artistic Perfection: The Musical Interpretation of Prayers

MAESTRO ELLI JAFFE[1]

Leonard Bernstein, the legendary composer and conductor, claimed that the conductor of a classical music orchestra must ensure that all the instrument players in his orchestra execute their notes properly; but it is even more important for the conductor to understand the musical intentions of the composer of the music his orchestra is playing. This is what classifies his artistry and stature.

> *Leib Glantz rightly deserves the title of the "Leonard Bernstein of Cantorial." Many cantors have composed great liturgical compositions, but Glantz possessed a unique musical language. He had amazing rhetorical capabilities that he was able to communicate to his generation as well as to future generations.*

Bernstein himself was the archetype of fundamental understanding of music. Leib Glantz rightly deserves the title of the "Leonard Bernstein of Cantorial." Many cantors have composed wonderful liturgical compositions, but Glantz possessed something more: a unique musical language. He had amazing rhetorical capabilities, and he was able to communicate these to his own generation as well as to future generations.

He was actually the first and only cantor to write a serious analysis on all of the facets of the ancient Jewish prayer modes, the *Nu'sach*.

---

1 Maestro Elli Jaffe was born in Jerusalem and graduated with distinction from the Rubin Academy in Jerusalem and the Royal Academy of Music in London. He has conducted all of Israel's major orchestras, and holds the title of honorary guest conductor of the Prague Symphony Orchestra. He is the artistic director of the Jerusalem School for Cantorial Art and the music director of the Jerusalem Great Synagogue choir. He published an instructional CD on Hebrew liturgy. As composer, he had his First Symphony performed by the Israel Philharmonic Orchestra (IPO), and his Wind Quintet premiered by the IPO's Wind Ensemble.

Glantz's compositions were complex, sophisticated and modernistic. He was a true intellectual who expressed his ideas with clarity. His amazing compositions would transport the listener to worlds that at first seemed to be far away from the familiar traditional *Nu'sach*. But as the composition developed, the listener could not fail to understand how deeply rooted in *Nu'sach* his compositions actually were.

The amazing thing about Glantz was that he truly succeeded in uncovering the ancient secrets of the *Nu'sach*. No one before him had succeeded in deciphering these secrets. This enabled him to navigate his compositions toward distant musical targets, with the confidence of a man who clearly knew where he was coming from and to where he wanted to go.

This deep knowledge, combined with his pedagogic talents, enabled him to create compositions that were ultimate lessons in *Nu'sach*. A great example of this is his fantastic composition *She'va Pe'amim A'ta* ("Seven Times 'Thou'"), in which he demonstrates seven sentences taken from seven different prayers, each containing the word *A'ta* (Thou), and each with its proper *Nu'sach*. This composition is written with such clarity that any musician can witness the amazing connections that exist between the different prayer modes.

After carefully analyzing the *She'va Pe'amim A'ta* composition, I have come to the conclusion that our *Nu'sach* is influenced by our ancient biblical cantillations.[2] The categories of different prayer modes, even though they are based on different scales and tones, are all characterized by similar, uniquely Jewish, musical movements. This is exactly what Glantz the composer was trying to teach us in this composition, and he conveyed this message not only by using very clear language, but also by accompanying it with extraordinary music.

Glantz possessed an amazing talent that enabled him to compose music that brought forth startling new interpretations of the texts of the prayers. This represented a totally new phenomenon. It was never done before with any kind of music anywhere in the world. He uncovered hidden meanings that existed in familiar words — meanings that we never clearly comprehended until hearing his musical interpretations.

The Midnight *Se'li'chot* Service, which has become such an important prayer in our cantorial culture, thanks to Leib Glantz, is threaded with mystical declarations and hidden meanings. Glantz

> *Glantz had this wonderful ability to provide, through music, startling new interpretations of the texts of the prayers. This was never done before. He uncovered hidden meanings that existed in familiar words — meanings that we never clearly comprehended until hearing Glantz's interpretation.*

2 Cantillations for the *To'rah*, the cantillations for the Books of the Prophets and the *Me'gi'lot* (Scrolls), as well other specific cantillations.

knew how to decipher these inner secrets. Consider, for example, the prayer *Le'chu Ne'ra'ne'na* ("Come, let us sing to the Lord"), which opens the *Se'li'chot* service. Glantz paints these words with a musical treatment that resembles a royal procession — one that seems to be marching towards the heavens. This stands in stark contrast to the "sobbing" mode, which was typical of many of the cantors of his time. However, his interpretation truly reflects the meaning of the words of *Le'chu Ne'ra'ne'na*:

> Come, let us sing to the Lord, and let us call out to the Rock of our salvation. Let us greet Him with thanksgiving; with praiseful songs let us call out to Him. Righteousness and justice are Your throne's foundation; kindness and truth precede Your countenance. Together let us share a sweet secret, and in the House of God let us stride with emotion.

In another composition from the *Se'li'chot* service, he uses *Sprechstimme*, a humble whisper, to express the words *Eich Nif'tach Peh* ("How dare we open our mouths in Your presence, Oh Lord"). Glantz's heroic innovations enhance the excitement we experience throughout this very emotional prayer. His ultimate target was to present us with a musical interpretation of every word.

The focal point of Glantz's cantorial creativity was his famous composition *She'ma Yis'ra'el* ("Hear O Israel"). This composition is considered one of the greatest cantorial works ever written, if not the greatest! When we listen to *She'ma Yis'ra'el*, we tend to say to ourselves: "Is it possible to sing this composition any differently? This inevitably must be the final interpretation and it cannot be performed in any other way." This reminds me of Beethoven's Fifth Symphony. The great composer Ludwig von Beethoven actually composed a number of different versions for his famous Fifth Symphony. I had the distinct honor to witness the written notes of these different versions. All of them were wonderful. However, when we hear the classical version that we all recognize today, we are convinced that Beethoven could not have written it any other way.

This is how I feel about Leib Glantz's *She'ma Yis'ra'el*. Here he exhibits his greatness as a composer. *She'ma Yis'ra'el* is a classic example of the sort of artistic perfection that Leonard Bernstein had in mind.[3]

3 See Elli Jaffe's essay "The Masterpiece *She'ma Yis'ra'el*" in Part 2 of this book.

18

The Great Innovator

CANTOR MAX WOHLBERG[1]

Music and cantorial have always been important aspects of Jewish life, both spiritually and socially. To the lover of synagogue music — Cantor Leib Glantz was unique.

Glantz's newest recording of the complete "Midnight *Se'li'chot* Service," accompanied by a male choir, was recorded live from the *Tif'e'ret Zvi* synagogue in Tel Aviv. This is an opportunity to appreciate this specific work, and to analyze the unique path Glantz has carved in the cantorial world.

If we review the most important cantors of the century, and try to analyze each one's distinctive qualities, we will come to the conclusion that most of these cantors were gifted with common talents and qualities, and each one seemed to excel with personal traits and typical characteristics: Cantor Alter Karniol — with his wide voice range and his outstanding trills; Yossele Rosenblatt — with his flexible voice and heartiness, his tender singing and his special falsetto; Zavel Kwartin — with the beauty of his soft tenor and his lyrical romantic expression; David Roitman — with his enthusiasm and refined musicality; Steinberg — with his sweet folkloristic style; Gershon Sirota — with his giant dramatic voice and lively temperament; Pinchas Minkowsky — with his gentleness of performance; Pierre Pinchik — with his mystical religiosity and Chasidic devotion; Moshe and David Kousevitzky — with their unique technical singing perfection; and of course Shmuel Vigoda and Moshe Ganchoff — each with their specific qualities.

---

1 Cantor Max Wohlberg (1907-1996) developed a scientific approach to the study of *Nu'sach* (cantillation, liturgical motifs and melodies). He acquired a unique position as an expert in the field of Jewish music and *Cha'za'nut*. As a composer of cantorial recitative, Max Wohlberg was recognized as most sensitive to the interpretive nuances inherent in liturgical texts. This article was published in English in "The Cantor's Voice" journal and in Hebrew in the Israeli daily newspaper "*Ha'A'retz*" in 1954.

From the very beginning of his cantorial career, Leib Glantz displayed an original approach. His voice is a most magnificent lyric tenor; however, he does not rely solely on his voice. The text and the interpretation of the words and ideas — these are for Glantz the essence of cantorial. His main focus is on the hidden meanings of the prayers. He tries to penetrate and discover the inner messages, creating music with amazing interpretations.

> *His voice is a most magnificent lyric tenor, however he does not rely solely on his voice. The text and the interpretation of the words and ideas — these are for Glantz the essence of cantorial.*

Glantz's intrinsic contribution to the art of cantorial is intellectual and not only emotional. The daring musical intervals, the surprising modulations and the exciting motifs are based on diligent research and cautious discretion. Only after this stage is resolved in his mind, does Glantz apply his illustrious artistic imagination and his charming compositional talents.

In addition to his profound musicality, Glantz is a true adherent to the *Nu'sach Ha'Te'fi'la*, the ancient Jewish prayer modes. He faithfully guards this tradition and its unique styles. In his wonderful recordings, such as *She'ma Yis'ra'el, Ez'ke'ra E'lo'kim, Le'chu Ne'ra'ne'na, Hash'ki'vei'nu,* and *Sho'mer Yis'ra'el,* pure *Nu'sach* is intertwined into them. This is the work of a true artist, applying every color of the rainbow. In every musical voyage, Glantz always seems to find the proper motif, through which he consistently finds the road back to the original *Nu'sach*.

Yet another virtue is Glantz's quality to diversify and change the style of his recitatives. He is daring and aggressive in his compositions *A'ta Nig'lei'ta* and *T'kah Be'Sho'far;* he portrays closeness to God in *Sho'mer Yis'ra'el* and *Av Ha'Ra'cha'mim*; he displays melodic and rhythmic pastoralism in *Te'vi'ei'nu,* and a colorful ballad mood in *Be'Tzeit Yis'ra'el.* Glantz's composition *U'Ve'Nu'cho Yo'mar* echoes like a Pentatonic recitation, and *Ha'loch Ve'Ka'ra'ta* is full of fun and joy. In *Ein Ke'Er'ke'cha* he becomes serious and dramatic, while in *A'hav'ti* he is seeking, agitated and desperate. Glantz's Chasidic melodies are also masterpieces in the spirit of the *Ad'mo'rim.*[2]

"Midnight *Se'li'chot* Service" is one of Leib Glantz's latest recordings. The music was composed for tenor and baritone, with organ accompaniment. It is an important asset in his synagogue repertoire. On this new LP record, Glantz opens the service with the choir humming an introduction before the festive *Ash'rei.* After the traditional *Ka'ddish,* there is a dramatic outburst of *A'ta He'tzav'ta* and the colorful *Nu'sach* of *Le'chu Ne'ra'ne'na. Eich Nif'tach Peh* is in a mood of despair and tears; *Ka'ma Yi'sar'ta'nu* — cries of grief and mourning; *El E'rech A'pa'yim* displays

---

2 *Ad'mor* is a title for Chasidic rabbis, which means "our master and teacher." Plural: *Ad'mo'rim.*

Glantz's creative choral talents; and in *Be'Mo'tza'ei Me'nu'cha* and *She'ma Ko'lei'nu* — we for an instant mistakenly think that he has lost his way, but soon realize that he is well on the way to the correct path of the *Nu'sach*. The lyrics and the softness of *Hi'ma'tzeh La'nu* lead to the lovely melody of *Te'vi'e'nu*. *Mach'ni'sei Ra'cha'mim* is the final prayer of the *Se'li'chot* service — a marvelous climax of religious exaltation.

In this *Se'li'chot* recording, Glantz again justifies his reputation as the "Cantor of Cantors." He is truly a great innovator.

I am convinced that if we succeed in molding for the future a generation of serious and intelligent cantors — that generation will choose Leib Glantz, the cantor, composer, researcher and pedagogue, as the main image to research, to study and to follow. In the history of Jewish music, Leib Glantz is the most daring and most original cantor that ever lived!

I am convinced that if we succeed in molding for the future a generation of serious and intelligent cantors — that generation will choose Leib Glantz, the cantor, composer, researcher and pedagogue, as the main image to research, to study and to follow. In the history of Jewish music, Leib Glantz is the most daring and most original cantor that ever lived!

19

Leib Glantz's *Se'li'chot*

CANTOR MAX WOHLBERG[1]

By the beginning of the twentieth century, the Chazanic recitative had acquired a precise character. Both in format and melodic content, it conformed to a fairly definite formula. It was of course inevitable that the melodic content was shaped by the personal predilection of each composer-executant. Some recitatives were characterized by abundant and involved *coloratura*, while others had a plaintive *Te'chi'na* (begging) quality. Some were tuneful, imbued with a folk-style charm; others possessed a spiritual lyricism, while some were set in a mood of mystic fervor. Yet, these differences notwithstanding, the essential character of the recitative remained unchanged.

With the arrival of Leib Glantz on the Chazanic scene, the recitative acquired previously unknown dimensions. Glantz brought to it an imaginative and daring manipulation of the Nu'sach modes and motifs; he introduced into our repertoire a novel concept of tunefulness and added a dynamic intensity unheard before.

With the arrival of Leib Glantz on the Chazanic scene, the recitative acquired previously unknown dimensions. Glantz brought to it an imaginative and daring manipulation of the

1 Cantor Max Wohlberg (1907-1996) was cantor, composer, theorist, collector of Jewish music and a central figure in the organization and education of the American Cantorate. He was head of the *Nu'sach* department at The Jewish Theological Seminary's Cantors Institute (1950-1988); He wrote a regular column entitled *"Pir'kei ha'zza'nut"* for "The Cantor's Voice" newsletter (1951-1963). Wohlberg profoundly influenced the education and standards of a generation of American cantors. This essay appeared as a preface to Leib Glantz's book *S'lichoth*, one of seven music books of the series "Selected Works *Rinat Hakodesh*," edited by David Loeb and prepared for publication by Yehoshua Zohar. It was published by the Tel Aviv Institute of Jewish Liturgical Music in conjunction with the Israel Music Institute, Tel Aviv, Israel, 1971.

Nu'sach modes and motifs; he introduced into our repertoire a novel concept of tunefulness and added a dynamic intensity unheard before.

A daring innovator and a bold iconoclast, he was also fortunate in possessing an incredibly flexible vocal apparatus, which permitted him to explore an endless number of delicate nuances and dynamic effects. His greatness, it seems to me, lay in three areas: artistic inventiveness, masterful manipulation of the *Nu'sach,* and relentless probing of the liturgical text. Carefully analyzing the words he was to sing, he searched for new meanings and for subtle shading inherent in the text. He then selected the appropriate mood dictated by the words. From there, imagination and musicianship took over, and creativity began.

> *His greatness lay in three areas: artistic inventiveness, masterful manipulation of the* Nu'sach, *and relentless probing of the liturgical text. Carefully analyzing the words he was to sing, he searched for new meanings and for subtle shading inherent in the text.*

The *Se'li'chot* service faithfully mirrors the artist at his maturity. Beginning with the humming motif drawn from the High Holiday morning service, to the concluding gem, *Mach'ni'sei Ra'cha'mim,* the mood ranges from poignant tenderness to impassioned outbursts. The music is characterized by melodic invention and subtle modulations, many of which were improvised during actual services. It is hoped that those who will be enabled to study the art of Leib Glantz through the medium of this publication, will be inspired to continue the work he so nobly pursued.

20

Musical *Chutz'pah* of a Genius

Cantor Jacob Ben-Zion Mendelson[1]

Some years ago, a beginning student came to my office for his first coaching session in *Cha'za'nut* and announced: "I want to study Glantz!" I told him: "You need to be able to walk, before you compete for Olympic Gold." Notice I didn't say run . . .

As a child, I was reared listening to *Cha'za'nut*. Mordechai Hershman, Yossele Rosenblatt, Zavel Kwartin, Pierre Pinchik and David Roitman were recorded staples. Berele Chagy, and the Kousevitzky brothers were the live models. I believed I had a handle on how the art form was to be presented. Then I came across that famous recording of Leibele Glantz singing *Te'fi'lat Tal* and *She'ma Yis'ra'el*, and my world was turned upside down! The musical *Chutz'pah* of this genius practically drove me mad! Let me try to explain why.

> *I came across that famous recording of Leibele Glantz singing* Te'fi'lat Tal *and* She'ma Yis'ra'el, *and my world was turned upside down! The musical* Chutz'pah *of this genius practically drove me mad!*

In *Te'fi'lat Tal*, Glantz opens: "*Dew... grant it to favor the land.*" He repeats the word "favor," the second time in a more urgent tone, rolling the Hebrew letter *Resh*, settling quietly, on the word "land."

---

1 Cantor Jacob Ben-Zion Mendelson was raised in Brooklyn, NY. He is a graduate of the American Opera Center at Julliard. He has taught at the Hebrew Union College, School of Sacred Music and the H.L. Miller Cantorial School at the Jewish Theological Seminary, both awarding him with Honorary Doctorates as cantor and composer. He served as President of the Cantors Assembly in 2003-4. He is the subject of the 2006 award winning documentary film *A Cantor's Tale* directed by Erik Greenberg Anjou.

In the next sentence, "*Designate us for blessing in your joy*," Glantz sings a remarkable, shocking, ascending *coloratura*, painting the words "designate us." Then with a sweeter, softer *coloratura* he highlights "blessing," with a lovely, calm, resolution for "in your joy." One can sense the smile in his eyes.

"*With abundant grain and wine by your bounty*" is sung with a simple pre-resolution phrase in the lowered seventh major triad. However, one perceives a certain patting of the belly for the word "abundant."

"*Re-establish (Jerusalem) the city of your desire*" is divided into three descending phrases, like teardrops.

In "*Your desire through dew*," "Your desire" is repeated. He does so very gently in G minor. Then, repeating the last word, he touches on the sixth note of the scale, mystically ascending upwards in the minor mode. Finally, in the last repetition of the word "Dew" he goes from minor, to another minor up a fourth, and incredibly changes into major, with a slight hesitation in order to emphasize, and then again back to minor, thereby creating a strong emotional effect.

What I have just described was only the first verse of the prayer. On the recording, Glantz sings the first and last verses. I distinctly remember lifting the needle of the Victrola record player, because I just had to hear it again and again before going on to the final verse.

"*Through dew bless (our) food*." Here Glantz repeats the word "dew" three times: First he establishes the key, then, in two ascending moves, with a strong accent on top, he pounds it into our heads. The third repetition leads into "bless our foods." One senses that Glantz is getting very emotional, however, it is but the tip of the iceberg.

"*In our bounty let there be no scarcity*." In the repetition of "In our bounty," Glantz unleashes a tri-tone chord that makes the hairs on the back of your neck stand up. In the second part of the phrase there is an amazing *coloratura* on the words "no scarcity."

> *In the repetition of "In our bounty," Glantz unleashes a tri-tone chord that makes the hairs on the back of your neck stand up!*

"*To the people you had led like sheep*," Glantz chooses to sing "To the people" twice. The first, with an even wilder *coloratura* than on the former "no scarcity." The second is just indescribable! This is not mere singing of difficult *coloratura*. This is "*Hish'tap'chut Ne'fesh*," a pouring out of the soul. Many great *Cha'za'nim* have sung with pathos, but Glantz's pathos is more effective because it follows such magical, pure musical moments. It is the *chiaroscuro*[2] of the musicianship and emotional abandon that gets Glantz's music to us like no one else!

"*Please fulfill her desire through dew.*" Appropriately, having said it all, Glantz ends the prayer in classical tradition, proceeding to the blessings of dew.

So, you want to study and emulate Glantz? All you need is to have a limitless tenor range, perfect musicianship, be a world class Hebraist, and have emotions that can roam freely. Good Luck!

---

2 *Chiascuro* is the art of using strong light and dark shadows to represent a pictorial image.

21

The Guardian of Israel: *Sho'mer Yis'ra'el*

Cantor Moshe Kraus[1]

Glantz's mastery of the *Nu'sach* (Jewish prayer modes) was immaculate. In his research, he succeeded in defining the *Nu'sach* melodies that we currently use in our synagogues as originating from the "songs that the Levite priests sang" in the Holy Temple in Jerusalem thousands of years ago.

He possessed a penetrating knowledge of the Hebrew language that enabled him to use music to interpret the texts of the prayers as could no one else. To

> *Glantz's mastery of the* Nu'sach *(Jewish prayer modes) was immaculate. In his research, he succeeded in defining the* Nu'sach *melodies that we currently use in our synagogues as originating from the "songs that the Levite priests sang" in the Holy Temple in Jerusalem thousands of years ago.*

him every word and every letter was important. Every word he sang, whether in Ashkenazic or Sephardic pronunciation was flawless.

"Sho'mer Yis'ra'el" ("The Guardian of Israel"), one of Glantz's greatest compositions, is a classical example of authentic *Nu'sach*. In the period before the Holocaust, I used to listen to Jews in Europe who were praying quietly behind the heating furnaces of their humble houses of

---

1 Cantor Moshe Kraus officiated in Sighet, Hungary, and was the last Chief Cantor of the famous *Shom'rei Sha'bbat* Synagogue in Budapest before being transported to Nazi concentration camps in Yugoslavia and later to Bergen-Belzen. After the Holocaust he emigrated to Israel, where he served as Chief Cantor of the Israel Defense Forces. Subsequently he officiated as cantor in Antwerpen, Mexico City, and Johannesburg. Since 1976 he has officiated as cantor in Ottawa, Canada.

prayer. They poured out their hearts praying the words of *"Sho'mer Yis'ra'el"* — uttering precisely the same *Nu'sach* as we can hear in Glantz's composition.

Glantz opens this composition by introducing himself to God the Almighty, as if declaring:

> I am a simple, humble Jew. I am in deep pain because of the grave situation of my brothers and sisters, the Jews of this world. I am speaking directly to you, God! You, the Guardian and Savior of Israel. I demand that you save the remnants of Your people, so that they may not perish. These are Your people — the same loyal people who pray every day of the year, uttering the sacred words *"She'ma Yis'ra'el"* ("Hear O Israel, God is our Lord, God is One").

After raising his voice, Glantz fearfully realizes that he had dared to shout towards God, the Almighty. He therefore swiftly changes his tone and begs forgiveness: "He who giveth mercy, Who is appeased by his people's prayers of supplication — please come forth and save this generation of Your people." There is no one else that can help us but God!

After raising his voice, Glantz fearfully realizes that he dared to shout towards God, the Almighty, so he swiftly changes his tone and begs forgiveness.

Glantz ends the prayer by offering to make peace with God: "Our Father, our Lord! Please have mercy upon us and answer our prayers. Give us justice, charity, and salvation."

What an amazing interpretation!

22

Ez'ke'ra E'lo'kim:
One of the Greatest Masterpieces of Cha'za'nut

Cantor Louis Danto[1]

I first met Leib Glantz at the *Chazonim Farband*[2] in New York City in 1947. He emphatically encouraged me to pursue a career as a cantor. Needless to say, he was very convincing. At the *Farband* meeting, Glantz presented an impressive lecture on his views regarding the opening blessing of the *Ha'llel* prayer service. All the cantors of that time customarily sang this blessing in the Minor mode. Glantz adamantly opposed this. Interpreting the actual words of the prayers, he convinced many of the cantors that were present that this blessing should be sung in the Major mode in order to emphasize the text that praised the Lord. Having successfully proved his point, he influenced many cantors to change their chants from Minor to Major.

A wonderful example of his unique approach to *Cha'za'nut* is his composition *A'hav'ti* ("I love that the Lord heareth my voice, my supplications"). The majority of this prayer is sung in *pianissimo*, greatly enhancing the interpretation of this intimate text, with the cantor talking directly to God.

Glantz's composition "*Ez'ke'ra E'lo'kim*" ("I remember, O God") from the closing *Ne'i'la* prayer service of *Yom Ki'ppur* (The Day of Atonement), is one of the greatest masterpieces of *Cha'za'nut!*

---

1 Cantor Louis Danto of Toronto, Canada, received an Honorary Doctorate in Music from the Jewish Theological Seminary in NY. Born in Poland, he studied voice and cello in the Minsk Conservatory and later in the Lodz Conservatory. Danto studied *Cha'za'nut* with Leo Lowe and Herman Zalis, and was a student at the *Mirr* Yeshiva. He has researched and discovered rare manuscripts of Jewish music in Eastern Europe.

2 *Chazonim Farband* — The Jewish Ministers Cantors Association of America.

> *Glantz's composition "Ez'ke'ra E'lo'kim" ("I remember, O God") from the closing Ne'i'la service of Yom Ki'ppur, is one of the greatest masterpieces of Cha'za'nut! . . . The musical and vocal interpretation is nothing short of genius.*

The musical and vocal interpretation of *Ez'ke'ra E'lo'kim* is nothing short of genius. The text of this prayer is made up of sentences, that when interpreted properly, require different combinations of music. The text begins with disaster, moves to an affirmation of faith and ends with a plea for mercy. Glantz finds wonderful musical ways to expose the differences between each of these sections.

The prayer opens with "I remember, O God, and I am deeply vexed" (*Ez'ke'ra E'lo'kim Ve'E'he'ma'ya*). Glantz instantly creates a mood signifying the destruction of the Holy Temple. He expresses deep emotion that enables the worshipper to grasp the immense tragedy of the destruction. Then, as if in a fantasy, he enables us to lament the fact that all the cities of the world remain erect while "Jerusalem, the city of God, is razed to the ground" (*Ir Ha'E'lo'kim Mush'pe'let Ad She'ol Tach'ti'ya*).

Then comes the firm affirmation: "Yet for all this, our faith in Thee does not falter" (*U'Ve'chol Zot A'nu Le'cha Ve'Ei'nei'nu Le'cha*). Here Glantz enrolls his amazing vocal ability to transmit the yearning and the hope of his people.

When he addresses this plea to God to give his people a "measure of mercy" *(Mi'dat Ha'Ra'cha'mim),* we actually feel the pain: "Every heart is faint and every head is weary" (*Ki Kol Le'vav Da'vai Ve'Chol Rosh La'Cho'li*). No one who hears Glantz's moving rendition of these words can remain indifferent. It is an authentic expression of collective pain, of broken hearts and of tears.

Singing with a weeping voice, Glantz begs the Lord to collect and conserve our tears, as if to remind God of our enduring suffering.

The final affirmation, in contrast, is sung in a very optimistic musical style: "For unto Thee our eyes turn evermore" (*Ki Le'cha Le'vad Ei'nei'nu Te'lu'yot*). This optimistic music leaves us with no doubt that God, and only God, is the one who can save His people.

23

A Breath of Fresh Air to the Entire Cantorate

CANTOR BENZION MILLER[1]

Who was Cantor Leib Glantz? Was he just another cantor or was he unique? Was he just another composer or was he a superb composer? Was he just another artist or was he a master artist? To me the name Leib Glantz is synonymous with the word genius.

Reminiscing back as far as I can remember, I always loved the cantorial masterpieces of Cantor Glantz.

How does one begin to explain the intricacies of this type of *Cha'za'nut?*

There were many great cantors and composers of cantorial compositions in Glantz's era. However, not one possessed his deep insight into the liturgy. Upon hearing most cantorial compositions or recitatives for the first time, one can almost immediately decide whether one enjoys listening to them and understands them. This is not the case with the compositions of Glantz. To fully comprehend the beauty and intricacy of his music, listening alone is not sufficient. One is required to study the composition carefully. Only then can one really appreciate the depth of his creations.

When I was just 15 years of age, being familiar with and loving the original works of Cantor Glantz, I heard his famous composition "*A'na Be'Cho'ach,*" for the very first time. At first I felt extremely disappointed. I recalled his famous recitatives "*She'ma Yis'ra'el*" and "*Tal.*" This was entirely different. However, there was something in this composition that kept haunting me

---

1 Benzion Miller is cantor of Young Israel Beth-El Synagogue, Borough Park, NY. He is a graduate of the Bobover Yeshivas in Brooklyn, New York and Bat Yam, Israel. He studied Music Theory and *solfège* under Cantor Samuel Taube of Montreal and Voice Production at the Champagne School of Music in Montreal.

> *There was something in this composition, A'na Be'Cho'ach, that kept haunting me for weeks. A certain motif kept on repeating in my head, a motif that I could not forget.*

for weeks. A certain motif kept on repeating in my head, one that I could not forget. Soon after, I had the good fortune to hear it once again, and concentrate on it seriously. Suddenly the music became clear to me and I connected with the depth of this illustrious composer.

I was not privileged to hear Cantor Glantz in person. My connection with him is solely through his recordings. His voice was extremely unique. It was very smooth and very high in range. His intonation was perfect. His *coloratura*, a very important component in cantorial music, was impeccably fluid and intricate, putting great emphasis on timing, pronunciation and punctuation of the text.

Glantz was a master composer. His works have a quality of abstract *Cha'za'nut*. His music was not intended for listening pleasure alone. In order to appreciate it fully, one needs to concentrate and connect with his amazing musical interpretations of the text.

"*A'na Be'Cho'ach*" ("We implore You, by the great power of Your right hand") was written by Rabbi Nechunia Ben Hakana, a rabbi who lived in the first century. This poetic prayer includes hidden secrets of Jewish mysticism. Glantz weaves a beautiful composition using various mystical motifs to express the hidden meaning of the text. Towards the end of the composition, as he proclaims *Shav'a'tei'nu Ka'bel U'She'ma Tza'a'ka'tei'nu* ("accept our supplications and hear our cry"), with special fervor, almost like a Chasidic Rebbe, Glantz raises his voice with a begging and emotional cry towards the Almighty.

Another aspect of Glantz's unique artistry is the setting to the Psalm "*Be'Tzeit Yis'ra'el Mi'Mitz'ra'yim*" ("When the people of Israel went forth out of Egypt"). We recite this Psalm in the *Ha'llel* portion of the synagogue prayer service on the blessing for *Rosh Cho'desh* (the blessing of the new month), on *Yom Tov,* the Jewish Festivals, and when reading the *Ha'gga'da* at the Passover *Se'dder*. Here Glantz displays his brilliance as an artist. By simply telling the story of the Exodus of the Israelites from Egypt, he places the listener in the middle of the episode itself. All one needs to do is shut one's eyes and envision the masses of men, women and children with their animals and personal possessions, exiting slowly out of Egypt. Glantz was such a master craftsman that he could make simple words visible and even tangible.

In his composition "*Ki Hi'nei Ka'Cho'mer*" ("As clay are we…that lies between the fingers of the potter") from the *Yom Ki'ppur* evening service liturgy, Glantz simply clarifies the text using music. When he reaches the words *Ken A'nach'nu Be'Yad'cha* ("So are we in Your hand, God"), he transforms into a Chasidic fervor, begging and pleading before the Almighty: *La'Brit Ha'beit, Ha'beit Ve'Al Tei'fen* ("Thy covenant recall and show Thy mercy"). He then completes each section with pathos, albeit softer: *Ve'Al, Ve'Al, Ve'Al Tei'fen La'Yei'tzer* ("God, do not act on impulse"). In the second stanza of this prayer Glantz shows his virtuosity with acrobatics and magnificent *coloratura*, while carefully remaining completely loyal to the text. Here again, when reaching the words *Ken A'nach'nu Be'Yad'cha* ("So are we in Your hand"), he reverts to a begging mode as in the first stanza.

I have yet to find another cantor who amazes me as does Leib Glantz. I find new aspects in his music every time I listen to him sing. There have been many people who have argued that *Cha'za'nut* is actually a primitive form of music. However, with the appearance of Leib Glantz on the cantorial scene, he completely disproved this mistaken theory.

Cantor Leib Glantz was a blessing and a breath of fresh air to the entire Cantorate.

> *I have yet to find another cantor who amazes me as does Leib Glantz. I find new aspects in his music every time I listen to him sing.*

24

The Brilliant Lion

CANTOR BENJAMIN MULLER[1]

The translation of Leib Glantz is "brilliant lion."

A brilliant lion is a wonderful description of Leibele Glantz, one of the greatest cantors of the Golden Age of *Cha'za'nut*. He possessed a brilliant voice, and his compositions are brilliant both musically and in the manner in which they originally and authentically convey the fervent expression of the Jewish soul.

> *Glantz possessed a brilliant voice, and his compositions are brilliant both musically and in the manner in which they originally and authentically convey the fervent expression of the Jewish soul.*

His music and his voice have the power of a lion, penetrating into the most hardened heart, awe inspiring by their majestic brilliance, beauty of tone and melodious musical line.

Cantors consider Leib Glantz not only as a brilliant composer and interpreter of the prayer texts, but also as a unique source of learning — elevating cantors to a deeper understanding of the meaning of fervor and purity of expression. By emulating Glantz's approach of engaging in a dialogue with the Almighty, a cantor can aspire to reach the highest spheres of interpretation of the prayers.

---

1 Cantor Benjamin Muller was born in Geneva, Switzerland, and officiates as cantor in the Shomrei Hadas Congregation in Antwerpen, Belgium.

I first encountered Glantz as a young child, by listening to his recordings. The impact on my singing and praying was enormous. I endeavored to adopt his unique style, avoiding artificial mannerisms and vocal prowess, but rather emphasizing the inner beauty and inspiration of the prayers.

Glantz would analyze each and every prayer and compare it with existing traditions. This led him to offer radical new melodies that he felt should replace melodies that were not appropriately anchored in the correct *Nu'sach,* or did not represent the essence of the prayer texts. He was a perfectionist and he remained authentic in every endeavor he took upon himself.

Besides being a musician of the highest stature, Glantz was blessed with an unusually high and flexible tenor voice. When listening to him sing, one gets the impression that his vocal possibilities were limitless — both in range and in dynamics.

Even though his music was highly expressive, Glantz had the utmost respect for tradition. Throughout his life he believed that his mission was to purify cantorial art by purging it from what he considered secular, popular, and foreign influences, that contaminated the purity and the authenticity of our traditional prayer modes.

Many of Glantz's compositions are considered to be the cream-of-the-cream of the art of *Cha'za'nut.* When carefully analyzed, every time one listens to them, one discovers new and exciting nuances. Glantz would fascinate the members of his congregation by suddenly speaking the words of the prayers without melody. It was as if he were talking directly to God the Almighty with such intensity and fervor that his listeners were swayed to far away worlds.

> *It was as if he were talking directly to God the Almighty, with such intensity and fervor that his listeners were swayed to far away worlds.*

Leib Glantz created Jewish music that was highly sophisticated compared to the traditional *Cha'za'nut* of his generation. However, I have no doubt that his music will live on in the hearts of the Jewish people for eternity.

25

A Glance at Glantz

CANTOR ARIE L. SUBAR[1]

"Letters are the path to words.
Words are the path to music.
But it is the heart and the soul that give life to the text."
— Leib Glantz

Is it possible to implement change in a profession that is deeply embedded in the status quo? Can one man go against centuries of placidity and transform not only the art, but also the attitude of his colleagues and audiences to accept innovation? These were the questions facing Cantor Leib Glantz as he first appeared on the cantorial stage early in the twentieth century.

Glantz was born in Kiev. He grew up surrounded by the aura of cantorial music and in the shadow of some of the greatest cantors of his time. His father was a well-known cantor, and young Leib quickly embraced Jewish music. He began to perform publicly when he was only eight years old. Leibele, as he was known, toured Europe conducting prayer services and appearing in concerts. Even then, those who were fortunate to hear him knew that he was on his way to becoming a driving force in the reformation of cantorial.

Glantz was well aware that most audiences, whether in concert or during prayer services, were not seeking innovation in cantorial. They merely required cantors who could deliver an enjoyable performance of the familiar melodies originating from the cantors who preceded them.

---

1 Cantor Arie L. Subar of Montreal, Canada, an expert on *Nu'sach Ha'Te'fi'la,* has organized conventions of the Council of Hazzanim of Greater Montreal and the Cantorial Council of America. He has issued numerous publications on *Cha'za'nut* and serves as Professor of Cantorial at the Montreal Cantorial Institute.

Glantz realized that most synagogue-going Jews were not *Me'vi'nim* (experts) when it came to Jewish liturgy. To his dismay, he also discovered that many cantors themselves were not knowledgeable regarding the authentic Jewish prayer modes (*Nu'sach*). Glantz's life mission was to transform the focus of cantorial from simple delivery to thought and knowledge.

Glantz complained that instead of singing the ancient modes, most cantors relied on more recent (eighteenth and nineteenth century) European compositions to placate their audiences. In his opinion, some of these melodies were inappropriate, as they originated from church hymns and other non-Jewish sources. He was vehemently opposed to introducing operatic themes or popular songs into the prayer service. To his mind, these transgressions were blasphemous. Traditional Jewish music was not only available, but also mandated to be used in prayer by Jewish tradition; therefore, it should be used accordingly.

With the establishment of the State of Israel in 1948, Glantz, a fervent and active Zionist, was inspired. The land and the people of Israel became his muses and inspired him to set forth on a journey to change cantorial forever.

Glantz felt that the prevailing attitude in cantorial lacked thought and depth. As a composer and researcher, he believed that the Pentatonic scale (five notes represented by the black keys on a piano starting from F sharp) was a quintessentially Jewish scale, as it is used in many traditional Jewish prayers and rituals, including *Ak'da'mut* (an eleventh century poem recited on the first day of the holiday of *Sha'vu'ot* before the reading of the *To'rah*), the cantillation for the *To'rah* reading, *Shach'rit* (morning prayer service) for weekdays, *Psu'kei De'Zim'ra* (introduction to *Shach'rit* for Sabbath and weekdays), *Shi'rat Ha'Yam* (the Song of Moses), and the blessings after the *Haf'ta'rah*, (readings from the Prophets following the *To'rah* reading).

> *With the establishment of the State of Israel in 1948, Glantz, a fervant and active Zionist, was inspired. The land and the people of Israel became his muses and inspired him to set forth to change cantorial forever.*

Glantz began composing and performing complex compositions, proving to the Jewish music world that original work that maintained the spirit of traditional Jewish music could be created. He opposed the then-popular technique of "sobbing" during services, especially where the prayer texts did not call for it. He wished to train the Jewish populace to contemplate and try to comprehend the text as well as its music. He wanted cantors to take the initiative and try to delve into the deeper meanings of the text, in order to expose their inner emotions and enable themselves to elevate their congregations to a higher spiritual level.

Leib Glantz lecturing on Jewish Music in Montreal, Canada, November, 1963.

Glantz never intended to entice other cantors to perform his own music. He earnestly wanted them to analyze the prayer texts and reach their own artistic conclusions, just as he did himself.

Glantz's approach puzzled many of his colleagues. They felt that changing the traditional ways they performed their cantorial music would not necessarily improve their popularity. They also realized that his compositions were relatively complex and required outstanding vocal capabilities.

But this was precisely Glantz's point. He argued that most cantors did not have the musical education of their great predecessors. To his mind, they could not explain the rules of the authentic prayer modes that they were employing, even if they were instinctively singing these modes correctly. This was especially true regarding such important prayers as *Tal* (Dew) and *Ge'shem* (Rain). Moreover, he held that the commonly used *Nu'sach* for the *Ha'llel* prayers was incorrect — as expressed in his famous 1961 debate with Israeli musicologist Menashe Ravina in the Israeli publications *Bat Kol*, a music Journal, and *Ha'Po'el Ha'Tza'ir*, a socialist weekly magazine. Glantz firmly believed that the *Ha'llel* service should be performed in the Mixolydian mode (a Major scale with the leading tone moved down by a semi-tone), but instead was mostly improperly performed by cantors in a Minor scale.

Glantz gleaned his knowledge from the works of the great cantors of earlier generations, such as Betzalel Odesser, Yerucham Hakatan, Nissan Belzer, Nissan Blumenthal, Pinchas Minkowsky and Avram Kalachnik-Berkovitch. He believed that cantors should revert to using the traditionally accepted *Nu'sach* as exemplified by these greats. He stressed the importance of the ancient musical heritage, and emphasized that traditional *Nu'sach* was essential in the performance of prayer.

Glantz exclaimed that cantorial was his true "romance." He boldly declared that his performance was not to satisfy the worshippers but for the glory of the Almighty. He stressed that cantorial was "the voice of God that not only cleaves with shafts of fire, but also with a gentle whisper" (Psalms 29).

With Israel, his muse, inspiring him, Glantz wrote books on traditional *Nu'sach*, and composed for choir, cantor and organ, as well as for prayer services during the yearly cycles. In addition, he wrote Hebrew and Yiddish songs. In his recordings, you can hear him sometimes as a dancing Chasid, while in others he is a philosopher. In some of his music he conducts discussions with his Creator, while in others he makes demands of Him. In every aspect of his work, it is clear that Glantz was a man of deep faith and conviction.

I had the privilege to attend one of Glantz's holiday services in the 1950s. It transformed my thinking, both about cantorial and about Glantz. During the service, I felt as if I was in a different sphere — that I was spiritually and physically elevated. It was a life-changing event that solidified my understanding of the relationship between text and music, and clarified the very important role the cantor plays in the spiritual elevation of the congregation.

> *I had the privilege to attend one of Glantz's holiday services in the 1950s, which transformed my thinking, both about cantorial and about Glantz. During the service, I felt as if I was in a different sphere — spiritually and physically elevated. It was a life-changing event that solidified my understanding of the relationship between text and music.*

A few weeks before his passing, Glantz was a guest of the Cantorial Council of Greater Montreal, for whom he lectured and performed in concert. I had the honor of hosting him in my home. The few days I spent with him were an experience I will never forget. His advice and constructive criticism of my own Sabbath performance helped elevate me to where I am today.

Glantz was prolific. He created compositions such as the romantic *Ha'loch Ve'Ka'ra'ta*; the mystical and philosophical *A'na Be'Cho'ach*; the simple *Sho'mer Yis'ra'el; Te'vi'ei'nu*, in which you hear him on his way to the Holy Mount of God; *U'Ve'Nu'cho Yo'mar*, composed in the Pentatonic mode; and the *Ash'rei* of the *Se'li'chot* service, praising and glorifying God. His focus on proper *Nu'sach* led him to introduce the authentic mode of the *Se'li'chot* service, which was not popular at the time, but is now used by most cantors. Glantz also composed a new melody for the popular *Cha'nu'ka* song *Ma'oz Tzur*, based on authentic Jewish scales. Sadly, the source of the music popularly sung while lighting the *Cha'nu'ka* candles by Jews around the world is from several Middle-Age church tunes and marches.

Glantz may have passed away in 1964, but his contributions are still felt today. Many cantors study his philosophy and follow him in an attempt to grasp the inner meanings of the words of the prayers. I am proud that in our institution, the Montreal Cantorial Institute, we promote the teachings of Leib Glantz. We know that Glantz was not just a great among the greats, but a giant in a category of his own. His insight, wisdom, spirit and individuality were incomparable, and they serve as an inspiration to many upcoming and practicing cantors.

The old Jewish adage "change is bad" has been replaced with study and understanding of the texts, leading to the creation of new Jewish compositions that are enjoyed by audiences worldwide. That is what Glantz really hoped for: to foster a deep connection between the texts and the music, which in turn makes cantorial more meaningful for all of us.

Music That Speaks to Yemenite and Sephardic Jews

C A N T O R   A V S H A L O M   Z F I R A[1]

As a child, I grew up on Yemenite and Sephardic music. In my youth, I also became acquainted with Jewish liturgical music of the Eastern European Ashkenazic style.

My mother was born in Yemen, in the city of Ta'izz. In 1914, as a young girl, her family emigrated to Palestine, bringing with her all the ancient traditions of the Jews of Yemen in prayer, music and dance. She was responsible for instilling in me a love for the wonderful Jewish Yemenite culture.

My father was also born in Yemen, in the city of San'a. When he was very young, his parents moved to Egypt, where he lived until his family emigrated to Palestine when he was 13 years old. He absorbed the traditions of the Sephardic Jewish community. In these communities, singing and prayer were mainly in the language of *Ladino.*[2]

When my parents married, they lived in Jerusalem in the ultra-orthodox neighborhood of *Mei'ah She'a'rim.* Strangely, they spoke fluent Yiddish,[3] as they would attend prayer services at several synagogues, mainly those of the Ashkenazic tradition. For this reason, as a child I was also exposed to Eastern European Jewish liturgical music.

1 Cantor Avshalom Zfira was born in Jerusalem to Yemenite parents. He studied at the Rubin Music Academy in Jerusalem and was a vocal student of Avraham Margalit and the distinguished opera singer Vitorio Weinberg. Zfira studied Ashkenazic cantorial with Cantor Noach Schall and successfully combines Sephardic and Ashkenazic music in his appearances. He is a cantor in Boca Raton, Florida.

2 Ladino is the language of some Sephardic Jews, especially those formerly living in Mediterranean countries. It is based on medieval Spanish, with an admixture of Hebrew, Greek, and Turkish words, and is written in modified Hebrew characters.

3 Yiddish is a language used mainly by Ashkenazic Jews in Central and Eastern Europe. It was originally a German dialect with words from Hebrew and several other modern languages.

As I became a student of music and prayers, I learned to distinguish between the musical cultures of the Jews of Yemen, Sepharad,[4] and Ashkenaz.[5] Later, in my research, I have been able to identify bridges and common denominators between these musical cultures.

I was fortunate to study music with opera singer Vitorio Weinberg. Weinberg was born in *Mei'ah She'a'rim,* Jerusalem, to a family of Chasidim. In the 1930's, he became one of the most distinguished opera singers of his time. He appeared in Milano in the La Scala Opera as well as in other leading opera houses around the world. He officiated as a synagogue cantor as well. Following his retirement from the opera, he assumed the position of vocal teacher and musical educator at the Rubin Music Academy in Jerusalem.

In 1963, I remember visiting him at his Jerusalem home. Weinberg offered to play for me a recording, declaring: "Listen very attentively to this music, because what you are about to hear is divine singing. There will come a day, when the Jewish people will rebuild the Holy Temple in Jerusalem, and *this* is the music that will be sung there!"

> *"Listen very attentively to this music, because what you are about to hear is divine singing. There will come a day, when the Jewish people will rebuild the Holy Temple in Jerusalem, and this is the music that will be sung there!"*

I was stunned by this exclamation! The recording was that of the cantor and composer Leibele Glantz, singing one of his most amazing compositions — *She'ma Yis'ra'el.* This was the first time I heard Glantz, and I was overwhelmed by the sounds that were coming from the record player. I wanted to hear more and more of his music, and the more I listened, the stronger I felt the thrill of spiritual exaltation. Glantz's music introduced me to a new world. It sounded to me like a musical "ingathering of the exiles" (*Ki'bbutz Ga'lu'yot*). All the different flavors of Jewish music from all the Diasporas seemed to be blending together.

As I researched his music, I recognized common motifs from songs and prayers from my Yemenite background. Traditional expressions from Sephardic and *E'retz Yis'ra'el* melodies were clearly evident.

---

4 Sephardic Jews are historically associated with the Iberian peninsula (Spain and Portugal), including those who were subject to expulsion from Spain by order of the Catholic monarchs Ferdinand and Isabel (as codified in the Alhambra decree of 1492), or from Portugal in 1497 by order of King Manuel I. The traditional language of Sephardim is Ladino. In the vernacular of modern-day Israel, Sephardi has also come to be used as an umbrella term for any Jewish person who is not Ashkenazi, including Jews from Arabia and Iran, sometimes defined as *Ei'dot Ha'Miz'rach* (from the East).

5 Ashkenazi Jews descended from the medieval Jewish communities of the Rhineland. Many later migrated eastward, forming communities mainly in Germany, Poland, Austria, and Eastern Europe between the tenth and nineteenth centuries. From medieval times until the mid-twentieth century, the *lingua franca* among Ashkenazi Jews was Yiddish, and they developed a distinct culture and liturgy influenced by interaction with the surrounding nations.

In the composition *She'ma Yis'ra'el* ("Hear O Israel"), Glantz's musical virtuosity creates a sacred mood by using clearly identifiable Sephardic motifs. *Sim Sha'lom* ("Grant Peace"), is a liturgical composition consisting of melodies that distinctly remind me of the Sephardic folklore that I grew up on in my childhood while attending several Sephardic synagogues in Jerusalem.

E'shet Cha'il ("Woman of Valour") is a song I particularly love. It reminds me of Yemenite songs and dance rhythms, and has Sephardic motifs as well. In this song you can easily identify Glantz's love and sensitivity of the many facets of Jewish tradition.

The song *Ve'Te'che'ze'na* ("We shall witness Your return to Zion") is representative of Glantz's *E'retz Yis'ra'el* style, and is strongly influenced by popular Israeli folklore. *Matai* ("When?") is a song that Glantz defines as "Palestinian." It is a beautiful combination of classical and popular motifs.

Dror Yik'ra ("Let freedom be proclaimed") is one of Glantz's most popular songs, written in the Talner Chasidim style. The music to the lyrics *She'vu Ve'Nu'chu Ve'Yom Sha'bbat* ("Rest on the Sabbath day"), and *She'eh Shav'at B'nei A'mi* ("Heed to the yearnings of my people"), are typical examples of Sephardic expression. It is a song that is happily sung during Sabbath and festival feasts both by Sephardic and Ashkenazic Jews all over the world.

Glantz's primary objective was to offer authentic interpretations to the meaning of every word and every phrase. He battled to prevent foreign contamination from seeping into the Jewishness of the melodies. These were issues of cardinal importance for him. At the same time he strove to create beautiful music that would inspire his listeners to pray or to rejoice.

Leib Glantz was a real idealist. His Zionist activism had a major impact on his life and on his musical creativity. He succeeded in using his great artistic gift to preserve and cherish the ancient traditional music and culture of the Jewish people.

In his research, Glantz traced the origins of Jewish music all the way back to the glorious days in history when the Jewish people were independently living together in the Promised Land, commonly sharing their religious and secular music. After the destruction of the Holy Temple in Jerusalem by the Roman Empire, almost 2,000 years ago, the Jewish people were exiled from the Holy Land to the four corners of the earth. Each Jewish community in the Diaspora maintained its Jewish culture and continued to practice traditional religious rites. Naturally, as time passed, each community in exile absorbed some of the local culture. This explains the distinctions that developed between Sephardic, Yemenite, and Ashkenazic liturgical music.

Leib Glantz, through his research, was convinced that since the origins of Jewish music were historically common to all the exiled Jewish communities, he could create music that represented the true ancient melodies. These melodies were based on musical scales unique to the Jewish people that were preserved for thousands of years as they were passed down from

> *Glantz, through his research, was convinced that since the origins of Jewish music were historically common to all the exiled Jewish communities, he could create music that represented the true ancient melodies . . . based on the musical scales unique to the Jewish people that were preserved for thousands of years.*

generation to generation. When the Zionist dream became a reality in the form of the independent State of Israel, Glantz seized the opportunity to settle in Tel Aviv and embark on a mission to create Jewish music based on the blending together of the melodies of the scattered communities of the Diaspora.

27

Bridging the Ashkenazic-Sephardic Gap

Cantor Aaron Bensoussan[1]

Cantor Leib Glantz, one of the great Cantors of *the Golden Age of Cha'za'nut*, was truly unique in his renditions and masterful compositions. They were often way ahead of their time. What astonished me upon hearing Glantz's music for the first time was that his compositions were drawn from many different musical traditions, masterfully woven together. This approach was certainly radical in his generation.

His music and style speak to my heart. As a Moroccan-born cantor, I grew up with Andalusian[2] and Arabic *Ma'ka'mat* modes.[3] I left Morocco at the age of fourteen and subsequently absorbed Ashkenazic music in New York. It is natural for me to understand and appreciate Glantz's complex style.

As I began to delve into the art of composition, I drew great inspiration from Leib Glantz. In my opinion, it is justified that *Nu'sach,* the ancient Jewish prayer modes, should reflect the

---

1 Cantor Aaron Bensoussan comes from a prominent rabbinic dynasty. His grandfather, Rabbi Haim Bensoussan, was the Chief Rabbi of Morocco and his great grandfather, Rabbi Avraham Bensoussan, was one of the Rabbis to emerge from the city of Fez, tracing the family back to a teacher of Maimonides. Aaron Bensoussan came to the United States in 1968 and studied in Yeshivas in Chicago and New York. He studied Sephardic liturgical music with his father and received formal cantorial and musical training at Queen's College, the Yeshiva University Belz School of Music and the Jewish Theological Seminary. Bensoussan combines expertise in both Ashkenazic and Sephardic styles and has created a unique blend of the two cultures.

2 Andalusia is a region of Southern Spain that contains magnificent Moorish architecture, including the historic towns of Seville, Grenada, and Cordoba. The name Andalusia is derived from the Arabic name *"Al An'da'lus,"* which refers to the parts of the Iberian Peninsula that were historically under Muslim-Moorish rule from 711 till 1492.

3 *Ma'ka'mat* is Arab Middle East music rooted in ancient traditions. It consists of very special melodic lines based on quarter note steps. Each *Ma'kam* has a distinctive sequence of notes in a specific range, with one or more tonics, and a melodic phasing unique unto itself.

influence of the various cultures in which the Jewish people lived during their history. It is perfectly legitimate to combine the different *Nus'cha'ot* of various Jewish communities of the Diaspora, especially since the Jewish people in Israel, our historic homeland, are living in a period of "ingathering of the exiles" (*Ki'bbutz Ga'lu'yot*).

Sephardic cantorial music emphasizes joyous melodies combined with the traditional *Nu'sach*.

> *Sephardic cantorial emphasizes joyous melodies combined with the traditional Nu'sach. Glantz, a great scholar of Jewish music, by way of his compositions and his unique style, taught his generation of cantors how this can be achieved.*

Glantz, a great scholar of Jewish music, by way of his compositions and his unique style, taught his generation of cantors how this can be achieved. He was firmly against the Chazanic custom of chanting the blessing of the *Ha'llel* prayer service in the gloomy Minor mode. He advanced the idea that cantors should sing the *Ha'llel* in the Major mode in order to reflect the joy of praising of the Lord.

I have written numerous compositions that are a reflection of the musical experiences that I was exposed to in the past. These compositions represent a fusion of modes and styles. Leib Glantz's musical research and his wonderful compositions are living proof that there is much in common between the Ashkenazic and Sephardic musical cultures. Glantz's compositions and style were far ahead of his contemporaries, but today, forty-four years after his death, it is clear that he created an original musical path, one that sings to the heart of both Sephardim and Ashkenazim!

28

A Combination of *To'rah* and Art

DR. CHAIM HARRIS[1]

When one tries to sum up all the deeds and enterprises of a whole culture in a period of one generation, with the intent to appreciate its spiritual assets and to include all its creative powers of that period, especially in the field of musical art, one assumes an enormous responsibility. Perhaps the known achievements did not receive their proper recognition, or perhaps some aspects were simply unknown or unnoticed.

In earlier generations great achievements were accomplished in the art of cantorial. Great cantors and composers created works that have not been duplicated in our generation. Only very few of today's cantors are rich with talent and musicality compared to the great cantors of earlier times, such as Kashtan, Weintraub, Tsalal, Blumental, Rozovsky, Gerovitz, Nowakowsky, and Minkowsky.

We might conclude that we are in a period of decline in the art of synagogue music, caused by the upheavals, destruction, and extinction that the Jewish people have experienced in this generation. However, the truth is that this pessimistic conclusion has no basis. Great artists are still among us. There are cantors today with great talent, who are highly knowledgeable in Jewish wisdom and in the art of music, that are equipped with the advantages needed to officiate with honor in our synagogues.

---

1 Dr. Chaim (Hyman H.) Harris is author of the Hebrew book *Tol'dot Ha'Ne'gi'na Be'Yis'ra'el* (Hebrew Liturgical Music — A Survey of Traditional Hebrew Music: Biblical Cantillation and the Music of the Cantors), published by Bitzaron, New York, 1950. This translated essay was originally published in Hebrew in *Bitzaron* — a quarterly review of Hebrew letters, *Riv'on Le'Sif'rut, Ha'gut, U'Mech'kar*, June-July 1958.

We must not overlook the supreme qualities of great cantors such as Rosenblatt, Kwartin, Pinchik, and others, each excelling in his unique way. However, as we analyze their work and their style, we find that they have not defined for themselves a characteristic new path, and did not uncover new directions that would distinguish them from the traditional treasures of their predecessors.

Great researchers of Jewish music, such as A. Z. Idelsohn, have written about the musical distinctions that differentiate between Jewish and non-Jewish music. It is obvious that ancient Jewish music was influenced by non-Jewish oriental music. The Jewish bible cantillation, on the other hand, is undoubtedly a true original remnant that survived to this very day, thanks to the sanctity of the *To'rah*. We can therefore assume that every synagogue melody that contains these typical movements is definitely of Jewish origin.

Unfortunately, most of the cantors of our generation are unwilling to adopt "the path of the *To'rah*" in the cantorial profession, as did their parents and teachers of the generation before them. In addition, in their efforts to charm their audiences, cantors create musical inventions and gyrations that cannot withstand criticism. Their common denominator is that they are performed as entertainment, as opposed to the original Israeli Holy Temple music, that will remain alive for the duration of the nation's history. This leads to the conclusion that every melody that is performed in the synagogue, that is intended to add to the original building blocks, will be viable as an inherent part of the ancient Jewish musical heritage. For this reason, it is the duty of every respectable cantor to immerse himself with profound knowledge of the spiritual history of the people of Israel, including its musical rules and traditions.

One of the great artists and cantors of this generation is Leib Glantz. He is the symbol of the perfect cantor who has all the attributes demanded by this holy office. Glantz sings with a beautiful and powerful voice, which rises high above that of a typical tenor. He has a capability to command complicated vocal decorations, in order to intensify and modify the melodic expressions of the ideas in the text, with movements, flourishes, twists, colors, and 'creases.' He is totally devoted to the exploration of the deeper meanings of the texts of the *To'rah*, the Jewish literature, and the Jewish culture. However, his heart and soul are dedicated to the music. Here Glantz found the roots of his soul, his true world, the domain where he could devote all of his energy and achieve his goals.

> *One of the great artists and cantors of this generation is Leib Glantz. He is the symbol of the perfect cantor who has all the attributes demanded by this holy office . . . His heart and soul are dedicated to the music. Here Glantz found the roots of his soul, his true world, the domain where he could devote all of his energy and achieve his goals.*

Early in childhood, Leibele, as he was fondly named, grew up in a very religious family in the Ukrainian city of Kiev, similar to the great cantors Rozovsky, Gerovitz, Minkowsky, and others. He learned cantorial from his father, Cantor Kalman Glantz. In addition to his fundamental education in Judaism, Jewish and secular music, he was well known as one of the leaders of the Zionist movement. He was blessed as a great speaker, writer, and editor.

I would like to describe the basic characteristics of the cantorial of Leib Glantz:

1. Glantz does not limit himself to any specific method or style set forth by his predecessors. He created a totally independent style that borrows from no one and acquires nothing from existing melodies.

> *Glantz does not limit himself to any specific method or style set forth by his predecessors. He created a totally independent style that borrows from no one and acquires nothing from existing melodies.*

2. As a child prodigy, who began performing in public at the age of eight, Glantz became an innovator, researcher, and a collector of all available Jewish musical material. He ardently studied this material, and after delving deeply into its secret attributes, he filtered, refined, processed, redesigned, and then created amazing new original melodies, firmly built on the solid foundations of the traditional Jewish prayer modes (*Nu'sach*). Glantz never lowered himself to the level of those in the congregation who favored superficial melodies that were externally pleasant but internally void of content or legitimacy. He was a creator of music that offered original content, richness of ideas, and deep penetration into the souls of his listeners. Glantz could grasp the essence of a melody as it came out from the mouths of simple Jews praying innocently in the synagogues, pouring out their hearts and souls, sweetening their pleas with tunes, with whispers, with secret exchanges from a praying man to his Lord, in the simplest of expressions.

3. Glantz was extremely successful in discovering the spring from which the Chasidic melodies emanated. He filtered out the foreign elements that penetrated the music, and created melodies that were built on the pureness of Chasidic ecstasy.

4. There were those who tried to criticize Glantz for supposedly dissenting from the accepted, traditional, melodic tunes of the Jewish prayer modes. Some even believed he broke the rules of cantorial, as set forth by the early cantorial composers. At first, it might have seemed that there was some logic in this, but the truth soon became very clear. These critics simply did not recognize the fact that this was a "contradiction for the sake of constructing a newer and stronger foundation." The truth must be stated clearly: Glantz, in his compositions and his chanting of the Jewish prayers, strictly maintains the traditional prayer

modes in the most meticulous way. What he succeeded in achieving was to remove the wild weeds, and follow the original seeds of the traditional prayer modes.

The same can be said of his Chasidic melodies. As he discovers the roots of the melody, he extracts its essence, modifies and improves it according to the rules of music, and comes up with a perfect composition. In addition to the musical talent with which select human beings are naturally born, there is still a need to obtain a serious musical education. This is where Glantz exhibited to us all that he was a man who could utilize both crowns by combining great knowledge (*To'rah*) with great art.

Leib Glantz's method and style in cantorial are clearly reflected in the last three compositions that appeared in print: *She'ma Yis'ra'el (Hear O Israel)* from the *Sabbath Mu'saf Ke'du'sha* prayer service, *Ve'Al Yi'dei A'va'de'cha* ("And by your servants, the prophets, it is written") from the New Year *Rosh Ha'Sha'na* service, and *U'Ve'Nu'cho Yo'mar* ("When the ark rested, Moses would say") from the Sabbath service. The *She'ma Yis'ra'el* and the *U'Ve'Nu'cho Yo'mar* melodies are characterized by traditional *Nu'sach,* with complex and clever modulations — the work of a true artist. In his masterpiece *Ha'loch Ve'Ka'ra'ta* ("Go and proclaim so that Jerusalem may hear"), Glantz proves to be an amazing improviser. He seems at first to be implementing the traditional melodies usually sung for the *Zich'ro'not* (Remembrance) verses of the High Holiday prayer services, but we suddenly realize that the melody gains a shade of "nobility," as the soft and gentle oriental coloration of the tune is so appropriate for the poetic content of the words of this prayer. As for the third composition, *U'Ve'Nu'cho Yo'mar* — here Glantz successfully applies the most beautiful harmony.

29

Cantor, Composer and Researcher

ALEXANDER URIA BOSKOVITZ[1]

In recent years I have seldom attended synagogue services. I was under the impression that the musical standard of cantorial and the dubious taste in which it was performed, were detrimental to any authentic spiritual experience.

However, I was recently invited to the *Tif'e'ret Zvi* synagogue in Tel-Aviv to hear Cantor Leib Glantz praying the *Mu'saf* prayer service on the *Rosh Ha'Sha'na* holiday. I must admit — it was truly an amazing spiritual and artistic experience.

A great cantor must possess the qualities of an artist, a composer and a virtuoso. He must master the complex traditions of cantorial music. The combination of these qualities in one and the same person is very rare. Most of the great cantors of the past stem from family lineage that guards its qualities as if they were professional secrets. They are the sons and grandsons of cantors — a biological heritage. This consolidation of musical talent frequently erupts in the form of secular musical giants — stars of concert halls and opera houses.

Leib Glantz is a third generation cantor — the son and grandson of famous cantors. From early childhood he absorbed the musical legacy of the Jewish people.

This tradition of sacred services enabled the Jews to guard their unique culture from some of the dangers of assimilation. There have been many assimilatory tendencies. One example is

---

1 Alexander Uria Boskovitz (1907-1964), composer and music critic. This article appeared in *"Ha'A'retz"* daily newspaper, Israel, 1957.

Leib Glantz working on a composition at his piano at home in Tel Aviv, Israel, 1958.

the Chasidic movement, which absorbed popular foreign music from its surrounding gentile communities. Another example is the *Has'ka'la,*[2] a movement that tried to "modernize" Jewish liturgy, by enabling Lutheran choral melodies to 'invade' the synagogues, mostly in Central Europe. However, by far the most damaging was the introduction of secular music into cantorial performances, most notably Italian opera.

Fortunately, counter to this assimilation process, a generation of cantors emerged that was endowed with artistic intuition and musical training. These cantors recognized the importance of *Cha'za'nut* as an authentic cultural and religious asset.

One of the most distinguished among these cantors is Leib Glantz. He studied composition in Kiev with the well-known Ukrainian composer, Reinhold Gliere. In America he continued his musical education with Aspinol, teacher of the great opera singers Enrico Caruso and Benjamino Gigli. When Glantz was offered enticing opportunities to become a star in the opera world, he withstood the temptation, realizing that his true mission in life was to be a cantor. He officiated in prominent American synagogues and appeared with great success on

---

2 *Has'ka'la* was a movement of enlightenment in Europe in the early nineteenth century, that sought to combine elements of Jewish tradition with modern secular thought in the belief that cultural assimilation would bring about a radical change in the situation of the Jews in the world.

radio and television. His unique compositions were recorded and made him famous worldwide. At the height of his career, in 1954, he and his family left the United States and settled in Israel — his lifelong dream as a fervent Zionist.

Glantz has a tenor voice that contends with ease with any technical complexi-

When Glantz was offered enticing opportunities to become a star in the opera world, he withstood the temptation, realizing that his true mission in life was to be a cantor.

ties. Even though he has marvelous virtuosity, his singing is never an end in itself — but rather a means to arouse deep religious emotion. Glantz composes nearly all the music he performs. He devoted years to penetrating research and unearthed the ancient origins and principles on which Jewish music is based. He has demonstrated that he belongs in the same category as A.Z. Idelsohn and Solomon Rosowsky, the most distinguished research scholars in the field of traditional Jewish music.

Glantz's famous lecture at the 1952 Annual Convention of the Cantors Assembly of America solidified his stature as a great scholar. In this lecture he analyzed the fundamental basis of traditional Jewish music — *Nu'sach Ha'Te'fi'la* — the Jewish prayer modes.

This *Nu'sach*, similar to the Arab *Ma'kam* and the Indian *Ra'ga* music, consists of short melodies, based on principal themes, on which variations can be made. The singer who knows the archetype of the melody may improvise and create melodies of his own, as long as the basic *Nu'sach* themes continue to be maintained. The *Nu'sach* contains motifs similar to those on which the cantillation of the *To'rah* is based. These motifs are the most ancient known sources of Jewish music. They actually provide a common basis for all Jewish music, although there are indeed variations among the different Jewish communities of the Diaspora.

Evidence of the antiquity of these cantillations and *Nu'sach* modes is the fact that they are based on the ancient Pentatonic and Mixolydian musical scales. The Pentatonic scale dates back to very early stages in human musical history. In European music it has since evolved into a twelve-tone scale, but in the music of some of the Asian cultures, such as the Chinese, it remained frozen in its ancient form. In the Jewish musical tradition, the Pentatonic scale evolved at a very early stage into a seven-tone scale — the Mixolydian mode. Indeed, both Idelsohn and Rosowsky researched and wrote about this.

However, Leib Glantz went several steps further. He discovered that Jewish musicians combined several Tetrachords in a unique and original manner (such as combining four continuous Pentatones), by "borrowing" scales from ancient Greek origins. Glantz defined and proved that these musical combinations were authentically Jewish.

There are two main types of prayer modes in cantorial music. The first are melodies with a recitative character that the cantor is forbidden to change. They are called *Nu'sach Mi'Si'nai*, or prayer modes dictated from the revelation at Mount Sinai. The second type of *Nu'sach* uses basic themes that the cantor is permitted to improvise on to compose his own compositions. It is much like variations on a hidden theme. Examples of *Nu'sach Mi'Si'nai* are the *Ak'da'mut* prayer, which is sung on the *Sha'vu'ot* holiday service, using the Pentatonic scale, the *Ye'kum Pur'kan* prayer from the Sabbath *Mu'saf* service and the *Ka'ddish* prayer from the final *Ne'il'a* service of *Yom Ki'ppur* (Day of Atonement). These are based on the Mixolydian scale. Glantz succeeded in identifying the original Jewish building blocks of these prayer modes, and thanks to him we are capable of maintaining the purity of Jewish liturgical music and of identifying the correct execution of the *Nu'sach*.

> *Glantz succeeded in identifying the original Jewish building blocks of these prayer modes, and thanks to him we are capable of maintaining the purity of Jewish liturgical music as well as identifying the correct execution of the* Nu'sach.

These pure traditional modes of the Hebrew liturgy are particularly important for Jewish or Israeli composers who seek inspiration from the musical past of our nation. Leib Glantz himself uses these motifs both in his liturgical and secular compositions, giving them an authentic Hebrew character.

I wonder if new "Israeli" prayer modes could be created by musicians or cantors of the newly independent State of Israel. Would these be accepted by the Jewish communities of the Diaspora? Leib Glantz believes that Israel is destined to become the musical center of the Jewish world. If this dream is to be fulfilled, the State of Israel will need to develop serious cantorial schools where authentic cantors and professional choirs would be trained to officiate in synagogues in Israel and around the world.

30

A Unique Musical Personality

Maestro Seymour Silbermintz[1]

I first met him at a gathering of music lovers and musicians on a hot summer evening in New York. As he entered the room, I knew at once that it was Leib Glantz. In a matter of but a few moments his personality established itself. Every person present felt as if they had known him for a long time. In reality, who had not heard him perform, either in person or via recording? Who in that room had not experienced the glowing warmth of his artistry? The same spirit that permeated his public performance seemed to emanate from his natural "off-stage" self. There were no mannerisms to note, only a friendly

> *As he entered the room, I knew at once that it was Leib Glantz. In a matter of but a few moments his personality established itself. Every person present felt as if they had known him for a long time.*

smile that made one feel at ease in his presence. It was as if he were exclaiming: "I like music and I like art, but above all, I love people." It was this feeling of relaxation, of security, of genuineness, that one also finds upon examination of his music.

At this meeting Cantor Glantz made some remarks that granted us an insight into his unique personality. In the midst of a heated discussion about the merits and faults of a certain approach to a particular artistic problem, he suddenly exclaimed: "Theory, pure theory. It won't work. It doesn't 'feel' right. We should not invent a theory and stubbornly insist that it

---

1 Seymour Silbermintz (1917-2000) was a legendary figure in the field of Jewish music for over sixty years, as an instructor, arranger and choral conductor. This article was published in 1952.

is the best and only way. First let your instinct guide you and then develop a theory from your initial intuitive reactions."

Attention to details clearly shows up in his written works. He doesn't throw notes together and come up with a composition. His approach is consistently sensitive. The notation on his musical scores shows that infinitesimal patience and care has been lavished upon them so that every subtle nuance of soulful expression is properly written down.

Glantz anticipates and successfully avoids the usual pitfalls, the melodic *clichés*, the hackneyed sequences and the trite of monotonous gymnastics of run-of-the-mill cantorial recitatives. Moreover, with only seeming occasional deviation from traditional modes, he infuses into his creations a truly original spirit. There is an inspiring aura about his works that clearly indicates: "Made by Leib Glantz." No one else could have written them. They bear his unmistakable stamp.

Such music could not have been written by a formula in order to prove some preconceived theory. Glantz undoubtedly composes according to his natural musical impulses in a way that turns out to be quite different from those of his contemporaries or predecessors in the cantorial field. He is an originator with a style all his own. He has captured the hearts of an audience that has become international in scope, achieving world eminence. He is considered the master of his profession.

> *Glantz is an originator with a style all his own. He has captured the hearts of an audience that has become international in scope, achieving world eminence. He is considered the master of his profession.*

Glantz is an innovator. He sounds different. At first it is not easy to absorb. Such style is not similar to anything one has ever heard: unfamiliar intervallic relationships; exciting modulations; colorful harmonies; melodic patterns that are clearly oriental in quality. There are interesting rhythmic figures, groups of repeated notes in quick succession, all supplementing the basic motifs of the liturgy. But, above all, there is a fundamental simplicity of style, relying on expressive interpretation of the text rather than on ornateness of design for effect.

Furthermore, in addition to Leib Glantz the cantor and Leib Glantz the composer, there is Leib Glantz the scholar. He has conducted a serious study of the music of the synagogue. His research has confirmed what first came to him as insight and later formed as a hypothetical theory. I am not at liberty to reveal the exact nature of Glantz's ideas in this realm (which he is preparing for publication), but I can say that I have found them to be truly original and revolutionary. As a matter of fact, they are so simple and clarifying that it is a wonder that other theoreticians in the field have not stumbled upon them before.

In the process of studying the Jewish prayer modes, the *Nu'sach*, he has come to the conclusion that *Nu'sach* cannot be understood in terms of the usual Major and Minor scales. In addition, Glantz refuses to recognize the standard tonics (basic tones) that please the Western ear. He replaces them with tonics and tone-groupings more enjoyable to the Eastern ear. This, he affirms, brings us closer to an understanding of the true *Nu'sach* that originated in the old scale forms borrowed from the ancient Greeks. These were transformed by Jewish musicians into original Jewish prayer modes. In time, however, changes and accretions have affected the liturgy. According to Glantz, it is imperative to revise some of the so-called "traditional" music and revert back to the early sources. He firmly believes that his discoveries will point the way to further research and discoveries. Judging by his determination and seriousness of purpose, he will leave a permanent mark, and a healthy one at that, on the future course of Jewish music.

One of Glantz's newest sheet music publications is a prophetic message to Jerusalem from the prophets Jeremiah and Ezekiel, titled *"Ha'loch Ve'Ka'ra'ta"* ("Go and proclaim so that Jerusalem may hear"). It possesses a very special meaning in our time and demonstrates the special 'Glantz technique' of combining the expected with the unusual, creating thrilling and fascinating Eastern sounds. The composition is appropriately dedicated to David Ben Gurion, the Prime Minister of Israel. An interesting sidelight is the fact that Glantz chose to provide both the Sephardic and Ashkenazi texts in these printed compositions.

Leib Glantz creates music that is hauntingly different. He opens a window to wider vistas and new horizons. This music represents a stimulating originality in the art of cantorial.

Leib Glantz creates music that is hauntingly different. He opens a window to wider vistas and new horizons. This music represents a stimulating originality in the art of cantorial.

31

In Memory of Leib Glantz

CANTOR NATHAN MENDELSON[1]

How shall we characterize this unique personality, this brilliant musician, this inspired *Cha'zan*, Leib Glantz?

We may characterize his life by the first verse of Psalm 147:2: "For it is good to sing praises unto our God, for it is pleasant, and praise is comely" (*Ha'lle'lu'ya Ki Tov Zam'ra E'lo'kei'nu, Ki Na'im Na'a'vah Te'hi'la*). How fitting in this connection is the second verse as well: "The Lord doth build up Jerusalem, he gathereth together the dispersed of Israel" (*Bo'neh Ye'ru'sha'la'yim Ha'Shem, Nid'chei Yis'ra'el Ye'cha'nes*). Indeed, we had all hoped for the fulfillment of the third verse: "Who healeth the broken in heart and bindeth up their wounds" (*Ha'Ro'feh Li'She'vu'rei Lev U'Me'cha'besh Le'Atz'vo'tam*).

But it was not to be. And here at this convention, we sit amongst his family and indeed all of Israel, as we mourn and lament the passing of this sweet singer of the songs of Israel (*Ne'im Ze'mi'rot Yis'ra'el*).

Leib Glantz was an idealist and a whole-hearted, warm personality. What was the secret of his life? What in *Cha'za'nut* fascinated him? Was it the thrill of being a *Shli'ach Tzi'bur*, the people's deputy in petition before the Lord? No doubt this was one element.

Was it the pursuit of the elusive scales of ancient Jewish music and the prayer modes, the *Nus'cha'ot*, associated with them, from which these scales are derived? It was this as well.

---

1 Cantor Nathan Mendelson (1907-1977) served as President of the Cantors Assembly (1951-1954). This eulogy was presented as part of a *Yiz'kor* service in memory of Leib Glantz at the 17th Annual Convention of the Cantors Assembly of America (New York, May 25, 1964).

Was it the curious, romantic, tragic, and inspiring history of the evolution of the *Cha'zan,* with all the roles he has played in the community in past ages, and all he does in the expanding picture of Jewish community life today? Was it all we anticipate from the *Cha'zan* in future days of glory? Again the answer is yes.

Leib Glantz demonstrated by his deeds as well as by his words, his readiness to toil and sacrifice for the advancement of our liturgical music, our folk music, and our art music in the land of Israel and abroad.

What were his striving, his inner compulsion, the springs of his being, the source of his perennial spring (*Ma'a'yan Mit'ga'ber*), which kept him young and fresh, even as he approached his older years? What was this inner urge? The answer is that it was his self-imposed role as the reviver of the dead (*Me'cha'yeh Ha'Mei'tim*).

Now what do I mean by this phrase? When we recite the 'Eighteen Benedictions' (*A'mi'da*), just before the Sanctification prayer (*Ke'du'sha*), we declare: "Blessed are You, O Lord, who revives the dead" (*Ba'ruch A'ta Ha'Shem, Me'cha'yeh Ha'Mei'tim*). Why do we say this? Who are these dead people whom the Lord is reviving? My friends and colleagues: the Lord is reviving us — the House of Israel.

We are all idealists and philosophers when it comes to theory. We set our ideals on a high and holy pedestal. However, when it comes to the point of dedicating our actions to the ideal and translating our ideals into actions, we are often sadly wanting.

Not so Leib Glantz! As our revered colleague and inspiring Cantor Israel Alter has stated, Leib Glantz was a man who was crazy (*Me'shu'ga*) for *Cha'za'nut*. He relinquished position, comfort, livelihood, and security in order to make Israel his home, and in that country to develop his sacred art. And he realized his ideal — thus sanctifying the name of the Lord. Leib Glantz created the miracle of the revival of the dead. He revived *Cha'za'nut!*

> *Glantz relinquished position, comfort, livelihood and security in order to make Israel his home and [there] develop his sacred art . . . He revived* Cha'za'nut!

Words lacking spirit are dead. When a man prays in the spirit of "mercy and petition" before the Divine Presence, the letters and words fly about, hover in the air, soar upward toward the Throne of Glory, and there they form wreaths and garlands on the brow of the Almighty. Israel was the spring of Leib Glantz's inspiration, his fountain of self-renewing waters that enabled him to achieve his greatest feats.

The cantor has always been a reflection of emotional crisis in Jewish life. Through his song often came to expression the full sweep of feelings that held sway over his people. Leib Glantz actually succeeded in breathing life into the words of our prayers. His music gave new meanings to ancient texts.

Glantz founded a school of *Cha'za'nut* in Israel. I am assured that this Cantors Assembly, of which he was an ardent supporter and co-worker, will do its share to perpetuate Leib Glantz's contribution to synagogue chant. Let us bear in mind the message he sent a year ago to the students of our Cantors Institute and to the members of the Cantors Assembly:

Dear Students of the Cantors Institute and members of the Cantors Assembly:

I send you these words from Israel as it is a little too distant for me to be with you tonight.

There was a time when Jewish life was full of religious content, and cantors grew organically out of the cultural soil of the community. At that time musical talent was all that needed to be added to Jewish knowledge, for a man to be able to fulfill the role of cantor and *Shli'ach Tzi'bur.*

In recent years, with the progressive alienation of the Jewish youth from Jewish education and Jewish sources, the cantor does not always come to this calling from a rich Jewish environment.

Therefore, it becomes more and more necessary that the future cantors acquire an appropriate Jewish and musical education in institutions specifically designed for this purpose. Among these institutions, the Cantors Institute of the Cantors Assembly is one of the distinguished pioneers. I am sure that the Cantors Institute will continue to give its students excellent training in the basic knowledge necessary to fulfill minimum needs and demands.

In this era, school, university, yeshiva and conservatory, are only first steps in the long road toward progress, enhancement, fulfillment and advancement of the art of cantorial.

Too many of our colleagues have ceased to strive for something new and different in the cantorial field. Much has become frozen. Too many have learned some elementary principles and have been content to offer them as the whole deal.

And just as minimum knowledge is not enough, a good voice is not enough either. A good voice has to be properly and permanently trained. One has to know how to sing properly — but one also has to know how to pray. There has to be *Ka'va'na* and *D'vei'kut* (mental concentration and closeness to God.) But there can be no *Ka'va'na* and *D'vei'kut* if there is no true understanding of Jewish prayer, of Jewish poetry, of

Te'fi'la. Even if a cantor knows Hebrew, it is not sufficient unless he understands the spirit, meaning and symbolism of the text.

And so we see that in order to be a good cantor, one must have knowledge, a trained voice, a deep feeling for prayer, willingness to continue to study, and a great love of the cantorial calling itself.

Accept my heartiest blessings for great success. Sincerely and comradely yours,

Leib Glantz

In all the aspects of his cantorial activity, Leib Glantz brought to bear the impress of a great soul. Let us do what we can that his soul may be bound in the bond of life.

Let me conclude with a story of the "unfinished *Ka'ddish.*" A dear colleague, Cantor Shlomo Gisser, who has just returned from Israel, has related to me what he gleaned about Leib Glantz's last days and last moments. Cantor Gisser visited Miriam, Leib's widow, and there he

The grave site of Leib and Miriam Glantz at Kir'yat Sha'ul cemetery in North Tel Aviv, Israel.

found still resting on Glantz's piano, the last composition which Leib Glantz had been working on. It was an unfinished composition of *Ka'ddish*. While he was writing it, he called out to Mrs. Glantz with a smile: "Well, as soon as I have finished composing the *Ka'ddish*, I am ready to die . . ."

> *"Well, as soon as I have finished composing the* Ka'ddish, *I am ready to die…"*

Leib Glantz died just a few days later, and never succeeded in finishing this new composition.

Fifth Annual Kavod Awards

The Cantors Assembly of America's Fifth Annual *Kavod* Awards (1964)
presented for outstanding contributions to the music of the Jewish people:

Cha'zan Leib Glantz
in memoriam
to a uniquely gifted *Cha'zan,* composer and scholar,
whose original and authentic contributions to the music
of the synagogue will help keep his memory alive and
fresh forever in the hearts of his colleagues and all who
love and perform the sacred music of our people.

32

Leibele Glantz's Great Musical Heritage

CANTOR SHOLOM SECUNDA[1]

It is hard to believe that Cantor Leib Glantz, the pedagogue, composer, idealist, Zionist and great scholar of Jewish music is no longer amongst the living.

Two days after I learned of his death, I received in the mail a letter from Glantz thanking me for the article I had written in the *Forward* newspaper about his Cantors Academy in Tel Aviv. This institution was very important and he devoted much of his energy to its success. In his last visit to America, shortly before his death, he stressed how important it was for all of us to support this academy in order to avoid the deterioration of cantorial art.

Glantz departed from America to Israel with great energy. He could have chosen to enjoy a much better economic situation for his family in the United States, but returned to Israel, declaring that Israel was the place where he flourished.

Glantz's career, with so many great accomplishments, was not always smooth and easy. He encountered hardships and difficulties that would have easily broken a less courageous man. He succeeded in overcoming every obstacle without ever bending his ideological principles.

---

1 Cantor Sholom Secunda (1894-1975) was a composer, arranger, director and critic who came to New York in 1907, and entered the Institute of Musical Art (later renamed the Juilliard School) where he trained with the famous composer Ernest Bloch. In the Yiddish theater he was a composer and director until the early 1970's. His compositions have been successful in Yiddish theater and in popular music with hit songs by such artists as the Andrews Sisters *("Bei Mir Bist Du Sheyn")* and Joan Baez *("Dona, Dona, Dona")*. In the 1940s, he began working in radio, and from 1946 he was the music critic for the *Jewish Daily Forward*. Secunda composed many Jewish liturgical compositions and regularly conducted performances of classical music with well-known musicians and opera singers. This article was published in the *Jewish Daily Forward* on January 13, 1967.

He fought like a giant and won his battles. As a cantor, he strongly adhered to the traditional *Nu'sach*. He would not agree to follow well-trodden paths of other famous cantors that he listened to and appreciated. He created for himself a totally new path, loyal to the ancient prayer modes, but not stagnating in the acceptable musical styles of the Eastern European Diaspora. He preferred the Middle Eastern style and atmosphere of the land of Israel and the motifs of our ancient forefathers.

As a wonderful composer, lecturer and writer, who was bold enough to express original and unique styles and theories, there were always those that held different opinions, even among his fellow cantors, composers and musicians. However, they would never miss an opportunity to hear him chant in the synagogue, the concert hall, or when he lectured, carefully studying his writings and his compositions.

> *We find ourselves continuously discussing and analyzing his style and his unique compositions. These will continue to occupy our thoughts, for he left for us a great musical heritage that will nourish the Jewish nation's religious and secular music for many years to come.*

Two years have gone by since Leibele passed away, but we find ourselves continuously discussing and analyzing his style and his unique compositions. These will continue to occupy our thoughts, for he left for us a great musical heritage that will nourish the Jewish nation's religious and secular music for many years to come.

33

How Unique Was Leib Glantz?

A<small>KIVA</small> Z<small>IMMERMAN</small> [1]

Cantor Leib Glantz was a unique phenomenon in the world of Jewish song and prayer. Cantorial was the true essence of his life. It surrounded him at all times, not only while chanting in the synagogue. He desired to pass this quality on to his students and to his audiences.

A cantor is not just a singer and the synagogue is not a theater. The cantor's art is the continuation of the musical traditions of the Levite priests who sang and played instrumental music in the ancient Holy Temple in Jerusalem two thousand years ago. An Italian or Russian opera singer is not required to be knowledgeable about his people's history. On the other hand, according to Glantz, a qualified cantor needs to be well versed in Jewish history, Jewish literature and the written and oral laws of the Jewish religion.

Leib Glantz was a great musician. As a young man in the Ukraine, he studied at the world famous Kiev conservatory with the leading Russian musicians of the era: composition with the distinguished composer Reinhold Gliere, piano with Professor Dombrovsky and Professor Nikolai Tutkovski, and Musical Theory and Harmony with Nikolai Lisenko. He was seriously preparing himself for a career as a classical music piano soloist. Eventually, he realized that he was destined to devote his life to his real passion — composing and singing cantorial music — "the song of songs" of his life — as he fondly described it.

---

1 Akiva Zimmerman is an authority on cantorial and Jewish music. Author of *B'Ron Yahad — Essays, Research and Notes on Hazzanut and Jewish Music,* The Central Cantorial Archive, Tel Aviv, 1988, and *S'harei Ron — The Cantorate in Responsa,* Published by Bron Yahad — Tel Aviv, 1992. In addition, Zimmerman authored a book about Cantor Moshe Kousevitzky and has lectured on Leib Glantz and on cantorial throughout the world.

> *"Come and hear this wonderful cantor whose singing is that of a man speaking to God..." His voice came to her ears as she entered the auditorium, and even before seeing his face, she was convinced that this was the man she would one day marry!*

His devoted wife, Miriam Lipton Glantz, a woman of great personality and intellect, grew up in an assimilated Jewish home, far removed from religious tradition. Sara Wachs, a close friend, once invited her to "come and hear this wonderful cantor whose singing is that of a man speaking to God." Miriam arrived at the concert hall shortly after Glantz had begun singing. Hearing Glantz's voice from afar as she entered the auditorium, and even before seeing his face, she was convinced that this was the man she would one day marry!

One of Glantz's most important compositions is *She'va Pe'amim A'ta* ("Seven Times 'Thou'"), in which he sings seven different prayers from seven different prayer services, all containing the word "Thou" (*A'ta*). In each of these prayers, Glantz seems to be speaking directly to God. Each and every one of the seven prayers is sung with its specific prayer mode, or *Nu'sach*: week-

days, Sabbath and holidays — each with its different flavor. Glantz, with his miraculous talents, illuminated the mystical connections between the different prayer modes, and formed a beautiful composition that has actually become a master class on the fundamentals of *Nu'sach*!

Leib Glantz was passionately active as one of the great leaders of the Zionist movement. His first visit to Palestine, or *E'retz Yis'ra'el* as it was called, was in 1930. His work as a writer, editor, lecturer, and fundraiser on behalf of the *He'Cha'lutz* and *Tse'i'rei Zion* movements, in Kiev, Kishinev, New York, Los Angeles and Israel, led to his participation as an elected delegate to eleven World Zionist Congresses. He sincerely believed that the Jewish people were destined to eventually achieve a national homeland, and fulfilled his family's dream by settling in Israel in 1954. Spirituality and idealism were far more important for Leib Glantz than material gains. He relinquished a much superior income in the United

States in order to fulfill his dream of living in Israel, and being involved with synagogue audiences that truly comprehended the texts of the Hebrew prayers that he was performing. Interestingly, eighty of Leib Glantz's 216 original compositions were composed in Israel.

When Glantz arrived in America in 1926, he was immediately recognized as a unique cantor. The famous Cantor David Roitman wrote about him: "There are hundreds of *Cha'za'nim* in America, but there is only one Leibele Glantz." When Glantz left New York to settle in Los Angeles in 1941, Roitman wrote to him again: "Leibele, there is not a second Leib Glantz in our generation, and I doubt there will ever be someone of your stature."

The famous Cantor and Professor Max Wohlberg wrote about the impact of Glantz on American and world cantorial:

> With the arrival of Leib Glantz on the *Cha'za'nic* scene, the cantorate acquired previously unimagined dimensions. Glantz brought imaginative manipulation of the *Nu'sach* and motifs, and introduced into our repertoire a noble concept of tunefulness and a dynamic intensity that was yet unheard of. He was also fortunate in possessing an incredibly flexible vocal apparatus that enabled him to explore an endless number of delicate nuances and dynamic effects. Glantz was a masterful manipulator of the *Nu'sach* and a relentless prober of the liturgical texts.

Professor Wohlberg believed that our generation of *Cha'za'nut* would be branded by the creativity of Leib Glantz!

In his wonderful composition *Sho'mer Yis'ra'el* ("Guardian of Israel"), Glantz expresses several moods of Jews while praying: crying out to God to "save the remnants of your people of Israel," begging the almighty that "thy people of Israel should not be abandoned and lost," abruptly demanding "our Father, our Lord, please have mercy upon us and answer our prayers, because we have no bad deeds."

The pinnacle of Leib Glantz's creativity was undoubtedly the music he composed for the complete Midnight *Se'li'chot* Service. He composed each and every one of the twenty prayers. As a young man in my twenties, I was fortunate to attend his synagogue on *Se'li'chot*. I listened in awe as Glantz sung. He stood on the *Tif'e'ret Zvi* synagogue pulpit for three solid hours, chanting his unbelievably unique compositions. I will never forget feeling as if Glantz, with his amazing tenor voice, was actually *talking* to God in the language of the liturgical poets *(Py'ta'nim)*. You could feel his voice penetrating

> *I will never forget feeling as if Glantz, with his amazing tenor voice, was actually talking to God in the language of the liturgical poets* (Py'ta'nim). *You could feel his voice penetrating into the hearts of the masses that swarmed to the synagogue to listen to him.*

into the hearts of the masses that swarmed to the synagogue to listen to him — an enormous audience of followers and admirers who adored him in Israel from 1954 for the last ten years of his life.

Glantz considered his cantorial work a mission. He would never accept the idea that cantorial was a form of entertainment. In a lecture Glantz presented at the 1959 conference of the Israel Music Institute in Jerusalem, he declared:

> We must fight against the current contempt that exists towards cantorial. It is Judaism itself that is being dishonored. We must not enable cantors to lower *Cha'za'nut* to the level of mass entertainment. Cantors must not succumb to sing only those compositions that are demanded by the masses. We must cleanse our cantorial art from foreign elements. We need to stubbornly guard our ancient traditions, and at the same time introduce new musical creations. This is the path to reviving our authentic Jewish cantorial art.

Leib Glantz was the most unique phenomenon in the world of *Cha'za'nut*! Will there appear another great cantor and composer of the stature of Leib Glantz in our generation? Unfortunately, Jewish communities similar to those that nurtured cantors like Leib Glantz have ceased to exist. The Jewish way of life of the Eastern European *"Min'cha and Ma'a'riv"* Jews, from which Glantz and his generation of cantors absorbed their inspiration — exists no more. Therefore, I wonder if it is conceivable that another great genius of the stature of Leib Glantz can possibly evolve.

34

A Pioneer in Jewish Liturgical Music

MACY NULMAN[1]

Leib Glantz was the only composer in Israel who was seriously interested in the fostering of synagogue music. He was an accomplished cantor who rejected the superficial brilliance that had crept into most of European, American and Israeli cantorial art.[2] He was imbued with the spirit of his ancient heritage and totally immersed in *D'vei'kut.*[3] All this, together with an abundant flow of creative genius, enabled him to contribute mightily to the building of a new era in Jewish liturgical music.

Glantz wrote on the importance of *D'vei'kut*:

> "Cha'za'nut *must always be spiritually and intellectually superior. The higher* Cha'za'nut *is removed from the mundane, the closer it will be to heaven.*"

> The word *D'vei'kut* is immersed in sound. True *Cha'za'nut* is a ritual purification in *D'vei'kut,* and is heavenly divine. Therefore, *Cha'za'nut* should never sink to the level of ordinary song. *Cha'za'nut* must always be spiritually and intellectually superior. The higher *Cha'za'nut* is removed from the mundane, the closer it will be to heaven.[4]

---

1 Macy Nulman is the former director of the Philip and Sara Belz School of Jewish Music of the Rabbi Isaac Elchanan Theological Seminary at Yeshiva University. He authored the *Encyclopedia of the Sayings of the Jewish People, the Encyclopedia of Jewish Prayer, Concepts of Jewish Music and Prayer,* the *Concise Encyclopedia of Jewish Music,* and *Essays of Jewish Music and Prayer.*
2 Peter Gradenwitz, *Music and Musicians in Israel,* Israeli Music Publications Limited, Tel Aviv, 1978, p. 122.
3 *D'vei'kut* (literally: "clinging") — profound concentration; spiritual attachment to, or unification with, the Divine; a communion with the Divine that removes one from physical awareness.
4 *Zeharim — In Memory of Leib Glantz,* Tel Aviv Institute for Jewish Liturgical Music, Tel Aviv, 1965, p. 218.

Glantz stood apart from the conventional and usual Chazanic pattern. His brilliant, high lyric tenor voice talked to God, pleaded, demanded, and always made an earnest appeal on behalf of the congregation. He created a style of his own and is remembered by posterity as a great innovator. He also fought vigorously to purify the Hebrew chant from alien elements.

Glantz was also an outstanding writer and researcher, He began to write on Jewish music when he was in Kishinev in the "*Un'zer Zeit*" Yiddish newspaper in 1924. In an article titled "The First Night of *Se'li'chot*" (*Layl Ri'shon Le'Se'li'chot*)[5] he describes the special mood of the people after the *Sha'bbat*, when the *Sha'mash* (the synagogue beadle) summons the worshippers to get up to come and pray the midnight *Se'li'chot* service. In this article, Glantz explains the inner meanings of key phrases in the *Se'li'chot* service, thus enhancing his musical interpretations.

In 1959 Glantz founded the Tel Aviv Institute for Jewish Liturgical Music and its Cantors Academy. At the inauguration ceremony Glantz declared:

> We shall strive to put an end to the lawlessness and recklessness in the field of Jewish music and prayer. We want to change the stature of the cantor in Israel and in the world. Not anyone who wishes to acquire the title *Cha'zan* should be permitted to do so. Not every person who has an untrained voice should be compared to a singer who has obtained a serious musical education. Those who adulterate the words of the prayers and poems (*Pi'yu'tim*) cannot serve as leaders of a congregation (*Shli'ach Tzi'bur*). Our objective is to teach our cantorial students the simple meanings in *Cha'za'nut*. They should know not only *what* to sing, not only *how* to chant the *Nu'sach* prayer modes, but *why* they sing specifically this *Nu'sach* and not another. The answers regarding these issues can all be found in our *Nus'cha'ot*, which contain musical explanations and musical logic. Those who are seriously interested in this knowledge can and will understand it. The *Nu'sach* contains clear language. One has simply to decipher its secrets.[6]

Much remains to be done in order to reclaim even a small part of the great output and ideas that Leib Glantz left with us. It is my hope and prayer that someone will undertake the direct continuation of his monumental work.

5 Cf. *Zeharim*, ibid, p. 113-117.
6 Cf. *Zeharim*, ibid, p. 201.

35

A Giant in the Cantorial World

CANTOR NATHAN STOLNITZ[1]

With the premature passing of the famous singer and composer Leib Glantz, the field of *Cha'za'nut* has lost a great creative power, who exerted substantial influence on the musical art forms of Jewish life, and who was a pillar of strength in the preservation of the Jewish musical tradition. He held high the banner and tirelessly encouraged his colleagues to new challenges, to raise the standard of liturgical art ever upward, so that the crown of cantorial art should win its true and rightful place.

Many have written about Glantz's musical and liturgical creativity, describing him as a phenomenon among cantors — a unique figure who established his own philosophy and doctrine of music.

> *Glantz was not only one of the most intellectually and creatively gifted cantors of our day. He did not confine himself to the limits of his sacred task within the synagogue, where he was the poet of the altar. He was also active in the sphere of Jewish national and communal life, being possessed of leadership qualities both in word and deed.*

Glantz was not only one of the most intellectually and creatively gifted cantors of our day, but was an influential and versatile personality on many fronts. He did not confine himself to the limits of his sacred task within the synagogue, where he was the poet of the altar, but was also

---

1 From "On Wings of Song," by Rev. Nathan Stolnitz, Artistic Printing Co. Ltd., Toronto, Canada, 1968. Reprinted from *The Jewish Standard*, Toronto, September 1, 1964. Nathan Stolnitz was a cantor and journalist.

Leib Glantz with Sara Wachs, his agent, manager and lifelong friend in Los Angeles, 1943.

active in the sphere of Jewish national and communal life, being possessed of leadership qualities both in word and deed. His activity in the Labor Zionist camp, as a writer and a thinker, commanded great respect.

Besides his numerous liturgical compositions, he composed Hebrew, Yiddish and Chasidic songs, lectured and wrote intensively on Jewish music.

For years he was among the leading pacesetters in cantorial circles in the United States and Canada, and was a frequent participant in professional conferences. He was blessed with many qualities that added luster to his cantorial vocation. This is confirmed by the recordings of his album *"D'vei'kut"* ("Hassidic Spirituals") which aroused enthusiasm among the greatest musical personalities and most famous intellectuals of our time, including the great musician Ernest I. Bloch and the scientist Dr. Albert Einstein, both of whom wrote him warm letters of admiration.

As an ardent lover of Zion throughout his life, Glantz fulfilled his dream by settling in Israel in 1954, where he assumed a prominent cantorial post in Tel Aviv. Among his newly won admirers were many of Israel's leaders.

When I visited Israel in 1961, I attended the Cantors Academy, which was established and led by Leib Glantz. I was inspired by his plans to raise the level of our liturgical craft.

Leib Glantz's warm and brotherly behavior, noble personality and great artistic influence, will remain forever implanted in the minds of all who knew and respected him.

36

Blazing Artistic Path of an Avant-Garde Cantor

CANTOR SAM WEISS[1]

For four years, beginning in 1916, Leib Glantz moved between the Ukraine and Besarabia, and began writing liturgical recitatives — the first of over 200 striking Jewish musical compositions uniquely suited to his own limber voice and fiery temperament. In 1920 he moved permanently from Kiev to Kishinev, where he composed his first settings of secular Hebrew poetry.

He came to America in the summer of 1926, blazing an artistic path for himself in city after city; critics, congregants and concert audiences raved about the startling and uplifting experience of listening to this avant-garde cantor. He communicated the nuances of every single word he sang with old-world piety, steeped in the traditional modes and patterns of synagogue song; yet he rarely proceeded along a predictable melodic path. Glantz stretched the classical cantorial art-form to its creative limits, using his lyric tenor voice in a dramatic and declamatory style with the eloquence of an orator. It was a style that made considerable aesthetic demands on the listener — with its angular vocal lines, chromatics, and

> *He came to America in the summer of 1926, blazing an artistic path for himself in city after city; critics, congregants and concert audiences raved about the startling and uplifting experience of listening to this avant-garde cantor.*

1 Sam Weiss is the cantor of The Jewish Community Center of Paramus, New Jersey. He is a noted recitalist, lecturer, and Jewish music consultant. This is an abridged version of his essay titled "Nine Luminaries of Jewish Liturgical Song," published in 2006.

occasional histrionic effects like *sprechstimme, glissando,* and sharp dynamic contrasts. Not all listeners cared for it. But those who were willing to listen carefully to his interpretations and improvisations were rewarded with a profound musical and religious experience. The first two compositions that he recorded for RCA in 1929, were talked about for years, and to this day have not lost their creative edge. *Shéma Yis'ra'el* and *Tal* revealed his remarkable poetic soul even to those not versed in Hebrew or the Jewish liturgical tradition, while those so versed marveled at his use of the traditional prayer modes (*Nu'sach*) for tonal exploration into areas untouched by his predecessors. In addition to synagogal works, the approximately 100 compositions that he recorded over his career included Hebrew and Yiddish art songs, as well as original settings of traditional Chasidic songs.

Glantz settled in Israel in 1954 to assume a pulpit in Tel-Aviv, which he held for the very creative and productive last decade of his life. A crowd of 4,000 people, impossible to accommodate, gathered to hear his first Midnight Penitential Service (*Se'li'chot*). In succeeding years the *Se'li'chot* services, whether heard at his synagogue or via national radio broadcast, became a widely-followed annual cultural event among Israeli music lovers. A compilation recording of some of these broadcasted services was issued in 1962. His musicianship, creativity and scholarship in the field of liturgical music also earned the respect of secular Israeli composers and critics, many of whom looked to his theories for guidance in formulating a national musical idiom.

> *His musicianship, creativity and scholarship in the field of liturgical music also earned the respect of secular Israeli composers and critics, many of whom looked to his theories for guidance in formulating a national musical idiom.*

37

The Dignity of Words

PROFESSOR SAUL PHILIP WACHS[1]

During my studies at the Jewish Theological Seminary's College of Jewish Music during the 1950s, I became aware of Leib Glantz's unique place in the cantorate through the lectures of our esteemed professor of *Nu'sach*, Dr. Max Wohlberg. Cantor Wohlberg, on more than one occasion, singled out Glantz as a shining example of artistic creativity in the service of the liturgy. In particular, he explained that it was Glantz's goal to excise the 18th century *Galant* style which had played a prominent role in synagogue chant since the days of the sons of Johann Sebastian Bach.[2] Glantz strove to restore *Cha'za'nut* to its ancient oriental foundations.

His greatest gift was his ability to interpret the words of the liturgy. Synagogue chant was intended to be "logogenic," that is, to enlighten and do justice to the word. In Judaism, the word is at the center of prayer. A great *Cha'zan* is one who can interpret the word creatively and thus enable the worshippers to sense a nuance that was not seen before.

Of the many examples of Leib Glantz's commitment to the word, I will cite his musical treatment of the word *A'ta* (Thou) in *Sho'mei'a Te'fi'la, A'de'cha Kol Ba'sar Ya'vo'u* ("All flesh shall come to You, O Lord who listens to prayer"). This is a liturgical poem (*Pi'yut*) from the Penitential Prayers of *Se'li'chot*. This word, so common in the liturgy, is the key word of a large section of this *Pi'yut*. His strong and forceful reiteration of the word *A'ta*, illuminates the con-

---

1 Cantor Saul Philip Wachs, Ph.D, is the Rosaline B. Feinstein Professor of Education and Liturgy at the Gratz College of Jewish Studies in Melrose Park, Pennsylvania.

2 *Galant* style is a Rococo style characterized by flourishes and frills, introduced by Carl Philipp Emanuel Bach and others during the 18th century. It was adopted by many cantors of that era and often led to an ignoring or distorting of the meaning of the Hebrew words they chanted.

nective thread that binds the sentences of that section through acknowledging God's awesome power, past and present.

This overarching goal for cantors was eloquently conveyed to the cantorate by Abraham Joshua Heschel, as part of an address to the members of the Cantors Assembly of America and later published in a book of Heschel's essays:

> "I should like to conceive *Cha'za'nut* as the art of *Si'ddur* exegesis, as the art of interpreting the words of the liturgy. Words die of routine. The cantor's task is to bring them to life . . . There is the liturgy but there is also an inner approach and response to it, a way of giving life to the words, a style in which the words become a personal and unique utterance."[3]

Cha'zan Glantz personified a commitment to an appreciation of what Heschel called the "dignity of words." Interestingly, Heschel tied the dignity of cantorial music to liturgical revival with a focus on gaining new insights into the meaning of the words of the liturgy.[4]

In 1955, I was fortunate to spend a semester in Israel in association with the Chaim Greenberg Institute. While I spent most of my time in Jerusalem, I visited Tel-Aviv frequently. I spent one *Sha'bbat* as the guest of my cousin Meir Noy, a composer, musicologist and music educator of note. Noy was engaged in the process of assembling what ultimately became the largest private collection of Jewish ethnic music in the world.[5] Meir informed me that musicologists who were generally not in the habit of attending the synagogue, being far from religious, would make frequent visits to the synagogue on Herman Cohen Street where Leib Glantz officiated. Aware of his ideas, they sought inspiration for their own efforts to contribute to an understanding of what should be the shape of Jewish music in Israel. Evidently, Glantz represented an intellectual approach to his craft which yielded a powerful emotional expression of the words of liturgy.

My experience at the *Tif'e'ret Zvi* synagogue confirmed the judgment of Cantor Wohlberg and countless others of Glantz's unique powers. As a fourth year student in the Seminary College of Jewish Music, I had prided myself on being able to follow and even

The experiences of Davening with Leib Glantz humbled me and made me realize how far I had to go in order to truly appreciate the richness of liturgical music and the possibilities of restoring Cha'za'nut to its Eastern origins.

---

3 Abraham Joshua Heschel, "The Vocation of the Cantor," in *The Insecurity of Freedom: Essays on Human Existence,* The Noonday Press, New York, 1967, pp. 242-253. The entire essay is instructive and pages 249-251 are especially relevant to cantors.

4 Ibid. p. 249.

5 Today, this collection is housed in the Noy-Wachs Archive in the National Library at the Givat Ram campus of the Hebrew University in Jerusalem. It was purchased from Meir Noy and donated to the University by Ellis and Peggy Wachs of Philadelphia.

anticipate the sequences that make up a cantorial recitative. The experiences of Davening with Leib Glantz humbled me and made me realize how far I had to go in order to truly appreciate the richness of liturgical music and the possibilities of restoring *Cha'za'nut* to its Eastern origins. Again and again he surprised me with his chanting. It was the word that was the center of his interpretations of the prayers.

Following one of the services I told him how deeply impressed I was. He confided in me that, sometimes, he was so lost in his "conversations with God" that he could not remember exactly what he had done at the *A'mud* (prayer pulpit). His words and the way in which he expressed them (almost with a sense of embarrassment) came from the heart. I never forgot them nor the subtle advice he was conveying to me as a young student of *Cha'za'nut.*

It has been my privilege for the past thirty six years to act as guest *Shli'ach Tzi'bur* (leader of the congregation in prayer) for the High Holidays at Kehillath Israel Congregation in Brookline, Massachusetts. During those services, I have tried to convey the richness of a few of Leib Glantz's compositions, particularly, *T'ka Be'Sho'far Ga'dol* ("Blow the Great Ram's Horn") from the High Holiday *Sho'fa'rot* prayer service and *Ez'ke'ra Elo'him Ve'E'he'ma'ya* ("I remember, O God, and I am deeply vexed") from the *Ne'i'la* service of the Day of Atonement. After hearing two recordings of his setting of *D'ror Yik'ra*, a Chasidic melody, one by the composer and the other by Cantor Leon Lissek, I decided this year to utilize this melody for the singing of *Me'lech El'yon* ("Superior King") at congregation Kehillath Israel. As I anticipated, the melody proved to be very accessible to the congregation and they were easily able to join in after the first two verses.

The Talmud tells us that when the words of a deceased scholar are repeated, his lips move in his grave.[6] I hope that when we seek to share the gifts provided to us by Leib Glantz, this great *Ba'al Te'fila*, a master of prayer, is granted a similar measure of satisfaction. He spoke to God in his own unique fashion and left us a treasure to challenge and inspire all who would merit the titles of *Shli'ach Tzi'bur* and *Ba'al Te'fi'la.*

> *He spoke to God in his own unique fashion and left us a treasure to challenge and inspire all who would merit the titles of* **Shli'ach Tzi'bur** *and* Ba'al Te'fi'la.

---

6 According to *Ma'se'chet Ye'va'mot* (97a) of the Talmud, Rabbi Yochanan thus exclaimed to Rabbi Shimon Bar Yochai. In Rashi's interpretation, the deceased scholar derives pleasure as though he continues his life in the world of the living.

Part Two

Analyses of Leib Glantz's Historical Significance as Cantor, Composer, Researcher, Pedagogue and Zionist Leader

The transliteration of Hebrew and Yiddish terms in this book has been created to make it easier for readers who do not speak these languages. Hebrew and Yiddish words appear in italics, begin with capital letters, and an apostrophe separates every syllable. The Hebrew and Yiddish words and sentences are followed by the English translation (in parentheses). Several authors of essays have used a different transliteration system; however, an effort has been made to use the same transliteration system throughout the book.

1

Harmonizing Theory with Creativity:
Cantor Leib Glantz's Musical Agenda

Amit Klein[1]

IN COLLABORATION WITH
Prof. Eliyahu Schleifer[2] and Prof. Edwin Seroussi[3]
Jewish Music Research Centre, Hebrew University, Jerusalem

"We were born either before our time, or too late, or perhaps both..."[4]

Eastern European *Cha'za'nut* or "cantorial art," the elaborated performance of Jewish liturgical music in and outside the synagogue services, is a unique phenomenon that developed gradually since the mid-nineteenth century. Inherent to *Cha'za'nut* is a dialectical movement between traditional patterns of synagogue chant that date back to medieval times and artistic creativity dictated by modern musical sensibilities. Therefore *Cha'za'nut* encapsulates both long-term memory and innovation. In the recording era, i.e. in the twentieth century, this field of religious Jewish music underwent further detachment from its synagogue roots, becoming a "genre" of commodified music that has well-defined markets, concert circuits, broadcastings, critics etc.

---

1 Amit Klein — Ph.D. student at the Music Department of Bar-Ilan University, Israel and researcher of Ashkenazi Cantorial music in the Jewish Music Research Centre at the Hebrew University of Jerusalem.

2 Eliyahu Schleifer — Associate Professor of Sacred Music and Director of Cantorial Studies at the Hebrew Union College — Jewish Institute of Religion in Jerusalem, and member of the Jewish Music Research Centre of the Jewish National and University Library in Jerusalem. Former President of the Israeli Musicological Society. Founder and first editor of *Israel Studies in Musicology*, the Journal of the Israeli Musicological Society. Author of various articles on Cantorial and Chasidic music.

3 Edwin Seroussi — Emanuel Alexandre Professor of Musicology, Chair of the Department of Musicology and Director of the Jewish Music Research Centre at the Hebrew University of Jerusalem. Former Head of the Department of Musicology at Bar Ilan University. Published numerous books and articles on Jewish and Israeli music, including *Popular Music in Israel* (with Motti Regev, 2004) and *Spanish-Portuguese Synagogue Music in Reform Sources from Hamburg* (1996).

4 Leib Glantz, in a letter to Cantor Israel Alter, as quoted in *Ze'ha'rim — In Memory of Leib Glantz*, The Tel Aviv Institute for Jewish Religious Music, 1965, page 9.

In the rich and multifaceted world of twentieth century *Cha'za'nut,* many outstanding figures shaped the cantorial art as we know it at the outset of the twenty-first century. Some cantors gained renown for the richness of their compositional skills, others attained fame for the incredible capabilities of their voice, and some will be remembered for their ability to strike a chord every time they passed before the *Tei'va* (cantor's stand). Among the giants of modern *Cha'za'nut,* Leib Glantz still stands out as a unique phenomenon: a synthesis of scholar, theoretician, composer and performer. This incredible coexistence of so many virtues in one individual is even more amazing if we understand that some of these virtues actually stood in opposition to each other. The image of the composer and performer is the image of the artist: creative, imaginative, burning with desire to spread out his virtuosity. The image of the scholar is that of the sage: venerable, moderate, wary of foreign influences and innovation. Holding fast to established traditions, while at the same time looking forward for growth and progress of *Cha'za'nut* as an artistic and religious endeavor, typified Glantz's career. He was the brilliant innovator and the formidable conservative.

> *Among the giants of modern* Cha'za'nut, *Leib Glantz still stands out as a unique phenomenon: a synthesis of scholar, theoretician, composer and performer.*

These seemingly incompatible contradictions are at the core of the present discussion of Glantz's work and personality. Fortunately, in teasing out these various forces one can rely on his own self-conscious assessments of *Cha'za'nut* which he often articulated in writing. This was Glantz the cantorial theoretician, a penchant rooted in his integrity and introspectiveness. Glantz reflected upon some fundamental traits which he considered essential to cantorial composition and to the cantor's role through his articles, lectures and speeches delivered across the years. This information sheds light upon the manner in which Glantz hoped to merge his drive towards innovation with his deep respect towards the time-honored traditions of Eastern Ashkenazi cantorial heritage. We shall attempt to draw on the theoretical work of Glantz in order to gain a better understanding of how he accomplished reconciling innovation with conservation, musical creativity with staunch preservation of fading or endangered traditions. In addition, we shall attempt to demonstrate how his theoretical ideas found expression in his unique compositional style.

Glantz the Theoretician

The preservation and glorification of the Eastern Ashkenazi cantorial heritage were a central aspect of Glantz's life-long activities.[5] Throughout his oral and written expositions, Glantz advocated theories which were directed to that end. Glantz was strong minded as to the proper position and character of *Cha'za'nut* in modern and yet traditional context and expressed his views vigorously. Three major themes stand out among his collected works, which provide three fundamental cornerstones of modern *Cha'za'nut: Nu'sach,* innovation and hermeneutics.[6]

Glantz repeatedly stressed the importance of the restoration and revival of the musical *Nu'sach* — the traditional Jewish musical formats of prayers — after a period perceived as decadent. He resolutely required that the synagogue be kept clear of foreign and assimilationist influences.

Glantz viewed the *Nu'sach* legacy as consisting of two major genres: the first one is a set of melodies, phrases and short musical motifs used by cantors as a basis for their recitatives, improvisations or compositions. The improviser or composer has full freedom to elaborate, develop and introduce modulations within the framework of each particular musical unit. The second genre differs from the first one; it consists of a group of fixed prayer melodies that have been associated with specific texts from time immemorial. These fixed melodies are not subject to improvisation, elaboration, or any major change. Called in the literature *"Ni'ggu'nim Mi'Si'nai"* ("tunes from Sinai"), they include some of the most important prayers of the liturgy and are always sung in a well-defined, crystallized form. Glantz insisted that the cantorial recitatives be based on this traditional repository of melodies which encapsulated the core of the Ashkenazi liturgical music tradition at least since the late medieval period.[7]

Glantz protested against alien influences on the prayer tunes and insisted upon cleansing *Nu'sach* from such tendencies and upon preserving the time-honored melodies that had been passed down through the generations.

Despite this conservatism, Glantz pursued innovation and musical creativity, which constitute his second principle of *Cha'za'nut*. On several occasions Glantz criticized the music of renowned cantors for being stagnant and lacking imagination. Cantorial art, according to

---

5 Another major enterprise of Glantz's was his political activity as an avid Zionist. During his early years in Eastern Europe, Glantz was one of the central activists of Zionist organizations such as *He'Cha'lutz* (The Pioneer) and *Tze'i'rei Tzi'on* (Zion's Youth) and wrote for several newspapers. He continued his Zionist cultural and educational activities in his years in the United States and Israel and served as a delegate to the World Zionist Congress eleven times.

6 Hermeneutics — the branch of knowledge that deals with interpretation, especially of the bible or literary texts.

7 L. Glantz, *"The Musical Basis of Nu'sach Ha'Tefi'la,"* Proceedings of the Annual Conference Convention of the Cantors Assembly of America, 1954, p. 17. For the *Mi'Si'nai* tunes see, A.Z. Idelsohn, *"Der Missinai-Gesang der deutschen Synagoge,"* Zeitschrift für Musikwisseschaft 8 (1926), 449-472; D. Katz, *"From Mount Sinai to the Year 6000: A Study of the Interaction of Oral Tradition and Written Sources in the Transmission of an Ashkenazi Liturgical Chant (Ak'da'mut),"* Rivista Internazionale di Musica Sacra, 20/1 (1999), pp.175-206, corrected version: supplement to 20/2 (2000).

Glantz, must demonstrate novelty and originality — within the boundaries of *Nu'sach*. In a letter to his colleague and friend, Cantor Israel Alter, he asks: "How is it possible to lead *Cha'za'nut* in the path of true inspiration, to seek the novel truth of *Cha'za'nut*, its noble yearnings for the truth, for the fiery inflaming notes, for the sacred sparks of fire rising heavenward? … How shall one haul the cart of *Cha'za'nut* from the banal marshes into the Temple of awe and noble exaltation as did Yeruham Ha'Katan Blindman [1798-1891], Baruch Schorr [1823-1904], Nissan Blumenthal [1805-1903], Abraham Kalechnik Berkowitz, [1846-1927], Bezalel Schulsinger from Odessa [1790-1861] and Baruch Kintzler — to introduce in it the ancient grace of the cantorial art and the beauty of the modern world [of music]."[8] This statement, incidentally, does not contradict his antipathy for alien musical motives, but apparently indicates his interest in utilizing modern musical styles within his creative process.

> *"How is it possible to lead* Cha'za'nut *in the path of true inspiration, to seek the novel truth of* Cha'za'nut, *its noble yearnings for the truth, for the fiery inflaming notes, for the sacred sparks of fire rising heavenward?"*

This paradox between the traditional and the contemporary is threaded through Glantz's writings. The historical role of the cantor, says Glantz, was two-fold: "First: the preservation, concentration and maintenance of the purity of the unique *Nu'sach*. Second: to keep the *Nu'sach* in motion, so that it would not become dull and routine, to inspire it with new spirit, true heartfelt passion, a fresh renewed course accorded to the era, but not to abuse this adjustment to make way to musical 'heresy.'" Cantors must not forget their historical destiny. They should bear in mind: "1) Not to let go of those Jewish vocal compounds, those Jewish sound-elements, the *Nu'sach* and the Jewish character; 2) Not to allow the *Nu'sach* to freeze, to congeal, to cool down… Stagnation in art means death! Art must extend, elevate, intensify. Art is dynamic! Art is a fiery flame, 'an unconsumed bush.' *Cha'za'nut* should be nourished with new musical ways, using the established foundations of the old and antique, and it must establish fresh and up-to-date [music]." [9]

The third fundamental of *Cha'za'nut* is its hermeneutical function. The cantor must harness his music to an interpretational end and must be able to illuminate the ancient texts with his musical interpretations. In order to cope with this role, the cantor, claims Glantz, must be learned, discerning and broad-minded. Vocal abilities and musical innovation by themselves

---

8 Eliezer Steinman, "*Sho'ra'shim U'Me'chi'tsot*" in E. Steinman, (Ed), *Ze'ha'rim — In Memory of Leib Glantz*. The Tel Aviv Institute for Jewish Religious Music, 1965, p. 68.

9 "*Cha'za'nut — 'Shir Ha'Shi'rim' Le'Am'cha Yis'ra'el*," *Cha'zu'nim Journal* (Yiddish), 1951, quoted in Steinman, *Ze'ha'rim*, p. 147 and p. 150; italics in the original.

would not suffice. Glantz portrays the cantor as a "perfect, flawless Jew, versed in the national heritage, ancient Hebraic lore, the Holy Scriptures and the Commentaries, *Ha'la'cha, Ha'gga'da* and *Mid'rash,* medieval literature — including the liturgical works, and contemporary Jewish literature."[10] If a well-founded Jewish identity and a thorough familiarity with the texts of the services are missing, even a highly talented musician will not be able to pour meaning into the holy texts of the liturgical order and to use music as a tool for insight and interpretation.

> *If a well-founded Jewish identity and a thorough familiarity with the texts of the services are missing, even a highly talented musician will not be able to pour meaning into the holy texts of the liturgical order and to use music as a tool for insight and interpretation.*

From Theory to Practice

Not only did Glantz lay theoretical foundations for the art of *Cha'za'nut,* he also pursued the ideas implied in his theories through practical means. This practical aspect of his life work was twofold — the mentoring of young cantors and the composition of original works. Glantz actively contributed to the education of novice cantors in accordance with his doctrine, and he was a vibrant participant in the foundation of the Tel Aviv Institute for Jewish Liturgical Music and the Cantors Academy *(Ha'A'ka'de'mi'a Le'Cha'za'nut)* in 1959. He served as musical director of these institutes until his sudden passing on January 27, 1964, and in these roles he implanted his ideas among his young disciples.

Whatever he preached to others, he fulfilled in his own *Cha'za'nut.* His compositions, as well as his performance of them, attempted to combine *Nu'sach,* innovation and interpretation, namely the traditional chant elements, and creative and innovative musical imagination in the service of text interpretation.

Glantz's approach to textual hermeneutics yielded musical interpretations that ranged from simple 'word painting' (if we may borrow a problematic concept from Renaissance music literature), to the deepest penetration into the Midrashic meanings of the prayers. Our task is to unveil the whole spectrum of his interpretation. Glantz insisted that cantors must be aware of the textual and contextual meanings of the liturgical texts, precisely because he expected *Cha'za'nim* to harness their music in an attempt to reflect and magnify textual meanings. This

---

10 "The Destination *of Cha'za'nut*" — A lecture at the Cantors Academy, quoted in *Ze'ha'rim — In Memory of Leib Glantz,* Steinman, E. (Ed.), p. 203.

is not to say that every musical maneuver must be geared towards an interpretation of the text, or that every textual idea must be reflected in a correlative musical gesture.

On the simplest level of interpretation, we can find many passages that could be explained as 'word painting' with a self-explanatory relationship between the signifier and signified. *"Be'Shuv A'do'nai"* (Psalm 126) is an illuminating illustration of this type of simple musical denotation. The melody assigned to the word *"Ke'Chol'mim"* ("like those who dream") conveys a feeling of reverie, while the phrase *"Az Yi'ma'le Se'chok Pi'nu U'Le'sho'nei'nu Ri'na"* ("Then was our mouth filled with laughter, and our tongue with singing") sounds unmistakably like a rolling laughter. However, through most of the ensuing discussion, we shall focus on the deeper and more abstract relationship between textual meaning and musical motifs in Glantz's work. In order to do so, we must delve deep into each composition. Three works of Glantz's complete *oeuvre* were selected for further study and analysis: *"Kol A'do'nai," "Bir'kat Ko'ha'nim"* and *"A'na Be'Cho'ach."*

'Kol A'do'nai' (Psalm 29, 7 from *Ka'ba'lat Sha'bbat*, the Friday evening service)

The *Nu'sach* of this prayer was published by Glantz in his anthology *"Ri'nat Ha'Ko'desh — Nu'sa'chei Te'fi'la."* Even though the book was edited after the passing of Glantz, the editor — Yehoshua Zohar — notes in the introduction that the various excerpts of *Nu'sach* are based on actual demonstrations delivered by Glantz to his students at the Cantors Academy of the Tel Aviv Institute for Jewish Liturgical Music. Zohar worked with Glantz for many years and served as his choir director; he can therefore be relied upon as authoritative with regard to Glantz's *Nu'sach*. The prayer also appears as a cantorial recitative in a volume of Sabbath Evening Prayers set to music by Glantz. Furthermore, the recitative was recorded by Glantz with minor deviations from the score.[11] The tonality of the *Nu'sach* versions is set to D whereas the tonality of the cantorial recitative is set one tone higher to E. Apparently, the higher recitative was to serve the more professional cantors. By comparing these two versions we may obtain a better understanding of Glantz's methodology as to the proper approach to *Nu'sach*. Moreover, we can get a hint of the legitimate enhancements of the basic scheme that Glantz suggests in order to add further dimensions to the piece and to invest it with a higher level of artistic sophistication.[12]

---

11 Recorded by RCA Victor Company, v-59004. May also be found in JNUL. National Sound Archives, Jerusalem, L39a. [Ed. note: The three compositions discussed in this essay can be heard on the two compact disks accompanying this book.]

12 It is worthwhile noting that Glantz's *Nu'sach* is itself more complex than those of his contemporaries who published compendia of musical notations (such as Y. L. Neeman), and his genuine touch is apparent even in his basic rendition of *Nu'sach*. Nevertheless, the juxtaposition of *Nu'sach* and cantorial recitative allows us a direct perspective on Glantz's views regarding the place of *Nu'sach* in *Cha'za'nut*.

Upon comparing the simple prayer-chant with the artistic composition, one may easily notice how Glantz preserves the basic structure of the *Nu'sach* in the art work. In spite of the differences between the different renditions in scope and in melodic style, their tonal structure is identical. **Table 1** shows that this piece modulates three times: first from Major to the parallel Minor, then from the Minor to the Major key on the fourth degree, and finally from there back down to the original key and mode. Not only does Glantz employ the same modulations included in the simple *Nu'sach*, but he also retains their exact position in relation to the text:

Table 1: Tonal structure of *Kol A'do'nai: Nu'sach* and cantorial recitative

Psalms 29, verse nbr.	Text	*Nu'sach* version	Cantorial version
7-8	*Kol A'do'nai Cho'tzev…Mid'bar Ka'desh*	D major	E major
9	*Kol A'do'nai Ye'cho'lel…O'mer Ka'vod*	D minor	E minor
10	*A'do'nai La'Ma'bul Ya'shav…Me'lech Le'Olam*	G major	A major
		D minor	E minor
11	*A'do'nai Oz…A'mo Va'Sha'lom*	D minor	E minor

In addition to the identical tonal structure, Glantz actively maintains the melodic contour of the *Nu'sach* by incorporating segments thereof in the composition, as shall be evidenced by the three following examples: First, at the outset of the composition, Glantz employs the same melodic motif for the words *Kol A'do'nai Cho'tzev La'ha'vot Esh* (**Figure 1**). Second, Glantz assigns an almost identical motif to the words *Ye'cho'lel A'ya'lot Va'Ye'che'sof Ye'a'rot* (**Figure 2**). Finally, at the point of modulation back to D minor, on the word *Me'lech*, the pitches of the *Nu'sach* (E-C, D-A) appear in the cantorial recitative (transposed up by a minor second, as previously noted) with a little embellishment splitting the motive (**Figure 3**).

Figure 1: *Kol A'do'nai Cho'tzev La'ha'vot Esh*

Nu'sach version

Cantorial recitative

Figure 2: *Ye'cho'lel A'ya'lot Va'Ye'che'sof Ye'a'rot*

Nu'sach version

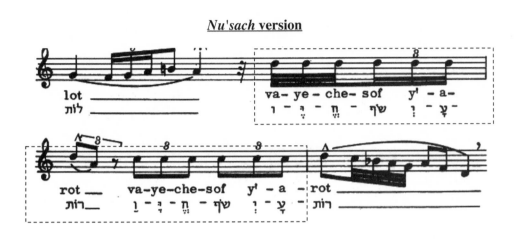

Cantorial recitative

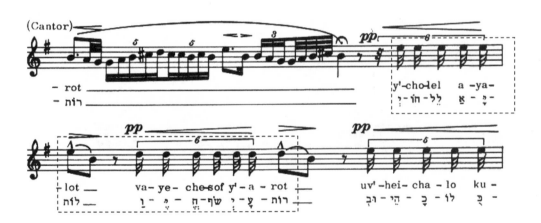

Figure 3: *Me'lech Le'O'lam*

Nu'sach version

Cantorial recitative

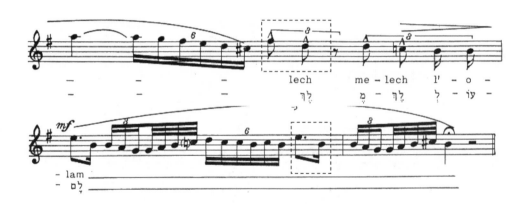

While Glantz adheres to the *Nu'sach* in his cantorial piece, he also gives vent to his creativity as he reinterprets the text through artful elaborations of the basic *Nu'sach*.

Already with the very first musical phrase (verses 7, 8), Glantz must have felt that the basic melody of the *Nu'sach* does not adequately express the magnitude of the scene described in the text. The verses of this Psalm refer to the might of God which is expressed in his dominion over the earth through his voice. Seven times throughout the psalm, God's voice is described in different forms of dominion ("The voice of the Lord is upon the waters … The voice of the Lord breaks the cedars," etc.). Likewise, verses 7 and 8 are praising the strength of God's voice ("The voice of the Lord flashes forth flames of fire. The voice of the Lord shakes the wilderness; the Lord shakes the wilderness of *Ka'desh*"). Moreover, according to the traditional Jewish interpretation, verses 7 and 8 describe the giving of the *To'rah* on Mount Sinai. The verses of the Pentateuch and the *Mid'rash* that the learned Glantz must have had in mind describe the giving of the *To'rah* on Mount Sinai as an awesome and inspiring theophany.[13] Glantz apparently sensed that this perception is not fully conveyed by the simplicity of the *Nu'sach*. After quoting the opening melodic theme of the *Nu'sach* (thus expressing his commitment to the venerable melody) Glantz departs to a different, more grandiose, direction in the second half of verse 8 in the words *Ya'chil A'do'nai Mid'bar Ka'desh*. After the recitation on the notes B and G# (which belong to the tonic chord) in the first part of the verse, Glantz diverts from the paved path of the *Nu'sach* to an original melodic climax. The recitative departs from the simple

> *Glantz diverts from the paved path of the* Nu'sach *to an original melodic climax. The recitative departs from the simple melody of the* Nu'sach *into a bursting statement on the might of God, with a climax on the tonic chord in the high register, developed by Glantz in an unconventional melodic movement.*

melody of the *Nu'sach* into a bursting statement on the might of God, with a climax on the tonic chord in the high register, developed by Glantz in an unconventional melodic movement. The diminished seventh A#— G is used — two notes not belonging to the basic scale (E major) — in order to enhance the climax by creating a sense of a diminished seventh chord leading to B, the dominant of E provided by the solution of the dissonance (**Figure 4**). Indeed, Glantz employs dissonant tension in his work to an extent that is greater than that of his contemporaries.

---

13 Exodus, chapter 19; TB *Sha'bbat* 88; TB *Ze'va'chim* 116 (1).

Figure 4: *Ya'chil A'do'nai Mid'bar Ka'desh*

At this point begins a long melismatic phrase on the words *Mid'bar Ka'desh* (**Figure 5**). This musical dramatization expresses the might of God at the scene of the giving of the *To'rah* and coincides with the depiction of trembling earth at that precise, dramatic event. This may be viewed as another instance of what we called "word painting": the agitated contour of the melody brings to mind a tremor *(Ya'chil)*.

Figure 5: *Mid'bar Ka'desh*

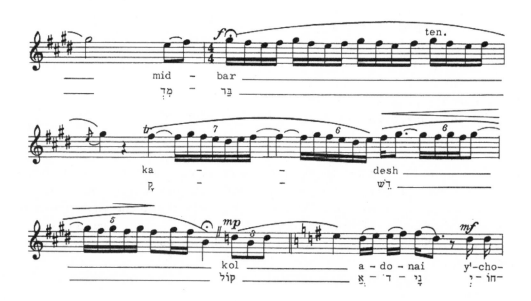

This melismatic phrase itself is unique and uncommon. Four notes only (D#-E-F#-G#) take part in the melisma. The structure of the melisma is fairly static and varies only with respect to the number of notes in use: starting with 3 notes in the first phrase, going through four notes in the second, and concluding with a trill on F#-G#, over a relatively long period of time (approximately 20 seconds). Conventional twentieth-century melismas in *Cha'za'nut* consist of a combination of sequences (a recurring motif transposed on consecutive pitches) and scalar passages (climbing up or down a scale). Glantz's melisma, in contradistinction, bears a different character: persistent, focused, perhaps even irritating, constantly repeating the same notes over and over again. Glantz's compositions include melismatic phrases of this kind; this style may reflect his personal traits: opinionated, clear-cut and unequivocal.[14]

One might expect that such a grandiose melismatic phrase would end on the tonic, and that it would properly conclude the first verse of the piece, by emphasizing the tonic (E), in a conventional manner. Surprisingly, though, Glantz chooses to finish the sentence on the dominant (B), demonstrating his avoidance of schematic conventions. His harmonic language is loose and unconstrained, and building up towards the tonic is not his main concern here.

The second verse of the composition may demonstrate another kind of deviation from the common *Nu'sach* into a personal style. The verse opens with a motif reminiscent of the *Nu'sach*. On the words *Ye'cho'lel A'ya'lot* ("The voice of the Lord causes the hinds to calve"), Glantz begins a recitation on E that abruptly jumps a fifth upwards and immediately returns (with a *glissando*) back to E. Sudden fluctuations in the melodic line interwoven among motifs taken from, or reminiscent of, the *Nu'sach,* are typical of Glantz's music and provide him another way of demonstrating musical creativity while maintaining the general scheme of the *Nu'sach.* The surprising and unexpected interval is further emphasized by the contrasting dynamics of *forte* and *piano* between the low the high notes (**Figure 6**).

> *Sudden fluctuations in the melodic line interwoven among motifs taken from, or reminiscent of, the* Nu'sach, *are typical of Glantz's music and provide him another way of demonstrating musical creativity while maintaining the general scheme of the* Nu'sach.

---

14 Occurrences of this melismatic style can be found in the two compositions discussed below ("*Bir'kat Ko'ha'nim*" and "*A'na Be'Cho'ach*").

Figure 6: *Ye'cho'lel A'ya'lot Va'Ye'che'sof Ye'a'rot*

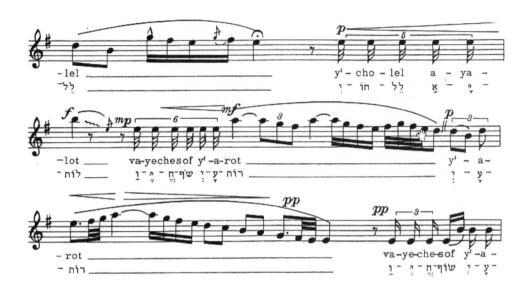

A similar leap upwards takes place further on in this musical phrase. Just as we expect to have arrived at the tonic (E), perhaps even to have reached the first clear cadence of the piece, on the word *Ye'a'rot* (D-B-D-E), Glantz draws back to the high note A, and only then does he return to the tonic E, one octave lower in a scalewise motion spanning over an octave and a half. Here, too, Glantz is revealed as an interpreter and not merely as a composer, for he expresses through his music the meaning of the words *Va'Ye'che'sof Ye'a'rot* ("strips the forests bare"). According to Rashi's[15] interpretation, God's stripping of the tall trees is an allegory of cutting down the heathens.

> *Glantz is revealed as an interpreter and not merely as a composer, for he expresses through his music the meaning of the words.*

The third sentence (verse 10), unlike its predecessors, opens with a cantorial innovation and then converges back to the traditional *Nu'sach*. It too, manifests Glantz's genuine treatment of

15 Rashi — Rabbi Solomon bar Isaac (1040-1105), a medieval French commentator on the Bible and the Talmud. His influential writings on the Bible examined the literal meaning of the text and used allegory, parable, and symbolism to analyze its non-literal meaning. His landmark commentary on the Talmud is a classic introduction to biblical and post-biblical Judaism.

Cha'za'nut. Glantz sets the words *A'do'nai La'Ma'bul Ya'shav* ("The Lord sat enthroned at the flood") as a cantorial recitative, in a speech-like manner; but, surprisingly, he does not wander around one pitch, as is the common practice in *Cha'za'nut*. Herein, Glantz introduces a new format to speech-like singing. Rather than employing a static melodic line unconstrained by rhythmic patterns or fixed meter, Glantz produces a similar static musical experience by maintaining a constant rhythm of sixteenth-notes all along the phrase (**Figure 7**). The sensation is one of a speech-like singing, even though the melodic line is dynamic. Needless to say, Glantz's unique performance of this composition contributes further to the atmosphere created by this technique.

During the remainder of verse 10 ("as King forever"), Glantz introduces a long melisma which corresponds to the word *Me'lech* ("King") in the score, and to the word *Le'O'lam* ("forever"), in the above-mentioned recording. Once again, this melismatic phrase demonstrates Glantz's unique aesthetic approach. The core of the melisma — which would have probably satisfied a somewhat more conservative cantor — is an interplay of the neighboring notes A-G#-A-G-A, but Glantz does not settle for that gesture. He expands the melisma by inserting an *arpeggio* on the A major chord that serves to intensify the strong dissonance G-G#, achieving an unconventional and distinctive musical effect.

Figure 7: *A'do'nai La'Ma'bul Ya'shav, Va'Ye'shev A'do'nai Me'lech Le'O'lam*

At the end of the composition, on the last verse of the Psalm, Glantz completely abandons the melody of the *Nu'sach* in favor of a classic cantorial finale. An intricate melismatic phrase reaches the subtonic degree and thereupon the final tonic.

Bar'chei'nu Va'Bra'cha — Bir'kat Ko'ha'nim (Priestly Blessing)

An additional liturgical composition by Glantz, *Bir'kat Ko'ha'nim,* notable for its refinement, is instructive for our present discussion. It clearly shows loyalty to the *Nu'sach* while ingeniously bringing the music to conform to the structure of the text. The innovative challenge here is greater because of the relative musical plainness of the *Nu'sach,* to which Glantz, as we recall, closely adheres. The traditional chant, provided in Glantz's *Nu'sach* book *"Ri'nat Ha'Ko'desh,"* is rather simple in nature and maintains the *Shtey'ger* (musical mode) *Nu'sach A'ha'va Ra'bah* throughout the composition, following the standard mode of the Sabbath morning prayers. The *Nu'sach* here does not fully convey the intricacy of the ritual and the structure of the text.

The text of *Bir'kat Ko'ha'nim* is divided into two major sections: a preamble, pleading with God to accept the Priestly Blessing; the Priestly Blessing itself, consisting of three separate verses, which constitute three distinctive blessings. Each of these three verses in turn consists of two segments (marked in **Table 2** below as A and B respectively).

The verses of *Bir'kat Ko'ha'nim* are among the oldest in continuous liturgical use. Archaeologists have found the words etched on silver scrolls on an amulet from the seventh century BCE. The words of the Priestly Blessing originate from the Book of Numbers 6:24-26:

- May the Lord bless you and keep you.
- May the Lord let His face shine upon you and be gracious to you.
- May the Lord look kindly upon you and give you peace.

The Hebrew text is built in an outstanding structure that cannot be indicated in any English translation. The verses progress from 3 to 5 to 7 words. The first two words in each blessing are a verb and then God's name, (**Table 2, Segment A**) then come the rest of the sentences one, three and five words respectively (**Table 2, Segment B**).

Table 2: Structure of *Bir'kat Ko'ha'nim*

Segment A	Segment B
Ye'va're'che'cha A'do'nai	*Ve'Yish'me're'cha*
Ya'er A'do'nai	*Pa'nav Ei'le'cha Vi'Chu'ne'ka*
Yi'sa A'do'nai	*Pa'nav Ei'le'cha Ve'Ya'sem Le'cha Sha'lom*

The challenge facing Glantz is, therefore, to design a musical framework that will correlate to this peculiar textual structure, while preserving the sense of the Sabbath morning *Nu'sach*. In the Ashkenazi tradition, two types of performance of the Priestly Blessing ceremony are customary: the first one, which is the common day-to-day practice in the Ashkenazi congregations of the Diaspora, is incorporated into the prayer of the *Cha'zan*, whereas in the second manner — which is practiced daily in the Land of Israel but in the Diaspora is reserved only to the High Holidays and the Three Festivals — the preamble is sung by the *Cha'zan* and the blessing itself is performed in alternation between the *Cha'zan* and the *Ko'ha'nim* (priests). While the *Ko'ha'nim* perform their responses, the entire congregation whispers a series of verses.[16]

Glantz's book *"Ri'nat Ha'Ko'desh"* provides two versions of the *Nu'sach* for *Bir'kat Ko'ha'nim* — a straightforward version, spare in melodic and tonal substance, for *Cha'zan* solo; and a richer version for *Cha'zan* and the *Ko'ha'nim*. Even though Glantz's cantorial composition *Bir'kat Ko'ha'nim* is designated to the solo cantor, Glantz relies on the *Nu'sach* version for *Cha'zan* and *Ko'ha'nim*. Thus he is able to adhere to the *Nu'sach* and yet to provide a traditional musical infrastructure upon which innovative ideas can be drawn. He begins by adopting the modal tonality of *A'ha'va Ra'bah* and the overall melodic outline of the opening section of the Priestly Blessing. Then, when he reaches the blessing proper, he modulates to the Minor mode, a melodic move that is also employed in his *Ri'nat Ha'Ko'desh* version for *Cha'zan* and *Ko'ha'nim*. He does this in order to demarcate the two segments of the blessing.

After modulating to the Minor mode, Glantz demarcates and subdivides the three separate verses-blessings. For that purpose he introduces a new method of synthesizing his novel music with traditional motifs. Schleifer points out that in the Ashkenazi communities, the officiating *Ko'ha'nim* used to chant their part of the blessing (i.e. their responses) in prolonged melodies (more than one melody to a word, at times). They did this in order to allow members of the congregation time to chant their complementary verses. Rather than employing the relatively frugal melody of the *Nu'sach* version, Glantz utilizes extended melodies that are usually sung by the *Ko'ha'nim,* melodies that were well-known to him. Thus he finds a compromise between his quest for musical substance that is rich enough to manipulate and his firm adherence to traditional legacies.

The melodies are utilized to delineate the three verses in the following manner: the first words of each verse are sung as metric melodies and the rest is chanted as a cantorial recitative which forms the natural continuum of the metric melody. For each verse, a metric melody is followed

---

16 *Bir'kat Ko'ha'nim* in the Ashkenazi tradition is thoroughly studied in E. Schleifer, *"The Priestly Blessing in the Ashkenazi Synagogue Ritual and Chant,"* Yuval 7, pp. 233-298.

by a cantorial recitative. The melodies delineate the separate verse-blessings by demarcating the beginning of each one (**Table 3**).[17]

Table 3: Structure of *Bir'kat Ko'ha'nim* — text and music

Section	Text	Music
Preamble	*E'lo'hei'nu Ve'E'lo'hei A'vo'tei'nu Bar'chei'nu Va'Bra'cha Ha'Me'shu'le'shet*	*A'ha'va Ra'bah Shtey'ger*
First blessing	*Ye'va're'che'cha A'do'nai Ve'Yish'me're'cha*	Metric melody in Minor
		Cantorial recitative
Second blessing	*Ya'er A'do'nai Pa'nav Ei'le'cha Vi'chu'ne'ka*	Metric melody in Minor
		Cantorial recitative
Third blessing	*Yi'sa A'do'nai Pa'nav Ei'le'cha Ve'Ya'sem Le'cha Sha'lom*	Metric melody in Minor
		Cantorial recitative

An additional advantage of incorporating the melodies of the *Ko'ha'nim* in Glantz's cantorial composition is the historical preservation of an infrequent ritual. As we noted earlier, the ordinary performance of the *Bir'kat Ko'ha'nim* in the Ashkenazi congregations of the Diaspora is in form of a prayer by the cantor, not a priestly ceremony; it therefore precludes the actual participation of the *Ko'ha'nim*. The liturgical occasions on which the priests actually took part in the ritual were relatively rare. Glantz uses the metric melodies in a way that is reminiscent of the singing of the *Ko'ha'nim* and thus calls the audience's attention to the festive, elaborate and ancient form of this ritual.

> *Glantz uses the metric melodies in a way that is reminiscent of the singing of the Ko'ha'nim and thus calls the audience's attention to the festive, elaborated and ancient form of this ritual.*

17 Note the difference in this regard between the score and the version recorded by Glantz. In the score, the first words of the third verse — *Yi'sa A'do'nai Pa'nav Ei'le'cha* ("The Lord shall lift up his countenance upon thee") — are designated to be sung by the cantor as a metric melody, followed by the recitative, as detailed above. In the recorded version, however, Glantz refrains from singing the metric melody and leaves it to the accompanying organ. Glantz himself (the cantor) enters at the beginning of the recitative. Since in the last blessing, the cantorial recitative starts at the very beginning of the verse and encompasses the name of God, it may be presumed that the reason for that difference lies in Glantz's reluctance to repeat the name of God.

Another way of conveying the essence of the traditional ceremony as it is conducted on festive occasions in Glantz's composition is the emphasis on the word *Ko'ha'nim* ("priests") that appears close to the end of the preamble, just before the beginning of the blessing itself. In the synagogue performance, the *Cha'zan* (or some other member of the congregation) calls out loudly *'Ko'ha'nim!'* as a signal to the priests to begin their blessing. Even though Glantz sings his composition solo, he mimics this introduction by dramatizing the word *'Ko'ha'nim'* in the preamble. Such dramatization is a common cantorial practice and can be found in compositions by Berele Chagy or Yehoshua Meislish.[18] However, Glantz further dramatizes this gesture by a sharp and sudden modulation to the Major mode followed by the immediate return to Minor at the beginning of the first verse-blessing.

This piece is indeed a shining illustration of Glantz's textual sensitivity and provides several other examples in that regard. The three verses-blessings form in themselves a fascinating textual structure. The length of the verses, however, is not constant but it grows serially: three words in the first verse, five in the second and seven in the last verse. This textual development is reflected in Glantz's music, which progresses alongside the text. The longer the blessing, the more melismatic and embellished does the melody become. The music further evolves in other ways, as the melodic line becomes more and more complex and the *tessitura* gradually expands.

Moreover, Glantz artificially extends the length of the verses exponentially in order to provide a longer platform for his melodic and melismatic development. He does so by the common cantorial routine of repeating some of the words of the second and third verses, as follows: the gap between the first and the second verses grows to six words, whilst the gap between the second and the third verses is duple (twelve words). Thus, a magnified prolongation is created to an extent of 3-9-21 words that allows enough room for musical elaboration (**Table 4**).

Table 4: Prolongation of the verse-blessings in *Bir'kat Ko'ha'nim*

Original verse	Nbr. of words	Prolonged verse	Nbr. of words
Ye'va're'che'cha A'do'nai Ve'Yish'me're'cha	3	*Ye'va're'che'cha A'do'nai Ve'Yish'me're'cha*	3
Ya'er A'do'nai Pa'nav Ei'le'cha Vi'chu'ne'ka	5	*Ya'er A'do'nai Pa'nav Ei'le'cha, Pa'nav Ei'le'cha, Pa'nav Ei'le'cha, Vi'chu'ne'ka*	9
Yi'sa A'do'nai Pa'nav Ei'le'cha Ve'Ya'sem Le'cha Sha'lom	7	*Yi'sa A'do'nai Pa'nav Ei'le'cha, Pa'nav Ei'le'cha, Pa'nav Ei'le'cha, Ei'le'cha Pa'nav, Pa'nav Ei'le'cha, Ei'le'cha, Ve'Ya'sem Le'cha, Le'cha, Ve'Ya'sem Le'cha, Le'cha, Le'cha, Sha'lom*	21

---

18 See *The Golden Age of Cantors — Musical Masterpieces of the Synagogue*, ed. Velvel Pasternak and Noah Schall, New York: Tara Publications, 1991, pp. 59-65 and pp. 130-130 respectively.

But this increase in intensity is already heralded in the preamble to the Priestly Blessing: The preamble goes as follows: "Our God and God of our forefathers. Bless us with the blessing tripled *(Me'shu'le'shet)* in the *To'rah* that is written by Moses your servant." Most believe that the correct way to punctuate this sentence is by putting a comma after the word *Me'shu'le'shet*. The meaning of the sentence so punctuated is that the blessing is threefold (consists of three different blessings) and that it appears (once) in the *To'rah*. Yet, some *Cha'za'nim* punctuate after the word *"To'rah,"* thus implying incorrectly that the Priestly Blessing appears three times in the *To'rah*.[19]

In his composition, Glantz finds a way to bridge between the two versions of the punctuation. Instead of preferring one option or the other, he divides the text into three, partly overlapping phrases, in the following manner:

1. Bless us with the tripled blessing;
2. The blessing tripled in the *To'rah;*
3. In the *To'rah* that is written by Moses your servant.

Some[20] have argued that Glantz evaded a clear stand on the issue of the punctuation of the preamble to the Priestly Blessing by reciting all possible forms. In our view, this explanation, which does not quite fit Glantz's general opinionated and unequivocal character, is uncalled for; after all, it is hardly conceivable that Glantz would have used an incorrect punctuation just to appease every possible point of view. In our view, the repetition and lingering serve a different purpose, one that rather coexists with Glantz's textual sensitivity.

As can be seen in the body of the Priestly Blessing, the ternary motif is central to the blessing. It is of sufficient significance to serve as the adjective used to describe the Priestly Blessing in the preamble, *Ha'Bra'cha Ha'Me'shu'le'shet* ("the tripled blessing"). Glantz draws our attention to this motif in the very beginning of the composition by dividing the text of the preamble around the word *Me'shu'le'shet* to three overlapping phrases. Furthermore, these three phrases of the preamble are constructed in a manner that resembles the subsequent tripartite form of the Priestly Blessing itself. As we have noted, the three verses of the Priestly Blessing expand in a serial manner (3-5-7 words), and Glantz's musical phrases are designed to reflect and intensify this prolongation by repeating words. So he does in the preamble too. First, Glantz lingers shortly over the last word of each phrase, prolonging each one in comparison to its predecessor. This slight difference is more noticeable in Glantz's recording than in the score. More importantly, the melodic line of the phrases rises progressively. The first phrase culminates in C, the second phrase in D#, and the third in E. Climbing the musical scale correlates to the incremental extension of the three verses and illustrates the evolving character of the composition (**Figure 8**).

---

19 Cantor Zvi Granatov in Leo Leov's composition, available on sound recording, JNUL, National Sound Archives, K-1958.
20 M. Sobol, *"Lif'nei Ha'Tei'va"* Israeli radio program on *Cha'za'nut*, on recording available with the authors.

Figure 8: *Bar'chei'nu Va'be'ra'cha Ha'Me'shu'le'shet Ba'To'rah Ha'K'tu'va...*

This interpretation illustrates the inter-connectedness of the musical structure and the textual structure and the intra-connectedness of the musical design in the Priestly Blessing by Glantz. The unity of text and music is a focal point of Glantz's philosophy and in this manner we should interpret the structure of this unique cantorial composition.

A'na Be'Cho'ach (Ka'bba'lat Sha'bbat, Friday evening service)

Glantz's profound understanding of the liturgical texts and contexts is further demonstrated in his setting of *A'na Be'Cho'ach*, which reveals an additional layer of Glantz's ability to compose his music in accordance with the special role of the prayer. Glantz was dissatisfied with the common practice of Eastern-European cantors designating a wail or whimper-like tune to every prayer, be it a lamentation or a *Gloria*. The all-too-common utilization of wailing and melismatic melodies suffered from the three flaws that Glantz so persistently stood up against:

1. It did not (always) align with the *Nu'sach*;
2. It created melodic lines that were dull and monotonous and lacked the much needed compositional renovation, and
3. It did not (consistently) reflect the meaning of the text and rarely provided an insight into the inner layers of interpretation that underlie the explicit meaning of the text.

Thus, Glantz sought new and innovative ways to express the spirit of the prayers through music. True to his own guidelines, Glantz composed the prayer *A'na Be'Cho'ach* in a very different style from other composers. The compositions of this text by Glantz's contemporaries, such as Leibele Waldman (1907-1969) or Moshe Kousevitzky (1899-1966), or by those of his predecessors, such as Abraham Kalechnik [Berkowitz], are quite standard in style and are no different from any other prayer composed as a plea or an imploration. Glantz's composition, as we shall see, is exceptional and one of a kind.

The prayer *A'na Be'Cho'ach* is exceptional in the scenery of the *Sha'bbat* evening prayers in particular and in the more general realm of prayer. Unlike the rest of the first part of the Sabbath evening prayers *(Ka'bba'lat Sha'bbat),* which consist mostly of a collection of Psalms, this prayer is Kabbalistic poetry, attributed to the *Ta'nna* Rabbi Nechunia Ben Hakana.[21] It consists of seven verses, each one comprised of six words, amounting to a total of forty-two words. The initials of the forty-two words represent the letters of one of God's names — 'The Forty-Two Letter Name' of Jewish mysticism. This highly sacred name is said to contain multiple covert meanings. It is thus not to be revealed to anyone until he becomes of certain age and unless he accomplishes a long list of virtues, such as humbleness, moderation, benevolence and others *(Tal'mud Bav'li, Ki'du'shin,* 71a). As a result, the meaning of the name was only known to few Kabbalists and one was not allowed to pronounce it straightforwardly. The text enshrouds the 'Forty-Two Letter Name,' and when it is chanted, the suppliant will be advised to depict and visualize the name embedded in the initials *(ab"g yt"z; kr"a st"n* etc.) and thus transport his mind from the realm of *A'si'ya* (action) to the realm of *Ye'tzi'ra* (formation).[22] The prayer is recited by certain congregations in the daily morning prayers after the *To'rah* portion called *Kor'ba'not* ("Sacrifices"), in the days of "Counting of the *O'mer*" and in the Sabbath evening prayers — all of them liturgical contexts of Kabbalistic importance.

Leib Glantz's spent his childhood in Chasidic courtyards, where he learned and assimilated Chassidic philosophy as well as its underlying Kabbalistic roots. The Kabbalistic context and implications of this prayer could not have passed him by. Glantz provides a glimpse to the mystery of the text by hinting at its concealed meanings.

Leib Glantz spent his childhood in Chasidic courtyards, where he learned and assimilated Chasidic philosophy as well as its underlying Kabbalistic roots. The Kabbalistic context and implications of this prayer could not have passed him by. Glantz provides a glimpse into the mystery of the text by

21 Rabbi Nechunia Ben Hakana — a *Ta'nna* (an authority quoted in the Mishna) of the second half of the First Century CE. He was a disciple of Rabbi Yochanan Ben Zakkai, the teacher of Rabbi Yishmael, Rabbi Akiva, and Rabbi Eliezer.

22 According to the *Ka'bba'lah* (e.g. Rabbi Chayim Vital in *"Sha'ar Ha'Ka'va'not"*), all of existence consists of four worlds — *A'si'ya* (action), *Ye'tzi'ra* (formation), *Bri'ah* (creation) and *A'tzi'lut* (dignity) — each world constituting a spiritual rank and a certain level of abstraction. The most degraded of all worlds is our perceptible world, the world of *A'si'ya.* According to Kabbalistic tradition, by reciting the Forty-Two Letter Name one may be transported to the world of *Ye'tzi'ra.*

hinting at its concealed meanings. The outward meaning of the text bespeaks a plea for salvation, but its underlying Kabbalistic connotation evokes the mystique of the 'Forty-Two Letter Name.' Glantz aspires to provide music that will not only reflect the banal straightforward plea but will also convey a more subtle mystical interpretation.

This goal is attained by introducing an unconventional singing style. The piece is neither an operatic recitative nor is it the classical cantorial recitative. The usual speech-like manner of traditional *Cha'za'nut* is grounded in a melodically static line recited in a flowing rhythm. The new style introduced by Glantz, however, reverses this formula: the rhythm is static whereas the melody is unconstrained. Glantz evidently delved into an active search for innovative forms of speech-mannered music, which would serve his purpose in this composition.

Two distinguishable rhythmic patterns can be viewed throughout the composition. The first pattern consists of three or four short notes, a longer note and a closing short note. The second pattern consists of a number of short notes ended by a longer note (**Figure 9**). There are, of course, minor variations on these rhythmical motifs, but the composition as a whole hinges upon the constant rhythmic movement. By contrast, the corresponding melodic line is extremely loose and unrestrained. The loose melodic line displays substantial dissonant intervals and unexpected turns of the melodic direction, commingled with extreme dynamic shifts and timbre diversification (running from shouts to *falsetto*).

Figure 9: The two rhythmic patterns

Another factor contributing to the special atmosphere of the composition is its special scoring (which appears in the written score but is not apparent in Glantz's solo recording of this composition). Unlike other compositions in the anthology *"Ri'nat Ha'Ko'desh,"* this piece calls for two choirs: an ordinary four part (SATB) choir[23] and a two part (TB) choir. The score includes detailed instructions as to the size and placement of the second choir: it should be small and must be positioned behind the principal choir and its main task is humming. Unquestionably, the make-up of the second choir, its position, and its role enhance the mysteriousness that enshrouds this composition.

As already noted, at the foreground layer of the poem is an imploration. This facet of the text also finds its way into Glantz's composition. The last part of the composition consists of a

---

23 SATB — abbreviation of the constitution of a choir consisting of the singing voices of soprano, alto, tenor, and bass required for a particular piece of music; TB — tenor and bass only.

> *The image envisioned as we hear Glantz audaciously confronting God may be that of Rabbi Levi Itzchak of Berdichev. Glantz approaches God in a familiar manner that is reminiscent of the practice of this Chasidic leader, who was known to accost God with protestations and grievances, or even with exasperation.*

recitation of the last verse of the poem — *Shav'a'tei'nu Ka'bel U'She'ma Tza'a'ka'tei'nu, Yo'de'a Ta'a'lu'mot* ("Accept our plea and hear our cry, O Knower of all secrets") that is repeated no less than six times. This persistent repetition of the same words over and over again transforms the pleading character of the text into a resolute demand. The abrupt dramatic shouting of the words *Shav'a'tei'nu Ka'bel U'She'ma* and the multiple repetitions of the verse, seem to generate a demand, perhaps even an impudent one (**Figure 10**); note the *Schprächgesang* style in the high notes. The image envisioned as we hear Glantz audaciously confronting God may be that of Rabbi Levi Itzchak of Berdichev. Glantz approaches God in a familiar manner that is reminiscent of the practice of this Chasidic leader, who was known to accost God with protestations and grievances, or even with exasperation.[24]

Figure 10: *Shav'a'tei'nu Ka'bel U'She'ma*

A'na Be'Cho'ach allows us to observe another way in which Glantz related to his fascination with the old *Nu'sach.* We have so far mentioned how Glantz was inspired by the *Nu'sach* in his compositional structure and melodic contour. We shall now explore how Glantz was inspired by the "tonal irregularity" of *Nu'sach,* a feature that he perceived as an old and "authentic" one.

---

24 Rabbi Levi Itzchak of Berdichev was known as *Sa'ne'go'ram Shel Yis'ra'el* (The Pleader of Israel). There are many tales depicting the unyielding manner in which he confronted God. Once, during the Day of Judgment, he abruptly halted his prayer and clamored to God: "God Almighty! Should you inscribe your people of Israel in the Book of Life, fine, as the saving of life overrides the holiday observance. Else, I, Levi Itzhak, Rabbi of Berdichev, forbid you the writing during the Holy Day" (*Encyclopedia Mich'lal,* vol. 9, pp. 114-115).

To those accustomed to Western music, the tonal complexities of *Nu'sach* are hard to recon-cile with the established patterns of tonal organization and voice leading. Like many other Jewish music scholars and *Cha'za'nim*, Glantz, too, tried to decipher the structural rationale of the *Nu'sach*.[25] Glantz set out to write a comprehensive treatise on the topic, which sought to reconcile the various motifs of each *Shtey'ger* and to set them in a series of sequential notes in the manner of the Western scales.[26] Even though Glantz died before accomplishing this task, he expressed his views on the matter in various works, all of which explore with endearment and appreciation the unique features of *Nu'sach* Ashkenaz that separate it from Western music.

In this regard as well, Glantz was unique among his contemporaries. Early *Cha'za'nut* that originated from the *Nu'sach* relied upon the motifs of the *Shtey'gers* and did not stray afar from their complex tonal structure. As time went by, cantors focused on the predominant Ashkenazi *Shtey'gers* (*A'ha'va Ra'bah, A'do'nai Ma'lach, Ma'gen A'vot*) as these were formally canonized in the late nineteenth-century and early twentieth-century literature on the subject and in the training institutions and communication media of *Cha'za'nim* (schools of cantors, periodicals of cantors' associations, printed methods, etc.). This canonization gradually reduced the incongruities that characterized the earlier practice of the Ashkenazi prayer modes. In twenti-eth-century *Cha'za'nut* we may be able to find a broad tonal diversity based upon modulations of the various established *Shtey'gers* and Major-Minor modes. However, it is rare to stumble upon instances of tonal incoherencies that were apparently abundant in early nineteenth-cen-tury *Cha'za'nut*, according to the scattered and fragmented written sources available to us that precede the imposing regularization initiated in the writings of cantor Joseph Singer (1841-1911) in the 1880s.

The following musical phrase, exemplary of nineteenth century *Cha'za'nut*, is not what we would expect to find in twentieth century cantorial compositions. The phrase is taken from the composition of *Cha'zan* Hirsch Weintraub (1811-1882) — *"Ki Ke'Shim'cha"* (**Figure 11**). Note how the phrase employs both G flat and G natural in close proximity to create a pecu-liar modality.

---

25 For Glantz's view on this subject see his lecture, *"The Musical Basis of Nu'sach Ha'Te'fi'la"* published in the Proceedings of the Annual Conference Convention of the Cantors Assembly of America, 1954, pp. 17-25. [Ed. Note: this lecture appears in Part 3 of this book.] For a sample of approaches to this complex subject see A. Z. Idelsohn *Jewish Music in its Historical Development*, chapters IV and VIII; B.J. Cohon, *"The Structure of the Synagogue Prayer-Chant,"* Journal of the American Musicological Society, vol. 3 (1950), pp 17-32; J. Frigyesi, *"Preliminary Thoughts Toward the Study of Music Without Clear Beat; the example of 'flowing rhythm' in Jewish 'Nusah,'"* Asian Music 24/2 (1993), pp. 59-88; and particularly the more recent views and bibliography in B. Tarsi, *"Toward A Clearer Definition of the Ma'gen A'vot Mode,"* Musica Judaica, vol. 16 (2001-2), pp. 53-79.

26 As Glantz himself notes in a recording of a lecture delivered at The Tel Aviv Institute of Liturgical Music, JNUL, National Sound Archives, Y03376A.

Figure 11: Hirsch Weintraub — *"Ki Ke'Shim'cha"*

Unlike many other twentieth century cantors, Glantz, who was familiar with older raw materials of *Nu'sach,* such as Weintraub's example, was eager to reestablish these kinds of motifs in contemporary *Cha'za'nut* composition. In his own work, Glantz often employed these nineteenth century 'modes.' For example, in the composition *"Kol A'do'nai"* discussed earlier, during the middle phrase in E minor, a sudden C# appears and is utilized not as a mere embellishment, but as an ingredient of the harmonic mainframe (**Figure 2**).

Returning to the composition under consideration, *"A'na Be'Cho'ach"* provides even more striking examples of such melodic "deviations" that are associated with older strata of *Cha'za'nut.* In the second verse, Glantz employs both E flat and E natural, D flat and D natural all in the same melodic phrase (**Figure 12**). The use of so many sharply contrasting notes in one phrase is a substantial departure from prevailing patterns of contemporary *Cha'za'nut* and creates a structure reminiscent of nineteenth century *Nu'sach.* Undoubtedly, the unique mystical atmosphere of *A'na Be'Cho'ach* served Glantz as fertile soil for his incursion into such "magical" and daring tonal adventures, linking his striking modernism with the oldest practices of *Min'hag Ashkenaz.*

Figure 12: *Sag've'nu Ta'ha're'nu* (from *A'na Be'Cho'ach*)

Concluding Thoughts

The success of the artistic cantorial creation lies in the reconciliation of the contradicting inclinations of faithfulness to the venerable traditions on the one hand and the urge for innovation on the other hand. No simple formula can be provided for such a complex undertaking. Even Glantz, a grandmaster of the art of *Cha'za'nut,* had to recruit to this task every bit of creativity in his possession. His success in this manner is beyond doubt, yet one of the reasons for it was his ability to find different degrees of balance between these traits. The fluctuation of his works between faithfulness to tradition and innovation in accordance goes hand in hand with the interpretational requirements of each text and within the constraints of the liturgical context.

In the first composition discussed (*"Kol A'do'nai"*) Glantz preserved the tonal frame of the *Nu'sach* and several of its melodic motifs, but replaced the modest melodic line with grandiose melismatic embellishments and surprising dissonant intervals in order to reflect the agitated atmosphere of the events described in the verses of Psalm 29. On the other hand, when the melodic substance of the *Nu'sach* was frugal (such as *"Bir'kat Ko'ha'nim"*), Glantz took greater liberty with the *Nu'sach*, perhaps because he could satisfy his conservativeness by importing other traditional resources, such as the prolonged melodies habitually sung by the priests. Finally, in the last composition discussed (*"A'na Be'Cho'ach"*), for which no distinctive *Nu'sach* exists, Glantz had to draw on his familiar knowledge of older *Nu'sach* structures in order to assimilate the mood of the *Nu'sach* in his original composition.

Glantz utilizes his music as a hermeneutical tool in diversified ways that again are compromises between the given *Nu'sach* and his inspired innovation. In the composition *"Kol A'do'nai"* Glantz utilizes his music in order to "paint" — quite ingeniously, one must say — certain words in the text. In the second composition, *"Bir'kat Ko'ha'nim,"* the musical structure mirrors the more abstract "ternary" construction of the text and the prolonged musical sentences enhance the terraced formation of the verses. The relation of music and text here is thus subtler than in the first composition. Finally, in the composition *"A'na Be'Cho'ach,"* the manner in which the music relates to the text is even more sophisticated and mysterious. The sonic atmosphere created by the double choir and the erratic *Nu'sach* (for contemporary ears, of course) attempts to mirror the hidden Kabbalistic traditions underlying this text.

Even though Glantz's compositions do not seem to follow one sustained guideline with regards to the equilibrium point between tradition and innovation, even though his adherence to the *Nu'sach* found expression in many varied ways, and even though he uses diverse musical techniques in order to interpret the texts, each and every one of his works bears the clear, identifiable fingerprints of their composer. His unique style of composition is clearly distinguishable and easy to recognize. The musical maneuvers that unmistakably characterize his music are different in shape, but they are all Glantz's and together they bring new spirit to the world of *Cha'za'nut*. Like other reformers, his audience, too, did not

> *His unique style of composition is clearly distinguishable and easy to recognize. The musical maneuvers that unmistakably characterize his music are different in shape, but they are all Glantz's and together they bring new spirit to the world of* Cha'za'nut.

instantly adopt Glantz. His new style of *Cha'za'nut* was hard to comprehend and like many other geniuses, he was not properly appreciated. He introduced a refreshing original scent to the scene of cantorial art, some may say too original. At the time he was viewed as extremely progressive and his newly introduced modalities and melodies were considered avant-garde dissonances.

Yet, we have tried to show here that he merged old and new so seamlessly that the different components of each work interact with each other in a perfectly harmonious way, even though they are seemingly antithetical. Indeed, this ability to unify divergent or antagonistic artistic forces is a hallmark of a great artist, and so Glantz can be considered one of the giants of the art of *Cha'za'nut*. As a great artist, he moved beyond the conventional boundaries of *Cha'za'nut*. But this move was characteristically achieved by exploiting and expanding the existent vocabulary, rather than by rejecting and discarding the contributions of the past. In this sense, although much of Glantz's work was

> *Indeed, this ability to unify divergent or antagonistic artistic forces is a hallmark of a great artist, and so Glantz can be considered one of the giants of the art of* Cha'za'nut.

strikingly creative, to the point of being considered revolutionary, he still was sensitive to the evolutionary aspects of the creative process. Returning to the motto by Glantz that was quoted in the beginning of this paper: "We were born either before our time, or too late, or perhaps both," Glantz was indeed the innovator who introduced a new melodic spirit to a world not yet prepared for it, while tenaciously adhering to the bygone legacies of the past.

Glantz can be considered as the Expressionist among East-European cantors. The Expressionistic artists and writers — we should be reminded — aimed to create a highly emotional atmosphere by extending selected features of objects and persons beyond their normal appearance. Some of them courted surrealism or tended to enhance the mystical aspects of life. Glantz did the same with the traditional *Cha'za'nut*. He extended traditional motifs and melodic gests much beyond their ordinary forms. Thus he created an artistic language that transcended even the highly emotional character of East-European cantorial art, and he reshaped it into a modern Expressionistic idiom. In this, Glantz's vocal art is similar to Marc Chagall's paintings and S.Y. Agnon's literary writings, both of whom utilized tradition to create modern art in an Expressionist spirit with surrealistic overtones. Glantz's musical creativity shows a striking resemblance to Agnon's literal imagery. Agnon's writings are steeped in the old Jewish lore from the Talmud to Chasidic tales, and yet the meaning is new and the usage revolutionary. One of the foremost critiques of modern Israeli literature, Gershon Shaked, called Agnon, the Nobel Prize laureate writer, "a revolutionary traditionalist."[27] Clearly, this appropriate oxymoron befits the cantor and composer Leib Glantz.

---

27 This indeed is the title of his book, Shaked, G. (1989).

References quoted

Avnon, Y. (Ed.). (1979). *Levi Yitzchak Miberditchev,* Encyclopedia Michlal, vol. 9, pp. 114-116. Tel Aviv: Yavneh. (Hebrew).

Cohon, B. J. (1950). *The Structure of the Synagogue Prayer-chant.* Journal of the American Musicological Society, vol. 3, pp 17-32.

Frigyesi, J. (1993). *Preliminary thoughts toward the study of music without clear beat; the example of 'flowing rhythm' in Jewish 'Nusah,'* Asian Music 24/2, pp. 59-88.

Glantz, L (1929) *Kol A'do'nai,* Cantor Leib Glantz, Tenor with Pipe Organ, Victor Company, v-59004. Also in JNUL, National Sound Archives, L39a.

Glantz, L. (1952). *Bir'kat Ko'ha'nim.* Sound recording, JNUL, National Sound Archives k-2228.

Glantz, L. (1954). *The Musical Basis of Nu'sach Ha'Te'fi'la.* Proceedings of the Annual Conference Convention of the Cantors Assembly of America, pp. 17-25.

Glantz, L. (1960). *Al Chi'nuch Cha'za'nim.* Duchan, vol. 1, pp 57-61.

Glantz, L. (1968). *Ha'llel* and *Tal* — a lecture including musical illustrations, in D. Loev (Ed), *Ri'nat Ha'Ko'desh — Ha'llel* and Three Festivals. Tel Aviv: Israel Music Institute.

Glantz, L. (no date). *Lecture at the First Conference of the Institute of Cantorial Art in Tel Aviv.* Sound recording, JNUL, National Sound Archives, Y03376A,

Idelsohn, A. Z. (1926). *Der Missinai-Gesang der Deutschen Synagoge.* Zeitschrift für Musikwisseschaft, vol. 8, pp. 449-472.

Idelsohn, A. Z. (1929). *Jewish Music in its Historical Development.* New York: Schocken Books.

Katz, D. (1999). *From Mount Sinai to the Year 6000: A Study of the Interaction of Oral Tradition and Written Sources in the Transmission of an Ashkenazi Liturgical Chant (Ak'da'mut).* Rivista Internazionale di Musica Sacra, vol. 20/1, pp.175-206, corrected version: supplement to 20/2 (2000).

Loev, D. (Ed) (1967). *Leib Glantz — Selected Works — Ri'nat Ha'Ko'desh — Friday Evening Service.* Tel Aviv: Israel Music Institute.

Loev, D. (Ed) (1971). *Leib Glantz — Selected Works — Ri'nat Ha'Ko'desh — Sabbath Morning Service.* Tel Aviv: Israel Music Institute.

Ne'eman, Y. L. (1968). *No'sah La'ha'zan — The Traditional Chant of the Synagogue.* Jerusalem: Israel Institute for Sacred Music. (Hebrew).

Schall, N. and Pasternak, V. (1991). *The Golden Age of Cantors — Musical Masterpieces of the Synagogue.* USA: Tara Publications.

Shacked, G. (1989) *S.Y. Agnon, A Revolutionary Traditionalist.* New York and London: New York University Press.

Schleifer, E. (2002). *The Priestly Blessing in the Ashkenazi Synagogue Ritual and Chant.* Yuval — Studies of the Jewish Music Research Centre, vol. 7 (Studies in Honour of Israel Adler), pp. 233-298.

Steinman, E. (Ed) (1965). *Ze'ha'rim — In Memory of Leib Glantz.* The Tel Aviv Institute for Jewish Liturgical Music. (Hebrew and Yiddish.)

Tarsi, B. (2001-2). *Toward A Clearer Definition of the Ma'gen A'vot Mode.* Musica Judaica, vol. 16, pp. 53-79.

Weintraub. Z.H.A. (1859). *Schire Beith Adonai: Tempelgesänge für den Gottesdienst der Israeliten / Componirt und Herausgegeben von H. Weintraub.* Leipzig: Breitkopf and Härtel.

Zimmerman, A. (1988). *B'Ron Ya'had — Essays, Research and Notes on Hazzanut and Jewish Music.* Tel Aviv: The Central Cantorial Archive. (Hebrew).

Zohar, Y. (1965). *Yehuda Leib Glantz — Ri'nat Ha'Ko'desh — Prayer Modes.* Tel Aviv: Israel Music Institute.

2

Music Theory as an Expression of Musical and Extra-musical Views Reflected in Leib Glantz's Liturgical Settings

Boaz Tarsi[1]

Among the more characteristic traits of conversations with Max Wohlberg that I recall was his tendency to fondly summon up nostalgia-laden memories of Cantors Assembly conventions of days gone by. These recollections frequently portrayed gatherings in one of the borsht-belt hotels of the Catskills for days of recharging, camaraderie, and frolicking. Clearly, joke-telling and sweating in the sauna were not the only activities. The volumes of conference proceedings from the 1950s and 1960s reveal a dynamic scene covering a wide spectrum of professional and scholarly concerns. The level of involvement and passion in these discussions is remarkable. But more important, perhaps, these documents provide a rare window into the perceptions, self-perceptions, and worldviews of the participants.

In the annual conference convention of the Cantors Assembly in 1952, Leib Glantz presented a talk on his overall perception of the music theory of the Ashkenazi liturgical repertoire.[2] Two years later Max Wohlberg lectured on a similar topic but also included in his presentation a rough survey of past attempts at creating such theory.[3] Almost twenty years after that,

---

1 Dr. Boaz Tarsi, an accomplished composer, is Associate Professor of Music at the Jewish Theological Seminary in New York, teaching courses on *Nu'sach* theory and the scales, modes and motifs of Ashkenazi chant. His main research areas are the theory of Ashkenazi liturgical music and the composer Arnold Schoenberg. He received his doctorate from Cornell University.

2 Leib Glantz, "The Musical Basis of Nusach Hatefillah," in *Proceedings of the Fifth Annual Conference-Convention of the Cantors Assembly of America and the Department of Music of the United Synagogue of America* (1952):16-25

3 Max Wohlberg, "The History of the Musical Modes of the Ashkenazic Synagogue and their Usage," in *Proceedings of the Seventh Annual Conference-Convention of the Cantors Assembly of America and the Department of Music of the United Synagogue of America* (1954):36-42.

both Glantz's and Wohlberg's lectures as well as the reactions to them were re-published together in the Journal of Synagogue Music.[4] This juxtaposition created a retrospective panel in which both papers and the reactions to them can be read sequentially.[5]

It is difficult to ascertain whether Wohlberg's paper was indeed directly intended as a reaction to Glantz's presentation or even just motivated by it. Regardless, after his review of past attempts at defining these prayer modes, Wohlberg devotes a few pages to Glantz's theory, specifically as presented in the 1952 lecture. He also refers to a theory by Joseph Yasser,[6] which in turn involves both Yasser and Glantz in a debate of sorts. This debate is reflected in the exchange of correspondence in the proceedings of the 1954 conference and the 1972 reprints.

Wohlberg's paradigm was primarily defined by motivic structure, and he takes issue with Glantz's scale-oriented approach. Indeed, there is practically no mention of motifs in the presentation by Glantz (or Yasser, for that matter). Yet it is safe to assume that Glantz was very much aware of the motivic aspect of this repertoire. He also must have been familiar with Avraham Zvi Idelsohn's work addressing motivic structures. Nevertheless, it seems that Glantz's objective was to explore how an overall scale-derived theory could be applied to the Ashkenazi liturgical repertoire. The following discussion proposes that this specific approach to the theory is one example of a general approach to this traditional repertoire. Although this approach was expressed mainly in musical terms, it is derived from an all-encompassing worldview and ideological stance. This affected Glantz's choices of repertoire examples, and at times resulted in specific types of adjustments in his settings of the traditional material.

> *Although Glantz's approach was expressed mainly in musical terms, it is derived from an all-encompassing worldview and ideological stance.*

Discussions of music theory that are highly influenced by preset paradigms, including worldviews and ideology, are not unique to the work of Leib Glantz. Even in the narrower field of the music theory of Ashkenazi liturgy, Glantz's work is not the first instance in which this tendency can be observed. In fact, his narrative echoes similar phenomena in the work of A.Z. Idelsohn, and even discourse that preceded Idelsohn.

---

4 *Journal of Synagogue Music* 4/1-2 (1972):31-61.

5 We should note that the Glantz-Wohlberg-Yasser correspondence had already been published in the proceedings of the 1954 convention (pp. 42-44). [Ed. note: This correspondence appears in Appendix 1 of this book.]

6 Wohlberg mentions Yasser's "theory of triple-key modes." The only available record I know of Yasser's attempt at applying this theory to Ashkenazi prayer music is a summary of a lecture, published as Joseph Yasser, "The Structural Aspects of Jewish Modality," *The Jewish Music Forum* 10 (1956):33-35.

The attempts of pre-Idelsohn nineteenth- and early twentieth-century cantors to form a music-theory elucidation of their discipline were constrained by the concepts and terminology that were available to them at the time, and viewing Ashkenazi liturgical repertoire in terms of scales is the dominating paradigm in these works.[7] In the absence of post-modern *sui generis* concepts and terminology, yet without retreating to the major-minor system, the default was almost always the "pseudo Greek" modal scales.[8] Beyond the limited theoretical tools at these cantors' disposal, there was also a two-pronged ideological stance that motivated the pseudo Greek scales explanation. One impetus was to reveal that Jewish prayer music was based on a coherent system just as much as church music and other traditional practices. The other motivating force was to demonstrate that just like ideas, literature, liturgy, philosophy, worldview, and other cultural variables, non-Jewish music too was derived, or even stolen, from Jewish origins. Glantz's scale-based theory, especially its "pseudo Greek modes" underpinnings, hearkens back to these pre-Idelsohn sources,[9] yet its extra-musical underlining and related ideology are different from theirs.

So far as resonating with Idelsohn is concerned, both Glantz and Idelsohn sought an explication of this repertoire within an overall meta-structure that can be depicted in one unifying set of principles. Idelsohn's paradigm strove to contain all Jewish music throughout history and throughout the world in one overall meta-tradition. The basic tenets of this paradigm are: that all Jewish music (regardless of geographical factors, different traditions, or sects) exhibits the same traits; that it is in essence a Near-Eastern discipline; and that Jewish prayer modes as we know them originated in the music of ancient-world Israel.

Glantz's and Idelsohn's meta-structure approaches are expressed somewhat differently in their respective works. One characteristic of Idelsohn's all-encompassing explanation of Jewish

7 A.M. Bernstein, Moritz Deutsch, Aron Friedmann, Josef Goldstein, Alois Kaiser and William Sparger, Isaak Lachmann, M. Markson and M. Wolf, Pinchas Minkowski, Samuel Naumbourg, Josef Singer, and Hirsch Weintraub. Interestingly enough, these are the very sources that Wohlberg reviews in his 1954 presentation. This too may point to a possible conscious or unconscious intent in Wohlberg's paper to provide a mirror of sorts to Glantz's presentation.

8 I am using the term "pseudo Greek modes" in reference to the nineteenth-century portrayal of seven Greek modal scales as they appear, for example, in the authentic modes in Glarean's system (Ionian, Dorian, Phrygian, etc.) I borrowed this term from Harold Powers, "From Psalmody to Tonality," in *Tonal Structure in Early Music*, Cristle Collins Judd, ed. (New York and London: Garland, 1998):337, note 19. Some of the pre-Idelsohn sources also address the same scale system as "church scales," for example, "*den alten Kirchentonarten*" in the introduction to Hirsch and Solomon Weintraub, *Schire Beth Adonai* (Leipzig: M.W. Kauffmann, 1901, First edition: Königsberg, 1859, no page number indicated). The church connotation here corresponds with the need to show a link to church music (in itself part of these sources' agenda as mentioned below).

9 One clearly manifested example of this pre-Idelsohn scalar perception is the notating of a one-octave scale as an illustration of various mode-names, found in abundance in Aron Friedmann, *Schir Lischlaumau* (Berlin: Deutsch-Israelitischen Gemeindenbunde, 1901). In this respect Glantz's similarity to the pre-Idelsohn perception is very graphically illustrated in Leib Glantz, *Rinat Hakodesh: Prayer Modes*, Yehoshua Zohar, ed. (Tel Aviv: Israel Music Institute, 1965). The same procedure — providing a musical example for the identified scales (although different from Friedmann's scales) — is prevalent throughout this collection. Whether Glantz was conscious of this graphic similarly to Friedmann's book is difficult to determine.

music is that it includes the entire repertoire throughout the world and through history. His inclusive approach is not only reflected in the attempt to establish one system to explain the entire repertoire. As a part of the paradigm described above, this "lumping" viewpoint is also expressed in the attempt to demonstrate that the different subgroups (sects, traditions, and geographical origins) all belong in the same category. On the other hand, the detail of the portrayal of this unity reveals a larger degree of variety, at least so far as the theory is concerned. For example, Idelsohn accounts for a significantly higher number of "modes" within the repertoire. Moreover, even when he identifies modes that he claims to be present across geographical and sectional boundaries, the constituent defining particles of these modes are different in each such tradition or geographical origin.

Glantz, on the other hand, seems to unify almost the entire repertoire under his one-scale meta-structure theory: the "*Yekum Purkon* mode," which will be discussed in detail below. In fact, in correspondence with Max Wohlberg,[10] he adds repertoire that he had previously placed under a separate modal scale (*A'ha'va Ra'bbah*) into the meta-scale of the *Yekum Purkon* mode. Moreover, even his definition of *A'ha'va Ra'bbah* is more inclusive than what is traditionally considered to be identified as an *A'ha'va Ra'bbah* scale.[11]

> *Unlike Idelsohn, there is no significant evidence suggesting that Glantz sought to implement his theory on any repertoire other than the Ashkenazi tradition.*

Finally, as we shall see below, material that he identified as pentatonic was also included in the *Yekum Purkon* mode by its association with *A'do'nai Ma'lach*. On the other hand, unlike Idelsohn, there is no significant evidence suggesting that Glantz sought to implement his theory on any repertoire other than the Ashkenazi tradition.

The parallel to the other aspect of Idelsohn's paradigm — seeking origins in antiquity — is, in Glantz's work, the notion that the Diaspora changed, in fact distorted, the original spirit and substance of the ancient, pre-exilic authentic version of Jewish prayer music.[12] Both the

---

10 Wohlberg, "The History of the Musical Modes of the Ashkenazic Synagogue and their Usage," p. 42.

11 This procedure in itself is an interesting demonstration of Glantz's process. In order to establish more unity among the repertoire, he creates one meta-category in which he can include material that otherwise would belong in three separate scales or modes: minor, *A'ha'va Ra'bbah* (and Phrygian), and an augmented 4th scale, most commonly known in this field as Ukrainian-Dorian (Glantz, "The Musical Basis of Nusach Hatefillah," pp. 21-23). The details of how he does this are beyond the scope of this comment. In summary we can observe the similarity to other instances, in which Glantz overlooks different tonics or defines the same one tonic for a variety of music sections, each of which, in fact has its own different tonic. See also Glantz's tonal identification of *O'chi'la La'El* and *Ak'da'mut* below.

12 Among other instances, this idea is prevalent in Glantz's lectures, particularly "A lecture on *Hallel* and *Tal*," on a vinyl record attached to the transcription as it appears in Leib Glantz, *Mivchar Yetsirot Rinat Hakodesh: Hallel Veshalosh Regalim, Selected Works Rinat Hakodesh: Hallel and Three Festivals*, David Loeb, ed. (Tel Aviv: Tel Aviv Institute of Jewish Liturgical Music in Conjunction with Israel Music Institute, 1968), unnumbered pages. This lecture is discussed in more detail below.

meta-structure notion and the desire for a pre-Diaspora authentic version are served well by a scalar explanation, particularly one that eschews the Western major-minor system, especially when it involves a "Greek"-modes undercurrent.

The following case-studies explore the details in a few instances in which Glantz's sincere and passionate drive regarding his musical theories, and the musical and extra-musical views they supported, affected his choices of repertoire examples, as well as denoted specific types of adjustments in his presentation of the traditional material.

Glantz's renderings of music for the liturgy appear both in written form and in recordings. Some of the recordings also have a transcribed version. It would be difficult to discern whether Glantz considered the versions he chose to keep in written form only, particularly those in his published books, to be better representatives of the tradition. It is therefore impossible to detect Glantz's divergences from conventional practice by comparing his own different versions to each other. Identifying points that significantly deviate from the tradition can only be done in sections of the liturgy in which the "correct" traditional version is more or less established and known. Yet much of the Ashkenazi traditional music has yet to be mapped out. A large portion of this repertoire has not yet been explored systematically; some of the material has a built-in high degree of freedom; and some of the liturgical sections are not featured in enough sources, or the available sources exhibit too much variety.

There are several ways to bypass this difficulty:

- Examine the parts of the liturgy in which the degree of freedom is relatively low.
- Choose liturgical sections whose musical tradition is well-established, known, and universally agreed upon.
- Examine prayer units whose music is featured in many sources that present a relatively uniform depiction and a high degree of consistency.
- Identify diversions from the tradition in places that use prayer modes whose definition has been sufficiently elucidated.

Thus the diversions from the traditional practice to which I point in this paper are fundamental, basic, and structural.

Some of Glantz's written depictions of his versions of Ashkenazi liturgical music are distinctly different from the majority of the written sources of this repertoire. The types of these alterations or adjustments vary. In the case of his *Ne'i'la Ka'ddish* depiction discussed below, these differences are reflected primarily in the use of a significantly abridged version, omission of some motifs and tonal markers, and the use of other motifs that may not be typical of this repertoire section. In other instances we see how these changes either echo a certain idiomatic use of the material (for example, juxtaposing the traditional idioms of one occasion with another), detours from or alterations to the traditional material, significant chromatic alterations, or using motifs in a function that is different from the one normally assigned to them. In all of these instances I believe the adjustments are made deliberately, to support his declared aesthetic or ideological approach.

It is important to realize that Glantz's choices concerning his presentation of the tradition and the changes and adjustments he made were neither arbitrary nor the result of random creative volition. In fact, I discovered that generally, variants that are only an expression of Glantz's creativity do not result in changes to the defining constituents of the tradition itself.

One such creative variant, for example, is in Glantz's setting of the liturgy for the announcement of the new month (*Bir'kat Rosh Cho'desh*).[13] Glantz's rendition is a classic example of an extensive use of traditional *A'do'nai Ma'lach* characteristics. Yet in measure 4 of page 93 and the last measure of page 94 we can observe a use of these characteristics "with a twist." At this point Glantz reaches a cadence on the 5th degree below the tonic, and in both places this cadence includes a specific approach to this scale degree.

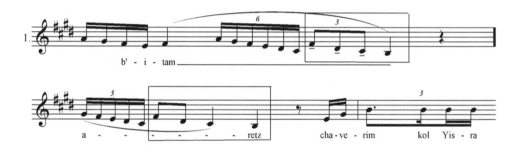

Here Glantz introduces a play on two of the constituent characteristics of this traditional mode as follows: one of the primary traits of *A'do'nai Ma'lach* is featuring pausal notes on the 5th scale degree. Thus Glantz's choice is not just any note, but specifically the 5th alluding to the traditional building block. Yet he does not use the typical 5th degree above the tonic but rather the one below it. Moreover, the way he approaches this note is one of the characteristic "frequently occurring variant" in a cadence. This variant, however, is not of a cadence for a pausal note but for an ending cadence on the tonic.[14] All of this, however, is still within the traditional defining constituents of the mode. The degree of freedom within this mode allows for cadences on various notes and for approaching these notes in any manner chosen. Thus

---

13 Glantz, *Rinat Hakodesh*, pp. 90-95.

14 For a discussion, analysis, and demonstration of these characteristics see Boaz Tarsi, "The *Adonai Malach* Mode in Ashkenazi Prayer Music: the Problem Stated and a Proposed Outlook based on Musical Characteristics," in *Proceedings of the Thirteenth World Congress of Jewish Studies*, http://www.lekket.com/articles/003000093.pdf (2001):10-11, 13-14, specifically characteristics "C" and "J."

Glantz indeed presents atypical motivic procedures with the realization that they are justified because of the built-in degree of freedom. Yet he does not use this freedom simply to compose arbitrary material. Rather, he uses the traditional building blocks themselves as the device for a creative change.

When Glantz changes fundamental defining elements, however, to the point of a qualitative departure, he does so with the genuine belief that these changes are necessary in order to adhere to his contentions about the tradition. These departures emanate from a larger overall view, paradigm, or perceptions, and at times, extra-musical contentions. To Glantz they are, in fact, corrective measures, taken in order to reveal the true uncorrupted version of the tradition. In other cases, in which these changes do not reveal an authentic version, Glantz still needs to depart from the tradition either in order to show what he views as the appropriate theory behind the practice or as corrective measures indicated by this theory. In this respect, Glantz's approach is common in a substantial body of work both within the tradition of Ashkenazi liturgical music as well as almost every other field of traditional, religious, or ethnic music throughout history. In addition, as I further discuss below, Glantz's procedure also expresses typical specific stylistic and ideological markers of his *zeitgeist*. We also need to keep in mind that both Glantz and the emerging "Mediterranean style" in Israel, which will be discussed below, are one instance among a dominating and wide-spread trend of turning to folk and quasi-folk "roots," including seeking indication for it in various modal qualities — however they interpret "mode" — in the second half of the nineteenth and into the twentieth century.[15]

> *When Glantz changes fundamental defining elements, however, to the point of a qualitative departure, he does so with the genuine belief that these changes are necessary in order to adhere to his contentions about the tradition. These departures emanate from a larger overall view, paradigm, or perceptions, and at times, extra-musical contentions.*

In the examined cases that follow, I concentrate on those fundamental basic changes and the possible perceptions, paradigms, worldview, and even ideology that constitute the driving force behind them. One of the most interesting examples of an overall paradigm's dictating fundamental changes to traditional material appears in Glantz's convention presentation from 1952. In presenting his scale-based theory, Glantz introduces what is *de facto* a modal scale,

---

15 This phenomenon, primarily an expression of *"Volksgeist,"* is reflected in a substantial body of work — research and prose, as well as music composition. Some notable cases among the multitude of possible examples are the philosophy of Johann Gottfried von Herder, the musicological work of Carl Dahlhaus and Robert Lachmann, and both the compositions and the research endeavors of Béla Bartók, Zoltán Kodály, and Leoš Janáček.

which he calls "*Yekum Purkon*," with which he connects a large portion of the repertoire. In the following quote Glantz strives to show how this scale can explain the music for the *Ne'i'la* service of *Yom Ki'ppur*:

> The original "Yekum Purkon" prayer of Sabbath "Musaf," as well as the other basic Sabbath tefillot, [are] shaped in the "Yekum Purkon" nusach… It is fascinating to observe that some of the "Mi-sinai" nuschaot, contain only one feature or one variation of this "Yekum Purkon" nusach — either the seven-step, ten-step, or thirteen-step line. As a striking example of the most elementary type of major scale, namely: the original Mixolydian seven-step, two tetrachord line, we can mention the famous "Neilah" Kaddish.[16]

He then provides a short example in which all the notes from this section of the *Ne'i'la* service are explained within the Mixolydian mode's scale.

How Glantz came to this conclusion seems clear. Indeed, if we were to consider the first (and in Glantz's example also the last) note as the first scale-degree and then arrange the note-collection in his example in an ascending sequential order, the resulting configuration would be a Mixolydian scale. This result, however, would be the outcome of a mechanical procedure that does not reflect the reality of the music. Specifically, in this example the section's beginning and even ending on a certain note does not exclude the possibility of a tonic on a different note. This tool — identifying a tonic that confirms a theory, rather than attempting to find the actual tonic — may be Glantz's most prevalent device. Other examples of this are his identifying the first note of *O'chi'la La'El* as the tonic in order to fit it into a raised 4th scale,[17]

16 Glantz, "The Musical Basis of Nusach Hatefillah," p. 19. [Ed. note: In the version of this lecture, as it appears in part 3 of this book, the transliteration of Hebrew words has been modified in order to be consistent with other essays and lectures included in this book.]

17 *Ibid.*, p. 23.

or the key-signature adjustment in *Ak'da'mut* in order to consider it Mixolydian.[18] The Mixolydian explanation for the *Ne'i'la Ka'ddish* also does not consider the possibility that one of the notes may be an alteration and therefore not a constitutional part of the scale (in Glantz's example the alteration manifests itself as B natural instead of B flat, thus making this note appear even more like a constitutional part of the scale).[19]

The application of Glantz's *Yekum Purkon* theory to the traditional music for *Ne'i'la*, however, required a number of changes and adjustments. This in turn resulted in a number of anomalies detected in his depiction of this liturgical section:

i.   The example he provides is extremely short. What in other sources requires several pages of music is here provided in one short line. One possible solution would be to assume that this line should be repeated, but there is no indication here that this should be done or how. The text that Glantz does provide in this musical example is only the very beginning of the *Ka'ddish* (up to "*Ve'Yam'lich Mal'chu'te*") and therefore does not address how his musical line would cover the entire text of the *Ka'ddish*, let alone the following *A'vot* and *G'vu'rot*.

ii.   Being this short, the example presents only three motifs, two of which are cadences. The fact that one of the cadences is in the assumed Mixolydian tonic and the other one is in minor a fifth above it, without its leading tone (see item iv), and that there is no additional musical material in the example, makes the Mixolydian explanation more likely. Most important, all of the definitive cadences in the minor key, and on a different tonic — so prevalent throughout the canon — are missing here.

iii.   By presenting a small amount of material, Glantz bypasses motifs or musical material that normally exist in this liturgical section and that do not follow the Mixolydian explanation.

iv.   Glantz consistently omits one particular note (in his example, this would be C sharp). This omission neutralizes a crucial factor that would support a different tonal explanation: a leading tone to minor, and a different tonic (D) from the proposed Mixolydian on G.

v.   The second motif (D-F-D in the second measure of Example 2) presents an atypical variant of the cadences in this section. Granted, this motif can still be considered an

---

18 See further discussion below and footnote 27.

19 The overall tonality of this version of the *Ne'i'la Ka'ddish* is in fact minor (if not for the anomalies mentioned below, this would be D minor in Glantz's example). Some of the elements that cannot be explained by the overall minor tonality are due to the presence of a major "lower extension" in this liturgical section (see Boaz Tarsi, "Lower Extension of the Minor Scale in Ashkenazi Prayer Music," *Indiana Theory Review* 23 [2002]:153-183).

acceptable variant in *Ne'i'la*, but Glantz's atypical variant omits the same leading tone mentioned above as well as makes this motif sound more like *Tal-Ge'shem* than *Ne'i'la*. In this sense, this motif undermines Glantz's other objective in this presentation — to illustrate the difference between *Tal-Ge'shem* and *Ne'i'la*.

vi.   There seems to be no support for this kind of "twist" on the *Ne'i'la Ka'ddish* in the literature. Unlike other instances (attributing the High Holiday "*A'vot*" section to Bezalel Odesser, by way of Avraham Kalechnik, or stating that his version of the *Tal-Ge'shem* music had been commonly practiced by Pinchas Minkowsky), Glantz does not mention from where such an unusual example is drawn. Another irregularity that makes it difficult to examine how Glantz would reconcile this example within the music of a *Ne'i'la* service, is that none of Glantz's cantorial books I know seem to provide a full setting of this liturgy.

These anomalies are interesting in and of themselves. Yet what concerns our point here is that all of them are necessary in order for the Mixolydian/ *Yekum Purkon* theory to work. I believe that behind these anomalies and adjustments lies a dominating paradigm that can be observed throughout Glantz's work. In the *Ne'i'la* case, this paradigm is best served by the theory Glantz presents in his lecture, and the anomalies are corrective adjustments that come to serve the theory.

This paradigm dominated Glantz's approach to the material, his thought-process, his presentations, and the music presented in his examples and liturgical settings. Here Glantz resonates with the pre-Idelsohn perceptions by utilizing a scale-derived explanation, and as such, one of the "pseudo Greek" modes. Concurrently, this theory is also in part tangential to Idelsohn's paradigm and in part overlaps with it. The Mixolydian-based theory that comes into full view with the foregoing adjustments serves the desired non-Western traits, (i.e., non-European, which for Glantz equals non-Diaspora).[20] At the same time it also serves as a cross-repertoire unifying factor for an overall meta-structure provided by the all-inclusive three variations format of this Mixolydian scale (see below).

The *Ne'i'la* example is one subtopic within a larger case Glantz makes in his 1952 presentation. This lecture is one of the most notable and involved demonstrations of Glantz's meta-structure approach. Fitting the *Ne'i'la* music into the given scalar explanation serves to demonstrate a link among several sections of the liturgical repertoire. The selections chosen are *Yekum Purkon* on Sabbath morning, most of the Passover *Ha'gga'da*, the *Bar'chu* for the Three

---

20 The claim for Middle-Eastern characteristics is somewhat more subtle in Glantz's output than it is in Idelsohn's. As we shall observe later below, it is expressed primarily in Glantz's following the prevailing tendency of his *zeitgeist*, especially in Israel, to identify or create traits that they considered "Eastern." In addition, both Idelsohn and the Israeli "Mediterranean style" mentioned below combined the Middle-Eastern traits and markers of antiquity by considering the former an indication of the latter.

Festivals *Ma'a'riv*, the *A'mi'da* for the morning of the Three Festivals, "*Ve'Ha'Ko'ha'nim*" from the *A'vo'da* service on *Yom Ki'ppur*, the beginning of the *A'mi'da* (*A'vot*) for the High Holidays, the *Ka'ddish* for the *Yom Ki'ppur Ne'i'la*, several *Mi'Si'nai* tunes, and several *Sha'bbat* prayers.

Another aspect of Glantz's *Yekum Purkon* mode and the Mixolydian scale is their connection to what is called in the cantorial field the "*A'do'nai Ma'lach*" mode.[21] Rendering the *Yekum Purkon* mode Mixolydian, and *A'do'nai Ma'lach* identical, is directly acknowledged in Glantz's 1952 conference presentation as well as in his 1961 radio lecture. As a direct result, the entire *Ka'bba'lat Sha'bbat* service is also added into this category. In addition, by way of his associating *A'do'nai Ma'lach* with the pentatonic scale, in his 1961 radio lecture "The Pentatonic Scales and the *A'do'shem Ma'lach Nu'sach*," Glantz also adds to this list the High Holiday *Ma'a'riv*, *Ak'da'mut*, several parts of the *Ha'llel*, portions of the *Ki'ddush*, the *Bra'chot* after the *Haf'ta'ra* reading, Sabbath *Ke'du'sha* for *Mu'saf*, *A'ta Nig'lei'ta* from *Rosh Ha'Sha'na Mu'saf*, and *Mi She'A'sa Ni'ssim* from *Bir'kat Rosh Cho'desh*. To this entire repertoire, all the material covered under *A'ha'va Ra'bbah* and Ukrainian-Dorian is also added due to these modes' association with the *Yekum Purkon* modal scale as mentioned above (see also footnote 11).

> *The mechanism by which Glantz's theory aims to apply to a substantial portion of the repertoire is by including all of it under the aegis of one unifying scale.*

The mechanism by which this theory aims to apply to a substantial portion of the repertoire is by including all of it under the aegis of one unifying scale. This scale can present itself in three progressive states: seven-note, ten-note, and twelve-note. In its seven-note state this scale is identical to the "pseudo Greek" Mixolydian modal scale. In its 10-note form a minor 10th is added, and in its complete thirteen-note configuration the scale comprises four major tetrachords superimposed one on top of the other:

---

21 For descriptions and discussions of *Adonai Malach* see for example, Hanoch Avenary, "The Concept of Mode in European Synagogue Chant," *Yuval* 2 (1971):11-21; Hanoch Avenary, "Second Thoughts about the Configuration of a Synagogue Mode," *Orbis Musicae* 9 (1986-87):11-16; Baruch Cohon, "The Structure of the Synagogue Prayer-Chant," *Journal of the American Musicological Society* 3/1 (1950):13-32; Avraham Zvi Idelsohn, *Jewish Music in its Historical Development*, New York: Henry Holt and Company (1929): *passim*; Avraham Zvi Idelsohn, *The Traditional Songs of the South German Jews*, Thesaurus of Hebrew Oriental Melodies, Volume 7, Leipzig: Friedrich Hofmeister (1933):xx-xxii; Joseph Levine, "Toward Defining the Jewish Prayer Modes; with Particular Emphasis on the Adonay Malakh Mode," *Musica Judaica* 3/1 (1980-81):13-15; Tarsi, "The *Adonai Malach* Mode in Ashkenazi Payer Music, Eric Werner, *A Voice Still Heard: the Sacred Songs of the Ashkenazic Jews*, University Park and London, The Pennsylvania State University Press (1976):46-61.

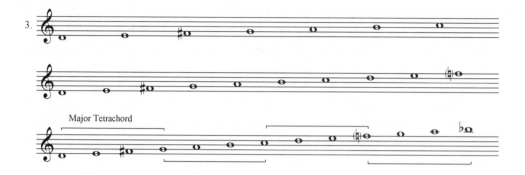

A depiction of the long version of this scale appears in the introduction to Glantz's 1965 collection, identified as the *A'do'nai Ma'lach* scale.[22] The only other examples of this scale I have found (with an added tetrachord below the tonic, thus totaling five tetrachords) are in works by Hanoch Avenary and Joseph Yasser.[23] All three instances mention this scale in their discussions of the *A'do'nai Ma'lach* mode. In Avenary's work this scale is used as an example of an artificially manufactured device that in fact does not explain the mode.[24] It is difficult to ascertain whether this five-tetrachord scale, specifically its top, actually exists in the practicum or the literature. I have only encountered one example that reaches this high segment of the *ambitus* in a hand-written transcription of Joseph Rosenblatt's "*Omar Rabi Elozor.*"[25] But at that highest part, Rosenblatt uses Ukrainian-Dorian, not the major tetrachord featured in the above-mentioned scale depictions. It might very well be that the overly extended range of this scale is, in Glantz's case, the result of incorporating the *A'do'nai Ma'lach* mode into the overall one-scale theory. Once this combination occurs, one must take into account the tetrachord below the tonic, which is fundamentally constitutional to *A'do'nai Ma'lach*. This in turn results in an extended *ambitus*, which may effect a range that is too large to actually exist in the practicum or to be found in written material.

It may very well be that the creation of a theory, with a sense of order and

> *It may very well be that the creation of a theory, with a sense of order and inclusiveness that makes everything fit together, is motivation enough and in itself the reason Glantz was so invested in showing its validity.*

---

22 Glantz, Rinat Hakodesh, introduction, no pagination.

23 Hanoch Avenary, "Second Thoughts about the Configuration of a Synagogue Mode"; Yasser, "The Structural Aspects of Jewish Modality."

24 In "Second Thoughts about the Configuration of a Synagogue Mode," p. 14 Avenary states that "[this scalar explanation should be] discarded [because it is merely the product of] the inquiry of a young composer from the contemporary avant-garde [who is ignorant of the points at issue]... as a stimulus for a creative process."

25 *Rare Collection of Cantorial Masterpieces*, assembled by the Toronto Council of Hazzanim, p. 22 (no date indicated).

inclusiveness that makes everything fit together, is motivation enough and in itself the reason Glantz was so invested in showing its validity.[26] Yet expressing this theory specifically in these scalar terms provides additional support for Glantz's overall view. It is the rationale for inter-connecting all of the liturgical sections mentioned above. Additionally, this creates a unifying factor and identifies a single governing principle, which establishes an overall meta-structure for the tradition. Furthermore, this scale, at least in its seven-note format, is identical to a "pseudo Greek" mode, and therefore fits in with the paradigm of non-Western or at least outside of the common practice major/minor depiction. Even further, Dorian as a replacement for minor, and Mixolydian for major is the basis for the "authentic, Hebraic, and antiquity-derived" music of that period (see further discussion below). In order to support this theory and his overall perception of the tradition, Glantz needed to choose examples that support it or create such examples. In other cases he had to overlook some traits or identify them as wrong or unauthentic, and at times Glantz would simply modify some of the material in order to adjust it to what he viewed as the correct version.

As I have mentioned briefly above (footnote 9), titling liturgical sections with their scale or mode, as well as providing a notated depiction of the scale on top of the music itself, is common throughout Glantz's work. It is interesting that in *Rinat Hakodesh* most of the material that exhibits clear features of *A'do'nai Ma'lach* is not titled at all, some material that may or may not occasionally include a flat 7 is titled "Mixolydian," and some material is titled in various other different ways. I have not yet come up with a discernible principle that explains these different title choices. Yet I do believe that the desire to show the presence of Mixolydian is the motivation behind giving this title (although without the notated scale illustration) to material that is normally considered neither *A'do'nai Ma'lach* nor Mixolydian. One typical example of superimposing a Mixolydian title is Glantz's *Ak'da'mut*.[27] The D major example is given an A major key signature, the extra G sharp this key signature brings in is neutralized within the body of the music, the first note, A, which is in fact the dominant of a regular D major tonality, is considered to be the tonic, and thus a selection in D major becomes A Mixolydian.

Perhaps the most ideology-derived aspects of Glantz's underlying perception, indeed at times bordering on an agenda, are expressed in his lecture entitled: "*Nu'sach Ha'llel* and *Tal.*"[28] In his analysis of the music for this liturgical section and as his opinion regarding the correct manner of singing it, he states: "What was the form of *Ha'llel* in the ancient Holy Temple? … It might

---

26 Glantz even made it a point to reaffirm his theory by reporting that he had found further supporting evidence in more cases, which he had examined after his 1952 presentation. (Wohlberg, "The History of the Musical Modes of the Ashkenazic Synagogue and their Usage," pp. 42-43.)

27 Glantz, *Rinat Hakodesh*, p. 106. This explanation is also essential for his discussion of *Ak'da'mut* in Leib Glantz, "The Pentatonic Scales and the '*Adoshem Malach*' Nusach," presented on "*Kol Yisrael*" radio, Israel, 1961.

28 Glantz, *Mivchar Yetsirot Rinat Hakodesh*, introduction, no pagination. This lecture was delivered by Glantz as a radio talk. It was the third of a six-lecture series on *Kol Yis'ra'el* radio station in Israel in 1961. All quotes from Glantz's oral presentations are based on my translation of the original Hebrew, on their published versions, or on translations supplied to me by the Glantz family.

be expected then, that this exalted verbal content would dictate a music form that is true to the original sources — authentic and appropriately jubilant." Glantz then berates the melancholic wailing manner in which cantors actually present this music. "'The heavens are the heavens of the Lord, but the earth He has given to mankind,' or 'To Thee I will offer a thanksgiving sacrifice' and so forth. What is there to bewail?" He goes on to state that the jubilant characteristic is in fact the authentic one. Glantz then connects the inappropriate wailing and crying character of such performance with the use of the minor scale. Moreover, he does not conceal his judgmental evaluation as he comments that the use of this scale is "unfortunate."

But Glantz ascribes the (inappropriate) wailing and sad character to "the entire tragedy of exile and the tragic and catastrophic situation of the Jews of the Diaspora." The musical indicator of this wailing is again the wrong use of the minor key, which is suitable to the (no longer applicable) tragedy of exile. He specifically addresses the Diaspora cantor who, by his tearful rendering "was sinning not only against the music, but, and that is the most important point, against the text and against the general spirit of the originally jubilant *Ha'llel*." He uses the Hebrew adjective "*Me'shu'bash*" ("corrupt, distorted, in need of correction") to describe this minor key, which results in "no thanksgiving and no praise, no song and no exultation. Instead there are only broken sounds and plaints, weak suffering voices. The more tearful the cantor, the greater his reputation."

> Glantz ascribes the (inappropriate) wailing and sad character to "the entire tragedy of exile and the tragic and catastrophic situation of the Jews of the Diaspora." The musical indicator of this wailing is again the wrong use of the minor key, which is suitable to the (no longer applicable) tragedy of exile.

Glantz calls for getting away from this corrupt version and its melancholic character. He seeks renewal of an ancient authentic Hebraic music for the liturgy and a return to what he claims is the true authentic pre-exile origin. The key to change and the counterindication for this "characteristic wailing and weeping" is consistent with his scale-derived paradigm. He says: "…after years of searching, examining and striving to find the musical truth about the *Ha'llel*, I have come to the recognition that the first blessing of the *Ha'llel* is not to be sung in the minor key." The correct musical antithesis to this Diaspora-derived wailing is the "Mixolydian scale, as well as… the pentatonic scale, which are the main and authentically original scales of our *nusach*."

Later in this lecture Glantz contributes the final ingredient for what he considers the appropriate, authentic version of liturgical music by invoking its Middle-Eastern character. In the final statement of his lecture Glantz interjects [Middle Eastern] Orientalism as well as the "new Jew" with his associated rural agricultural traits. Concurrently, this same short statement manages succinctly to re-state identifying the proposed version as the correct one, its need to be removed from the major/minor system, its ancient, almost mythological roots ("*Mi'Si'nai*"), and an urgent call to implement change.

> The original Jewish *Tal* must be garbed in "oriental" dress — in oriental scales. The cantor must do everything he can to divest himself of those ordinary major and minor keys. The agricultural village life of our country must be given the proper and true musical expression in our prayers. The *nusach* from Sinai must be revived, perhaps in a modernistic manner, but in a clear and concrete fashion.

The core of the pre-Diaspora approach that Glantz presents is essentially the same as Idelsohn's search for antiquity. Glantz supports the pre-exile perception and points to its association with a non-Westernized version of major and minor in statements such as "major and the Jewish minor contain something characteristic and specific, something that survived from the ancient modes of the oriental peoples, that is not to be found at all in the modern West European scales." The Mixolydian-derived *Yekum Purkon* theory we have examined earlier is one sub-case of this approach.[29] Thus while Glantz's ideology is somewhat tangential to Idelsohn's, his technical solution (the "pseudo Greek" modes, and a theory based on scales alone) emulates the pre-Idelsohn theories as discussed above.

Beyond the meta-structure-"pseudo Greek mode"-scalar framework, I found two other devices by which Glantz strives to achieve this pre-exile, authentic, and non-Western sound. Both are common traits of the so-called "Mediterranean style" of Glantz's era.[30] The most important point for our discussion concerning this multi-faceted phenomenon may be summed up in Alexander Boskovitz's contention that "melancholy music of northern Europe [would be] out of place in Mediterranean countries" and that "cantorial liturgy and folk songs of the Jewish Diaspora would not fit the spirits of the *Yeshuv* in Palestine."[31]

---

29 Other cases involve identifying within this repertoire Aeolian, Phrygian, and Dorian as replacement for minor and Mixolydian as replacement for major. Another expression of the same aspect is Glantz's using the old insider's title for *A'ha'va Ra'bbah* as "*freygish*," which Glantz takes a step closer to the Greek modes by translating it into English as "Jewish Phrygian" (*Rinat Hakodesh*, pp. 69, 79; on p. 90 the Hebrew title indicates — in Hebrew script — *Freygish*, while the English title is "Phrygian").

30 This style, its many-fold implications, and its role in music (both art and popular) and culture in Palestine during the first half of the twentieth century is beyond the scope of this paper. A few selected samples among the abundant discussions of "Mediterraneanism" in music of that era include Philip Bohlman, "The Immigrant Composer in Palestine, 1933-1948: Stranger in a Strange Land," *Asian Music* 17/3 (1986):147-167; Philip Bohlman, *The Land where Two Streams Flow: Music in the German-Jewish Community of Israel* (Urbana: University of Illinois, 1989); Philip Bohlman, *The World Center of Jewish Music in Palestine 1936-1940: Jewish Musical Life on the Eve of World War II* (Oxford: Clarendon, 1992); Philip Bohlman, "Inventing Jewish music," *Yuval* 7 (2002):33-74; Shai Burstyn, "Inventing Musical Tradition: the Case of the Hebrew (Folk) Song" in *Proceedings of the International Conference, Rethinking Interpretive Traditions in Musicology, Orbis Musicae* 13 (1999):127-136; Jehoash Hirshberg, *Paul Ben-Haim his Life and Work* (Jerusalem: Israeli Music Publication, 1990); and Jehoash Hirshberg, *Music in the Jewish Community of Palestine 1880-1948* (Oxford: Clarendon, 1995).

31 Hirshberg, *Music in the Jewish Community of Palestine 1880-1948*, p. 263. [Ed. note: *Yeshuv* refers to the Jewish population, including the pre-Zionist Jewish community known as the Old *Yeshuv*, which lived in Palestine before the State of Israel was proclaimed in 1948.]

In the lecture on *Ha'llel* and *Tal* Glantz suggests that a specific chromatic alteration is not only the key for rejuvenation from the wailing Diaspora character of this liturgical section, but that it is in fact its proper and truly authentic version. This is based on an interchange between minor and major, which affects one repeating motif, as the following example demonstrates:

It is clear that Glantz's choice of this specific device to create a sense of antiquity and, more important, to redirect the musical material back to its Middle-Eastern roots, is influenced by his *zeitgeist*. This interchangeable chromatic alteration (B flat/B natural in example 4) is one of the traits of the emerging new Israeli style of music in the beginning and middle of the twentieth century, which strives in a similar manner to Glantz's, towards an "Oriental," "nationally authentic" repertoire. Just as in Glantz's approach to the liturgical tradition, the Mediterranean style clearly resonates with the nineteenth-century perception of modality as a marker of "the folk."[32] In its own particular way, this emerging style combines such modality with Western common practice brought in from Europe and with "Oriental" elements found in Arab or Bedouin music, as well as with Jewish music of non-European origins with particular affinity to the music of Yemenite Jews. (The narrative of that era — not the least of which influenced by Idelsohn's ideas — was dominated by the romantic notion that the Yemenite Jews best represent the original Hebrews and that Jewish Yemenite culture in general, and music in particular, constitute the most accurate representation of antiquity and authenticity.)

Glantz's chromatic interchange underlies both a modal approach typical of the Mediterranean style (through the allusion to Dorian as discussed below), and "Oriental" characteristics. As a Middle-Eastern trait this alteration is intended as a device to approximate the sound of quartertones of Arab music. Shai Burstyn, of Tel Aviv University, discusses instances of chromatic alteration in Israeli songs that are identical to Glantz's and identifies their assigned role in inducing a Middle-Eastern character. "Resembling the oriental soundscape by chromatic fluctuation must have been in the air, for we find it in several other contemporary songs."[33] Among many such cases, Burstyn cites Yedidiah Admon's *Shir Ha'Ga'mal* (1927) and Mordechai Zeira's *Hi'ne A'cha'le'la* (1927). The alterations between F and F# in the first and C and C# in the second are identical to the alteration between B flat and B natural in example 4.

---

32 In this respect both Glantz and the emerging "Mediterranean style" in Israel are another example of the dominating *Volksgeist* trend mentioned in footnote 15.

33 Burstyn, "Inventing Musical Tradition," p. 130.

The chromatic alteration interchange in Glantz's example of *Tal-Ge'shem* may also be linked to another device by which Middle-Eastern character was attempted in Israeli songs of that era. Given that the tonic of the *Tal-Ge'shem Ka'ddish* is located a fifth below the ending note of the altered motif, the altered scale degree is 6. Raising the 6th degree in a minor scale renders it identical to the scale structure of Dorian in the "pseudo Greek" modal system. Indeed Glantz formally identifies several sections in his liturgical collection as "Aeolian-Dorian" and provides a notated example of a one-octave minor scale, in which the 6th degree is both minor and major.[34] Just as using Mixolydian instead of major was a device to induce the Middle-Eastern, non-European, and ancient character, so was the replacement of minor with Dorian. "Neutralizing the hegemony of the major and minor scales was a most effective, and therefore a most prevalent, means of attaining the new Hebrew *melos*… [chromatic alterations] led back to the frequent employment of Mixolydian rather than major, and Dorian and Aeolian rather than minor."[35] Examples of this technique are abundant; among them are Mordechai Zeira's *Ka'to'nu Me'od*, David Zehavi's *Ye'su'sum Mid'bar Ve'Tsi'a*, Imanuel Zamir's *Me'ga'dim Le'Re'i*, Mark Lavri's *Ma Mi'Lay'la Ba'Cha'ni'ta* (from his opera *Dan Ha'Sho'mer*), and Daniel Sambursky's *Shir Ha'E'mek*.

Another element that Glantz viewed as a marker for Hebraic pre-exile authenticity is the pentatonic scale. I am not sure how aware he was of the various theories that associate pentatonic scales with earlier and/or "primitive" musics.[36] But just like the other ideology-derived technical devices he shared with his contemporaries in Israel, the presence of pentatonic scales was

---

34 Glantz, *Rinat Hakodesh*, p. 107-108. A similar alteration also appears on p. 34 in a *Ka'bba'lat Sha'bbat* setting for *Kol A'do'nai*.

35 Burstyn, "Inventing Musical Tradition," p. 131. Similar phenomena are discussed and demonstrated in Herzl Shmueli, *Hazemer Hayisraeli Iyunim Besignono, Mivnehu Umahuto (The Israeli Song)* (Tel Aviv: Hamerkaz Leltarbut Velechinuch, Hasifriya Lemusika, 1971), particularly the fourth chapter entitled "*Hasulamiyut Balachan Hayisraeli* (the scalar traits of the Israeli melody)," pp. 143-155.

36 Theories of this and similar ideas abound. Among the classic examples is Curt Sachs, *The Rise of Music in the Ancient world* (New York: Norton, 1943).

> *The presence of pentatonic scales was a trait he sought to demonstrate throughout the repertoire. Like the other characteristics he associated with the authentic original version of this repertoire, pentatonic scales were indications of both authenticity and of Hebraic, pre-exilic antiquity.*

a trait he sought to demonstrate throughout the repertoire. Like the other characteristics he associated with the authentic original version of this repertoire, pentatonic scales were indications of both authenticity and of Hebraic, pre-exilic antiquity. Two specific tools for establishing the pentatonic scale as an indication of antiquity are linking it with biblical cantillations (following an idea originally expressed by Idelsohn) and associating it with the *Mi'Si'nai* tunes (which are enshrined in an almost mythological aura of antiquity):[37]

...the various forms of the ancient pentatonic scale. How great is the difference between the reading of the Torah on Shabbat — pentatonic major — and the reading of the Haftara — pentatonic minor.[38]

On the Sabbath morning... the "P'sukei D'zimrah" [are sung] in a pure pentatonic or 5-step line. This nusach can definitely be traced to the Biblical cantillation... The "Akdamut" prayer of Shavuot can also be clearly understood through the application of the plain and simple pentatonic line. It too has remained... it is considered to be a "Mi-sinai" nusach...[39]

The pentatonic scale and the identification of repertoire sections as pentatonic are prevalent throughout Glantz's work. Moreover, in his 1961 radio lecture, "The Pentatonic Scales and the *'A'do'nai Ma'lach' Nu'sach*," he links the pentatonic scale to *A'do'nai Ma'lach* and therefore also to the *Yekum Purkon* theory (this also further serves the meta-structure concept).

We observed earlier that in his work Glantz does not always identify the tonality or modality of every liturgical section. Yet in *Rinat Hakodesh* he specifically adds the title "pentatonic" at

---

37 The *Mi'Si'nai* tunes were never considered actually to come directly from the time of antiquity. Nevertheless, there is still a question as to their time origin. Many other facets of this phenomenon, and even its definition and which melodies are covered under this rubric, have yet to be pursued. For a sample of discussions of these tunes, some of which must be read critically, see Hanoch Avenary, "Mi-Sinai Niggunim" in *Encyclopedia Judaica* 12 (1971):151-153; Idelsohn, *Thesaurus* vii:xxix-xxxvi, and viii:xv-xvii; Joseph Levine, "The Musical Trope System of Ashkenazic Prophetic Reading," *Musica Judaica* 5/1 (1982-83):43-44; Joseph Levine, *Synagogue Song in America*, (Crown Point: WhiteCliffs Media, 1989):44-54; and Eric Werner, *A Voice Still Heard: the Sacred Songs of the Ashkenazic Jews* (University Park: Pennsylvania State University, 1976):26-43 and *passim*.

38 Glantz, *Rinat Hakodesh*, introduction, no pagination.

39 Glantz, "The Musical Basis of Nusach Hatefillah," pp. 18-19.

the top of twelve different repertoire segments.[40] These sections are not always, in fact, pentatonic, and are at times adjusted so that the note-collection they present can be similar to a pentatonic scale. A striking example of the desire to identify pentatonic characteristics in the repertoire, to the point of not only an occasional change but a real adjustment of the defining motivic material, is his example of the second version for the *Sha'bbat Ma'a'riv Bar'chu.*[41]

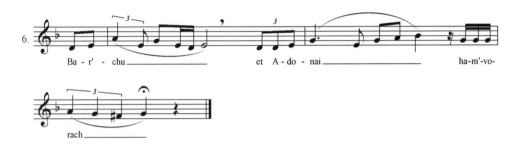

This example constitutes a fundamental deviation from the traditional version.[42] Moreover, one of the striking traits that results from this deviation is a jazz-like sound, quite foreign to this repertoire (especially the progression G-E-D-E-D-D-E-G-E-G-A-Bb in measures 1-2). Yet this version is not simply the result of Glantz's free use of his own composed material. Analysis reveals that Glantz does not begin the phrase with the traditional motif. He does not, however, merely make up his own motif; rather, he borrows a motif that normally opens a pre-concluding paragraph in this section and uses it on the opening *Bar'chu* text. In its normal form, this motif would comprise the notes D-E-A-E-G-F-E-D-E. Yet Glantz eliminates the F note. By doing so he turns the note-collection in this motif into a pentatonic scale, thus shaping this motif into the variant as it appears in the first eight notes of example 6. Once he has established a pentatonic environment, Glantz concludes the phrase in its traditional cadence (G-A-Bb-G-A-G-F#-G). The juxtaposition of the opening motif borrowed from a different function of the phrase, adjusted to fit a pentatonic scale, with the traditional ending cadence creates a collision between the F and F#. It also creates a clash of sorts between the different traditional motifs (now misplaced and altered), which, in turn, also results in the above-mentioned unusual "jazzy" sound.

40 "Pentatonic," pp. 17, 21, 23, 104; "Minor pentatonic," pp. 13, 19, 20, 24, 42; "Major pentatonic," pp. 15, 24, 27. This title is by far the most prevalent of Glantz's modal, tonal, and scalar titles.

41 *Rinat Hakodesh*, pp. 42-43. Glantz provides three different versions for this liturgical occasion: the first he titles "minor," the second "Pentatonic (minor)," and the third "Choral major." These versions parallel Joshua Ne'eman's "Nusach A" (Lithuanian), "Nusach B" (Central European), and "Nusach C" (Volhynian) in Joshua Ne'eman, *Nosah Lahazan: The Traditional Chant of the Synagogue According to the Lithuanian-Jerusalem Musical Tradition, Vol. II.,* (Jerusalem: Israel Institute for Sacred Music, 1968/69):26-37.

42 Glantz's second version ("*Arvit* 2") sets out to demonstrate the minor version of this *Bar'chu* — the most prevalent version in both Israel and the U.S., which in all likelihood is an East European, Polish-Lithuanian practice. See Boaz Tarsi, "Observations on Practices of *Nusach* in America," *Asian Music* 33/2 (2000):180-192.

As I already demonstrated, Glantz's creative use within the boundaries of the tradition involved a play on the constituents of traditional modes. But even in the cases in which Glantz's changes result in a fundamental deviation from the tradition, they still involve some reference to the traditional parameters. For example, the changes to the Friday night *Ma'a'riv* discussed above, entail borrowing material from one location in the paragraph and using it elsewhere, as well as changing the motif's function from an opener of a pre-concluding *Bra'cha* phrase to an opener of the entire service and a call for prayer. In the *Ne'i'la Ka'ddish*, these changes constitute what in Glantz's eyes would be "cleansing" it of impurities — weeding out the components that murky up the picture that emerges from the theory. In the same example, the changes also involve borrowing a motivic variant from a different occasion (*Tal-Ge'shem*). In the quasi-repetition of the *A'mi'da* on Friday night these changes are expressed in using the Saturday morning *A'vot* music for *Bir'kat She'va* (a practice that now seems to prevail in North America), and in moving one norm of performance — cantorial recitative — from its customary location in the *Re'tse* paragraph to the previous paragraph (*Ma'gen A'vot Bi'Dva'ro*, which is normally sung as a metrical tune).[43] Many other creative innovations can be observed abundantly throughout his liturgical settings, both in terms of ornamental additions and in an innovative way of using existing traditional motifs.

The research of traditional Ashkenazi liturgical music relies heavily on written material in cantorial manuscripts and books. Yet any information drawn from this source material has to be interpreted through the mindset of its author. It is extremely rare to find a source in which so much additional information is available beyond the musical evidence alone. In this respect, the work of Leib Glantz provides a unique opportunity to extract a genuine and clear picture of the various aspects at play in the evolution of a traditional source. Studying Leib Glantz brings into light much information about how to read a work through the prism of a very specific era, and about very specific and known tools of adaptation. Moreover, this adaptation is done by an individual who is both an insider practitioner as well as an outside-educated professional. We also know what the purpose of the adaptation is and as such, it provides a rare view into both the characteristic markers of an era and as a model of adaptation, its origins, and its outcome. In addition, Glantz's theory serves as a bridge of sorts between Idelsohn's

> *This adaptation is done by an individual who is both an insider practitioner as well as an outside-educated professional. We also know what the purpose of the adaptation is and as such, it provides a rare view into both the characteristic markers of an era and as a model of adaptation, its origins, and its outcome.*

---

43 See Boaz Tarsi, "Toward A Clearer Definition of the *Magen Avot* Mode," *Musica Judaica* 16 (2001-2002):68-70.

work, later studies, and onto the threshold of postmodern paradigms, while at the same time also tying in the pre-Idelsohn perceptions. But most importantly, the total sum of his *oeuvre* and his own documented process can facilitate a case-study of how to read the written documentations within the canon of Ashkenazi liturgical music and can provide a springboard onto further explication of this tradition.

3

The Uniqueness of the Chazanic Art of Leib Glantz

CANTOR DR. SHOLOM KALIB[1]

> *Leibele Glantz, as he was endearingly referred to by masses whom he enthralled by his fiery, often mystical and extraordinarily imaginative approach to Cha'za'nut, was unquestionably among the foremost practitioners of the chazanic art of the zenith period of its history.*

Leib Glantz, or Leibele Glantz, as he was endearingly referred to by masses whom he enthralled by his fiery, often mystical, and extraordinarily imaginative approach to *Cha'za'nut,* was unquestionably among the foremost practitioners of the chazanic art of the zenith period of its history. Leibele Glantz was among the last of the chazanic giants of that era, as well as one who stood out in a manner which differed from even his most illustrious contemporaries, due to his personality as well his rare vocal and musical gifts, resulting in his unique approach to his sacred calling.

As is true of the chazanic art in general, a full appreciation of that of Leibele Glantz can be had only by a listener who is familiar with the religious attitude of the congregations of the past for whom his *Cha'za'nut* took shape. In addition, it must be a listener who has an intimate knowledge of the prayer text at hand along with its traditional *Nu'sach* (basic chant) and

---

1 Cantor Sholom Kalib received his doctorate degree in Music Theory from Northwestern University. He began conducting synagogue choirs at age 14, and assumed a cantors position at age 20. He was a cantorial teacher at the Jewish Music Institute of the College of Jewish Studies (today the Spertus Institute) in Chicago, and is the author of *The Musical Tradition of the Eastern European Synagogue.* He is Professor Emeritus of Eastern Michigan University.

accepted norms of extension though *Cha'za'nut* (the cantorial art), as well as the significance and atmosphere of the liturgical occasion on which a particular prayer is being intoned.

Inasmuch as a full awareness of this "picture" has long ceased to exist in the minds of worshippers in the overwhelming majority of synagogues worldwide, most twenty-first century listeners, by far, are unprepared to understand — let alone appreciate — the *Cha'za'nut* of Leibele Glantz without background knowledge of a number of key factors which were central to the culture in which it functioned and flourished.

The place of worship, the synagogue, was in former times perceived as the House of God, a *Ma'kom Ka'dosh* (a holy place) which worshippers approached and entered with a profound sense of awe, as a place in which His presence was perceptible. The

prayer leader, whether the lay *Ba'al Te'fi'la* or the professional *Cha'zan,* was viewed as the *Sh'li'ach Tzi'bur,* the community's representative in public prayer to God. High Holiday *Pi'yu'tim* (liturgical poems) — such as *Ya'rei'ti,* near the beginning of the reader's repetition of the *Shach'rit A'mi'da* of the First Day of *Rosh Ha'Sha'na,* and *A'ti'ti* in the parallel place for the Second Day of *Rosh Ha'Sha'na; Hi'ne'ni He'A'ni Mi'Ma'as,* preceding the *Mu'saf A'mi'da* of *Rosh Ha'Sha'na* and *Yom Ki'ppur;* and *He'ye Im Pi'fi'yot,* preceding *O'chi'la La'El,* in the *Mu'saf A'mi'da* of *Rosh Ha'Sha'na* and *Yom Ki'ppur* — dramatically attest to this perception of the *Sh'li'ach Tzi'bur.* The *Sh'li'ach Tzi'bur* assumed his role veritably with trepidation and as a grave responsibility, and the congregation placed its hope and trust in the sincerity, piety and effective plea brought by him before the Almighty on its behalf and on behalf of the entire House of Israel. Therefore, adherence to traditional *Nu'sach,* as well as truly heartfelt prayer and meaningful musical interpretation of the liturgical texts, were assumed sacred obligations on the part of the *Sh'li'ach Tzi'bur,* and were expected — nay required — by a God-fearing, knowledgeable and highly critical congregation of worshippers.

Every *Cha'zan,* in the traditional sense of that title, performed according to the requirements of that value system. Those who most effectively touched the hearts of the masses through exceptional vocal, musical and/or interpretive skills achieved fame and wide recognition. Each of the relative few who achieved such status possessed a combination of artistic assets which distinguished him in a manner unique *vis-à-vis* all others. The uniqueness of Leibele Glantz, formed by particular characteristics which distinguished him from all other *Cha'za'nim* known

> *The uniqueness of Leibele Glantz, formed by particular characteristics which distinguished him from all other Cha'za'nim known to this writer who preceded or followed him, stems first from the depth of intensity of his passion in liturgical singing.*

to this writer, who preceded or followed him, stems first from the depth of intensity of his passion in liturgical singing. From this metaphoric tree trunk, ever present in his chanting, branches extended in numerous directions.

His renditions project his inner sense of awe described in the Talmudic dictum, *Da Lif'nei Mi A'ta O'med* ("Know before Whom you stand"), which appears above the Holy Ark in many synagogues. Glantz's delivery reflects the ideal *Sh'li'ach Tzi'bur* in a style once referred to as *Zogachtz,*[2] literally "telling" or "speaking," which term implies devotional chanted discourse with the Creator.

Glantz's musical-liturgical creations were meticulously, painstakingly planned and notated to the minutest detail, including microtonal inflections, as seen in Example 1 below (m. 4, second note) and in Example 3 (m. 5, first note). Most amazingly, despite such detailed pre-planned writing, his singing comes off with such conviction that if his notations did not exist, listeners would in all probability staunchly maintain that each recitative could only have been improvised.

Most *Cha'za'nim,* including the greatest, tended to downplay quickly paced *parlando* passages, rendering them not infrequently almost totally unimpassioned. Glantz, by contrast, typically executed such passages with deep emotion and temperament.

Chazanic artistry comes to the fore at every level of dynamic nuance within his deeply impassioned approach to addressing the Almighty. Most typically, it is manifest in dramatic, fiery and ecstatic delivery, as if addressing the Master of the Universe, distantly perceived in the heavens above. At other times his delivery comes off as the Jews' profoundly felt, collective cry for mercy across history. Yet at other times — unique to Glantz's delivery — it comes off as an angry protest of the Jew across history for his suffering and persecution. Sharply contrasting to all

---

2 *Zogachtz:* See Sholom Kalib, *The Musical Tradition of the Eastern European Synagogue,* vol. I, part I [2002, Syracuse University Press], 161-62.

these is the quasi-whispered intimate prayer to the Father in heaven, now perceived as close by, on the earth below, as it were.

This impassioned approach branches out still further to various expressions of meditation and/or mystical awe which, in turn, leads to highly sophisticated musical innovations, reflecting his conservatory training in his native Ukraine in the 1920's. These include striking usages of chromaticism,[3] surprising unorthodox melodic intervals, subtle interchanges of modes, and decidedly Eastern-style vocal inflection and expression.

All the above-mentioned techniques bring about startling digressions from basic *Nu'sa'chim*. Despite these characteristic Glantzian digressions, however, he remains fiercely loyal and devoted to the traditional *Nu'sach,* first of all, by his absolute reliability to return to the *Nu'sach* at hand by concluding a passage or phrase with the utmost basic and authentic expressions of that *Nu'sach*. When doing so, he brings the return with the depth of passion so characteristic of his delivery in general. Moreover, precisely when he introduces the mentioned digressions, he strongly gives convincing expression to what this writer has termed the qualitative aspect of *Nu'sach,*[4] that is to say, to the spirit and ambience of the text, in the verbal sense as well as that evoked by the liturgical occasion on which it is intoned.

Examples 1 through 5 below illustrate the techniques mentioned, and bring into relief various aspects of Glantz's temperament and musical imagination. (The sources of the examples are given below.)

Example 1, the opening bars of his celebrated recording of *Ein Ke'Er'ke'cha* (from the *Sha'bbat Shach'rit* service) display his use of chromaticism and manipulation of modes. In m. 2, the

---

3 Chromaticism — in music, a standard key and most modes consist of seven staple tones within a given octave. The octave, however, contains twelve semitones (half-steps). The term chromaticism denotes selected use of the five non-staple tones to embellish or substitute any of the staple ones in the interest of musical variety as well as heightened emotional expression.

4 See Sholom Kalib, *The Musical Tradition of the Eastern European Synagogue,* vol. 1 [2002, Syracuse University Press], 100-101.

descending chromatic line, c'—g, renders mystical expression to the words, "None can compare to You."

From the initial key of C major, the d' in m. 3 (third quarter) through the a in m. 4 (third note) initially alludes to D minor via the descending line, d'—c'—b flat—a, but continues on via the descending line, b natural—a flat—g, to effect an overall d'—g descent along the G major-third Phrygian mode, thereby landing on the dominant note (fifth scale-degree, g) of the original key of C major. This digression from the *Nu'sach* is immediately "rectified" by the clear return to the original key in the ensuing m. 5ff.

Example 2, a passage from *Ash'rei* (Psalm 145) of the first *Se'li'chot* service preceding *Rosh Ha'Sha'na*, illustrates highly unorthodox melodic intervals and intensive use of chromaticisms. The textual phrase, *Ve'Zo'kef Le'Chol Ha'Ke'fu'fim* ("God upholds all who are fallen and straightens up those who are bent down"), is set in the authentic-range E major-third Phrygian mode, the dominant (fifth scale-degree) of the overall key of A minor, a characteristic turn within the traditional *Nu'sach* of *Ash'rei* of *Se'li'chot*.

The passage, set for choir in Glantz's *Ri'nat Ha'Ko'desh* (see Sources, below), begins with the tone-painting of the word *Ve'Zo'kef* ("and straightens up") through the ascending leaps, e—b and e—c', followed by the respective descending leaps, b—e and c'—d (in mm. 1—2), landing on d, the subtonic scale-degree of the E major-third Phrygian mode. The momentary expression of D major on this subtonic note (in m. 3) is a typical move within a number of *Nu'sa'chim* based on the major-third Phrygian mode. However, the introduction of the b flat in m. 4 requires comment. This chromaticism is indeed included at times as part of a momentary turn to the major-third Phrygian mode on the fourth scale-degree (a) within an overall E minor mode (e.g., b flat—a or d'—c sharp—b flat—a).[5] As employed here, however, it

5 See Kalib: *The Musical Tradition of the Eastern European Synagogue*, 132.

constitutes a startling digression from the norm. In this instance, the resultant upward thrust from f sharp—b flat, followed by the downward leap to f sharp suggests the "straightening up" by the Almighty of those bent down. Bringing this about via the ascending and descending diminished-fourth interval (f sharp—b flat), however, is a typical Glantzian mystical expression.

The return to the E major-third Phrygian tonic note, e, normally achieved via a descending scale-passage to it, is brought about here once again by a Glantzian-style return to b flat in m. 6, followed by the almost fully chromatic descent to the cadential e, but across g natural rather than the g sharp of the major-third Phrygian mode! The unequivocal E major-third Phrygian mode is re-introduced in the ensuing turn of mm. 7—8. The remainder of the example, from the turn of mm. 8—9 until the end, first brings a sequential repetition of the mystical diminished-fourth motive of mm. 4—5 in mm. 9—10, this time within the major-third Phrygian mode. Bars 11—12 bring back the content of mm. 6—7 followed by the d—A—d—e interior cadential motive characteristic of a number of *Nu'sa'chim* in the major-third Phrygian mode. The cadential e (first note in m. 14) is extended by yet another ascending-descending fourth-motive. This time, however, it is the perfect-fourth diatonic succession within the major-third Phrygian mode (cf. mm. 4—5 and 9—10).

The totality of the entire example reveals much of how chromaticism and manipulation of modes and *Nu'sach* convey the depth of emotion and imagination that characterize and distinguish the musical-liturgical style of Leibele Glantz.

Example 3, a passage from *Le'cha A'do'shem* (from the *Se'li'chot* service) illustrates usages of highly uncommon melodic leaps.

In the passage, *A'sher Be'Ya'do Ne'fesh Kol Chai Ve'Ru'ach Kol Be'sar Ish* ("For His is the soul of every living being and the spirit of all human flesh"), Glantz renders passionate expression, beginning in the high *tessitura,* g'—f sharp', concluding in a submissive *pianissimo* lower-middle range, in a style drenched in the spirit of *Se'li'chot* services characteristic of innumerable *Cha'za'nim,* executed here by Glantz with ideal beauty and authenticity. Glantzian touches, however, are manifest in the uncharacteristic descending and ascending ninth- and tenth-leaps, e flat'—d—e flat' and f'—d—e flat' in mm. 4—5, and in the ascending and descending seventh-leaps, d—c' and f'—g, in m. 7.

Example 4, also from *Le'cha A'do'shem* (from the *Se'li'chot* service) illustrates Glantz's use of the Pentatonic scale and Eastern-style vocalisms and expression.

The passage *Ha'Ne'sha'ma Lach* is set in a traditional-style opening ascent from the middle-range g to the upper g' in mm. 1—2 (first note) and concluding shift from the opening G minor mode to the parallel G major-third Phrygian mode in mm. 4—5, heard in renditions by countless *Cha'za'nim.* The unequivocal Glantzian touches, however, are the sudden intrusion of the Pentatonic motivic pattern, g'—f natural—d'—c'—d' in m. 1 (third quarter)—2 (first note), and in the uncommon Dorian-sixth scale-degree, e natural, within the otherwise unequivocal G minor mode of mm. 2 (last quarter)—3, brought out with decided Eastern expression, also typical of the so-called Mediterranean style of the folk musical idiom of the early days of the *Ye'shuv* in pre-statehood *E'retz Yis'ra'el,* as is the mentioned Pentatonic motive.

Example 5, a passage from *Eich Nif'tach Peh* (also from the *Se'li'chot* service), illustrates intensive chromaticism and the use of *Sprechstimme.*

The heavily chromatic movement in the quasi speech-like approach at the beginning of *Eich Nif'tach Peh* ("How can we open our mouths before You…[In what way can we pour out our prayers]?") reveals yet another aspect of Glantz's temperament. The speech-song effect introduced here reflects Glantz's feeling that the words here defy any ordinary melodic means of rendering them appropriate expression. Hence he turns to *Sprechstimme*, the half-speech half-song technique introduced by Arnold Schoenberg, including its characteristic notational style, as seen in mm. 4 (last note)—5.

All these would be unthinkable without the vocal capability and musical knowledge, skill and imagination possessed by Leibele Glantz. Although his voice was essentially a lyric tenor in quality, it came off as decidedly powerful in *forte* and dramatic passages. He displayed amazing agility in his *coloraturas* and exceptional gracefulness in his vast dynamic range, within which he shifted with ease from the softest *pianissimo* to his sudden bursts of *fortissimo*, and vice versa.

Although his voice was essentially a lyric tenor in quality, it came off as decidedly powerful in **forte** *and dramatic passages. He displayed amazing agility in his* **coloraturas** *and exceptional gracefulness in his vast dynamic range within which he shifted with ease from the softest* **pianissimo** *to his sudden bursts of* **fortissimo**, *and vice versa.*

Finally, his stunning innovative manipulation of modes, uncommon melodic intervals and use of chromaticism reflect not only the conservatory training of his youth, but his life-long probing into the origins and course of development of our traditional synagogue music, as well as its musical-theoretical foundation.

He was the consummate pulpit artist, great singer and interpreter of our sacred liturgical music, who, through his rare vocal talent and scholarly investigation brought out in writing and in sound the heart and depth of the total Jewish musical religious-historical experience.

Sources

Example 1. Leib Glantz, Selected Works, *Rinat Hakodesh*, ed. David Loeb (Tel Aviv Institute of Jewish Liturgical Music in Conjunction with Israel Music Institute, 1971), volume 3, *Sha'bbat*, 9–10 (mm. 1–10).

Example 2. *Rinat Hakodesh*, volume 5, *Se'li'chot*, 31–34.

Example 3. *Ibid*, 79 (m. 6, last note)–81 (m. 2, first note).

Example 4. *Ibid*, 83 (m. 7, last quarter)–84 (m. 3, third quarter).

Example 5. *Ibid*, 87 (mm. 4–8, third quarter).

4

Creativity, Passion, Intensity and Conflict

DR. KALMAN GLANTZ[1]

There were three aspects to my father's career: cantorial, politics and musicological research. All of these three pursuits brought Leib Glantz recognition but also involved him in controversy. On all three subjects, he had fiercely-held views. His music challenged his audiences to listen in new, unfamiliar ways. His politics were out of sync with

> *His music challenged his audiences to listen in new, unfamiliar ways. His politics were out of sync with his music, and his research challenged widely-accepted beliefs.*

his music, and his research challenged widely-accepted beliefs, often on shaky, if thought-provoking, grounds. All this made for a life that contained, in Winston Churchill's phrase, triumph and tragedy. For his family, it was sometimes a rough ride, but Glantz never wavered in his convictions.

Music and the Audience

There is a paradox at the heart of Leib Glantz' music. On the one hand, he was a classical East European cantor, immersed in tradition, bathed in Chasidic music from infancy, and heir to

---

1 Dr. Kalman Glantz — the elder son of Miriam and Leib Glantz is a psychologist in Cambridge, Massachusetts, and author of *Exiles from Eden — Psychotherapy from an Evolutionary Perspective,* W.W. Norton and Company, New York, 1989 (with John K. Pearce), and *Staying Human in the Organization — Our Biological Heritage and the Workplace,* Praeger Publishers, Westport, Connecticut, 1992 (with J. Gary Bernhard).

such deeply Orthodox giants of his time as Nissi Belzer and Pini Minkowsky. He was passionately devoted to the old ways, and sought the roots of Jewish music in centuries past.

On the other hand, he was a trained musician who studied piano and composition at the Kiev Conservatory with, among others, the Russian composer Gliere. This training enabled him to develop original variations on the old themes (the *Nu'sach*), variations that are particularly prominent in his improvisations. Glantz's unique style was thus a blend of innovation and tradition. The combination earned him fame, if not fortune, and an enduring reputation among musicians, connoisseurs and intellectuals.

As a result, those who write about Glantz note his passion for the ancient *Nu'sach* but also hail him as the pioneer of a "new way" in cantorial. How to resolve this contradiction?

One way to understand it is to look at the relationship between Blues and Jazz. The Blues was the music of poor musicians who were largely self-taught and who belonged to a persecuted minority. It was a folk art. Jazz used Blues themes to create a much more complicated music.

> *In a way, Glantz started a Jewish jazz. But there were no followers, because the really talented musicians of the next generation got into American music. Fifty years earlier, George Gershwin might have written for the synagogue and Al Jolson really might have been a cantor.*

Cantorial was the Blues of the Jews of Eastern Europe. Glantz grew up with these Blues, but he was a creative artist in a world that was changing. Like the musicians who created Jazz, he took the old themes and did different things with them. His variations were new; the themes weren't. And so the paradox is resolved: the old exists in the new.

In a way, Glantz started a Jewish Jazz. But there were no followers, because the really talented musicians of the next generation got into American music. Fifty years earlier, George Gershwin might have written for the synagogue and Al Jolson really might have been a cantor. So, though he didn't like to think so, Glantz represents the end of an epoch, not a new beginning. He left no followers. Not even imitators. Such, I think, is the verdict of history, from which there is no appeal.

The merging of the old with the new created problems for him over the course of his career. Some people liked the old, some the new. Relatively few really appreciated both.

The innovations were not the only element of his approach to prayer that created problems. Glantz was a scholar of Hebrew and of the liturgy. He was not merely a singer; he was an interpreter. He did not produce sounds in order to impress or please. He uttered interpretations of the text — a commentary, much like the commentary of, say, Rashi.[2] To understand what Glantz was doing, listeners had to understand the words of the prayers.

For Glantz, the ideal listener or congregant was someone who knew Hebrew, was immersed in Jewish sacred literature, and was brought up on cantorial music. Only that listener could really appreciate the musical subtleties with which he illuminated the text of the prayers. Such listeners were not always numerous in his congregations.

These problems weren't apparent in the first two phases of Glantz's career. That career can be divided into four phases:

1. Eastern Europe (1898-1926);
2. New York (1926-1941);
3. Los Angeles (1941-1954); and
4. Israel (1954-1964).

On records, only the last three periods are available, but we can assume that the music of the New York period was similar to what Glantz would have been singing in Eastern Europe.

The Eastern European Period (1898-1926)

The Kiev where Glantz was born, in 1898, was a hotbed of Chasidism and a center of cantorial music. The ordinary synagogue goers were steeped in Jewish tradition and knew the meaning of the prayers. Any child with talent generally gravitated towards the music of the synagogue. Glantz first davened a prayer service at age 4, at the Talner Synagogue in Kiev, where several generations of his ancestors had been cantors. When he was eight, he began to tour the Ukraine and Russia with his father. These appearances continued until he reached puberty and his voice changed.

He fled Kiev permanently in 1920, in order to escape from serving in the Bolshevik army, and ended up in Kishinev, Besarabia. The Jews of Kishinev, like those of Kiev, were totally immersed in tradition, so he had no problem being understood. In 1926, as the communists enhanced their persecution of the Jews and of the Zionist activists in particular, he left for America, with the idea of ending up in Palestine. But *A'li'yah* would have to wait. New York was a hotbed of cantorial and Glantz became part of the *Golden Age of Cha'za'nut.*

---

2 Rashi — Rabbi Solomon Bar Isaac (1040–1105), a medieval French Jewish commentator on the Bible and the Talmud. Rashi's commentary on the Pentateuch (printed in 1475) is considered the first dated Hebrew book ever published. His commentary on the Talmud covers the *Mish'na* with the *Ge'ma'ra*. His influential writings on the bible examined the literal meaning of the text and used allegory, parable, and symbolism to analyze its non-literal meaning.

The New York Period (1926-1941)

The New York period was actually little more than an extension of the Eastern European phase; the audience was the same. It was composed mostly of immigrants brought up on Jewish culture in European ghetto communities. Their primary identification was Jewish, not American. They spoke Yiddish and they knew the Hebrew of the prayers. They compared cantors the way people today compare basketball players and rock stars. Everybody had a favorite. People would travel from Brooklyn to the Bronx to hear a new cantor.

These were the people with whom Glantz had been brought up. He was one of them. He reminded them of the cantors they had heard in their youth. They recognized him, knew what he was doing, and appreciated the subtleties of his art.

During this period he was a free-lance cantor, traveling around the world to wherever he was in demand: a Sabbath in New York, a concert in Johannesburg, a High Holiday in Philadelphia. His agent, the legendary Sara Wachs, just had to sit back and take the bookings. RCA signed him and put him on the Red Seal label, then the top of the line.

The ten numbers he recorded for RCA made him known all over the world. Chief among these was his signature piece, *Shema Yis'ra'el*, recorded near the beginning of his American career. What is most astonishing about this piece is the utter abandon and the vocal risk-taking. I know it's a record, but I'm always afraid. I have to keep rooting for him to make it and I'm always relieved when he does.

Glantz's interpretation of this text hinges on the tense of the verb "to hear." It's the imperative tense. Hence Glantz issues a clarion call: "Hear O Israel." It's a command. No hesitation, no doubts.

Another piece from this period, *Tal*, the prayer for dew, is perhaps the best demonstration of how to use the traditional *Nu'sach* of a prayer as the basis for variations. The organ starts with the traditional *Nu'sach* of *Tal*, after which Glantz improvises on that theme. Each sentence of the prayer is a different improvised variation.

The style, intensity and vocal quality of all the RCA recordings are similar to those in *Shema Yis'ra'el*. We will see that change significantly in the next period.

The Los Angeles Period (1941-1954)

Glantz's life as a free-lance cantor came to an end when I was 4, in 1941. My sense is that this marked the end of cantorial as the national music of the Jews. At any rate, my father took a position at Sinai Temple in Los Angeles, where the audience was largely second generation.

The members of Sinai Temple saw themselves as Americans. They looked down on immigrants and on ghetto culture. They were Jewish, of course, but as a religion, not as a culture or nationality. They wanted to be like everyone else. They weren't really comfortable with music that sounded foreign.

Glantz's cantorial was affected. It got toned down. I vaguely remember discussions about this between my father and mother. The gap between what he wanted to do and what the listeners could grasp bothered him. He felt unappreciated, out of his element. He longed to get back to New York. If you listen to records from this period, the difference is obvious.

A good example is his composition *Be'Rosh Ha'Sha'na*. The words are simple, if somewhat portentous: "On *Rosh Ha'Sha'na* our fate will be written." Glantz sings this with a good deal of reserve. The voice production is sweeter, less impassioned. There is less intensity, more smoothness. The beginning of this piece is a very singable melody, quite suitable for a congregational sing-a-long.

Another good example is *A'hav'ti*, from the *Ha'llel* service. This was actually recorded on a trip to New York from Israel, and to my mind represents a blend of periods three and four. The

Presentation of Scroll of Registration in the Jewish National Fund Golden Book of Honor to Maestro Arturo Toscannini in recognition of his noble stand against Nazism (Los Angeles, 1945).

voice production, the quietness, is pure period three (Los Angeles), but the poetic interpretation of the text is more aimed at the Israeli audience.

A glimpse into Glantz's interpretative style can be gained by listening to the different ways the word "hear" is treated in *She'ma Yis'ra'el* and in *A'hav'ti*. In *She'ma Yis'ra'el,* as stated before, Glantz is stern and stentorian, as he reminds the people of Israel that *A'do'nai* is their Lord. In *A'hav'ti,* the verb "hear" is in the conditional tense. The words mean: "I would really like it if you would hear my voice." It's a request, addressed to a superior being, for attention and consideration, on the part of someone who is a loving devotee. To each prayer, Glantz assigns music that highlights the different relationships expressed in the texts.

Perhaps the best example of the Los Angeles style is a hard-to-find recording of *U'Ve'Nu'cho Yo'mar.* This is part of a Passover program recorded for a radio station in Los Angeles. Restraint is the watchword: don't overdo it. One can almost sense a desire not to be too foreign. Glantz doesn't actually betray his principles by, for example, introducing operatic or pop music themes into the prayers, but he certainly has tailored his style to the audience of the moment.

The Israeli Period (1954-1964)

When Glantz moved to Israel, in 1954, he moved back into his element. For the people there, Judaism was a total way of life. The Eastern European Jews and the American immigrants understood the Hebrew of the prayers. In Israel, everyone spoke Hebrew and understood every nuance of interpretation, every new idea that Glantz expressed in a tone or a change of dynamics.

The response to Glantz's decision to settle in Israel was quite extraordinary. The streets in front of the Synagogue had to be blocked off for the first *Se'li'chot* service. People were desperate to get in. One person in the crowd threatened the ticket-taker with a knife, and among the people who had tickets were some of the most prominent musicians, politicians, writers and scholars of Israel. All the newspapers carried stories about the event.

The Israeli public provided Glantz with a chance to re-experience the fame and adoration that was his during the magical days of Kiev, Kishinev and New York. Not surprisingly, the

> *The streets in front of the Synagogue in Tel Aviv had to be blocked off for the first* Se'li'chot *service. People were desperate to get in. One person in the crowd threatened the ticket-taker with a knife, and among the people who had tickets were some of the most prominent musicians, politicians, writers and scholars of Israel.*

response of the Israeli people stimulated him to produce some of his best work. In listening to the works of that period, what is most striking is the return of the intensity, the raw emotional and religious fervor.

Perhaps the most interesting, and difficult, piece from this period is *Eich Nif'tach Peh*. The words mean: "How can I dare to open my mouth before Thee?"

Glantz does not sing these words. Rather, he uses *sprechstimme* — spoken voice. Why? By not singing, Glantz signals that he dare not open his mouth, at least not in the usual way. This is the kind of interpretation that dazzled the scholars and writers. Only an audience who knew Hebrew perfectly could grasp what Glantz was doing here, and then only as a kind of *post facto* revelation: "My goodness, he didn't sing because he didn't dare to!"

Music and Politics

My father was, by conviction, a Labor Zionist. This was a source of much trouble for him, but he never changed his view to advance his career.

Glantz had been active in Zionist politics in Kiev, and almost immediately after he made his escape to Kishinev, he became a member of the Central Committee of *Tze'i'rei Tzi'on*, a faction of the Labor Zionist movement. He established at this time friendships with many of the people who would eventually become the political leaders of *Ma'pai*, the Labor party in Israel, including the Speaker of the *Kne'sset* Yoseph Sprintzak, and the Party leader Akiva Guvrin. Two of his close friends from that period, Yitzchak Ben-Zvi and Zalman Shazar, eventually became Presidents of the State of Israel. In Kishinev Glantz continued to perform as a cantor, but he did so primarily to make a living and to raise money for Zionist causes.

Most Labor Zionists were atheists. *Tze'i'rei Tzi'on,* my father's faction, was anti-Communist but had a socialist ideology, and most of the members were in rebellion against various aspects of religious Judaism in Eastern Europe. As a result, Glantz lived in two worlds, worlds that were often dismissive of each other.

So far as I know, the anti-religious character of the Labor Zionist movement didn't bother my father. For him, Zionism and Judaism were one. Having a State *was* Judaism. To be a Jew was to want a State. He was religious; if other Zionists weren't, that could be overlooked. In fact, he stopped bugging me about my own religious views and practices as soon as he had me safely ensconced in Israel.

But while his participation in Labor Zionist politics didn't create ideological conflicts within him, the fact is that his political activism was very costly to him. The time he could have spent promoting his career, or making money performing weddings, he preferred devoting to late night discussions in the offices of the party, and to writing political articles in the Yiddish press. He avoided spending time with people who were prominent in synagogue life. In the Diaspora, these tensions played out behind the scenes. Few people outside party circles knew he was an activist. But when he arrived in Israel, it became a major, and very public, issue.

The salary my father had accepted to become the cantor of the *Tif'e'ret Zvi* synagogue wasn't enough to buy a decent apartment, so the Municipality of Tel Aviv, which was at that time controlled by the General Zionist Party, voted to give him a loan at favorable terms, arguing that it would be good for tourism. The newspapers of the religious parties immediately made this into an issue, the first hint that my father's politics were going to get him into trouble in Israel.

Because of his politics, Glantz was never cantor of the Great Synagogue of Tel Aviv, a stronghold of the religious parties. The religious papers ran articles accusing him of being irreligious. When a non-religious critic wrote that Glantz had "immortalized a text" of the prayers, a religious journalist objected strongly, arguing that the text was already immortal.

Perhaps an incident that happened to me can convey the intensity and pervasiveness of these conflicts. During Glantz's time in Israel, the religious parties politically controlled the Post Office, and virtually all the employees were conspicuously religious. One day I walked into a Post Office in Jerusalem to mail a letter. The clerk, noting the return address, asked me if I was Leib Glantz's son.

When I said yes, he said: "So why aren't you wearing a *Yar'mul'ka*?"[3] Before I could answer, a voice from the rear of the room piped up: "Why should he, when his father doesn't either?" Naturally, I felt guilty about fanning the flames of religious intolerance and even more about the possibility of jeopardizing his job, which was at that time paying for my education.

Eventually these political conflicts divided *Tif'er'et Zvi* synagogue, whose president had brought Glantz to Israel. This man, Yitzchak Raziel, was overthrown in what amounted to a coup, and my father's contract could not be renewed.

Researching the *Nu'sach*

One wouldn't think that researching the origins of synagogue music would be a contested area, but it was and is. This was a subject on which my father had especially strong convictions. He was extremely concerned — upset, would be more accurate — about the fact that Western

---

3 *Yar'mul'ka* — a skullcap worn by religious Jews.

musical themes and scales such as Major and Minor had crept into synagogue music. In his opinion, the original *Nu'sach* of the prayers was being obscured by the music of the various peoples among whom the Jews lived. This he saw as a great tragedy.

Glantz thought it might be possible, through a process of comparison and elimination, to reconstruct the pure music of the Jews, perhaps even the music of the Second Temple. Who knows?

He apparently got started on this enterprise in his youth when he happened to visit a synagogue of the Karaites in Kiev. What he heard was a revelation to him. The Karaites, a sect that was founded in the eighth century C. E., rejected the Talmudic and Rabbinic traditions. They recognized only the authority of the *To'rah*. Glantz concluded that their music might also reflect a tradition going back to the time of the *To'rah* and thus perhaps even to the Temple of Solomon. From then on, Glantz tried to figure out what the original *Nu'sach* of each prayer might have been.

That introduced an almost moral dimension into the music. He wasn't just trying to create something beautiful, or expressive, or meaningful. He was trying to get it *right*. And if there is a right way, there is also a *wrong* way.

Was he right? I certainly can't say. But it is interesting that long before he moved to Israel, his research had given his music more of a Sephardic sound than was common in Eastern Europe and America. He felt that this vindicated his vision.

On at least one occasion, this business of right and wrong became a problem even for him. He had written and recorded some music for *Be'Tzeit Yis'ra'el*, a *Ha'llel* prayer, using the Pentatonic scale. It was a piece that I loved, and it was very popular. But one day his research indicated to him that the Pentatonic wasn't appropriate for *Ha'llel*.

Conflict! What to do? Very uncharacteristically, he asked for my opinion: "Should I scrap the piece?" I said "No." He looked troubled, but ended up keeping it in the repertoire. This may be the only time I ever influenced him.

———

What was the secret of Glantz's appeal? At his best, Glantz entered a trance-like state — a state of mystical union — when he began to pray. In this state, he was not singing or performing. He

> *What was the secret of Glantz's appeal? At his best, Glantz entered a trance-like state — a state of mystical union — when he began to pray. In this state, he was not singing or performing. He was floating in communion with the text and with God; nothing else existed.*

was floating in communion with the text and with God; nothing else existed. He literally became the *Shli'ach Tzi'bur* — the messenger of the people. And he would provide members of the congregation with a similar, trance-like experience. The voice — the sound — was only a part of this experience. True, his voice would ring out with amazing resonance and freedom. But sound was not his concern. What was important to him was the message he was carrying to God. As a result, he provided those who understood him with a unique experience, something that was both musically *and* intellectually authentic.

5

Se'li'chot: A Wonderful Mixture of Ancient and Modern

CANTOR PINCHAS SPIRO[1]

The lamented Cantor Leib Glantz is better known to most synagogue musicians through his recordings than through his printed works. With the posthumous publication of his major work, the *Se'li'chot* prayer service, an important new dimension has been added to his influence. Although his *Se'li'chot* service contains unusual elements, they should not come as a surprise to those who have studied his works through the years. There seems to be a consistent evolution in his style, and the *Se'li'chot* service can be regarded as its logical and crowning culmination.

In attempting to evaluate the legacy that *Cha'zan* Glantz left to contemporary *Cha'za'nut* in this outstanding service, the following fundamental consideration comes to mind. To say that Glantz sought and found a perfect blend between music and word is not quite enough. The overriding impression is that he placed the greatest emphasis on the words of the prayers and on their deep meaning and interpretation.

When we consider the fact that the Chasidic background of Glantz was by far the most affecting influence that shaped his musical personality and style, we find here a great paradox. On the one hand we have as a dominant factor the complete sense of freedom of expression, the *Dvei'kut,* the abandon and the total lack of inhibition — all characteristic influences of Chasidism. On the other hand, contrary to the basic Chasidic philosophy, we find an almost

---

1 Cantor Pinchas Spiro attended the Juilliard School of Music and graduated from Syracuse University in 1952. He received his Cantorial Ordination from the Jerusalem Cantorial Institute and has authored numerous books in the field of Jewish liturgical music. This essay (abridged) appeared in the Journal of Synagogue Music, September, 1968, following the publication of *S'lichot Service for Cantor, Chorus and Organ,* by Leib Glantz, edited by David Loeb, published by the Hallel V'Zimra Association, Montreal, Quebec, Canada, 1965.

> *The melodic line is so subordinated to the needs of the words that in some instances it disappears completely. The dominant and most impressive feature of the Se'li'chot service by Leib Glantz is his use of a "singing-speaking" style of declamation where nothing matters but the true and pure interpretation of the text.*

complete lack of pure melodies that have an independent life of their own. The melodic line is so subordinated to the needs of the words that in some instances it disappears completely.

The dominant and most impressive feature of the *Se'li'chot* service by Leib Glantz is his use of a "singing-speaking" style of declamation where nothing matters but the true and pure interpretation of the text. In several instances, *"sprechstimme"* (literally, "spoken voice") is used with only a vague sense of pitch. Such extreme instances, when music seems to give in altogether, occur only in a few short phrases in the service, but a modified extension of this technique of speaking-singing-declamation (reminiscent of Alban Berg's style) constitutes the major feature of the entire service. It is an effective tool that affords the *Shli'ach Tzi'bur* (messenger of the congregation, the leader in prayer) the opportunity for a most direct expression and interpretation of highly emotional and dramatic passages and to communicate them to the congregation with a shattering impact. This, after all, is the most important role of the *Shli'ach Tzi'bur.*

Contrary to impression, this style is far from simple or easy to adopt. Only a man with the fantastic vocal, musical and scholarly talents of Glantz could have perfected it. To be able to utilize this technique effectively, a cantor must possess natural musicianship of the highest order that will prevent him from veering off helplessly into unrelated tonalities. He must also be fully versed in the text, its deep meaning and its historical and philosophical implications. Above all, he must possess an innate piety that will enable him to communicate his sincere feelings and intentions to his congregation. When done improperly, this sublime form of expression can easily degenerate into cheap theatrics. There is an additional practical difficulty to the utilization of this trail-blazing style, a difficulty that has to do not with the qualifications of the cantor but with those of his worshippers. Since this style discourages the inclusion of mere pretty melodies that exist for their own sake, it would require a congregation that fluently speaks and understands the Hebrew language to appreciate it and to react instantly and spontaneously to all the nuances that its spokesman is trying to communicate to them. The fact that Glantz wrote this service in Israel for an Israeli congregation explains, in part, its effective use and acceptance there.

The great cantor-composers who have left their mark on *Cha'za'nut* through their recordings can be divided into two categories. There are those whose music can easily be utilized by others in the profession with only slight modifications. The number of their compositions that are in current use can measure their influence. On the other hand, there are a few whose creations are uniquely tailored to their own individual musical personality and talent to such an extent that attempts to adapt them usually end in frustration. Their influence is subtle, but deeper and more affecting even if it is not quite as tangible. The late *Cha'zan* Glantz belonged to that second group. This fact explains why even a thorough examination and study of the printed score of his *Se'li'chot* service may leave one with a vague and not completely satisfying impression.

Fortunately, Leib Glantz left us a magnificently recorded version of the same service (Midnight Selichot Service, Famous Records, FAM-1015). It is most highly recommended as an indispensable companion to the printed score to anyone who wishes to discover the important contribution that this great genius has made to the *Cha'za'nut*

of today and tomorrow. Listening to this recording while following the printed score was for this reviewer a deeply moving and unforgettable experience that left him limp and emotionally drained. It was an experience that transcended by far the mere pleasure of hearing the magnificent voice of Glantz with its phenomenal range and incredible flexibility. Having previously struggled to make sense of the printed score, it was now amazing and truly awe-inspiring to see the dry notes and the seemingly meaningless passages come to life with such irrepressible vitality and with such intense power. Old familiar words and phrases suddenly assumed new and unexpected meaning, and conveyed a variety of new emotions — raw and uninhibited. The total effect is a curious and wonderful mixture of the old-fashioned and the daringly new. Almost completely absent are the folksy rhythmical tunes that made *Cha'za'nut* such a popular art and which, at the same time, halted its development and arrested its growth. Gone, to a large extent, are the arbitrary Chazanic *clichés* and formulas whose destination and character are so familiar and so predictable. Instead, we have a freewheeling melodic line that seems to blaze new and exciting trails in previously uncharted grounds. Uninhibited and unrestrained, it proceeds daringly to vividly draw a variety of new pictures and to convey new moods and emotions. Alternately, it is expressing fear, mystery, anger and hurt. Alternately, it is arguing, pleading, shouting, whispering and talking. But, at the same time, there is always the comforting presence of the pure and authentic *Nu'sach,* which is the hallmark of Leib Glantz's art. It acts to reassure the listener and to cushion the jarring effect of the unfamiliar manner of expression and the daring innovations. Particularly deliberate and effective is the pure and unadulterated *Nu'sach* conclusion of most of the selections. They give the listener the warm feeling of having arrived home after an exciting and adventurous exposure to the elements. The printed score of the *Se'li'chot* service contains a brilliant preface by Cantor Max Wohlberg, which eloquently sums up its outstanding virtues.

No *Cha'zan* should be without this book!

Let us reiterate our conviction that the *Se'li'chot* service by Leib Glantz is a towering achievement and indeed a milestone in the development of contemporary *Cha'za'nut*. It is an extremely important work that will, no doubt, influence the future course of cantorial and will enshrine the memory of *Cha'zan* Leib Glantz in our grateful hearts.

> *The* Se'li'chot *service by Leib Glantz is a towering achievement and indeed a milestone in the development of contemporary* Cha'za'nut. *It is an extremely important work that will, no doubt, influence the future course of cantorial.*

6

"How Shall We Open Our Mouth Before Thee?"

CANTOR ABRAHAM LUBIN[1]

The last two decades of the nineteenth century and the first three decades of the twentieth century witnessed the arrival of some of the great cantorial masters to the shores of the United States. These cantorial artists, who arrived primarily from East European countries, possessed extraordinary vocal, creative and improvisatory musical talents which served them well in their rendition of the traditional liturgical prayers of the synagogue.

The greatest among these cantors were extremely popular with the Jewish masses and worshippers who appreciated the depth of the emotional impact their prayer interpretations made on them during the Sabbath and Festival services. The worshippers literally "worshipped" these cantors as the popular "stars" and folk heroes of their day.

Among these great cantors was Leib Glantz, or as he was lovingly known "Leibele" Glantz. Glantz shone as the most creative and unique cantor-composer in the midst of this panoply of shining cantorial artists. He was a unique performer of the cantorial masterpieces of the East European tradition and the single most original composer of a body of liturgical music that has never been surpassed before or since. As a composer of liturgical song Leib Glantz was *sui generis.*

Although Glantz stemmed from a similar tradition of learning and exposure to the cantorial chants of the East European synagogue as his other talented colleagues and peers, nevertheless,

---

1 Cantor Abraham Lubin graduated from the Jews' College Cantorial School and studied secular music at the London College of Music. He is a Bachelor of Music graduate of the College Conservatory of Music of the University of Cincinnati, Master of Music with distinction at De Paul University and Doctor of Music from the Jewish Theological Seminary of America. Cantor Lubin is also a distinguished composer, educator, lecturer and researcher of Jewish music. He is a past president of the Cantors Assembly (1995-97) and past editor of the Journal of Synagogue Music.

> *Glantz shone as the most creative and unique cantor-composer in the midst of this panoply of shining cantorial artists. He was a unique performer of the cantorial masterpieces of the East European tradition and the single most original composer of a body of liturgical music that was never surpassed before or since.*

he grew and developed his artistry in a style all his own, uniquely Glantzian. He elevated his creative efforts to an art form that other musicians and composers, from totally different genres of music, were drawn to appreciate and to be inspired by the uniquely original performance of his own liturgical works.

In our attempt to understand Glantz among the traditional school of cantor-composers of Jewish liturgical music, one could compare him in certain ways to the great twentieth-century composer, Arnold Schoenberg (1874-1951). Schoenberg, considered one of the seminal musical figures of his time, was unique among the classic Western composers of the twentieth century. Just as Schoenberg loosened the grip of traditional tonality and explored new ways of working the twelve notes of the chromatic scale, Leib Glantz explored completely new tracks and paved a new path in rendering the "traditional" modes of East European liturgical song. Like Schoenberg, Glantz conceived and created a most original and revolutionary approach to the interpretation of the liturgical texts of the prayer book in ways never attempted before.

Among his many works, perhaps his greatest creation is his Midnight *Se'li'chot* Service. This service is chanted on the Saturday midnight just before the High Holy Days. A live recording of this service took place at the *Tif'e'ret Zvi* synagogue in Tel Aviv. A publication of the musical score for cantor and choir was published by the *Hallel V'Zimra* Association, Montreal, Canada in 1965, and also by *The Tel Aviv Institute of Jewish Liturgical Music* in conjunction with *Israel Music Institute,* Tel Aviv, in 1971.

A brief analysis of two of the prayers in this collection will give us an appreciation of his uniqueness and originality.

The prayer *Eich Nif'tach Peh* ("How shall we open our mouth before Thee, Thou Who dwellest on high?") begins this eleventh century liturgical poem of the *Se'li'chot*. It is interpreted by Glantz in a most moving manner. He relates each word of the text with its full meaning and seeks to find the exact musical interpretation for every given word and phrase. The first word *Eich* — "How" is indicated in the score to be sung in a *Sprechstimme* — *ad libitum,*[2] as well as in the breakdown of the tonic scale.

---

2 *Ad libitum* — at the discretion of the performer. Used chiefly as a direction, giving license to alter, omit, or improvise a part (Latin).

This *"Sprechstimme"* (half speaking and half singing) musical idea is reminiscent of Arnold Schoenberg, who created it and used it often in his own works. Glantz begins to sing the word *Eich* ("How") in *piano* (softly), in an ascending chromatic scale, quickly reaching the upper octave pitch of A marked "ff" (*fortissimo*). He then proceeds to descend more than a full octave chromatically from the A to the Ab in short order. This is followed with the words: *Be'Ei'lu Fa'nim Nish'poch Si'chim* ("In what manner shall we pour forth our prayers?"). This is done in descending notes that are marked to indicate the vagueness of the pitches, again in *Sprechstimme* style.

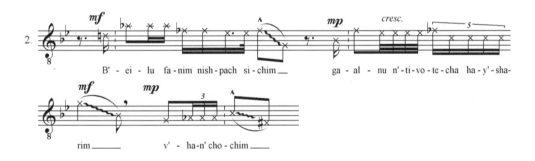

The text continues: *Ka'mah Yi'sar'ta'nu Al Ye'dei Tzi'rim U'Shlu'chim, Lo Hik'shav'nu La'Mo'rim Ve'Lishmo'a La'Mo'chi'chim* ("How often didst Thou admonish us through envoys [prophets] and messengers! Yet we did not hearken to our teachers, nor listen to our rebukers"). These impassioned words, crying out so effectively as if speaking to God directly, are treated with a burst of expressiveness stressing the words: *Lo Hik'shav'nu* ("We did not hearken"):

Ka - ma_____ yi - sar - ta - nu al y' - dei tsi - rim u - shlu - chim

lo hik - shav - nu_____ lo hik - shav - nu ka - ma yis - sar -

ta - nu al y'-dei tsi - rim u-sh'-lu-chim___ lo hik-shav-nu la-mo - rim lo hik-shav-nu la mo rim la mo

rim _____ v' - la - mo - chi - chim ___

A sudden shift, without musical preparation, occurs when Glantz moves from G minor to G major as he reaches the following words: *Por'chei Am'cha A'sher l'veil Sho'cha'chim, Tze'fer Va'E'rev La'ma Matz'li'chim?* ("The oppressors of Thy people, who bow to *Ba'al*,[3] why do they prosper morning and evening?"):

Por-chei am-cha a - sher l'-veil sho-cha - chim _____ por-chei am-cha a-

sher l'-veil sho-cha-chim tse - fer va - e - rev la-ma la-ma la - ma mats - li - chim

He also clearly articulates, in a musical gesture of a question, the word *La'ma* ("why"). When he reaches the words *Sho'chen Ad* ("He Who dwells in eternity"), Glantz prolongs the duration of the note for *Ad* ("eternity") and stretches himself, musically as it were, by indicating

3 *Ba'al* — a Canaanite idol/god (Hebrew).

an unusual marking on the note with a 1/4 sign and an arrow upward for the note to be sung a quarter-note lower than the indicated pitch. Surely we are confronted here with Glantz searching for a musical nuance, wherever it takes him, in order to find the exact musical means to interpret accurately the meaning and sense of the word or phrase.

The prayer that follows in the liturgy is *El E'rech A'pa'yim A'ta U'Va'al Ha'Ra'cha'mim Nik'rei'ta...* ("Thou art a God slow to anger, and art called God of mercy"). We have here a complete and dramatic contrast in the interpretation of this prayer from the previous prayer. Here it is submissive and sung practically throughout with a soft *pianissimo* in very hushed tones. Only very briefly does he indicate an "mf" (*mezzo forte*) or "f" (*forte*) marking in his written notes. The entire rendition transforms us into a mood reflective of God's attribute of mercy and compassion, rendered in the softest of musical gestures and caressing every word, relative to the sentiment of a forgiving and merciful God.

Eil Erech Apayim

(Example 6)

Leib Glantz

Glantz constantly tested his creative juices to find just the right way, unconventional though it might be, in order to be true to the sacred texts and to find the hidden and mystical meaning of the words he interpreted at the *A'mud* (cantor's pulpit) from where he stood and led his people in prayer.

Leib Glantz singing in Tel Aviv, Israel, 1955.

7

A Dialogue with the Almighty!

CANTOR NAFTALI HERSTIK[1]

There is a story in the Talmud about a great rabbi, Yonatan Ben Uziel, whose intensity of learning and concentration was so great that if a bird flew over his head while studying, it would go up in flames. That was similar to my impression of Leib Glantz when I heard him for the first time in my life — a vision of burning flames shooting in all directions.

I was merely eight years old when my late father, Cantor Moshe M. Herstik, took me to a service led by Leib Glantz at the *Tif'e'ret Zvi* synagogue in Tel Aviv. It was *Sha'bbat Rosh Cho'desh* (Sabbath of the new month) and in the midst of the *Ha'llel* prayer, Glantz suddenly exclaimed: *Lo A'mut Ki Ech'yeh, Va'A'sa'per Ma'a'sei Yah* ("I shall not die, but live, and recount the works of the Lord"). It was as though he was engaged in a "dialogue" with the Almighty. It was so daring that one felt that Glantz was ready to sacrifice his life on behalf of his congregation. It was total dedication: *Me'si'rut Ne'fesh.*

> *It was as if he was engaged in a "dialogue" with the Almighty. It was so daring that one felt that Glantz was ready to sacrifice his life on behalf of his congregation.*
> *It was total dedication!*

---

1 Cantor Naftali Herstik — Chief Cantor of the Jerusalem Great Synagogue since 1979. He studied at the Ponivesz Yeshiva, Kfar Chasidim, Israel, and graduated from the Royal College of Music in London. He is the Director of the Tel Aviv Cantorial Institute.

Rabbi Joseph B. Soloveitchik, in his book "The Lonely Man of Faith," described the ultimate form of prayer as standing before the Almighty and speaking directly to Him. Hence the direct form *"Ba'ruch A'ta"* ("Blessed are You").

Listening as a teenager to Leib Glantz's live radio broadcasts of the *Se'li'chot* service,[2] or as an adult to the reissued recordings, I cannot escape feeling that Glantz was talking directly *to* God, or even talking *with* God. It is no wonder that so many households in Israel were glued to their radios for the annual Saturday midnight live broadcast of the *Se'li'chot* service, in order to listen to Leib Glantz.

> *Listening as a teenager to Leib Glantz's live radio broadcasts of the* Se'li'chot *service, or as an adult on the reissued recordings, I cannot escape feeling that Glantz was talking directly* to *God, or even talking* with *God.*

I have always felt that it would be hard to imagine the musical form of the first night of *Se'li'chot* prior to the Leib Glantz era. He created in that prayer service a new dimension, radically different from whatever preceded. It is similar to what was said of Maria Callas and Enrico Caruso — that the world of opera that preceded them was not the same as it was following them.

How does Glantz differ from his predecessors? What are the special tools with which Glantz created such a revolution?

We must establish from the very beginning that Glantz was a great exponent of *Nu'sach Ha'Te'fi'la*. He was an ardent warrior in the battle to maintain these traditional prayer modes as the basis of all liturgical music. It is therefore even more significant, even astonishing, to realize that Glantz's "revolution" took place *within* the boundaries of traditional *Nu'sach*.

In an article written by Leib Glantz himself on the occasion of the Fiftieth Anniversary of the Jewish Ministers Cantors' Association of America (New York, December 1947), Glantz defines the cantor as "a unique creation of Jewish life." That very article highlights Leib Glantz's perception of the ideal cantor — a true *Shli'ach Tzi'bur*. In this article, Glantz refers to the biblical term of *"A'man"* — the artist:

> The definition of the word "artist" in the bible is remarkable. Each time I read the portion of the bible which deals with the artist, I am thrilled by the term which is used to describe him: *"Cha'cham Lev"*: He who has wisdom of the heart — that is

---

2 *Se'li'chot* service — Jewish penitential poems and prayers, especially those said in the period leading up to the High Holy Days. *Se'li'chot* refers to both the service itself and to each of the liturgical poems — *Pi'yu'tim* — that compose the service.

how the bible describes the artist! The term *"Chochma"* in Hebrew means many things: scholarship, wisdom, knowledge and even plain good sense. The biblical distinction between intellectual wisdom and emotional wisdom constitutes a striking definition of art, for it recognizes that art penetrates directly into the heart and often speaks more deeply than words and scholarly definitions. In Jewish prayer services, *"To'rah"* and *"A'vo'da,"* intellectual and emotional wisdom — the wisdom of the mind and the wisdom of the heart — go hand in hand.

Glantz, a true artist and a great scholar, successfully employed all the God-given gifts with which he had so richly been endowed: musical creativity, outstanding vocal ability, an inquisitive mind, and insurmountable energy and feeling.

From *Ash'rei*,[3] the very first word of the *Se'li'chot* service, one is impressed by Glantz's penetrating thought and profound original interpretation of the text. Above all, he creates a unique atmosphere that elevates his listeners towards readiness to pray before the Creator during the period of *Ha'Ya'mim Ha'No'ra'im* — the "Days of Awe." Such is his choral introduction to *Se'li'chot*, which is interwoven with the modes and moods of the High Holiday spirit, encompassing the entirety of prayer from *P'su'kei D'Zim'ra*[4] to *Ne'i'la.*[5] One immediately senses Glantz's clever way of using the Relative Major in order to brighten up the somber mode of the minor chords, hinting at the regal *Mal'chu'yot* element of *Rosh Ha'Sha'na*, the Jewish New Year holiday.

Part of his innovation in the *Nu'sach* of *Se'li'chot* is the use of the aforementioned Relative Major as early as the word *"Od"* in his opening of the *Ash'rei* prayer and in his well-known composition *"Le'chu Ne'ra'ne'na."* It would be impossible to analyze here all of Glantz's uses of modes and scales in his *Se'li'chot* service, but I would mention that unlike the limited modes of the "conventional" *Nu'sach* of the *Se'li'chot*, Glantz skillfully maneuvers among a whole range of traditional modes, from what he calls Major and Minor Pentatonic, to *Yish'ta'bach* and *A'do'nai Ma'lach*, to *A'ha'va Ra'bbah* and *Av Ha'Ra'cha'mim*, to Natural Minor and Harmonic Minor.

It is very interesting to follow Glantz's unique use of the choir as an integral part of his service. I firmly believe that on the one hand Glantz wanted to create an effect of *Shi'rat Ha'Le'vi'im* (the Levites singing in the ancient Holy Temple in Jerusalem) — hence the use of minimalist harmony and open fifths, his unusual emphasis of basses over the tenors, and the descending upper line against the ascending lower line. On the other hand Glantz wanted to create *Shi'rat Ka'hal* (congregational singing) in all its forms — *Te'hi'lim Zo'gn, Ta'cha'nun, Ze'mi'rot, Shi'rat Ha'llel* and so forth. This might be the explanation for the choir singing a great

---

3 *Ash'rei* — happy are those who dwell in His house.
4 *P'su'kei D'Zim'ra* — ("Verses of Song"), designed in many ways as a warm-up to the central prayers of the service.
5 *Ne'i'la* — the final prayer service of *Yom Ki'ppur* — the Jewish Holy Day of Atonement.

deal in unison, octaves, two-part harmony, and repetition of certain motifs in "strategic" places in the service.

However, the most outstanding feature of Glantz's *Se'li'chot* is his ability to carry the worshipping congregation through every kind of mood and emotion in the liturgy. He could "paint" a vivid and picturesque view of the creation in *"Le'cha Sha'ma'yim,"* a gloomy mood in *"Ki'Chlot Ko'che'inu,"* the trumpets' call to assemble in *"Le'chu Ne'ra'ne'na"* and *"Ki Vei'ti Beit Te'fi'la Yi'ka're Le'Chol Ha'A'mim,"* and supplication in *"HaN'sha'ma Lach"* or *"Re'tze A'ti'ra'tam."*

> *The most outstanding feature of Glantz's* Se'li'chot *is his ability to carry the worshipping congregation through every kind of mood and emotion in the liturgy.*

Leib Glantz described his beloved colleague, Cantor David Roitman, as *"Me'sho'rer Ha'A'mud"* (the poet of the synagogue pulpit), thus distinguishing Roitman from other *Cha'za'nim*. Without doubt, the same can be said of Leib Glantz himself. His portrayal of the text and his interpretive powers were reminiscent of the great poets of years past, who had a magical effect on their listeners and whose words often carried the moral strength of prophets (*"El E'rech A'pa'yim A'ta"* and *"Mach'ni'sei Ra'cha'mim"*). Glantz the poet was a master of timing and rhythm. His deliberate use of repeated words and split phrases, his sense of rhythmic form, and his measured approach to each musical detail are the tools of a master poet.

One cannot distinguish Leib Glantz — the staunch Zionist activist, the fiery speaker and the great orator — from Leib Glantz the cantor. He was truly a great orator at the *"A'mud"* (cantor's pulpit) as well. His deep insight into the texts and his powerful oratory are astonishing in the dramatic outbursts of his composition *"Eich Nif'tach Peh Le'fa'ne'cha."* Glantz often used his wonderful oratory powers as another means of interpretation in the musical tradition of *Sprechgesang* (spoken song). It is a tool with which Glantz creates tension and expectation of his "coming back" to the more traditional, more familiar modes and tunes. I actually witnessed that "sigh" of joy and relief by the worshippers when Glantz *Kummt Zu'rik A'heim* (arrived back home).

What inspired Leib Glantz to become so unique were his dedicated Chasidic upbringing and his deep faith in *Ne'tzach Yis'ra'el*.[6]

He was very individualistic in his creative approach to *Te'fi'la*, and at the same time he was totally loyal to the "traditional *Nu'sach*." Most of the time, he successfully melded the two

---

6 *Ne'tzach Yis'ra'el* can be understood in two ways. It can mean the "Eternal One of Israel" — God. It can also mean "the eternity of Israel" — the survival of the Jewish people, in spite of persecution and assimilation.

> *Like many other geniuses before him, Glantz was frequently misunderstood. In his lifetime, many considered his approach too radical. However, as time went by, his enormous contribution to the world of Cha'za'nut is today recognized by all.*

elements into a cohesive expression. Yet like many other geniuses before him (and he was definitely an *I'lui* — a genius), Glantz was frequently misunderstood. In his lifetime, many considered his approach too radical. However, as time went by, his enormous contribution to the world of *Cha'za'nut* is today recognized by all.

During the course of every academic year at the Tel Aviv Cantorial Institute, some young student will come to me, his head still spinning, and he will tell me excitedly that he had just listened to Glantz's *Se'li'chot* for the first time and that it was a life changing event.

I am thankful to the Almighty for the privilege of having known Leib Glantz personally, having heard him in *Te'fi'la*, and having shared conversations with him when I was merely fifteen years old. I hope that thanks to my years of experience at the *A'mud*, I have grown to better understand those conversations, and that I now have greater insight into the Glantz phenomenon, so that I can help the next generation appreciate the greatness of Leib Glantz the *Cha'zan*, the musician, the composer, the poet, the orator, the man whose *Te'fi'lot* (prayers) could at once soar with fiery intensity, and just as quickly could float on heavenly softness. Most importantly, I want the next generation of *Shli'chei Tzi'bur* (leaders of congregations) to see Leib Glantz as I see him — a prime example of *Sa'ne'go'ram Shel Yis'ra'el*[7] — a true advocate, pleading before God on behalf of the people of Israel.

---

7 *Sa'ne'go'ram Shel Yis'ra'el* — Moses was considered the "advocate" of the Israelites when, according to the bible, he spoke to God in Egypt. Rabbi Levi Yitzchak from Berdichev, one of the legendary figures of Chasidism (1740-1810), was also called *Sa'ne'go'ram Shel Yis'ra'el*, because of his consuming love of God and his people. He became known as the "defender of the people of Israel" as he would argue with God, charging Him with being too stern a father to His children, pleading for an end to the prolonged exile from Zion.

8

The Masterpiece: *She'ma Yis'ra'el*

MAESTRO ELLI JAFFE[1]

The legendary cantor, Leib Glantz, was a central pillar of the world of cantorial music. Glantz was not only a magnificent performer, but was also a musician of the highest stature. His com-positions are characterized by pro-found intellect, clarity of expression, and above all — daring innovations, which were strictly in line with tradi-tional cantorial concepts; his monu-mental work took the form of old wine in new vessels.

> *Glantz was not only a magnificent performer, but also a musician of the highest stature. His compositions are characterized by profound intellect, clarity of expression, and above all — daring innovations, which were strictly in line with traditional cantorial concepts.*

He was a master of the Jewish prayer modes, the *Nu'sach,* and in his research he displayed amazing knowledge of the ancient origins of Jewish music.

One of his most impressive composi-tions is *She'ma Yis'ra'el* (Hear O Israel). Glantz created a musical interpretation of each and every word of the prayer, bringing the *Ke'du'sha* prayer service to the level of a royal ceremo-ny.

---

1 Elli Jaffe was born in Jerusalem and graduated with distinction from the Rubin Academy in Jerusalem and the Royal Academy of Music in London; he has conducted all of Israel's major orchestras, and holds the title of honorary guest conductor of the Prague Symphony Orchestra. He is artistic director of the Jerusalem School for Cantorial Art and conductor of Jerusalem's Great Synagogue choir. He has published an instructional compact disk on the Hebrew liturgy. As composer, the Israel Philharmonic performed his First Symphony, and his Wind Quintet was premiered by that orchestra's wind ensemble.

In my following analysis I would like to highlight some of the elements of Leib Glantz's penetrating interpretation of this famous prayer.

There are several musical triplicities in Glantz's *Shéma Yis'ra'el*. In the opening word *"Shéma,"* there are three fundamental steps:

1. An opening two-tone declaration (example 1);
2. A cyclic melody, rising in tempo (example 2);
3. An ending trill that leads to a lasting tone (example 3).

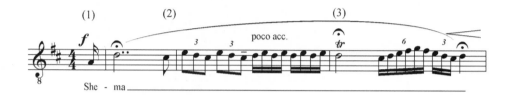

In my opinion there are several reasons for this theme:

First, in the *To'rah,* the word *Shéma* is spelled in a very special way: the last letter in this word — the Hebrew letter *Ei'yen* — is printed in a larger font compared to the other letters in the word. The same is true of the letter *Da'let* in the word *E'chad.* Interestingly, these two letters comprise the Hebrew word *Ad* (pronounced "aid") which means "witness." I assume that Glantz wanted to musically emphasize the belief that the Lord will reign forever and that we, his people, are destined to be his witnesses.

Secondly, *Shéma* is a call to everyone: listen and "hear." The first call — a prolonged note — is directed towards those who are near. The second is to those who are farther away. Interestingly, this is the exact interpretation of Rabbi Shimshon Raphael Hirsch.[2]

Then, with a cyclic rising tempo, ending with another prolonged note, all Israel become *one,* which explains the use of the words "Hear O Israel," rather than "Hear O Israelites."

Rashi,[3] the great Jewish commentator, claimed that God, who is *one,* would eventually be *one* God not only to Israel, but also to all the nations of the world, as stated in the biblical prophe-

---

2 Rabbi Shimshon Raphael Hirsch (1808–1888) was a German rabbi and a chief exponent of Neo-Orthodoxy. As rabbi in Frankfurt-am-Main, in 1837 he wrote in *Ho'reb* that the reason for the Jews' existence was, in keeping with biblical teachings, to exemplify the righteous life for the entire world as revealed by God.

3 Rashi (1040–1105) — Jewish exegete, grammarian, and legal authority was born in Troyes, France. The name by which he is known is an acronym of Rabbi Shlomo bar Yitzchak. He studied in Worms and Mainz, taught and wrote commentaries to most of the Bible and Talmud. Distinguished by great clarity, they are among the most inclusive and authoritative in Jewish exegesis.

cies of Zephania and Zecharia. Glantz's musical interpretation follows this same line of thought. He sings the opening in a continuous tone, which represents the God of Israel; he follows with a cyclic melody with rising tempo to represent the process of God's becoming Lord of all nations; and then he moves to a final continuous note singing *A'do'nai* is our God, *A'do'nai* is one.

Here, the word *She'ma* is expressed by Glantz in a quiet tone, a preamble to the words *A'do'nai E'lo'kei'nu*, as if it were a secret between God and the Israelites: "Come together my people for I will reveal myself before you."

The word *She'ma* is then sung as if it were the "sound of the great *Sho'far*"[4] (*U'Ve'Sho'far Ga'dol Yi'ta'kah*), but the word *Yis'ra'el* is uttered in a "silent voice" (*Kol De'ma'mah Da'kah*). The Magid of Kotzk[5] is quoted to have said: "When the great *Sho'far* is blown, a silent voice can be heard!" By accepting God's rule, the people of Israel are able to appreciate both the silent and the vibrant sounds of the *Sho'far*. Interestingly, the word *"She'ma"* in Glantz's music resembles the three steps of the traditional blowing of the *Sho'far*, which are *"Te'ki'ah," "Te'ru'ah,"* and *"She'va'rim."*[6]

In Glantz's composition, the word *Yis'ra'el* consists of three "steps" — three rising tones (example 4), which is another instance of triplicities:

The Hebrew Scriptures consist of three main parts: The *To'rah* of Moses, the *Prophets*, and the *Writings* (*To'rah, Ne'vi'im, Ke'tu'vim*). By the same token, the people of Israel comprised three defined groups: *Ko'ha'nim, Le'vi'im* and *Yis'ra'el*.[7] Surely, Glantz had these elements in mind

---

4 *Sho'far* — A trumpet made of a ram's horn, blown by the ancient Hebrews during religious ceremonies and as a signal in battle, now sounded in the synagogue during *Rosh Ha'Sha'na* and at the conclusion of the *Yom Ki'ppur* prayer services.

5 Rabbi Menachem Mendel Morgenstern of Kotzk, better known as the Kotzker Rebbe (1787-1859), was a Chasidic leader. Having acquired impressive Talmudic and Kabbalistic knowledge at a very young age, he was well known for his incisive down-to-earth philosophies, and sharp-witted sayings.

6 The *Sho'far* is blown in three distinct sounds: The *"Te'ki'ah"* is a plain deep sound ending abruptly; the *"Te'ru'ah"* is a trill, and the *"She'va'rim"* is composed of several connected short sounds.

7 *Ko'ha'nim* were the priests at the Holy Temple, assumed to be direct male descendants of the biblical Aaron, brother of Moses. Aaron was a member of the Tribe of Levi, so all *Ko'ha'nim* are Levites, as tribal membership passes via patrilineal descent. However, not all Levites are *Ko'ha'nim*. Most of the Holy Temple services (such as the sacrifices) were conducted by *Ko'ha'nim*. The Levites who were not *Ko'ha'nim* (those who descend from Levi, the son of Jacob, but not from Aaron) provided a variety of other Temple roles, most notably music and songs (Psalms) to accompany the Temple ceremonies, as well as a variety of other duties. The majority of Jews are called *Yis'ra'el*. They are neither *Ko'ha'nim* nor Levites.

when creating this composition. Especially intriguing is the unique movement on the second of the three notes, which seems to emphasize the Levites. Could the reason for this be that the Levites were in charge of singing and music in the Holy Temple?

The composer created an interesting separation between the words *A'do'nai* and *E'lo'kei'nu* (example 5):

Before Glantz's interpretation, these words were traditionally sung together, and immediately followed by *A'do'nai E'chad* (example 6):

One might wonder why Glantz chose to separate these words in the manner he did, considering that they don't correspond with the biblical cantillations for this text.

However, if we turn again to Rashi's commentary, we find a striking parallel to Glantz's interpretation! Rashi writes that God is *our* Lord *now*, and not the Lord of the nations who pray to idols; but in the future our Lord will be the sole God of *all* people. The words *She'ma* and *E'chad* (example 7) were given by Glantz a strikingly similar musical character:

The same can be said of the similarity between the musical character given to the words *Yis'ra'el* and *E'lo'kei'nu* (example 8):

Glantz sings *Yis'ra'el* and *E'lo'kei'nu* in a typically introverted style. The word *E'lo'kei'nu* serves Glantz as a bridge connecting the past — the God of Israel alone — with the future, as the God of all nations. It takes musical form as a rising melody, beginning from the word *E'lo'kei'nu* and reaching a climax in the words "God is one" (*A'do'nai E'chad*). This is Glantz's way of describing the *process* that will lead to the recognition of God's superiority by the nations of the world. This is also the wonderful way in which Glantz, a great Jewish scholar in his own right, exemplifies, with such a magnificent and moving melody, the comments of Rashi, written 900 years earlier.

In the fourth chapter of *The Chronicles of Rabbi Eliezer,*[8] the Rabbi states that the *She'ma Yis'ra'el* is, in fact, a declaration by the people of Israel of their belief in the concept of the unity of God. Glantz expresses this ancient commentary by using a royal grand opening, something that sounds as if it were being performed before an enormous crowd in the presence of a king. Interestingly, this opening is *not* in the Mixolydian mode[9] (example 9), the mode that characterizes the rest of the composition. It actually begins in the classic Major scale[10] (example 10), which is typical of almost all prayers dealing with the concept of Kingdom:[11]

Using the classic Major scale exemplifies the fact that declaring *She'ma Yis'ra'el* is, according to the *Ge'ma'ra*[12] (in *Ma'se'chet B'ra'chot*), a declaration of the unity of God. In a way it reminds one of operatic music. However, Glantz remained loyal to the authentic *Nu'sach*, withstanding the temptation to create operatic melodies so characteristic of royal scenes.

In the second part of *She'ma Yis'ra'el*, Glantz reverts to the Eastern European style of cantorial, applying the Mixolydian mode. He seasons the music with gentle chromatics[13] that produce meaningful effects. The transfer to the Mixolydian mode is achieved by lowering the sixth tone (extended Mixolydian), and the seventh tone (example 11):

8   Rabbi Eliezer Ben Horkonus, one of the great teachers of the *Mish'na*, lived in the last period of the Second Temple. *Pir'kei Rabbi Eliezer*, written in Italy shortly after 833 CE, chronicles his ideas.

9   Mixolydian Mode — A medieval mode whose scale pattern is that of playing G to G on the white keys of a piano.

10 Major scale — A diatonic scale in which the intervals between the degrees are each one tone, except for the intervals between the third and fourth and between the seventh and eighth, which are each a semitone.

11 For example: the *Ma'a'riv* service for *Rosh Ha'Sha'na*, the *Se'der Mal'chu'yot* of the *Mu'saf* service of *Rosh Ha'Sha'na*, removing the *To'rah* scrolls on the Sabbath service (*Ein Ka'mo'cha…Mal'chut'cha Mal'chut Kol Ha'O'la'mim*), etc.

12 *Ge'ma'ra* — a rabbinical commentary on the *Mish'na*, forming the second part of the Talmud. It originates from the Aramaic word *Ge'ma'ra* — "completion."

13 Chromatics — the use of all 12 musical tones, especially for heightened expressivity. A standard key or mode principally employed 7 tones, leaving 5 tones for discretionary use.

In the next portion of the composition Glantz exhibits the depth of his genius as an interpreter. In the list of God's attributes, his emphasis is on the word "He" (*Hu*), and not on the attributes such as "our Lord," "our Father," "our King," and "our Deliverer" (*E'lo'kei'nu, A'vi'nu, Mal'kei'nu, Mo'shi'ei'nu*). Glantz emphasizes the word "He" as if to say: "It is He and no one else!"

The first "He" is sung in a circling and descending sequence. Glantz uses a technique to illustrate the statement: "You are our Lord in the heavens and on earth," with tones descending from higher to lower (example 12):

When he arrives at the words "our Lord" (*E'lo'kei'nu*), he repeats the word "He," and emphasizes each and every syllable, as if shuddering and trembling (example 13):

When Glantz reaches the second attribute, "our Father" (*A'vi'nu*) is expressed in a more worldly manner, somewhat like the sweet voice of a father talking to his child. Here the word "He" is repeated three times, but when he comes to the word *A'vi'nu,* there is a definite culmination, as if realizing that "father" there is only *one*…(as in example 14):

The words "our Lord" (*E'lo'kei'nu*) end on the fifth tone of the scale (example 15):

According to Rashi's interpretation, mentioned above, the word *E'lo'kei'nu* is similar in musical character to the word *Yis'ra'el* (from the first part of the composition): In the future *all* nations will eventually recognize that "God is one and His Name is one" (*A'do'nai E'chad U'Shmo E'chad*). However, as this goal has yet to have been fulfilled, the word *E'lo'kei'nu* remains similar in musical character to the word *Yis'ra'el*.

The third attribute, "He is our King" (*Hu Mal'kei'nu*), is similar in musical character to the word *She'ma*, stating the acceptance by the nation of Israel of the obligation to serve the King of the heavens. The word "He" (*Hu*) is characterized by the cyclic lowering and rising melody (example 16):

As in the word *She'ma,* this describes God's kingdom as a kingdom that rules the entire universe. The words "He is our King" (*Hu Mal'kei'nu*) are sung twice, first reminding us of the earlier words "He is our Lord" (*Hu Elo'kei'nu*), but the second mention of these words puts the ending on the fifth tone, similar, as above, to the words "He is our Lord" (example 17):

Glantz is describing the two virtues of the King: the first represents the virtue of justice (*Mi'dat Ha'Din*) and the second represents the virtue of mercy (*Mi'dat Ha'Ra'cha'mim*). The same chromatics express a glimpse towards the third part of the composition — "When will You reign?" (*Ma'tai Tim'loch?*), as if to say: "You are the King — please reign over us!"

This leads us to the third part of *Shema Yis'ra'el* — and to the third attribute — "He is our Deliverer" (*Hu Mo'shi'ei'nu*). Three times "He" (*Hu*) is repeated — the third transfers us to a prayer mode, as if to say we have passed the first two "redemptions" (*Ge'u'lot*) (as in example 18), and now we await the third and last redemption: "God the Almighty — you are called upon to complete your commitment to be our Deliverer" (example 19):

At this point in the composition Glantz moves to the Eastern European mode of his Chazanic art — a prevalent occurrence in many of his compositions. Notwithstanding the fact that the words "He will let us hear" (*Ve'Hu Yash'mi'ei'nu*) describe an actual situation, and not a plea (*A'na, To'shi'ei'nu*), still the musical character remains similar to "When will You reign in Zion?" (*Ma'tai Tim'loch Be'Tzion?*). This sentence — "He will again let us witness His mercy" (*Ve'Hu Yash'mi'ei'nu Be'Rach'mav Shei'nit*) — is repeated twice: first as a plea (example 20), then in an optimistic musical line, expressing belief that the salvation and deliverance will occur "in the presence of all living" (*Le'Ei'nei Kol Chai*):

This royal conclusion reminds us of the opening of *Shema Yis'ra'el,* even in its Eastern European style, transferring us again to the Major scale (example 21), as if Glantz wants to declare, "In the eyes of all nations God displayed His righteousness" (*Le'Ei'nei Ha'A'mim Gi'la Tzid'ka'to*):

At the end of the composition, again with triplicities, Glantz unravels a surprise, when singing "to be Your God" (*Le'hi'yot La'chem La'lo'him*). The words "to be Your" (*Le'hi'yot La'chem*) are repeated twice: first, in a way that is musically similar to the word *Yis'ra'el* (example 22) — an expression of Rashi's interpretation, and then a second time with a musical expression of the word *She'ma* (example 23). In a final third time, Glantz stresses the word *La'chem,* with a musical movement that is similar to the opening *She'ma:*

The final words of this prayer are actually part of a longer phrase: "I have redeemed you from this final (exile) as from the first, to be Your God" (*Hen Ga'al'ti Et'chem Ach'rit Ke've'Rai'shit, Li'hi'yot La'chem La'lo'him*). This longer phrase is traditionally sung in Sephardic synagogues during the *Ke'du'sha* (Sanctification) of the Sabbath *Mu'saf* prayer service. In Israel, Glantz officiated as cantor of the Sephardic *Tif'e'ret Zvi* synagogue in Tel Aviv. He expressed his musical interpretation of these words as follows: after the first two "redemptions" (*Ge'u'lot*), there was a third redemption. The final tones of the word "Your" (*La'chem*) remind us musically of the word *She'ma* that leads to the acceptance of God's Kingdom by "all the living" (*Kol Chai*), in accordance with Rashi's famous interpretation.

She'ma Yis'ra'el [14] is one of the greatest masterpieces in Jewish liturgy. It shows what a great composer, blessed with deep intellectual capacities, can achieve. This is not only great Jewish cantorial music. It is music that appeals to lovers of beautiful and meaningful music throughout the world!

She'ma Yis'ra'el *is one of the greatest masterpieces in Jewish liturgy. It shows what a great composer, attributed with deep intellectual capacities, can achieve. This is not only great Jewish Cantorial music. It is music that appeals to lovers of beautiful and meaningful music throughout the world!*

14 The composition *She'ma Yis'ra'el,* composed and sung by Leib Glantz, can be heard on the compact disk accompanying this book (CD 1).

9

Supplication and Forgiveness – Genius and Divine Singing

MAESTRO MORDECHAI SOBOL[1]

The approach of a creative artist to composing a text that is both elated and joyful is totally different from the artistic approach to composing a text of supplication. The extent to which a composer is able to preserve a unique and uniform artistic level is what makes the difference between a good cantor and a great one.

> *In his unique approach to texts, Leib Glantz succeeded in preserving a high artistic level of composition and performance, placing him as the first among the first of cantors.*

In his unique approach to texts, Leib Glantz succeeded in preserving a high artistic level of composition and performance, placing him as the first among the first of cantors.

The composition *"Ez'ke'ra E'lo'kim Ve'E'he'ma'ya"* ("I remember, O God, and I am deeply vexed") from the *Se'li'chot* of the *Yom Ki'ppur Ne'i'la* prayer service, exemplifies all the elements we mentioned above. I will try to analyze this composition by identifying the amazing correlations between the text of this prayer and Glantz's musical interpretations.

The following is the translated text of *Ez'ke'ra E'lo'kim Ve'E'he'ma'ya:*[2]

---

1 Dr. Mordechai Sobol is a leading force in the world of Jewish liturgical music. He is the Music Director and Conductor of the Yuval Symphony Orchestra and Chorus, as well as the Israel Philharmonic Orchestra in its Jewish liturgical series. Dr. Sobol, who was born in Israel, was a student of the legendary cantor Shlomo Ravitz. He holds a doctoral degree in Jewish Music and is an important composer, conductor and orchestrator.

2 This liturgical poem *(Pi'yut)* was composed by Amittai Ben Shephatiah in the late ninth century. The translation is from "High Holiday Prayer Book," compiled and arranged by Rabbi Morris Silverman, Published by The United Synagogue of America, The Prayer Book Press of Media Judaica, Inc., Bridgeport, Connecticut, 1951.

I remember, O God, and I am deeply vexed
When I see every city built on its own site,
While Jerusalem, the city of God is razed to the ground;
Yet for all this, our faith in Thee does not falter.

O attribute of mercy, be moved compassionately toward us;
Supplicate your possessor, the Eternal,
And entreat for mercy for your people.
"For every heart is faint and every head is weary."

On the thirteen attributes of God, do I rely,
And on the flowing tears of contrite hearts;
Therefore have I poured out my prayer to Him who searcheth hearts.
In these do I have faith, and in the merit of the fathers.

O Thou who hearest weeping, hear Thou us.
And do Thou pour our tears in Thy heavenly urn.
Deliver us; forgo Thy dread decrees,
For unto Thee our eyes turn evermore.

Thou sittest on Thy judgment seat enthroned on high...

This penitential hymn is from the liturgical poem *A'do'shem A'do'shem El Ra'chum Ve'Cha'nun* ("The Lord, the Lord is a God full of compassion"). It is different from all other penitential hymns, as in this one there is vigorous energy, even though the text is an exact repetition of the hymn *Mal'a'chei Ra'cha'mim* ("Angels of Mercy") of the *Se'li'chot* prayer. However, here the logic is different: it is not that the Lord is unwilling to listen to our pleas, but it is impossible for us to make requests of God at a time when our hearts and souls are suffering from the pain of exile. Then comes the prayer *Ye'hi Ra'tzon Mil'fa'ne'cha...* ("O Thou who hearest weeping, hear Thou us, and do Thou pour our tears in Thy heavenly urn..."). This prayer of the *Ne'i'la* service becomes a direct conversation from our painful hearts, with our Creator, the King of the Universe, who commands all living beings. There is no one to advocate on our behalf, and therefore we address God directly, hoping He will accept our prayers and supplications and will ensure a decent life, by including us in the signing and sealing of our fate just before the gates of the heavens are closed at the end of the Holy Day of Atonement.

Glantz creates an atmosphere for the whole composition in the very first words. A leap of the fourth interval ascending from the original foundation in the Phrygian mode towards the mother Minor scale of the mode creates an effect of declaration that fades into a mystical memory, as if to say: "I remember the beautiful city of God, as compared to its state of destruction in present times, and this causes me to weep." At the very mention of tears and sadness — Glantz proceeds to the basic note of the Jewish Phrygian mode *(Phry'gish)*, known as the *"A'ha'va Ra'bbah" Shtey'ger,* which characterizes our prayers, especially the array of musical supplications:

In the next sentence — *Bir'o'ti Kol Ir Al Ti'lah Be'nu'yah* ("When I see every city built on its own site"), another leap up to the mother Harmonic Minor scale, then a gradual sequential ascent of a tonality system arriving onto a secondary peak in the words *Al Ti'lah Be'nu'yah,* with an emphasis on the words "built on its own site," sung on one note and in short emphasis. On the other hand, the sentence *Ve'Ir Ha'E'lo'kim Mush'pe'let* ("While [Jerusalem,] the city of God is razed to the ground"), begins a gradual descent until the words *Tach'ti'ya* ("the depths of the abyss"), again with an accented emphasis on one note — this time the treatment of the subdominant of the mother Minor original scale, as a parallel to *Kol Ir Al Ti'lah Be'nu'yah* — but this time not at the peak but at the lowest degradation:

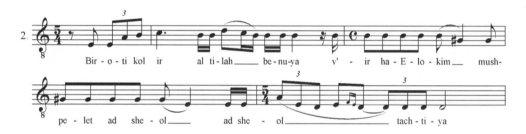

In the sentence *U'Ve'Chol Zot A'nu Le'Ya Ve'Ei'nei'nu Le'Ya* ("Yet for all this, our faith in Thee does not falter"), it will start again on the fourth note of the Jewish Phrygian mode, towards the Harmonic Minor — its close relative scale, and in it the words *Ve'Ei'nei'nu Le'Ya.* Glantz stretches and extends the tones, until arriving to the home base of the mode, this time in the upper Tetrachord or the upper part of the scale, and from here he then will land on the Minor scale, as if saying "'all will be clear in the end." Following this opening, Glantz is now ready to develop the musical theme:

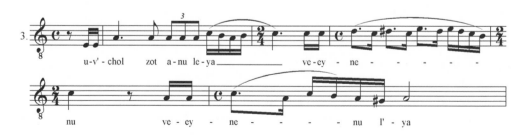

In the second stanza, *Mi'dat Ha'Ra'cha'mim A'lei'nu Hit'gal'ge'li* ("O attribute of mercy, be moved compassionately toward us"), Glantz begins to create an array of musical supplications, as the anguished word *Ra'chamim* pierces the heart. The word *Hit'gal'ge'li* rolls upwards and downwards as if saying, "If there is mercy in heaven we are in need of it now. We are your children and we beg for compassion, the compassion of a father towards his sons":

Ve'Lif'nei Ko'neich ("and cast our supplication before the Creator") sets the purpose and the function of *Mi'dat Ha'Ra'cha'mim* (the quality of compassion) to reach the Throne of God and bring before Him our supplications. This finds expression in the consecutive melody's extended sequence up to the word *Ha'pi'li* (cast), which Glantz will use for the idea of emphasizing tones on one note:

The words *U'Ve'ad A'mech Ra'cha'mim Sha'a'li* ("and entreat for mercy Your people") again establishes the purpose of what *Mi'dat Ha'Ra'cha'mim* must accomplish: our hearts are in anguish because of the long and painful exile, which tears us away from the city of our forefathers, making our heads weary (*Ve'Chol Rosh La'Cho'li*). Glantz's stressing of the word *La'Cho'li* is created by short tones on one note, ending the first chapter of the composition and making a full musical circle:

Thus we arrive at one of the most emotional texts in the *Ne'i'la* service. It would seem that this tearful text, *Ve'Ta'tzi'lei'nu Mi'Kol Ge'zei'rot Ka'shot, Ach'za'ri'yot* ("Deliver us; forgo Thy dread decrees"), would call for tearful music. Indeed many cantors who have composed music for this text, each in his own way and according to his specific musical skills and vocal abilities, offered such a musical interpretation to these words. Glantz was not content to dwell on the word *Ve'Ta'tzi'lei'nu,* but instead began his musical interpretation earlier, enabling us to comprehend the meaning of *Sho'me'ah Kol Bich'yot* ("O Thou who hearest weeping"). Glantz preferred to talk rather than to sing this to the Almighty, filling with unique musical content his function as a *Shli'ach Tzi'bur* (leader of the congregation in prayer), demanding of God "life and not death" for his people.

His splendid interpretation of the two-word phrase *Kol Bich'yot* ("the sound of weeping") — represents four sets of silent mystical weeping. From one cry to the next, he uses separate half tones in descending sequences, meaning that from the Harmonic Minor basic scale Glantz uses a formula of dotted eight notes resting on the minor tonic with sixteen notes below the basic tonic note. In this way Glantz starts with the lower 3rd, which is the 6th note of the scale, and then moves to the 5th note. Thus he continues descending with chromatic moves, until he is established on the minor tonic, and here again, he uses rhythmic patterns on the tonic:

At this point Glantz "rolls up his sleeves" and begins an emotional ascent to the climax of this musical work with the words *Ve'Ta'tzi'lei'nu Mi'Kol Ge'zei'rot Ka'shot, Ach'za'ri'yot* ("Deliver us; forgo Thy dread decrees"). This ascent is not without dwelling on the underlying meaning of the words *Dim'o'tei'nu* ("our tears") on one hand, and *Be'Nod'cha Li'hi'yot* ("in Thy heavenly urn") on the other.

The *A'ha'va Ra'bbah Shtey'ger* was built by Glantz on the basis of the Minor scale as the mother scale. Thus, the mother Minor scale becomes the foundation of the dominant modality, which strives towards a new Harmonic Minor — a 4th higher from the previous Minor scale.

So far we have shown that the composition opened with the *A'ha'va Ra'bbah* mode (*Shtey'ger*) on E Phrygian (Jewish *Phry'gish*). This Phrygian is drawn into the harmonic of A minor, which contains within it the original E *Phry'gish Shtey'ger*. And now, with a 4th higher, the A minor turns into A *Phry'gish,* which immediately is drawn into a new tonality of D Harmonic Minor, which again contains within it the earlier A *Phry'gish*. Glantz then repeats and emphasizes the word *Ve'Ta'tzi'lei'nu* ("and You will save us"), as he exits from a minor chord formula D — F — A, while creating a momentary pause (a musical comma) on the third F.

From this point Glantz immediately continues answering *Ve'Ta'tzi'lei'nu Mi'Kol Ge'zei'rot Ka'shot* ("deliver us, forgo Thy dread decrees") until the final answer with the word *Ach'za'ri'yot* ("Thy dread decrees"). Here Glantz creates a sort of turning musical maneuver in a brilliant fast moving *coloratura* within the interval of a 3rd on the words *Ki Le'cha Le'vad* ("for only unto Thee"), again and again with the touch of the 5th:

It is at this moment that Glantz creates one of the most surprising and original endings in Jewish liturgical music by combining the ending of this prayer *Ki Le'cha Le'vad Ei'nei'nu Te'lu'yot* ("for only unto Thee our eyes turn evermore") with the opening of the next prayer *El Me'lech Yo'shev Al Ki'sei Ra'cha'mim* ("Thou sittest on Thy judgment seat enthroned on high") — the *Shlosh Es'reh Mi'dot* (the Thirteen Divine Attributes), that are proclaimed as the congregation rises to their feet. This musical ending is not sung as a continuation of the sobbing scale, not the Jewish *Phry'gish* and not the Harmonic Minor, but as a majestic ending in Major, as Glantz expresses confidence that our fate will be positive and the King of Kings, who is the master of forgiveness and mercy, will forgive the sins of his faithful:

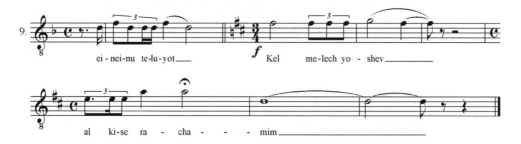

This amazing composition[3] is undoubtedly a classical, penetrating and complex lesson in the art of *Cha'za'nut,* in the art of cantorial performance, and especially in the deep interpretation of this prayer text. It is a master class in translating the words into the language of music.

The title of this essay represents my conclusion that this unbelievably authentic composition, establishes Leib Glantz as the genius of the divine music of the Jewish people.

> *This amazing composition [Ez'ke'ra E'lo'kim] is undoubtedly a classical, penetrating and complex lesson in the art of* Cha'za'nut, *in the art of cantorial performance, and especially in the deep interpretation of this prayer text. It is a master class in translating the words into the language of music, [and] establishes Leib Glantz as the genius of the divine music of the Jewish people.*

---

3 The composition *Ez'ke'ra E'lo'kim,* composed and sung by Leib Glantz, can be heard on the compact disk accompanying this book (CD 1).

Leib Glantz with male choir in prayer service in New York, 1936.

10

Leib Glantz's Impact on The Art of *Cha'za'nut*

CANTOR MOSHE SCHULHOF[1]

> *There are those rare visionaries, individuals who possess such creativity, coupled with immense courage, that ultimately impact their art form for generations to come.*

As in every art form, there are those who excel in presenting their art to the world and who live on through their works for eternity. Beyond that, there are those rare visionaries, individuals who possess such creativity, coupled with immense courage, that ultimately create an impact on their art form for generations to come. Generally, these artists and composers are considered "ahead of their time" and may be confronted with opposition during their lifetimes. Ultimately, their thoughts and visions succeed in steering the art form into new paths to the point where anyone who comes later finds himself building upon their innovations.

In the world of classical music, such individuals included the likes of Bach, Mozart, Beethoven, Stravinsky or Hindemith; and in the world of fine arts — geniuses such as Leonardo Da Vinci, Michelangelo, Rembrandt, El Greco, Monet, and Picasso. Each one changed his art for all eternity.

Similarly, the art of the cantor has evolved through the years. The roots of this art can be traced back to ancient times when the cantillation of the bible was begun, leading to the early

---

1 Cantor Moshe Schulhof studied cantorial and opera in the New York and Montreal conservatories. He is a composer and teacher of *Cha'za'nut* and *Nu'sach* at the Academy of Jewish Religion in New York. He performed in Israel with the Israeli Philharmonic Orchestra.

development of the ancient Jewish prayer modes (*Nu'sach*). Among the first to "pour old wine into new vessels" in past centuries were Solomone Rossi (1570-1630), Salomon Sulzer (1804-1890) and Louis Lewandowski (1823-1894). They began to incorporate Western European choral music into the synagogue service, using age-old motifs. Synagogue composers, such as David Nowakowsky (1848-1921), Abraham Dunajefsky, Nissi Belzer (1824-1906), and "Pitzsche" Abrass (1820-1896), wrote choral harmonies to traditional Eastern European *Cha'za'nut*. This continued in the twentieth century by notable composers such as Sholom Secunda, Max Helfman, and Max Janowsky. Present day composers continue to build upon these earlier works.

In Eastern Europe, in the late eighteenth century, a new phenomenon began developing — the virtuoso cantor; the art of the cantor reached beyond the walls of the synagogue onto the concert stage. In that sense, *Cha'za'nut* has emerged not only as a form of worship, but also as entertainment. Indeed cantors were often referred to as *"O'med Kunts'ler"* (artists of the pulpit). One of the earliest of this type of cantor was the eighteenth century Cantor Yoel Dovid Strashunsky (1816-1850), known as the Vilner Balabesl. Other notables were Yerucham Hakatan (Blindman) (1798-1891), Solomon Rozumni (1866-1904), Avraham Berkovitz (Kalachnik), and Jacob Bachmann (1846-1905).

In order for these extraordinary cantors to have a vehicle with which to present their phenomenal vocal and musical talents, music had to be composed. Hence, some of these artists were not only great singers but great composers, as well. Four individuals stand out, in my humble assessment, as innovators of the so-called *"Golden Age of Cha'za'nut"*: Yossele Rosenblatt, Zavel Kwartin, Moshe Kousevitsky, and Leib Glantz. To appreciate the impact of Leib Glantz on cantorial art, it is essential first to understand the contribution of the other three great personalities.

Yossele Rosenblatt (1882-1933) possessed a voice of rare beauty that sounded almost like a cello. His compositions are full of melody, sophisticated but simple; they appeal both to the lovers of *Cha'za'nut* and to the uninitiated. He was the Verdi of *Cha'za'nut*.

Zavel Kwartin (1874-1952), with his magnificent baritone, was the master of the predictable. His music was genuinely Jewish. He taught us how to be dramatic without veering away from the road of *Nu'sach* and old-fashioned *Cha'za'nut*.

Moshe Kousevitsky (1899-1966) created a style based upon vocal acrobatics. Because he possessed an enormous voice that had nearly limitless range and flexibility, he created and adapted compositions that would show off the brilliance of his voice and technique. Every cantor today would like to sound like Kousevitsky. Unfortunately, the road is littered with the corpses of ruined voices of Kousevitsky wanna-bees. Yet his style survives.

Leib Glantz (1898-1964) was different. I never had the honor to meet him personally, nor to hear him sing in a live performance. It was my privilege to serve as the cantor of *Sha'a'rei Te'fi'lah* synagogue in Los Angeles for eight years, on the same pulpit that he had graced prior to his making *A'li'ya* to Israel in 1954. During my years at *Sha'a'rei Te'fi'lah*, I heard many members of the congregation warmly reminiscing about his days as their cantor. I also had the pleasure of spending hours with his wife, Miriam, listening to her describe Glantz's unique approach to *Cha'za'nut*.

I was first exposed to his music as a teenager while studying *Cha'za'nut* and *Nu'sach* with Noah Schall, who had me listen to Leib Glantz's *Se'li'chot* Service. The *Se'li'chot* was one of Glantz's last recordings. It was recorded live for Israeli Radio at a synagogue service in Tel Aviv's *Tif'e'ret Zvi* synagogue. This was the completely mature Glantz, and it was radically different from anything I had ever heard before.

> *I was first exposed to Glantz's music as a teenager while studying* Cha'za'nut *and* Nu'sach *with Noah Schall, who had me listen to Leib Glantz's* Se'li'chot *Service.*

My first reaction was very negative! I felt that it was way over my head. Noah Schall raved about Glantz's genius while enjoying my bewilderment. He took it as a challenge to make me see what Glantz was about, and to teach me to understand and appreciate his genius. Mrs. Glantz once described Glantz's approach to cantorial: Glantz believed that the music was an accompaniment to the text. Basically, he was not looking to create pleasing melodies, to show off his range or his phenomenal *coloratura*. These were just vehicles to be used only when they could interpret the meaning and the spirit of the text, the *Nu'sach*, and the atmosphere of the prayer.

Before Glantz made this the cornerstone of his cantorial, it was usually the other way around. The music was of primary importance, very often having very little connection to the text. Glantz, on the other hand, wasn't concerned about how melodic, beautiful, or entertaining the music was. It was meant to stir you, even to disturb you if the text called for it. Above all, this music was intended to bring you to deeply understand what the author of the prayer was trying to say to God.

In order to listen or to sing Glantz's music, one is required to be in a completely different mindset. One cannot listen to Glantz casually, especially to his later compositions. He needs to be studied and absorbed. As a novice listener, one has to listen to him a number of times after which one can appreciate his genius.

His style evolved throughout his lifetime. His first recordings (1929-30) contain some of his most famous compositions: *She'ma Yis'ra'el, Te'fi'lat Tal,* and *Ki Hi'nei Ka'Cho'mer.* Though highly original, these were just the first stirrings of what was beginning to develop. Since these compositions are relatively conventional, they remain part of the standard repertoire of every cantor of note, and are sung as part of their popular repertoire. They are always "crowd pleasers."

As he further crystallized his approach, in his middle era, his most notable recorded composition was *"Sho'mer Yis'ra'el."* Here Glantz began with a typical *Nu'sach* melody that a simple Jew would pray in the synagogue in every morning service. He slowly built up intensity upon that motif. The listener becomes caught up in this growing intensity and is deeply moved. At the same time, he becomes almost disturbed. I

Sinai Temple, Los Angeles, California, 1942. Leib Glantz officiated as chief cantor at Sinai Temple from 1941 till 1945.

recall being introduced to this number by Cantor Arie Subar of Montreal, an avid fan of Glantz. He heard Glantz sing *Sho'mer Yis'ra'el* at a concert, and became so emotionally shaken that he had to leave the auditorium! Indeed, every time I hear this composition, I am still in absolute awe. I have yet to hear anyone other than Glantz sing it.

All great innovators begin their careers in one era and end in another. The middle period is the bridge between the two. It was a very prolific time for Glantz. Not only did he write *Cha'za'nut* but also *Zmi'rot* (songs) that are sung at many *Sha'bbat* dinner tables. A great example is the ever-popular Chasidic melody *D'ror Yik'ra*.

His style reached its full bloom during his last ten years in Israel (1954 until his passing in 1964). In Tel Aviv he enjoyed an audience that clearly understood the Hebrew language. This audience was capable of comprehending what he was trying to do. Indeed, many of the people who became Glantz fans were beginning to regard "conventional" *Cha'za'nut* as somewhat superficial. It was during this period that his unique style came into full maturity.

With an audience capable of understanding the words, Glantz was able to provide ever-deeper interpretations of the prayers, finding hidden meanings and illuminating both the explicit and implicit content. He accomplished this by venturing into new musical areas rarely explored. He used chromatics (12 tone scales), as well as modern musical concepts of tonality. He would use diminished and augmented intervals, and even atonal expressions. He introduced *"Pshat"* (deeper interpretations, literal meanings), as well as expressionism into his music. At times Glantz would "refresh" the *Nu'sach* by veering far away from it, then returning to it, preventing monotony and reinforcing it anew.

His colossal vocal abilities enabled Glantz to venture vocally to wherever his creative mind took him. Though his voice was unique, his style and philosophical approach have deeply influenced all who came after him. Even some of his contemporaries in their later years began to use his concepts. Indeed, we hear a lot of "Glantzism" in the latter years of cantors such as Moshe Ganchof, Shlomo Mandel, and Moshe Kraus.

> *His colossal vocal abilities enabled Glantz to venture vocally to wherever his creative mind took him. Though his voice was unique, his style and philosophical approach have deeply influenced all who came after him.*

Contemporary composers of liturgical music are currently writing music with modern harmonies, mainly because Glantz proved that one could still be rooted in tradition and at the same time be thoroughly modern. The music performed at Jerusalem's Great Synagogue is a study of how tradition and modernism can be successfully combined — an example set by Leib Glantz.

My cantorial compositions are extremely influenced by Glantz's teachings. I write music to enhance the text, while endeavoring to be emotionally stirring, musically interesting, yet true to the *Nu'sach*. Glantz opened up my imagination and showed me the limitless horizons of creativity, while at the same time remaining true to tradition. I may even write atonally, while at the same time being tonal. I can venture from one mode into another key using any note on the original scale as the new tonic of a new scale. I can use chromatics, dissonant intervals, large interval jumps; in short, I can go fearlessly wherever my imagination takes me, thanks to the path shown by the immortal genius of Leib Glantz. He will forever be an integral part of the continuous development and metamorphosis of cantorial and Jewish Music.

11

The Music of Leib Glantz

POST-ROMANTIC AND EXTENDED INSTRUMENTAL TECHNIQUES

CANTOR SIDNEY S. DWORKIN [1]

Much has been said about Leib Glantz the cantor, the composer, the *Ba'al-Nu'sach* [2] and the Zionist.

His unique cantorial style has captivated aficionados of *Cha'za'nut* [3] for decades; his compositions have challenged the cantorial world from the time of their inception; he has been greatly respected for his adherence to traditional *Nu'sach Ha'Te'fi'la*; [4] and he has been admired for his love of the land of Israel and his musical creativity, capturing the flavor of the budding State of Israel through the writing of numerous Hebrew songs.

Beyond the spiritual underpinnings of Glantz's inspiration, there is yet another area of accomplishment which, in my opinion, provides an extraordinary insight into the depths of his musical expression. I am referring to Leib Glantz the musician.

The son and grandson of cantors, and himself a child prodigy from age eight, Glantz was also trained as a classical [5] pianist. He had the opportunity to study music and composition in his native Kiev with a number of Russian masters of the day, most notably the renowned

---

1 Sidney S. Dworkin is Cantor Emeritus of Congregation *Sha'ar Ha'Sho'ma'yim* in Montreal, Canada and past President of the Council of Chazanim of Greater Montreal. He is a graduate of McGill University in Music, majoring in Voice, Violin and Music Education, and he has a Masters Degree in Social Work.
2 *Ba'al-Nu'sach* — Master of prayer modes.
3 *Cha'za'nut* — the art of the cantor, cantorial.
4 *Nu'sach Ha'Te'fi'la* — the musical prayer modes appropriate for texts emanating from specific services and related melodies.
5 Classical music refers to the genre of music that encompasses the more specific historical periods of music known as Baroque, Classical, Romantic, etc.

composer Reinhold Gliere (1875-1956). Early in his adult life, Glantz was faced with a choice: to pursue his potential as a pianist, or to dedicate himself to his people and his tradition as a *Shli'ach Tzi'bur.*[6] As history records, he chose cantorial, but his classical music background led him to explore cantorial composition in a manner that remains unique to this day.

A number of techniques that Glantz employed in composing and/or singing a cantorial recitative[7] point to his grounding in, and familiarity with, classical form, nuance, performance practice, and period-related trends. Some of these techniques are not normally associated with vocal music, but rather suggest a musical line that could easily have been written for an instrument. Others are indicative of Glantz's determination, be it deliberate or subconscious, to develop his own unique characteristic style. In essence, this moved his composition into a realm that might aptly be classified as "post-Romantic." The "quasi-classical" compositions that were more or less the order of cantorial composition of the *"Golden Era of Cha'za'nut"* (roughly the first half of the twentieth century) contained trace elements of the Baroque, Classical and Romantic periods. It was Glantz alone whose music reverberated with the sound of a new era.

> The *"quasi-classical" compositions that were more or less the order of cantorial composition of the "*Golden Era of Cha'za'nut*" contained trace elements of the Baroque, Classical and Romantic periods. It was Glantz alone whose music reverberated with the sound of a new era.*

Here follows a discussion of some of these techniques.

Sonata Form

As a trained pianist, *Sonata* form would have been second nature to Glantz. Commonly used in the first and last movements of piano *sonatas* by the great classical composers, the first and second themes are presented in what is known as the Exposition section. There follows a Development section, then a Recapitulation section repeating the original themes, and finally the *Coda* (see *Coda* section below) to conclude the piece.

---

6 *Shli'ach Tzi'bur* — messenger of the people (representing the congregation in prayer).

7 A recitative has been defined as a type of vocal writing, normally for a single voice, which follows the natural rhythms and accentuation of speech and its pitch contours. A "cantorial recitative" likely acquired its descriptive title owing to the chant-like interpretations of prayer texts, featuring free-flowing melodic material, for the most part devoid of rhythmical structure. From a musical standpoint, while a genre in its own right, the elaborate embellishment and vocally challenging nature of a "cantorial recitative" as composed by Glantz and others, can best be understood by the layman as comparable to an operatic *aria.*

In contrast, a cantorial recitative has no such defined structure. It attempts to interpret a prayer text where there are usually no repeated words in the text itself and no later repetition of thematic material introduced at the beginning of the composition. This should not be confused with the practice of using one phrase as a rhythmical refrain that returns after each *recitativo* section. This was a later development in the cantorial repertoire, probably for its value in concert, and not one employed by Glantz in his cantorial compositions.

However, one can see a defined structure in Glantz's approach to composition, indicative of his formal musical training. In his treatment of *Bir'kat Ko'ha'nim,*[8] he opens with what can be called the first theme or motif on the word *Elo'kei'nu* (F—C—A) followed by a descending *coloratura* passage (see *Coloratura* section below), ascending to the cadence on the words *Ve'Elo'kei A'vo'tei'nu* ("and the God of our fathers"). The piece develops inspirationally, drawing upon the melody of *duchenen* (The Priestly Benediction). Remarkably, Glantz then presents a musical recapitulation of the first motif on the word *Ve'Ya'sem* (F—C—A) followed again by the *coloratura* passage, this time in a shorter rhythmic variant on the word *Le'cha* (to thee). The *Coda* follows to conclude the piece.

Coda

The purpose of the *coda*[9] is to achieve a stronger sense of finality to conclude a piece of music. Professional cantors are familiar with the standard type of ending — *Al Ye'dei Da'vid Me'shi'ach Tzid'ke'cha* ("by the hands of David, your righteous Messiah"), which would constitute a *coda* to a cantorial recitative.

---

8 *Bir'kat Ko'ha'nim* — the Priestly Benediction, also called *duchenen.*
9 *Coda* — a concluding musical section that is formally distinct from the main structure.

In classical music, other than driving to the end of a piece using fragments of the central theme(s) or simply a series of dynamic progressions, it is not uncommon to implant a totally new musical idea distinct from the piece up to that point. A wonderful example of this type of *coda* is found in Josef Strauss' Concert Waltz, *Mein Lebenslauf Ist Lieb und Lust* Op. 263. Here we find the composer concluding his piece by switching from the 3/4 waltz rhythm to introduce a charming 6/8 melody that serves as the focal point of the *coda*.

Glantz institutes the very same type of *coda* at the conclusion of his composition *Az Be'Kol* ("Then with a loud sound"). He inserts a 4/4 melody (the only rhythmic phrase in the recitative) on the fifth, fourth and third of last bars on the words *Le'U'ma'tam Ba'ruch Yo'me'ru* ("Facing them, blessed they say"). Similarly in his composition *Hash'ki'vei'nu* ("God, make us lie down in peace"), Glantz again presents a lone rhythmic melody on the words *Ha'Po'res Su'kat Sha'lom Alei'nu Ve'Al Kol A'mo Yis'ra'el* ("He who spreads the shelter of peace over us and over all His people, Israel"), to form the first part of a somewhat longer *coda*.

Coloratura

As with most of the star cantors of the *Golden Era,* Glantz had a highly developed *coloratura.*[10] In part, he used it in the traditional manner, by making use of runs and culminating patterns familiar to those versed in the cantorial arts. Glantz, however, also introduced some fresh, vibrant and very different runs, runs that in fact are more reminiscent of instrumental movements than of vocal ones. Some of these are among the most difficult runs in the cantorial repertoire. The human voice has a practical quality range of a little less than two octaves, while a violin has an effective range of over three octaves. With this in mind, notice the structural similarity of the following phrase from Glantz's composition *A'sher Bi'Dva'ro* (At Thy word bringest on the evenings) alongside a passage from Johannes Brahms Violin Concerto in D major, Op. 77.

> *Glantz introduced fresh, vibrant and very different runs, runs that in fact are more reminiscent of instrumental movements than of vocal ones. Some of these are among the most difficult runs in the cantorial repertoire.*

---

10 *Coloratura* — the extemporary or written decoration of vocal melody in the shape of runs, *roulades* and *cadenzas* of all kinds.

Example 1: Glantz: *A'sher Bi'Dva'ro*[11]

Example 2: Brahms: Violin Concerto in D major Op. 77

Another interesting example of instrumental-sounding *coloratura* is the scale-like pattern employed by Glantz in the composition *Bir'kat Ko'ha'nim* (The Priestly Blessing), as follows:

Example 3: Glantz: *Bir'kat Ko'ha'nim*

At first glance, one might think that this phrase could be likened to a vocal exercise. I would like to suggest, however, that scale quotations of this type are a common occurrence in piano literature. A typical example is provided here from the *Mephisto Waltz* S.513 of Franz Liszt.

---

11 Examples of Leib Glantz's music herein have been transcribed from actual recorded performances by Glantz, which may differ from printed versions published after his death.

Example 4: Liszt: *Mephisto Waltz*

Staccato

The use of the singing voice quite naturally lends itself to *legato* phrasing, but Glantz sometimes does something quite different. In *Bir'kat Ko'ha'nim*, in the first portrayal of the words *Ya'er Pa'nav Ei'le'cha* ("May God turn His face to thee"), Glantz comes out of a fast *coloratura* passage with a three-fold glottal attack on the word *Pa'nav* ("His face") in a descending pattern (A—G—F) thereby creating a *staccato* effect.[12] Again, this passage would be more representative of an instrumental line than a vocal one.

Subito Piano/Subito Forte

These tactics[13] are quite common in orchestral music but uncommon in solo singing. In this regard, Glantz uses his voice very much like an instrument. The effect is a very wide contrast in tone color and dynamics.[14]

Examples of *subito piano* occur in the composition *MiM'kom'cha* ("From Your place, our King, You will appear") on the words *Tim'loch Be'Tzion* ("When will You reign in Zion?") and *Be'Shi'rei U'ze'cha* ("In the songs of Your might"); in the composition *Te'fi'lat Tal* ("The prayer for dew") on the word *Ye'hi* ("Let there be"); in the composition *She'ma Yis'ra'el* ("Hear O Israel") on the

---

12 *Staccato* — detached notes, i.e. the opposite of *legato* (a smooth connection between notes).
13 *Subito Piano/Subito Forte* — literally: suddenly soft/suddenly loud (i.e. from one note to the next).
14 Variation and contrast in force and intensity (as in the spectrum from *pianissimo* to *fortissimo*/very soft to very loud).

opening *Yis'ra'el* and in the composition *Ash'rei* ("Blessed are they") on the word *Od* ("forever"). *Subito forte* can be found in *MiM'kom'cha* on the word *Ma'tai* ("When?") in the first and third repetitions, on the words *Ve'Ei'nei'nu Tir'ena* ("and our eyes will witness"), on the words *Al Ye'dei Da'vid* ("by the hands of David") and in *Be'Tzeit Yis'ra'el* ("Upon the Israelites' exodus from Egypt") on the words *He'Ha'rim Ra'ke'du Che'Ey'lim* ("The mountains skipped like rams").

Glissando

While it may not be unusual to find a cantor slide from a climactic high note down to the final tonic to conclude a piece *(portamento),* the kind of chromatic [15] *glissando* [16] presented by Glantz on the word *Ve'Yish'me're'cha* (and guard you) in his composition *Bir'kat Ko'ha'nim* is a lengthy linear movement which is clearly synonymous with a stringed instrument such as a violin. The chromatic nature of this ascending and descending musical line is additionally something which is much more likely to be found in an *avant-garde* composition.

Example 5: Glantz: *Bir'kat Ko'ha'nim*

As always, Glantz's intention was to emphasize the meaning of the words. The awe-inspiring nature of the blessing, which the Almighty can bestow upon an individual, is beyond our comprehension, and as such is reflected through this unusual vocal chromatic *glissando*.

Sprechstimme

Sprechstimme [17] is a technique that probably derived from opera; the earliest known use is found in Engelbert Humperdinck's opera *Königskinder* in 1897. Later, *Sprechstimme* appeared more particularly in Operetta and also amongst the Second Viennese School composers including Arnold Schoenberg (1874-1951) and his pupils.

A spoken word, phrase, or exclamation is woven in between melodic phrases, thereby enhancing the singer's ability to communicate with his audience as if he were conversing, imploring

---

15 The Chromatic scale is one that uses nothing but semitones.

16 *Glissando* — taken from the French *Glisser*; to slide. A series of adjacent notes up or down the scale.

17 *Sprechstimme* — a form of dramatic declamation between singing and speaking.

— crying out as much as singing. Some splendid examples of this technique can be found on a series of Eurodisc recordings featuring the German tenor Rudolf Shock singing the operettas of Strauss, Lehar, von Suppé and the Jewish Hungarian composer Emmerich Kalman. In more recent times there is no better example of *Sprechstimme* than Rex Harrison's performance in the Broadway musical "My Fair Lady."

Two cantors adopted the use of *Sprechstimme* in their cantorial recitatives: Glantz and Pierre Pinchik. Both utilize this technique skillfully, connecting the spoken fragments to the melodic phrases that preceded or followed them, but Glantz added a mysterious mystical element, which created more of a "mood" rather than a mere "effect."

Among the numerous examples of *Sprechstimme* found in Glantz's delivery, the opening of *MiM'kom'cha* begins with the spoken words *Ba'ruch Ke'vod* ("Blessed be God"). Similarly, the beginning words of the composition *Hash'ki'vei'nu* ("God, make us lie down in peace"), are delivered in *Sprechstimme* and so, later on, are the words *Ve'Ha'gen Ba'a'dei'nu* ("Shield us"). The most poignant examples of *Sprechstimme* are found at the outset of *Eich Nif'tach Peh* ("How can we open our mouths before Thee?") and in the composition *A'hav'ti* ("I love when God hears my voice") from the *Ha'llel* prayer service, where Glantz intersperses the spoken style throughout the piece, to express the powerful contrasting themes of despair and consolation.

Intervals

In many ways it is in the area of intervals[18] where Glantz's unique style is established. The fascination with chromatic intervals, modal borrowing, trills, use of the tritone, and the outlining of dissonant harmony are all part of the Glantz sound. One gets the feeling that he was deliberately manipulating sound; experimenting with forbidden fruit, as it were.

> *It is in the area of intervals where Glantz's unique style is established. The fascination with chromatic intervals, modal borrowing, trills, use of the tritone, and the outlining of dissonant harmony are all part of the Glantz sound. One gets the feeling that he was deliberately manipulating sound; experimenting with forbidden fruit, as it were.*

The Oxford dictionary of music says of the tritone: "it is a difficult interval to sing and hence usually avoided in composing vocal music." Yet it is precisely the tritone (or augmented fourth) that Glantz chooses to portray the words *O'yev, De'ver, Ve'Che'rev* (enemies,

---

18 Intervals — the numerical distance between any two notes reflecting their difference in pitch.

plague, and sword) in *Hash'ki'vei'nu*. He does so to emphasize the dread implicit in the words "enemy," "plague," and "sword."

The trill is understood as a vibration causing the alternation of two musical tones a scale degree apart. The rapidity of Glantz's trill heightened the intensity of any given passage. Good examples of this technique are found as part of the opening *She'ma* ("Hear") in *She'ma Yis'ra'el* and on the final *Ba'ruch* (*Yo'mei'ru*) in the composition *Az Be'Kol*. The trill was an important vocal ornament in the eighteenth century, but not in Glantz's time. It is, however, a vital element in the repertoire of Classical and Romantic piano *concerti*. Perhaps this was another inherent carry-over from Glantz's training as a pianist.

Although firmly committed to the Jewish prayer modes in his composition, Glantz occasionally visits less common modal territory resulting in an augmented variety of musical colors. An intriguing example of this is found in the use of the Dorian mode throughout the opening section of *Az Be'kol*.

Further, the use of "accidental"[19] notes has always been a means of creating a more richly varied palette. Glantz's music is no exception. Through the use of chromatic intervals, sequences and phrases, he creates astonishing images of awe and wonder. There are countless examples of chromatic movement in Glantz's compositions.

As mentioned earlier, under the heading of *Glissando*, there is the unusual chromatic phrase in the *Bir'kat Ko'ha'nim* composition (**Example 5**). Another such unique chromatic phrase occurs on the word *MiM'ko'mo* ("From His place") in the composition *MiM'kom'cha*, where Glantz wavers back and forth on the minor second (the notes E and D#). The context of this chromatic interval, along with the preceding sequential phrase, conjures up a wondrous illustration of the limitless parameters of God's abode.

Chromatic sequences are also most interesting. Look at the following example from *Az Be'kol*. It is the first note in each grouping (illustrated by the arrows below) that forms the chromatic sequence.

Example 6: Glantz: *Az Be'kol*

mit - na - s' - im____ l' - u - mat s' - ra - fim____

---

19 Accidental notes are notes that are not part of the prevailing key.

The use of dissonant harmony moving toward atonality[20] began to take root even amongst late-Romantic classical composers making use of chromatic melody lines and chord progressions while still anchored in a tonal context.

Melodic tension is created when Glantz jumps to a minor seventh interval on the word *Av'de'cha* ("Your servant") in the composition *Bir'kat Ko'ha'nim*. The A flat, borrowing from the fourth mode of F harmonic minor (*Mi'She'Bei'rach*, or "Ukrainian-Dorian"), is held against the subdominant (B flat major) establishing a conflicting dissonant effect for the plagal cadence (IV-I resolution).

Of course, dissonant harmony or the use of chromatic notes, in and of themselves, do not necessarily interfere with the overall feeling of tonality or tonal harmony in a given piece. Even as far back as 1785, Mozart used chromatic intervals that were considered radical at the time in the opening of his so-called *Dissonance Quartet*, KV465.

Look at the similarity in the chromatic opening of Glantz's *Ein Ke'Er'ke'cha* ("There is none like You") as compared to the opening cello statement in the third movement of Brahms' Double Concerto in A minor, Op. 102. Both of these attractive chromatic melody lines are still very much rooted in a tonal context.

Example 7: Glantz: *Ein Ke'Er'ke'cha*

Example 8: Brahms: Double Concerto in A minor, Op. 102

It is also worth noting Glantz's occasional use of microtones, an interval that is smaller than a semitone (the semitone being the smallest interval used in Western music), indicated by arrows over the notes[21] (as in **Example 7**).

---

20 Atonality is music that is not based on harmonic and melodic relationships revolving around a key center.
21 Charles Heller, *What to Listen for in Jewish Music*. (Toronto: Ecanthus Press, 2006) pp. 276.

Opera and the Rolled R

Those who have studied Italian opera know that an Italian R is a rolled R (known as the alveolar trill in the IPA [International Phonetic Alphabet], symbolized by the [ř]) such as in pronunciation of [Ř]*econdita A*[ř]*monia*, the tenor aria from Puccini's opera *Tosca*. A Modern Hebrew R is a much more guttural sound; the French R somewhere in between.

Glantz must have had a keen interest in Italian opera aside from the pianistic aspect of his classical grounding, since he quite regularly uses a strong Italian R in his pronunciation, seemingly for emphasis.

We find the use of the rolled R in *Hash'ki'vei'nu* on the words *De've*[ř], *Ve'che*[ř]*ev* and in his *MiM'kom'cha* on the words *ti*[ř]*e'na, Ka'da'va*[ř] and *Ha'Amu*[ř].

While we are on the subject of opera, could it be coincidental that the phrase below (example 9), from *Le'chu Ne'ra'ne'na* ("Let us sing to the Lord"), seems extremely similar to **Example 10**, an excerpt from the tenor aria *M'appari Tutt'amor* in Friedrich von Flotow's opera *"Martha"*?

Example 9: Glantz: *Le'chu Ne'ra'ne'na*

Example 10: *M'appari Tutt'amor* aria from Friedrich von Flotow's opera *"Martha"*

The influences that shape a composer's music are many, and Glantz was very much a product of his environment. He was exposed to the great European musical tradition and found a place for its richness in his music. The influence of his Russian musical schooling, and the effect of his greatest professor, Reinhold Gliere can be felt as well. Consider the melody line of Glantz's

Glantz was exposed to the great European musical tradition and found a place for its richness in his music. The influence of his Russian musical schooling and the effect of his greatest professor Reinhold Gliere can be felt as well.

Sim Sha'lom ("Grant peace"). He begins in the upper register in a very insistent dramatic manner, very deliberate and emphatic. The performance style, more even than the melodic line itself, rings of the folk element — not dissimilar to the *Russian Sailor's Dance* in Gliere's famous ballet score *"The Red Poppy."*

Gliere was said to have drifted away from the Russian nationalist school and began introducing Impressionistic elements into his music. The Impressionist period in music began in France in the late nineteenth century and continued through the middle of the twentieth century. Likened to the art of Claude Monet (1840-1926) and Pierre Auguste Renoir (1841-1919), whence the term Impressionism is derived, Impressionist composers like Claude Debussy (1862-1918) and Maurice Ravel (1875-1937) were essentially romantic composers who expanded harmonic detail to bring a more vivid color to their music. The use of the whole-tone scale took precedence over Major and Minor scales, and various other new techniques were introduced in an effort to create an effect in their works focusing on tone color and atmosphere rather than strict musical form. Glantz, who was born in 1898, was evolving musically during the height of the Impressionist period.

While some elements of Impressionism are reflected in Glantz's music (the use of the Greek modes as alternative scales, mood creation and dissonant intervals), there seems a much stronger tendency toward his identification with Expressionism, particularly in his later compositions.

Expressionism, another musical movement that borrowed its title from the art of painting, emerged roughly during the same period. Expressionism focused on an outpouring of emotional angst. The psychological theories of Sigmund Freud, the First World War, and later the Great Depression, all reflected the mindset of the time and likely influenced Expressionist development. "Whereas Impressionism sought to represent objects of the external world as perceived at a given moment, Expressionism, proceeding in the opposite direction, sought to represent inner experience."[22]

The highly distinctive Expressionist composers Arnold Schoenberg (1874-1951), and his pupils Alban Berg (1885-1935) and Anton Webern (1883-1945), sought to "distort reality for emotional effect."[23] Their music underwent three evolutionary periods, initially characterized by Post-Romantic expanded tonality, later a totally chromatic atonality, and finally Schoenberg's twelve-tone compositional technique (serialism).

Glantz's use of extreme contrast in dynamics, lengthy chromatic phrases, and emotion-laden *Sprechstimme* all point to the influence of Expressionism.

---

22 Donald Jay Grout, *A History of Western Music, 5th ed.* (New York: W. W. Norton and Co., 1996) pp. 735.
23 "Expressionism." See *Wikipedia:* <http://en.wikipedia.org/wiki/Category:Expressionism>.

With the unfolding of the twentieth century came a rapid and dramatic evolution of musical development. As in the field of classical music, by the middle of the century, the *"Golden Era of Cha'za'nut"* had peaked and begun to wane.

Historically, Leib Glantz was the luminary figure of his time — his cantorial compositions representing the final metamorphosis of the *"Golden Era."* In addition to his vocal brilliance and personal creativity, the fusion of the traditional cantorial art form with the evolving sounds and trends of period-related classicism, as well as the influence of instrumental music, made Leib Glantz's enigmatic and innovative style unique amongst his peers — a virtual beacon highlighting a pathway toward the future. He was the sole exponent of what can respectfully be called "Progressive Twentieth Century Cha'za'nut." As Glantz himself once remarked, it would take several generations before his music was understood.

> *Leib Glantz was the luminary figure of his time — his cantorial compositions representing the final metamorphosis of the "Golden Era." In addition to his vocal brilliance and personal creativity, the fusion of the traditional cantorial art form with the evolving sounds and trends of period-related classicism, as well as the influence of instrumental music, made Leib Glantz's enigmatic and innovative style unique amongst his peers — a virtual beacon highlighting a pathway toward the future.*

Leib Glantz singing at a concert in Tel Aviv, Israel, accompanied by pianist and composer Nachum Nardi (1947).

12

The Glantz/Pinchik Conundrum

DR. JOSEPH A. LEVINE[1]

His son saw Cantor Leib Glantz (1898-1964) as representing "the end of an epoch, not a new beginning; he left no followers, not even imitators."[2] Yet, the cantor most like him in pouring the flame of Chasidic fervor into new musical vessels, his fellow Ukrainian Pierre Pinchik (1895-1971), enjoyed that sincerest form of flattery from the beginning, and continues to do so. Why should this be? Why did Glantz's *Cha'za'nut*, whose excellence equaled Pinchik's in every respect and actually exceeded it in vocal brilliance, lead to a dead end while his rival's style inspires copycats to this day, over a generation after they had both departed this world?

They were born three years apart at a time when Judaism's mystical stream had been reduced to a trickle, until the Yiddish playwright Shin Anski opened its floodgates with his dramatic legend, *The Dybbuk*, in 1920. An eyewitness reported on its opening night at the Eliseum Theater in Warsaw:

> It became pitch black. Before me I saw an old Ta'llit (prayer shawl) soaked in tears. In the thick darkness I saw a tall young Chasid, with a prayer book and a candle. He looked afar off, there where nothing comes to an end. When the second curtain rose in the prayer house, I heard broken, torn sounds, an unclear melody; notes which moan; ecstatic communing with God; notes which are drawn from generations and generations, slowly, very slowly. They sing slowly and rock with nervous speed. This

---

1 Dr. Joseph A. Levine has taught Sacred Music at the Jewish Theological Seminary in New York, the Academy for Jewish Religion in Riverdale, and the School of Jewish Liturgical Music at the University of London. He served on the Rabbinical Assembly Mahzor Committee and is editor of the Journal of Synagogue Music.

2 Ezra [Jerry] Glantz, in a retrospective on his father's career, marking the 100th anniversary of Glantz's birth. *Proceedings of the Cantors Assembly Jubilee Convention* (New York: Marriott at the World Trade Center), 1998:18.

Leibele Glantz and Pierre Pinchik, singing in choir in a synagogue in 1903. (Bottom row, Glantz, age 5, fifth from left; Pinchik, age 7, third from right, with Star of David). Both Glantz and Pinchik later immigrated to the United States to become famous cantors.

lasted quite a long time, before they spoke the first word. It was almost like a big overture, but without an orchestra. And I must admit that no orchestra in the world and no composer could draw one in, into the mystical Chasidic atmosphere, better than did the movements and the torn notes of these Jews.[3]

This was the atmosphere in which Pierre Pinchik and Leib Glantz grew to young manhood. They both arrived in the United States in 1926, and almost simultaneously achieved international fame: Pinchik with his recording of *Ra'za De'Sha'bbat* ("The Mystery of Sabbath") and Glantz with his recording of *She'ma Yis'ra'el* ("Hear, O Israel"), both on the RCA Victor label. Glantz's *She'ma Yis'ra'el* was the first of the two compositions to be published, in 1949, while Pinchik's *Ra'za De'Sha'bbat* waited another fifteen years before it appeared in a book of his recitatives in 1964. *She'ma Yis'ra'el* was published first because it is the most accessible — and therefore the most frequently performed — of all Glantz's works. It is also more familiar-

---

3 Yiddish operetta composer Joseph Rumshinsky (1881-1950), cited in Nahma Sandrow, *Vagabond Stars* (New York: Harper and Row), 1977:219.

sounding and less exotic (read: Chasidic) to American Jews. Part of the *Mu'saf Ke'du'sha* (Sanctification prayer of the Additional prayer service) on Sabbaths and Festivals, its text in the Glantz recording is the standard Ashkenazic, non-Chasidic version.[4]

Pinchik's rightly celebrated *Ra'za De'Sha'bbat*, which Glantz admired greatly,[5] is a setting of the mystical Aramaic preamble to Friday Night *Ma'a'riv* proper. It proclaims the union of God's "Presence" (*She'chi'na*) with the Holy One in the Heavenly Kingdom, simultaneous with Sabbath's arrival in the mundane world. Its text, from the *Zo'har* (Book of "Splendor," Jewish mysticism's primary source),[6] appears in the Chasidic rite that Glantz and Pinchik knew from childhood. Pinchik specifically chose it as his entrée to a worldwide audience, including the ultra-pious. The music, as well as his performance of it, treats each word with the respect due a visionary insight into the profound meaning of being at One: through our welcoming the Sabbath "below," the Glory Throne is prepared for the One Above. In *She'ma Yis'ra'el*, on the other hand, Glantz set forth his own exquisitely musical interpretation of a laudatory modal chant pattern (*Nu'sach*) that his fellow-cantors had been singing for decades and still do, in traditional synagogues. In effect, his recording "froze" that version,[7] making it common coin for generations of *Cha'za'nim* to use at auditions, concerts and worship services.

> In She'ma Yis'ra'el *Glantz set forth his own exquisitely musical interpretation of a laudatory modal chant pattern* (Nu'sach) *that his fellow-cantors had been singing for decades and still do, in traditional synagogues. In effect, his recording "froze" that version, making it common coin for generations of* Cha'za'nim.

The perception of Glantz's and Pinchik's lyric tenor voices by audiences did not vary that greatly. If Pinchik's voice was sweeter in tone, Glantz's was wider in range. If Glantz's could produce a more shattering *fortissimo*, Pinchik's could melt stone with its *pianissimo*. If Pinchik's could move you to fear of Heaven, Glantz's' could stir you to fear of sin. If Glantz's could induce you to feel shame, Pinchik's could raise you to a state of exaltation. If Pinchik's could

---

4 The Chasidic variant beginning after *Hu Mo'shi'ei'nu* ("He is our Savior"), used by Sephardim as well, actually makes more sense than the Ashkenazic version because it spells out what is being promised in the phrase that follows in both rites, "He will again proclaim on our behalf" — *Ve'Hu Yash'mi'ei'nu: Hu Yo'shi'ei'nu Ve'Yig'a'lei'nu Shei'nit* ("He will again redeem us") *Ve'Yash'mi'ei'nu Be'Ra'cha'mav Le'Ei'nei Kol Chai Lei'mor* ("and will mercifully proclaim the following before all living beings"), "*Hen Ga'al'ti Et'chem A'cha'rit Ke'Rei'shit*" ("Behold, I have redeemed you in the end as I did in the beginning").

5 Ezra [Jerry] Glantz, *Cantors Assembly Proceedings*, 1998, p. 16.

6 Compiled by Moses Ben Shemtov de Leon in the thirteenth century; part III, Book of Exodus, *Pa'ra'shat Te'ru'mah:*135a-135b.

7 For this telling analysis of the long-term effect that definitive cantorial phonograph recordings of universally used texts, by star cantors like Glantz, had on Chazanic creativity — I am indebted to Henry Sapoznik, curator of the Cantorial Recordings Collection at YIVO in New York; private communication to the writer, November, 1985.

inspire you to regular *To'rah* study, Glantz's could convince you that prayer is heard. And if we reversed every component in the foregoing equations, the analogy would still ring true — like the sound of their voices.

Pinchik and Glantz both held aloft the torch of Chasidism as they stood before the *A'mud,*[8] yet they guarded its flame differently because of their individual temperaments. In prayer, Glantz was passionate and intense,[9] never officiating without the accompaniment of a choir.[10] Pinchik appeared more gentle and withdrawn, preferring to guest-officiate alone on Sabbaths, while keeping worshippers on the edge of their seats by constantly thwarting expectations through the element of surprise.[11] When people attempted to touch the Torah with the corners of their prayer shawls as he carried it from the Ark at the front of the synagogue to the centrally situated *Bi'mah* (reading platform), he would shroud the scroll with his own extra-large *Ta'llit,* as if protecting it from harm (in seemingly calculated re-enactment of Mark Chagall's painting, *Rabbi with Red To'rah*).[12]

Glantz, a stickler for propriety, used less dramatic methods. He'd catch a congregation unaware through sudden changes of mode rather than with eye-catching theatrical gestures, and he achieved the same end: maintaining the momentum of worship. Away from the *A'mud,* he researched and taught. The instructional material he compiled for students at the cantorial school he established and directed in Tel Aviv[13] offers countless examples of this subtle musical legerdemain. **Example 1**[14] shows a passage from the third of three modes that Glantz wanted students to learn as variants of basic *Nu'sach* for chanting the Friday night *Ma'a'riv* service. This excerpt from *Ve'Sham'ru* ("Let the children of Israel observe the Sabbath throughout their generations") moves the natural-Minor mode *Ma'gen A'vot* ("Our Forebears' Shield") on D (Glantz calls it a "Choral Major" mode), to the lowered-7th Major mode *A'do'nai Ma'lach* ("God Reigns") on D, to *A'do'nai Ma'lach* on

> *For a musician like Glantz, hearing his students seamlessly execute passages was a dream come true; for the students, attempting to get it right must have been a nightmare...*

G, to *A'do'nai Ma'lach* on F, and back to *Ma'gen A'vot* on D — all within eight measures. For a musician like Glantz, hearing his students seamlessly execute passages like this one was a dream come true; for the students, attempting to get it right must have been a nightmare...

---

8 Prayer lectern.

9 Ezra [Jerry] Glantz, *Cantors Assembly Proceedings,* 1998, p. 15.

10 Akiva Zimmermann. *Be'Ron Ya'chad,* Itzhak Alfassi, ed. (Tel Aviv: The Central Cantorial Archive), 1988:217.

11 The writer's impression of Friday night and Shabbat morning services that Pinchik led at the Stone Avenue Talmud Torah in Brooklyn, NY during the Spring of 1957.

12 1930; now hanging in the Tel Aviv Museum, *Beit Ha'Te'fu'tsot.*

13 The Tel Aviv Institute of Jewish Liturgical Music was established in 1959.

14 Leib Glantz. *Ri'nat Ha'Ko'desh,* Yehoshua Zohar, ed. (Tel Aviv: Israel Music Institute), 1965:48.

Example 1. The opening of Glantz's *Ve'Sham'ru* for Friday night, in "Choral Major":

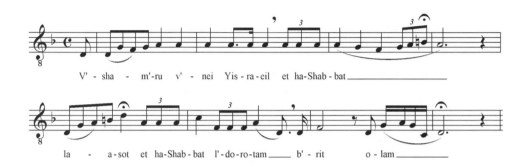

It wasn't the way Glantz (or anyone else) would normally chant *Ma'a'riv Le'Sha'bbat* in real life, but rather, a theoretical construct that he came up with "after years of searching, examination, and striving to find the musical truth."[15] Built on "two competing modes, the Aeolian and the Dorian"[16] — one with a flatted 6th degree and one with a natural 6th degree — Glantz labels it "*Nu'sach* from Sinai...established melody that no cantor has the right to alter in any way whatsoever."[17] Still, the music of Example 1 is unclear. Its key signature indicates that the 6th degree (B) should be flatted. Yet, of eight occurrences in the whole piece, the B is raised six times when ascending, flatted once when ascending and flatted once when descending. Where, then, does the Aeolian mode (B natural) end, and the Dorian mode (Bb) begin? And what specific *Nu'sach* from Sinai is the one that dictates when exceptions are to be made?

Glantz maintained that the Mixolydian (the segment G—G^1 of a diatonic scale) and the Pentatonic (a 5-tone scale to the octave, having no semitones — and starting on different tones, yielding five different modes) are the chief scales of our *Nu'sach*. He offers what he claims is the "traditional" Festival *Cha'ti'ma* (cadential motif) as proof. See **Example 2, *Ve'E'met A'do'nai*** ("God's truth is forever," *Ha'llel* Psalm 117).[18]

Example 2. Glantz's "traditional" *Festival Cha'ti'ma* motif from the *Ha'llel* service:

---

15 Leib Glantz. *Ha'llel and Three Festivals*, David Loeb, ed. (Tel Aviv: Institute of Jewish Liturgical Music), 1968:13.

16 *Ibid.*, p. 18.

17 *Ibid.*, p. 15.

18 *Ibid.*, p. 14.

Most authorities who cite this Festival ending for blessings or paragraphs do so as follows (**Example 3**).[19]

Example 3. The Festival *Cha'ti'ma motif* as transmitted by most authorities:

Other authorities avoid the argument by retaining only a portion of the motif's descending melismatic[20] run (bracketed), concluding before its final note (**Example 4**).[21]

Example 4. The Festival *Cha'ti'ma motif* — with melismatic run in partial form:

Motifs, after all, are the building blocks of our *Nu'sach*;[22] scales were derived *from* them much later, as a means of categorization. The C# and Bb (raised 7th / lowered 4th degrees in a natural minor mode on D) in Example 3 may also appear in any other liturgical passage, no matter in which of the three principal prayer modes it is being sung: *A'do'nai Ma'lach; Ma'gen A'vot,* or *A'ha'va Ra'bbah* (major, with lowered 2nd and 6th degrees). For the sake of convenience I have elsewhere labeled any similarly altered passage as Ukrainian/Dorian, which I categorize as one of three secondary prayer modes.[23] One might also define Ukrainian/Dorian as an augmented-4th Dorian mode.[24] Its characteristic motif — the melismatic run of Example 3 —

19 H. Weintraub (1859:#116b), L. Lewandowski (1871:#73), A. Baer (1877:#791), M. Wodak (1897:#404), A. Friedmann (1901:#250), S. Sulzer (1905:#195), A. Z. Idelsohn, Vol. VIII (1932:#102), B. Z. Hoffman (ca. 1960:58), S. Ravitz (1964:136), I. Alter (1979:33), A. Y. Weisgal (Levine 1981:#408), N. Schall (1990:53-54).

20 Melismatic — a group of notes sung to one syllable of text.

21 A. Berkovitch (Kalechnik; ca. 1900:86), G. Ephros (1948:174, 1.), A. Katchko (1952:#195), M. Nathanson (1974:40).

22 Abraham Z. Idelsohn. "Songs of the Babylonian Jews," in *Thesaurus of Hebrew Oriental Melodies*, Vol. II (Berlin: Benjamin Harz), 1923:27-28).

23 Joseph A. Levine. *Synagogue Song in America* (Northvale, NJ: Jason Aronson), 2001:112-115.

24 Sholom Kalib. *The Musical Tradition of the Eastern European Synagogue*, Vol. I, part 1 (Syracuse, NY: Syracuse University Press), 2002: Example 133b.

generally starts on the 5th degree in *A'do'nai Ma'lach*. **Example 5**, *Ye'chad'shei'hu* ("May the Holy One bless this new month" from the Sabbath Morning *To'rah* Service)[25] shows the Ukrainian/Dorian motif in a run that will be expanded by moving up to the octave from the 5th degree in *A'do'nai Ma'lach* on G, before descending all the way down to the tonic, in virtuosic style.

Example 5. Zavel Kwartin's *Ye'chad'shei'hu in A'do'nai Ma'lach*: Ukrainian/Dorian motif expanded from 5th up to octave and down to tonic, in virtuosic style:

Example 6, *Pe'er Ve'Cha'vod* ("God is acclaimed in beauty and glory," Sabbath and Festival *Shach'rit*)[26] in the second principal prayer mode — *Ma'gen A'vot* — on F#, shows the Ukrainian/Dorian motif starting on a 5th degree that's been temporarily lowered for the sake of a passing modulation, rising a fifth to the supertonic that's also been temporarily lowered, and then descending to the supertonic.

---

25 *Idem*, citing Zavel Kwartin, *"Ye'chad'shei'hu," Shiroth Zebulon* (New York: self-published), 1938:40.

26 Eliezer Gerovitch. *Schirei Simroh* (Rostow on Don: self-published), 1904:#19.

Example 6. Eliezer Gerovitch's *Pe'er Ve'Cha'vod* **in** *Ma'gen A'vot* **— Ukrainian/Dorian motif starting on temporarily lowered 5th and supertonic degrees:**

Example 7, *Ve'Lo Ne'ta'to* ("You gave the *To'rah* to Israel"), from the Sabbath *Shach'rit A'mi'da* service),[27] shows the Ukrainian/Dorian motif in *A'ha'va Ra'bbah* ("God's love for Israel is great"), last of the three principal prayer modes, also identifiable as a major-third Phrygian, i.e., a G—A flat—B—C—D—E flat—F—G^1 scale.[28] Here, the Ukrainian/Dorian motif rises from 4th-to-6th degree and descends to the subtonic — a replica of the classic version by most authorities **(Example 3),** but in a different mode.

27 Salomon Sulzer. *Schir Zion*, Joseph Sulzer, ed. (Frankfurt am Main: J. Kauffmann Verlag), 1922:#87.

28 Sholom Kalib. *The Musical Tradition of the Eastern European Synagogue*, Vol. I, part 2 (Syracuse, NY: Syracuse University Press), 2002:133-134.

Example 7. Salomon Sulzer's *Ve'Lo Ne'ta'to:* **classic Ukrainian/Dorian motif in** *A'ha'va Ra'bbah* **prayer mode, from 4th-to-6th degrees and down to subtonic:**

We now return to Leib Glantz's understanding of the Ukrainian/Dorian motif. In defending his unique version of it — the same notes that we have come to expect but without a raised 4th and lowered 3rd degree — he decries the fact that "almost all cantors sing the passages of the *Ha'llel* service in the Harmonic Minor...the peak of melancholy."[29] The melancholy Harmonic Minor to which Glantz alludes is, of course, none other than our poignant Ukrainian/Dorian motif. In Glantz's usage —**Example 2** — it displays all the color of an albino in a snowstorm. A dab of C# and a touch of Bb would have imparted a shade of longing to the chant, an emotional highlighting of the Psalm text it purports to tone-paint — our people's most universal aspiration — that the day speedily comes when all nations will praise God, Whose truth will last beyond the end of time. Halleluyah!

Any song expressing that hope needs all the yearning we can give it — until it becomes a reality. It's not as if Glantz himself never used the Ukrainian/Dorian mode/motif/coloring in *Ha'llel*, where, according to him, it doesn't belong. **Example 8,**[30] *Ki Chi'latz'ta Naf'shi Mi'Ma'vet* ("You have delivered my soul from death," *Ha'llel* Psalm 116) cites the motif repeatedly — seven times partially and twice in full.

29 Glantz, *Ha'llel and Three Festivals*, 1968, p. 14.
30 *Ibid.*, pp. 78-80.

Example 8. Glantz's use of Ukrainian/Dorian: *Ki Chi'latz'ta Naf'shi Mi'Ma'vet* **from the prayer** *"A'hav'ti"* **from the** *Ha'llel* **Service:**

Glantz's counterpart, Pinchik, never felt the need to teach *Nu'sach* or to enter into a discussion of its theoretical underpinnings. Nor did he ever hold a full-time position after his six years of serving as Chief Cantor at the Great Synagogue in Leningrad from 1920 to 1925. The Communist authorities granted him the privilege of that high religious function so long as he agreed to set anti-religious song lyrics to music. Typically, he chose well-known synagogue melodies like *A'tah E'chad* ("You are One" from the Sabbath *Min'cha* service) and *Ti'kan'ta Sha'bbat* ("You ordained the Sabbath Day" from the Sabbath *Mu'saf* service).[31] Tiring of this game by 1926, he emigrated to the United States where, from his arrival, he concertized widely, recorded extensively and officiated regularly as a guest *Cha'zan*. When he raised or lowered modal degrees, he usually did so in order to change key, and he executed the transition so swiftly that it was virtually undetectable. **Example 9,**[32] *Be'Rosh Ha'Sha'na* ("On New Year the

31 Zimmermann, Akiva, *Be'Ron Ya'chad*, 1988, pp. 371-372.

32 Recorded anonymously at a High Holy Day service that Pinchik led in the mid-1950s at an unknown location, transcribed by Sholom Kalib, presented at the Cantors Assembly's annual convention in 1999 and published in a subsequent article, *"Nu'sach in the Eastern European Synagogue: Its Diverse Elements and Interdependence with Cha'za'nut,"* Journal of Synagogue Music, Vol. 27, No. 1, Fall/Winter 2000:24.

decree is written"), from the High Holy Day *Mu'saf* service, modulates almost imperceptibly from D *Ma'gen A'vot* to D *A'ha'va Ra'bbah*, to E *A'ha'va Ra'bbah*, and to E *Ma'gen A'vot*, in its opening fourteen measures.

Example 9. The opening of Pinchik's *Be'Rosh Ha'Sha'na*, showing four swift and almost imperceptible modulations:

Leib Glantz could command the rapt attention of a worshipping congregation just as effectively, without modulation, by reiterating a figuration similar to Pinchik's *Be'Rosh Ha'Sha'na Yi'ka'tei'vun* in a single key, but with a steadily increasing amount of embellishment. In addition, he intuitively sustained a quasi-psalmodic parallelism[33] in his phrasing, whereby he himself "answered" each musical thought in the antecedent half of a verse by its slightly varied "echo." He often did this in sections where he wanted the freedom of moving rapidly without having to wait for choral replies. Inevitably, worshippers davening[34] along in an undertone would fill the gap with impromptu hums or harmonized words. This type of solo call and unrehearsed response very much resembles the antebellum Gospel "Callers" in black church-

33 Levine, *Synagogue Song in America*, 2001, pp. 7, 29, 34.
34 This anglicized verb developed from Yiddish *daven'n*: "praying"; half aloud, half to oneself.

es, who could inspire worshipful cries of "Amen," "Halleluyah" or "Tell it, Brother" from the pews, by example alone.[35] Moreover, Glantz achieved this effect even in the versions of his compositions that he condensed, simplified and transposed downward for his students.

Example 10; *Sho'mer Yis'ra'el* ("Guardian of Israel"), from the *Ta'cha'nun* section of weekday *Shach'rit and Min'cha* services, gives the opening five phrases of his famous recording.[36] Each phrase sounds as if it could be part of a learning session between master and pupil, in conformity with the Talmud's advice concerning teaching techniques: Pose the question according to subject; give the answer according to rule.[37] I've therefore transcribed them in psalmodic half-verses with semi-bar lines and no fixed meter, the rhythm to be determined solely by stresses and number of syllables. Verse segments are marked 1a/1b, 2a/2b, etc.

Example 10. The opening of Glantz's *Sho'mer Yis'ra'el* recording, transcribed as psalmodic-style half-verses with no fixed meter; rhythm to be determined by stresses and number of syllables. Verse segments are marked 1a/1b, 2a/2b, etc:

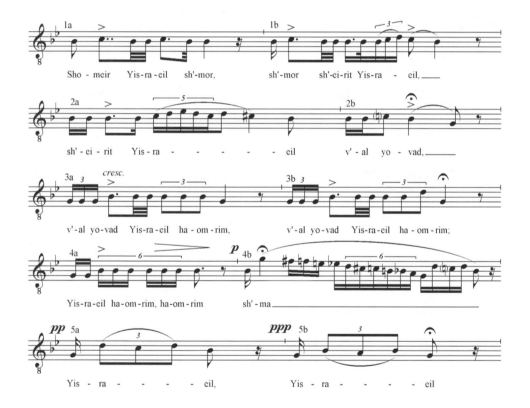

35 Nat Hentoff, *"The Joyous Power of Black Gospel Music,"* citing David Stowe, *How Sweet the Sound* (Cambridge, MA: Harvard University Press), 2005; *Wall Street Journal*, March 29, 2006.

36 Leib Glantz. *Sho'mer Yis'ra'el*, Hebraica Records (RCA Camden Label, ca. 1930) LPZ-H70P 3658, side 2, track 4; transcribed by the writer.

37 *Sho'el Ke'In'ya'no, Mei'shiv Ka'Ha'la'cha*; *Mish'na A'vot*, 5:10.

For a version that novices could manage comfortably, Glantz pitched the recitative a 4th lower, in D minor, reduced the number of verse-equivalents from five to four, streamlined the *coloratura* runs, and condensed the number of notes from ninety-one to seventy-two. Notwithstanding these simplifications, **Example 11**[38] retains the balanced parallelism of its fuller recorded prototype, along with the tension that's needed to hold every pair of phrases together in a kind of dynamic reciprocity.

Example 11. The opening of Glantz's student-version *Sho'mer Yis'ra'el*, still transcribed as parallel psalmodic-style half-verses marked 1a/1b, 2a/2b, etc:

It's been said that "the originality of Chasidism lies in the fact that mystics who…had discovered the secret of true *D'vei'kut* (closeness to God) turned to the people with their mystical knowledge…and undertook to teach the secrets to all men of good will."[39] By the same token, the uniqueness of Chasidic-born cantors Pierre Pinchik and Leib Glantz lies in their having taken the raw emotion of the Chasidic *Shti'bl* (prayer room), preserved its essence through their innate musicality, and brought it to mainstream synagogues in a form that was at once musically accessible and aesthetically impeccable. They not only mined the ore of their childhood; they refined it into pure gold!

38 Glantz, *Ri'nat Ha'Ko'desh*, 1965, p. 18.
39 Gershom G. Scholem. *Major Trends in Jewish Myticism* (New York: Schoken Books), 1941:342.

For over thirty years Leib Glantz's father had served as *Ba'al Te'fi'la* (prayer leader) in the *Beit Mid'rash*[40] of the Talner Chasidim, as had Leib's grandfather and great-grandfather. The Talner dynasty was known for its joyful *Ni'gu'nim* — melodies requiring no words — that part of Chasidic lifestyle most emulated by Jews of other persuasions. Almost every great European-born *Cha'zan* of the twentieth century was either reared in a Chasidic environment, or familiarized himself sufficiently with its musical practice to imbue his own singing with the same

> *The uniqueness of Chasidic-born cantors Pierre Pinchik and Leib Glantz lay in their having taken the raw emotion of the Chasidic Shti'bl (prayer room), preserved its essence through their innate musicality, and brought it to mainstream synagogues in a form that was at once musically accessible and aesthetically impeccable.*

infectious spirit when it was required. And should a *Cha'zan* have been reared in Northern Europe's more austere Lithuanian centers of Jewish learning, where they studied Talmud "with two thumbs" — as it were — he would still have spent a significant part of his childhood singing *Ze'mi'rot*, quasi-liturgical hymns of Chasidic flavor around the family table on Sabbaths and Festivals.

As a child, Leib Glantz had imbibed the dual nature of Chasidic song: meditative, in order to attain *D'vei'kut*; and ecstatic, in the form of *Ri'kud* (*Ni'gu'nim* that lent themselves to frenzied dance). In his middle years (1931-1947) he set to music a poem that Israel's third president, Zalman Shazar, had written in his youth. In it a young Chasid speaks of his love for Dvoirele, a girl he has only glimpsed at a *Me'la'veh Mal'ka.*[41] He knows that his feelings can never come to fruition, as the Rebbe[42] has matched her with another, but still, he fantasizes over what might have been. Shazar, a man of letters[43] who had been raised in a Chasidic family, poured memories of an earlier personal disappointment into the poem.[44]

---

40 *Beit Mid'rash* was a "study hall" adjacent to the synagogue where daily learning and prayer took place. During the months of cold weather, which in Eastern Europe usually prevailed from October through May, people in small towns prayed in the *Beit Mid'rash* on Sabbaths and Festivals as well, since it was heated. On the High Holy Days and possibly the *Sha'vu'ot* festival, which fell during the warmer months, services were held in the unheated synagogue.

41 *Me'la'veh Mal'ka* — "The ushering out of the Queen," the community's bittersweet leave-taking of the Sabbath — with food, drink and song. In Chasidic circles it was often held in the Rebbe's home.

42 Rebbe — a Chasidic spiritual leader akin to a rabbi— and often ordained as such — but usually more charismatic.

43 Most notably through *Morning Stars,* an autobiographical memoir, by Shulamith Schwartz Nardi, tr. (Philadelphia: Jewish Publication Society), 1967.

44 Zimmermann, Akiva, *Be'Ron Ya'chad,* 1988, p. 220.

Glantz began his setting of the poem with a typical melodic invention in Chasidic style — *Mach'sha'va Shel Ne'gi'na Be'Cha'si'dut* [45] — a *D'vei'kut Ni'gun*. The Arabic world knows this genre of mystical, non-rhythmic prelude as a *tartil,*[46] and although Glantz keeps it wordless until near the very end, the music sings its own three-part fantasy of a love that might have been. Part A, hushed and anticipatory, imagines the Chasid's first encounter with the beloved. Part B tone-paints an unrestrained outburst: his declaration of devotion to her. Part C, sublime and blissful, envisions the consummation of their love. The last part could well serve as a paragon of Ukrainian/Dorian "poignancy" coloration, against whose use in *Ha'llel* and the Three Festivals (Example 3) Glantz so vehemently objected (**Example 12**).[47]

Nothing in Pierre Pinchik's Chasidic *oeuvre* compares with Leib Glantz's *Dvoirele* in emotional range and power. Pinchik's characteristically muted palette and restrained dynamic bear a much closer resemblance to Glantz's fourteen Chasidic settings of texts from Sabbath table songs and High Holy Day penitential pleadings, in musical idioms such as Bratslaver, Lubavitcher, Talner and Israeli. The collection, *Cha'si'dim Be'Ri'nah — Chasidic Spirituals,*[48] presents an ideal artistic blending of the gentleness and exuberance that is endemic to the Chasidic *métier.* By composing the settings in this manner Glantz returned to his roots after years of overturning mountains with his more *bravura* style.

> *Nothing in Pierre Pinchik's Chasidic* oeuvre *compares with Leib Glantz's* Dvoirele *in emotional range and power.*

A case in point: he lavishes upon a cheerful little ditty of a *Ze'mi'ra — Dror Yik'ra* ("On the Sabbath, God frees each of us from toil")[49] — the same lyrical inventiveness shown in any of his more grandiloquent works. He even manages to incorporate the filler syllables preferred by Talner Chasidim: *ai-dee-di-dee, ai-dee-di-dee, ai;* but he organizes the material into a classic A-B-A song form. That is different from habitual Chasidic practice with *Ni'gu'nim* set to liturgical words. These are always sung after the service is over (to avoid *Haf'sa'ka,* the prohibition against interrupting prayer).[50] Usually, a selection is repeated over and over again, climbing a

---

45 A description I've borrowed from the musical imagination of another Chasid at heart, Chazan Abba Yosef Weisgal (1885-1981), whose *"Ni'gun A'bba"* closely resembles Glantz's *Ni'gun* from his song *Dvoirele* (Joseph A. Levine, *Emunat Abba,* New York: Cantors Assembly, 2006:#250).

46 Abraham Z. Idelsohn. *Jewish Music in Its Historical Development* (New York: Henry Holt and Co.), 1929:25.

47 *Cantor Leib Glantz: Songs Sacred and Secular — Hebrew Spirituals/Hassidic Ecstacy* (Recorded 1931-47), Musique Internationale, cassette CM 514, 1988, side 1, 2nd number.

48 Hebraica Records LP J08P-2731-20732 (New York: RCA Victor), 1948.

49 *Ibid.,* side 2, track 3.

50 Sam Weiss, *"Congregational Singing in Chasidic Congregations,"* Journal of Synagogue Music, Vol. 30, No. 1, Fall 2005:100.

Example 12. The introductory three-part *D'vei'kut Ni'gun* from Glantz's song, *"Dvoirele"*:

half-tone in pitch and several decibels in volume with each succeeding chorus until the singing becomes too high and too loud for comfort, whereupon it drops an octave and the volume abates so that the process can begin all over again. Glantz treated *Dror Yik'ra* as an art song, to be sung and not danced, although its melody could be construed as that of a *Ri'kud*. It's certainly too sprightly for a *D'vei'kah Ni'gun*, and therein lies the challenge. It needs to be performed while standing perfectly still — as if one were moving! **Example 13**[51] gives the melody line of its middle (B) section, which features filler syllables preferred by the Talner Chasidim.[52]

Example 13. The middle section of Glantz's *Dror Yik'ra*, featuring filler syllables preferred by the Talner Chasidim:

Pinchik's treatment of the *Mu'saf* prayer *U'Ve'Yom Ha'Sha'bbat* ("On the Sabbath Day")[53] comes closest to Glantz's *Dror Yik'ra*, in that both of these dance-like settings are the only ones in which either composer allowed himself the liberty of using filler syllables in a published liturgical text. Granted that Glantz had limited his use of *ai-dee-di-dee, ai-dee-di-dee, ai*, to a *Ze'mi'ra* that is sung at home or in a concert hall; Pinchik took the process beyond quasi-liturgical texts, and potentially, into the synagogue itself (**Example 14**).

Example 14. Pinchik's filler syllables in *U'Ve'Yom Ha'Sha'bbat* — a liturgical text that could be sung during worship:

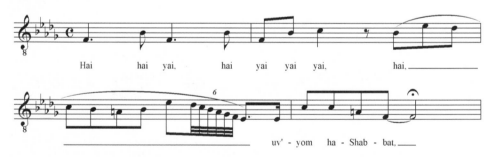

51 Glantz, *Cha'si'dim Be'Ri'nah*, 1948, side 2, track 3.

52 The singing of *Ni'gu'nim* by filler syllables rather than through words stems from a Chasidic belief that the souls speaks directly to God through melody, whereas words only serve to interrupt its emotional outpouring. Furthermore, words limit the melody's duration; when they run out, it is over. But wordless melody — sung to non-semantic filler syllables — can go on endlessly (according to the early Chasidic master, Shneur Zalman of Liady, cited in Abraham W. Binder, "Jewish Music," *Jewish Encyclopedia Handbooks*, New York: Central Yiddish Cultural Organization, 1952).

53 Pierre S. Pinchik. *The Repertoire of Hazzan Pinchik, Vol. I — Hazzanic Recitatives with Piano-Organ Accompaniment* (New York: Cantors Assembly), 1964:56.

Another area in which Pinchik and Glantz pioneered was the judicious sprinkling of *leitmotifs* throughout their compositions, melodic figurations in the voice and in the accompaniment that permanently fixed the piece's theme in listeners' minds. The leading motifs were adapted either from Bible-reading tropes (*Ta'a'mei Mik'ra*) or from age-old synagogue chants. **Example 15** quotes the *leitmotif* of Pinchik's *Ra'za De'Sha'bbat*,[54] a

Another area in which Pinchik and Glantz pioneered was the judicious sprinkling of leitmotifs *throughout their compositions, melodic figurations in the voice and in the accompaniment that permanently fixed the piece's theme in listeners' minds.*

combined paraphrase of two *Te'a'mim* for chanting prophetic readings (*Haf'ta'rot*): *Se'gol* and *Re'vi'a.*[55]

Example 15. Derivation of Pinchik's *Ra'za De'Sha'bbat* theme from two *Haf'ta'ra* tropes:

The underlying theme of Leib Glantz's *Bir'kat Ko'ha'nim* (Priestly Benediction) simulates the lengthy wordless refrain that worshippers sing along with the cantor in traditional synagogues, after the *Ko'ha'nim* conclude each section of their tripartite blessing. The sources from which Glantz may have derived inspiration for his own noble four-part creation are documented in **Example 16**. None of these sources approach the grandeur, solemnity and "rightness" for the occasion that Glantz has achieved in adapting them for his elaborate *leitmotif.* He plucked fragments of *Nu'sach* from the liturgy, biblical cantillation motifs from *Ta'a'mei Mik'ra*, idiomatic turns of phrase from Yiddish folk songs and Chasidic *Ni'gu'nim*. All of these elements he combined — whether consciously or intuitively — with "Mediterranean"-style Zionist paeans to the Land of Israel that were then being written by pioneer settlers in Palestine under the British Mandate. Glantz had always been an ardent and supportive member of *Tze'i'rei Tzi'yon*, a Labor Zionist youth organization that promoted *A'li'ya*,[56] and their hymns may have provided the seed that begat his old/new chant for *Bir'kat Ko'ha'nim.*[57]

---

54 *Ibid.*, pp. 78-80.

55 Levine, *Synagogue Song in America*, 2001:81, Example 5.2,b.

56 *A'li'ya* —"Going up" to live in the ancestral homeland; Zimmermann, Akiva, *Be'Ron Ya'chad*, 1988, p. 218.

57 *Ri'nat Ha'Ko'desh*, Hebraica Records (RCA Camden) LPZ-H70P 3658, side 1, track 5. *Bir'kat Ko'ha'nim* can be heard on the compact disks accompanying this book.

Example 16. Glantz's *leitmotif* for *Bir'kat Ko'ha'nim* — with possible sources appearing under each of its four parts:

At a 1960 Executive Council meeting of the Cantors Assembly that took place in New York, Pinchik and Glantz happened to arrive at the same time as two-dozen other attendees. Glantz went to one side of the room and sat down; Pinchik seated himself as far on the other side as possible. For two hours neither took cognizance of the other's presence, and when the meeting broke, they left without even a nod of mutual recognition.[58] Perhaps this shared disdain, at least on Glantz's part, stemmed from disapproval of Pinchik's bachelor lifestyle[59] that he felt did not measure up to what a cantor should be: "an intellectual, a scholar, a model for the congregation, a spiritual leader."[60] In fairness it must be noted that Pinchik as well had just reason for keeping his distance, as his repeated attempts to contact Glantz went unanswered.[61]

> *Glantz went to one side of the room and sat down; Pinchik seated himself as far on the other side as possible. For two hours neither took cognizance of the other's presence, and when the meeting broke, they left without even a nod of mutual recognition.*

Sigmund Freud seems to have been correct in assessing the biblical injunction to love one's neighbor as oneself, as "a commandment which is really justified by the fact that nothing else runs so strongly counter to the original nature of man."[62] Among countless similar examples,

---

58 I thank my lifelong friend Solomon Mendelson, a past president and Program Chairman of the Cantors Assembly, for this historical footnote.

59 A fact the writer can attest to, having interviewed *Cha'zan* Pinchik in his Manhattan hotel room in May of 1948, for *Commentator*, at that time the monthly magazine of Yeshiva University's Talmudical Academy High School.

60 Ezra [Jerry] Glantz, in a personal communication to the writer, April 2006.

61 *Idem.*

62 Sigmund Freud, *Civilization and Its Discontents*, translated from the German and edited by James Strachey (New York: W. W. Norton), 1961:59.

witness the American Civil War of 1860-1865 or the Iraq-Iran War of 1980-1988 for proof. Contemporary realist painter David Hewitt, who views the world as an increasingly global school, has given us a hint for understanding the "conundrum" of this essay's title. In his 1989-1992 series, *Between Cultures*, Hewitt makes the point that we are more comfortable with our neighbor if he or she does not get too close.[63]

Pinchik and Glantz may have kept a comfortable distance between them, but historically they came very close to participating in a modern miracle: the revival of Jewish worship through Chasidic *Ni'gu'nim*. Towards the very end of their lives, by an unlikely coincidence, the example of their unabashedly Chasidic practices at the *A'mud* and on recordings would prove a godsend to North American synagogue practice, which had run out of ideas by the late 1960s. The current ongoing neo-Chasidic revival started when a Tel Aviv theatrical troupe semi-staged an hour-long medley of *Ni'gu'nim* that had been provided with vernacular lyrics. The song genre was invented late in the eighteenth century by Rabbi Yitzchak Eizik Taub of Kalev,[64] who so loved the pastoral ballads of his native Hungary, that he would adjust their words and melodies to sound more Jewish.

> *Pinchik and Glantz may have kept a comfortable distance between them, but historically they came very close to participating in a modern miracle: the revival of Jewish worship through Chasidic Ni'gu'nim.*

An ode to the wild woods, to a far-away Rose[65]

— became —

A plea to the She'chi'na[66]
So far away,
To end the long Exile
This very day…

(See **Example 17**).[67]

---

63 Quoted in Edward Rubin, *"Reconstructing Reality,"* Art and Antiques, April 2006:43.

64 Rabbi Yitzchak Eizik Taub of Kalov, Hungary (1751-1821). The first Chasidic Rebbe in Hungary, known as "the Sweet Singer of Israel," he composed many popular Chasidic melodies. Often he adapted Hungarian folk songs, adding Jewish words. He taught that the tunes he heard were really from the Holy Temple in Jerusalem, and were lost among the nations over the years, and he found them and returned them to the Jewish people.

65 Abraham Z. Idelsohn. *"Songs of the Hasidim,"* Thesaurus of Hebrew Oriental Melodies, vol. X (Leipzig: Friedrich Hofmeister), 1932:#192, I.

66 *She'chi'na* — God's presence.

67 *Idem*, #192, II.

Example 17. Yitzchak Eizik Taub of Kalev's Judaized Hungarian pastoral ballad:

During its adaptation, the wistful Hungarian folk melody was rewritten in a mode normally used for studying Talmud,[68] and its words transformed from a shepherd's longing for his beloved Rose into a Jew's yearning for God and the long-awaited final Redemption. Israeli composer Dan Almagor borrowed Rav Yitzchak of Kalev's Judaized version, along with a dozen other fervently devotional dialogues with God that were cut from the same mold. He strung them together as a series of dramatic tableaus, wedding *Ni'gu'nim* — with and without lyrics — to a story line told by alternating narrators. The premiere performance of *Ish Cha'sid Ha'yah* ("Once There Was A Chasid") proved so irresistible that a recording of it was released,[69] and within a year, Jewish theatrical companies began staging their own productions all over North America.

Cantors quickly appropriated the underlying idea and used it to enliven their repertoire of congregational refrains with Chasidic bits and pieces. They soon realized that such tired old Chasidic standbys as *Ve'Ta'her Li'bei'nu* ("Purify Our Hearts") were no longer sufficiently upbeat in comparison, so they commissioned new ones to be written to folk-rock rhythms. Israeli songwriters, eager to supply the mushrooming demand, complied with a complete list of neo-Chasidic *Ni'gu'nim* over the ensuing decades. Recordings and sheet music of annual Chasidic Festivals sold briskly all over the world, and especially well in the United States and Canada. These were followed by live performances featuring several generations of young Israeli artists who unknowingly helped pay off countless sponsoring congregations' mortgages through benefit concerts. Very quickly, cantors discovered that many of their formerly jaded congregants were spontaneously singing along with the new refrains. Chasidic-style tunes (set to rock rhythms) were the catalyst; they gave late twentieth-century American worship a boost of adrenaline that has lasted until this writing and gives no indication of slackening. To

---

68 The *Ler'n Shtey'ger* or Study Mode; Levine, *Synagogue Song in America*, 2001:117-119.

69 *Once There Was A Chasid*, LP AP-332 (Tel Aviv: Yaakov Agmon, 1968); text reproduced by the Hebrew Cultural Council of Philadelphia, 1969.

circumvent the difficulty encountered by Reform parishioners who could not follow the unfamiliar Hebrew lyrics, an alternate means of lay involvement was introduced: mass handclapping.

In a strange turnabout, the only synagogues now distinguished by a lack of handclapping are Chasidic ones, where such activity — along with dancing — is reserved for after worship (see note 50). A visit to almost any other type of service, including Modern Orthodox, is liable to include not only rhythmic applause but also stomping of feet and grabbing of shoulders, particularly in the uninhibited atmosphere of Southern California. This writer once wandered into a Friday Night Conservative "happening" in suburban Los Angeles, which bore an eerie resemblance to the Solidarity Service envisioned some sixty years earlier by novelist Aldous Huxley.[70]

> "Men and women…ready to be made one, to lose their separate identities in a larger being. The first Solidarity Hymn was a brief haunting melody, repeated plangently to a pulsing rhythmic accompaniment, and visceral in its effect… Ultimately the participants form a dancing circle with hands on the preceding person's hips, shouting in unison and beating the insistent refrain."

In addition to these elements came the rhythmic applause that an electronic organ reinforced until the hip-hugging circle snaked its way out of the sanctuary and into an adjoining auditorium where a roaming accordion took over.

Leib Glantz and Pierre Pinchik did not live to witness all of this excess. Like a first-stage rocket, the power segment that supplies initial thrust for the entire voyage, their journey came to an end just as the neo-Chasidic revival entered outer space and began to circle the Jewish world.

Leib Glantz and Pierre Pinchik did not live to witness all of this excess. Like a first-stage rocket, the power segment that supplies initial thrust for the entire voyage, their journey came to an end just as the neo-Chasidic revival entered outer space and began to circle the Jewish world. Other factors would enter once the movement had attained orbit speed: Klezmer, Reggae, Fusion, Rap, etc. But it all began with an Israeli composer rediscovering a *Ni'gun* written by a Hungarian Chasid 200 years before, and seeing possibilities in it.

---

70 *Brave New World* (1932), cited in Joseph A. Levine, *Rise and Be Seated — The Ups and Downs of Jewish Worship* (Northvale, NJ: Jason Aronson), 2001:167.

What if that Israeli composer — Dan Almagor — in search of *Ni'gu'nim* before his big break-through, had dropped by for *Me'la'veh Mal'ka* inspiration in a certain Rebbe's *Beit Mid'rash* in Tel Aviv, where Pierre Pinchik — grey-haired in retirement and wearing his favorite beige cardigan, blue shirt and red tie — sat and quietly regaled the gathered Chasidim with *Ze'mi'rot?* Surely, one of the *Ni'gu'nim* Pinchik sang that Saturday night could have been the meditative refrain in Chasidic style that he had used as a *leitmotif* whenever he led the week-day *Ma'a'riv* service (**Example 18**).[71]

Example 18. Pinchik's meditative refrain in Chasidic style for the weekday *Ma'a'riv* service:

Or suppose that Dan Almagor, in search of ways to spotlight the *Ni'gu'nim* he had rediscov-ered, had heard Leib Glantz — reinvigorated since resettling in the Land of Israel — daven the midnight *Se'li'chot* service before *Rosh Ha'Sha'na* in Tel Aviv's *Tif'e'ret Zvi* synagogue? There, the idea already forming in Almagor's imagination — to dramatize a series of Chasidic God-dialogues — would have been validated as doable by Glantz's one-on-one with the Creator in the fourth strophe of *Be'Mo'tsa'ei Me'nu'cha*,[72] the *Se'li'chot* service's centerpiece:

> *"Zo'cha'lim Ve'Ro'a'dim Mi'Yom Bo'e'cha,*
> *Cha'lim Ke'Mav'ki'ra Mei'Ev'rat Ma'sa'e'cha."*[73]

Glantz tone-painted the opening words over and over, with each "repetition" minutely varied so as to evoke the doomsday fear that Jews customarily felt during this curtain raiser for the annual Day of Judgment. It was the liturgical equivalent of Yitzchak Eizik of Kalev's *"She'chi'na, She'chi'na"*: at first a trembling acknowledgement of personal inadequacy before the Throne of Justice, then a halting presentation of legal precedents, and finally a heart-

---

71 The writer's approximation of a melody that he — and others — had heard Pinchik sing with the congregation before every blessing in a concert weekday *Ma'a'riv* service. According to a report in *Yedi'ot Acharonot* (June 3, 1956), Pinchik had followed Glantz to Israel for a visit of several months.

72 An anonymous alphabetical acrostic, as in *Se'li'chot*, edited by Louis Feinberg (New York: Behrman House), 1954:15.

73 "Groaning like one in travail, Thy children remain helpless before Thee."

in-hand plea for divine relief on behalf of the entire congregation. **Example 19**[74] cites the opening portion of that musical brief.

Example 19. The opening section of Glantz's *Zo'cha'lim Ve'Ro'a'dim* from the midnight *Se'li'chot* service:

With each succeeding stanza, Glantz's case petition before the Heavenly Tribunal gained in confidence until, with the cadence of his final refrain (**Example 19a**) — *Lish'mo'a El Ha'Ri'na Ve'El Ha'Te'fi'la* ("Hear our song and our prayer"), he stamped the emotion-laden argument with his own idiomatic *Cha'ti'ma* (cantorial "signature") and brought the entire congregation into joining a beloved cadential phrase in the proper "*Nu'sach* from Sinai" (see note 17).

---

74 *"Se'li'chot* 1958," *Cantor Leib Glantz — High Holiday Moods*, (Chicago: Musique Internationale), cassette CM 516, 1993: side B. [It can be heard on the compact disks accompanying this book.]

Example 19a. *Ve'El Ha'Te'fi'la,* the cadential *"Nu'sach* from Sinai" phrase of Glantz's final *Lish'mo'a El Ha'Ri'na* refrain:

It was precisely the kind of ritual moment that Dan Almagor would successfully replicate on the stage of the Israel Teachers Union Building in Tel Aviv — less than a decade later — and thereby open a door that has yet to close. There may be no direct link between the high Chazanic art evidenced in Glantz's and Pinchik's *D'vei'kut Ni'gu'nim* and the neo-*Ri'kud* hits that poured forth from Israeli Chasidic Festivals during the next quarter-century. Yet the affinity between Pinchik's meditative refrain from the weekday *Ma'a'riv* service (**Example 18**) and Yitzchak Eizik of Kalev's *She'chi'na, She'chi'na* (**Example 17**) is undeniable.

So is the kinship of Glantz's cadence "From Sinai" for the final *Lish'mo'a* with Almagor's *Mich'tav La'Ra'bi* ("A Letter to the Rebbe"), the *finalé* from *Ish Cha'sid Ha'ya* (**Example 20**):[75]

"Le'Fe'lach Mo'hi'lov, La'Ir La'di, La'Ra'bi Ha'Ka'dosh, Reb Shne'ur Zal'man."[76]

Example 20. "A Letter to the Rebbe," the *finalé* from Almagor's *"Ish Cha'sid Ha'ya"*:

---

75 *"Once There Was A Chasid,"* 1968, Side 2:12.
76 "To the Mohilov district; To the city of Liady; For the Holy Rabbi Shneur Zalman."

Along with the 1950s' example of old-time piety that Chasidic survivors of the Holocaust[77] set for an American Orthodoxy that had gone Modern,[78] the 1960s' nostalgia for our great-grand-parents' Eastern European folkways[79] as depicted by philosophers Martin Buber and Abraham Joshua Heschel,[80] the 1970s' desire of small prayer groups *(Cha'vu'rot)*[81] for the warmth of Chasidic worship, the continuing popularity of the Broadway musical *Fiddler on the Roof*[82] and the lasting influence of guitar-strumming Rabbi Shlomo Carlebach,[83] Leib Glantz and Pierre Pinchik played no less a role in rescuing late twentieth-century synagogues from the lingering Victorian rationalism that had been strangling them. This, I believe, is their true legacy, the one by which history will judge them. The less-traveled road they took — before its time had come — also leads to an answer for this essay's opening question: why is Pinchik still imitated, and Glantz not?

> *Leib Glantz and Pierre Pinchik played a role in rescuing late twentieth-century synagogues from the lingering Victorian rationalism that had been strangling them. This, I believe, is their true legacy.*

It has to do with a changing *Zeitgeist* in America, from acquiescent patriotism to anti-establishment activism, which occurred at the height of protest against the Vietnam War. Its watershed was reached in the summer of 1968, when national television cameras caught police in a particularly bloody reaction against young people demonstrating outside the Democratic Party Convention in Chicago. Overnight, respect for authority evaporated all across the cultural horizon, including the foursquare religious anthems that a generation of parents who grew up during the Great Depression of the 1930s had been singing during worship. Rock rhythm was about to cross the threshold of America's churches, and Chasidic *Ri'ku'dim* (dances) were set to approach the Holy Ark in American synagogues.

Decades before, Glantz and Pinchik had spread a red carpet of *D'vei'kut Ni'gu'nim* that Israeli folk-rock settings of liturgical refrains would now follow — straight to the hearts of congregants

77 Levine, *Rise and Be Seated*, 2001:149-151.

78 Haym Soloveitchik, *"Rupture and Reconstruction — the Transformation of Modern Orthodoxy,"* Tradition, Summer 1994:65-130.

79 Mark Zborowsky and Elizabeth Herzog, *Life Is with People* (1952), New York: Schocken Paperback, 1962, throughout.

80 Martin Buber, *Tales of the Hasidim: The Early Masters* (New York: Schocken, 1947); *The Later Masters* (New York: Farrar, Strauss and Young, 1948); Abraham Joshua Heschel, *The Earth Is the Lord's* (New York: Harper), 1966.

81 Bernard Reisman, The *Havurah* (New York: Union of American Hebrew Congregations), 1977, *passim*; and personal communication to the writer, October 1995.

82 Book by Joseph Stein, lyrics by Sheldon Harnick, music by Jerry Bock (New York: Sunbeam), 1964.

83 Liner notes for CD, *In the Palace of the King* (Santa Monica, CA: Vanguard), 1965; Jeremy Gaisin, *"The Immortality of Shlomo Carlebach and His Music,"* Commentator (New York: Yeshiva University, 11/25/02.

tired of being told what to do and how to do it during services. Their elders had sat and listened as Pinchik and Glantz's generation of star cantors performed on their behalf. Glantz's sky-high pyrotechnics had proved daunting even for his professional colleagues; Pinchik's more down-to-earth approach lent itself much more easily to emulation by amateurs. As illustration: Pinchik's gentle *Ma'oz Tsur* in Chasidic style,[84] though singable by everyone

> *Glantz's sky-high pyrotechnics had proved daunting even for his professional colleagues; Pinchik's more down-to-earth approach lent itself much more easily to emulation by amateurs.*

back in the 1930s, had still been lively enough to provide a missing link with the syncopated new ballads from Israel, beginning with the very first Chasidic Song Festival prizewinner, *O'seh Sha'lom.*[85] Because it gave worshippers an organic part to play in the service (singing as a community to conclude the *A'mi'da* or the Readers *Ka'ddish*), that groundbreaker literally took the process of "Chasidifying" the liturgy a dance-step beyond anything that Glantz or Pinchik would have dared attempt in their day.

---

84 *The Art of Cantor Pinchik*, cassette GRC 234 (Brooklyn, NY: Greater Recording Company), 1973, B:3.

85 Nurit Hirsh (1969), *The Best of the Chasidic Song Festivals*, compiled and edited by Velvel Pasternak (New York: Tara), 1989:53.

13

"He Who Strikes Flames of Fire"

"Cho'tzev La'ha'vot Esh"

Cantor Benjamin Z. Maissner[1]

On my *Bar Mitz'va*,[2] *A'don*[3] Leib Glantz gave me a book as a gift that I treasure to this very day: *"Mil'che̊met Ha'Shich'rur"*: The History of Israel's War of Independence. The inscription in the book, in his own handwriting, was truly the highlight of my *Bar Mitz'va*. Years later I realized the significance of this book: it was given to me by an ardent Zionist who combined love for Israel and its people with his art.

Several people influenced my development as a musician and cantor. First and foremost were my two uncles. The first was cantor Israel Alter, who instilled in me discipline and accuracy in the execution of the *Nu'sach*.[4] Alter was a very close friend and colleague of Leib Glantz, and they enjoyed great mutual respect for each other's cantorial attributes.

The second was my uncle David Brenner, an outstanding *Ba'al Te̊fi'la*,[5] a great friend of Glantz, and the founder of the Israeli cantorial music society *"Likud Cho've'vei Ne'gi'na,"* after whom I affectionately named my own choral chamber group in Toronto: *"La'chan."* Others to whom I owe thanks are Cantor Shlomo Ravitz and my Hebrew teacher Arye Lebel.

---

1 Cantor Benjamine Z. Maissner was born in Tel Aviv in 1944. Since 1980 he has served as cantor and Music Director of Holy Blossom Temple in Toronto, Canada. He earned his Masters degree in Music from Temple University, and has taught vocal and cantorial at the Hebrew Union College in NY, Cincinnati and Jerusalem, where he was awarded an honorary Doctorate of Music.

2 *Bar Mitz'va* — thirteenth birthday ceremony when Jewish boys assume religious obligations.

3 *A'don* = Sir.

4 *Nu'sach* — The ancient Jewish Prayer Modes.

5 *Ba'al Te̊fi'la* — a layman, but experienced leader of synagogue prayers, usually very knowledgeable in *Nu'sach*.

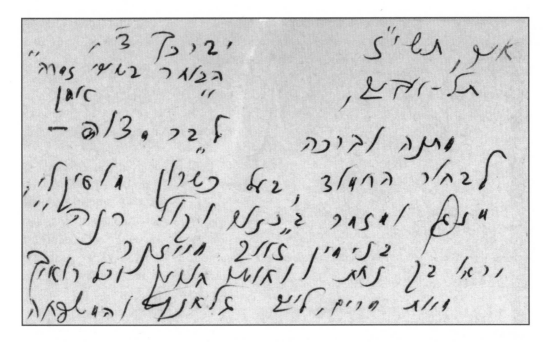

The inscription written by Glantz in the book *"Mil'che'met Ha'Shich'rur"* that Leib Glantz gave Benjamin Maissner as a Bar Mitzva gift in 1957: "May God bless you, he who chooses song! To the *Bar Mitz'va* boy Benjamin Zeev Maissner, a gift and a blessing to a wonderful young man, who posseses musical talent, plays the violin and sings with a lovely voice. May your parents and all who see you be gratified. Leib Glantz, Miriam and all of the family."

I was a ten-year-old when I first met Leib Glantz. The Glantz family had just arrived in Israel. They lived in Tel Aviv just around the corner from my parents' home. I used to tag along with my uncle Brenner and Glantz, as they would walk home together from the synagogue. I loved to listen to their conversations about cantorial. At the time I probably understood very little, but I must have absorbed some of it subconsciously.

I loved to attend the countless prayer services at the *Tif'e'ret Zvi* synagogue on Sabbaths, Festivals, High Holy Days and *Se'li'chot*[6] services. I was always seated only a short distance away from Cantor Glantz's pulpit. What might have been seen at the time as blurred and forgotten experiences actually became subconsciously embedded into my identity as a cantor. It was only decades later that I realized how it all crystallized into a structured art form.

---

6 *Se'li'chot* — a midnight prayer service conducted on the Saturday night before the Jewish New Year, *Rosh Ha'Sha'na*, consisting mainly of Jewish penitential poems and prayers seeking forgiveness.

In *"Ze'ha'rim,"* a 1965 book in Hebrew about the life and creativity of Leib Glantz, I discovered a detailed account of those ten years between 1954-1964. It helped me to bring back memories and to relive some of those wonderful experiences.

I remember myself as a small boy in the *Tif'e'ret Zvi* synagogue, standing close to the choir, next to the cantor's podium. I was mesmerized by the ecstasy that evoked loud emotional responses from the worshippers.

> *I remember myself as a small boy in the* Tif'e'ret Zvi *synagogue, standing close to the choir, next to the cantor's podium. I was mesmerized by the ecstasy that evoked loud emotional responses from the worshippers.*

I relived moments at concerts and lectures, always impressed by Glantz's brilliant mind as he skillfully maneuvered through complicated compositions with amazing vocal abilities, combining them with profound knowledge of the Hebrew language and the secrets of liturgy.

I cherish the memories from the *Ne'i'la* prayer service.[7] Sitting very close to Glantz on the cantor's pulpit, near conductor Yehoshua Zohar's choir, I could notice the subtle body language and intimate nuances of communication between Cantor Glantz and Conductor Zohar. I could sense the carefully planned musical passages that they sang in such a calculated fashion.

I was impressed by the awesome intonation of *Od Ye'ha'le'lu'cha Se'la* ("they are ever praising Thee") at the opening of the *Se'li'chot* service, and the yearning of *Al Ta'az'vei'nu Le'Et Zik'na* ("cast us not away in our old age!"). I can recall my body trembling as Glantz waved his hands, shaking in ecstasy, as he called out *Eich, Eich Nif'tach Peh* ("How can we open our mouths before Thee?"), or *Ma'rom! Ma'rom! Ma'rom!* ("Merciful one in the heavens!").

Fantasy images of a child would overcome me as I could sense Glantz wandering off into far away worlds, describing God as one who "crushes the heads of Leviathan" (*Ata Ro'tzatz'ta Ra'shei Li'via'tan)*, or the anxiety and mystery of phrases such as *Zo'cha'lim Ve'Ro'a'dim* ("groaning like one in travail, they remain helpless before Thee") from the *Se'li'chot* service poem *Be'Mo'tza'ei Me'nu'cha* ("at the close of the Sabbath, our voice we raise"), revolving into the beautiful refrain *Lish'mo'a El Ha'Ri'na Ve'El Ha'Te'fi'la* ("to listen to our song and our prayer").

I remember the feeling of exultation as I listened to Glantz's classic compositions such as *She'ma Yis'ra'el* ("Hear O Israel!") from the *Ke'du'sha Mu'saf* service, or *Ein Ke'Er'ke'cha* ("There is none to be compared unto Thee!") from the Sabbath morning *Shach'rit* service.

---

7 *Ne'i'la* — The final service of *Yom Ki'ppur*, the Day of Atonement.

It was so puzzling to hear the tranquil opening tones of *A'hav'ti Ki Yish'ma A'do'nai Et Ko'li* ("I love the Lord because He heareth my voice and my supplications") from the *Ha'llel* service. At first one experiences a mood of optimism, then suddenly one is in the center of a giant storm as Glantz cries out towards God: *A'na A'do'nai Mal'ta Naf'shi* ("O Lord, I beseech Thee, deliver my soul"). This is followed by the proclamation *Shu'vi Naf'shi Li'M'nu'chai'chi* ("return unto thy rest, O my soul") in a unique speaking voice. Then, in such a refreshing mode, he would sing *Sho'mer Pe'ta'im Ha'Shem* ("the Lord preserveth the simple folk"), moving on to resolve the prayer with a typical Major cadence. I remember the happy rejoicing feeling as Glantz practically danced to the words *Et'ha'lech Lif'nei Ha'Shem Be'Ar'tzot Ha'Cha'yim* ("I shall walk before the Lord in the land of the living")! Glantz would always find the way to "arrive home" safely with the genuine *Nu'sach* conclusion of the *Ha'llel* service, declaring: *A'ni A'mar'ti Be'Chof'zi — Kol Ha'A'dam Ko'zev* ("even when I said in haste — all men are liars"). *A'hav'ti* greatly influenced my composition *Sim Sha'lom*, to which I will refer later.

The music of *A'na Be'Cho'ach* ("Please, by the force of Your great right hand") was so intimately true to the meanings of every word of the text. The exaltation and inner fervor of *Ka'bel Ri'nat A'me'cha* ("accept the prayer of Your people"), the elevation and awesomeness of *Cha'sin Ka'dosh* ("Mighty, Holy One"), and the ecstasy of *Shav'a'tei'nu Ka'bel U'Shma Tza'a'ka'tei'nu* ("accept our prayer, and hear our cry") were way beyond human imagination. The climax of *A'na Be'Cho'ach* is the mysterious and haunting final tones: *Yo'de'a Ta'a'lu'mot* ("God, who knows all the world's mysteries")!

> *The music of* A'na Be'Cho'ach *("Please, by the force of Your great right hand") was so intimately true to the meanings of every word of the text.*

I witnessed the whole congregation sighing with teary eyes when "Leibele" lovingly poured his heart out in *Shma Ko'lei'nu* ("Hear our voice, O Lord") and *Al Tash'li'chei'nu Le'Et Zik'na* ("cast us not away in our old age, when our strength faileth"), on *Yom Ki'ppur's* sacred hour of *Kol Nid'rei*.[8] It made a lasting impression on me as a young man.

At the time I was too young to understand the deeper meanings of *D'vei'kut*[9] and *Ka'va'na*,[10] but I felt those exalting sounds of *A'na Ha'Shem Ho'shi'a Na, Hatz'li'cha Na* ("Save, we beseech

---

8 *Kol Nid'rei* — The opening prayer of *Yom Ki'ppur,* The Holy Day of Atonement: "All our unfulfilled vows to God shall be absolved."

9 *D'vei'kut* — closeness to God.

10 *Ka'va'na* — mental concentration during Jewish prayer.

Thee, O Lord, make us prosper") at the conclusion of the *Ha'llel* service, which exposed Glantz's profound *Cha'si'dic*[11] fervor.

In this essay I would like to reflect on the great impact Leib Glantz had upon my personal development as a cantor.

Leib Glantz possessed great musical skills. His vocal capabilities were limitless, and he was driven by passion in every fiber of his body and soul. Today, after more than four decades as a cantor, I have come to the realization that it was Glantz who shaped my identity. He created within me a deep understanding and appreciation of cantorial art.

> *Today, after more than four decades as a Cha'zan, I have come to the realization that it was Glantz who shaped my identity.*

I find myself intoning hidden phrases such as *Me'loch Al Kol Ha'O'lam* ("O Lord, reign on the whole world") on *Rosh Ha'Sha'na, Me'lech Al Kol Ha'A'retz* ("The Lord shall be King over the whole earth"), and *T'ka Be'Sho'far Ga'dol Le'Che'ru'tei'nu* ("Sound the great *Sho'far* for our freedom") — all in declamatory *parlando*, and recitative style. These came to me from Glantz.

I frequently fantasize about the subtle meanings of prayers such as *A'vi'nu Mal'kei'nu* ("Our Father, our King") or about the joyous melodies of the *Ha'llel* service, even in the compositions of Max Helfman, Max Janowski, Israel Alter or Moshe Ganchoff. I constantly try to keep in mind the importance of rendering the right inflection of each prayer. My images were molded by the images that Glantz created. I was inspired by his fiery emotions.

Over the years I have come to recognize similarities between my own compositions and those of Glantz. Musical phrases and melodic sequences have been directly influenced by Glantz's musical compositions. I will try to illustrate this by comparing compositions in the following examples.

A first example is of the simple *Cha'si'dic* fervor of a Glantz *Ni'ggun*[12] *Ho'du La'A'do'nai Ki Tov* ("O give thanks unto the Lord for He is good") from the Glantz book *"Ha'llel"* and Three Festivals" (p. 88-89):

---

11 Chasidism — a mystical Jewish movement founded in Poland in the 18th century in reaction to the rigid academicism of rabbinical Judaism, emphasizing emotion, dance and music.

12 *Ni'ggun* — a Hebrew term that means "humming tune," usually, religious songs and tunes.

Example I   *Ho'du La' A'do'nai*   L. Glantz

or: *Tit'ga'dal* from Glantz's book "Songs" (p. 14):

Example I (cont'd)   *Tit'ga'dal*   L. Glantz

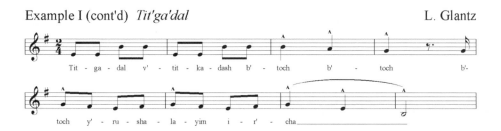

Glantz demonstrated *D'vei'kut* — inner joy, exaltation, and optimism. In my own phrasing of *Ha'Yom Te'am'tzei'nu* ("Today You will adopt us"), from the conclusion to *Rosh Ha'Sha'na* and *Yom Ki'ppur Mu'saf* services, in both musical lines A and B, I felt that same exaltation:

Example Ia   *Ha' Yom*   B. Maissner

In *Nach'pe'sa D'ra'chei'nu* ("We shall seek our path"), from Glantz's book "Songs" (p. 35), the opening melody has enchanted me since childhood.

Example II   *Nach' pe'sa D'ra'chei'nu*   L. Glantz

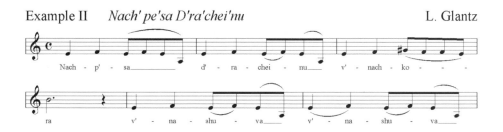

The opening *Ni'ggun* of my composition *Ve'Hu Ra'chum* ("And He is merciful"), although not of the same thematic material, contains a similar message of pastoral tranquility:

To my surprise, and in a totally different musical context, I found the following line in *Tal,* the prayer for dew: *A'yu'ma A'sher Hi'sa'ata Ka'Tzon* ("Bestow Thy favor on the people whom Thou didst lead like a flock"). See the Glantz book "*Ha'llel* and Three Festivals" (p. 100):

This is very similar to my *Ho'shi'a Ha'Me'lech Ya'a'nei'nu* ("May the King answer us on the day we call") from my composition *Ve'Hu Ra'chum:*

In a short segment from *Tik'u Va'Cho'desh Sho'far* ("Sound the *Sho'far* on the new moon") on *Rosh Ha'Sha'na* Eve, I have always been singing the High Holiday motif in a Glantz style. I recall the following phrase *Mi Ya'ale B'Har A'do'nai* ("Who shall ascend the mountain of the Lord?") from the prayer *Le'Da'vid Miz'mor,*[13] from the Glantz book "High Holidays" (p. 9):

---

13 *Miz'mor Le'Da'vid* — King David's psalm (Psalm 24).

Example IV   *Tik'u Va'Cho'desh Sho'far*   B. Maissner

Example IVa   *Mi Ya'ale B'har A'do'nai*   L. Glantz

In 1971, in Tel Aviv, I dedicated the song *Shi'rat A'ha'vah* to my daughter, Shira. *Shi'rat A'ha'vah* and a later melody composed for the poem *Be'ta'le'lei O'rah* ("with firmament of light" — from a Passover liturgical poem of Sephardic tradition). They were influenced by Glantz's *Be'Rosh Ha'Sha'na* (On New Year's Day):

Example V   *Shi'rat A'ha'vah*   B. Maissner

Example Va   *Be'ta'le'lei O'rah*   B. Maissner

In Glantz's book "High Holidays" (p. 45-55):

Furthermore, I believe that *Shi'rat A'ha'vah* (measure 55) — *Ve'Od Ha'Pa'am Ef'ro'chim A'zu'vim* ("and again the chicks are abandoned") has similarities to *Ki Mi'dey Dab'ri Bo Za'chor Ez'ke're'nu* ("My beloved child — even when I speak harshly of him, I still remember him with affection") in *Ha'loch Ve'Ka'ra'ta* ("Go and proclaim so that Jerusalem will hear!") from his "High Holiday" book (p. 96-97):

When I attempted to write the opening phrases to *Min Ha'Mei'tsar* ("Out of the depths I called upon the Lord"), from the introductory passages for the *Sho'far*[14] service, I had in mind many of Glantz's playful ideas with chromatic and accidental treatment. For example, while finishing the phrase with the traditional *Mi She'Bei'rach* mode[15] of *Zam'ru Le'Mal'kei'nu Za'mei'ru* ("Sing unto our King, sing praises"):

14 *Sho'far* is a ram's-horn trumpet used by ancient Jews in religious ceremonies and as a battle signal. In the synagogue it is sounded on *Rosh Ha'Sha'na* and *Yom Ki'ppur* prayer services.

15 *Nu'sach Mi'She'Bei'rach* — one of the Jewish prayer modes.

Example VII   *Min Ha'Mei'tsar (Sho'far Intro)*   B. Maissner

Za mei - ru___ lei-lo-him___ za - mei-ru   za - m'-ru l'-mal-kei - - - nu   za - mei - ru

Ma'lach Elo'him Al Go'yim ("God reigns on all nations") was also undoubtedly influenced by a Major key treatment of Glantz's approach to the effect of the moment:

Example VIIa   *Ma'lach Elo'him Al Go'yim*   B. Maissner

Ma - lach E-lo-him al go - yim   E - lo - him ya-shav___ al ki - sei___kod - sho

In the case of *Elo'him Ya'shav Al Ki'sei Kod'sho* ("The Lord sat on His holy throne"), my ending of the phrase is in the cantillation motif of *Shi'rat Ha'Yam* ("the Song of the Red Sea").

In *Rosh D'var'cha E'met* ("The beginning of Thy word is truth"), which was written in a typical High Holiday prayer mode, I was encouraged to express in a playful way the phrase *Sas A'no'chi Al Im'ra'te'cha K'mo'tse Sha'lal Rav* ("I rejoice at Thy word as one that finds great spoils"), in order to enhance its joy and brightness.

Example VIII   *Rosh D'var'cha E'met*   B. Maissner

Rosh   d'-va-r'-cha_____   e - met,___ u - l'-o - lam kol mish - pat tzid-ke-cha

sas___ a - no - chi   al   im - ra-te-cha,   k' - mo - tse sha - lal_____ rav

Glantz would often raise a note by a half tone to give it a bright Major feeling. One of the characteristics of Glantz's style is the interchange between Major and Minor keys. A typical example can be found in the prayer for Dew, *Te'fi'lat Tal*. In Glantz's book *"Ha'llel and The Three Festivals"* (p. 98), at the end of one of the paragraphs, he sings *Be'Tal...Be'Tal* as follows:

Example IX   *Tal*   L. Glantz

Tal_____   b' - tal_____

This minor change between Eb and E natural gave the entire *Tal* prayer a brighter and fresher approach, especially if compared to the traditional East European "wailing" or "sobbing" style. The change completely alters the nature of the prayer to a more authentic Hebraic-Israeli tribal motif. These changes of tonalities and brightness of color have embedded themselves within the consciousness of every cantor since Leib Glantz presented them in his compositions and recordings.

In my own attempts to write liturgical compositions I have discovered that such moves surface subconsciously. The bright and optimistic nature of a phrase in which I try to express the text is directly influenced by his method. My *Sim Sha'lom* ("O Lord, grant peace for Your people") demonstrates this point. *Bar'chei'nu A'vi'nu* ("Bless us all alike, our Father") leads into *Ki Ve'Or Pa'ne'cha* ("indeed by the light of Thy countenance"):

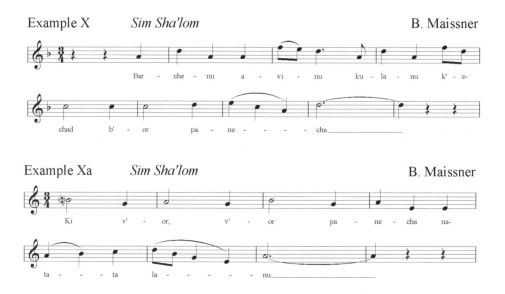

In the tonality of D minor, this switch to a subdominant major is a welcome change from the ongoing sad, contemplative *Ma'gen A'vot* mode.[16] Hints of these effects and musical movements can be found throughout the repertoire published in Glantz's Song Book. For example, section B of *Tit'ga'dal* ("Mayest Thou be exalted and sanctified in Jerusalem Thy city") (p. 14-15) as well as in the *"Cha'si'dic Cha'bad"* version of the composition *A'ta Yo'de'a* (p. 30-31). Another clear example of a refreshing modulation can be found in the earlier mentioned song — *"Nach'pe'sa D'ra'chei'nu"* (Song book, p. 35), where the treatment of the melody is predominantly in Minor, but towards the end of the song (Section B) it brightens up with a Major tonality (page 38):

16 *Nu'sach Ma'gen A'vot* — one of the Jewish prayer modes.

Example XI   *Nach'pe'sa D'ra'chei'nu*   L. Glantz

While the recapitulation section in this song is intoned in A major, the phrase that follows —
Ki Ye'min'cha Pe'shu'ta Le'Ka'bel Sha'vim ("Your hand is extended to accept those who repent")
is back in A minor. Notice that in the second half of the phrase, Glantz uses segments of the
Ukrainian-Dorian mode:[17]

Example XIa   *Ki Ye'min'cha*   L. Glantz

I attribute my dance-like treatment of the text in *Pit'chu La'nu* ("Open the gates for us") to
Glantz's famous song *D'ror Yik'ra* ("Let freedom be proclaimed"). Though far from being a
direct quote in musical form and analysis, the dance-like *Sha'a'rei O'ra, Sha'a'rei Gi'la, Vra'cha,
Hod Ve'Ha'dar* ("Enlightening gates of happiness, blessings of grandeur and splendor") is
engraved in my mind as I recall the joy Glantz created in *D'ror Yik'ra*, especially in the phrase
Yin'tzor'chem Ke'mo Ba'Vat ("He will guard you like the apple of the eye"):

Example XII   *D'ror Yik'ra (Z'mir'ot Sha'bbat)*   L. Glantz

17 Ukrainian-Dorian Mode — the musical mode represented by the natural diatonic scale D—D containing a minor 3rd and
minor 7th, with a raised 4th.

Example XIIa   *Pit'chu La'nu (Ne'i'la)*   B. Maissner

The following phrases represent the unique creativity and the precious style of a man who achieved the highest level of musical and religious interpretation of the Jewish sacred texts. To me, the paradigm example of this is expressed in the spoken words of the prayer *Mach'ni'sei Ra'cha'mim* ("Angels of mercy") — the concluding prayer of the midnight *Se'li'chot* service. I cannot forget how Glantz's words, music and ecstasy tore my heart out as a young man praying in the synagogue!

> *I cannot forget how Glantz's words, music and ecstasy tore my heart out as a young man praying in the synagogue!*

In this wonderful composition — *Mach'ni'sei Ra'cha'mim* — the angels are called upon to plead on our behalf before God. It brings shivers to my spine when I hear Glantz's mysterious, haunting, quiet and subdued voice, calling upon *Mal'a'chey El'yon*, the angels above, to bring forth our plea for God's mercy — *Hach'ni'su Ra'cha'mei'nu Lif'nei Me'lech Mit'ra'tze Bi'Dma'ot* ("the forgiving King who gladly accepts our tears"). Glantz maneuvers the text in *parlando,* a semi-spoken song style, arriving at the passage *Hish'tad'lu Ve'Har'bu Te'chi'na U'Va'ka'sha Lif'nei Me'lech* ("intercede for us and multiply supplication and petition before the King"). I cannot forget the way he cried out, demanding of the angels *Haz'ki'ru Le'Fa'nav To'rah U'Ma'a'sim To'vim Shel Shoch'nei A'far* ("remind God of the good deeds of His earthly mortals"); *Ma'her A'nei'nu Elo'hei Yish'ei'nu* ("speedily answer us, our redeeming God").

The final tones of this prayer no longer remain in the sphere of our world! Glantz seemingly emerges to his personal "palace" of musical fantasy. He utters the final words *Ve'Ho'shi'a Be'Ra'cha'me'cha Me'shi'ach Tzid'ke'cha Ve'A'me'cha* ("save us, our redeemer"). He returns to us, with perfect *Nu'sach,* and in complete astonishment, we rejoin him in a conventional cadence of our own earthly world.

See Glantz's book *"Se'li'chot"* (p. 122):

Glantz's dramatic and intimate composition *A'hav'ti* ("I love the Lord because He heareth my voice and my supplications"), from the *Ha'llel* service (see his book "*Ha'llel* and The Three Festivals," p. 76-77), influenced my ideas and musical motif in *Sim Sha'lom* ("grant peace"), especially his rendering of the words *A'na A'do'nai Mal'ta Naf'shi* and *Shu'vi Naf'shi…Ga'mal A'lai'chi* ("O Lord, save my life! Be again at rest, O my soul, for the Lord has dealt kindly with you"), as shown in the following example:

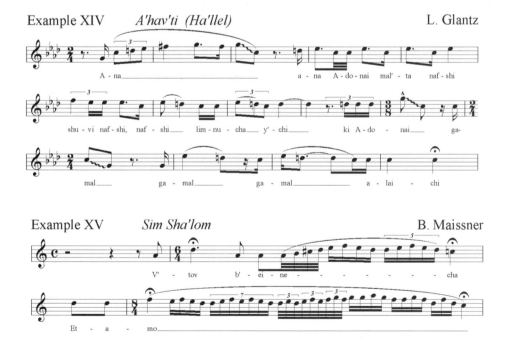

Similar ideas may be found in the conclusion of *Yir'u Ei'nei'nu... Ve'Al Kol Ma'a'se'cha* ("our eyes will witness...all Your great deeds"). This outpouring of ecstasy, which I believe I received directly from Glantz, found refuge in many of my melodic curves and rhythmic motifs.

Example XVa — *Yir'u Ei'nei'nu* — B. Maissner

A great example of Glantz's intellectual treatment of prayer text can be found in his exemplary composition, the mystical melody of *Bir'kat Ko'ha'nim* ("The Priestly Blessing"). Notice the words *Ye'va're'che'cha...Ve'Yish'me're'cha* ("He will bless you and save you") from Glantz's book "Sabbath Morning Service," p. 92:

Example XVI — *Bir'kat Ko'ha'nim* — L. Glantz

I later realized that this same flavor found in Glantz's *Bir'kat Ko'ha'nim* is very similar to Theme B of *Be'ta'le'lei O'rah* and in its following thematic developments:

Example XVIa   *Be'ta'le'lei O'rah (Tal)*   B. Maissner

Example XVIb   *Be'ta'le'lei O'rah (Tal)*   B. Maissner

Example XVIc   *Be'ta'le'lei O'rah (Tal)*   B. Maissner

It is amazing how similar melodic material of open 5th and 4th create such archaic, Hebraic and authentic characteristics of typical Oriental [Middle Eastern]-Israeli style, so strongly connected to the land of Israel. Years ago when searching for some melodic opening to an English text of our "Martyrology Service"[18] on *Yom Ki'ppur,* I found myself in similar spheres. My composition "Night of Mankind" from the *Yom Ki'ppur* Martyrology begins calmly: "If the voice of the prophet…" then continues with expressions of horror: "…made of martyrs children's bones." This is really the pinnacle of Glantz's influence upon my musical thinking.

Example XVII   Night Of Mankind *(Yom Ki'ppur* Martyrology) B. Maissner

---

18 Martyrology Service is a section of the Day of Atonement services in memory of the death of ten Rabbis who sanctified God's Name during the Bar Kochba revolt against the Roman Empire in the year 131 of the Common Era.

I recently realized a discovery that was evidently dormant for most of my life. It exemplifies the importance of Leib Glantz's impact upon me. Glantz's composition *Mi Cha'mo'cha* ("Who is like Thee, O Lord?"), which I remember vividly from my childhood, when I had sung it so many times without full awareness, found its way into my own compositions of *Mi Cha'mo'cha* and *Yir'u Ei'nei'nu* ("Our eyes will witness"):

The following recitative of the same *Yi'ru Ei'nei'nu* undoubtedly has its roots in the fiber Glantz had impressed upon my entire cantorial philosophy:

Finally, my sweetest musical memory is that of *Do'di Ze'chor Li Shik'ley Ef'ron* ("my beloved, recall my merit of the shekels Abraham gave Efron") from *the Mu'saf* service of *Sha'bbat She'ka'lim.*[19] These musical moments linger in my memory as the focus of Glantz's message. Here he said it all. Indeed, this composition was the essence of his singing *Ne'sha'ma,*[20] his true yearning soul.

Mach'ni'sei Ra'cha'mim and *Dodi Ze'chor Li Shik'ley E'fron* were two distinct liturgical moments that changed my entire approach to the art of cantorial music. Glantz sang these prayers with melodies that have actually haunted me for the rest of my life!

Leib Glantz was the paradigm mentor of *Cha'za'nut* in our time. Lovers of cantorial adore his glorious voice, his tears, and his joyful music. Every person who was privileged to hear him praying was affected and moved by his passion and his intimate interpretations of the prayer texts. Moreover, there is not one cantor or *Ba'al Te'fi'la* in our time who has not been directly or indirectly influenced by the legacy left for us by Leib Glantz. Consciously or subconsciously, every improvisational sequence in today's cantorial art contains the ingredients originally created by Leib Glantz.

---

19 *Sha'bbat She'ka'lim* — the Sabbath when the *To'rah* chapter *She'ka'lim* is read in the synagogue.
20 *Ne'sha'ma* — soul.

Leib Glantz embraced the entire scope of Jewish liturgy. As *Cha'zan*, composer, superb musician, poet, dramatist, actor, academician, teacher and most of all *O'hev Tzi'yon*, a lover of Zion, his life was dedicated to a sacred mission. He possessed the quality to heal the souls of his listeners. He provoked anger and made demands of the Almighty. He succeeded in bringing the aura of heaven to earth, so that we mortals could share a glimpse of what the creatures and angels surrounding God's chariot might experience. Glantz evoked in us the deepest of human emotions. We experienced pain as he reminded us of the destruction of our people, our communities and our Holy Temple. His ascending, chromatic rising and falling wailing, made us tremble with anxiety, fear and awe. His pastoral passages of *Ka'va'na* and *D'vei'kut* made us dwell upon the meaning of life.

> *He provoked anger and made demands of the Almighty. He succeeded in bringing the aura of heaven to earth, so that we mortals could share a glimpse of what the creatures and angels surrounding God's chariot might experience.*

His voice was medicine to my soul, food for my thoughts, a platform to aspire to and, in a way, an insurmountable height to be achieved. His image lives within me with my every breath, every song, and every prayer. This giant of a musical and vocal genius remains for me "*A'don* Glantz" as I used to address him in my childhood. I will forever remember that warm intimate handshake after each and every prayer service with the blessing of *Yi'shar Ko'cha'cha*[21] and his warm hugs at my *Bar Mitz'va*, handing his gift to me with his own handwritten blessing.

Indeed, as he wrote to me in the *Bar Mitz'va* book — "*Ha'Bo'cher Be'Shi'rei Zim'ra*" — He chose *my* life's melody.

---

21 *Yi'shar Ko'cha'cha* — Congratulations! Well done!

14

The Anatomy of Greatness

CANTOR CHAIM FEIFEL[1]

What is the force behind the greatness of Cantor Leib Glantz?

When I think of Glantz's direction and achievements I am reminded of the prophesy of Isaiah Chapter 40:

> "Speak to the heart of Jerusalem and proclaim to her that the time of exile has been fulfilled. Prepare the way of the Lord, make straight the crooked way in the desert and smooth out the rough places... Climb to the highest mountain and raise your voice with strength, lift your voice and do not be afraid."

Glantz was most probably inspired by these prophetic words. His creative genius paved a fresh path that will enhance the future of *Cha'za'nut*.

I was fortunate to have had the opportunity to share many hours with Glantz. It was at a time when I was very young. Today, with hindsight, I better understand the person who gave me the opportunity to glimpse his creative energies. Most people only knew him through his recordings. Some actually heard him chant at synagogue services. Only a few knew him on a personal level as a creative individual. I was one of those fortunate people.

---

[1] Cantor Chaim Feifel is a graduate of the Cantorial School of the Jewish Theological Seminary in New York. Upon graduation he spent a year in Israel, studying at the Rubin Academy of Music and privately with Cantor Leib Glantz. He served as cantor of various congregations in the U.S. for 20 years and received a Masters degree in Rehabilitation Counseling. Following *A'li'ya* to Israel, the Feifel family was one of the pioneers of the Sinai city of Yamit. He is a highly respected teacher of *Cha'za'nut* at the Tel Aviv Cantorial Institute (TACI) and at the Cantorial School of the Hebrew Union College in Jerusalem.

When I think of Leib Glantz the first words that enter my mind are "creativity" and "energy." He had an abundance of both. He imbued me with both of these qualities and these shaped my life and my career as a *Cha'zan*.

Glantz rarely spoke about his own career and the process by which he achieved his goals. However, one could absorb a lot of his flow through his teaching. His lectures revealed his energy to fulfill his goals. I learned from him that in order to be creative, I must ask questions in order to clarify my objectives. I must never take anything for granted. In the onset of our meetings I was somewhat stressed by his unending questions that were at times difficult to answer. Today, fifty years later, I realize that his questions gave me strength to learn and find my deeper self, enabling me to feel in harmony with his unique cantorial approach and to express the *Te'fi'la* (prayers) in a most meaningful way.

Glantz's method of work was very microcosmic: everything that he created was executed with consciously clear thought. This awareness enabled him to bond the past with the present, so as to create gateways to the future.

> *Glantz's method of work was very microcosmic: everything that Glantz created was executed with consciously clear thought. This awareness enabled him to bond the past with the present, so as to create gateways to the future.*

He didn't function in a vacuum. He expanded the roots he derived from his youth under the influence of his father and other early traditional experiences. He felt a need to broaden these roots in order to enhance his professional and creative growth. He did so by investigating the deeds of other great cantors. His inquisitiveness led him to find sources that would broaden his views. Glantz would mention the names of *Cha'za'nim* such as David Roitman, Pinchas Minkowsky, Yerucham Hakatan, Israel Alter, Bezalel Odesser [Schulsinger] and other cantors who inspired him. I believe that these men had great influence on Glantz and became an important source which enabled him to expand his roots and lead to his own creative development.

He was also involved in research, discovering lost traditional prayer elements that he wished to reintroduce to their respectable place in the *Te'fi'la*. His inquisitiveness directed him to visit different synagogues and study other traditions. There he hoped to find ancient authentic sources of prayer chants. He observed that during the years in the Diaspora all kinds of foreign elements crept into our prayer services. One of his primary aims was to diminish their presence. He promoted his research by giving lectures to professionals and non-professionals, hoping that through his research and discoveries he would reintroduce these ancient sources

Levi Eshkol, Prime Minister of Israel, with A. Rosenblatt and Leib Glantz, at the opening of the Tel Aviv Institute for Jewish Liturgical Music and the Cantors Academy, Tel Aviv, 1959.

as he developed a new trend in synagogue chant. Cantor Glantz combined these discoveries with his own creative forces to enhance his own compositions.

He was an ardent Zionist. His conviction and commitment to Zionism was so strong that he decided to live out his years in *E'retz Yis'ra'el*. His return to Zion was a fulfillment of a dream. While in Israel he remembered his early years in the *Ga'lut* (Diaspora) and the maudlin qualities that *Cha'za'nim* had been expressing for centuries. It was difficult for him to accept the extensive sobbing, typical of the East European chant. Glantz recognized the reason for this sadness. He realized that the crying was a reflection of the suffering of the Jewish people throughout the centuries. Yet he felt that once our people returned to the shores of our forefathers, establishing an independent state, it was time to diminish the sadness and implant a greater amount of joy into our prayers. Glantz would often become upset when listening to cantors crying in prayers that were totally positive in nature, or when observing the demise of the traditional *Nu'sach*. He was even more astounded to observe that *Ba'a'lei Te'fi'la* and *Cha'za'nim* in synagogues had forgotten the *Nu'sach,* thus corrupting our historical musical connection with our past. His aim was to develop and introduce new elements into the

> *His aim was to develop and introduce new elements into the worship that would evolve into an Israeli Nu'sach, combining the age old traditions with new ideas, clearly reflecting our return to our historical homeland.*

worship that would evolve into an Israeli *Nu'sach*, combining the age old traditions with new ideas, clearly reflecting our return to our historical homeland.

Leib Glantz belonged to a rare breed of people. He was a fighter, and no matter what challenge he had chosen for himself he would have succeeded in his aims and reached his goal. I admired his perseverance, facing obstacles and setbacks without hesitating, until finally realizing his goals. Glantz chose to direct his energies to bringing new life to synagogue chant. His single mindedness and his faith in his goals strengthened his capacity to adhere to his chosen path. Glantz, beyond doubt, was a true rebel, totally immersed in his chosen path. A rebel can be described as a person who is unhappy with present conditions and invests all his energies to bring about change. Glantz kept growing and climbing to new worlds, integrating all his energies into a solid path leading towards a unified goal.

The process of integrating his inner forces made his creations ever more complex. The more complex he became, the more his compositions created a greater gap between himself and the common worshipper. He traveled so deeply into the heavenly spheres that the average person at the time found it difficult to appreciate his language and creative ideas. He truly envisioned raising the level of worship for everyone; however, in his lifetime he succeeded in touching but a small group of educated people who were capable of cerebrally grasping his intentions. The ordinary worshipper could neither comprehend the level of his works nor could he be emotionally moved by his innovations. The typical worshipper, in his simplicity, wanted to hear the same sounds that he heard throughout his lifetime, unwilling to deal with extreme changes. In spite of this, Glantz continued in his struggle against rejection, believing that eventually it would enhance synagogue worship.

Glantz was fortunate that he received much support from the more educated cantors who were intellectually capable of appreciating his creative insights. This intellectual and professional support was critical in order for him to continue in his path. In addition, he received great support from the worshippers who actually came to his synagogue to hear him chant. When Cantor Glantz chanted services, the synagogue was always fully packed to the point of standing room only. Glantz was successful in turning his creativity into action. Above and beyond his innovative creations, while on the pulpit, Glantz would give himself up completely to the spirit of the prayers and released a passion that was absolutely hypnotic and electrifying. He could lift the worshipper to an elevated spiritual plane. The emotions that emanated from him were uplifting and exciting, employing multitudes of colors, moods and variations of *Nu'sach* that were never heard before. Once the worshipper caught on to Glantz's penetrating expressions, his meaning became clearly understood and appreciated and the old styles of chanting became mundane to their ears. Unfortunately, not enough people had the opportunity to fall under his novel spell when he chanted. Had he found workable pathways to spread his ideas and meaning, his approach to *Te'fi'la* would have eventually become more universal in his lifetime.

The deep integration of his intent and his lofty creative powers drove him more and more to become individualistic. However, a creator cannot spread his intentions successfully without followers. In many ways, he was a one man show. He needed the support of the multitudes. As an individualist, the greatness of his accomplishments and creative work could not be dispersed amongst ordinary worshippers. He was unable to create followers who would bring his message to the throngs. In order to achieve this he needed to develop community leaders in order to promote his aims. At times Glantz was frustrated due to the fact that other musicians, cantors and singers were able to disperse their ideas among the ordinary worshippers. Perhaps these men succeeded because they used a language that was simpler and easier to relate to.

Glantz realized that he could not be successful in bringing his ideas to the common worshippers without the help of others. He therefore founded a school for *Cha'za'nim*, hoping that in time his students would prove to be his emissaries in bringing his ideas to the masses. Over the years, those of his students who became cantors did advance his musical ideas. He also succeeded in preparing cantorial teachers who promote the principles that he devised and believed in. Eventually, new generations of cantors are beginning to enhance their *Te'fi'la* in the spirit that Glantz created.

Cantor Glantz reached a level of expression that no *Cha'zan* can emulate. He stands alone above all others. Time has a way of promoting difficult creative ideas and making them more acceptable to the common ear. There is no doubt that he was ahead of his time. Today his early compositions such as *She'ma Yis'ra'el, Bir'kat Ko'ha'nim,* and *Sim Sha'lom* have become quite popular amongst *Cha'za'nim* and are sung quite frequently. His newer creations are rarely performed. In order to sing these newer works successfully, the *Cha'zan* has to have a very solid background in classical singing. His newer creations speak a poetic language which is absolutely beautiful. In the beginning of his career, Glantz used an innovative Chazanic style that he nurtured from youth. As time progressed, Glantz's early creative process broadened and developed into a poetic style. In many of his later chants he diminished the

> *Glantz reached a level of expression that no* Cha'zan *can emulate. He stands alone above all others. Time has a way of promoting difficult creative ideas and making them more acceptable to the common ear. There is no doubt that he was ahead of his time.*

use of the old Chazanic styles and turned the *Te'fi'la* into pure poetry. When I listen to Glantz's compositions such as *Mach'ni'sei Ra'cha'mim, A'hav'ti,* and *A'na Be'Cho'ach* — I feel as if I am listening to beautiful musical poetry that ties in deeply with the depth of emotion and true essence of the text. For Glantz, the interpretation of the word was the most essential aspect of his creative process.

Glantz was well aware of his objectives. He followed his path with dedication and resolve. He engaged every aspect of his mind and spirit. He never doubted, regretted, or feared the path that he chose. His psychic energies were in full bloom, directing him on a harmonious path toward what he believed in. He would never surrender his goals. On the contrary, he relentlessly smoothed out the rough places on his chosen path and gained courage to flow onward, developing a greater understanding of his powers. His unique capacity to unify concepts, his capacity for deep reflection, and his ability to turn theory into action are the keys to understanding his greatness. He went forward in his chosen path with total abandon and complete involvement. Glantz did not know the meaning of boredom. I believe that he found great joy and satisfaction in his creative achievements. He would not indulge in projects that were not truly authentic. He would not allow himself to fall into the trap of creating just what the common worshipper desired to hear. He was truly authentic by being intrinsically motivated, believing in the value and importance of his mission. His intensity and love of what he was doing created greatness. His sharp awareness of everything he did musically supremely added quality to his goals.

Leib Glantz is a highly esteemed member of the "Cantorial Hall of Fame." His name is well known throughout the Jewish world for the greatness of his contributions. The creative flow that Glantz created is becoming an important part of our existing traditions, adding new energies to enhance the meaning of *Te'fi'la.*

Cantor Glantz died at the height of his creativity. I can't begin to imagine where he would have led us had he continued to live. His school would have expanded, drawing people to him from all over the world in order to study his methods and absorb his spirit.

People like Leib Glantz never die. Their spirits continue to flow for ever and ever, enriching others to follow in their footsteps and enhance the traditions that they created.

> *People like Leib Glantz never die. Their spirits continue to flow for ever and ever, enriching others to follow in his footsteps and enhance the traditions that he created.*

15

Present Day Problems in the Performance Practice
of the Works of Leib Glantz

Maestro Raymond Goldstein[1]

Unlike some of the more "popular" cantors of the *"Golden Age of Cha'za'nut,"* Leib Glantz not only was capable of writing music but was also highly articulate and true to his own transcriptions of his cantorial compositions.

Going through his archive at the Tel Aviv Cantorial Institute, it is interesting to note how the composer adjusted himself to the forces at hand, whether it was in the United States or later, in Israel. The earlier liturgical works were written for cantor and SATB (mixed choir, often with organ/piano accompaniment). The later ones were written for cantor and TTBB (male choir), a cappella.

During his lifetime, Bloch and Transcontinental Music Publications published a number of single compositions, mostly for cantor and piano. After his death, Israel Music Institute published a collection of his compositions called *"Selected Works Ri'nat Ha'Ko'desh"*:

Volume 1:   *Nu'sa'chei Te'fi'la* (Prayer modes for solo cantor);
Volume 2:   *Te'fi'lot Leil Sha'bbat* (Friday Evening Service);
Volume 3:   *Te'fi'lot Sha'bbat* (Sabbath Morning Service);
Volume 4:   *Ha'llel Ve'Sha'losh Re'ga'lim* (*Hallel* and Three Festivals);
Volume 5:   *Se'li'chot* (Penitential prayers);

---

1 Raymond Goldstein is the associate conductor and resident composer-arranger for the Jerusalem Great Synagogue choir. Born in Cape Town, South Africa (1953), he has served since 1978 on the faculty of the Rubin Academy of Music in Jerusalem, and since 1991 on the faculty of the Tel Aviv Cantorial Institute.

Volume 6: *Ya'mim No'ra'im* (High Holidays)[2];
Volume 7: *Shi'rim* (Songs)[3].

Reviewing all the available recordings, from 78 RPM records to LP's (33-1/3 RPM) to cassettes (the latter, based in part on live and radio recordings issued by Musique Internationale), one is made painfully aware of the lack of completeness as to what was written and later published and what was actually recorded, making one grateful for the private collections of transcriptions [from the recordings] made by master transcribers like Noach Schall and Shmuel Baruch Taube.

As a cantor, Glantz was primarily a melodist with much ingenuity, originality and inventiveness: for example, his use of the ascending and descending fourth and fifth intervals as well as his tendency to emphasize accented, non-essential notes in a given chord, exemplified his own unique brand of *Nu'sach*. Like any great composer, two bars of Glantz's music immediately inform us as to the author of the piece.

> *As a cantor, Glantz was primarily a melodist with much ingenuity, originality and inventiveness... Two bars of Glantz's music immediately inform us as to the author of the piece.*

Glantz is not for the faint-hearted. His main concern was for *Pei'rush Ha'Mi'la* — interpretation of the word — the inner understanding of each prayer. However, Glantz's harmonic palette was based on traditional Western harmony and sometimes failed to bring out the inner beauty of some of his works. Basic harmony from the romantic tradition was to prove inadequate when harmonic difficulties arose because of the innate twists and turns of classical Hebrew prayer modes. This led to a frequent reliance on the use of the diminished chord as a panacea to any harmonic problem.

It is interesting to compare the original editions of *She'ma Yis'ra'el* and *Dror Yik'ra* with Dr. Hanan Winternitz's reworking of the same piece for the collected edition published after Glantz's death. On various recordings recorded by Glantz himself, when the accompanist was also a professional arranger, such as Vladimir Heifetz, the accompaniment is of a much higher standard, as Glantz had to acquiesce to the request of the accompanist and perhaps of himself.

It is not this writer's intention to delve into the re-workings of David Loeb's settings that were done and published after Glantz's death; suffice it to say that they bear no real harmonic

---

2 Volumes 2–6 were edited and rearranged by David Loeb.
3 Volume 7 (Songs) was edited by Maestro Yehoshua Zohar. The piano accompaniments were rearranged by Dr. Hanan Winternitz.

relationship to much of the original unpublished manuscripts (and recordings done by Glantz himself). They are, by and large, modernistic in approach and unfortunately do not enhance the religious character of Glantz's compositions, thus rendering them as rather useless and difficult to perform and to be appreciated by our present day "traditional" audiences.

Loeb writes those compositions with keyboard for organ with pedal accompaniment (3 staves), making it impractical unless performed on some organ in a well-equipped auditorium and/or church! Few auditoriums for the modern *Cha'za'nut* lovers have organs with pedals and many Conservative and Reform temples have dispensed with the pedal organs in favor of modern manual electric keyboards. At any rate, most of Glantz's compositions would have been deemed as too "heavy" for them.

Alas, we have but few cantors capable of performing these magnificent recitatives today and many of those who are capable of performing them will have learned the material by rote (from the recordings themselves). Unfortunately, too many of our traditional cantors have never developed excellent sight-reading abilities or the assurance of interpreting works from scores alone!

Singing Glantz's material in the synagogue is feasible. However, it is more difficult in the concert hall. Glantz's vocal writing is for high agile tenors with a deep understanding of the cantorial *coloratura*. His work would never find place with baritones and basses. This writer has had the privilege over the years to arrange from scratch a number of recitatives for various concerts with internationally renowned cantors. Like Cantor Yossele Rosenblatt before him, Glantz actually inspires a good arranger to use his own inventiveness to create good harmonic background for these compositions.

> *Glantz's vocal writing is for high agile tenors with a deep understanding of the cantorial* coloratura.

A practical solution to all of the above would be:

1. Publish a collected edition of all the recitatives *sans* accompaniment. The edition should include some grave omissions (like the early *Le'chu Ne'ra'ne'na* and the famous *Sho'mer Yis'ra'el*), culled from Glantz's own musical manuscripts

2. Publish an edition for voice and piano of the famous cantorial recitatives (based largely on the existing vocal scores with subtle harmonic changes where really deemed necessary) that would supplement the secular and patriotic songs (as already rearranged by Dr. Hanan Winternitz).

3.   Publish a new "practical" edition of the best of the choral compositions, arranged for
      cantor and TTBB (male choir).

In the archives there are still compositions and melodies that have remained in manuscript and
were also never recorded.

At this stage in time there is a different perception as to what the emphasis for publication
should be than what prevailed immediately after Glantz's death in 1964. A full thematic catalog with *incipits* should be made available for researchers and performers. These publications
would then rekindle the flame that was lit by the wonderful originality personified in the art
of Leib Glantz.

16

The Theory of the Jewish Prayer Modes

Maestro Yehoshua Zohar[1]

The Tel Aviv Institute for Jewish liturgical Music was established in 1959 under the leadership of the late Cantor Leib Glantz. The aim of this institute was to educate a generation of modern cantors, enlightened by Jewish culture, who would possess a general as well as a musical education. These cantors were to become knowledgeable in the secrets of their profession, and would be capable of restoring the glory of the Hebrew melody to its former state.

Leib Glantz developed his art on firm theoretical foundations that he established after many years of deep and thorough research. His students were required to recognize the melodic line upon which every prayer was based. This was the way to ensure that the cantor would not deviate from the *Nu'sach* and would be able to create new melodies within the framework of that *Nu'sach*.

Together with the teaching of theoretical foundations, the future cantors received practical instruction. Leib Glantz would present each prayer, indicating the melodic line on which it was based. This is how the chapters of

> *Glantz developed his art on firm theoretical foundations that he established after many years of deep and thorough research. His students were required to recognize the melodic line upon which every prayer was based.*

---

1 Yehoshua Zohar, Musicologist and conductor of Cantor Leib Glantz's choir at the *Tif'e'ret Zvi* synagogue in Tel Aviv from 1955 till 1964. These words were the foreword of the Leib Glantz book "*Ri'nat Ha'Ko'desh — Nu'sa'chei Te'fi'la* (prayer modes), edited by Yehoshua Zohar, published by The Tel Aviv Institute for Jewish Liturgical Music in conjunction with the Israel Music Institute, Tel Aviv, 1965.

Shach'rit, Min'cha and *Ar'vit* for weekdays, *Ka'ba'lat Sha'bbat, Ar'vit* for *Sha'bbat* in three modes, *Shach'rit* and *Mu'saf* for *Sha'bbat, Ar'vit* and *Shach'rit* for *Sha'losh Re'ga'lim,* and also *Se'der Ha'llel,* were formed and are presented in the book *Ri'nat Ha'Ko'desh,* which is dedicated to defining the ancient Jewish prayer modes.

Glantz disdained the idea of educating a generation of "imitating cantors" who would copy his prayers and those of others. His energy was totally devoted to creating a new type of cantor who would feel comfortable within the wonderful array of *Nu'sa'chim* and melodies, and who would always know where he was musically standing and to where he was headed.

> *Glantz disdained the idea of educating a generation of "imitating cantors" who would copy his prayers and those of others. His energy was totally devoted to creating a new type of cantor who would feel comfortable within the wonderful array of* Nu'sa'chim *and melodies.*

That is the reason why Glantz did not compose a textbook for his students, as did his great predecessors, Baer, Wodak, and others, who left no room for individualistic expression, but rather handed over to the cantor a prepared and complete framework which did not demand of the student anything but perseverance in the study of enormous quantities of musical material.

Glantz, on the other hand, taught his students both the foundations and the building materials: the musical structure of the *Nu'sa'chim* as well as ways to use them. In this way, they were able to distinguish between the various forms of the ancient Pentatonic scales, the differences between the Sabbath reading of the *To'rah* in Pentatonic Major and the reading of the *Haf'ta'ra* in Pentatonic Minor. It would seem that it is the same melodic line, but the difference is in the central pivotal tone. The Pentatonic Major pivots on the tone F, and sometimes on C, whereas the Pentatonic Minor pivots on D. These differences can be found in the various prayers.

The *Bir'kot Ha'Sha'char* for weekday services are sung in the Pentatonic Minor, whereas the *A'vot* for *Shach'rit,* and the ending of the prayer *"A'lei'nu Le'Sha'bey'ach"* are sung in the Pentatonic Major.

Glantz clarified the text of *"Ye'kum Pur'kan"* or *"A'do'shem Ma'lach"* for the Friday evening service, in a line composed of seven to thirteen tones, aided by the Tetrachord theory that he himself developed.

It is possible to distinguish four Tetrachords, each of which is built according to 1 - 1 - 1/2 steps (i.e., a Major Tetrachord), and each of which starts with the final tone of the preceding

Yehoshua Zohar, Glantz's choir conductor, speaking at the President of Israel's 1965 reception on the occasion of the publication of the book "*Zeharim — In Memory of Leib Glantz.*"
From left: Y. Zohar, Prof. Yehuda Even-Shmuel Kaufman, Mrs. Shazar, President of Israel Zalman Shazar, Miriam Glantz and S.Z. Shragai.

Tetrachord. The result is a line consisting of thirteen tones in which appear F sharp, F natural, and B flat. The use of this line in prayers is possible in one of the three following forms:

a. Seven tones (parallel to the Mixolydian mode);
b. Ten tones;
c. Thirteen tones.

In *Ka'ddish* for the *Ne'i'la Yom Ki'ppur* service, or in the reciting of the *Ha'gga'da* for the Passover *Se'dder*, the line with seven tones is used.

An example of the use of the ten-tone line is *Bar'chu* for *Ar'vit* and *U'Mi'pnei Cha'ta'ei'nu* from the *A'mi'da*, both from the *Sha'losh Re'ga'lim* prayer service.

The line composed of thirteen tones is used in *A'vot* for the High Holy Days, which is one of the most difficult prayers for the cantor to execute.

In this way, Glantz presented and explained the context of the prayer *A'ha'va Ra'bbah* and its variations, *O'chi'la La'El, Ma'gen A'vot* and its variations, *Yish'ta'bach* (from *Shach'rit* for Sabbath), *Mi She'bei'rach* (*Mu'saf* for Sabbath), *A'ta Zo'cher* (*Mu'saf* for *Rosh Ha'Sha'na*), *Shach'rit* for *Rosh Ha'Sha'na,* and the *Nu'sach* for *Te'fi'lat Tal* and *Te'fi'lat Ge'shem.*

Each prayer has its place within one of the above frameworks. The educated cantor who knows each prayer's place in the service will maintain the fine tradition of our ancient *Nu'sach* prayer modes. This cantor will never fail, and even more important, will never cause the worshippers of his congregation to falter.

Before he could complete the mission he took upon himself to rehabilitate the art of cantorial music and prayer, Leib Glantz's life work was cut short. On this first anniversary of his death, we accompany this important publication with the hope that this book will enable cantors and lovers of cantorial to recognize and understand the value of their art and their calling, and will lead them to engage in profound study, so that they can follow in the steps of their great scholar and teacher — Leib Glantz.

Part Three

Writings and Lectures of Leib Glantz

The transliteration of Hebrew and Yiddish terms in this book has been created to make it easier for readers who do not speak these languages. Hebrew and Yiddish words appear in italics, begin with capital letters, and an apostrophe separates every syllable. The Hebrew and Yiddish words and sentences are followed by the English translation (in parentheses). Several authors of essays have used a different transliteration system; however, an effort has been made to use the same transliteration system throughout the book.

In several of the articles, essays, and lectures that appear in Part 3, the term "Oriental," that was used in the first half of the twentieth century to describe Middle Eastern Jews, culture and music, should be understood as it is currently used, as "Eastern" or "Middle Eastern" (Eastern Jews, Eastern culture, Eastern music, and so forth).

1

The Musical Basis of *Nu'sach Ha'Te'fi'la*

LECTURE AT THE FIFTH ANNUAL CONVENTION OF THE CANTORS ASSEMBLY, 1952[1]

LEIB GLANTZ

When cantors ask themselves, "What is the musical basis of *Nu'sach Ha'Te'fi'la?*"[2] — they are seeking first and foremost a viable method, a method which will enable them to understand what they are doing in and with our musical tradition and which will help them to do it with more assurance, more clarity and more confidence.

The day is past when the cantor lived in an environment in which the Jewish musical heritage was an organic part of his being and when the musical tradition permeated every moment of his life, from the chanting of the *Mo'deh A'ni* in the early morning to the *She'ma* he said before retiring. Today, the cantor must learn his art as a separate and often isolated element in his musical education. To do this, he cannot be satisfied merely with knowing the historical basis or the archaeological findings of scholars. These are important, interesting, and significant, but we need something more specifically useful in our actual work.

If we are to retain the purity and beauty of our musical services, where every prayer has its traditional setting and every holiday its specific musical aroma, we must find a way to transmit

---

1 Lecture by Leib Glantz on May 6th, 1952, at the session devoted to Cantorial Studies, at the Fifth Annual Conference-Convention of The Cantors Assembly and The Department of Music of the United Synagogues of America at The Concord Hotel, Kiamesha Lake, New York.

2 *Nu'sach* – an Aramaic term derived from the Hebrew root *Sach. Nu'sach* is a melodic pattern or prayer mode governing the traditional chanting of the prayer texts. The melodies of the prayers were transmitted informally from generation to generation, and collated into a body called *Nu'sach.* Chanting the prayers according to given melodic patterns and modes was traditional and obligatory. The motifs are subject to repetition and omission and may generally be altered and varied, affording ample opportunity for improvisation. The plural of *Nu'sach* is *Nus'cha'ot.* [Source: *Concise Encyclopedia of Jewish Music,* by Macy Nulman, McGraw-Hill Book Co., NY, 1975].

the knowledge of the subtleties and the differences between the *Nus'cha'ot*. We cannot depend upon memory or mechanical imitation and repetition alone.

Our music has many subtle variations and it is only too easy for the cantor to get lost in a labyrinth. Think for a moment of the similarity between the *Ka'ddish* of the *Ne'i'la* service and the *Ka'ddish* of the prayers of *Tal* or *Ge'shem*.[3] They are both from the group called *"Mi'Sinai" Nus'cha'ot* and some of their intervals are identical.

> *Our music has many subtle variations and it is only too easy for the cantor to get lost in a labyrinth.*

Nevertheless, the differences are significant. In a culture where every Jew was familiar with the appropriate *Nu'sach*, memory, habit, training and tradition kept the cantor within the proper framework, along with his whole congregation. How few are today the worshippers who know the difference.

We must develop a system by which we may be able to teach the basic musical line for each *Nu'sach* with which the cantors work. I have been thinking along these lines for a long time and I should like to present to you some of my observations. I have found them very useful in providing me with a theoretical basis in terms of which I can understand and differentiate the various *Nus'cha'ot*. I have not yet determined a satisfactory line for all of them, but I believe that this line of inquiry has already brought into the light some of the secrets of how the *Nus'cha'ot* are built. In certain of the *Nus'cha'ot,* where I was able to work out complete and correct lines or scales, the similarities, the differences and the confusions between them were clarified. Elements that formerly had to be described as accidental, or capricious, found their place in a regular pattern.

Before we begin our analysis of the *Nus'cha'ot* in terms of musical intervals, lines, modes and scales, let us first briefly review the concept of *Nu'sach* itself. The Jews used this term in the same way as did other Eastern peoples, such as the Arabs and the Hindus. They used it to describe a short musical line, a musical group, or a musical phrase, which was the basis of their melodies. Once the performer knew these short musical lines, he was left to himself to improvise and elaborate upon that basic line.

The Jewish people developed two types or groups of *Nus'cha'ot*. The first type fits the description as given above more exactly. It is a group of musical phrases built upon the biblical cantillation modes.[4] The cantors use these *Nus'cha'ot* as a basis for their recitatives, improvisations

---

3 *Ge'shem* and *Tal* — rain and dew.

4 Biblical cantillation modes — the art of chanting the *To'rah* is over two thousand years old and evolved from a solely oral tradition, to a formalized system of musical notation that we now call trope, *Ta'a'mim*, or musical cantillation. This biblical cantillation system is made up of 28 signs and each sign stands for a specific musical pattern or melodic motif.

or compositions. The improviser or composer had full freedom to elaborate, to develop, to introduce modulations, within the framework of the particular musical line. Examples of such *Nus'cha'ot* are the *"A'do'nai Ma'lach" Nu'sach* of Friday night, which is identical with the *"Ye'kum Pur'kan" Nu'sach* of Saturday morning, the *"Ma'gen A'vot" Nu'sach,* the *"Yish'ta'bach" Nu'sach* of Saturday morning, and the *"A'ha'va Ra'bbah" Nu'sach.*

There is a second type, also called *Nus'cha'ot,* which differs from the first group, because it consists of a group of *fixed prayer melodies* that have been associated with certain texts from time immemorial. These fixed melodies are not subject to improvisation, elaboration or any kind of change. They are always sung in the definite crystallized form. These are called *"Mi'Sinai"* melodies, or "melodies from Sinai" and they include some of the most beloved and important prayers of the liturgy. Of course, even the fixed melodies vary in different parts of the world. The Oriental [Middle Eastern], the Sephardic, and the Ashkenazic communities have crystallized different melodies for the same texts.

Poetic legend has it that God himself sang these melodies to Moses on Mt. Sinai, when He gave him the *To'rah.* To our forefathers it was unthinkable that God should not reveal Himself in music. How lofty an origin does our tradition ascribe to the music of our prayers!

Although legend and folklore place the origin of the *Mi'Sinai* prayer melodies even further back in the mists of history than the biblical cantillations, musicological research has demonstrated that these *Mi'Sinai* melodies developed later — in the Diaspora. The first group, the musical lines based upon the biblical cantillation modes, has history that goes back at least 2400 years. Both the biblical modes and the *Mi'Sinai* melodies were exposed to many different influences and to many different cultures in their long history, but their main features have remained the basis of synagogue music to this day.

> *Although legend and folklore place the origin of the* Mi'Sinai *prayer melodies even further back in the mists of history than the biblical cantillations, musicological research has demonstrated that these* Mi'Sinai *melodies developed later — in the Diaspora.*

In any discussion of the origin of Jewish music, full recognition must be given to the great musicologist, Avraham Zvi Idelsohn (1882-1938), who in the short span of his life succeeded in proving that the biblical cantillation modes were well preserved in their raw state by the Oriental [Middle Eastern] Jewish communities. He also proved that the Byzantine and the Western Christian world inherited and utilized the same modes in their Gregorian chants. There is also a contemporary musicologist, Shlomo Rosowsky (b. 1878), who is making tremendous contributions in the study of biblical cantillation. A few others are engaged in this field and we are beginning to see light on all of these mysteries of the Jewish contribution to the art of music.

I do not belong to that school of thought that believes that the roots of a culture are necessarily the same as the flowers and the fruits of a culture. It is very important to know the roots and the sources. It is just as important to cherish and to value the manifold developments of a culture throughout its entire history.

There is a danger, it is true, that strange and illegitimate elements often find their way into a culture. These must be discriminated against and eliminated wherever possible. But in the dynamic life of a people, much is absorbed from the outside, assimilated and transformed into the true image of that people and that culture.

In our enthusiasm for the tremendously important scientific researches into the musical origins of our *Nus'cha'ot*, we may tend today to overestimate the importance of that part of our musical heritage that was frozen at a very primitive level by the Eastern Jewish communities. There is a tendency among certain circles to minimize much of the dynamic musical development of the Ashkenazic and Eastern European musical culture, while overestimating the value of that portion of our musical heritage that was kept in the "deep-freeze" by the Eastern Jewish communities. If we had relied upon the Eastern Jewish communities alone for our music, we would find ourselves today with only a few bare roots. If I may be allowed to draw a parallel, although no analogy is perfect, the Eastern Jewry played almost the same role in Jewish music as the *Karaite*[5] sect played in the freezing of Jewish *Ha'la'cha*[6] on the basis of the Five Books of Moses alone.

If the biblical cantillation modes may be considered the *"To'rah She'Bich'tav"* (written law) of Jewish music, then the later development of the *Nus'cha'ot* by the different communities, especially by Ashkenazic and Eastern European Jewries, may be likened to the *"To'rah She'Ba'al Peh,"* the oral commentary and interpretation of the raw material of the biblical cantillation.

The dynamic vitality of the Ashkenazic Jewry and later the Jewry of the Eastern European countries, which created the Rabbinic literature, the *Ka'bba'la*,[7] the Chasidic movement, the great modern Hebrew and Yiddish literatures, that same vitality also flourished in the field of music. It continued to create and to re-create, change and interchange, and also to weave-in new threads, new intervals, new musical lines, and even one great new *Nu'sach*, the *A'ha'va Ra'bbah Nu'sach,* into the Jewish liturgy.

We must recognize that just as the time came for the Talmud to be recorded and published, so the time has come when Jewish music can no longer withstand the great onslaughts of accidental singing. The time of *Ge'ni'za* (archiving) of Jewish music has arrived. The cantor and the composer must have the true musical line for each and every prayer. We must stop the guesswork and replace it with true understanding of the elements of cantorial creativity.

> *The time has come when Jewish music can no longer withstand the great onslaughts of accidental singing . . . We must stop the guesswork and replace it with true understanding of the elements of cantorial creativity.*

Let us now begin to look into the nature of our *Nus'cha'ot*. On the one hand, it is clear that they cannot be understood in terms of the crystallized Major and Minor scales of Western music. On the other hand, an analysis of the *Nus'cha'ot,* in terms of the biblical cantillation modes alone leads us into a labyrinth of such complexity that only the most articulate and skillful of musical scholars can find his way around.

5 *Karaites* — a Jewish sect founded in the eighth century and located chiefly in the Crimea and nearby areas, and in Israel, which rejects rabbinical interpretation in favor of a literal interpretation of the scriptures.
6 *Ha'la'cha* — Jewish law and jurisprudence, based on the Talmud.
7 *Ka'bba'la* — the ancient Jewish tradition of mystical interpretation of the Bible, first transmitted orally and using esoteric methods (including ciphers). It reached the height of its influence in the later Middle Ages and remains significant in Chasidism.

If I may be permitted to paraphrase a popular expression, "The Greeks had a line for it." Although it may be historically true that the Greek modes themselves were shaped upon the biblical modes, there is no doubt in my mind that the Greek modes offer the most useful lines for the understanding of our own musical formations.

The basic element of the Greek mode is the Tetrachord, a line of four steps. Various modes are different combinations of different Tetrachords.

Certain Jewish prayers can be analyzed in terms of known and recognized Greek modes. They can be understood by simply following the five-step (Pentachord), seven-step (Heptachord), or eight-step (Octachord) lines of the Greek modes.

There are others, however, which remain incapable of being so easily described. These, of course, are the ones that present the real problem to us. My observation is that the Ashkenazic Jews created new scales based upon new combinations of the elements of the Greek modes. We can find *Nus'cha'ot* based on a ten-step line, a twelve-step line, and a thirteen-step line, all of them new combinations of three or four Tetrachords in varying sequence.

> *The Ashkenazic Jews created new scales based upon new combinations of the elements of the Greek modes.*

It would not be possible in a single lecture to analyze every important prayer in the liturgy. This would require a series of lectures. In this presentation, we will have to limit ourselves to only a few examples.

On Sabbath morning the *Ba'al Shach'rit*, who usually precedes the cantor, sings the *Psu'kei De'Zim'ra* in a pure Pentatonic, or five-step line. This *Nu'sach* can definitely be traced to the biblical cantillation, but for all practical musical purposes, the modern musician can understand it as a *Nu'sach* built on the pure and simple Pentatonic line. This portion of the Sabbath service was most often chanted by a layman rather than by a professional cantor. Therefore it retained the simplicity of the original, and was not subjected to the musical development that other *Nus'cha'ot* experienced.

ILLUSTRATION 1

1a) *P'su'kei De'Zim'ra* **phrase:**

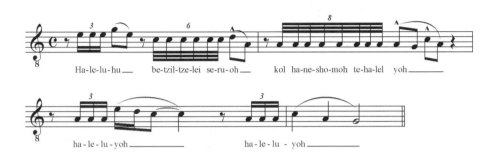

1b) The Pentatonic line:

The *Ak'da'mut* prayer of the *Sha'vu'ot* festival service can also be clearly understood through the application of the plain and simple Pentatonic line. It, too, has remained in an elementary form, because it is considered to be a *Mi'Sinai Nu'sach,* and as such was not subject to development. Of course, certain *Ba'a'lei Kri'ah* (masters of musical reading of the *To'rah*) may add some western intervals to the *Ak'da'mut,* but the Pentachord is so prominently dominating in it, that we can easily discard those additions as accidental and definitely ascertain the right line upon which it is built. To mention at least one more type of prominent prayer built on the Pentatonic, let us not forget the *A'vot* of the weekday *A'mi'da,* which is definitely sung in the Pentatonic all over the world, although different communities sing the entire weekday *A'mi'da* (which follows after the *A'vot*) in a different musical line. The *A'vot* remains the same Pentatonic in almost every place where Jews conduct prayer services.

ILLUSTRATION 2

2a) The *"Ak'da'mut"* **phrase:**

2b) The Pentatonic line:

2c) The *"A'vot"* of the weekday *A'mi'da:*

Let us now look at the *Nu'sach* of the *A'do'nai Ma'lach* of the Friday night service, which is identical with the *Ye'kum Pur'kan Nu'sach* of the Saturday morning service. The name *Ye'kum Pur'kan* was used mostly by Eastern European cantors. It is the most typical Major *Nu'sach* of the Jewish liturgy. This *Nu'sach* is used in almost every prayer that is sung in the Jewish Major scale. The most important of these are the *A'vot* of the Sabbath and festival morning services, and the *Na'a'ritz'cha* of the *Mu'saf* service.

When we apply the Greek Mixolydian mode, which consists of two conjunctive Tetrachords, the last note of the first Tetrachord, forming the first note of the second Tetrachord of this mode, forms a line of the following intervals:

one-tone,   one-tone,   one-half-tone.

ILLUSTRATION 3

3a) *Ye'kum Pur'kan* elementary short phrase:

3b) The Mixolydian mode:

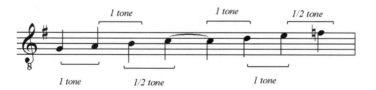

But when we look deeper into the *Ye'kum Pur'kan Nu'sach,* we find two prominent peculiarities:

1. When we proceed above the second Tetrachord, we must use Bb instead of B natural.
2. We use F# instead of F natural when we proceed below the first Tetrachord.

These two peculiarities have "tormented"' my thoughts for a long time. I am happy to present a solution to this problem:

The Jews added an identical Tetrachord on top of the second Tetrachord, and then added another identical Tetrachord below the first. The first addition creates a ten-step line, or a three-Tetrachord line, upon which some of our *Mi'Sinai Nus'cha'ot* are built. The second addition creates a thirteen-step line or four-Tetrachord line, upon which other *Mi'Sinai Nus'cha'ot* are built. We may compare it to a two-car train to which a car was added in front and another similar one added in the back.

ILLUSTRATION 4

4a) The 10-step *Ye'kum Pur'kan* line:

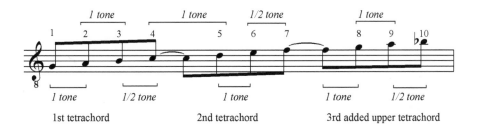

4b) The 13-step *Ye'kum Pur'kan* line:

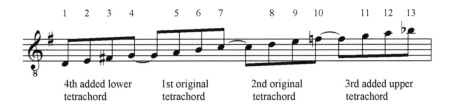

The original *Ye'kum Pur'kan* prayer of the Sabbath *Mu'saf* service, as well as the other basic Sabbath prayers, which are shaped in the *Ye'kum Pur'kan Nu'sach,* contain in themselves all of the features mentioned above. It is fascinating to observe that some of the *Mi'Sinai Nus'cha'ot*

of fixed prayer melodies, contain only one feature or one variation of this *Ye'kum Pur'kan Nu'sach* — either the seven-step, ten-step, or thirteen-step line. As a striking example of the most elementary type of Major scale, namely — the original Mixolydian seven-step, two Tetrachord line, we can mention the *Ka'ddish* prayer of the *Ne'i'la* service of *Yom Ki'ppur*.

Please keep this in mind. This analysis refers only to the *Ka'ddish* prayer of the *Ne'i'la* service. Although the *Ka'ddish* prayer for *Ge'shem* (rain) and *Tal* (dew) contain many elements of the same melody, it is definitely built on another line that we shall discuss later.

If we start the *Ne'i'la Ka'ddish* prayer from the G, while bearing in mind the seven-step line, and we work only within these seven steps, we can never lose the pattern of the *Nu'sach* of the *Ne'i'la* service.

ILLUSTRATION 5

5a) The *"Ne'i'la Ka'ddish"* phrase:

5b) The Mixolydian 7-step line:

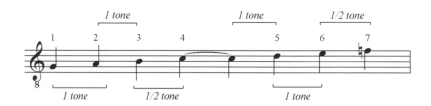

Another striking example of the seven-step major line is the *Nu'sach* of the *Ha'gga'da* (the story of the Exodus of the Israelites from Egypt) for *Pe'ssach* (Passover holiday*)*. With the exception of the melody for the "Four Questions," *Ma Nish'ta'na* ("Wherefore is this night distinguished from all other nights?"), which I venture to call a *Mi'Sinai* prayer melody, as it is almost an exact imitation of the biblical cantillation, the rest of the *Ha'gga'da* can be analyzed and understood much more easily in terms of the two Tetrachord, seven-step Major line.

ILLUSTRATION 6

6a) *"A'va'dim Ha'yi'nu"* (from the Passover *Ha'gga'da*):

A- vo-dim ho - yi - nu le-far-oh be-mitz-ro - yim etc.

6b) The Mixolydian 7-step line:

1   2   3   4   5   6   7

6c) *"A'dir Hu"* (from the Passover *Ha'gga'da*):

A - dir hu   bo- chur hu   cho- sid hu   za- kai hu   bim-hei - ro bim-hei - ro b'yo-

mei-nu be-ko-rov   Eil   be-nei   Eil   be-nei   be-nei   veis-cho be - ko - rov

A unique demonstration of the ten-step line is the *Ba're'chu* prayer of the evening Festival service. It is unique because the entire evening *Ma'a'riv* service of the festival is performed by the Ashkenazic and Eastern European communities in a Minor key. The *Ba're'chu,* curiously enough, starts with a Major, and climbs up to the Bb at the end of the third Tetrachord. This same three-Tetrachord line runs through the Festival morning *A'mi'da Nu'sach.*

ILLUSTRATION 7

7a) *"Ba're'chu"* for Festival evening services:

Bo   -   re chu   es   A - do - noy   ha-me-vo - roch

7b) The Festival *"A'mi'da"* morning service phrases:

u - mi - p' - nei   cha - to - ei - nu   go - li - nu me - ar - tzei - nu

ve - ho - fa_____ ve hi no-sei_____ o - lei - nu   le-ei - nei_____ kol   chai

7c) The three Tetrachord, 10-step line, *Ye'kum Pur'kan Nu'sach:*

1st tetrachord   2nd tetrachord   3rd added tetrachord

An even more striking example of the three-Tetrachord line, is the first part of the *Ve'Ha'Ko'ha'nim* prayer from the *A'vo'da* ceremony of *Rosh Ha'Sha'na* and *Yom Ki'ppur*. This is a fixed prayer melody, a *Mi'Sinai Nu'sach,* and is one of the most difficult for any cantor to understand or to analyze. I am glad to say that since I discovered the two-fold *Nu'sach* of the *Ve'Ha'Ko'ha'nim* prayer, I find it easier and more interesting to chant.

The secret of the *Ve'Ha'Ko'ha'nim* lies in the fact that it is built on two different *Nus'cha'ot*. The first part is based on the ten-step *Ye'kum Pur'kan Nu'sach*. However, it has its own particular combination of Tetrachords, in which the third Tetrachord is added below the first instead of above the second line. This gives us a line from D to F (above the octave).

If we start the *Ve'Ha'Ko'ha'nim* from G in the Jewish Major scale, one might be misled into thinking that this is the basic tonic of this musical scale. But we are amazed to learn in the course of chanting the *Nu'sach* that the tonic stems from the D below. Suddenly, in the middle of the *Ve'Ha'Ko'ha'nim*, we find a modulation from the Major of the *Ye'kum Pur'kan Nu'sach* to the *Nu'sach* of the *A'ha'va Ra'bbah*, which I shall discuss later.

ILLUSTRATION 8

8a) *"Ve'Ha'Ko'ha'nim"* (first part) built on the three Tetrachord, 10 step-line of the *Ye'kum Pur'kan Nu'sach*:

8b) *"Ve'Ha'Ko'ha'nim"* (second part) — modulates to *A'ha'va Ra'bbah Nu'sach*:

Please note that this *A'ha'va Ra'bbah* part has no augmented second interval in the second Tetrachord, which we will discuss later when we take up the special members of the *A'ha'va Ra'bbah* family.

Another type of *"Ve'Ha'Ko'ha'nim"* also modulates into *A'ha'va Ra'bbah* but in the first lower Tetrachord and not in the second as we have seen above.

8c) A second type of *"Ve'Ha'Ko'ha'nim"*:

The last and most important illustration of the *Ye'kum Pur'kan Nu'sach* in its entirety, namely the thirteen-step line, embracing all the four Tetrachords, I found in one of the greatest fixed prayer melodies, the *A'vot* of the High Holidays. I sometimes allude to this *Nu'sach* as an 'escalator' melody, for the rising thirteen-step line makes it the most difficult of all prayers.

As a child, I used to pity my grandfather and my father, who were both cantors, when they entangled themselves in that melody and had difficulty finding the way back to the tonic. When I grew older, I begged every cantor and every *Ba'al Te'fi'la* (prayer master) to demonstrate the *A'vot* for me in an effort to get at the mystery of its structure.

One of the oldest *Ba'a'lei Te'fi'la*, whom I met in a small town near Odessa, sang the *A'vot* for me in a most peculiar fashion. He assured me that he had heard it from Bezalel Odesser (1790-1860), the famous cantor and *Ba'al Te'fi'la*, who was considered the father of *Nu'sach Ha'Te'fi'la* for the Eastern European *Cha'za'nut* of the nineteenth century.

When I was sent by my father to Kishinev in order to hear the famous cantor, Avraham Berkovitch-Kalechnik, that cantor again sang the *A'vot* in the same manner as the old man mentioned above. On asking Kalechnik about the origin of the *A'vot* that he sang, he told me that it was given to him as an authentic *Nu'sach* from the mouth of Bezalel Odesser. Lately, while looking for an example of a *Mi'Sinai Nu'sach* in the thirteen-step line, I found in the *A'vot* version of those two people, the complete thirteen-step *Ye'kum Pur'kan* line. In the *A'vot*, as well as in the *Ve'Ha'Ko'ha'nim*, we discover that the Major melody is suddenly cut off and modulates into the same *A'ha'va Ra'bbah Nu'sach*. If one knows the full thirteen-step line of the *Ye'kum Pur'kan Nu'sach* and the *A'ha'va Ra'bbah* line as well, he is always on solid ground when he executes this complicated prayer.

The *A'vot* always presents an additional vocal difficulty to cantors, for its proper presentation requires a voice of considerable range.

This is clear as soon as you realize that it is based on a line of thirteen steps, each one playing an important role in the *Nu'sach*. The cantor should know which is the lowest of the thirteen steps in order to make it possible for him to climb up to those in the highest Tetrachord.

ILLUSTRATION 9

9a) *"A'vot"* **of the High Holidays (first part) built on a four Tetrachord, 13-step** *Ye'kum Pur'kan* **line:**

9b) Modulation of the *"A'vot"* **into** *A'ha'va Ra'bbah:*

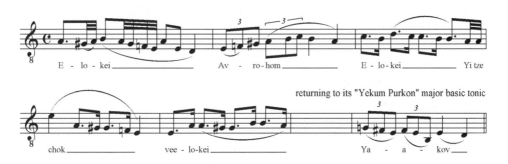

9c) The 13-step line used in this *"A'vot":*

9d) The *A'ha'va Ra'bbah* **line used in the** *"A'vot":*

Please note again that in the second Tetrachord of the *A'ha'va Ra'bbah Nu'sach* there is no augmented second interval.

I mentioned the *A'ha'va Ra'bbah Nu'sach* in passing as being one of the parts of the *Ve'Ha'Ko'ha'nim* and of the *A'vot*. Let us look into its structure for a moment. Musicologists tell us that there is no trace of this *Nu'sach* in the biblical cantillation. Therefore, it is looked upon by some people as being under suspicion of illegitimacy. Some say it is a gypsy mode, others that it is a copy of the Hedjaz or the Tartaric music. Still others think that the Jews took it over from the Ukrainians. Whatever its birth, I think no one can deny that the *A'ha'va Ra'bbah Nu'sach* has become a love child in the family of Jewish *Nus'cha'ot*. We have molded and transformed it into our own true image.

It is generally considered that the tonic of this *Nu'sach* is E. That is why it is also called the Phrygian, or as the Eastern European cantors called it, Phrygish. The name probably was accepted because the medieval Phrygian mode also begins with E. The most important feature of this *Nu'sach* is the fact that the second interval has an augmented second. However, there is another feature in this *Nu'sach,* which is even stranger than the augmented second. This is the fact that when we go down below the E, we must sing D and C# instead of C natural, which again creates the peculiar situation that within one scale we have C natural and C#, and D natural and D# as well.

My answer to this is the same. The Jews did something of their own to an existing mode. We added a Tetrachord of another type below the tonic. The original two Tetrachords both have the following intervals:

> half-tone,   tone and-a-half,   half-tone.

The connection between the Tetrachords is a disjunctive one. This means that the beginning of the second Tetrachord does not start with the last note of the first. The added Tetrachord, added down below the tonic is a major Tetrachord. Its intervals are:

> one-tone,   one-tone,   half-tone.

This then gives us the following line of 12 tones:

> (A, B natural, C#, D) (E, F, G#, A) (B, C natural, D#, E).

Anyone who is acquainted with the way that cantors treat the peculiar patterns of the *A'ha'va Ra'bbah Nu'sach* will admit that the most interesting feature, besides the augmented second, is the additional strange Tetrachord, which was hooked on to the other two. It is this that gives it the specific Jewish flavor, which you cannot find in any other formation.

These features are easily recognizable in the prayer *Be'Mo'tza'ei* of the *Se'li'chot* service and in many other prayer-melodies of the weekday, Sabbath, High Holidays and Festival services.

The entire *A'mi'da* of both *Shach'rit* and *Mu'saf* services on Sabbath is sung in the *A'ha'va Ra'bbah Nu'sach*.

ILLUSTRATION 10

10a) The basic line of the *A'ha'va Ra'bbah Nu'sach*:

10b) The addition of a Major Tetrachord below the tonic:

10c) A typical *A'ha'va Ra'bbah* cantorial phrase built on a three Tetrachord, 12 step line:

10d) The complete 12-step line in *A'ha'va Ra'bbah*:

Here of course we should remember that some of the members of the *A'ha'va Ra'bbah* family omit the D# in the second Tetrachord and we have the augmented second only in the first lower Tetrachord.

A specific example of the *A'ha'va Ra'bbah Nu'sach* is the *Yit'ga'dal* prayer of the High Holiday *Mu'saf* service. It is another fixed *Mi'Sinai* prayer melody that is made up of a combination of two basic *Nus'cha'ot*. The first one is definitely in the *A'ha'va Ra'bbah Nu'sach*. The second part is in the regular *Ma'gen A'vot Nu'sach*, which I shall analyze later.

ILLUSTRATION 11

11a) The beginning of the High Holiday "*Ka'ddish*" in E mode of the *A'ha'va Ra'bbah Nu'sach*:

11b) The second part of the "*Ka'ddish*" in *Ma'gen A'vot* (Aeolian mode) in A:

It is also interesting to note that the *A'ha'va Ra'bbah Nu'sach* has several expressions and formations. One of the most attractive of these is the kind of *A'ha'va Ra'bbah Nu'sach* which runs through the famous High Holiday prayer, *O'chi'la La'El*. I therefore call this type by the name *O'chi'1a La'El Nu'sach*. This prayer has a *Mi'Sinai* melody, which is both strange and beautiful. Its peculiarity consists of two features:

* It drags the basic tone down below the E, and it lands on the D;
* The second Tetrachord, going upward, omits the interval of the augmented second, which it had in the first Tetrachord. It is obviously a different Tetrachord that is a plain Minor, with the following steps:

> (A B C D)

When we construct the entire mode from these two Tetrachords going upward from D to D, we get the full line of the *O'chi'la La 'El Nu'sach*, which has all the flavor and all the peculiarities of the *A'ha'va Ra'bbah Nu'sach*. However, the augmented second interval appears here not between the second and the third step, but between the third and fourth step, since the basic tone here is not E, but D. And. of course, as I said before, that augmented second interval appears only in the first Tetrachord and disappears in the second one.

A similar *A'ha'va Ra'bbah Nu'sach* is found in the latter part of the *A'vot,* in *A'ta Gi'bor Le'O'lam A'do'nai,* which is also built on the D tonic instead of the E. The same is true of the *O'chi'la La'El Nu'sach* principle.

ILLUSTRATION 12

12a) The *O'chi'la La'El* branch of the *A'ha'va Ra'bbah Nu'sach*:

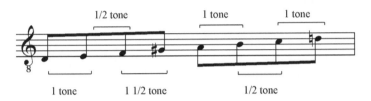

12b) The *O'chi'la La'El* phrase:

12c) *"A'ta Gi'bor"* and other later parts of the *"A'vot"* have the same musical line as the *O'chi'la La'El* (as in illustration 12b).

The *A'ha'va Ra'bbah Nu'sach,* in all of its manifestations, has become so dear to the Jewish people that it is an almost inescapable pattern in many folk songs and in many Chasidic *Ni'gu'nim* (melodies). Among these are *"Ei'li Ei'li"* and *"The Re'bbes Ni'gun."* It is interesting to see that when Louis Lewandowski (1821-1894) succeeded in freeing himself entirely from German influences, he created one of his best and most authentically Jewish compositions — *"Ki Ke'Shim'cha"* — in the purest *A'ha'va Ra'bbah Nu'sach.*

One of the greatest of the contemporary Jewish and universal composers, Ernest Bloch (1880-1959), also could not escape its charm. His *"Tzur Yis'ra'el"* composition is a real gem in that same *Nu'sach.*

When we approach another basic *Nu'sach,* the *Ma'gen A'vot* of Friday night, we know that this one is definitely linked with the biblical cantillation. It is generally treated as a D mode with Bb in it. But again and again, I must emphasize that we can better understand it by applying the Aeolian mode as its basic musical line. This line does not require any accidentals (as the D line would), requiring the use of the Bb. Of the *Mi'Sinai* melodies built on the *Ma'gen A'vot Nu'sach,* let me mention at least two: *She'ma Yis'ra'el* at the opening of the Ark on the High Holidays, and the *P'tach La'nu Sha'ar* of the *Yom Ki'ppur Ne'i'la* service.

ILLUSTRATION 13

13a) The *Ma'gen A'vot* (Aeolian mode):

13b) *"She'ma Yis'ra'el,"* opening the Ark on the High Holidays:

13c) *"P'tach La'nu Sha'ar"* (*Yom Ki'ppur Ne'i'la* service):

The original *Ma'gen A'vot Nu'sach* branched out into many variations. It created a whole family of the Jewish Minor scale. I shall illustrate briefly just five of the many members of this family:

- *Yish'ta'bach* of the Sabbath *Shach'rit* service;
- *Mi'She'Bei'rach* of the Sabbath *Mu'saf* service;
- *A'ta Zo'cher* of the *Rosh Ha'Sha'na Mu'saf* service;
- the *Shach'rit* service of *Rosh Ha'Sha'na* morning; and
- the *Ge'shem/Tal Nu'sach*.

The *Yish'ta'bach Nu'sach* can be easily understood when it is seen as an eight-step line, from E to E, built upon two Tetrachords of the plain Greek Dorian or the medieval Phrygian mode.

The East Europeans modulated very easily from the *Yish'ta'bach* weekday *Nu'sach* to the *A'ha'va Ra'bbah Nu'sach*, even in the middle of the *Yish'ta'bach* prayer itself.

ILLUSTRATION 14

14a) The *"Yish'ta'bach"* **phrase (Sabbath morning):**

14b) The Greek Dorian or medieval Phrygian mode:

14c) Modulating from *Yish'ta'bach* to *A'ha'va Ra'bbah* in Eastern European synagogues:

Be - ro - chos ve - ho - da - os me - a - to ve - ad o - lom_____

The only change they make is from G natural to G#.

A really striking branch of the Minor family is the great *A'mi'da Nu'sach* from the *Rosh Ha'Sha'na Mu'saf* service, the *Mal'chu'yot, Zich'ro'not* and *Shof'rot*. I do not agree with the contention of some, that this *Nu'sach* is identical with the *Mi'She'Bei'rach Nu'sach* of the Sabbath *Mu'saf* service. The differences appear to be very slight but they are the result of two separate and distinct musical lines. Furthermore, they each create a different mood and impression.

Both are built from D to D on the white keys of the piano. They both use the Bb on the sixth step. The difference lies in this: The *Mi'She'Bei'rach* has an augmented second between the F and the G#, and is therefore likened to the Ukrainian-Dorian. It is considered to be the result of Slavic interference.

ILLUSTRATION 15

15a) The *"Mi She'bei'rach"* phrase (Saturday morning *Mu'saf* service) in D mode:

Mi she-bei-rach a - vo-sei - nu Av - ro - hom Yitz - chok ve - Ya - a - kov

* Editor's note: In the original article, a mistake was made by the printer and the starred note above was printed as a Bb and not a B natural. Glantz, in a later printing, corrected the mistake. The corrected version is above.

15b) The *Mi She'bei'rach Nu'sach* line (Ukrainian/Dorian):

The *A'mi'da Nu'sach* of *Rosh Ha'Sha'na,* which some cantors call the *A'ta Zo'cher Nu'sach,* is distinguished from the *Mi'She'Bei'rach Nu'sach* by avoiding the augmented second and also by frequent modulation into the Major scale built on its third step.

There is another great feature of the *A'ta Zo'cher Nu'sach.* It is closely related to the *Shach'rit Nu'sach* of the *Rosh Ha'Sha'na* service, also a prominent member of the Minor scale family. Each is built on two Tetrachords with the following intervals:

<u>one tone</u>, <u>half-a-tone</u>, <u>one tone</u>.

The difference lies in the fact that in the *Shach'rit Nu'sach* there is an additional Tetrachord placed below the basic D on the conjunctive principle: the beginning of the second Tetrachord is the last tone of the first Tetrachord. This line is:

(A B C D)   (D E F G),

whereas in the *A'ta Zo'cher Nu'sach,* the same Tetrachord is placed on top of the basic Tetrachord on the disjunctive principal, which gives the line:

(D E F G)   PLUS   (A B C D).

All three Tetrachords are Minor and have identical intervals.

ILLUSTRATION 16

16a) The *"A'ta Zo'cher"* phrase — D mode modulating into *Ye'kum Pur'kan Nu'sach* from its third step (F):

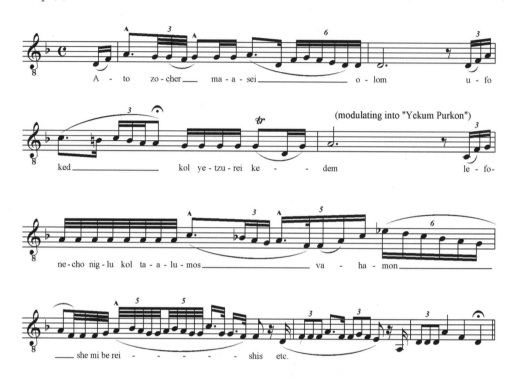

16b) The D line of *"A'ta Zo'cher"*:

16c) The F line of the *Ye'kum Pur'kan* — Mixolydian transposed from G:

16d) The *Shach'rit Nu'sach*:

Finale in Shacharis
the same as in Musaf

16e) The added Tetrachord:

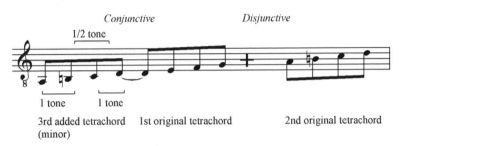

The last illustration for which we shall have time today and which will conclude the description of the Jewish Minor scale family is an analysis of the *Nu'sach* of *Ge'shem and Tal*. The pure Greek Phrygian mode, otherwise known as the medieval Dorian, from D to D gives us the clue to this *Nu'sach*. The difference between the original *Ma'gen A'vot Nu'sach* and the *Ge'shem* or *Tal Nu'sach* lies in one interval. This interval appears between the fifth and the sixth step. If we build the *Ma'gen A'vot Nu'sach* from D to D, there must be a Bb on the sixth step.

When we build the same line for *Ge'shem or Tal,* we notice a struggle between the B natural and the Bb. I think that the B natural is the prevailing feature of the *Ge'shem/Tal Nu'sach.* Years ago, when I recorded my composition *"Tal"* for the RCA Victor recording company, I dared to use the B natural in a revolutionary way, although at that time I could not yet theoretically explain why I did it.

Today I believe that I can give the full reasoning. The following illustration for the *"Af Brie"* — the *Pi'yut* (liturgical poem) that is a real *Mi'Sinai/Ge'shem Nu'sach*, shows clearly how the B natural pushes forward and struggles for its recognition.

ILLUSTRATION 17

17a) *"Af Brie" (Ge'shem Pi'yut) Nu'sach* **built on D (both B natural and Bb are features of this** *Ge'shem Nu'sach.*

17b) The D line which forms the *Ge'shem-Tal Nu'sach:*

As we could see from the above illustration, both the Bb and the B natural manage to live together in this *Nu'sach.* That is why, if we want to be true to its particular two-fold flavor, we must emphasize that double feature in the concluding phrase of the *Nu'sach:*

> Bb, A, B natural, G, A.

From this we can see the tremendous difference between the *Ka'ddish* of *Ne'i'la* and the *Ka'ddish* of *Tal.* One only has to know that the *Ne'i'la Ka'ddish* is based on the elementary *Ye'kum Pur'kan* Jewish Major, which is understood when we have in mind the Mixolydian mode, and that the *Ge'shem/Tal Nu'sach* is based on a Minor scale and is a branching out of the *Ma'gen A'vot Nu'sach.*

———

In conclusion, I should like to make one general remark. I do not claim to know all the secrets of all the *Nus'cha'ot*. All I can say is that knowing this much, we shall be able to proceed further. The material is fascinating, the theme is so dear, the problem so important, that we should try to study our wonderful *Nus'cha'ot* with patience and love. We are entrusted with the task of guarding our musical heritage; therefore we must also carry forward and develop it.

We are entrusted with the task of guarding our musical heritage; therefore we must also carry forward and develop it. The future of Jewish music depends on us.

The future of Jewish music depends on us. It depends on the degree of our own deepening of our studies, and also our teaching it to the entire Jewish people.[8]

---

8 Ed. Note: See Appendix 1 for comments on Leib Glantz's lecture by Cantor Max Wohlberg. Wohlberg lectured to the delegates of the 7th Annual Cantors Assembly Convention in June, 1954, on "The History of the Musical Modes of the Ashkenazic Synagogue and Their Usage." This is followed by Glantz's reply in a letter to Wohlberg.

2

The Essence of *Cha'za'nut*

LEIB GLANTZ[1]

The Chasidic movement cannot dominate the prayers of the synagogue. In Chasidic *Kloy'zen* (prayer rooms) and *Shtib'lach* (small houses of worship and study) I have witnessed *Cha'si'dim* who were Davening (praying) totally without *Nu'sach* (Jewish prayer modes). They "created" their own "*Nu'sach.*" I was in Uman, where I heard Bratzlaver cantors in the synagogue of the great Rebbe himself, singing beautifully. But there was no *Nu'sach* in their prayers!

In this conference today, I truly enjoyed hearing speakers talk about the reading of the *To'rah* and the cantillation melodies in which they are sung. However, we must not limit our discussion regarding *Nu'sach* to these alone. If we do so, we will not be able to demystify the secrets of our prayers. There was a time when writers of encyclopedias did not know what to write about *Nu'sach Ha'Te'fi'la* because they really had no explanation, no knowledge. As a matter of fact, even the greatest and most famous cantors did not know how to explain the theoretical aspects of *Nu'sach*, even though they actually prayed using the correct modes.

> *Even the greatest and most famous cantors did not know how to explain the theoretical aspects of* Nu'sach, *even though they prayed using the correct modes.*

I must admit that 20 years ago, if I had been asked how I analyze what I was singing, I would not have been capable of answering! My father and grandfathers, all cantors, definitely could not analyze the *Nu'sach* that they sang.

---

1 Lecture by Leib Glantz at *Ha'Ma'chon Le'Mu'si'ka Da'tit*, The Institute for Jewish Music (today called "Renanot"), Jerusalem, December 8, 1958.

In theory, the cantor improves and beautifies the prayer service, organizes the service, raises it to a level of *Hit'la'ha'vut* (enthusiasm), and to an enlightened musical level. Therefore, an analysis of cantorial music must begin with the personal human attributes of the cantor.

Cha'za'nut is not just a musical profession. It is not just a trade. It is wisdom *(Choch'ma)*. Wisdom in all its aspects: wisdom, understanding and knowledge. The integral mission assigned to the cantor consists of demands that are not necessarily musical. A cantor is undoubtedly a singer. However, a singer is definitely not a cantor, even when he performs cantorial music in a synagogue. A classical soloist, highly respected by great conductors, can be a wonderful soloist, but he is not a cantor. The greatest Italian opera

Leib Glantz praying at *"O'hel Shem"* **concert hall in Tel Aviv in January, 1947 (front page photo of** *"Ha'Olam Ha'Zeh,"* **a weekly journal).**

singer, in order to excel, is not required to be knowledgeable about the Italian people, their history, their customs and their culture. The cantor, on the other hand, must be a complete Jew in spirit and soul. He must be a scholar of Jewish history, ancient Jewish literature, the written and oral *To'rah,* the *Ha'la'cha* (interpretation of the laws of the Scriptures), and the *Mid'ra'shim* (Jewish commentaries on the Hebrew Scriptures). He must be familiar with the literature of the Middle Ages, including its *Pay'ta'nim* (poets) and *Pi'yu'tim* (liturgical poems). He should be familiar with modern Hebrew literature. This Jewish consciousness is the primary basis for the wisdom of *Cha'za'nut,* and serves as the principle attribute of the cantor's mission.

A second attribute, one that is no less important, is the cantor's standard of morality. Many singers and artists conduct their lives in what is often called "bohemian" lifestyle. They frequently indulge in alcohol and unrestrained social behavior. This kind of lifestyle does not disqualify the secular artist. Cantors, as leaders of their communities, are measured according to their morality. Their behavior must be a model for the public. A cantor is not just another member of the community, but an example to be followed. His singing must originate from holiness and purity.

A third important aspect of the *Cha'zan* is his credo *(A'ni Ma'amin)*. He must be loyal to his people and to their holy values. His religious faith must be unabridged; he must believe in the words he is uttering, as he is required to be an interpreter of those texts.

Here is an episode to illustrate the important difference between the secular artist and the *Cha'zan*. A few days ago, the Israel Composers Association, of which I am a member, presented a composition by one of its members, an Israeli composer, at an affair called "The Composer's Stage." Before proceeding to play this truly beautiful symphonic composition, the composer found it necessary to stand up and declare before his fellow Israeli composers that his music is not Israeli music because he considered himself a "cosmopolitan musician," and furthermore, it is not religious music because he was a self-declared atheist...

This artist felt the need to make this kind of declaration, and none of his fellow Israeli composers felt shocked by it! Perhaps some even identified with his words.

In my heart I quietly said to myself that this is a classic example of the difference between a cantorial composer and a secular composer. With that kind of declaration the cantor would immediately cause himself to be disqualified, not necessarily by the rabbis, but by himself as well. A cantor must be a person of religious faith and a person of national loyalty in heart and soul.

Let us now move on to the musical fundamentals of *Cha'za'nut*.

A cantor, as opposed to a regular singer, must become a musician of the highest level — one who is knowledgeable both in universal music and especially in original Jewish music. When I was a child, I remember my father declaring that the most humiliating thing for a cantor was when it was mentioned that he could read musical notes! Can you believe this? What is a cantor supposed to master if not the ability to read musical notes? You must have heard people praising a cantor because he sings even though he cannot read notes! Who then is required to read notes? A tailor? A shoemaker? A merchant? Obviously this is the A B C of the cantor! Have you ever heard of a violinist or a pianist that does not know how to read notes? A serious cantor needs to master not only musical notes, but also theory, harmony, counterpoint, choir conducting, orchestration, and an elementary capability of playing a musical instrument.

Of course the cantor must professionally develop his voice. Those times have passed when cantors could sing at the level of an amateur. Today's public can easily distinguish between cultured and non-cultured singers.

If a cantor has attributes of an improviser, he must be well aware of what is allowed and what is forbidden in improvisation. Improper improvisation can get a cantor into trouble. If a cantor does not have improvisational capabilities, he should learn to excel in executing recitatives and compositions of others. If that is the case, then he needs to become an expert in the art of execution. This demands serious study. This cantor must not just learn to imitate other cantors. The gramophone or the recording cannot teach him how to execute cantorial compositions. He needs to learn the general style of each composer, and styles of music in general. If an operatic aria is sung in the style of a cantorial recitative, it will create laughter in the audience. There are great differences in style among the different operas and different arias. The same is true in Chazanic prayer. Even the greatest opera singer, if he sings a cantorial recitative in the style of *La Traviata,* will be ridiculed by an intelligent audience.

> *Even the greatest opera singer, if he sings a cantorial recitative in the style of* **La Traviata,** *will be ridiculed by an intelligent audience.*

Each and every creative cantor has his own exclusive style. Louis Lewandowski cannot be performed in the style of Zeidel Rovner. Nissan Belzer cannot be sung in the style of David Nowakowsky. There was a great cantor and conductor, Arie Leib Roitman, who was famous for his great talent to sing every cantor's compositions in the style of each composer, while adding his own spirit and temperament.

Lewandowski composed cantorial music in the style that was performed in the synagogues of Vienna, but he would conduct Nissan Belzer's composition *"Ke'Gav'na"* in Belzer's style, even though their styles were completely different. This is what the art of performance is all about.

Now I will refer to the topic: What are the musical fundamentals of creative *Cha'za'nut?* The times have passed when the synagogue congregation was the cantor's sole "professor" regarding the *Nu'sach* of the prayer services. The "university" of the *Cha'zan* was the regular chanting of simple members of the congregation. There was no theoretical analysis and no specific singing style.

The wonderful Cantor Zevulun (Zavel) Kwartin was known for his great *Nu'sach.* Where did he learn this *Nu'sach?* What did he know about the principles, the theory of the *Nu'sach* that he was using? The answer is that he knew nothing! I personally asked him for explanations. Why was he singing with certain *Nus'cha'ot* in this prayer and that prayer? He admitted that he could not reply! He simply had no idea!

Nu'sach *was a secret passed on from generation to generation, and even though [the cantors] could not analyze it, they performed it perfectly and properly.*

The theoretical essays of the cantors of the end of the nineteenth and beginning of the twentieth century (50 years ago) on *Nu'sach* have no useful value for us because they simply did not have any research or theoretical basis on which to build! It was a mystery. They simply did not know how to theorize. *Nu'sach* was a secret passed on from generation to generation, and even though they could not analyze it, they performed it perfectly and properly, because the atmosphere and the lifestyle of the Jewish people at that time was immersed in the synagogue and in the *Nu'sach* of the prayers. That is where they learned it.

However, today most of the members of congregations cannot differentiate between one *Nu'sach* and the other. A few years ago I succeeded in proving this point to a group of very famous cantors and composers. I invited them to listen to my prayers at a large and famous orthodox synagogue in New York. It was the holiday of *She'mi'ni A'tze'ret,*[2] and I purposely sang the prayer for rain *(Te'fi'lat Ge'shem)* in the *Nu'sach* of the *Yom Ki'ppur Ne'i'la* service... Not one person from the congregation stood up and protested! Fifty years ago the congregation might have stoned to death a cantor who did such a terrible deed! He would definitely have been ridiculed.

The foregone conclusion is that we must seriously research the original Hebrew prayer modes, and develop a clear musical and musicological theory. If we do not achieve this, our *Nu'sach* will be forgotten and distorted, not only by the congregations but by the cantors as well. We need to define the lines, the modes and the scales of the tones and semi-tones and the intervals upon which each *Nu'sach* is built. Without this we are lost in the dark.

It is amazing to me when I hear Jewish musicians and musicologists in the United States who totally deny the existence of authentic original Jewish music. In my opinion these are signs of assimilation. Even here in Israel there are serious Israeli composers of classical music who have expressed their doubts as to the existence of Jewish music! This amounts to musical assimilation.

Throughout my life I have been convinced of the existence of ancient Jewish music — even at a time when I was not yet capable of analyzing it. I felt it in my heart and in my soul. I would listen to music in general and then I would listen to Jewish music and I realized that there was an enormous musical difference in the structure upon which the Jews built their *Nu'sach.*

---

2 *She'mi'ni A'tze'ret* — the eighth day holiday immediately following the seven day *Su'ccot* holiday.

Regarding the music of the cantillation of the bible *(Ta'a'mei Ha'Mik'ra)*, there is no doubt that these are among the primary building blocks of Jewish music. But these are not the only primary sources. At a time when there were no other forms of music, these melodies were already in existence and served as the proper musical interpretation of the biblical texts. However, we must not allow ourselves to be confined to these alone. The basic line of the cantillation of the bible is the Pentatonic line. However, the Pentatonic line has so much more than what is actually used in the cantillation of the bible. The same tones miraculously create totally new melodies! It is very clear that the Pentatonic and not the cantillation of the bible created the music of the *Haf'ta'ra*!

In conclusion, we must be able to define scales on which we can build the different *Nus'cha'ot*. We must be capable of creating a situation whereby any intelligent musician can understand and build any *Nu'sach* without being confronted with complications.

3

Cha'za'nut : The Israeli Song of Songs

LEIB GLANTZ[1]

Cha'za'nut *is my true love!*

Cha'za'nut is my true love!

Cha'za'nut expresses sorrow, happiness, devotion and the sanctification of the Lord. It is the voice of joy and happiness that accompanies the intimate pleasures of the Jewish family life. It serves as the echo of Jewish mourning — the music of grief and the groans of pain and sorrow.

Cantorial melodies seem to originate from the heavens, expressing the most exciting and enthusiastic aspects of praising the Lord — a musical endeavor to tell sacred stories using divine prayer modes.

The idea of *D'vei'kut* — closeness to God, devotion, and ecstasy — is expressed through music. Cantorial music is surrounded by devotion. It is capable of spiritually raising its listeners above and beyond the mundane.

Historians try to comprehend the miracle of the survival of the Jewish people and the Jewish culture. This, in spite of the fact that the Jewish people endured seven stages of hell, everlasting

---

1 This article was originally written in Yiddish in *'Cha'za'nim Journal,'* New York, 1951. It was translated into Hebrew in *"Ze'ha'rim — In Memory of Leib Glantz,"* published by the Tel Aviv Institute for Jewish Liturgical Music, 1965.

Diasporas, humiliations, inquisitions, pogroms, oppressions, tortures, and slaughters! The secret of Jewish vitality can be explained by their consistent reliance on two perennial pillars:

- Their natural impulse to consistently study the *To'rah*, sharpening and discerning their minds;
- Their perpetuated practice of soul searching, intuitiveness, vitality, experience, elation, and yearning for spiritual holiness, achieved by pious religious worship.

Beyond the wisdom of the *mind* there is wisdom of the *heart*. The *To'rah* defines the first artist of the Jewish people, Bezalel, as "*Cha'cham Lev*" — wise of heart. Words alone cannot express all of our feelings. God and divinity are concepts superior to the human mind. There is a limit to human knowledge and understanding. However, the wisdom of the heart is superior to the wisdom of the mind. Melodies can enable us to discover paths that cannot be defined by words.

> *Melodies can enable us to discover paths that cannot be defined by words.*

Before the destruction of the Second Temple, there existed a Jewish slogan: "Let us come before God *with song*." In Jerusalem and later in the various Diasporas, a musical theme for prayers, pleas, conversations with God, and complaints toward God had developed in Jewish houses of prayer — the synagogues. This was the fountain from which Jewish prayer modes stemmed. Jewish prayer was musical. Just before the prayer of *Bar'chu* we state that God Himself had chosen song as the highest level of praise, and therefore Jews proclaim every single day: "Song and praise, *Ha'llel* and music, from now until eternity."[2] This prayer ends with the musical phrase: "God the Almighty, who chooses song and music."[3]

At first the Jews interpreted the *To'rah* through cantillation, a chanting or reciting of the bible with prescribed musical phrases indicated by notations. These musical notes were indicated on each word. They represented a whole tune, and not just a single tone, as in the modern scores of today. This scale was based on a set of five descending tones called Pentatones, which are deeply rooted in Jewish music, and sung by every Jew, even if he does not realize he is doing so. The Pentatonic scale does not contain any distilled major or minor, or groups of tunes combining four or five notes. Jews read the *To'rah* and pray their prayers with these same five tones. As long as Jews exist, it is improbable that they will deviate from this musical path.

In addition to the cantillation of the *To'rah*, many modes and traditions served as the basis for the *Nu'sach*, each used for specific prayer services. A complete web of folklore creations was formed, each with its own intricate logic.

---

2 *Shir U'Shva'cha, Ha'llel Ve'Zim'ra, Me'A'ta Ve'Ad O'lam.*
3 *Ha'Bo'cher Be'Shi'rei Zim'ra.*

Every one of these prayer modes is built on different tonal systems and combinations of scales, which represent a treasure of Jewish cultural originality.

These original combinations of Tetratones and Pentatones became subconsciously comfortable and circumscribed within the Jewish ear, so much so that it is almost impossible for Jews to free themselves from this music. They have a "biological connection" to these tones.

Many traditional tunes and prayer modes would have been lost had it not been for the instinct of survival so embedded in the nature of the Jews. With the creation of the profession called the "*Cantorate of Israel,*" cantors took upon themselves the duty of conserving the Jewishness of the prayers despite the disastrous storms and calamities of Jewish life in the Diaspora.

The first cantors were extremely ethical and moral, very talented and imaginative. They were poets, composers, and creators of unique texts. Instating them into the prayer books sanctified these texts. This process of writing poems and composing appropriate music for them within the strict rules of the Jewish prayer modes was called cantorial music, or, in Hebrew, *Cha'za'nut.*

After the period when the prayer books were completed, cantors assumed new roles: to preserve the holy prayer modes, ensuring that they would not solidify and freeze, nor become routine and monotonous. Cantors were to continue to inject passionate new versions, while guarding the music from contamination by foreign elements.

A Jewish musician who desires to be true to his cultural heritage must go to synagogues and listen to the prayers. Before I set out to compose my composition *Sho'mer Yis'ra'el,*[4] a prayer that follows the *Tach'nun* prayer of the weekday service, I literally devoted months to standing discretely in different synagogues in New York's East side, among old Jews who attended the *Ka'ddish* mourning prayers. I listened to them very carefully in an effort to discover the authentic origins of the *Nu'sach*. I believe this enabled me to capture the true spirit of *"Sho'mer Yis'ra'el."*

I have no doubt that in the future, a Jewish symphony will be composed that will be compared to the great symphonies composed by the likes of Beethoven and Bach. I am confident that the roots of this symphony will stem from cantorial music, inevitably based on the ancient prayer modes of song and prayer that were created in our glorious past.

The establishment of the State of Israel in 1948, and the trend to emphasize the Jewish essence of Israel, will hopefully create a new stream of love and admiration for cantorial music.

4 *Sho'mer Yis'ra'el* — "The Guardian of Israel."

I strongly believe that the *Song of Songs* of the people of Israel, as well as of the Jews of the Diaspora, will rise in the future toward a period of impetus and momentum. Until this happens, our cantors must not water down our true Jewish art. They must keep in mind two basic principles:

- Never distance themselves from the original Jewish vocal combinations, tonal units, prayer modes and Jewish character of their performance;
- Never let this *Nu'sach* freeze or become paralyzed. Paralysis in art means death.

The cantor must be in love with his art! He must never stop developing and enhancing it. He must delve deeply into its depths, modify, pamper and glorify it, and constantly look for new ways to express its beauty.

> *The cantor must be in love with his art!*
> *He must never stop developing and*
> *enhancing it.*

4

We Must Not Let *Cha'za'nut* Perish!

Leib Glantz[1]

There is a new generation in Israel — a generation that is not only neglecting, but rejecting one of our most sacred cultural heritages: our original religious music — *Cha'za'nut*.

People of mediocre taste are actively depleting the stature of our traditional music. They are cultivating a fashion of cantorial recordings for the sole purpose of cheap entertainment. At the same time, our writers, poets, artists, intelligentsia, as well as our religious scholars, are becoming indifferent towards this great cultural asset.

Some consider themselves *"secular"* — careful not to be stigmatized, God forbid, with a trace of Judaism from the past. Religious scholars are engulfed in a peculiar snobbism, totally ignoring our popular original art.

In America there is a trend to impose musical assimilation — an effort to copy Protestant ways of prayer. "Modern" Rabbis are introducing spoken prayers, declamations, and translations into English, totally neglecting our original ancient Jewish prayer modes.[2] Jewish men and women sit politely in these synagogues, hardly uttering a word, lacking even a trace of Jewish song or Hebrew inspiration.

Should not this worry us? Can we afford to let this cultural treasure disintegrate before our eyes? Is it not our holy duty to wake up and struggle for our nation's musical soul, especially in this historical period "When the Lord restores the fortunes of Zion"?[3]

---

1 Translated from the Israeli newspaper *"Da'var,"* 1957.
2 Prayer modes — *Nu'sach Ha'Te'fi'la.*
3 Psalms 126 — *Shir Ha'Ma'a'lot — Be'Shuv A'do'nai Et Shi'vat Z'ion.*

How can it be that in the State of Israel not even one great choir with a national artistic vision has been formed? This kind of choir should be creating authentic interpretations of our ancient melodies, presented in modern forms through the voices of choir singers similar to the great choirs of David Nowakowsky and Louis Lewandowski?

How can we explain that wonderful musicians such as Nissan Belzer and Zeidel Rovner have not appeared in this generation of national renewal? Belzer and Rovner used to travel with enormous choirs on horse carriages, during hot summer months as well as rainy winters, in order to bring musical bliss to their fellow brothers. They performed a holy mission, enthusiastically singing the great compositions of Baruch Schorr of L'vov, Pinchas Minkowsky and David Nowakowsky of Odessa, Avraham Berkovitz-Kalechnik of Kishinev, and Solomon Sulzer of Vienna.

It is not surprising that a cantor such as Baruch Schorr could enrich lives with his penetrating interpretation and amazing harmonization of the *Ka'ddish*[4] of the High Holidays, the *Kol Nid'rei*[5] and the *A'vo'dat Ha'Ko'ha'nim*[6] of the *Yom Ki'ppur* services! It is no miracle that Zeidel Rovner created such a beautiful musical interpretation of *Me'loch Al Kol Ha'O'lam Ku'lo*[7] — an interpretation that is unparalleled to this very day.

If love and appreciation for our wonderful Jewish music disappear, creativity and quality of performance will disappear as well. It is as if I hear a divine voice whispering in my ear: "How can we refrain from singing the song of the Lord in our *own* liberated land of Israel — the song of so many generations — the eternal song of the people of Israel?"

> *How can we refrain from singing the song of the Lord in our own liberated land of Israel?*

We must not allow our wonderful cantorial art to perish!

---

4 *Ka'ddish* — Consecration; prayer.
5 *Kol Nid'rei* — the opening prayer of the evening Day of Atonement service.
6 *A'vo'dat Ko'ha'nim* — liturgy for the *Mu'saf* service on the Day of Atonement.
7 *Me'loch Al Kol Ha'O'lam Ku'lo* — May God Reign over the whole world.

The Cantor — A Unique Creation of Jewish Life

Leib Glantz[1]

Is the cantor a singer, a composer, a musical interpreter, a "deputy of the people" *(Shli'ach Tzi'bur),* a "messenger to God," or is he all of these together? The difficulty of defining the role of the cantor lies in the fact that the institution of "the Cantorate" or *"Cha'za'nut"* is a completely Jewish phenomenon, a unique and specifically Jewish creation. It is, therefore, difficult to compare the Cantorate with the existing institutions of other religions.

We find the institution of priests *(Ko'ha'nim)* among the Egyptians, the Phoenicians, the Indians and other nations that were in existence at the time of the creation of the Jewish priesthood. The Cantorate, however, is distinctly and originally Jewish, and in order to understand it we must read the bible again and observe the very roots of Judaism in the days of its birth.

The definition of the word "artist" in the bible is remarkable. Each time I read the portion of the bible that deals with the "artist," I am thrilled by the term that is used to describe him: *Cha'cham Lev* — he who has the wisdom of the heart. The term *"Choch'ma"* in Hebrew means several things: scholarship, wisdom, knowledge and plain good sense. The biblical distinction between intellectual *Choch'ma* and emotional *Choch'ma* constitutes, therefore, a striking definition of art, for it recognizes that art penetrates directly into the heart and often speaks more deeply than words and scholarly definitions.

> *Music in itself is a religious miracle. It cannot be explained in words — neither its meaning nor its influence.*

Music in itself is a religious miracle. It cannot be explained in words —

---

1 Article published in the Golden Jubilee Journal of the Jewish Ministers Cantors' Association of America, New York, 1947.

neither its meaning nor its influence. For example, genuine musical audiences are in fact religious audiences — if not consciously, then certainly emotionally and instinctively. There is often religiosity in the heart even when the mind denies it, and the most radically minded person is often intensely religious, although often unaware of it. The religious feeling that is created and that responds to *Chochmat Lev* exists in many places and in many hearts and souls, for the "Wisdom of the Heart" may not be clearly defined, but it is always rich and deep and reaches more people than the "Wisdom of the Mind."

The Jewish prayer book brilliantly acknowledges the kinship between music and religiosity. It contains a remarkable daily prayer in which God is proclaimed as "the one who chooses music" *(Ha'Bo'cher Be'Shi'rei Zim'ra)*. This description of God as a lover of music is based on many manifestations of Jewish religious expression that we find throughout Jewish history, from the days of the bible through the ceremonial services in both Holy Temples in Jerusalem *(A'vo'da)*, up to the early days of the synagogues of the Diaspora.

The very word *Ne'vu'ah* (prophecy) became synonymous with the word for music in the bible. *"Ha'Ni'ba'im Be'Chi'no'rot"* in Hebrew means "men who prophesied with their harps." The "Psalms of David" were in reality a series of poetic lyrics set to music, sung by large choirs and accompanied by large orchestras. At the time of the first Temple, an entire Jewish tribe, the Levites, were trained and consecrated to serve as singers and musicians at religious services. At the Holy Temple in Jerusalem, each and every day had its special musical program, the so-called "Song of the Day" *("Shir Shel Yom")*. The Talmud uses a significant phrase to describe the contribution of the Levites who "spoke through Song" *(Ve'Dib'ru Ha'Le'vi'im Be'Shir)*. In Jewish religious services *"To'rah"* and *"A'vo'da,"* intellectual and emotional wisdom, the wisdom of the mind and the wisdom of the heart, go hand in hand. That is why the Jewish liturgy calls upon us constantly to sing and to exult in singing. The very first call to the people of Israel on the Friday night service is: "Let us sing to God" *(Le'chu Ne'ra'ne'na)*, "Sing unto the Lord a new song," and "Sing unto God, all the earth." These and other passages are short quotations from the Jewish liturgy, which is full of references to song and to music as a medium of religious expression. The musical cantillation of the bible may be responsible not only for the preservation of the ceremony of the reading of the bible itself in the synagogue, but also for the preservation of the fundamentals of original Jewish music.

When Ezra and Nechemia led the Jewish people back to their homeland from their first captivity in Babylon, they did not neglect to take with them *"Klei Shir"* which they significantly called "instruments of song," implying by this term that these instruments were played only as an accompaniment to the main performers, the singers. At the time of the Second Holy Temple, religious musical performance was at its highest point of development. As many as 4,500 persons permanently participated in these exaltations and the pilgrims, the *"O'lei Re'gel"* who used to come to Jerusalem for the festivities from all parts of the country, witnessed ecstatic and jubilant ceremonies accompanied by mass singing and mass playing.

> *After the destruction of the Second Temple, among the great cultural losses was the lamentable loss of the wonderful Jewish melodies. Even the melody of the Song of Songs was lost forever.*

After the destruction of the Second Temple, among the great cultural losses was the lamentable loss of the wonderful Jewish melodies. Even the melody of the Song of Songs was lost forever.

The Great Temple at Jerusalem was gone and the "little Temple" *(Mik'dash Me'at),* the small synagogues, were slowly and quietly founded. With the birth of the synagogue, the institution of the Cantorate came into existence. Had there been trained professional cantors in the very earliest days of the Diaspora, we might not have lost most of our precious musical heritage. What has been saved, has been saved by the Cantorate, who have had the mission to preserve what was Jewish in music and in song for the last 1,800 years. The earliest cantors, who were also called *"Pay'ta'nim"* (from the Greek word for poet), were not only singers and composers. They were actually poets as well.

These poets inspired the synagogue worshippers with their creation of new liturgical texts, called *"Pi'yu'tim."* These new lyrics, which were set to new musical compositions, brought consolation and spiritual elevation to the great masses of Jewry. For 1,800 years, cantors officiated in place of the Levites of the Temple, performing the *A'vo'da* services for their people with all their heart and soul. The Jewish people recognized them as their *Shli'chei Tzi'bur* (leaders of the congregation), who inspired them with voice and song and who helped to preserve the love of the people for their ancient religious music.

It is significant that those who compiled the prayer book for the Day of Atonement, *Yom Ki'ppur,* included a special prayer dedicated to the cantor alone in which he introduces himself, humbly and with deep humility, as the deputy, frightened and overwhelmed, and declares: "Here am I, poor in deed and in fear of He who rules the world. Here I come to stand before Thee and to ask for mercy for Thy people" *(Hi'ne'ni He'Ani Mi'Ma'as).* This is why the cantor cannot be just a singer or a composer. He must be conscious of the fact that he constitutes a link between the generations of Jewry. He must feel that he has a mission — to preserve the very soul and very heart of Judaism by preserving its cherished melodies and the *A'vo'da* in musical form.

Having traveled widely, I have been pleasantly amazed to hear — in Constantinople, in Africa, in Palestine, and in other distant places — almost the same *"Le'cha Do'di"* on Friday night services, or the same *"Tal"* or *"Ge'shem"* (prayers for dew or rain), as I had heard in my grandfather's synagogue in Kiev, in the Ukraine. Jewish song of the synagogue stretches its wings across oceans and continents, saying *"Sha'lom A'lei'chem"* to the scattered Jews of the world. Jewish modes and melodies lie deep in the hearts of Jews whether they will it or not. What would our Sabbath be like without its melodies? Who would have preserved these melodies if it were not for the cantor, the lover of both Sabbath and song?

It is not a mere coincidence that the author who recently completed a great scientific work on the origins and content of the musical cantillation of the bible is none other than the son of a great cantor. I refer to Cantor Solomon Rosovsky of Riga (born in 1878). It is the cantor's soul in him that is guiding him and deepening his love for this ancient and complex subject. Most of the great compositions for the synagogue were written by great cantors and composers. Music for the synagogue should be written by people who devote their lives to synagogue music. The cantor-composer is the guardian of original Jewish music, the *"Sho'mer Ne'gi'nat Yis'ra'el,"* the one who preserves the national treasury of Jewish song and Jewish music.

The strength of a true cantor is not only in his music. The cantor should be, rather must be, a Jewish idealist.

The cantor who sincerely lives and feels the passages of the *Ki'not* (Elegies) on *Tish'ah Be'Av* (the ninth day of the month of Av commemorating the destruction of the Holy Temple in Jerusalem), the chapters of the *Se'li'chot* (Penitential poems), the majestic prayer *A'ta Nig'lei'ta* of *Rosh Ha'Sha'na*, the recreation of the ancient *A'vo'da* service on *Yom Ki'ppur*, or the heart breaking *Shlosh Es'rei Mi'dot* (The Thirteen Attributes) of the *Ne'i'la Yom Ki'ppur* service, cannot be an artist alone. A cantor who prays truly for the restoration of Zion must also assume his role in the rebuilding of Palestine. A cantor who seriously believes in the texts of the prophets,

A cantor who prays truly for the restoration of Zion must also assume his role in the rebuilding of Palestine.

that speak of social justice and social idealism, must today take part in furthering these ideals. A cantor who is called upon to eulogize the murdered millions of European Jewry cannot distance himself from the daily tasks involved in rescuing those who can still be saved. A cantor can convince, motivate and influence others only if he himself is moved to action. This is why a cantor is not only a singer, not only a performer, not only a minister and messenger to God. He is all of these combined together. He is a unique personality in Jewish life — a creation of generations of Jewish life in the Diaspora.

With the restoration of the Jewish State, the cantors of the world must assume a great role in the restoration of our sacred Jewish music.

6

The Origins of Traditional Jewish Music

Leib Glantz

Ladies and gentlemen — dear listeners!

When one approaches the task of revealing the interesting and complex musical and textual issues of the Jewish prayer modes, the *Nu'sach,* one finds oneself encumbered by various difficulties that at first seem almost impossible to overcome.

Some of our radio listeners are professional musicians, while most of the listeners will need to make an effort to comprehend what they hear, without the benefit of a musical education.

Therefore, in the following six radio lectures I will try to ease the burden on the ears of the non-professional musicians among the listeners. I will try to limit the number of technical musical terms used. Nevertheless, the existing musical explanations are sufficient to decipher the secrets of Jewish music and its historic development. This first lecture will serve as an introduction to the subject, and will deal with the origins of traditional Jewish music.

Jewish liturgical music is the primary, original, and authentic research source for the study of *all* Jewish music. The principle key to deciphering Jewish liturgical music is the bible cantillations *(Ta'amei Ha'Mik'ra),* and the musical scales and modes upon which they were constructed.

The Jews were "partners" with peoples of other cultures in using some of these ancient musical scales, and this is perfectly natural and healthy, since they did not live in a vacuum, but

---

1 First of six radio lectures by Leib Glantz, broadcast by *Kol Yis'ra'el,* the Israel Broadcasting Authority, 1961.

among the people and the melodies of those cultures. However, even though they had an impact, Jewish music did not assimilate nor alienate itself from its distinct national character.

In fact, Jews contributed much of their own to this "partnership." No other human group in the world has used these scales in the manner that the Jews did. The Jewish musicians actually altered these musical scales and attached to them a unique character, so much so that it can be

> *The Jewish musicians actually altered these musical scales and attached to them a unique character, so much so that it can comfortably be stated that they enriched the music of the world with typical colors, with original formulas, with unique rhythm, and with an original Jewish implementation.*

stated that they enriched the music of the world with typical colors, with original formulas, with unique rhythm, and with an original Jewish implementation.

Some of the greatest performing artists in the world are Jewish: great pianists, violinists, conductors and opera singers. However, these Jewish musicians did not limit themselves to the performance of "foreign" music, according to the claims of some assimilationists among us, as well as certain antisemites. The answer to these claims can be found in the words of our national poet, Chaim Nachman Bialik: "If your soul wishes to know where is the spring from which your brothers absorbed their knowledge…go to find it in the synagogue…"

This is definitely true if we remember the prayer modes we learned at our synagogues and houses of learning *(Ba'tei Ha'Mid'rash),* especially when we listen to the reading of the *To'rah,* the Prophets and the *Me'gi'lot* (scrolls).

A good example can be heard in the musical melody that opens the daily radio broadcasts in Israel on this *"Kol Yis'ra'el"* station:

This melody is actually the first musical phrase in the reading of the *To'rah:*

That is the tune to the words of Genesis: "At the beginning God created the heavens and the earth." This melody is the foundation for the creation of the different *Nus'cha'ot*. It repeats itself in different forms in all of the prayers and liturgical hymns *(Pi'yu'tim)*. It has the potential to serve as a firm basis for a Jewish musical genius to compose a typical Jewish symphony of classical music.

The *Nu'sach* for the Sabbath *Psu'kei De'Zim'ra* (Recitation Verses) is as follows:

The foundation of this *Nu'sach* also exists in the melody of the reading of the *To'rah*. Let us listen to the Blessing of the Wine *(Ki'ddush)* on the Sabbath eve feast:

Music defines this as the "Pentatonic scale." The foundation of this scale has a Major base:

There is no doubt whatsoever that the Pentatonic scale was being used in the most ancient Jewish music as far back in history as the songs that the Levites used to sing in the Holy Temple. It is a fact that the tribe of Levi, whose life was dedicated to religious rites, was in charge of Jewish liturgical music for a period of approximately 1,000 years.

During the musical reading of the *To'rah*, we hear sentences ending in a slightly different melody, or different *Nu'sach*. This repeats itself throughout the reading of the *To'rah*. For example:

The above example is exactly the same way we sing the last phrase of the *To'rah:*

This phrase is completely in Minor, as opposed to the beginning of the reading of the *To'rah*, which, as I mentioned, is completely in Major. We hear this same melody from every *Bar Mitz'va* youth when he stands up to sing the *Haf'ta'ra*. The melody is built specifically on the Pentatonic Minor:

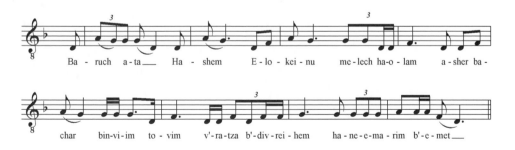

You might be surprised to learn that there is another transformation to this same melody: "The Song of Songs" *(Shir Ha'Shi'rim)*. However, in the Song of Songs we find both the

Major and the Minor in the same phrase. This *Nu'sach* begins with Minor and ends with Major:

Shir ha-shi-rim a-sher lish-lo-mo_ y'-sha-kei-ni min-shi-kot pi-hu ki-to-

vim do-de-cha mi-ya-yin la la la la la la la la la la la la la la la la la la

la la la la la la la la la la la la_ la la la

Clearly, the beginning is Minor and the ending is Major — just the opposite as in the reading of the *To'rah*.

This leads me to the conviction that in order to use the correct *Nu'sach,* it is not sufficient only to use Hebrew texts or even biblical texts. Great classical composers such as George Frideric Handel (1685-1759), Joseph Haydn (1732-1809), Johann Sebastian Bach (1685-1750), and others composed music to texts of the Jewish Bible; however, their music cannot be considered Jewish music. Even Felix Mendelssohn (1809-1847), who was supposedly Jewish, did not succeed in creating authentic Jewish music!

The key to creating typical Jewish compositions is the ancient *Nu'sach.* These synagogue prayer modes are capable of flowing into the souls of original composers who, in the future, may create typical Jewish melodies and rhythms.

> *I call upon Jewish composers, especially those in Israel, to come to the synagogues and listen carefully to the music of Jews at prayer. This will invigorate and enrich them, and lead them to the creation of monumental music.*

I call upon Jewish composers, especially those in Israel, to come to the synagogues and listen carefully to the music of Jews at prayer. This will invigorate and enrich them, and lead them to the creation of monumental music.

We have defined the primary origin of Jewish music — the synagogue. However, there is another vital force driving Jewish song: the traditional Jewish home, with its holiday feasts that are natural continuations of the synagogue services. The melodies (*Zmi'rot*) of the Sabbath and Holiday feasts, the singing of grace after meals *(Bir'kat Ha'Ma'zon)*, the Sabbath ending *Hav'da'la* ceremony, the Passover *Ha'gga'da* songs, and the *Pu'rim* and *Cha'nu'ka* holiday melodies — all comprise an intimate collection of typical Jewish music.

A good example of this transformation is the prayer *Ve'Sham'ru* that we sing in the synagogue. This melody is also sung at our festive Sabbath and holiday feasts at home with the song *"Kol Me'ka'desh."* I will now demonstrate a portion of the *Ve'Sham'ru:*

Now listen to the transformation of *Ve'Sham'ru* in the melody of *"Kol Me'ka'desh Shvi'ie"* ("Whoever duly observes the Sabbath"), which I composed while in Jerusalem on one of my visits to the Holy land, before my family and I settled in Israel. In this recording, Mark Lavry is conducting the Tel Aviv Chamber Orchestra.[2]

[*"Kol Me'ka'desh"* — composed and sung by Leib Glantz.]

---

2 *"Kol Me'ka'desh"* — composed and sung by Leib Glantz can be heard on compact disk (CD number 2) that accompanies this book.

This same transition occurs with other melodies that have passed from the synagogue to the home. Listen to Cantor Yossele Rosenblatt's composition *"Ra'chem Na"* ("Have mercy") from the *Bir'kat Ha'Ma'zon* (the grace after meals). It is based on the Major and Minor Pentatonic *Nu'sach:*

[*"Ra'chem Na"* — recording sung by Cantor Yossele Rosenblatt.]

Another composition, by Cantor Zavel Zilberts, gives us a similar view of the Jewish home on Saturday night, during the *Hav'da'la* ceremony that brings the Sabbath to a conclusion. *Hi'nei El Ye'shu'a'ti, Ev'tach Ve'Lo Ef'chad* ("Behold, God is my deliverance; I will trust and will not be afraid").

["*Hav'da'la*" — recording composed by Cantor Zavel Zilberts, sung by Cantor Richard Tucker.]

Finally, let us listen to Cantor David Moshe Steinberg singing *"Yis'me'chu"* (*Yis'me'chu Ve'Mal'chut'cha Shom'rei Sha'bat Ve'Kor'ei O'neg* — "Those who observe the Sabbath and call it a delight shall rejoice"), which is both a prayer in the synagogue and a melody sung at home during family feasts:

[*"Yis'me'chu"* — recording sung by Cantor David Moshe Steinberg.]

In this first of six radio lectures, I have presented a general introduction on the Jewish prayer modes *(Nus'cha'ot Ha'Te'fi'la)*. In the next lectures we will discuss several other prayer services and go into more detail.

7

The *Nu'sach* of the Passover *Ha'gga'da*

LEIB GLANTZ

Ladies and gentlemen — dear listeners!

My first lecture was a general introduction on the origins of traditional Jewish music. I emphasized its main scale — the Pentatonic scale, which contains five tones and four intervals. It is the primary and original scale upon which the Jewish prayer modes, the *Nus'cha'ot,*[2] were based. The cantillation of the bible (*Ta'a'mei Ha'Mik'ra)* is also based on the Pentatonic scale, as well as the reading of the *To'rah,* the *Haf'ta'ra,*[3] the *Me'gi'lot* (scrolls), and many *Nus'cha'ot* of the different prayers of the Jewish people. With this scale it is possible to compose melodies that are totally different from each other — some with a Major background and others with a Minor background. They can be joyful melodies as well as sad melodies, in accordance with the text. This is the key to understanding other scales.

In today's lecture, I will try to present a topic that is connected with this very day. This Sabbath we got a taste of the music of the *Ha'gga'da*[4] of *Pe'ssach.*[5] We might consider today's prayer services as a final "rehearsal" before the "drama" of the *Se'dder*[6] in which we celebrate

1 Second of six radio lectures by Leib Glantz, broadcast by *Kol Yis'ra'el,* the Israel Broadcasting Authority, 1961.

2 *Nus'cha'ot* — the ancient Jewish prayer modes.

3 *Haf'ta'ra* — A selection from the Prophets, read in synagogue services on the Sabbath following the reading from the *To'rah.* It usually has a thematic link to the *To'rah* reading that precedes it. The *Haf'ta'ra* is sung in the synagogue with cantillation according to a unique melody (not with the same cantillation melody as the *To'rah.)*

4 *Ha'gga'da* — the text recited at the *Se'dder* of the Jewish Passover, including a narrative of the Exodus of the Israelites from Pharaoh's Egypt.

5 *Pe'ssach* — The Passover holiday.

6 *Se'dder* — a Jewish ritual service and ceremonial dinner celebrated on the first night of Passover (in Israel) or the first two nights of Passover (in the Diaspora).

the exodus of the Israelites from Egypt. Therefore, we shall discuss the melodies of the Passover holiday.

This holiday is actually presented to us in four different versions:
- The Passover holiday *(Chag Ha'Pe'ssach);*
- The holiday of unleavened bread *(Chag Ha'Ma'tzot);*
- The holiday of freedom *(Chag Ha'Chei'rut);*
- The holiday of spring *(Chag He'A'viv).*

There are also four musical aspects of Passover, representing four different moods:
- The general *Nu'sach* of *Sha'losh Re'ga'lim* (the three pilgrimage festivals);
- The reading of the *Ha'gga'da* on the night of the *Se'dder* feast;
- The *Ha'llel* prayer — rejoicing in God;
- *Bir'kat Tal* — the blessing for dew.

On the first night of Passover the synagogue glows with joy. There is a sense that the evening *Ma'a'riv* prayer service is but a prelude to the upcoming enchanting drama that will follow the synagogue service in our homes. This anticipation towards the festive event of the *Se'dder* creates a unique tension in the synagogue. The first melody of the holiday service for the familiar words *"Bar'chu Et Ha'Shem Ha'Me'vo'rach"* ("Bless the Lord who is to be praised") is greatly different from the melody used for the same words on weekdays, Sabbaths, *Rosh Ha'Sha'na* and the *Kol Nid'rei* services. The musical *Nu'sach* used on this night is a ceremonious and beautiful melody:

> *On the first night of Passover the synagogue glows with joy. There is a sense that the evening* Ma'a'riv *prayer service is but a prelude to the upcoming enchanting drama that will follow the synagogue service in our homes.*

1. Bar - - chu   et Ha - shem _____ ha - m'vo - rach __

From a professional musician's standpoint, the musical origin of this melody is a scale of seven tones called the Mixolydian mode. It includes two Tetrachords connected and equal to each other; two lines of four tones:

The truth must be stated: this mode is not originally Jewish. It is one of the Greek musical modes. However, the Jewish people transformed it into an independent Jewish mode, by adding a third Tetrachord, so that instead of a line of seven tones, they created a totally new mode, consisting of three Tetrachords and ten tones, as follows:

It is worth mentioning that in this line there is a B natural below and also a Bb above. In this form we sing all of the synagogue prayers of the Passover night *Ma'a'riv* service. The first word — *"Ba're'chu"* — we sing in B natural and immediately afterward we sing the second and third word *(Et A'do'nai)* in Bb. The same is true for all the endings of the prayers of this service, such as the endings of the *Cha'tzi Ka'ddish* that precedes the *Te'fi'lat She'va,* the ending of the *Ki'ddush* (blessing of the wine), and others:

It is important to note that in the *Cha'tzi Ka'ddish* we add one extra tone:

That was the *Nu'sach* of *Sha'losh Re'ga'lim.*

At the completion of the *Ma'a'riv* service at the synagogue, we arrive at home and sense this great anticipation. Tensions are high as we get ready for an extraordinary feast. This night is different from every other night in the Jewish home. The family members and their invited guests excitedly congregate together, all dressed in their finest holiday clothes *("Big'dei Mal'chut").* The master of the house appears like a king, the mother a queen, the sons and daughters princes and princesses. Everyone gathered around the table is anxious to fulfill any role bestowed upon him

In this artistic ceremony, commemorating the great Exodus of the Israelites from Egypt thousands of years ago, there is a "stage" with special decorations: the table of the feast, with a special Passover plate, wine glasses, the prophet Eliahu's (Elijah's) special wine cup, and many other features. All these elevate the moods of the participants and create a wonderful artistic atmosphere.

> *In this artistic ceremony, commemorating the great Exodus of the Israelites from Egypt, thousands of years ago, there is a "stage" with special decorations.*

or her. In this artistic ceremony, commemorating the great Exodus of the
Israelites from Egypt thousands of years
ago, there is a "stage" with special decorations:

The most exciting aspect is the singing of the traditional Jewish music. The *Ha'gga'da* has its special *Nu'sach*. It is full of joy, sometimes dramatic and sometimes humorous. It is very intimate. The children tend to raise their voices above those of the elders. There are soloists and choruses. Every Jewish home is celebrating the *Se'dder* feast, and all together the whole community of Jewish people around the world band together, singing the songs of Exodus and freedom! Every Jew in every generation must consider as if he himself were part of the Exodus from Egypt. How very symbolic!

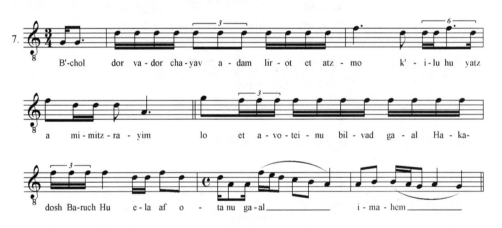

What then is the foundation of the typical music of the *Ha'gga'da?* It is the familiar mode from the synagogue prayers of *Sha'losh Re'ga'lim* — the Mixolydian mode. However, there is one small, if very important, difference. The recurring melody is Mixolydian, but it is different from that sung in the synagogue during the *Ma'a'riv* service: in place of the Bb above, which we emphasize in the synagogue prayer, we end the melodies with B natural below:

I will now sing some of the songs of the *Ha'gga'da:* Let us begin with *"A'va'dim Ha'yi'nu":*

We sing the names of the ten plagues God rendered upon the Egyptians *(E'ser Ha'Ma'kot):*

The "concert" continues in full force following the grace after meals *(Bir'kat Ha'Ma'zon)*. Song after song is built on the same Mixolydian mode. For example *"A'dir Hu":*

The song *"Chad Gad'ya,"* which contains both humor and deep philosophical ideas:

It is very important to note that there are a few songs in the *Ha'gga'da* that are not based on the Mixolydian mode, such as the Four Questions traditionally "asked" by the youngest son — the *"Ku'shi'yot,"* or *"Ma Nish'ta'na Ha'Ly'la Ha'Ze Mi'Kol Ha'Lay'lot?"* ("Why is this night different from all other nights?"). The melody here reverts to the basic Pentatonic scale, which, of course, is the musical basis for the reading of the *To'rah* and the *Haf'ta'ra*. What is the explanation for this "reversion"? It is not just a simple coincidence. The answer is really very simple. Small children are always those who sing these Four Questions. They are taught to sing this by their school teachers (who frequently are also those who read the *To'rah* in the synagogue, using the Pentatonic scale). These teachers/readers of the *To'rah* are not musicians, and therefore are not bound by the strict rules of using the general *Nu'sach* of the *Ha'gga'da*. They teach the children to sing *"Ma Nish'ta'na"* in the same melodic *Nu'sach* as they teach them to recite the *To'rah*, the Prophets, and the *Ge'ma'ra*.[7] Therefore, the Pentatonic *"Ma Nish'ta'na"* song became set in the minds of young and old alike. I will sing this *Nu'sach* to illustrate:

The musical assets of the Passover *Ha'gga'da* frequently get "lost" due to all sorts of additions and mistaken falsifications. However, we must take into account the fact that in different periods of Jewish history, Jews were obliged to perform their *Se'dder* feasts secretly and under clandestine conditions. An important example is the Marranos — the Jews in Spain and Portugal who, during the dreaded Inquisition, were forced to convert to Christianity, or if they refused, were to be burned at the stake. In other periods, violent pogroms were carried out against the Jews purposely on the night of the Passover *Se'dder*. Obviously, these catastrophes influenced the tone of the *Se'dder* songs, introducing sounds of sobbing, fear and anxiety. Having said this, it can be stated that in general, the *Ha'gga'da* melodies remained joyfully based on ancient modes that are rich with Eastern charm.

Finally, I will now sing *"Ve'Hi She'Am'da,"* a song I composed under the influence of my family's singing at our *Se'dder*. This song is built on the ancient Dorian mode[8] that is partly in Major and partly in Minor. The Minor is from the first to the sixth tone, and the sixth is Major:

---

7 *Ge'ma'ra* — a rabbinical commentary on the *Mish'na* (oral tradition of Jewish law,) forming the second part of the Talmud.
8 Dorian Mode — the mode represented by the natural diatonic scale D–D (containing a minor 3rd and minor 7th).

14.

V'-hi she-am-da la-a-vo-tei-nu v'-la-nu v'-la - nu she - lo e-chad bi-l'-vad bi-l'-vad a-

mad a-lei-nu she - lo e-chad bi-l'-vad bi-l' - vad a-mad a-lei-nu l'-cha-lo-tei-nu l'-

cha - lo - tei - nu e - la she-b'-chol dor va-dor dor va-dor om-dim a-lei-nu l'-

cha-lo-tei-nu l' - cha-lo-tei - nu v' - Ha-ka-dosh Ba-ruch Hu ma-tzi-lei-nu mi-ya - dam

mi-ya-dam Ha-ka-dosh Ba-ruch Hu ma-tzi-lei-nu mi-ya - dam___ mi-ya-dam v' -

Ha-ka-dosh Ba-ruch Hu ma-tzi-lei-nu mi-ya-dam___ mi-ya-dam v' - Ha-ka-dosh Ba-ruch Hu ma-tzi-

lei-nu mi-ya - dam mi-ya-dam v' - hi she-am-da la-a-vo-tei-nu v'-la-nu v'-la - nu she -

lo e-chad bi-l'-vad a-mad a-lei - nu she - lo e-chad bi-l'-vad bi-l' - vad a-mad a-lei-nu l'-

cha-lo-tei-nu l' - cha-lo-tei - - nu e - la she-b'-chol dor va-dor o-m'-

dim a-lei-nu l'-cha-lo - tei-nu   l' - cha - lo - tei   -   nu   v' - Ha-ka-dosh Ba-ruch Hu ma-tzi-

lei-nu mi-ya - dam   mi - ya-dam   v'-Ha-Ka-dosh Ba-ruch Hu ma-tzi-lei - nu   mi-ya - dam__ mi-ya-

dam v'-Ha-ka-dosh Ba-ruch Hu ma-tzi-lei-nu mi-ya - dam   mi-ya-dam v'-Ha-ka-dosh Ba-ruch Hu ma-tzi-

lei - nu   mi - ya - dam___   mi - ya - dam_____

8

Nu'sach Ha'llel and Tal

THIRD KOL YISRAEL RADIO LECTURE[1]

LEIB GLANTZ

Ladies and gentlemen — dear listeners:

In this lecture I should like to discuss the prayers *Ha'llel* and *Tal*. Let us consider a characteristic fact that is eminently worthy of our attention. When we enter an Orthodox synagogue,
either in Israel or in the Diaspora, the first thing we notice is the sad, almost tearful, tones.
One might get the impression that all Jewish liturgy sounds sad, even when the text expresses joy and thanksgiving.

We must wonder how the *Ha'llel* was performed in the ancient Holy Temple. The great
Rambam[2] wrote that "The reader sings the *Ha'llel* and the congregation responds after every
passage: *'Ha'lle'lu'yah.'* The congregation thus answers *'Ha'lle'lu'yah'* one hundred and twenty
three times. When the cantor sings, *'Ba'ruch Ha'Ba,'* the congregation responds: *'Be'Shem
Ha'Shem.'"* [3]

It might be expected that this exalted verbal content would appropriately call for jubilant
music. Unfortunately that is not the case. Almost all cantors sing the passages of *Ha'llel* in the
Harmonic Minor. The "peak" of melancholy is reached in conjunction with phrases like "The

---

1 Third of six radio lectures by Leib Glantz, broadcast by *Kol Yis'ra'el,* the Israel Broadcasting Authority, 1961.
2 Moses Maimonides (1138-1204) — Rabbi Moshe Ben Maimon (Rambam) — religious scholar, mathematician, astronomer,
  and commentator on the art of medicine, his influence has spanned centuries and cultures. He was born in Spain and educated by his father, a Jewish judge. Eventually settling in Cairo, he became court physician to two Viziers of Egypt. Rambam codified the Talmud and in *Guide for the Perplexed* (1190) attempted to reconcile Aristotelian philosophy with Jewish theology.
3 Rambam, *Mish'ne To'rah, Su'cca* III:10.

heavens are the heavens of the Lord, but the earth He has given to mankind," or "To Thee I will offer a thanksgiving sacrifice." What is there to bewail?

I have intensively studied this perplexing question and have found two explanations:

- The first explanation is extremely simple: for many generations the situation of the Jews of the Diaspora has been tragic and catastrophic; Jewish blood had flowed like water. Attention to the verbal content of the prayers was neglected. The synagogue services became a suitable opportunity for the Jews to pour out their hearts in lamentation, to cry out and complain to the Almighty about their bitter plight;

- The second explanation is not quite as simple. Its source lies precisely in the music formula of the *Ha'llel*. The origin of this *Nu'sach* is rooted in the very first blessing: "He who has sanctified us with His commandments and ordained on us the reading of the *Ha'llel*." The cantor opens the *Ha'llel* blessing in what seems to be a pure Minor key, but actually it is only an illusory Minor, and as a result both the cantor and the congregation continue with this deceptive Minor throughout most of the passages of the *Ha'llel*. There is no thanksgiving and no praise, no song and no exultation. Instead, there are broken sounds and plaints, weak suffering voices. The more tearful the cantor, the greater his reputation...

> *The more tearful the cantor,*
> *the greater his reputation . . .*

The great European "Choral Cantors," such as Solomon Sulzer[4] and his followers, reacting against this characteristic lachrymosity, changed the key from the Harmonic Minor to the classic West European Major. It was as though they were saying: What is the matter with you wailing "Ost Juden,"[5] that you weep with tears while singing *Ha'lle'lu'ya*? Go sing *Ha'lle'lu'ya* in a Major key, a la Mozart or Schubert.

The truth of the matter is that neither of these approaches found the proper path to the original Jewish *Nu'sach* of the *Ha'llel*. I am convinced that both the Jewish Major and the Jewish Minor contain something characteristic and specific, that survived from the ancient modes of

---

4 Solomon Sulzer (1804-1890) was born in Austria. After acquiring a conservatory education in composition and singing, Sulzer became the first musician in modern times to create a synagogue liturgy of the highest aesthetic standard by combining the cantorial heritage with forms and performance techniques of modern European music. He composed some of the greatest synagogue music. Sulzer officiated as cantor at the Seitenstettengasse Temple in Vienna. He tried to find a "middle road" path that would preserve the essential elements of Jewish musical traditions, but clothe them in modern Austrian garb; that, he believed, would please the older generation, and at the same time provide an idiom to which the younger acculturated Austrian Jews could relate. People flocked from all over Europe to the synagogue to hear Sulzer and his choir.

5 "Ost Juden" — Jews from the East.

the Oriental [Middle Eastern] peoples, that is not to be found at all in the modern West European scales.

After years of searching, examining and striving to find the musical truth about the *Ha'llel*, I have come to recognize that the first blessing of the *Ha'llel* is not to be sung in the Minor key, but is actually a direct continuation from the end of *Te'fi'lat Ha'She'va*, from the *Nu'sach* of the *Sha'losh Re'ga'lim*[6] prayer service to the beginning of the blessing of *Ha'llel*.

I shall now sing for you the *Nu'sach* of *Te'fi'lat Ha'She'va*, finishing with the last blessing *Ha'Me'va'rech Et A'mo Yis'ra'el Ba'Sha'lom* ("O Lord, who blesseth His people of Israel with peace"). Let us try to listen as musicians, and hear how we pass over to the *Ha'llel* blessing. This will prove the validity of this hypothesis.

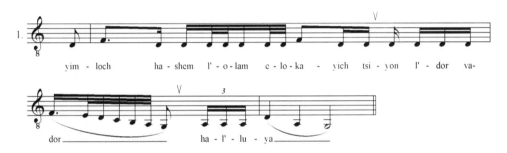

For instance we finish with:

We begin *A'ta Ve'char'ta'nu*:

---

6 *Sha'losh Re'ga'lim* — the three festivals of *Pe'sach, Sha'vu'ot* and *Su'ccot.*

And now you can hear that we are already in the Minor. And we end with:

And immediately after that we begin the *Ha'llel* blessing:

Yes, but it sounds Minor.

The entire *Tefi'lat Ha'She'va* is sung in the *Nu'sach* of *Sha'losh Re'ga'lim,* or in other words, in the Mixolydian mode. Throughout this entire prayer we are moving back and forth between the fifth and the seventh:

On the basis of this movement, we construct this entire unusual *Nu'sach.* Instead of simply touching this seventh here, just as a step in the Mixolydian scale, we build for ourselves a new, truly Minor basis, from D to F, and we thereby abandon the *Nu'sach* entirely, and virtually never return to it.

One trespass leads to another, and this passing musical deviation led to an actual departure from the basis, which is G in the Mixolydian mode, and an unnatural attachment to a new basis: D minor:

Instead of:

lik - ro_____ et ha - ha - lel_____

When this is done in the prayer *U'Mi'pnei Cha'ta'ei'nu* ("because of our sins"), at least it has a certain logical justification in the text:

u-mip - nei - cha-ta - ei - nu ga - li - nu me-ar-tse - nu   v' -nit -ra chak - nu me-al   ad-ma-te - nu

The entire tragedy of exile has found its expression in this text, and the Minor key suited it in every sense. But when this musical deviation passed on to the jubilant *Ha'llel,* the cantor was sinning not only against the music, but — and that is the most important point — against the text and against the general spirit of the *Ha'llel.*

Moreover, in the *Shmo'neh Es'reh* prayers, the cantor is accustomed, at least at the end of every blessing, to return to the regular recurring melody of the *Nu'sach* of *Sha'losh Re'ga'lim.* This is not the case with the *Ha'llel.* Here he has really lost the "essential point," which most cantors term: the "*Nu'sach* from Sinai."

> *When this musical deviation passed on to the jubilant* Ha'llel, *the cantor was sinning not only against the music, but — and that is the most important point — against the text and against the general spirit of the* Ha'llel.

We shall now attempt to explain what is the "*Nu'sach* from Sinai," and what is the "general *Nu'sach,*" in the terminology of cantors. The "*Nu'sach* from Sinai" is the established melody that no cantor has the right to alter in any way whatsoever. The "general *Nu'sach,*" on the contrary, although it is indeed built on the same scales as the "*Nu'sach* from Sinai," allows the cantor leeway to create new melodies, sometimes going quite far in transitions from one key to another, and from one tonality to another. He may create spontaneous improvisations, or he may prepare in advance a modern composition belonging to any period in the world of music, but he must return to the basis, to the "*Nu'sach* from Sinai," to the established, recurring melody whose very presence is the distinguishing feature of any given *Nu'sach.*

There are three fixed rules to every passage of prayers:

A. The scale or mode on which it must be built;
B. The recurring melody (for example, the *"Nu'sach* from Sinai"*);
C. The proper interpretation of the words.

Two great cantors have shown us the correct path: Cantor Bezalel Odesser-Schulsinger (1790-1860) from Odessa, in Eastern Europe, who was a great pioneer in the rediscovery of the *Nu'sach;* and Cantor Abraham Baer (1834-1894) from Germany, in Western Europe, who published his *Nus'cha'ot* in a monumental volume entitled *"Ba'al T'fi'llah — Der Practische Vorbeter,"* which was originally published in Frankfurt-am-Main in 1877.

Bezalel Odesser usually taught *Nu'sach* orally. However, from Bezalel's students we learned that he would conclude the first blessing of *Ha'llel* in the *Nu'sach* of the Festival *Shmo'neh Es'reh*.

Abraham Baer, in his 1877 book, recorded two *Nus'cha'ot* of the *Ha'llel* blessing: one (the corrupt one) in Minor, and the other clearly in the *Nu'sach* of *Sha'losh Re'ga'lim*. More significantly, Baer recommended that cantors conclude every single passage of *Ha'llel* with this *Sha'losh Re'ga'lim Nu'sach*.

I will now sing part of my composition for cantor and choir. In the framework of *Te'fi'lat Tal,* I tried to combine the scale, the *Nu'sach*, and my interpretation of the text of this prayer:

In order to complete this picture of the *Ha'llel*, it is worth mentioning some additional, perhaps fortuitous, but extremely characteristic facts: in several places in the *Ha'llel*, even those readers and cantors who ordinarily sing the entire *Ha'llel* in Minor momentarily abandon the Minor and, to a certain extent, transfer into the Mixolydian scale, as well as into the Pentatonic scale, which are the main scales of our Jewish *Nus'cha'ot*. For example:

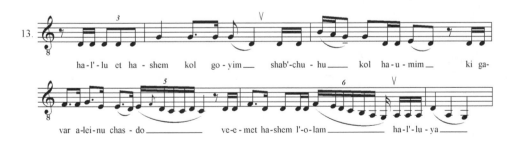

Or:

ze ha-yom a-sa ha-shem na-gi-la v'-nis-m'-cha___ vo___ ze ha-yom a-sa ha-shem___

___ na-gi-la v'-nis-m'-cha_____ v'-nis-m'-cha vo___

In the prayers *Ho'du* and *A'na*, several cantors attempt to introduce differing melodies, some of them quite typical, which are constructed on the ancient modes. One of them, which is more important than the others, is:

ho-du la-shem ki_____ tov___ ki_____ l'-o-lam_____ chas - do___

ki_____ l'-o-lam_____ chas - - - - do_____

I find it necessary to introduce some small changes to this melody, and thus make it entirely acceptable from a Jewish musical standpoint. After this small change, we have before us a pure ancient Oriental [Middle Eastern] melody. For example:

ho-du la-shem ki_____ tov___ ki_____ l'-o-lam_____ chas - do___

ki l'-o-lam_____ chas - - - - - - do

In addition to this melody, I would like to sing another melody of my own — *Ho'du* and *A'na*. We sing this at the *Tif'e'ret Zvi* synagogue, and the whole congregation joins in the singing along with the cantor and choir. This melody is based on the Dorian mode that begins in Minor and continues in Major:

17.

A - na a-na a-na___ Ha - shem___ ho - shi-a - na   a - na a-na a-na___

ha - shem___ ho - shi-a - na   a - na a-na a-na___ ho - shi - a

ho - shi-a - na   a - na a-na a-na___ Ha - shem___ ho - shi - a

na   a - na a-na a-na___ Ha - shem hatz - li-cha na   a-

na a-na a-na___ Ha - shem hatz - li-cha___ na   a - na a-na a-na___

Ha - shem___ hatz - li-cha na   a - na a-na a-na___ Ha - shem___

rall.

hatz - - - li - cha na

Let us now move to an analysis of *Tal,* the prayer for dew, or as it is sometimes called, the *Tal* blessing (*Bir'kat Ha'Tal*). I should like to stress at the outset that we are limiting this discussion to the *Nus'cha'ot* of Ashkenazic Jewry. I would not dare to analyze the *Nus'cha'ot* of the prayers of the Sephardic Jewry (*Ei'dot Ha'Miz'rach*). I believe that experts will arise among the Sephardic communities themselves, and they, and only they, will be capable to do this research and analysis both professionally and correctly.

In the *Nu'sach* of *Tal* as sung by the Sephardic communities there is quite a considerable difference both in the text and in the music. As regards the *Tal* prayer among the various Ashkenazic communities, it should be stressed that *Tal,* as well, has a "*Nu'sach* from Sinai" and a "general *Nu'sach.*" The "*Nu'sach* from Sinai," the basis of *Tal,* is sung to the text of the *Cha'tzi Ka'ddish,* at the beginning of the *A'vot* prayer in *Te'fi'lat Ha'She'va* and in the first *Pi'yu'tim* (liturgical poems), such as *Be'Da'a'to* and so forth.

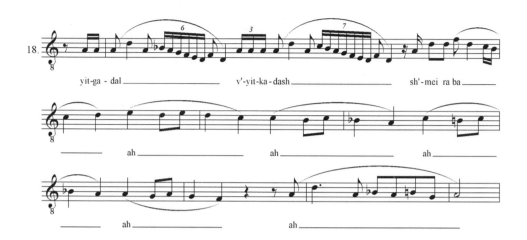

18.

yit-ga - dal _____ v'-yit-ka - dash _____ sh'-mei ra ba _____

_____ ah _____ ah _____ ah _____

_____ ah _____ ah _____

The "general *Nu'sach"* is used in the wonderful final text of *Tal Ten Le'ra'tsot Ar'tzach* ("Dew — grant it to favor Your land").

What did the Jews of the Diaspora do? When they finished singing the *Ka'ddish,* the *A'vot* and the first *Pi'yu'tim* of *Tal,* they abruptly abandoned this wonderful jubilant melody and began to chant the *Tal* in the mournful Harmonic Minor with the leading tone. The jubilation ended and was supplanted by the fashionable weeping. It is now almost impossible to distinguish between the *Tal* prayer and any other prayer of the Sabbath, the weekday, or the holiday. The stereotype is there: a bit of simple Minor, a bit of *Nu'sach A'ha'va Ra'bbah,* and what is most important, the entire congregation weeps, in exaggerated, sobbing tearfulness. There is no relation to the

> *The Jews of the Diaspora abruptly abandoned this wonderful jubilant melody, and began to chant the* Tal *in the mournful Harmonic Minor. The jubilation ended and was supplanted by the fashionable weeping.*

general spirit of the wonderful poem that was written by Rabbi Eliezer Hakalir in the seventh century. This is a poem that preserves for eternity a picture of the agricultural way of life in our own country. The prayers for *Ge'shem* (rain) and *Tal* (dew) are about water and dew, about blessed rainfall "that the earth, in pride and glory, may be filled with fruit." It is a poem describing the "precious dew, that makes the mountains sweet!"

The Jews living in the Diaspora for so long evidently forgot about these aspects of life. They had troubles and suffered persecution. Riots and blood libels were held against them. So, naturally, their conclusion was: "Let us weep even when singing *Tal.* Let us shed tears and sob and complain about our bitter fate." It was as though they were saying: "House of Jacob — come ye and let us weep!"

What then is the mode on which the lovely, wonderful *"Nu'sach* from Sinai" of *Tal* was constructed? This *Nu'sach* was actually built on two modes, intermingled but also competing with each other. One is the Aeolian mode, definitely not the Harmonic Minor, with the leading tone. The second is the Dorian mode. If we construct this *Nu'sach* in two competing modes, a line like the following will result:

Now let us hear what is done to the *Nu'sach* of *Tal:*

It is easy to hear what I have done above. I have pointed out both the Bb and the B natural at the end of the *Nu'sach*. This is what is wrongly done with the "general *Nu'sach*": it is entirely neglected and is sung as an ordinary prayer in an ordinary Minor key, or even sometimes in the *A'ha'va Ra'bbah Nu'sach.*

To my great joy, I discovered that the famous nineteenth century Cantor Pinchas Minkowsky, from the Brody synagogue in Odessa, who was a very modern, choral, almost Reform cantor, knew how to guide his choir and his congregation when chanting the prayer *Tal Ten* — in the "general *Nu'sach.*"

I use the words "to my great joy" because when I composed my composition *"Tal Ten"* (the two portions of *Tal* that are in my recordings), I did not realize that Minkowsky had done so as well. At that time, I could not bear this neglect, and at the very beginning I sang the words *E'lo'kei'nu Ve'E'lo'kei A'vo'tei'nu* in the *"Nu'sach* from Sinai":

Incidentally, the Chasidim selected this text and clothed it in various and sundry melodies. Indeed there are melodic kernels of *Nu'sach* in many Chasidic tunes. These are tunes that are sung at the Rabbi's table, and songs that are sung before and after the study of the *To'rah*. Some of these tunes are even sung at festive meals, often accompanied by Chasidic dancing with devotion and transcendent ecstasy. But as much as these songs may beautify our family life in the home, they should not be brought into the synagogue to supplant the appropriate traditional *Nu'sach*.

The original Jewish *Tal* must be garbed in "Eastern" dress — in Eastern scales. The cantor must do everything he can to divest himself of those ordinary Major and Minor keys. The agricultural village life of our country must be given the proper and true musical expression in our prayers. It is very important that the *"Nu'sach* from Sinai" be revived, perhaps in a modern manner, but in a clear and concrete fashion.

9

Nu'sach A'ha'va Ra'bbah

FOURTH KOL YISRAEL RADIO LECTURE[1]

LEIB GLANTZ

Ladies and gentlemen — dear listeners!

In this lecture we will talk about the Jewish prayer mode we call *"A'ha'va Ra'bbah."* This mode is exactly what its name expresses: It is full of unlimited love (*A'ha'va*). In this *Nu'sach,* we not only address the Lord with the words *"A'ha'va Ra'bbah A'hav'ta'nu"* ("With great love You have loved us"), but we ourselves address this mode with great affection, as if to warmly declare our love. There is a continuous, spiritual romance between the people of Israel and this *Nu'sach.* Somehow, our souls are strongly connected to it.

> *There is a continuous, spiritual romance between the people of Israel and* Nu'sach *A'ha'va Ra'bbah.* **Somehow, our souls are strongly connected to this** Nu'sach.

This love is a musical love, at times gentle and at times stormy. It is as if the Jews have musical chords of *"A'ha'va Ra'bbah"* deep inside their souls. We use this *Nu'sach* on different occasions, sometimes happy, but also in tragic moments of our lives, such as in our memorial service *Yiz'kor,* in the prayer *El Ma'leh Ra'cha'mim* ("O Lord, who art full of compassion").

Our first meeting with this *Nu'sach* is in the weekday evening *Ma'a'riv* service:

---

1 Fourth of six radio lectures by Leib Glantz, broadcast by *Kol Yis'ra'el,* the Israel Broadcasting Authority, 1961.

V'-hu ra - chum y'-cha-peir a-von v'-lo yash - chit v'-hir-ba l'-ha-shiv a-
po v'-lo ya-ir kol cha-ma-to____ Ha - shem ho-shi-a ha-me-lech ya-a-nei-nu v'-
yom kor - ei - nu

Then we find the *"A'ha'va Ra'bbah"* at the beginning of the Sabbath morning *Shach'rit* service, but in a totally different form. The words that we use with this *Nu'sach* are glorious. They describe our imagining the singing of angels in heaven: "All open their mouths in holiness and purity, with song and psalm, while they bless and praise, glorify and revere, sanctify and ascribe sovereignty to the name of the Divine King!"

From a musical standpoint, we begin singing in Major (a continuation of *Tit'ba'rach La'Ne'tzach*), and then we move on to the parallel Minor and end with the *A'ha'va Ra'bbah Nu'sach*:

V' - chu - lam pot - chim et pi-hem bik-du - sha uv-to-ho-ra b'-shi-ra u-v'-zim-
ra u-m'-var-chim u-m'-shab-chim u-m'-fa-a - rim____ u-ma-a-ri-tzim u-mak-di-
shim____ u - mam - li - chim____

This same *Nu'sach* is applied differently in our most dramatic and exciting prayers — whether universal, national, or personal. For instance, when we sing *Le'El Ba'ruch Ne'i'mot Yi'te'nu...Zmi'rot Yo'me'ru Ve'Tish'ba'chot Yash'mi'u* ("To the blessed God they offer melodious strains; they utter hymns and make their praises heard"), we immediately move to nationalistic requests, I would even call them Zionist requests: "O cause a new light to shine upon

Zion…arise to the help of Israel…and deliver Judah and Israel according to Your promise" (*Or Cha'dash Al Tzi'on Ta'ir…Ku'ma Be'Ez'rat Yis'ra'el…U'P'deh Ki'Ne'u'me'cha Ye'hu'da Ve'Yis'ra'el*).

As we come to the first *Ke'du'sha* prayer, *Nak'di'shach* or *Ne'ka'desh* ("we will sanctify Thy name"), we musically imagine the whispers of the angels: "As pleasant secret words of sacred angels…calling one onto the other, declaring: 'Holy, Holy, Holy is the Lord!'" (*Ke'No'am Si'ach Sod Sar'fei Ko'desh… Ve'Ka'ra Zeh El Zeh Ve'A'mar: Ka'dosh, Ka'dosh, Ka'dosh…*). And so we continue till the end of this prayer, with the final words: "Blessed art Thou, O Lord, who blessest Thy people Israel with peace" (*Ha'Me'va'rech Et A'mo Yis'ra'el Ba'Sha'lom*), sung in the *A'ha'va Ra'bbah Nu'sach*. Blessings, prayers, thanks, requests, and imaginary descriptions — all are sung in the *A'ha'va Ra'bbah Nu'sach*.

However, with the opening of the sacred Ark of the *To'rah* scrolls at the synagogue, after we have sung, in a totally different *Nu'sach*, the words *Ki A'yin Be'A'yin Yir'u Be'Shuv A'do'nai Tzi'on* ("For they shall see eye to eye when the Lord returneth to Zion"), we again return to the *A'ha'va Ra'bbah Nu'sach* with words of plea and supplication: *Av Ha'Ra'cha'mim, Hu Ye'ra'chem* ("Father of mercy, have mercy")! It is as if all of a sudden we were engulfed with musical longing and nostalgia to sing the beloved *A'ha'va Ra'bbah Nu'sach* once again. Even when we come to a festive prayer, such as the blessing of the new month (*Bir'kat Ha'Cho'desh*), we begin the prayer *Ye'hi Ra'tzon* ("May it be Thy will, O Lord") with the *A'ha'va Ra'bbah Nu'sach*, expressing both blessings and pleas.

It would be difficult in this short lecture to list all the prayers that are sung in the *A'ha'va Ra'bbah Nu'sach*. We can conclude however, that this *Nu'sach* dominated most of our Jewish prayers and liturgical poems (*Pi'yu'tim*).

If it were true that this *Nu'sach* is just an "adopted son" of the Jewish people, then the people of Israel were very good at the "art" of adoption. The Jews fell in love with this adopted "child," nourished it, and turned it into their dearest son (*Ben Ya'kir Ve'Ye'led Sha'a'shu'im*). Some secular musicologists have claimed that the mode on which the *A'ha'va Ra'bbah Nu'sach* is built is not Jewish but foreign — Gypsy, Armenian, or other. My answer to them is very simple: **They are wrong!**

> *Some secular musicologists have claimed that the mode on which the* A'ha'va Ra'bah Nu'sach *is built is not Jewish but foreign — Gypsy, Armenian, or other. My answer to them is very simple:* **They are wrong!**

Let us analyze the *A'ha'va Ra'bbah Nu'sach*. We may just discover that it is Jewish in its origin.

The following statements are intended for professional musicians, and for those who are not musicians, please forgive me for a moment. We all recognize that the *A'ha'va Ra'bbah Nu'sach* is built on a mode that cantors call "Phrygish." This name is derived from a Greek mode known as "Phrygian." There is an important difference between the two. The second interval in the "Phrygish" mode is augmented, and instead of the E – F – G – A that is sung in the "Phrygian" mode, in the cantorial mode we sing: E – F – G# – A. It is true that this augmented interval is used by several other cultures; however, the Jews introduced into it major changes that created an authentic and "kosher" Jewish mode.

Basically, the Jews frequently use the augmented second not only in its first Tetrachord, but also in the second Tetrachord, which means that we sing in this row as well: E – F – G# – A – B – C – D# – E.

It is interesting to point out that in Eastern European congregations that use *Nu'sach* Sepharad in their synagogue prayers, the Psalm *Le'Da'vid Miz'mor* ("Of David, a psalm") is sung in the evening *Ma'a'riv* service of the New Year (*Rosh Ha'Sha'na*) and on the *Kol Nid'rei* service of the Day of Atonement (*Yom Ki'ppur*) with extraordinary festivity. Here is how we sing this psalm:

This is typical *A'ha'va Ra'bbah Nu'sach*, and in both its Tetrachords, the second is definitely augmented. As a matter of fact, Joel Engel, the famous Jewish musician, succeeded in grasping the typical spirit of Jewish song in the Psalms, and had the actors of the Israeli National Theater *Ha'bi'ma* sing its tunes in the classic play, *"The Di'bbuk."* This is how the actors in the play hummed:

This humming is without doubt based on the *A'ha'va Ra'bbah Nu'sach,* on the augmented second in both Tetrachords of the "Phrygish."

In addition, I will illustrate two typical Jewish melodies from the spirit of two great Jewish cantorial composers: Pinchas Minkowsky and Yerucham Hakatan.

Minkowsky's melody laments over the destruction of the Holy Temple in the amazing liturgical poem from the *Yom Ki'ppur* service, "When our Holy Temple was destroyed" (*U'Mi'She'Cha'rav Beit Mik'da'she'nu*). This melody employs the augmented second in both Tetrachords of the *A'ha'va Ra'bbah Nu'sach.*

Yerucham Hakatan's melody is also based on this principle. The words "Let our hearts cleave to Thy commandments" (*Ve'Da'vek Li'bei'nu Be'Mitz'vo'te'cha*) are from the *A'ha'va Ra'bbah* prayer. In other words we have the *A'ha'va Ra'bbah Nu'sach* in the *A'ha'va Ra'bbah prayer*. This is so appropriate for this nineteenth century genius of all cantors.

However, this is not the most important Jewish modification in the *A'ha'va Ra'bbah Nu'sach*. If it were just for this modification alone, we would not be able to relate this mode specifically to the Jewish people. We could possibly be satisfied with being just partners with other cultures. However, the Jews introduced a fundamental and original modification that was purely Jewish: they added an additional Tetrachord that begins from the fifth tone below the E, which is A. In other words, the "Phrygian" and the "Phrygish" combined together. This new Tetrachord is totally different: it does not employ an augmented second. This Tetrachord, which begins on A and continues B – C# – D – E is very surprising because it is a Major Tetrachord, as opposed to the first two Tetrachords that are clearly "Phrygish."

Cantors traditionally begin the *A'ha'va Ra'bbah Nu'sach* not from the tone E, but from the tone A (the fifth tone below the E):

This is a very peculiar and typically Jewish line! The music of no other culture has anything similar to this.

I will now illustrate this with a melody by the famous nineteenth-century cantor from Kishinev, Avraham Berkovitz-Kalechnik. The words are: "You did not give it, Lord our God, to the nations of the lands" (*Ve'Lo Ne'ta'to A'do'nai E'lo'hei'nu Le'Go'yei Ha'A'ra'tzot*):

This complete recitative is built purely on the three Tetrachords that we spoke of earlier. It is important to happily point out that the Chabad Chasidic movement succeeded in creating a melody called "*The Rebbe's Ni'ggun*," which is attributed to Rabbi Shneor Zalman Shneerson Miliadi. It is based on the pure *Nu'sach* of *A'ha'va Ra'bbah*, and includes all three of its Tetrachords. I believe this melody will forever remain the symbol of the authentic experience of the Jewish people in the Diaspora, who drew from the great eternal spring of original Jewish music:

Before ending this fourth lecture of the series, I would like to point out that in several Jewish communities, the second chapter of the *Ki'not* [2] is also sung according to the *A'ha'va Ra'bbah Nu'sach*.

Ani Ha'Ge'ver Ra'ah O'ni Be'She'vet Ev'ra'to; O'ti Na'hag Va'Yo'lech Cho'shech Ve'Lo Or; Ach Bi Ya'shuv Ya'ha'foch Ya'do Kol Ha'Yom ("I am the man who has known affliction under the rod of His wrath; me He drove on and on in unrelieved darkness; on none but me He brings down His hand again and again without cease"):

In this melody we add another typical and unique supplement to the *A'ha'va Ra'bbah Nu'sach*: at the end of the last musical phrase you can hear the additional F# followed by F natural:

2 *Ki'not* — special prayers recited on the holiday of *Tish'ah Be'Av* (the ninth day of the month of *Av*) — a day of fasting and prayer in remembrance of the destruction of the Holy Temple and other calamities that occurred to the Jewish people.

The Yiddish song *"Ei'li Ei'li"* has become very popular with the Jewish people, primarily because it also is based upon this beloved *A'ha'va Ra'bbah Nu'sach:*

Ei - li   Ei - li_____   la - ma   a - zav - ta - ni

The same is true of the Saturday night *Hav'da'la* prayer (the ceremony at the conclusion of the Sabbath). The popular melody *Ve'Ta'her Li'bei'nu* ("Cleanse our heart"), and the Israeli song *Ha'va Na'gi'la* ("Let us rejoice") are also based on the *A'ha'va Ra'bbah Nu'sach!* In general, this *Nu'sach* can be found in many places in the Jewish prayers. I will point out just a few of the more important ones:

- In the last part of the prayer *Ve'Ha'Ko'ha'nim* ("And the priests") from the *A'vo'da* prayer of *Yom Ki'ppur*, which is called *Nu'sach Mi'Sinai* (prayer mode from Sinai), the last musical phrase is distinctly in the *A'ha'va Ra'bbah Nu'sach:*

- At the beginning of the prayer *Kol Nid'rei* (the opening prayer on the evening of *Yom Ki'ppur*):

- At the beginning of the *Ka'ddish* prayer for the High Holidays:

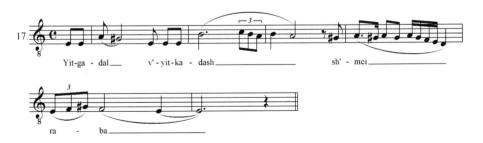

Yit-ga - dal___   v' - yit-ka - dash_____   sh' - mei_____

ra - ba_____

- In most of the texts of the *Se'li'chot* prayers.

I will now play my composition for the prayer *Mach'ni'sei Ra'cha'mim, Hach'ni'su Ra'cha'mei'nu Lif'nei Ba'al Ha'Ra'cha'mim!* ("Angels of mercy, bring our plea for mercy before him who is the source of all mercy"). Here is a direct appeal for assistance from the angels of heaven. This composition is based on the three Tetrachords that were mentioned earlier.[3]

---

3 The *"Mach'ni'sei Ra'cha'mim"* recording — composed and sung by Leib Glantz can be heard on compact disk [CD number 2] that accompanies this book.

10

Nu'sach A'do'nai Ma'lach and the Jewish Major

Fifth Kol Yisrael radio lecture[1]

Leib Glantz

Ladies and gentlemen — dear listeners:

In the former radio lectures we discussed the fact that many of the Jewish prayer modes, the *Nus'cha'ot Ha'Te'fi'la*, are based on the Major melodies that express happiness and joy. I also pointed out that the Jews of the Diaspora, having suffered from great hardships, strayed away from the Major and sang in Minor as a way of expressing their sorrow and misery.

In those lectures we brought forth the very important example of the biblical cantillations, which embody the primary source of both the Jewish Major and the Jewish Minor — the Pentatonic scale. In addition, when discussing *Nu'sach Sha'losh Re'ga'lim* (the three Festivals) and the *Ha'gga'da* for the *Passover* holiday *Se'dder,* we proved that they are based totally on the Mixolydian mode.

However, we did not cover the whole spectrum of important *Nus'cha'ot* on which most of our prayers are built, both in Major and Minor. In this lecture I will concentrate on the Jewish Major.

In classical music, the musicians use the customary crystallized Major scale that stems from the Ionian mode.[2] It ends with a leading tone from the seventh *(Septima)* to the octave, and it is easily harmonized:

---

1 Fifth of six radio lectures by Leib Glantz, broadcast by *Kol Yis'ra'el*, the Israel Broadcasting Authority, 1961.
2 Ionian mode — a medieval musical mode whose scale pattern is that of playing C to C on the white keys of a piano. This scale is identical to a Major scale.

Do re mi fa so la si do

Ancient cultures, including the Jewish people, used shorter musical lines compared to the customary Major scale in order to enlarge the space of the leading tone to the octave from a half step to a whole step. They omitted the tone leading from the seventh to the octave. In order to emphasize the Major in the Jewish *Nu'sach*, they tended to use the Pentatonic and Mixolydian scales. These *Nus'cha'ot* are found in several services throughout the year, including Sabbath, Festival and High Holiday prayers.

A good example is the *Ma'a'riv* evening service for the New Year (*Rosh Ha'Sha'na*), and the *Kol Nid'rei* service on the eve of the Day of Atonement (*Yom Ki'ppur*). The cantor sings the Jewish Major continuously and specifically in the Pentatonic mode. However, during the many generations in which the Jewish people were scattered all over Europe, the worshippers added an additional melody to these prayers. Interestingly, this melody became so ingrained in the prayer services that sometimes it became even more dominant than the proper melody sung by the cantor.

> *The cantor sings the Jewish Major continuously and specifically in the Pentatonic mode. However, during the many generations in which the Jewish people were scattered all over Europe, the worshippers added an additional melody to these prayers. Interestingly, this melody became so ingrained in the prayer services that sometimes it became even more dominant than the proper melody sung by the cantor.*

A famous professor of Musicology and Oriental Music in Los Angeles decided to send his class of university students, most of whom were not Jewish, to my synagogue to listen to the *Kol Nid'rei* service. He desired them to witness what he described as "Jewish Oriental music." Following the holiday, my friend the professor questioned me, asking: "Is it possible that the refrain of the worshippers in the *Kol Nid'rei* service is really a representation of Oriental Jewish *Nu'sach?*"

I must admit that at the time I really did not know what to reply. Until this professor raised the question, I was not aware of the fact that this refrain was not a proper Jewish melody for the High Holiday evening services. After researching the issue, I realized that the main melody, as sung by the cantor, was the proper melody that defines the *Nu'sach*.

It is interesting that even though the cantor sings this *Ma'a'riv* service in the Pentatonic Major, the worshippers in the congregation stubbornly refrain in the classical Major, as if there was a musical "duel." Somehow the worshippers seem to have gained the upper hand, as it became more popular than the real *Nu'sach*! Let me offer an example:

That is the typical Jewish Pentatonic melody. Here now is an example of the worshippers' reply:

That is the adjunct melodic refrain. It is not typical and not Oriental [Middle Eastern]. The famous Jewish musicologist and cantor, Abraham Zvi Idelsohn,[3] made a serious effort to prove that this adjunct melody was adopted by the Christians from Jewish music. The Christian musicologists, on the other hand, claimed that this melody was originally Christian. In my research, I have come to the conclusion that this melody is only slightly similar to the relevant Christian melody, and the truth is that it is neither Jewish nor Christian. More importantly, in my opinion, it really holds no importance in regard to original Jewish music!

Another interesting example of the Jewish Major is connected to Rabbi Meir Bar Yitzchak, an eleventh century Jewish poet, who was also a famous cantor. He wrote an Aramaic poem called *Ak'da'mut*,[4] which is sung on the festival of *Sha'vu'ot*.[5] He also composed a beautiful melody for *Ak'da'mut*, which, amazingly, is totally based on the Pentatonic Major:

---

3 Abraham Zvi Idelsohn (1882–1938) was a prominent Jewish ethnologist and musicologist, who conducted several comprehensive studies of Jewish music around the world. Born in Latvia, he trained as a cantor. He worked briefly in both Europe and South Africa before immigrating to Palestine in 1905 and establishing a school of Jewish music in 1919. In 1922 he moved to Cincinnati, Ohio to take a position as professor of Jewish music at Hebrew Union College and published important books on Jewish music.

4 *Ak'da'mut Mi'lin* (or *The Introduction*) is a prominent *Pi'yut* (Jewish liturgical poem) recited annually on the *Sha'vu'ot* Festival. It was written by Rabbi Meir Bar Yitzchak of Worms, Germany, who lived in the eleventh century. *Ak'da'mut* consists entirely of praise for God and is written in Aramaic. *Ak'da'mut* has 90 verses in total. Its language is terse and complicated, and it is replete with references to *To'rah* and Talmud. The encoded message from the author is that a Jew never stops learning *To'rah*. When one finishes, one must start anew. This message was appropriately chosen for *Sha'vu'ot*, since the holiday commemorates the Jew's acceptance of the *To'rah* on Mount Sinai.

5 *Sha'vu'ot* — a major Jewish festival held fifty days after the second day of Passover. It was originally a harvest festival, but now also commemorates the giving of the Law (the *To'rah*). It is also called Pentecost and Feast of Weeks.

4. Ak-da - mut__ mi-lin v' sha-ra-yut shu-ta av-la sha-kil - na har - man ur-shu - ta

However, the traditional Jewish readers of the *To'rah (Ba'a'lei Kri'ah),* when singing *Ak'da'mut,* add a flavor of their own, thus creating a false melody. It is an Oriental [Middle Eastern] melody with the flavor of the classical Major. Musicians can easily hear this "duel" between the original and the false. Here is an example of the way *Ak'da'mut* is sung:

5. Ak-da - mut__ mi-lin v'-sha-ra-yot shu - - ta av-la sha-kil - na har-

man__ u - r' - shu - - - - ta

There is a typical Jewish Major, a true musical delight for the *Sha'vu'ot* festival. Knowledgeable cantors apply this charming melody to other prayers of this holiday, such as *Mi Ka'mo'cha* ("Who is like Thee?"), *Ho'du* and *A'na* from the *Ha'llel* service, portions of the *Ki'ddush* (blessing of the wine), and other prayers. This melody sounds as though it contains the smell of vegetation… so appropriate for the agricultural aspects of *Sha'vu'ot* (the Festival of the First Fruits).

Following is another fine example of the Pentatonic Major that reminds us of our constant yearnings for the Jewish Major in early Jewish melodies. This is from the very end of the *Haf'ta'ra*[6] and in the last blessings of the *Maf'tir.*[7] The body of the *Haf'ta'ra* is traditionally sung in the Pentatonic Minor:

6.

However, the final part of the *Haf'ta'ra* and all the blessings that follow are sung in the Pentatonic Major — the favorite mode of the ancient Jewish people:

6 *Haf'ta'ra* — A selection from the Prophets, read in synagogue services on Sabbath following the reading from the *To'rah.* It usually has a thematic link to the *To'rah* reading that precedes it. The *Haf'ta'ra* is sung in the synagogue with cantillation according to a unique melody (not with the same cantillation melody as the *To'rah*).

7 *Maf'tir* — informally it refers to the final section of the weekly reading on Sabbath and holiday mornings; technically, it means the person who is called to read that section.

Let us now discuss the Mixolydian mode. Many *Nus'cha'ot* have originated from it. It is definitely not a coincidence that the Jewish people, on *Yom Ki'ppur,* chose to sing the most festive and dramatic instances of their holiest day in the Mixolydian Major and not in Minor. This is true of prayers such as the *Ka'ddish,*[8] the *A'vot,* and the first prayers of the *Ne'i'la* service (the closing service of the Day of Atonement).

This *Nu'sach* is built only on the two original Tetrachords of the Mixolydian mode. Here is the introduction:

This is pure Mixolydian mode. However, it is another instance where the worshippers "added" something of their own. In the *Ne'i'la* service, in place of the Mixolydian Major the congregation sings in an extraordinary Minor melody that is not based on the original *Nu'sach.* This is how the congregation sings:

We must not forget that in the *Ne'i'la* service, the original Jewish modification in the *Mach'zor* (the High Holiday prayer book) had yet to appear, since the Mixolydian mode, with only two

---

8 *Ka'ddish* — Jewish doxology (hymn of praise to God) that is usually recited in Aramaic at the end of principal sections of all synagogue services. Originally recited in the rabbinical academies, it later became a regular feature of the synagogue service. The prayer expresses, in addition to the praise of God, the plea for the speedy realization of the messianic age. The prayer's association with the arrival of the Messiah and the resurrection of the dead led to its becoming the prayer of mourners. There are four other forms of the *Ka'ddish* used in worship services.

Tetrachords, appears in the music of several other nations as well, and not only in Jewish music. The beautiful melody is Jewish, even though the mode itself is not. However, Jews were not satisfied with that mode.

In one of my earlier lectures, I gave examples of Jewish prayer modes that consist of three Mixolydian Tetrachords. A good example is the *Nu'sach* of *Bar'chu* for *Sha'losh Re'ga'lim* (the three festivals of *Pe'sach, Sha'vu'ot* and *Su'ccot).* I would like to emphasize that the *Nu'sach Mi'Sinai* itself, the most holy of all the different *Nus'cha'ot,* which has a totally independent and unique melody, is based on the Mixolydian Major mode. It consists of three Tetrachords and ten tones. This is a pure Jewish mode. Let me give you an example of the *Ve'Ha'Ko'ha'nim Nu'sach,* from the *A'vo'da* service of *Yom Ki'ppur:*

It is important to remember that at the end of the prayer *Ve'Ha'Ko'ha'nim* we change over to the *A'ha'va Ra'bbah Nu'sach,* that we discussed in the last lecture.

However, there is an even more important Jewish "invention." This is the creation of a total Major *Nu'sach,* based on the Mixolydian mode, consisting of four Tetrachords and thirteen tones. In the cantorial world this *Nu'sach* has three equivalent names:

1.   In Eastern Europe it is called *"Nu'sach Ye'kum Pur'kan";*
2.   In Western Europe it is called *"Nu'sach A'do'nai Ma'lach";*
3.   The *Cha'si'dim* call it *"Nu'sach Ye'tza've Tzur Chas'do"* — a name taken from one of the Sabbath feast melodies *(Zmi'rot).* In Yiddish this is pronounced *"Ye'tzu've De'Chaz De'Gust"* ("May God grant his love to his people").

Let us now listen to the complete line-up of the four Tetrachords and its thirteen tones:

It is important to emphasize that in this mode there is, on the one hand an F#, and on the other — an F natural. There is also the use of a B natural and also a Bb. This offers the composer tremendous possibilities of melodic variations and colors.

Interestingly, non-Jewish musicians find it very difficult to comprehend this, and every time they hear this kind of melody, they comment that there must have been some mistake...

There are many prayers that we sing in the *Ye'kum Pur'kan* or *A'do'nai Ma'lach Nu'sach*. It would be difficult to list all of them in this lecture. I will mention just a few of the more important ones:

1. All of the prayers of the Friday night *Ka'bba'lat Sha'bbat* service till the end of the prayer *Bo'ie Ve'Sha'lom.* In Western Europe they even continue this *Nu'sach* till after the prayer *A'do'nai Ma'lach:*

2. In the *A'vot* (the first three blessings of the *A'mi'da* prayers, when the cantor chants the Sabbath and Festival *Shach'rit* and *Mu'saf* prayer services):

3. The *Ye'kum Pur'kan* prayer itself.
4. The *Mi She'A'sa Ni'ssim* and *Ye'chad'she'hu* prayers of the *Bir'kat Ha'Cho'desh* (the blessing of the New Month).
5. The prayers *Ke'ter Ke'du'sha* and *Nak'di'shach* ("We will revere and sanctify Thee") from the Sabbath *Mu'saf* Sanctification service.
6. The prayer *A'ta Nig'lei'ta* ("Thou didst reveal Thyself in a cloud of glory unto Thy holy people") from the New Year (*Rosh Ha'Sha'na*) *Mu'saf* service.

Even regular synagogue worshippers who are not accustomed to being leaders of the prayer services find themselves chanting this *Nu'sach* to themselves even before the cantor finishes singing each prayer. The Jewish Major has grasped their hearts and they are connected to it with blind love, whether they are aware of it or not!

It is therefore clear why the Yiddish song *"A Cha'zan'dl oif Sha'bbes"* has become so popular, even though its lyrics are a bit vulgar. The melody itself is totally *Nu'sach A'do'nai Ma'lach* (or *Ye'kum Pur'kan*). It is exactly the *Nu'sach* of the prayer *Zar'a'cha Cha'ya Ve'Ka'ya'ma:*

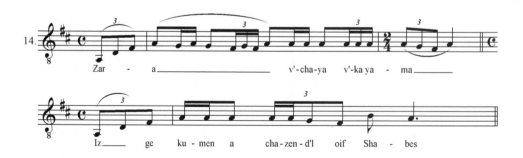

Even more characteristic is the fact that this *Nu'sach* is etched into a very important prayer — the *A'vot* of the *Shach'rit* and *Mu'saf* services of the High Holidays. There we find all four Tetrachords in the most obvious of forms. This is actually the *Nu'sach Mi'Sinai*, which is totally and independently Jewish.

Many *Ba'a'lei Te'fi'la*, and even some cantors who are not musically trained, fail in their execution of the High Holiday *A'vot* chant, only because they are not quite aware of how complex and complicated it really is. They need to realize that the chant needs to be opened in a very low tone, because as they rise to the higher stages of this lengthy mode, their voice can actually choke, and they are in danger of temporarily losing their voice! In this case they will find it almost impossible to return to the *Nu'sach*.

Finally, let us listen to some portions of typical compositions that are sung in the Jewish Major *Nu'sach*.

First, from the composition of Cantor David Nowakowsky — *"Ke'du'shat Ke'ter"*:

Let us now compare David Nowakowsky's composition with one of my compositions — *She'ma Yis'ra'el*, which is based on the Mixolydian Major as well:

Next we will listen to *"Sham'ah Va'Tis'mach Tzi'on,"* composed by David Eisenstadt of Warsaw, and sung by Cantor Gershon Sirota, who perished in the Warsaw Ghetto. This composition is also based on the *A'do'nai Ma'lach Nu'sach*:

Maestoso in 4

17.

Sha - m'ah va-tis-mach __ tzi - yon va-ta-gel _____ na va-ta-gel-na b'not Y'-hu-da l'-maan mish-pa-te-cha A-do-shem ___ Ki a-ta Ha-shem el-yon ___ al kol __ ha-a - retz m'od _____ na-a-lei - - ta al kol __ e - lo-him o-ha-ve A-do - shem ___ _ sin - u __ ra __ sin-u _____ ra sho - mer ___ naf-shot cha-si-dav ___ sho - mer _ naf-shot cha-si-dav _____ mi - yad ___ r'-sha-im mi-yad ___ r'-sha - im _ ya-tzi-

The last example you will hear is a brand new composition that I have written, which has never yet been performed. The name of this composition is *"Mi She'A'sa Ni'ssim"*:

cha-vei-rim cha-vei-rim cha-vei - rim _____ kol _____ Yis - ra - el cha-vei-

rim cha-vei-rim cha-vei-rim _____ kol _____ Yis-ra-eil _____

cha-vei - rim _____ cha-vei-rim Yis-ra-eil kol _____ Yis - ra - eil _____

cha-vei-rim cha-vei-rim cha-vei-rim cha-vei-rim kol _____ Yis-ra - eil _____ v'-no-

mar v'-no - mar v'-no - mar _____ A - mein _____

11

The Jewish Minor

SIXTH KOL YISRAEL RADIO LECTURE[1]

LEIB GLANTZ

Ladies and Gentlemen — dear listeners:

In the last lecture we concentrated on the Jewish Major. This time we will discuss the Jewish Minor. Before we go into detail, I would like to point out a very important issue that was mentioned earlier. The Jewish people, living in the Diaspora, have an inclination to "abandon" the Major *Nu'sach* and to replace it with Minor melodies that express bitterness and melancholy.

We have established earlier that all the prayers of the *Ka'bba'lat Sha'bbat*[2] service are sung in the different Mixolydian Major modes. However, we must remember that in the final prayer — *Ha'vu La'A'do'nai Bnei Ei'lim* ("Give to the Lord, O heavenly beings"), we transfer from Major to Minor. There are cantors who neglect the Major altogether throughout the prayer of *Ha'vu La'A'do'nai Bnei Ei'lim,* but cantors and scholars with musical knowledge are content with opening with Major and only in the second half of the prayer, with the words *Kol A'do'nai Ye'cho'lel A'ya'lot* ("The voice of the Lord whirls the oaks"), proceed to sing in Minor. As a typical example, I will play my composition *"Kol A'do'nai Cho'tzev La'ha'vot Esh"* ("The voice of the Lord strikes flames of fire"), a composition that opens in Major, changes to Minor, makes a modulation to Major with the words *A'do'nai La'Ma'bul Ya'shav* ("The Lord sat enthroned at the flood"), and ends returning to Minor. Evidently, this represents the will of the Jews living in the Diaspora, far away from their homeland.[3]

---

1 Sixth and last radio lecture by Leib Glantz, broadcast by *Kol Yis'ra'el,* the Israel Broadcasting Authority, 1961.

2 *Ka'bba'lat Sha'bbat* — the Friday night service welcoming the Sabbath.

3 *"Kol A'do'nai"* — composed and sung by Leib Glantz can be heard on compact disk (CD number one), which accompanies this book.

This piece clearly proves how difficult it was for the Jews in the Diaspora to maintain the Major *Nu'sach,* and how they escaped from time to time to the Minor.

However, in the Minor *Nus'cha'ot* the opposite is true. They clearly include within them the parallel Major as an integral part. Pure Jewish Minor almost does not exist. Major melodies add a special Jewish charm to our Minor. The explanation is very simple: The Jewish Minor of the biblical cantillations is a consequence of the Jewish Major. These biblical cantillations are sung in the Pentatonic Major. They have evolved from the readings of the *To'rah,* and are sung in the Pentatonic Minor. Therefore, the ancient Jewish Major and Minor are bound together and continuously absorb from each other.

> *The ancient Jewish Major and Minor are bound together and continuously absorb from each other.*

What are the different Jewish Minors? Basically, the original Minor comes from the Pentatonic scale and from the *Nu'sach* of the *Haf'ta'ra.* This *Nu'sach* was completely preserved in the prayers of the weekday services of *Shach'rit* and *Min'cha.* There are two reasons for this:

* These services come immediately following the Sabbath, and the *Haf'ta'ra* melodies are fresh in our memory;
* These services were usually led by simple worshippers and not by the cantors, so the cantors did not introduce changes.

Other *Nus'cha'ot* built upon modes and scales but *not* originating from the Pentatonic are:

* *Ma'gen A'vot;*
* *Yish'ta'bach;*
* *Keil A'don;*
* *Mi'She'Bei'rach.*

These all have a common characteristic: even though their base is Minor, their Minor disappears in favor of the parallel Major. Sobbing during prayer was not in the nature of the ancient Jewish worshippers. The opposite was true: they constantly looked for ways to get back to Major melodies in their prayers. Here is an example of *"Va'Ye'chu'lu":*

1.

Va - y'-chu - lu ha-sha-ma-yim v'-ha-a - retz v' - chol tz'-va-am va-y'-

chal E-lo-kim ba-yom ha-shvi-i m'-lach-to a-sher a-sa__ va-yish-bot___ ba-yom hash-vi-

i mi-kol m'-lach-to a-sher a-sa___ va-y'-va-rech E-lo-kim et yom hash-vi-i vay-ka-

desh o-to___ ki vo-sha-vat mi-kol m'-lach-to a-sher ba-ra E-lo - kim___ la-a-

sot___ Ba - ruch a - ta__ A-do - shem E-lo - kei-nu ve-lo-kei a-vo-tei - nu E-lo-

kei Av-ra - ham___ E-lo - kei Yitz - chak___ ve-lo - kei___ Ya-a - kov___ ha-

Keil ha-ga-dol ha-gi-bor v'-ha-no-ra Keil el - yon ko-nei sha-ma-yim va-a - retz

The same is true of *Nu'sach Ma'gen A'vot:*

2a.

Keil ha-ho-da-ot a - don ha-sha - lom___ m' - ka-

desh___ ha-sha - bat___

2b. Ka-d'-shei-nu b'-mitz-vo-te-cha v'-tein chel-kei — nu b'-to-ra-te cha v'-ta-heir li-bei-nu l'-ov-d'-cha — be-e-met v'-han-chi-lei — nu A-do-shem E-lo-kei nu b'-a-ha-va uv-ra - tzon sha-bat — kod - she-cha Ba-ruch a-ta A-do-shem m'-ka-deish — ha-sha-bat —

Nu'sach Ma'gen A'vot wanders musically between Minor and Major. Many composers, both cantorial and secular, have composed beautiful music built on this *Nu'sach*. Anton Rubinstein,[4] a Russian Jewish composer who converted to Christianity, was considered musically *more* Russian than most of his Russian contemporary musicians. However, even having become almost totally assimilated, in the wonderful chorus melody of his famous opera "Demon," he could not "biologically" free himself from the *Ma'gen A'vot Nu'sach*. This melody is clearly a copy of *El Ha'Ho'da'ot A'don O'lam* from the *Ma'gen A'vot Nu'sach*:

Yish'ta'bach and *Keil A'don* are also constant Minor *Nus'cha'ot* in our prayer services. However the modes upon which they are built change from time to time. Mostly we hear two modes that seem to be "competing" with each other:

4 Anton Grigorevich Rubinstein (1829-94) was a Russian pianist and composer, who in 1862 founded and directed the St. Petersburg Conservatory. He composed operas, symphonies, concertos and chamber works and was considered one of the world's greatest pianists of his era.

The first mode is the Phrygian:

The Phrygian is best represented by the lowered second tone of the scale in the first interval (C natural):

The second is the Dorian mode that is best represented by the raised sixth tone of the scale (F natural):

The *Yish'ta'bach Nu'sach,* which is also the *Nu'sach* of *Ve'Sham'ru, Hash'ki'vei'nu,* and many other prayers, is unique because on its fourth tone of the scale we seem to be building Major modulations. As a matter of fact there is really no modulation at all. It is clearly a continuation of the Dorian mode in its major sixth tone of the scale.

On the other hand, in the *Keil A'don Nu'sach,* the Major is two steps under its Minor base. As an example, I will sing *"E'lo'him Ziv,"* a composition by Cantor Teper, a renowned cantor and composer. He opens with the *Keil A'don Nu'sach* two steps lower, in other words, in Major:

M' - lei - im __ ziv_____ um-fi - kim_____ no - ga
m' - lei - im ziv_____ u-m'-fi - kim_____ no - - - ga na-
e zi-vam b'-chol ha-o-lam_____ s'-mei-chim b'-tzei-tam v'-sa - sim b'-vo-am_____ o-
sim_____ b' - ei - ma r' - tzon ko - nam_____

I wrote my own composition *"Ein Ke'Er'ke'cha"*[5] in a similar manner:

Ein ein ein k'-er-k'-cha_____ v'-ein v'-ein zu - la - te - cha
e - fes e-fes bil-t'-cha u - mi u - mi u - mi do - me __ lach

I opened *"Ein Ke'Er'ke'cha"* in Major and ended the composition in the *Keil A'don Nu'sach,* which is a Minor *Nu'sach* that contains Major as well. In order to prove how much the Major and Minor are bound together in our Minor *Nus'cha'ot,* it is worth noting the wonderful melody of *Me'gi'lat Ei'cha* (The Book of Lamentations). At the very tragic moment, on the ninth day of the Hebrew month of *Av,* as the Jewish people are lamenting over the destruction of the Holy Temple and the loss of their homeland, they sing in a Minor that is totally blended with Major. Actually, the opening musical phrase of *Me'gi'lat Ei'cha* is totally Major, and the final Minor of this *Nu'sach* is not of a sobbing nature, but noble, composed, restrained

---

5 *"Ein Ke'Er'ke'cha"* — composed and sung by Leib Glantz can be heard on compact disk (CD number one) that accompanies this book.

> *Within this aristocratic melody we witness the national pride of a people wailing over their bitter destiny in a most respectable manner.*

and subdued. There is no primitive shouting. This quiet and gentle *Nu'sach* of *Ei'cha* is evidence of the character of the Jewish people before they were exiled to the four corners of the earth. Within this aristocratic melody we witness the national pride of a people wailing over their bitter destiny in a most respectable manner:

Major and Minor, and again Major and Minor…

Another very "noble" Minor is the one we sing in the *Ne'i'la* service of *Yom Ki'ppur*. In the liturgical poem *Pe'tach La'nu Sha'ar Be'Et Ne'i'lat Sha'ar* ("Open Thou the gate, O Lord, even as it swingeth closed"), the prayer is expressed in a very tense and dramatic atmosphere, but sung in a very humble Minor. Jews in the synagogue are in the last moments of their "Day of Judgment," still maintaining their courage and national pride. This *Nu'sach* is built on the Aeolian mode[6] whose mark is the seventh degree of the scale without the tone leading to the octave of the Harmonic Minor (the octave going up is one whole step, as opposed to the Harmonic Minor — which is a half step):

---

6   The Aeolian mode formed part of the music theory of ancient Greece, based around the relative natural scale in A (that is, the same as playing all the 'white notes' of a piano from A to A). The Aeolian mode consists of the same components as the Major mode with the Minor's sixth scale degree as its tonic. As the Aeolian mode forms the natural Minor scale (also known as the descending melodic Minor scale), it is among the most frequently used diatonic modes in Western music.

It is worth mentioning that the *Nu'sach* for *Sim'chat To'rah* (the holiday of the Rejoicing of the Law) could logically be expected to express happiness in an exaggerated way. However, the main *Nu'sach* for this service is noble and restrained. In the prayer *A'ta Har'ei'ta La'Da'at* ("You have learned to know that the Lord is God"), we hear Major and a gentle Minor. It sounds as if it is declaring that we must refrain from going overboard in our rejoicing:

Even in the main melody, the motif of the *Shach'rit* service for the High Holidays stands out. We sing the Major and Minor closely bound together:

Another important Jewish Minor *Nu'sach* is *Mi'She'Bei'rach*. This *Nu'sach* inspires the services of the High Holidays as well as those of the Sabbath and Festivals. It is built on a mode that is common not only to the Jews but to other cultures as well — the Dorian-Ukrainian mode.[7] Some musical historians, mostly non-Jewish or assimilating Jews, consider this mode as totally Dorian-Ukrainian. The *Mi'She'Bei'rach Nu'sach,* noted by the first of its two Dorian Tetrachords, contains the raised fourth degree:

7 Dorian-Ukrainian mode — The raised 4th degree of this mode lends it its characteristic profile. It often forms the basis of the *Doina* (Romanian and Jewish-Romanian improvised lament), but is commonly found as well in forms of Klezmer music (instrumental folk music developed in Eastern European Jewish communities).

Let us listen to the original prayer that gave its name to this *Nu'sach* — *Mi'She'Bei'rach* ("He who blessed"):

Another prayer, which is built on *Nu'sach Mi'Si'nai,* also uses the raised sixth tone of the Dorian Tetrachord, is *O'chi'la La'El* from the High Holiday service:

Notice that the fourth tone of the scale is raised one half step. In the *O'chi'la La'El Nu'sach* we also sing parts of the *A'vot* from the High Holiday services, as well as several liturgical poems. For instance: *Me'lech O'zer U'Mo'shi'a U'Ma'gen:*

Therefore the Jews have a very legitimate claim that this *Nu'sach* is Jewish. They can definitely claim at least a "partnership" with others of the Dorian-Ukrainian mode.

Also, from this *Mi'She'Bei'rach Nu'sach* stemmed an important part of the *Nu'sach* of *Mal'chu'yot*, *Zich'ro'not* and *Sho'fa'rot* (Sovereignty, Remembrance and Trumpet verses). The difference between these two is the fact that on the High Holidays, we also employ other types of Minor, such as Phrygian, Dorian and Aeolian. The most significant attribute of the High Holiday *Nu'sach* is, once again, that the Minor frequently makes way for the Mixolydian Major, mainly for specific pauses and endings of the verses of the *Mal'chu'yot*, *Zich'ro'not* and *Sho'fa'rot*:

I will now demonstrate the melodies sung by the worshipping congregation as they answer the cantor, both in Major and in Minor. When the cantor sings in Major, the congregation answers in Major; when he sings in Minor, they answer in Minor:

It is evident that the worshippers know these High Holiday melodies…

Even the wonderful melody of the *Ka'ddish* for the *Se'li'chot* service and for the *Mu'saf* service of the High Holidays, that opens with the *A'ha'va Ra'bbah Nu'sach*, moves on to Minor, then trends toward Major modulations, and then returns to Minor, in a very typical Jewish way. This holy *Ka'ddish* seems to be taking an "excursion" between the Minor, the Major and the *A'ha'va Ra'bbah Nu'sach* to such an extent that it is almost impossible to define.

The great French composer Maurice Ravel (1875-1937), even though he was not Jewish, sensed the sacredness of our *Ka'ddish* perhaps even more than many Jewish composers.[8]

The melody of *Kol Nid'rei* from the *Yom Ki'ppur* evening service, charms us and causes our souls to tremble. There is no justification for the opinions expressed by certain musicologists

8 At this point in the lecture Glantz plays a recording of a section of Ravel's *Ka'ddish*.

> *The melody of* Kol Nid'rei *from the* Yom Ki'ppur *evening service, charms us and causes our souls to tremble. There is no justification for the opinions expressed by certain musicologists that condemn this* Nu'sach *as if it were an assimilation that is far from the Jewish spirit. The opposite is true: the* Nu'sach *of* Kol Nid'rei *is totally Jewish.*

that condemn this *Nu'sach* as if it were an assimilation that is far from the Jewish spirit. The opposite is true: the *Nu'sach* of *Kol Nid'rei* is totally Jewish. In fact, it stands to reason that the *Kol Nid'rei* text was preserved for eternity thanks to the melody of *Kol Nid'rei*!

Nu'sach Kol Nid'rei is a musical journey from mode to mode, going from *A'ha'va Ra'bbah* to Minor, and from Minor to Major, and back. The ending of this enchanting melody is totally in Major. It is therefore understandable why the great German composer Ludwig van Beethoven (1770-1827) fell in love with this sacred melody and immortalized it in one of his most monumental compositions, the String Quartet Number 14 in C# Minor.[9] In its sixth movement, *Adagio quasi un poco andante,* the viola clearly plays the *Nu'sach* of *Kol Nid'rei* over the background of the violins.[10]

This is the last of these six radio lectures. I would therefore like to offer some concluding notes. The Jewish people were unfortunately divided and scattered in numerous Diasporas and ghettos all over the world. However, in spite of this, they wisely preserved their precious asset of original Jewish music. Thanks to the nationalistic and religious atmosphere of the synagogue and the traditional life of the Jewish home, we were fortunate to save a good portion of the melodies and *Nus'cha'ot* of our forefathers. We must be very careful never to neglect this precious national asset. Each and every one of our prayers, holiday *Z'mi'rot* (hymns) and Chasidic *Ni'gu'nim* (tunes) contains something of the eternal glory of the Jewish people.

I call upon our great composers to draw inspiration from this source and compose authentic, original Jewish compositions.

---

9 The String Quartet No. 14 in C# minor, opus 131, by Ludwig van Beethoven was completed in 1826. This quartet, which is dedicated to Baron Stutterheim, was Beethoven's favorite and is considered the best composition Beethoven had written until then.

10 At this point in the lecture Glantz plays a recording of Beethoven's String Quartet No. 14 in C# Minor.

12

The Passover *Se'dder*

"Ve'Hi She'Am'da La'A'vo'tei'nu Ve'La'nu"

L<small>EIB</small> G<small>LANTZ</small> [1]

The Passover *Se'dder* [2] enjoys a prominent place in our lives not only because of its sanctity, but also because on this festival Jewish families stage a theatrical play in their homes. Indeed, the *Se'dder* has all the characteristics of a play.

The "stage" is the table of the feast, with its covered *Ma'tza* [3] and glasses of wine. Every person has a role. Exciting things happen: the Four Questions [4] that are "asked" by the youngest children, the mysterious entrance of the Prophet Eliyahu, the dripping of the wine from the glasses to the plates in remembrance of the Ten Plagues that befell Pharaoh and the Egyptians — all dramatic activities in which all the participants unite to become one ensemble, each performing his or her "role" in support of the "leading character" — the head of the family.

The most important aspect of the *Se'dder* is the "reading," rather the singing, of the *Ha'gga'da*. In my view, the music of the *Ha'gga'da* is authentically Jewish. It is based on original ancient Eastern melodies. A great "miracle" happened to our ancestors and to us: the music of the *Se'dder* did not become assimilated with foreign elements and remained almost totally original and authentic.

1 Translated from the Israeli daily newspaper *"Da'var,"* 1956.
2 *Pe'ssach Se'dder* — the Passover Festival feast and the reading of the *Ha'gga'da,* the story of the Israelites as slaves in ancient Egypt, and their redemption and Exodus into the Sinai desert led by Moses.
3 *Ma'tza* — unleavened bread that the Israelites, who escaped in haste, had to eat on their journey into the Sinai desert after fleeing from Egypt. In memory of those days, observant Jews are forbidden to eat bread during the seven days of Passover (eight days in the Diaspora), only *Ma'tza*.
4 *Ku'shi'yot* — the Four Questions that are sung by the youngest children at the *Se'dder* feast, in which they pose the question: "Why is this night of Passover different from all other nights?"

The musical "reading" of the *Ha'gga'da* is based on the ancient cantillation of the *To'rah.*[5] Even the Four Questions are not simply "asked" but are sung. The basis of this song is the same musical mode that we use when studying the *Ge'ma'ra*[6] — the mode we call *Nu'sach Pei'rush Ra'shi* (the mode of the *Ra'shi* commentary). This mode is the musical basis for the ancient five-tone Pentatonic scale. It is obviously different from the seven-tone or eight-tone scales. The reading of the *To'rah* is based on this Pentatonic scale, which we inherited from our Jewish ancestors of the Second Holy Temple in Jerusalem.

I am very skeptical about the idea expressed by some musicologists that this scale was originally Greek. As a matter of fact, it just might be the other way around: that the Jews, with their special music for praying and for reading the *To'rah* in the Holy Temple in Jerusalem influenced the Eastern world in general and the Greeks in particular.

This musical reading or singing of the *Ha'gga'da* using ancient scales has miraculously survived to this day. When we analyze our prayer modes, beginning from the weekday prayers and ending with the final *Ne'i'la* service of *Yom Ki'ppur*, we constantly discover the Pentatonic scale and its natural development — the Mixolydian mode. The Jews decorated the scale, built upon it original "grafts" and created numerous unique melodies. The melodies of *A'dir Hu, Ki Lo Na'eh, A'va'dim Ha'yi'nu* and others are undoubtedly based on Jewish scales. It is truly gratifying to me that even in the mode of the *Ha'gga'da* we discover the same fundamental Pentatonic and Mixolydian scales that we use in our synagogue prayers!

---

5 *Ta'a'mei Ha'Ne'gi'na* and *Ta'a'mei Ha'Mik'ra* — the musical cantillation of the *To'rah.*

6 *Ge'ma'ra* — The second part of the Talmud, consisting primarily of commentary on the *Mish'na*, which is the collection of Jewish laws written by Jewish scholars in Palestine and Babylon in 200–500 AD).

We might mistakenly think that Jews of different Diaspora origins "read" the *Ha'gga'da* differently — each with their own *Nu'sach*. However, all the versions are built on exactly the same foundation. What is amazing is that this happens naturally, with variants naturally passing down from generation to generation and from family to family.

In Israel, every archaeological discovery that is dug up from the soil is celebrated. In the same manner we must rejoice in this discovery that the melodies of the *Ha'gga'da*, that "stood by our fathers and us" (*"Ve'Hi She'Am'da La'A'vo'tei'nu Ve'La'nu"*), miraculously survived in the voices of our people, in the towns of Judah, in the streets of Jerusalem, and in the Jewish homes of the Diaspora.

> *We might mistakenly think that Jews of different Diaspora origins "read" the* Ha'ga'dah *differently — each with their own* Nu'sach. *However, all the versions are built on exactly the same foundation. What is amazing is that this happens naturally, with variants naturally passing down from generation to generation and from family to family.*

13

Te'fi'lat Tal — The Prayer for Dew

LEIB GLANTZ[1]

The most musically interesting Passover prayer is *Te'fi'lat Tal,* the prayer asking God to bless the fields with dew. It is based on an ancient Eastern musical mode and retains the originality and beauty of an Eastern song. The preservation of this composition was most fortunate. Two thousand years have passed since the Jews were exiled and dispersed all over the world. We were subjected to the influences of many nations among whom we lived, yet we continue to pray for dew and rain to fall over the distant lands of Israel! This attests to the eternal bond of the Jewish people with their holy land of Israel.

The *Ha'llel* prayer service, on the other hand, suffered greatly at the hands of musical assimilationists. Israelite pilgrims coming from all corners of the Holy Land as they marched toward the holy city of Jerusalem intoned this prayer. The *Ha'llel* consists of a colorful array of musical compositions, including the original Hebrew *Ha'lle'lu'yah* as rendered by the Levites.[2]

Many cantors today do not perform the *Ha'llel* ceremony using its original Eastern theme (*Nu'sach*). Fortunately, certain cantors, imbued with respect and appreciation for authentic sources of our tradition, succeeded in rescuing some of the original melodies, especially *Tal* and the *Nu'sach* of the *To'rah* reading — the biblical cantillations.

---

1 Originally published in the Bulletin of the Western Jewish Institute, Los Angeles, California, in April 1951.

2 Levites — a religious caste among the ancient Hebrews, descended from Jacob's son Levi and figuring prominently in the bible. Of the twelve tribes, they are the only one who received no allotment of land; instead they received revenues from certain cities, and each city had its quota of Levites to support. With the unification of worship at the city of Jerusalem, the Levites became servants of the Holy Temple. Their hereditary assignments included performing the musical functions at the Temple.

Leib Glantz in his cantor's attire in Kishinev, Bessarabia (today part of Moldava), age 22, in 1920.

14

The Music of the *Sha'vu'ot* Festival
— Blessing the First Fruits

LEIB GLANTZ[1]

It is not a coincidence that the prayer modes (*Nus'cha'ot*) for reading the *To'rah* on weekdays, Sabbaths, and festivals are all built upon one ancient scale — the Pentatonic scale. This is a scale with only five tones and four intervals:

The Pentatonic Scale

The same can be said of the *Me'gi'lot* (scrolls), which are read in the synagogues on the holidays of *Pe'ssach* (The Song of Songs), *Sha'vu'ot* (Ruth) and *Su'ccot* (Ecclesiastes). The reading, or singing, of these scrolls in the synagogue is based on the Pentatonic scale as well. The Jews were not the only ones who used this ancient scale, but the Jews rejuvenated, glorified, and sanctified it.

From an artistic point of view, it is amazing how this scale, which seems so confined and limited, enables us to design musical forms of the most diverse and complex nature.

In addition to the Pentatonic scale, the Jews added other unique scales, bustling with musical richness. But the original source, the Pentatonic scale, has remained the fundamental building block of this music throughout the centuries.

---

1 Translated from the Hebrew Israeli daily newspaper *"Da'var,"* 1956.

The Pentatonic scale is salient in the music of *Sha'vu'ot*. This holiday has two elements: one spiritual and one worldly. The spiritual element is the celebration of the revelation of the *To'rah*. The worldly element is a celebration of nature — the Festival of the First Fruits (*Chag Ha'Bi'ku'rim*). The people of Israel succeeded in blending into this holiday both the element of *thought* and the element of *labor.*[2] This blending is reflected in the fact that we use the Pentatonic scale both in the melodies of the celebration of the *To'rah* and in the melodies of the Festival of the First Fruits. This music was sung in the fields, the vineyards and the wine cellars.

As we read the *Me'gi'la* of Ruth, the scent of the fields rises not only from the idyllic poetic text, but also from the peaceful, calming melodies — the sounds of nature, soil and harvesting.

These Pentatonic songs seem naïve and simplistic, but those who know the charms of the Orient [Middle East] discover in them a philosophical depth, a creative rural reality, combining sadness and happiness, openness and concealment, innocence and dreaming, as well as thought and feeling.

> *These Pentatonic songs seem naïve and simplistic, but those who know the charms of the Orient discover in them a philosophical depth, a creative rural reality, combining sadness and happiness, openness and concealment, innocence and dreaming as well as thought and feeling.*

Hundreds of years after the *Nus'cha'ot* appropriate to the reading of the *To'rah* and the *Me'gi'lot* had crystallized, a great poet named Rabbi Meir Ben Yitzchak Nehorai, who was a cantor in Worms, Germany, in the eleventh century (and a contemporary of Rashi[3]), composed the wonderful poem *Ak'da'mut Mi'lin Ve'Sha'ra'yut Shu'ta* ("I utter these words as a prelude to this discourse"). The poem is about the happiness that will come upon the Israelites and the calamity that will be the destiny of those who persecute them. It is an expression of the eternal optimism of the Jewish people. Interestingly, the melody, which was also composed by the poet himself, is based on the Pentatonic scale.

The *Ak'da'mut* is sung on the *Sha'vu'ot* Festival, just before the reading of the *To'rah*. We read it in Aramaic,[4] just as it was written by the poet, and exactly in the melody the poet himself

---

2 *To'rah Ve'A'vo'da.*

3 Rashi (1040–1105) — a French Rabbi who taught and wrote commentaries to most of the Bible and Talmud with great clarity, considered the most inclusive and authoritative in Jewish exegesis.

4 *Aramaic* — a Syrian dialect of a Semitic language that was used as a *lingua franca* in the Near East from the sixth century BCE. It gradually replaced Hebrew as the language of the Jews in those areas, only to be later supplanted by Arabic in the seventh century CE.

> *The Ak'da'mut melody is pure Pentatonic. I believe this melody somehow helped the Jews appreciate the importance of this poem. There is always a spiritual connection between a nation and its music.*

composed. The melody is pure Pentatonic. I believe this melody somehow helped the Jews appreciate the importance of this poem. There is always a spiritual connection between a nation and its music.

It is also worth noting that the blessing of the wine, the *Ki'ddush* for the Three Festivals of *Pe'ssach*, *Su'ccot* and *Sha'vu'ot,* is actually sung in the same *Ak'da'mut Nu'sach.*

The *Nu'sach* of *Ak'da'mut*

Unfortunately, the secular songs of the Festival of the First Fruits were lost. These were sung in the days of the First and Second Temple, before and after the holiday, with "harps and singing and dancing in the fields and in the vineyards."

That "singing" was undoubtedly based on the same melodies, or very similar ones, upon which we built our singing and playing of musical instruments in the Holy Temple. After the destruction of the Temple, the Jewish people continued to sing these festive songs in our synagogues in the Holy Land as well as in the Diaspora.

A nation that denies its own musical prayer modes, its *Nu'sach,* denies its soul. I truly believe that in our renewed country of Israel there will someday rise from amongst our people an Israeli composer who will draw from the eternal musical fountain of our nation, and will compose modern Jewish symphonies that will be popular both in Israel and in the world at large.

15

Rosh Ha'Sha'na —
A Festive Day That Provokes Thought

Leib Glantz[1]

There are two kinds of "Days of Awe" (*Ya'mim No'ra'im*): *Rosh Ha'Sha'na* (the Jewish New Year) and *Yom Ki'ppur* (the Day of Atonement). There is a big difference between the two, both in spirit and in character.

The *To'rah* clearly points to this distinction: *Yom Ki'ppur* is defined as the day "God will forgive your sins" (*Ki Va'Yom Ha'Zeh Ye'cha'per A'lei'chem*). However, on *Rosh Ha'Sha'na* — "Blow the *Sho'far* on the new moon, at the beginning of the month, for our day of festival" (*Tik'u Va'Cho'desh Sho'far, Ba'Ke'seh Le'Yom Cha'gei'nu).*

In the *Mach'zor,* the prayer book used on *Rosh Ha'Sha'na,* the emphasis of the text is not on praying and asking for mercy. It concentrates on introspective thought. We reflect on our prayers. We think about our world. We ponder about the essence of life and death. We dwell on our past, going as far back as the Genesis and the Generation of the Great Flood (*Dor Ha'Ma'bul).* We try to contemplate the future of our people and the future of humanity.

When I analyze the wonderful poem of Rabbi Amnon of Mayence[2] — *U'Ne'ta'neh To'kef Ke'du'shat Ha'Yom* ("We shall observe the mighty holiness of this day"), I notice the absence of any begging for mercy. There is something more burning, more intense, and more penetrating. In *U'Ne'ta'neh To'kef* we hear a poet's artistic description and bold imagination of the Kingdom of the Heavens: "Thou unfoldest the records and the deeds therein inscribed that tell their story" (*Ve'Tif'tach Et Se'fer Ha'Zich'ro'not U'Me'E'lav Yi'ka'reh*).

---

1 Translated from the Hebrew daily newspaper *"Da'var"* — 1959.
2 Tradition ascribes this poem to Rabbi Amnon of Mayence (Mainz), who in 1196 reportedly uttered these words in his dying moments as a martyr, affirming his faith in God.

> *We have strayed far away from the penetrating philosophical ideas of the great philosophers of our past. It seems that our generation has chosen to simplify the meaning of our spiritual and cultural wealth to a primitive level that borders on ignorance! There is no need to shout or sob! After all, this is a festive day.*

This monumental poem stimulates me to call out to all the cantors and Jewish composers of our era and beg of them: Do not cry and do not lament on this glorious day of *Rosh Ha'Sha'na*! We have strayed far away from the penetrating philosophical ideas of the great philosophers of our past. It seems that our generation has chosen to simplify the meaning of our spiritual and cultural wealth to a primitive level that borders on ignorance! There is no need to shout or sob! After all, this is a festive day. The poetry of the prayers of *Rosh Ha'Sha'na* is glorious. The poets who wrote these poems employed thought and passion. Every word was a painting, a song, a philosophy. Sadly, many of us moan, sigh, flatter and plead as if we were beggars knocking on a door.

16

The Music of *Yom Ki'ppur*

LEIB GLANTZ[1]

As a child, before I could speak, and before I learned how to spell — I instinctively sensed that music, whether instrumental or vocal, was a wonderful form of communication.

As I grew older and began reflecting on the different paths of human language, I began to comprehend the secrets of harmonic musical tones. Music became the special "dialect" that I feel exists between man and God. It is like a ladder reaching up from earth into the heavens. Whether a gloomy melody or a happy song — both can elevate us from mundane surroundings to spiritual highs.

> *As a child, before I could speak, and before I learned how to spell — I instinctively sensed that music, whether instrumental or vocal, was a wonderful form of communication . . . Music became the special "dialect" that I feel exists between man and God. It is like a ladder reaching up from the earth into the heavens.*

Yom Ki'ppur, the Day of Atonement, is a day in which the People of Israel devote themselves to purify and sanctify their "contaminated" souls. For one whole day, from the opening *Kol Nid'rei* prayer[2] until the final service of *Ne'i'la*[3] — a crisis takes place, as man comes close to

---

1 Translated from Yiddish from the newspaper *"Der Tag,"* New York, 1940.

2 *Kol Nid'rei* — Aramaic, meaning 'all vows.' This prayer opens the evening service of the Jewish Day of Atonement, *Yom Ki'ppur*. It is customary for this prayer to be repeated three times, and it is a declaration of the community that all vows made to God that have not been fulfilled are thereby cancelled.

3 *Ne'i'la* is the concluding prayer of the Day of Atonement, performed very close to sunset.

God, and God to man. This is a ceremony that is performed in the most beautiful of languages — the language of music!

The congregation convenes in customary white gowns, anticipating the declaration of the cantor from Psalms (97:110): *Or Za'ru'ah La'Tza'dik* ("Light is sown to the righteous"). Then comes the bold statement that it is "permitted to pray with those who have transgressed" — perhaps hinting at the underground cellars of the Jews in Spain, who were terrorized to relinquish their religion under the ruthless tyranny of the Spanish Inquisition.[4] The *Kol Nid'rei* prayer is then sung before the open doors of the Holy Ark, witnessed by the *To'rah* scrolls held in the arms of pious biblical scholars.

The melody chosen by the Jews for *Kol Nid'rei* has been suspected of being a foreign musical intrusion that eventually became sanctified by the people themselves. Others claim that it is actually a remnant of the music of the Holy Temple! Whatever the truth, the music of *Kol Nid'rei* has become one of the great symbols of the Jewish nation.

---

4 The Spanish Inquisition was an ecclesiastical court established in Roman Catholic Spain in 1478 and directed originally against converts from Judaism and Islam but later also against Protestants. It operated with great severity until suppressed in the early 19th century.

17

The Sin of *"Ma'oz Tzur"*

LEIB GLANTZ[1]

The *Cha'nu'ka* holiday[2] annually reminds us that for centuries the Jewish people lived as minorities among other nations, and had to struggle constantly in order to avoid integrating the customs and culture of those among whom they lived.

Among the Jewish people were those who sought to assimilate. There was also what might be described as *unintentional* assimilation.

In our music this assimilation actually occurred. Current "Israeli" songs that are sung in Hebrew are frequently just imitations of Cossack, Gypsy and Wallachian melodies. In our concert halls and on the radio we hear melodies "borrowed" from Russia, Romania and Hungary as well as from American Jazz and Arabian Debka melodies.

This in itself is not necessarily a bad thing, as long as it does not affect our cantorial tradition, which represents an original cultural treasure of the Jewish people. Lately, we find ourselves praying in the synagogue or listening to cantorial music on the radio, as if we are listening to an *aria* from an opera.

One of the most popular Jewish holiday melodies, a tune sung throughout the Jewish world, is *"Ma'oz Tzur"* ("O mighty rock of my salvation, to praise Thee is a delight"), which accompanies the blessings of the *Cha'nu'ka* candles on the eight nights of the holiday. Shocking as it

---

1 Translated from the Israeli daily newspaper *"Da'var,"* 1956.

2 *Cha'nu'ka* — an eight-day Jewish holiday commemorating the rededication of the Temple of Jerusalem in 165 BCE by the Maccabees after its desecration by the Greek-Syrians.

may sound, the origins of this traditional "Jewish" holiday song are three famous German melodies:

- A German Lutheran Choral hymn from the fifteenth century;[3]
- A German song from the sixteenth century;[4]
- The *cantionales* from Magenza and other *cantionales* (fifteenth and sixteenth century).[5]

Can this really be our "national" *Cha'nu'ka* song?

> *In order to correct this "sin," I have composed a melody for* Ma'oz Tzur *that is based on the original* Nu'sach *of the traditional blessings of the* Cha'nu'ka *candles.*

In order to correct this "sin," I have composed a melody for *Ma'oz Tzur* that is based on the original *Nu'sach* (prayer mode) of the traditional blessings of the *Cha'nu'ka* candles. This *Nu'sach* has been a Jewish legacy for generations. The melodic composition of the music and its rhythm strictly adhere to the special spirit of the *Cha'nu'ka Nu'sach,* free of foreign influence or imitation. Hopefully, this *Ma'oz Tzur* will capture the hearts of those who yearn for true authentic culture in Israel.[6]

---

3 An adaptation of an old German folk song *"So weiss ich eins, das mich erfreut, das pluemlein auff preiter heyde,"* also adapted by Martin Luther for the opening of his church chorale *"Nun freut euch, lieben Christen g'mein"* ("Now rejoice, all you dear Christians, together").

4 A popular German battle song, "Benzenauer," which was originally sung in 1504.

5 Especially Protestant chorales in Central Europe *cantionales.*

6 *"Ma'oz Tzur"* — composed and sung by Leib Glantz can be heard on compact disk (CD number one) that accompanies this book.

18

"From The Depths I Call Upon You, O Lord!"

LEIB GLANTZ[1]

In ancient times, when worship of idols was the norm, one nation, the radically monotheistic sons of Abraham, was capable of perceiving the abstract and accepting the absolute — a God that did not resemble any image and could not be seen or touched.

How then did these ancient people conduct their prayers? No formal texts were at their disposal. No prayer books such as the *Si'ddur*[2] or *Mach'zor*[3] were available. How then did they express the deepest feelings from their hearts and souls?

"From the depths I call upon You, O Lord!" hails the author of the Psalms. How did the Israelites reach out from such "depths"?

From the *To'rah* we learn that Moses "implored the Lord" (Exodus 32:11), "prayed to the Lord" (Numbers 11:2), and "cried out to the Lord" (Numbers 12:13). We must wonder how Moses "prayed," how he "cried out."

Moses was described as a leader who expressed his feelings *together* with the whole community: "Moses and the children of Israel *sang a song* unto Thee with great joy!" And "Then Moses and the Israelites *sang this song* to the Lord." This represented communal singing of a whole

---

1 Translated from the Hebrew daily newspaper *"Da'var,"* 1957.

2 *Si'ddur* — the prayer book used by Jews all over the world, containing a set order of daily prayers for weekdays, Sabbaths and special prayers. Some of the earliest formal printed Jewish prayer books date back as early as the tenth century. Most contain only text and no musical notation; the melodies, some of which are ancient, have been passed down orally from generation to generation.

3 *Mach'zor* — the special prayer book used by Jews on the High Holidays of *Rosh Ha'Sha'na* and *Yom Ki'ppur*. Some Jews also make use of specialized *Mach'zors* on the three Pilgrimage Festivals: *Pe'ssach, Sha'vu'ot, and Su'ccot.*

nation as they "praised and extolled God, offered hymns, songs, praises, blessings and thanksgivings."

As we can observe from the biblical texts, the Israelites did not pray with words alone. They accompanied their prayers with music. We can assume that the singing of the prayers was spontaneous and improvisational.

In the early stages of their existence, the Israelites had to overcome the existing phenomenon of numerous "gods." Their religious leaders declared before the world that there was only *one* God, "who was first and foremost, and nothing existed before God's creation."

At the same time, the prayer of the individual — the prayer that one performs within one's self — existed from the beginning of man's history.

Leib Glantz lighting the *Cha'nu'ka* holiday candles in a Jerusalem concert, 1956.

We may ask ourselves how an individual expressed his pleas and supplications when his soul was in agony, broken hearted, or when he felt thankful and joyful. There are clues describing the prayers of the individual. One of the most outstanding stories is the description of the praying of Hannah, the wife of Elkanah (Samuel 1:1):

> "In her wretchedness she prayed to the Lord, weeping all the while. As she kept praying before the Lord, Eli, the priest, observed her mouth. Hannah was praying in her heart; only her lips moved, her voice could not be heard." In Hannah's words: "I have been pouring out my heart to the Lord."

If not praying with words, there might be a silent voice, a sigh, a quiet melody or even a quivering of the lips. According to the great Jewish writer, Isaac Leib Peretz, it is even acceptable to *whistle* one's prayers. The Chassidic Rabbi Nachman from Bratzlav would encourage Jews to dance while praying, both in private and in public. The Ba'al Shem Tov, the initiator of Chasidism, was observed in prayer to have shouted *Ta'teh Zi'sser* ("sweet father" — in Yiddish). According to Rabbi Levi Yitzchak from Bardichev, the same Ba'al Shem Tov poured out his heart in prayer before the Almighty in foreign languages. Jews have traditionally prayed with song and melody.

Moses, when praying, did not use words alone. In the bible it says: "Give ear, O heavens, let me speak…May my discourse come down as rain, my speech distill as dew…"

On the *Rosh Ha'Sha'na* holiday, more than on any other day of the year, we renew and eternalize the wonderful description from the prayer *A'ta Nig'lei'ta*: "From the heavens they heard Thy voice…and all the people perceived the thunders…causing them to hear the majesty of Thy voice and Thy holy words from the flames of fire."[4]

When praying alone, a person is free to improvise any expression of feelings without bonds of communal *"Nu'sach."* However, when one's heart opens, the divide between people is removed and melodies create a spiritual bridge between heaven and earth. Words alone, even the most sublime, are not capable of creating a holy bond between man and God. The power of song emphasizes and enriches the yearnings of our hearts and enables us to express our deepest feelings and emotions.

> *Words alone, even the most sublime, are not able to create the holy bond between man and God. The power of song emphasizes and enriches the yearnings of our hearts and enables us to express our deepest feelings and emotions.*

"My soul thirsts for You, my body yearns for You," is a statement that, when spoken, loses much of its forcefulness. These beautiful words from the author of the Psalms, when expressed with music, enhance the words with deeper meanings. The longing, the yearning and the spiritual thirst penetrate and undergo a metamorphosis.

The communal prayers of any congregation are rooted in the melodies of each nation. Observe the words of the *Se'li'chot* midnight service prayer *Mach'ni'sei Ra'cha'mim*: "Angels of mercy, bring our plea for mercy…Ye in charge of prayer, submit our prayer to Him…Ye in charge of lamentation…of tears…intercede for us, and multiply supplication and petition

---

4 *"A'ta Nig'lei'ta…Min Ha'Sha'ma'yim Hish'ma'a'tam Ko'le'cha…Be'Ko'lot U'Vra'kim A'lei'hem Nig'lei'ta…Va'Tash'mi'em Et Hod Ko'le'cha Ve'Dib'rot Kod'she'cha Mi'La'ha'vot Aish."*

before the King, the high exalted God." Could we faithfully approach God's angels and plead before them with words alone, without the melodies that seem to enable us to communicate with them?

We also use visual imagination to create musical expressions. In the prayer *U'Ne'ta'neh To'kef* ("We will observe the mighty holiness of this day"): "The great *Sho'far* is sounded, and a still small voice is heard...with great noise, mighty and strong..."[5] We actually visualize in our imagination the wonderful words of the prophet in the name of the Lord: "I will remember My covenant with you in the days of your youth...Is not Ephraim My beloved son, My beloved child...?"[6] Our musical imagination enables us to describe the vision of the coming of the Messiah with melodies that sound as if they are coming from another world.

> *Musical expression truly has the power to lift us beyond our mundane world, enabling our souls to soar into the heavens!*

We describe the image of God and the celestial entourage on the "Day of Judgment" with the words: "Thou pass and record, count and visit every living soul, appointing the measure of every creature's life and decreeing its destiny."[7] Musical expression truly has the power to lift us beyond our mundane world, enabling our souls to soar into the heavens!

---

5 *U'Ve'Sho'far Ga'dol Yi'ta'ka Ve'Kol De'ma'ma Da'ka Yi'sha'ma...*

6 *Ve'Za'char'ti A'ni Et Bri'ti O'tach Bi'mei Ne'u'ra'ich Va'Ha'ki'mo'ti Lach Brit O'lam...Ha'Ben Ya'kir Li Ef'ra'yim Im Ye'led Sha'a'shu'im...*

7 *Ken Ta'a'vir Ve'Tis'por Ve'Tim'neh, Ve'Tif'kod Ne'fesh Kol Chai, Ve'Tach'toch Kits'va Le'Chol B'ri'ya, Ve'Tich'tov Et Gzar Di'nam.*

19

Address to the Delegates of the Eighth Annual Conference-Convention of The Cantors Assembly of America (May, 1956)

LEIB GLANTZ

Dear colleagues and friends,

I know how eager you are to hear something encouraging from Mother Israel. I am glad that I am able to convey to you good news.

I know that no words can enable you to grasp the full impact of the dream that is developing into a fascinating reality — a reality that for many years has consisted of difficulties, sorrows, obstacles, and sometimes even pain. I realize that, not long ago, both you and I were frightened because of our awareness of the dangers to the existence of Israel. We would also tend to exaggerate the inherent difficulties existing in the Israeli society.

I am happy to tell you that for the first time, Israel is lifting the weight of her accumulated troubles and beginning to rejoice and celebrate. I consider myself a very privileged person to be able to be part of Israel at this time.

One of Israel's greatest events to date was the celebration of its eighth Independence Day. The sight of thousands of people thronging the streets, glorying in their happiness and freedom, has left upon me an unforgettable impression.

One had to witness the entire diplomatic corps presenting itself before the President of the State of Israel, offering him the respect and recognition accorded to the leaders of all nations, in order to grasp the full meaning of the miracle that has become a reality for the Jewish people in our generation. It was very exciting to observe that our own ambassador of the United States of America, as well as the ambassadors from Britain, Russia, and other great countries came to the Presidential reception in Jerusalem to pay their respects.

I took part in memorials for the fallen heroes of Israel who gave their lives so that we could live here in peace. The parents of the dead soldiers were crying but not despairing. The President of my synagogue, Yitzchak Raziel, who lost his only son in the 1948 War of Independence, said *Ka'ddish* with deep sadness. However, you could sense the pride he felt in his son's sacrifice. Other bereaved parents said they would not hesitate to send their remaining sons and daughters to fight for the same cause — if Israel ever needed them again.

One of the sustaining and uplifting influences for the Jewish people here in Israel is cantorial music, for which there is great love. In my life I have seen enthusiasm for cantorial music in Kiev, Kishinev, Berdichev, Warsaw, New York, Los Angeles, Mexico, London, and Johannesburg, but nowhere is the response of the people so spontaneous, so deeply and truly felt, as it is here in Jerusalem, Tel Aviv, and Haifa.

> *I have seen enthusiasm for cantorial music in Kiev, Kishinev, Berdichev, New York, Warsaw, Los Angeles, Mexico, London, and Johannesburg, but nowhere is the response of the people so spontaneous, so deeply and truly felt, as it is here in Jerusalem, Tel Aviv, and Haifa.*

I would like to take this opportunity to encourage you to attach the same importance to the study of the Hebrew language as you do to that of Jewish music. True *Cha'za'nut* includes the authentic interpretation of the text of the Hebrew prayers. One of the main reasons for the enthusiasm of the Israeli people for *Cha'za'nut* is their understanding of the Hebrew language. Here there is no need to translate the liturgy into a foreign language.

Please accept my heartiest congratulations and my hope that the results of your deliberations at the Eighth Cantors Assembly Convention will be most successful.

Sincerely yours,

Leib Glantz

PROGRAM of the FIFTIETH ANNIVERSARY CONCERT of the
JEWISH MINISTERS CANTORS' ASSOCIATION
OF AMERICA, INC.

Metropolitan Opera House, New York
TUESDAY EVENING, DECEMBER 9, 1947

Joseph Rumshinsky, Conductor

PART I.

STAR SPANGLED BANNER — HATIKVOH

PSALM ONE HUNDRED ....L. LEWANDOWSKI
Ensemble

KINDLING OF THE CHANUKAH LIGIHTS
Cantor Maurice Erstling

HANAYROS HALOLU ....J. RUMSHINSKY
Ensemble

YISMACH MOSHE ....J. RUMSHINSKY
Ensemble
Soloist . . . Cantor Berele Chagy

HABAYT MISHOMAYIM ....M. GANCHOFF
Cantor Moshe Ganchoff

RIBONO SHEL OLOM ....S. VIGODA
Cantor Samuel Vigoda

VENOMAR LEFANAV-AV HARACHAMIN (In S'fardith) .....L. GLANTZ
Cantor Leib Glantz

PSALM ONE HUNDRED EIGHTEEN ....ABRAS-RUMSHINSKY
Ensemble
Soloists . . . Cantor Moshe Ganchoff, Cantor E. Zaslavsky

OZ YOSHIR ....J. RUMSHINSKY
Ensemble
Soloists . . . Cantor A. Shapiro, Cantor E. Zaslavsky,
Cantor A. Goldenberg

PART II.

HEYE IM PIFIYOS ....Z. ZILBERTS
Ensemble
Soloists . . . Cantor A. Shapiro, Cantor H. Brockman,
Cantor H. Gertler, Cantor A. Goldenberg

MIDAS HORACHAMIM ....KAPOV-KAGAN
Cantor Kapov-Kagan

TIKANTO SHABOS ....B. CHAGY
Cantor B. Chagy

PSALM ONE HUNDRED TWENTY-SIX ....BIRENBAUM-ZILBERTS
Ensemble

HAVDOLOH ....Z. ZILBERTS
Ensemble
Soloist . . . Cantor Kapov-Kagan
Alexander D. Richardson . . . Accompanist

Program of the 50th Anniversary Concert of the Jewish Ministers Cantors' Association
at the Metropolitan Opera House, New York, 1947.

20

The Uniqueness of Chasidic Music

LEIB GLANTZ[1]

It is an honor to be the first speaker to open this important discussion on Chasidism.[2] I am excited, as I know that all nine lecturers who will speak after me are very knowledgeable about this subject and I am confident that I will learn a great deal from listening to their presentations.

In order to comprehend the uniqueness of the Chasidic melody, it is important to understand the meaning of Chasidism as a way of life. I am sure the scholars who are present here today are well versed on this subject. Therefore, I would like to go directly to my discussion on the music of Chasidism by defining the elements that are included in Chasidic song.

In any music there are three main elements: melody, rhythm and interpretation. Melodies can be defined as the meandering tones that flow through time. It is relatively easy for us to distinguish between different melodies.

Rhythm is the second element. In music there are many different rhythms, such as 2/4, 3/4 and 4/4. The same melody can be performed using different rhythms and tempos. Obviously, the chosen rhythm strongly influences the character of the melody.

---

1 Leib Glantz presented this lecture in Yiddish at a conference on Chasidism at the Jewish Teachers Seminary in New York in November, 1963. Cantor Chaim Feifel transcribed the music and Dr. Fred Heuman translated the recorded lecture from Yiddish.

2 Chasidism is an influential mystical Jewish movement founded in Poland in the eighteenth century in reaction to the rigid academicism of rabbinical Judaism. The movement declined sharply in the nineteenth century, but fundamentalist communities developed from it, and Chasidism is still a force in Jewish life, particularly in Israel and in New York.

Leib Glantz after presenting a concert at the Mann Auditorium *(Hei'hal Ha'Tar'but)*, **Tel Aviv, Israel, 1958.**

The third element is interpretation. The player of an instrument or the singer can determine the character of a melody according to his or her inner spirit. Symphony conductors present the same classical music of Beethoven or Brahms, but each interprets the musical notes of the same composer in totally different ways.

Let us now consider how the Jewish people applied these three elements to their music.

But first we must establish the existence of specific Jewish music. There are those whom I would describe as "assimilationists." These are people who claim that "Jewish music" simply does not exist. These are mainly individuals who do not bother to visit synagogues and are basically removed from Jewish life. They know very little about Jewish musical traditions and, in general, possess little understanding about the music of minorities. At the same time, they seem to be very knowledgeable about "international" music. They write articles in French, in English, in Hebrew, and even in Yiddish — in which they do not recognize the existence of Jewish music.

As an individual who has studied the subject intensively, I can tell you that I am totally convinced of the existence of specifically Jewish music. This music is built on unique lines that belong distinctly to the Jewish people and to no other people. Melodies can be compared to trains. They travel on specific tracks. Jewish melodies employ very specific lines such as the Pentatonic scale and several other unique scales that are not used by any other culture.

> *I am totally convinced of the existence of specific Jewish music. This music is built on specific lines belonging distinctly to the Jewish people and to no other people.*

I will endeavor to present some examples. If you listen to the Israeli national radio station *Kol Yis'ra'el* ("The Voice of Israel"), you will find that every morning they play a special melody that opens their daily broadcasts. The theme of this melody is derived from the cantillation used in the reading of the bible: "In the beginning God created the heaven and the earth" — the opening words of the *To'rah*:

This music is distinctly Jewish. The cantillation is built on the Pentatonic scale that has become the foundation for the development of Jewish music. It is used extensively in synagogue chant.

Here is another example: when a thirteen-year-old *Bar Mitz'va* youngster chants the blessings of the *To'rah* or the reading of the Prophets, the melodies he sings are clearly Jewish melodies. When the Psalms are chanted in the early part of the Sabbath prayer service before the prayer *"Sho'chen Ad"* ("He who dwells for eternity"), the Pentatonic scale appears again:

Unfortunately, many worshippers consider this part of the service relatively unimportant. However, it is sung in a melody that is part of the Pentatonic scale, which is truly a Jewish national treasure.

Many *Ba'a'lei Te'fi'la* (masters of prayer) confuse the chanting of weekday Psalms with the chanting of Sabbath Psalms. This very morning I prayed at a nearby New York synagogue where the improper modes were sung, and the congregation was totally unaware of the musical differences between the two services.

Let us now discuss the "Talmud" mode of singing:

You will never hear Gentiles using that line of music. However, if you listen to any child reciting the Four Questions (*Ar'ba Ku'shi'yot*) during the Passover *Se'dder*,[3] you will find that he is singing the same melody that is traditionally used while studying the Talmud in a Yeshiva.

When we listen to the Israeli radio we hear a distinctly Jewish melody. However, when we tune in to the radio here in the United States, what we hear is a different melody, such as the following:

Interestingly, if only we add another phrase to these three notes — we actually end up with a Jewish melody:

Jewish musicians should be aware of these basic facts so that they will be able to create cantatas, chamber music, symphonies, and oratorios based on uniquely Jewish musical modes.

Many songs have been written using synagogue modes. The melody for the Yiddish song "*A Cha'zan'dl oif Sha'bbes*" is sung in the same mode used by the cantor in the synagogue when he chants the prayer "*Ye'kum Pur'kan*" ("May there come forth redemption from Heaven"), which is recited before the replacement of the *To'rah* scrolls in the Ark during the Sabbath service, after the reading of the *To'rah*:

---

3 *Se'dder* — a feast held on Passover in Jewish homes during which the story of the Exodus from Slavery in Egypt is retold and reenacted, reading and singing from the *Ha'gga'da*.

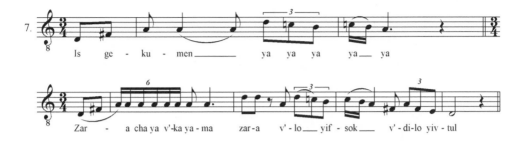

Jews have been hearing this mode in the synagogue throughout their lifetime, and it has been lovingly etched into their hearts. Another fine example of this is the song "*Ei'li Ei'li*":

Many non-Jewish singers love to sing this song. It is based on the synagogue prayer mode (*Nu'sach*) of *A'ha'va Ra'bbah* ("Great Love").

My time for this presentation is limited, so I will sing for you a few authentic Jewish themes. Let us begin with the melody for the *Ka'ddish* (prayer sanctifying God) in the closing *Ne'i'la* service of *Yom Ki'ppur* (the Day of Atonement):

This melody is built on lines very similar to those of the *Ka'ddish* sung in *Bir'kat Ge'shem* (the prayer for rain), yet each has characteristics that make it different and they both end different-ly:

There is a story about a cantor who suddenly, in the midst of the synagogue prayer service, forgot the proper melody. His wife, who was sitting in the woman's gallery (*Ez'rat Na'shim*), realized the situation and began to sing loudly in Yiddish, using the appropriate melody, with the words: "If you don't know the melody, and you can't sing it — then don't officiate as a cantor..."

11. M' - veis nit   u - m'ken nist   nemt men zich zoch   nish   un - ter

In addition to the existence of distinct Jewish melodies, there is distinct Jewish rhythm. When we listen to different recordings of the same song, we notice how rhythmic changes give the same melody a different character. Rhythm is a most important factor in the expression of a song, and you can identify Jewish music by its specific rhythm.

> *Rhythm is a most important factor in the expression of a song, and you can identify a Jewish song by its specific rhythm.*

It is the same with interpretation. When a German singer sings Richard Wagner's music, it sounds German. When a Jewish singer sings Wagner, it sounds totally different. Likewise, if a Frenchman sings a German song, the song will sound French, and an Englishman will give it yet another interpretation. Interpretation is a very important aspect of expression of music.

In Chasidic music, interpretation is critical. One of the most important aspects of Chasidic interpretation is that it often brings the singer into a state of ecstasy. Many of the classical cantors had the capacity to reach this ecstasy when they chanted prayers before their congregations in synagogues. Ecstasy is a universal characteristic that can be found in all kinds of music. In Black spiritual music you clearly experience ecstasy in the highest of forms.

However, Chasidic song is highly expressive. Its unique forms lead to ecstasy in ways that prove very difficult for many non-Jewish singers.

The examples I presented earlier, such as the child asking the Four Questions, the opening melody for the reading of the *To'rah*, or the Yiddish song "*A Cha'zan'dl oif Sha'bbes*," do not, however, possess the element of ecstasy.

When Chasidim sing, they sing with *cleaving*, meaning they become very emotionally involved. The Chasidim of Chabad, who felt that through singing they became closer to God, originally coined this term. Many Chasidic songs originated from melodies of the synagogue. Chasidic families consider singing at Sabbath and holiday feasts as an essential part of Chasidic life. The Chasid returns to his home from the synagogue prayers and enlightens his home with song. He sings special songs for the sanctification of the wine, songs during the meals and songs of grace at the end of the meal. In the Chasid's life, these family feasts represent a substitute for the sacrificial altar that once existed in the Holy Temple in ancient Jerusalem. Singing is a means to elevate the family's spiritual level.

> *[The Chasid considers the feast table something of a] substitute for the sacrificial altar that existed in the Holy Temple in ancient Jerusalem. Singing is a means to raise his family's mood to a higher spiritual level.*

Every Chasidic dynasty has created its unique brand of music. Each has its own composers devoted to developing that group's unique style. For instance, Shneur Zalman of Liady, the first *Re'bbe* of Chabad, created what is known as *"The Re'bbe's Ni'ggun"* which I will sing for you shortly. When we analyze their melodies, it is obvious that the Chasidim used the same Jewish scales and modes that are used in our synagogue prayers.

Let's listen to *"The Re'bbe's Ni'ggun"*:

ya___ya ya   a ya   ya ya ya   ya ya ya   ya   a ya ya yai   ah   ah_____ ah__

a ya ya ya ai___ai yai yai yai yai yai ai yai   ya ya ya ya yai_____ ah_____ ai yai

ai   yai   yai_____   bom bom bom bom yai   ai   dai dai dai__

ai   dai   dai   dai   ai   dai dai dai   ai   dai dai da   da

"*The Re'bbe's Ni'ggun*" contains the elements that make a song special: melody, rhythm, and meaningful interpretation.

In the Middle Ages, the Jewish people were led to believe that the Messiah's appearance was imminent. Many believed that Shabtai Tzvi (1626-1676) was this Messiah. The Jewish people prepared themselves to make great sacrifices in his honor. When eventually he converted to Islam, it was considered a tremendous catastrophe. The Messiah's "appearance" and the disillusionment that resulted caused such depression that many Jewish people actually considered committing suicide! However, the *Ba'al Shem Tov* and his Chasidic movement successfully restored the healthy state of mind of these people by guiding them to recapture a feeling of optimism and belief in a brighter future.

These Chasidic *Re'bbes* possessed some attributes characteristic of psychologists. Although they acquired no formal training, they had the capacity to heal people by guiding them to an optimistic approach to their daily problems. Their "medicine" was in the form of offering advice, consolation and, above all, utilizing the power of melody. The *Ni'ggun* (Chasidic melody) had a way of mysteriously healing people. When the *Re'bbes* engaged in singing and dancing, their followers became engulfed in ecstasy to the extent that they were capable of casting aside the burdens of their daily lives, and entering into a mystical state of mind that transported them into a spiritual sphere.

After the death of Nachman,[4] their *Re'bbe,* the Bratslaver Chasidim decided not to appoint a successor. They preferred that the *Re'bbe* remain their spiritual leader even after his death. Today, they are the only Chasidic dynasty that remains without a living spiritual leader.

---

4 Rabbi Nachman of Bratzlav (1770-1811) was founder of the Chasidic sect known as the "Bratzlaver Chasidim." He was the great grandson of the Ba'al Shem Tov — the father of Chasidism. Originally he settled in Bratzlav (Ukraine), from where he disseminated his teachings. He was considered an independent and ardent thinker. He moved to Uman (Ukraine), where he lived till his death. His grave and synagogue in Uman are the focus of annual pilgrimages.

I would like to share with you my personal experiences with the Bratslaver Chasidim. During the First World War, as a young boy, I traveled with my father to the city of Uman where the famous *Re'bbe* was buried. My experience at the Bratslaver synagogue Sabbath prayer service is one I will forever cherish. The Chasidim sang and danced uninterruptedly for three solid hours. They gathered me to dance with them. The prayer "*Le'cha Do'di*" ("Come my beloved to meet the Sabbath") continued for an hour, and the prayer "*Ve'Sham'ru*" ("They shall observe the Sabbath") went on for at least half an hour. There were elderly Jews with beards and long black coats who somehow found the inner strength to sing and dance throughout the whole service. They sang with great Chasidic fervor and seemed as though they lost recollection of where they were. Admittedly, I did not possess their endless energy. The next day I joined some of them on a march to the local cemetery. It happened to be the *Re'bbe's Yahr'zeit*[5] and I was curious to see how the memorial service would be conducted. The atmosphere was loaded with optimism. In place of mourning, the Chasidim came to sing and dance with joy in their hearts. Their song was therapeutic. I honestly felt its capacity to heal. There and then I realized how much power was contained in the musical "medicine" that the *Re'bbes* created.

The Moditzer *Re'bbe* was another Chasidic leader who created joyous song and dance that had a healing effect.

A *Ni'ggun* ascribed to the *Ba'al Shem Tov* — the father of the Chasidic movement — is "*Kol Me'ka'desh She'vi'i*." I will now sing my composition based on the same lyrics:[6]

The *Ba'al Shem Tov* was obviously not a physician but, according to his disciples, he proved to be a healer of those who were overwhelmed by troubles, sorrow and pain.

The opponents of Chasidism criticized the Chasidic *Re'bbes* for not emphasizing the importance of study. However, those same critics clearly envied the capacity of the Chasidim to sing and dance with ecstasy. Even these opponents would traditionally sing and dance in honor of the *To'rah* on the holiday of *Sim'chat To'rah*.[7] Here is an example of this:

---

5 *Yahr'zeit* — the anniversary of a person's death.

6 *Kol Me'ka'desh She'vi'i* — composed and sung by Leib Glantz, can be heard on Compact Disk (CD number 2) that accompanies this book.

7 *Sim'chat To'rah* — A festival celebrating the Law of Moses and the completion of the year's cycle of reading the *To'rah* and its subsequent new beginning, observed on the 22nd or 23rd day of the Hebrew month of *Tish'rei*.

14.

ze she no ga che sa pa - ro   u va so u va b' - tzi - da   ze she no ga

As you can hear, this singing of the opponents of Chasidism was far from having any therapeutic character. Their singing simply lacked the same authenticity as that of the ecstatic Chasidim.

Two very important Chasidic composers should be mentioned: Joseph Talmar and Hershel Talshiner. They were in constant competition with each other as they presented their songs during the Sabbath. Every Saturday night they would write down the musical notes of the songs that had been sung during that Sabbath.

The Talner *Re'bbe* was famous for his success in healing hundreds of cases of mental illness through song. Miraculously, by joining the singing and dancing, many troubled people were helped back to normalcy. Was the Talner *Re'bbe* a doctor? Obviously not. However, the psychiatrists of today recognize that there is healing power in song and dance.

> *The psychiatrists of today recognize that there is healing power in song and dance.*

There were times in the past when Chasidim abandoned Jewish musical sources and began to copy non-Jewish motifs. Unfortunately, the same can be said of numerous synagogue cantors. It is unacceptable to allow our treasured cultural and religious heritage to be tarnished by elements of foreign music. It is the duty of the Jewish people to guard and preserve our authentic and original Jewish modes.

Near my childhood home in Kiev (Ukraine), from time to time we would hear Chasidim marching down the street singing songs that sounded as though they were being sung by foreigners. Here is an example of beautiful Gentile music that crept into Chasidic singing:

15.

B'-tzeit Yis-ra-eil mi-mitz-ra-yim beit Ya-a-kov mei-am lo-eiz ha-yi-ta Y'-hu-da l'-kad-sho Yis-ra-eil____ mam-sh'-lo-tav b'-tzeit Yis-ra-eil__ mi-mitz-ra-yim beit Ya-a-kov mei-am lo-eiz ha-y'-ta Y'-hu-da Y'-hu-da l'-kad-sho Yis-ra-eil mam-sh'-lo-tav ha-y'-ta Y'-hu-da Y'-hu-da l'-kad-sho

To counter the last song, which I would like to define as "contaminated" Chasidic music, I would like to sing for you my composition "*Hu Yif'tach Li'bei'nu*" ("He shall open our heart") — a Chasidic interpretation of a Bratzlaver melody that is authentic, as well as melodically and rhythmically appropriate:

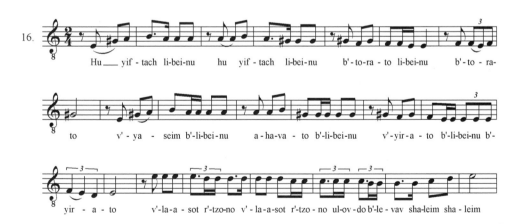

16.

Hu__ yif-tach li-bei-nu hu yif-tach li-bei-nu b'-to-ra-to li-bei-nu b'-to-ra-to v'-ya-seim b'-li-bei-nu a-ha-va-to b'-li-bei-nu v'-yir-a-to b'-li-bei-nu b'-yir-a-to v'-la-a-sot r'-tzo-no v'-la-a-sot r'-tzo-no ul-ov-do b'le-vav sha-leim sha-leim

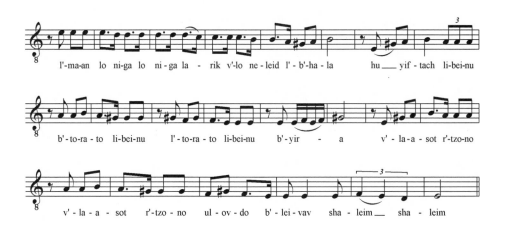

l'-ma-an lo ni-ga lo ni-ga la - rik v'-lo ne-leid l'-b'-ha-la hu __ yif-tach li-bei-nu

b'-to-ra-to li-bei-nu l'-to-ra-to li-bei-nu b'-yir - a v'-la-a-sot r'-tzo-no

v'-la-a-sot r'-tzo-no ul-ov-do b'-lei-vav sha-leim __ sha-leim

I will now play for you a Moditzer Chasidim melody "*Ho'du La'Shem*" ("Give thanks to God for all is well"), which is a very happy tune. I would like you to feel in your heart the joyfulness of this melody:

Ho - du la - shem ki __ tov ki __ l'-o - lam l'-o - lam chas -

do ya ba ba ba ba ba ya ba ba ba ba bam ya ba ba ba ba ba ba ba ba ya ba ba ba ba bam

bam yo - mar __ na beit A - ha-ron ki __ l'-o - lam

chas - do ho - du la - shem ki __ tov ki l' - o - lam

chas - - do ya ba ba ba ba ba ya ba ba ba ba

ya ba ba ba ba ba ba ba ya ba ba ba ba bam

Now I would like to introduce a Chasidic melody of the *Gur* Chasidim:

In conclusion, I would like to emphasize the fact that Chasidic music has never lost its power to heal those who are broken-hearted. This power exists even when some elements of the song are foreign to Jewish sources. The melody might be foreign, but the Jewish rhythm and the interpretation still remain authentically embedded in the song.

In Israel, Chasidic music is flourishing. There are multitudes of Jews in Tel Aviv who are dancing to the tunes of the *Moditzer* Chasidim. In Jerusalem you can witness similar experiences with the *Gur* Chasidim. The same spirit can be witnessed among the *Lubavitcher* Chasidim in Brooklyn, New York, or in Kfar Chabad in Israel. Chasidic melody and rhythm have mystical powers that can cure troubled people (as well as people in trouble) in every aspect of life.

Chasidism and Chasidic song will remain a very important element of Jewish life. My greatest wish is that Chasidism will not bypass its authentic Jewish musical sources and replace them with foreign songs and marches. I pray that Chasidic music will remain totally Jewish and will continue to combine its three musical elements — melody, rhythm, and interpretation.

Appendices

Correspondence Between Max Wohlberg and Leib Glantz Regarding Leib Glantz's 1952 Lecture "The Musical Basis of *Nu'sach Ha'Te'fi'la*"

Cantor Max Wohlberg[1] delivered a lecture to the delegates of the 7th annual Cantors Assembly Convention, which took place in New York in June 1954. In his lecture "*The History of the Musical Modes of the Ashkenazic Synagogue, and Their Usage*," Wohlberg made several comments regarding a lecture delivered two years earlier by Leib Glantz to the delegates of the 5th annual Cantors Assembly Convention, which took place in New York in May 1952, on the subject "The Musical Basis of *Nu'sach Ha'Te'fi'la*."

Following are Max Wohlberg's comments, and the letter of reply from Leib Glantz:

Comments from Cantor Max Wohlberg's lecture:

"In an effort to find a theoretical basis for our modes, two men have concurrently reached a partially similar result: Cantor Leib Glantz, in his lecture "The Musical Basis of *Nu'sach Ha'Te'fi'la*," which was presented at our convention in 1952, and Dr. Joseph Yasser, in a hitherto unpublished paper, "*The Structural Aspect of Jewish Modality.*"

Cantor Glantz points to the Pentatonic elements in the music of the synagogue and then marshals numerous musical illustrations to prove that the construction of our modes is Tetrachordal, conjunctive or disjunctive. Thus, the *Ye'kum Pur'kan* mode originally encompassed the two conjunctive Tetrachords G-A-B-C and C-D-E-F. To these were added one Tetrachord above: F-G-A-Bb and one below: D-E-F#-G. The Tetrachords of the *A'ha'va Ra'bbah* mode are E-F-G#-A - B-C-D#-E. To these was added below the E the Tetrachord A-B-C#-D.

---

1 Cantor Max Wohlberg (1907-1996) was born in Hungary and emigrated to the U.S. at age 16. He served as Cantor in six American synagogues for 40 years. He was a Professor of Cantorial, composer of Jewish music, and author of "The Music of the Synagogue" and many scholarly articles on all phases of Jewish music. He played an important role in the *Chazonim Farband*, The Jewish Ministers Cantors Association of America, and, together with Leib Glantz, was one of the founders of the *Cantors Cultural Society* in New York in 1930. He was the President of the Cantors Assembly from 1948 to 1951. Wohlberg developed a system for scientific teaching of *Nu'sach Ha'Te'fi'la* and in 1951 oversaw its institution at the Cantors Institute of the Jewish Theological Seminary.

The *Ma'gen A'vot* mode is built on A-B-C-D   E-F-G-A. This *Aeolian* mode branched out into many variations:

- One of these is the *Yish'ta'bach* mode: E-F-G-A   B-C-D-E (*Phrygian*).
- Another is the *Mi'She'Bei'rach* mode: D-E-F-G# A-B-C-D (Ukrainian-Dorian).
- A third is the *A'ta Zo'cher* mode: D-E-F-G   A-B-C-D, to which was added below A-B-C-D, making the Tetrachords conjunctive in the lower part and disjunctive above. In this group also belongs the *Tal/Ge'shem Nu'sach*.

I find myself unable to see eye to eye with Cantor Glantz regarding this theory, on two general grounds:

1. The justification of the theory itself (these objections apply partly also to Dr. Yasser's theory);
2. The transcription of his musical illustrations.

If the Glantz theory is correct, then Tetrachord was added to Tetrachord and thus the melody was extended. If this were the case, then the melodic line ought to exhibit some Tetrachordal characteristics, limitations, or breaks, whereas the truth is that most of the essential *Nu'sach*-motifs extend beyond a given Tetrachord. If the Tetrachordal theory were correct, then the fourth should have served as the dominant note in the scale, whereas we find the fifth doing that service. As far as synagogue music is concerned, I cannot subscribe to the Tetrachordal theory as advanced by musicologists relating to the development of general music (see article on "Scales" in *Grove's Dictionary of Music*). Even if that theory were correct, our *Nus'cha'ot* show clear evidence of either post-Tetrachordal age or total independence of Tetrachordality. Personally, I side with the latter probability.

As proof of the fact that Jews needed no Tetrachordal additions to indulge in wide-ranged melodies, we need but consider the cantillations of the bible. Furthermore, it is more likely and requires less credulity to suppose that melodic incursions took place throughout history without previous benefit of Tetrachordal adjustments and considerations than to presume that melodies were adopted only when they confirmed to a definite Tetrachordal pattern. In order to explain a structural peculiarity in the *A'ha'va Ra'bbah* mode, it is necessary, as Cantor Glantz states, to add a Tetrachord of another type below the tonic. However, may I point to two other collateral motifs of the *A'ha'va Ra'bbah* mode, hitherto overlooked, which I shall name as the *Az Mi'Si'nai* and the *Chem'dat Ya'mim* motifs? Neither of these can be accommodated into any of the hitherto synthetically constructed modal scales. The *Az Mi'Si'nai*, as incidentally the *Yish'ta'bach* mode, modulates temporarily to the major built on the fourth step of the scale. The *Chem'dat Ya'mim* mode is likewise a major motif. It is, however, based on the subtonic (see examples 14, 15).

Consideration ought also to be given the fact that a scale in no way is sufficiently descriptive of the characteristic motifs of a given mode. Thus, one may be able to place the *A'ta E'chad* and the *Ma'gen A'vot* in one scale. That scale, however, will not give us the peculiar differences between these two dissimilar modes, or take such unlike modes as the *Za'ra Cha'ya* and the *Ka'ddish* for the *Ne'i'la* service, both of which are assigned to the *A'do'shem Ma'lach* scale.

I now turn to the written musical illustrations that accompany the Glantz lecture. Illustration number 7, both A and B (Example 16), contain what seems to me as errors in the transcriptions. In the second measure of example A, the E should be flat, and most likely, the F should be sharp. In the last measure of example B, the B should be flat. I consider Cantor Glantz to be in error in placing these two items: *Bar'chu* for the festival evening service, and *U'Mi'pnei Cha'ta'ei'nu* in the *Yek'um Pur'kan* mode.

In illustration number 15 (example 17) Glantz uses the *Mi'She'Bei'rach* mode, which is normally saved for a later appearance, on the first words of the passage. By the way, the B should be natural in the first measure.

Finally, I cannot accept the contention of the author that the major sixth is a prominent element in the *Ge'shem/Tal* mode. I can justify its appearance on artistic grounds, but cannot accept its dominancy or even equality within the mode. Careful analysis of illustration number 17 (example 18) will reveal that Cantor Glantz, perhaps subconsciously, supports my view. Please observe whenever a B natural is used, it is on the weak beat of the measure. A far more convincing case of dualism could be made in the case of the festival *Ma'a'riv* mode where both a major and a minor third have equally legitimate claim."

———

Following is Leib Glantz's reply in the form of a letter:

Dear Cantor Wohlberg:

Thank you for sending me the one and a half pages of your paper dealing with my theory of *Nu'sach Ha'Te'fi'la*. I shall be very happy to comment upon the points you discuss. Before I begin, I want to thank you deeply for your wonderful words about my work in the last issue of the *Cantors Voice*. I always read your column with great interest and never fail to find the discussion scholarly, serious, and offering much food for thought. I was thrilled and moved to find your generous comments about me.

I should have liked to have had the opportunity to read your whole paper [lecture], for I am sure it would have been easier for me to answer your points. Since I do not have before me the positive elements of your paper, I must confine my remarks to the section you sent to me in which you find errors in, or disagreement with, my theory.

First, regarding the "errors":

Illustration 7-A of my paper:[2]

If I were writing E flat in the *Bar'chu* and even F sharp, in the festival *Bar'chu*, there would be no problem at all about the *Nu'sach* of the festival *Bar'chu*. It would simply be a Western Harmonic Minor. I discussed the problem with many great cantors, including the late Cantor Avraham Berkovitz-Kalechnik, and it also appears in the writings of Pinchas Minkowsky, that the festival *Bar'chu* is a problem just because it starts with B major in the first phrase, minor B in the second phrase, plus F natural and E natural. The answer lies in the fact that the *Bar'chu*, as well as the ending of the *Bra'chot* of the *Ma'ariv* service, are the only remnants of the festival *Nu'sach*, which is so clearly recognizable in the festival morning service. It is definitely a ten-step *Ye'kum Pur'kan Nu'sach*. Its line is three Tetrachords: G-A-B-C(C)-D-E-F(F)-G-A-Bb. Read the *Bar'chu* and you will find all these peculiarities: B natural in the lower phase, B flat above, F natural and E natural. A *Mi'Si'nai Nu'sach* cannot and should not be changed. The *Ma'a'riv* is in minor but the *Bra'chot* retain again the ten-step *Ye'kum Pur'kan*.

Illustration 7-B:

Your criticism is easy to answer. The error is yours. The B flat is there. The lower B must be natural in accordance with the point made above. Since I do not have your whole paper [lecture] before me, I do not know what musical line you ascribe to the festival *Nu'sach*. However, I can tell you that in my further studies since my paper was first presented in 1952, I have found more internal evidence of the close relationship between the *Ye'kum Pur'kan* and *A'ha'va Ra'bbah* modes, and have many more examples of *Mi'Si'nai Nus'cha'ot*, which corroborate this theory.

Illustration 15:

Here, my dear colleague, you are perfectly correct. However, the error is not mine, but that of the "*Bu'chur Ha'Se'tzer*" [the printer's copyist] as they used to say in the rabbinical literature. The copyist put the B natural in the second phrase, and also in the B of the first phrase of the *Mi'She'Bei'rach* line, but he omitted it in the first phrase. Thank you for calling it to my attention.

---

2 These four illustrations (7A, 7B, 15, & 17) may be viewed in the above-mentioned lecture by Leib Glantz "The Musical Basis of *Nu'sach Ha'Te'fi'la*," in Part 3 of this book.

Illustration 17:

Your remark that the most significant feature of the *Ge'shem/Tal Nu'sach*, which is the B natural, is that it falls on the weak beat, is irrelevant in my opinion. In many *Mi'Si'nai Nus'cha'ot* the same thing occurs. That is why we, the students of Jewish *Nu'sach* have to dig so carefully to find the hidden features of the *Nus'cha'ot*. The fact that we have B natural and B flat in succession in this *Nu'sach* is the real demonstration and illustration of the *Nu'sach*. Actually, it is its manifestation.

Since I have not had the opportunity to read and to study carefully the major features of your paper, I shall reserve comment on those remarks that you did send me relating to the theory in general. I look forward to further occasions, both personal and professional, to continue these discussions. From all our studies there will surely come a systematic, valid and viable analysis of the great cantorial heritage. I can only say that I did not find a single reason for doubting my theory. I am sure that my theory is now stronger than it originally was when written in 1952.

May I wish you and all our colleagues the greatest success in your deliberations. I am really sorry that I am unable to be with you this time.

Sha'lom U'Vra'cha,

Leib Glantz

Reinhold Gliere:
Leib Glantz's Distinguished Music Teacher

In January 1945 musical circles all over Russia celebrated the seventieth birthday of Reinhold Gliere (1875-1956), who was the Chairman of the Union of Soviet Composers, and one of the most influential teachers of modern times. Greetings from conductors such as Leopold Stokowski (1882-1977) and artists such as Jascha Heifetz (1901-1987), congratulated the "Father of Soviet Composers," as he was generally known.

Born in Kiev, Reinhold Moritzovich Glière was the second son of a master wind instrument maker, Ernst Moritz Glier (1834-1896), who emigrated from Saxony to Kiev, where he married Józefa (Josephine) Korczak (1849-1935), the daughter of his Jewish master instrument teacher from Warsaw. Gliere was baptized on January 19, 1875 in the Protestant Lutheran Church of Kiev.

He became an accomplished violinist while still a child. At age sixteen, in 1891, he was accepted to study at the Kiev School of Music. After three years, he entered the Moscow Conservatory and studied violin, harmony, counterpoint, and composition.

His compositional technique was quickly recognized by his teachers and he won several prizes for his early works, including his First String Sextet which was awarded the prestigious Glinka Prize from a jury consisting of Nokolai Rimsky-Korsakov, Alexander Glazunov and Anatoly Liadov. The respected Russian scholar and critic Professor Leonid Sabaneiev wrote:

> "His chamber compositions show him to have been an absolute master of form, and a virtuoso in his control of the resources of musical composition and expression."

In June 1902, as a young composer who had just graduated from the conservatory, Gliere's teacher Sergei Tanayev recommended him to the parents of young 11-year-old Seryozha Prokofiev to be his music teacher. During Gliere's second stay with Prokofiev, they worked enthusiastically on the composition of the child's third opera, "The Feast During the Plague." Explaining musical forms and harmony, Gliere roused the interest and the curiosity of his young pupil. Both pupil and teacher loved improvisation.

In a letter[1] from Prokofiev's mother Mariya Prokofieva to Sergei Taneyev, dated September 11, 1902, she writes:

"Recently, Reinhold Moritzevich [Gliere] has left our house, leaving the best memory behind him. He is irreplaceable as an instructor. He has so much tact and patience! With his knowledge and love of music, he could always get Seryozha interested and incline him to composition."

In November, Seryozha, now a year older, brought to Taneyev in Moscow seven songs and a symphony, the crown of his creative achievement in the first summer of studies with Gliere.

Gliere graduated from the conservatory with a one-act opera "*Earth and Heaven*" (based on the writings of Lord Byron), and accepted a teaching post at the famous Gnessin School of Music in Moscow. There he composed his second symphony, which he dedicated to his co-student and great friend Serge Koussevitzky (1874-1951). Gliere also spent three years (1905-1908) in Berlin studying with the famous conductor and composer Oskar Fried, and from that time became increasingly popular as a conductor of symphonic works.

His third symphony, "*Ilya Muromets*," which he dedicated to Alexander Glazunov (1865-1936), was published in 1911. This monumental work earned him worldwide renown; in America it became one of the favorite items in the extensive repertoire of Leopold Stokowski (1882-1977).

From 1913 to 1920 Gliere served as Director of the Kiev Conservatory, where he taught composition to several musicians who eventually became famous. Among them was Leib Glantz, who was considered his favorite student. Dr. Chaim Bar-Dayan, a childhood friend of Glantz, who was his co-student at the Kiev Conservatory, wrote in his memoir "Growing Up with Leibel in Kiev and Kishinev":

"In 1917, the year of the Communist Revolution, the great composer Reinhold Gliere, head of the prestigious Kiev Conservatory of Music, offered to teach Glantz composition. Gliere was very close to Glantz, considered him a musical genius, and encouraged him to dedicate himself to musical composition."[2]

Gliere was encouraged by the Soviet Government to conduct a study of the folklore and folk music of the Republic of Azerbaijan, with the objective of reviving their ancient national

---

1 As quoted in "Prokofiev — His Life and Times," by Natalia Savkina, Paganiniana Publications Inc., NJ, 1984.

2 Another well known Ukranian musician who was a teacher of Leib Glantz was Nikolai Appolonovich Tutkovski (1857-1931). Tutkovski, who was born in Kiev, taught piano from (1881-1890). He was appointed professor at the famous St. Petersburg Conservatory (1888-1890), where he taught History of Music. In 1893 he erected his famous Kiev Music School, which he directed for many years. He was renowned for his monumental literary work "A Study of Harmony" (1905), and his Symphonies "Pensee Elegiaque" and "Bacchanale Bohemienne." Glantz studied piano under Tutkovski.

Reinhold Gliere, Leib Glantz's distinguished music teacher.

music. He moved to the capital, Baku, and from there visited towns and villages on the shores of the Caspian Sea. He composed an Azerbaijanian opera "*Shah Senen*" based on a sixteenth-century Azerbaijanian fable. This opera, completed in 1925, is considered the first Soviet grand opera. A similar period of research in the Republic of Uzbekistan produced the musical drama "*Gulsara,*" and the opera "*Leili and Medjnun.*" Gliere then composed a choreographic poem "*Zaporozhtsy,*" based upon the national music of the Ukraine. His most important work is the famous ballet "*The Red Poppy.*"

Gliere enjoyed throughout his life the highest esteem of his fellow countrymen. He was awarded numerous awards, including the title "People's Artist of the Soviet Union," the "Order of the Red Banner," the "Soviet Order of Merit," and the degree of Doctor of Sciences (Research in Art). Gliere was apolitical and conservative in the cause of music. He was not active in the various musico-political groups of the early Soviet Union. Since all these eventually foundered, it has made of him, in retrospect, nothing less than a hero. However, at the time, he was criticized for his lack of involvement and lack of political direction.

He was a man of great intellect and personal charm, and an important social figure. Although many of his compositions are based upon the national music of various republics of the Soviet Union, they all bear the stamp of his own particular style of craftsmanship, and their popularity in Russia is probably due to his great understanding of his people's taste in music.

When the musical historians of the future review the twentieth century, they will find that Reinhold Gliere's greatest service to his art was in his work as a teacher of composition. He had always possessed a remarkable power of drawing out the real genius in his pupils and of inspiring them with all the best traditions of Russian music. Such brilliant composers as Sergei Prokofiev (1891-1953), Aram Khachaturian (1903-1978), Nicolai Miaskovsky (1881-1950), and Leib Glantz (1898-1964) were his devoted students and followers.

Sources:

[1] S. K. Gulinskaja, *Reinhold Morizevich Glier,* Moscow *"Musika"* 1986 (Russian).

[2] Stanley D. Krebs, *Soviet Composers and the Development of Soviet Music,* London, 1970.

[3] S. Bugoslawski, *R.M. Glière,* Music-Section, State Publishing House, Moscow, 1927.

[4] Natal'ja Petrowa, *Reinhold Morizevich Glier 1875-1956,* Leningrad, 1962 (Russian).

[5] Igor Belza, *R.M. Glier, Sovjetskij kompositor,* Moscow, 1962 (Russian).

[6] Boris S. Jagolim, *R.M. Glier, A catalog of works,* Moscow, 1964 (Russian).

[7] Natalia Savkina, *"Prokofiev — His Life and Times,"* Paganiniana Publications Inc., NJ, 1984.

[8] Alexandria Vodarsky-Shiraeff, *"Russian Composers and Musicians,"* Greenwood Press, NY, 1940.

Leib Glantz's Recording History

The process of sound recording (phonography) was invented by Thomas Alva Edison in 1877. The first cantors who are known to have been recorded were Cantor Felix Asch from Berlin, who immortalized a verse of the prayer *Kol Nid'rei* in 1902, and Cantor Gershon Sirota in 1903. Soon after, Zavel Kwartin was recorded as well. These recordings utilized the "acoustic" recording technique.

The distinguished Cantor Pinchas Minkowsky sternly criticized Sirota and Kwartin as the "*Gramophone Cha'zo'nim.*" He felt that the concept of recording cantorial synagogue music diminished its majesty and dignity, as well as the dignity of the cantor.

Following the First World War, many of the great European cantors immigrated to the United States. Well known among these were Mordechai Hershman, Zavel Kwartin, David Roitman and Yossele Rosenblatt. They were followed by Leib Glantz, Ben Zion Kapov-Kagan, Pierre Pinchik, Samuel Vigoda and others. The records that they recorded in America established these cantors as cultural stars in the Jewish world.

In the early 1920's the U.S. recording industry was dominated by two companies: the Victor Record Company and the Columbia Record Company.

After his arrival in New York in 1926, Leib Glantz engaged the services of Sara Wachs as his agent and manager. She dedicated her life to his success, arranging concert tours and synagogue appearances. She was responsible for creating most of Glantz's recordings, and frequently invested her own funds in order to bring them to light. Sara Wachs proved to be a loyal friend to the Glantz family throughout her life and deserves credit for enhancing Leib Glantz's career.

In 1928, following the development of "electrical" recording, Glantz signed a contract to record his compositions with RCA Victor on their prestigious "Red Label" series.

The first compositions Glantz recorded were 12 inch records, with 78 RPM (revolutions per minute). The duration of each side of the record was approximately four minutes. Therefore, the compositions needed to be "trimmed" into the available time span. Most recordings of that period were accompanied by an organ or by various instrumental ensembles. Glantz's liturgical recordings at RCA were accompanied by pipe organ, and the secular selections by piano. None were accompanied by other musical instruments.

These early compositions were recorded in a building in Camden, New Jersey, which was known as the "Old Church Building." It originally was a church and it possessed outstanding natural acoustical qualities. RCA recorded most of its cantorial recordings in this building during the early "electrical era." Glantz, as well as cantors Pinchik, Kwartin, Vigoda and Malavski were usually accompanied by Solomon Braslavsky on organ or piano.[1]

In total, Glantz recorded ten compositions that he arranged for the four minute durations of these records. His famous "*Shéma Yis'ra'el*" composition was limited to four minutes even though the original composition was considerably longer. Another example was "*Tal,*" where Glantz sang only the first and last of the six verses of the prayer. The other four minute liturgical compositions were: "*Kol A'do'nai,*" "*Ein Ke'Er'ke'cha,*" "*Av Ha'Ra'chamim,*" "*Bir'kat Ko'ha'nim,*" "*Le'chu Ne'ra'ne'na,*" "*Sho'mer Yis'ra'el,*" "*Ki Ke'Shim'cha*" and "*Ki Hi'neh Ka'Cho'mer.*"

"*Shéma Yis'ra'el*" and "*Tal*" became tremendously popular all over the world and represented a commercial success for RCA. Glantz recorded with RCA Victor another record with two of his secular compositions "*A'cha'rei Mo'ti,*" a Hebrew poem by Chaim Nachman Bialik, Israel's national poet, and "*D'voi're'le,*" a Yiddish poem by Zalman Shazar, who later became President of the State of Israel.

In the mid 1930's, RCA reissued some of their cantorial recordings in an album called "Golden Voices of Israel." The album included six 78 RPM discs, which RCA presented as the greatest compositions of the most famous cantors in the world. This best-selling album included Glantz's "*Shéma Yis'ra'el*" and "*Tal.*" The other cantors were Pierre Pinchik, Zavel Kwartin, Yossele Rosenblatt, Samuel Vigoda and Ben Zion Kapov-Kagan. The inclusion of these six cantors in this very successful RCA album made Leib Glantz an internationally famous recording artist.

Glantz recorded new compositions in 1940 with the Musicraft Record Company, a company owned by Samuel Puner. These were smaller 10 inch records that enabled only three minutes of recording time on each side. Therefore, compositions such as "*Mach'ni'sei Ra'chamim*" and "*Ez'ke'ra E'lo'kim*" needed to be shortened in comparison to Glantz's synagogue renditions. Incidently, this album was distributed by the socialist Yiddish newspaper *The Jewish Daily Forward.*

The Musicraft recordings do not possess the acoustic qualities of the RCA site in Camden, New Jersey, as they were conducted in the small confines of a radio studio. This studio did not

---

1 Incidently, Solomon Braslavsky was the choir conductor of the synagogue in Uman, Ukraine, where both Glantz and Pinchik are photographed singing together in the choir as small children (see page 267).

have RCA's magnificent pipe organ. The accompaniment used an electric organ, which lacks the majestic sounds of the RCA recordings.

Glantz, as opposed to other recording cantors, had a unique style. No one was capable of producing Glantz's vocal sounds. Sophisticated listeners, who were attracted to other than the "regular" cantorial sounds, were immensely attracted to the intellectual and artistic qualities of his cantorial music.

In 1942, Glantz signed a contract to produce several recordings with Asch Recordings in New York. The studio did not have an organ, so Glantz was accompanied on piano by Abe Ellstein. Since Asch, the owner, was mainly interested in folklore, Glantz's renditions were folkloric: liturgical, Yiddish and Hebrew (or "Palestinian" as it was then referred to). He recorded six compositions.[2]

The Asch recordings are influenced by Glantz's work in this period as cantor of a Conservative synagogue (Temple Sinai in Los Angeles). They are sung in a calm, subdued, manner, much different from his earlier recordings.

In the years following the Second World War, Glantz recorded for Besa Recording Company, which was owned by Cantor Sidor Bilarsky. Besa recorded eight compositions of Chasidic *D'vei'kut*[3] which they named "Chasidic Ecstasy."

Glantz recorded his interpretations of Chasidic melodies with a semi-improvised piano accompaniment by Nahum Nardi.[4]

In the recording of his composition "*Tal*," there is a distinct Palestinian (*E'retz Yis'ra'eli*) character. When recording for Musicraft, this aspect was much less noticeable than in the Asch recordings. The same can be said of Glantz's Besa recordings, where he sings in Hebrew Sephardic pronunciation — the same as is spoken in modern Israel. There were very few cantors who were capable of singing with the Sephardic pronunciation. Glantz, a scholar of Hebrew as well as an active Zionist from his earliest days, wrote and spoke Hebrew fluently.

During his 1949 concert tour of Israel, Glantz recorded "*Kol Me'ka'desh*" as part of an Israeli album titled "*O'neg Sha'bat*." He was accompanied by the Tel-Aviv Chamber Orchestra, conducted by Mark Lavry. Glantz composed this song, based on traditional modes, with a mystical combination of Israeli and Chasidic motifs.

---

2 See the list of these recordings in the Discography — Appendix 4.

3 *D'vei'kut* (Hebrew) — attachment to God; devoutness; devotion; coupled with sublime joy.

4 Glantz's agent and manager, Sara Wachs, was also the agent of Nachum Nardi, who was a distinguished Israeli pianist and composer.

In 1951, Glantz recorded two albums of *Cha'za'nut*, in Ashkenazic pronounciation. The first was "*Shir Cha'dash*" — New Liturgical Chants. The second was "*Kol Yom Ha'Din*" — High Holiday Moods. These were released by Reena Record Corporation — a company owned by Theodore Granik, who was a graduate of the Teachers Institute of the Jewish Theological Seminary. Granik, an avid Hebraist, produced recordings of Hebrew songs for Jewish children.

Glantz immigrated to Israel in the summer of 1954. In 1957, Sara Wachs re-issued his RCA recordings, after arranging for RCA to execute the technical recording and transformation of the 78 RPM masters to tape and then creating an LP (33-1/3 RPM long playing format). RCA also agreed that the records would appear under the RCA label. Wachs created the jacket of this album with artwork designed by the famous artist Saul Raskin. She labeled the series of albums "Hebraica Records." This first album of the series was named "*Ri'nat Ha'Ko'desh.*"

Subsequently, on the occasion of Glantz's 1958 concert tour of the United States and Canada, Sara Wachs organized studio recording sessions for Glantz in New York, where he recorded two additional albums of *Cha'za'nut*. "*Tif'e'ret Te'fi'la*" included a new version of "*Mach'ni'sei Ra'cha'mim,*" "*Sim Sha'lom,*" "*Hash'ki'vei'nu,*" "*Yiz'kor,*" and "*She'va Pe'a'mim A'ta.*" "*Ha'llel Ve'Zim'ra*" included Glantz's newest compositions — "*A'hav'ti,*" "*A'na Be'Cho'ach,*" "*U'Ve'Nu'cho Yo'mar,*" "*Be'Tzeit Yis'ra'el,*" "*Te'vi'e'nu,*" and "*B'rich Shmei.*" Most of these compositions were created in Israel.

In addition, Glantz recorded an album of Chasidic songs, "*Cha'si'dim Be'Ri'na,*" and an album of Hebrew art songs, "*Cha'zon Ve'Shi'ra*" ("Vision and Sound"). This last album was produced under the "Famous Records" label, a recording company founded by Saul Karp.

"Famous Records" also produced a double LP album — "Midnight *Se'li'chot* Service" — which consisted of live recordings made by "*Kol Yis'ra'el*" (the Israeli Broadcasting Authority). These recordings were broadcast live in Israel directly from the *Tif'e'ret Zvi* synagogue in Tel Aviv. They continue to be broadcast by "*Kol Yis'ra'el*" every year on the *Se'li'chot* holiday.

After Glantz's death in January 1964, the "Israel Music" recording company issued two compact discs: "Pearls of Jewish Liturgical Music — Cantor Leib Glantz" (ICD-5027), consisting of 13 of his compositions, and "Midnight *Se'li'chot* Service," (ICD-5095), a technically improved version of the "Famous Records" LP, consisting of all twenty compositions of the live synagogue service.

All of Leib Glantz's recorded compositions can be heard on the internet by logging on to the website of Florida Atlantic University (FAU) — the Judaica Sound Archives (JSA):

http://faujsa.fau.edu/glantz/glantz_albums.php

This recording history was compiled with the kind assistance of Barry Serota.

Discography of Leib Glantz's Audio Recordings

RCA Victor (Red & Black Seal labels):

R.C.A. Victor – 78 RPM

Tal – V-59001A
Shéma Yisrá'el – V-59001B

Accompaniment: Solomon Braslavsky, organ.
Camden, New Jersey – February 20, 1929.

Lé'chu Ne'rá'ne'na – V-59004A
Kol A'do'nai – V-59004B

Accompaniment: Abe Ellstein, organ.
Camden, New Jersey – July 15, 1929.

Bir'kat Ko'ha'nim – 9884A
Ein Ke'Er'ke'cha – 9884B

Ki Hi'nei Ka'Cho'mer – 9699A
Ki Ke'Shim'cha – 9699B

Accompaniment: Solomon Braslavsky, organ.
Camden, New Jersey – March 19, 1930.

A'cha'rei Mo'ti – 1149A
D'voi're'le – 1149B

Accompaniment: Solomon Braslavsky, piano.
Camden, New Jersey – July 28, 1932.

Sho'mer Yisrá'el – 11467A
Av Ha'Ra'cha'mim – 11467B

Accompaniment: Solomon Braslavsky, organ.

Camden, New Jersey – August 23, 1932.

[In the mid-1930's, RCA Victor reissued Leib Glantz's recordings of *Shéma Yisrá'el* and *Tal* on a six disc album (78 RPM), titled "*Golden Voices of Israel,*" including cantorial renditions from Pierre Pinchik, Zavel Kwartin, Yossele Rosenblatt, Samuel Vigoda, and Ben Zion Kapov-Kagan].

Album of Cantorial Chants

Musicraft Recording Corp., NY – 78 RPM

New York, NY – 1940.

Az Be'Kol – RS-838A
Mach'ni'sei Ra'cha'mim – RS-841B
Ez'ke'ra E'lo'kim – RS-842A

Accompaniment: Organ.

(This album was specially recorded for "The Jewish Daily Forward" and distributed by this New York newspaper. It included six compositions of which three were sung by Leib Glantz.)

Asch Recordings

Asch Recordings, NY – 78 RPM

New York, NY, ca 1942.

Hash'ki'vei'nu – H-6021A
Sim Sha'lom – H-6021B

A'da'rim – H-6022A (Asaf Halevi, Shlomo Weisfish, Julius Chajes)

Ma'tai? – H-6022B

Ich Bin A Yis'ro'el – H-6023A
A Din Toi're Mit Got – H-6023B

Accompaniment: Abe Ellstein, piano.

Hebrew Spirituals/Chassidic Ecstasy

Besa Record Co., NY – 78 RPM

New York, NY, 1947.

A'ta Yo'de'a – H-28-701A
Nach'pe'sa – H-28-701B

Ri'bon Ha'O'la'mim – H-28-702A
Al Tiz'kor – H28-702B

U'Ve'Yom Ha'Sha'bat – H-28-703A
E'lo'kei'nu Kad'shei'nu – H-28-703B

D'ror Yik'ra – H-28-704A
Ash'rei'nu – H-28-704B

Accompaniment: Nachum Nardi, piano.

O'neg Sha'bbat (Oneg Shabbat)

Israel Music Foundation, NY – 78 RPM
/ LP 33-1/3 RPM

112-IMF-54 / LP4-8 – Tel Aviv, Israel,
1949.

Kol Me'ka'desh

Accompaniment: The Tel Aviv Chamber
Orchestra conducted by Mark Lavry.

This album was published as a tribute to
the poet Chaim Nachman Bialik. It
includes six songs of which *Kol Me'ka'desh*
is composed and sung by Leib Glantz.

Shir Cha'dash – **New Liturgical Chants**

Reena Record Corp., NY – 78 RPM / LP
33-1/3 RPM

LP3A/B – New York, NY, 1951.

C501A/B; C502A/B; C503A/B

A'mar Ra'bbi E'la'zar

Le'Da'vid Miz'mor

Ha'beit Mi'Sha'ma'yim

Accompaniment: Organ.

Kol Yom Ha'Din – **High Holiday
Moods**

Reena Record Corp., NY – 78 RPM /
LP 33-1/3 RPM

C-3 C506A/B; C507A/B; C508A/B

CLP-5A/B – New York, NY, 1951.

Be'Rosh Ha'Sha'na

Te'ka Be'Sho'far

Ez'ke'ra E'lo'kim

Accompaniment: Organ.

Golden Voices of Israel

RCA Victor (Israel) – LP 33-1/3 RPM

E4VP-8497/8498 (LPT-1017) –
Published by *Ha'Aretz* Israeli Daily
Newspaper in Tel Aviv, 1955.

She'ma Yis'ra'el

Tal

Ri'nat Ha'Ko'desh (Rinat Hakodesh)

RCA Victor/Hebraica Records, N.Y. –
LP 33-1/3 RPM

H70P-3657/58 (HBR-LP1) – Published
in New York, NY, 1957.

Kol A'do'nai

Ein Ke'Er'ke'cha

Av Ha'Ra'cha'mim

She'ma Yis'ra'el

Bir'kat Ko'ha'nim

Te'fi'lat Tal

Le'chu Ne'ra'ne'na

Ki Ke'Shim'cha

Ki Hi'nei Ka'Cho'mer

Sho'mer Yis'ra'el

A'cha'rei Mo'ti (lyrics by Chaim Nachman Bialik)

Dvoi're'le (lyrics by Zalman Shazar)

This LP is a re-issue of the original RCA recordings of 1929-1932.

Tif'e'ret Te'fi'la (Tiferet Tefilah)

RCA Victor/Hebraica-Records, NY – LP 33-1/3 RPM

J70P-8279/80 (HBR-LP2) – New York, NY, 1958.

Mach'ni'sei Ra'cha'mim

Yiz'kor (El Ma'leh Ra'cha'mim) (In memory of the victims of the Holocaust)

She'va Pe'a'mim "A'ta"

Ha'loch Ve'Ka'ra'ta

Hash'ki'vei'nu

Sim Sha'lom

Accompaniment: Vladimir Heifetz, organ.

Ha'lel Ve'Zim'ra (Hallel V'Zimrah)

RCA Victor /Hebraica Records, NY – LP 33-1/3 RPM

J08P-3403/04 (HBR LP4) – New York, NY, 1958.

A'hav'ti

A'na Be'Cho'ach

U'Ve'Nu'cho Yo'mar

Be'Tzeit Yis'ra'el

Te'vi'e'nu

B'rich Sh'mei

Accompaniment: Vladimir Heifetz, organ.

Cha'si'dim Be'Ri'na (Chassidim B'Rinah)

RCA Victor/Hebraica Records, NY – LP 33-1/3 RPM

J08P-2731/32 (HBR-LP3) – New York, NY, 1958.

A) Bratslav Chasidim Style

Tit'ga'dal

Le'Dor Va'Dor

Yis'mach Mo'she

U'Ve'Yom Ha'Sha'bat

E'lo'kei'nu Kad'shei'nu

B) Ba'al Shem Tov Style

Ri'bon Ha'O'la'mim

C) Israeli-Yemenite Style

Le'cha Do'di

D) Israeli Chasidim Style

Ash'rei'nu

E) Talner Chasidim Style

Hu Yif'tach Li'bei'nu

D'ror Yik'ra

E'shet Cha'yil

F) Lubavitcher Chasidim Style

A'ta Yo'de'a

Al Tiz'kor

Nach'pe'sa

Accompaniment: Vladimir Heifetz, piano.

Cha'zon Ve'Shi'ra – **(Chazon V'Shirah)**
Shi'rei O'ma'nut **("Vision & Sound")**

Famous Records Inc., NY - LP 33-1/3 RPM

K70P-7472/73 (VS501) – New York, NY, 1958.

Mi A'ni – (lyrics: Yaakov Fichman)

Sho'sha'na – (lyrics: Saul Tchernichovsky)

Yod'li Yod'li – (lyrics: Zalman Schneur)

Om'rim Yesh'na E'retz – (lyrics: Saul Tchernichovsky)

Al Ha'She'chi'ta – (lyrics: Chaim Nachman Bialik)

Ma'tai? – (lyrics: traditional)

Be'Shuv Ha'Shem – (lyrics: traditional)

Nit'shu Zla'lim – (lyrics: Saul Tchernichovsky)

Om'rim Li Ei'nech Ya'fah – (lyrics: Yaakov Rimon)

Ve'Te'che'ze'na – (lyrics: traditional)

He'ma Ka're'u Ve'Na'fa'lu – (lyrics: traditional)

Great Cantors of The Present

Celebrity Records, NY, LP 33-1/3 RPM

S-1003

Sho'mer Yis'ra'el

This LP was published in the late 1950's.

Midnight Selichot Service in Israel

Famous Records Inc., NY – two LP records 33-1/3 RPM

FAM-1015A/B & FAM-1015C/D

Introduction and *Ash'rei*

Te'hi'la Le'Da'vid

Ka'ddish

Le'cha Sha'ma'yim

Le'chu Ne'ra'ne'na

A'sher Be'Ya'do

Eich Nif'tach Peh

El E'rech A'pa'yim

Ta'a'vor Al Pe'sha

Be'Mo'tza'ei Me'nu'cha

Zo'cha'lim Ve'Ro'a'dim

Yo'tzer A'ta

Ma'rom

P'ne Na

Re'tze A'ti'ra'tam

Hi'ma'tze La'nu

Te'vi'ei'nu

She'ma Ko'lei'nu

Ha'shi'vei'nu

Al Tash'li'chei'nu Mil'fa'ne'cha

Al Tash'li'chei'nu Le'Et Zik'na

Mach'ni'sei Ra'cha'mim

This LP album was originally published in 1963 and consists of a compilation of parts of the Selichot Services, recorded live in the "Tiferet Zvi" synagogue in Tel Aviv, by Kol Yisrael, the Israeli Broadcasting Authority, from 1954 to 1962. The choir is conducted by Yehoshua Zohar. Israel Music (IMC 1037) reproduced this recording in 2001 on a tape cassette titled "Midnight Selichot Service" — Leib Glantz. Finally, Israel Music produced an improved version on Compact Disk (ICD 5095). See details below.

Leib Glantz – *Miz'mor Shir Le'Yom Ha'Sha'bbat*

Eastronics Ltd. (RCA Victor) – tape cassette and LP 33-1/3 RPM

ISK-1015/ISR-1015 – Tel Aviv, Israel, (approx. 1970)

A'na Be'Cho'ach

B'rich Sh'mei

U'Ve'Nu'cho Yo'mar

Sim Sha'lom

Le'cha Do'di

E'shet Cha'yil

D'ror Yik'ra

Tit'ga'dal

Le'Dor Va'Dor

Yis'mach Mo'she

U'Ve'Yom Ha'Sha'bbat

This LP/ tape cassette is a reproduction of earlier LP recordings. Later re-issued on a tape cassette by Israel Music (IMC-1016).

Leib Glantz – *Ha'llel Ve'Sha'losh Re'ga'lim*

Eastronics Ltd. (RCA Victor) – tape cassette and LP 33-1/3 RPM

ISK-1018/ISR-1018 – Tel Aviv, Israel – approx. 1970

Bir'kat Ko'ha'nim

A'hav'ti

Av Ha'Ra'cha'mim

She'ma Yis'ra'el

Hash'ki'vei'nu

Mim'kom'cha*

Be'Tzeit Yis'ra'el

Tal

*The rendition of *Mim'kom'cha* was published for the first time on this LP.

Leib Glantz – *Ya'mim No'ra'im*

Eastronics Ltd. (RCA Victor) – tape cassette and LP 33-1/3 RPM

ISK-1020/ISR-1020 – Tel Aviv, Israel – approx. 1970

Le'chu Ne'ra'ne'na

Mach'ni'sei Ra'cha'mim

Le'Da'vid Miz'mor

Ki Ke'Shim'cha (E'met Ki A'ta Hu Yotz'ram)

Ha'loch Ve'Ka'ra'ta

Ki Hi'ne Ka'Cho'mer

Te'vi'e'nu

This LP/tape cassette is a reproduction of earlier LP recordings.

The Best Cantorial Works of Cantor Leib Glantz

Greater Recording Company, Inc., – tape cassette / LP 33-1/3 RPM

GRC-242 / LP: AAB-1117 & tape cassette: AAB-1118 – Brooklyn, N.Y. – (tape 1973, LP 1972).

She'ma Yis'ra'el

Tal

Kol A'do'nai

Ein Ke'Er'ke'cha

Av Ha'Ra'cha'mim

Le'chu Ne'ra'ne'na

Bir'kat Ko'ha'nim

Sho'mer Yis'ra'el

This LP/tape is a re-issue of RCA recordings.

Concert of Synagogue Music – Cantor Leib Glantz (1898-1964)

Musique Internationale – tape cassette

CM 513 – Chicago, 1988.

A'ni Ma'a'min (1)

Shir Miz'mor Le'A'saf (1)

El Ma'leh Ra'cha'mim (1)

Ka'ddish (1)

Mach'ni'sei Ra'cha'mim (2)

Re'tze (Composed by Yitzchak Schlossberg) *(3)*

Tzur Cha'yei'nu (3)

Ve'Al Ku'lam (3)

Sim Sha'lom (3)

(1) Recorded by Kol Yisrael in 1958.
(2) Recorded by Kol Yisrael at a concert in 1958.
(3) Recorded by Kol Yisrael at a Concert on August 19, 1952. Conductor: Israel Fuchs. Accompanied by the choir of the Great Synagogue of Tel Aviv. Pianist: Aryeh Graff.

Songs Sacred & Secular – Hebrew Spirituals/Hassidic Ecstacy

Musique Internationale – tape cassette

CM 514 – Chicago, 1989.

A'cha'rei Mo'ti (1) – (lyrics: Chaim Nachman Bialik)

D'voi're'le (1) – (lyrics: Zalman Shazar)

A Din Toi're Mit Got (Ka'ddish) (2) – (lyrics: Reb Levi Yitzchak Berdichever)

A'da'rim (3) – (Asaf Halevi, Shlomo Weisfish, Julius Chajes)

Ma'tai? (3)

Hash'ki'vei'nu (3)

Sim Sha'lom (3)

U'Ve'Yom Ha'Sha'bbat (4)

Kad'shei'nu (4)

D'ror Yik'ra (4)

Ash'rei'nu (4)

Ri'bon Ha'O'la'mim (4)

Al Tiz'kor (4)

A'ta Yo'de'a (4)

Nach'pe'sa (4)

Recordings from 1931 to 1947. Piano accompaniments by Nachum Nardi, Solomon Braslavsky and Abe Ellstein.
(1) Re-issued from RCA recordings.
(2) Never released "off-take" from Asch recordings.
(3) Re-issued from Asch Recordings.
(4) Re-issued from the album "Hebrew Spirituals/ Hassidic Ecstasy."

Prayer and Song – *Shi'ra U'Te'fi'la* – Cantor Leib Glantz

Musique Internationale – tape cassette

CM 515 – Chicago, 1992.

Mach'ni'sei Ra'cha'mim (1)

Ez'ke'ra E'lo'kim (1)

Az Be'Kol (1)

Ich Bin A Yis'ro'el (lyrics: Efraim Auerbach) *(2)*

Ho'ra (2)

Hi'nei Bor'chu – (lyrics: Julius Chajes) *(2)*

A Din Toi're Mit Got (Berdichever Ka'ddish) (2)

Kol Me'ka'desh (3)

Bor'chu (4)

She'ma (4)

A'do'nai Ze'cha'ra'nu (4)

Da'yei'nu (4)

U'Ve'Nu'cho Yo'mar (4)

Chad Gad'ya (4)

She'va Pe'a'mim "Ata" (5)

(1) Re-issue of "The Album of Cantorial Chants."
(2) "Off-takes" from the Asch Recordings.
(3) Re-issue from the album "*O'neg Sha'bbat.*"
(4) Passover Program for CBS radio, with the Sinai Temple Choir (organ: Lillian Klass).
(5) Re-issue from the LP "*Tif'e'ret Te'fi'la.*"

High Holiday Moods – Cantor Leib Glantz

Musique Internationale – tape cassette

CM 516 – Chicago, 1994.

Ash'rei (1)

A'ta Po'rar'ta (1)

A'sher Be'Ya'do (1)

Zo'cha'lim Ve'Ro'a'dim (1)

P'ne Na (1)

Re'tze A'ti'ra'tam (1)

Al Tash'li'chei'nu Mil'fa'ne'cha (1)

Al Tash'li'chei'nu Le'Et Zik'na (1)

Le'Da'vid Miz'mor (2)

Me'loch (3)

(1) Highlights from the live *Se'li'chot* Service of 1958 in Tel Aviv.
(2) Private recording of the composition published in the album *Shir Cha'dash* at a concert in Israel.
(3) Private recording of Zeidel Rovner's composition at a concert in Israel.

Golden Voices of Israel: *Ko'lot Ha'Za'hav Shel Yis'ra'el*

Israel Music – Compact Disk

ICD 5004 – Neve Monoson, Israel. 1989

She'ma Yis'ra'el

Tal

Golden Voices of Israel: Songs and Prayers for Sabbath

Israel Music – compact disk

ICD 5010 – Tel Aviv, Israel. 1993.

Le'cha Do'di

D'ror Yik'ra

Golden Voices of Israel: The High Holidays – *Miv'char Te'fi'lot La'Ya'mim Ha'No'ra'im*

Israel Music – compact disk

IM CD 31473 – Neve Monoson, Israel, 1994.

Mach'ni'sei Ra'cha'mim

Mysteries of The Sabbath – Classic Cantorial Recordings: 1907-47

Yazoo Records – compact disk

Yazoo 7002 – LC 5762 – New Jersey, USA, 1994

She'ma Yis'ra'el

Pearls of Jewish Liturgical Music – Cantor Leib Glantz

Israel Music – compact disk

ICD-5027 – Israel, 1995

Hash'ki'vei'nu

Mim'kom'cha

Bir'kat Ko'ha'nim

Sim Sha'lom

Be'Tzeit Yis'ra'el

A'hav'ti

Av Ha'Ra'cha'mim

Tal

She'ma Yis'ra'el

Le'chu Ne'ra'ne'na

Mach'ni'sei Ra'cha'mim

Ki Ke'Shim'cha (E'met Ki A'ta Hu Yotz'ram)

Ki Hi'ne Ka'Cho'mer

This CD is a reissue of previous existing commercial recordings.

The Promised Land – *Om'rim Yesh'na E'retz*

Israel Music – tape cassette/CD

IMC 1511/ICD 7005 – Tel Aviv, Israel, 1995.

Om'rim Yesh'na E'retz – (lyrics: Saul Tchernichovsky) *(1)*

Sho'sha'na – (lyrics: Saul Tchernichovsky) (1)

A'cha'rei Mo'ti – (lyrics: Chaim Nachman Bialik) (2)

Al Ha'She'chi'ta – (lyrics: Chaim Nachman Bialik) (1)

A'da'rim (Asaf Halevi, Shlomo Weisfish, Julius Chajes) (3)

(1) Re-issue from "*Cha'zon V'Shi'rah.*"
(2) Re-issue from the RCA recording.
(3) Re-issue from Asch recording.

She'ma Yis'ra'el: **Cantor Leib Glantz – Original Recordings**

I.M.C. – Israel Music International – tape cassette

MC-118 – Bnei Brak, Israel, 1995.

Ez'ke'ra E'lo'kim

Be'Shuv Ha'Shem

She'ma Yis'ra'el

Bir'kat Ko'ha'nim

A'na Be'Cho'ach

Ve'Te'che'ze'na Ei'nei'nu

Le'chu Ne'ra'ne'na

Sho'mer Yis'ra'el

D'ror Yik'ra

Original recordings on reel tape, filtered and technically improved by Dr. Mordechai Sobol at I.M.C., Bnei Brak.

Yor'zeit – Yiz'kor

Israel Music – compact disk

ICD 5038 – Tel Aviv, Israel, 1996.

E'met Ki A'ta Hu Yotz'ram (Ki Ke'Shim'cha)

Songs from The Book of Psalms – *Shi'rim Mi'toch Te'hi'lim*

Israel Music – compact disk

ICD 5048 – Tel Aviv, Israel. 1998.

Be'Shuv Ha'Shem

Prayers from The Book of Psalms – *Te'fi'lot Mi'Toch Te'hi'lim*

Israel Music – compact disk

ICD 5049 – Tel Aviv, Israel, 1998.

A'hav'ti

She'ma Yis'ra'el – **The Cantorial Project**

Israel Music – compact disk

ICD-4001, Tel Aviv, Israel. 1998.

She'ma Yis'ra'el

In this compact disk, Arik Rudich combines Cantor Leib Glantz's voice singing Glantz's composition "*She'ma Yis'ra'el,*" with his own electronic music, thus creating a very modern version of this prayer.

Leil Shi'mu'rim – **A Collection Of Prayers for Passover and *Se'fi'rat Ha'O'mer***

Israel Music – compact disk

ICD 5089 – Neve Monoson, Israel, 2001.

Tal

Be'Tzeit Yis'ra'el

Midnight Selichot Service

(Israel Music – compact disk)

ICD 5095 – Neve Monoson, Israel, 2001.

Introduction and *Ash'rei*

Te'hi'la Le'David

Ka'ddish

Le'cha Sha'ma'yim

Le'chu Ne'ra'ne'na

A'sher Be'yado

Eich Nif'tach Peh

El E'rech A'pa'yim

Ta'a'vor Al Pe'sha

Be'Mo'tza'ei Me'nu'cha

Zo'cha'lim Ve'Ro'a'dim

Yot'zer A'ta

Ma'rom

P'ne Na

Re'tze A'ti'ra'tam

Hi'ma'tze La'nu

Te'vi'ei'nu

She'ma Ko'lei'nu

Ha'shi'vei'nu

Al Tash'li'chei'nu Mil'fa'ne'cha

Al Tash'li'chei'nu Le'Et Zik'na

Mach'ni'sei Ra'cha'mim

This CD is a re-mastered and edited version of the original 1963 "Famous Records" LP, executed by Mordechai Sobol of I.M.C. (International Music Company), Bnei Brak, Israel. Eventually it was issued by Israel Music in Tel Aviv in 2001.

Gems of the Synagogue – Rare Cantorial Treasures – *A'shi'ra Na Le'Ye'di'dai*

Israel Music – compact disk

ICD – 5117 – Tel Aviv, 2004
Edited by Akiva Zimmerman.

Az Be'Kol (Ra'ash Ga'dol)

The Glory of Sabbath – Songs and Prayers

Israel Music – compact disk

ICD 5132 – Tel Aviv, Israel, 2005.

U'Ve'Yom Ha'Sha'bbat

In Those Days At This Time – *Ba'Ya'mim Ha'Hem Ba'Zman Ha'Zeh* (2)

IMC – International Music Company (Israel) – compact disk

MCD-222 – Bnei Brak, Israel, 2006.

Bir'kat Ko'ha'nim

Arranged and conducted by Dr. Mordechai Sobol, the Cantors Choir and the S.F.Y. Philharmonic Orchestra present a new accompaniment. In this recording, Leib Glantz's voice, singing the original 1930 RCA recording of *Bir'kat Ko'ha'nim*, was technically "cleared" of its original organ accompaniment, and a new accompaniment of 50 male voices of "The Cantors Choir" and the "S.F.Y. Philharmonic Orchestra" were added.

Ein Ke'Er'ke'cha

Noam Productions (*Noam Hafakot*) – compact disk

CDH-261 – Jerusalem, Israel. 2006. Edited by Akiva Zimmerman.

Ein Ke'Er'ke'cha (1)

Sho'mer Yis'ra'el (1)

Ba'rech A'lei'nu (2)

Te'ka Be'Sho'far (2)

Tzur Cha'yei'nu; Ve'Chol Ha'Cha'yim (3)

Ma'a'riv weekday service (Nu'sach Cha'nu'ka) (4)

Hash'ki'vei'nu weekday service (Nu'sach Cha'nu'ka) (4)

A'kav'ya Ben Ma'ha'la'lel O'mer (5)

Hu Yif'tach Li'bei'nu (4)

A Din Toi're Mit Got (Berdichever Ka'ddish) (4)

Yiz'kor (El Ma'lleh Ra'cha'mim) (In memory of the victims of the Holocaust) (6)

Ha'loch Ve'Ka'ra'ta (7)

Be'Shuv Ha'shem (8)

Ta'not Tza'rot Lo Nu'chal (Composed by Pinchas Minkowsky) *(9)*

Mi She'A'sa Ni'ssim (9)

(1) Re-issued from original RCA recordings.
(2) Kol Yisrael radio recording of excerpts of a special *Min'cha* prayer service in honor of Zvi Pinkas, on August 20th, 1952, at the Tel Aviv Synagogue "Beth El." Choir conducted by Israel Fuchs.
(3) Kol Yisrael radio recording of a concert on August 19th, 1952. Choir of "Beth El" Synagogue, conducted by Israel Fuchs. Pianist: Aryeh Graff.
(4) Kol Yisrael radio recording of a live *Cha'nu'ka Ma'ariv* prayer service and concert on December 22th, 1954 at the Tiferet Zvi Synagogue in Tel Aviv. Choir conducted by Schlomo Goldhour.
(5) Recorded at the funeral of Knesset chairman Yosef Sprinzak (January 1959).
(6) Recorded Live in Tel Aviv.
(7) Re-issued from the LP "*Tif'e'ret Te'fi'lah.*"
(8) Re-issued from the LP "*Cha'zon V'Shi'rah.*"
(9) Kol Yisrael radio recording – examples from a lecture given by Leib Glantz in 1962.

The Complete Cantorial Collection – *Mei'tav Pir'kei Ha'Cha'za'nut*

Israel Music – set of three compact disks

ICD-9002/1, ICD-9002/2, ICD-9002/3 – Tel Aviv, Israel, 2006.

She'ma Yis'ra'el

Tal

Mach'ni'sei Ra'cha'mim

Le'cha Do'di

D'ror Yik'ra

Great Voices of The Century – Cantorial Gems (Volume 3)

Period Records/Everest Records Production – LP 33-1/3 RPM VV-30542 – SC 860 B – New York, NY

Av Ha'Ra'cha'mim

The Man Who Spoke To God

Two compact disks attached to the book
"The Man Who Spoke To God"

Non commercial – 2008

<u>CD 1</u>:

She'ma Yis'ra'el

Te'fi'lat Tal

Kol A'do'nai

Bir'kat Ko'ha'nim

Ein Ke'Er'ke'cha

Ki Hi'ne Ka'Cho'mer

Sho'mer Yis'ra'el

Ez'ke'ra E'lo'kim

She'va Pe'a'mim "A'ta"

Ha'loch Ve'Ka'rata

A'hav'ti

Be'tzeit Yis'ra'el

Ma'oz Tsur*

<u>CD 2</u>:

A'na Be'Cho'ach*

U'Ve'Nu'cho Yo'mar*

Le'chu Ne'ra'ne'na

Eich Nif'tach Peh

Be'Mo'tza'ei Me'nu'cha

Zo'cha'lim Ve'Ro'a'dim

Yo'tzer A'ta

Ma'rom

P'ne Na

Re'tze A'ti'ra'tam

Te'vi'ei'nu

She'ma Ko'lei'nu

Mach'ni'sei Ra'cha'mim

Kol Me'ka'desh

D'ror Yik'ra

D'voi're'le

A'cha'rei Mo'ti

* Private non-commercial recordings.

*This Discography was compiled with the
kind assistance of Noam Brown.*

List of Compositions by Leib Glantz

Friday Night Prayer Service

1. *Le'chu Ne'ra'ne'na* (version 1)
2. *Le'chu Ne'ra'ne'na* (version 2)
3. *Le'chu Ne'ra'ne'na* (version 3)
4. *Le'chu Ne'ra'ne'na* (version 4 – Tel Aviv, 1956)
5. *Miz'mor Shir* (congregation)
6. *Ha'vu La'A'do'nai* (Tel Aviv, 1956)
7. *A'na Be'Cho'ach* (Tel Aviv, 1955)
8. *Le'cha Do'di* (Version 1 – Los Angeles, 1941)
9. *Le'cha Do'di* (Version 2 – Tel Aviv, 1956)
10. *A'do'nai Ma'lach Gei'ut La'veish* (Tel Aviv, 1957)
11. *Ra'za De'Sha'bbat* (Los Angeles, 1943)
12. *Ba're'chu* (version 1 – Los Angeles, 1946)
13. *Ba're'chu* (version 2 – Tel Aviv, 1956)
14. *A'ha'vat O'lam* (Tel Aviv, 1956)
15. *She'ma Yis'ra'el* (version 1 – Los Angeles, 1942)
16. *She'ma Yis'ra'el* (version 2 – Los Angeles, 1943)
17. *She'ma Yis'ra'el* (version 3 – Tel Aviv, 1956)
18. *She'ma Yis'ra'el* (version 4 – Tel Aviv, 1957)
19. *E'met Ve'E'mu'na* (Tel Aviv, 1963)
20. *Mi Cha'mo'cha* (version 1 – Los Angeles, 1942)
21. *Mi Cha'mo'cha* (version 2 [w/children solo] – Tel Aviv)
22. *Hash'ki'vei'nu*
23. *Ve'Sham'ru* (Tel Aviv, 1958)
24. *Ma'gen A'vot*

25. *A'mar Ra'bbi E'la'zar* (Los Angeles, 1943)
26. *A'don O'lam* (version 1 – Tel Aviv, 1955)
27. *A'don O'lam* (version 2 – Tel Aviv, 1958)
28. *Yig'dal E'lo'him Chai* (Los Angeles, 1944)
29. *Kol Me'ka'desh She'vi'i* (*Ze'mi'rot Le'Sha'bbat,* Los Angeles, 1947)

Sabbath *Shach'rit* Prayer Service

30. *Ein Ke'Er'ke'cha* (New York, 1938)
31. *El A'don* (version 1 – Congregation singing (Los Angeles, 1941)
32. *El A'don* (version 2)
33. *El A'don* (version 3)
34. *Ve'Chu'lam Me'kab'lim A'lei'hem* (Tel Aviv, 1960)
35. *Et Shem; Ka'dosh; Ba'ruch* (version 1)
36. *Et Shem; Ka'dosh; Ba'ruch* (version 2)
37. *Ha'Me'cha'desh Be'Tu'vo* (Tel Aviv, 1961)
38. *Mi Cha'mo'cha* (version 1)
39. *Mi Cha'mo'cha* (version 2)
40. *Az Be'Kol* (version 1 – New York, 1940)
41. *Az Be'Kol* (version 2)
42. *Yis'mach Mo'she* (Los Angeles, 1953)
43. *Ve'Lo Ne'ta'to* (New York, 1952)
44. *B'rich Sh'mei* (version 1 – Los Angeles, 1952)
45. *B'rich Sh'mei* (version 2 – Tel Aviv, 1958)
46. *Ve'No'mar Le'fa'nav* (New York, 1938)
47. *Av Ha'Ra'cha'mim Am A'mu'sim* (New York, 1938)

Sabbath *Mu'saf* Prayer Service

48. *Mi She'A'sa Ni'ssim* (Tel Aviv, 1962)
49. *Ha'Ne'e'ha'vim Ve'Ha'Ne'ïmim (Haz'ka'rat Ne'sha'mot)* (NY, 1940)
50. *U'Ve'Nu'cho Yo'mar* (Los Angeles, 1944)
51. *Cha'tzi Ka'ddish* (unfinished, Tel Aviv, Jan. 17, 1964)
52. *She'ma Yis'ra'el* (from *Ke'du'shat Ke'ter*, NY, 1930)
53. *Do'di Ze'chor Li* (*Pa'ra'shat She'ka'lim*, Tel Aviv, 1958)
54. *Ti'kan'ta Sha'bbat* (Tel Aviv)
55. *U'Ve'Yom Ha'Sha'bbat; Yis'me'chu* (Los Angeles, 1949)
56. *T'zur Cha'yei'nu* (Congregation, Los Angeles, 1945)
57. *Ve'Al Ku'lam; Ve'Chol Ha'Cha'yim* (Congregation, Los Angeles, 1943)
58. *Bir'kat Ko'ha'nim* (New York, 1930)
59. *Sim Sha'lom* (Los Angeles, 1944)
60. *Ein Ke'E'lo'hei'nu* (Tel Aviv, 1954)
61. *A'lei'nu Le'Sha'bei'ach* (Tel Aviv, 1955)

The Three Festivals Prayer Services

62. *Va'Ye'da'ber Mo'she* (*Ar'vit*, Tel Aviv, 1957)
63. *Re'bo'no Shel O'lam* (*Se'fi'rat Ha'O'mer*, Tel Aviv, 1955)
64. *Ki'ddush Le'Sha'losh Re'ga'lim* (Tel Aviv, 1960)
65. *A'ta Ve'char'ta'nu* (*Shach'rit*, Los Angeles, 1953)
66. *Ya'a'le* (*Shach'rit*, Los Angeles, 1953)
67. *Ha'lle'lu'ya Ha'lle'lu* (*Ha'llel*, Tel Aviv, 1956)
68. *Be'Tzeit Yis'ra'el* (*Ha'llel*, Tel Aviv, 1955)
69. *A'do'nai Ze'cha'ra'nu* (*Ha'llel*, Los Angeles, 1944)

70. *A'hav'ti Ki Yish'ma A'do'nai* (*Ha'llel*, Tel Aviv, 1956)
71. *Ha'lle'lu Et A'do'nai* (*Ha'llel*, Los Angeles, 1951)
72. *Ho'du La'A'do'nai; A'na A'do'nai* (*Ha'llel*, Tel Aviv)
73. *Pit'chu Li* (Los Angeles, 1951)
74. *Ho'Sha'na Le'Ha'ka'fot* (Los Angeles)
75. *Va'Ye'hi Bi'Ne'soa Ha'A'ron* (Los Angeles, 1943)
76. *A'do'nai, A'do'nai, El Cha'nun Ve'Ra'chum* (Los Angeles, 1952)
77. *She'ma Yis'ra'el* (for *Sha'vu'ot*, Los Angeles)
78. *Te'fi'lat Tal; Te'fi'lat Ge'shem* (New York, 1929-30)

Passover *Se'dder* (*Ha'gga'da*)

79. *Ve'Hi She'Am'da La'A'vo'tei'nu* (Tel Aviv, 1958)
80. *Sh'foch Cha'mat'cha* (Tel Aviv, 1958)
81. *U'Ve'Chen Va'Ye'hi Ba'Cha'tzi Ha'Ly'la* (Tel Aviv)
82. *Ki Lo Na'eh* (Tel Aviv)
83. *Cha'sal Si'dur Pe'ssach* (Tel Aviv)
84. *A'dir Hu* (Tel Aviv)
85. *E'chad Mi Yo'de'a*
86. *Chad Gad'ya*

Se'li'chot* Midnight Prayer Service

87. The opening melody (introduction) of the *Se'li'chot* service
88. *Ash'rei*
89. *Te'hi'la Le'Da'vid* (Tel Aviv, 1960)
90. *Cha'nun Ve'Ra'chum* (Tel Aviv, 1957)
91. *Le'ho'di'a* (Tel Aviv, 1957)
92. *Le'chu Ne'ra'ne'na* (version 1 – Los Angeles, 1944)
93. *Le'chu Ne'ra'ne'na* (version 2 – piano, Los Angeles, 1945)
94. *Eich Nif'tach Peh* (Tel Aviv)

95. *El E'rech A'pa'yim; Ta'a'vor Al Pe'sha* (Tel Aviv, 1961)

96. *Be'Mo'tza'ei Me'nu'cha* (Los Angeles, 1952)

97. *Zo'cha'lim Ve'Ro'a'dim* (Los Angeles)

98. *Yo'tzer A'ta* (Los Angeles)

99. *Ma'rom Im Atzimo*

100. *P'ne Na*

101. *Re'tze A'ti'ra'tam*

102. *Lish'mo'a El Ha'Ri'na*

103. *El Me'lech Yo'shev* (Tel Aviv, 1959)

104. *Hi'ma'tze La'nu*

105. *Te'vi'ei'nu*

106. *She'ma Ko'lei'nu* (Tel Aviv, 1959)

107. *Ha'shi'vei'nu* (Tel Aviv, 1959)

108. *Al Tash'li'chei'nu Mil'fa'ne'cha* (Tel Aviv, 1959)

109. *Al Tash'li'chei'nu Le'Et Zik'na* (Tel Aviv, 1959)

110. *Mach'ni'sei Ra'cha'mim* (piano accompaniment, New York, 1940)

111. *Mach'ni'sei Ra'cha'mim* (choir accompaniment, Tel Aviv, 1958)

Rosh Ha'Sha'na Prayer Services

112. *Tik'u Va'Cho'desh Sho'far (Ar'vit)* (Tel Aviv, 1956)

113. *Le'Da'vid Mizmor (Ar'vit)* (New York, 1951)

114. *Hi'ne'ni He'A'ni Mi'Ma'as (Mu'saf)*

115. *U'Ne'ta'neh To'kef* (Tel Aviv, 1957)

116. *E'met Ki A'ta Hu Da'yan; U'Ve'Sho'far Ga'dol* (Tel Aviv, 1961)

117. *Be'Rosh Ha'Sha'na* (version 1, Los Angeles, 1944)

118. *Be'Rosh Ha'Sha'na* (version 2, Tel Aviv)

119. *U'Te'shu'va U'Te'fi'la U'Tze'da'ka* (Los Angeles, 1944)

120. *Ki Ke'Shim'cha: E'met Ki A'ta Hu Yotz'ram* (New York, 1929)

121. *U'Ve'Chen Ten Ka'vod* (on board a ship to Israel, 1954)

122. *U'Ve'Chen Tza'di'kim*

123. *U'Mi'pnei Cha'ta'ei'nu*

124. *Ve'Ka'rev Pe'zu'rei'nu; Va'Ha'vi'ei'nu* (Tel Aviv, 1957)

125. *Me'loch* (Tel Aviv, 1960)

126. *Ha'loch Ve'Ka'ra'ta* (Los Angeles, 1949)

127. *Ve'Te'ra'eh Le'fa'ne'cha*

128. *A're'shet Se'fa'tei'nu* (Jerusalem, 1961)

129. *Ha'lle'lu'ya* , Psalms 150 (Tel Aviv, 1957)

130. *Te'ka Be'Sho'far Ga'dol*

Yom Ki'ppur Prayer Services

131. *Ki Va'Yom Ha'Zeh* (*Ar'vit*, Tel Aviv, 1957)

132. *Ya'a'le Ta'cha'nu'nei'nu* (*Ar'vit*, Los Angeles, 1950)

133. *S'lach Na A'sha'mot* (*Ar'vit*)

134. *Ze'chut Ez'rach; Sa'lach'ti* (*Ar'vit*)

135. *Ki Hi'nei Ka'Cho'mer* (*Ar'vit*, New York, 1929)

136. *Al Cheit She'Cha'ta'nu* (*Ar'vit*, Tel Aviv, 1955)

137. *Ve'Al Ku'lam E'lo'ha Se'li'chot* (*Ar'vit*, Los Angeles, 1951)

138. *Hi'ne'ni He'A'ni Mi'Ma'as* (*Mu'saf*, Los Angeles, 1950)

139. *Ve'Chach Ha'ya Mo'neh* (*Mu'saf*, Los Angeles, 1941)

140. *Ez'ke'ra E'lo'kim Ve'E'he'ma'ya* (*Ne'i'la*, New York, 1940)

Miscellaneous Prayers

141. *Yir'uh Ei'nei'nu* (*Ar'vit La'chol*, Tel Aviv, 1955)

142. *Ha'lle'lu'ya, Shi'ru La'A'do'nai Shir Cha'dash* – Psalms 149, (*Shach'rit*, concert)

143. *Ha'beit Mi'Sha'ma'yim* (*Shach'rit,* Los Angeles, 1948)
144. *Sho'mer Yis'ra'el* (*Shach'rit,* New York, 1933)
145. *Va'A'nach'nu Lo Nei'da* (*Shach'rit*)
146. *Mi Ke'Am'cha* (Tel Aviv, 1961)
147. *Al Ti'ra Mi'Pa'chad Pit'om* (*Mishlei,* Tel Aviv, 1959)
148. *La'Me'na'tzei'ach LiV'nei Ko'rach* – Psalms 85 (concert, Tel Aviv, 1961)
149. *She'va Pe'a'mim A'ta* (concert, New York)
150. *Miz'mor Le'Da'vid* (*Haz'ka'rat Ne'sha'mot*) (Tel Aviv, 1960)
151. *El Ma'leh Ra'cha'mim* (*Haz'ka'rat Ne'sha'mot*) (Los Angeles, 1946)
152. *Miz'mor Shir Cha'nu'kat Ha'Ba'yit* – Psalms 30 (Tel Aviv, 1957)
153. *Ma'oz Tzur* (Chanuka, Tel Aviv, 1956)
154. *Al Ha'Ni'ssim* (Chanuka)
155. *She'ma* and *Bar'chu* (Purim)
156. *Yir'uh Ei'nei'nu* (Purim, Tel Aviv, 1954)
157. *Sho'sha'nat Ya'a'kov* (Purim)
158. *Te'kes Ni'su'im* (Wedding Ceremony)

Chasidic Melodies (*Ni'ggu'nim*)

159. *D'ror Yik'ra* (Talner, Los Angeles, 1948)
160. *E'shet Cha'il* (Talner, Tel Aviv, 1954)
161. *Hu Yif'tach Li'bei'nu* (Talner)
162. *Le'cha Do'di* (Yemenite, Tel Aviv, 1956)
163. *Tit'ga'dal Ve'Tit'ka'dash* (Brazlaver, Tel Aviv, 1955)
164. *Le'Dor Va'Dor* (Brazlaver, Los Angeles, 1952)
165. *E'lo'kei'nu Ka'de'shei'nu* (Brazlaver, Los Angeles, 1948)

166. *Re'eh Na Be'On'yei'nu* (Brazlaver, Tel Aviv, 1961)
167. *Ash'rei'nu* (Israeli, Los Angeles)
168. *A'ta Yo'dei'a* (Chabad, Los Angeles, 1948)
169. *Al Tiz'kor* (Chabad, Los Angeles, 1948)
170. *Nach'pe'sa* (Chabad, Los Angeles)
171. *E'li'ya'hu* (Chabad, Tel Aviv, 1962)
172. *Ri'bon Ha'O'la'mim – Ni'ggun Ha'Ba'al Shem Tov,* (Los Angeles, 1948)
173. *Ma'tai?* (Los Angeles, 1944)

Hebrew Songs

174. *A'cha'rei Mo'ti* (Lyrics: Chaim Nachman Bialik, Kishinev, Besarabia, 1923)
175. *Yam Ha'D'ma'ma* (Bialik, Kishinev, Besarabia, 1923)
176. *Al Ha'Schi'ta* (Bialik, Los Angeles, 1943)
177. *Za'ri'ti La'Ru'ach An'cha'ti* (Bialik, Kishinev, Besarabia, 1923)
178. *K'vish* (Zalman Schneur, Los Angeles)
179. *Yod'li, Yod'li* (Zalman Schneur, Los Angeles)
180. *Om'rim Yesh'na E'retz* (Saul Tchernichovsky, Kishinev, Besarabia, 1924)
181. *Sho'sha'na* (Saul Tchernichovsky, Los Angeles, 1951)
182. *Nit'shu Z'la'lim* (Saul Tchernichovsky)
183. *Kol Dich'fin* (Saul Tchernichovsky)
184. *Om'rim Li Ei'nech Ya'fa* (Yaakov Rimon, Kishinev, Besarabia, 1925)
185. *Mi A'ni?* (Yaakov Fichman, Kishinev, Besarabia, 1925)

186. *Al Re'im She'Hal'chu* (Yaakov Fichman, Tel Aviv, 1957)
187. *Ge'shem Ly'la* (Yaakov Fichman, Tel Aviv, 1958)
188. *La'Me'na'tzei'ach Mis'ped* (Zalman Shazar, Tel Aviv, 1956)
189. *Od Be'Gan E'den* (Yaakov Cohen, Tel Aviv, 1960)
190. *Al Se'fod (Ha'Ne'e'ha'vim)* (David Shimoni, New York, 1940)
191. *Ron Le'va'vi* (Bracha Kopstein, Tel Aviv, 1960)
192. *He'ma Ka're'u Ve'Na'fa'lu – Shir Le'Za'hal* (Tel Aviv, 1957)
193. *Be'Shuv A'do'nai Et Shi'vat T'zi'on* – Psalms 126 (New York, 1940)
194. *Ve'Te'che'ze'na (Shir He'A'sor Le'Yis'ra'el)* (Tel Aviv, 1958)
195. *Le'D'gan'ya Shir Miz'mor* (Oded Avisar, Tel Aviv, 1960)
196. *Ze'mer Shir La'Ki'nnus Ha'Shvi'i (Kin'nus Ha'Po'el)* (Yossi Gamzu, Tel Aviv, 1960)
197. *Be'Ar'tzei'nu Or Va'Ziv* (Tel Aviv, 1954)
198. *Ha'Zor'im Be'Dim'ah* – Psalms 126 (Tel Aviv)
199. *U'tzu Ei'tza* (Tel Aviv, 1957)
200. *A'ni Le'Do'di (Shir Ha'Shi'rim 7, Tel Aviv)
201. *Kol Do'di He'nei Zeh Ba (Shir Ha'Shi'rim 8,* Tel Aviv, 1960)
202. *A'na Ha'lach Do'dech; Yo'mam Ha'She'mesh Lo Yich'beh* (Unfinished, January 14, 1964)

Yiddish Songs

203. *Dos Tze'bro'che'nor De'cha'le* – The Broken Roof (Zalman Rosental, Kishinev, Besarabia, 1924)

204. *S'is a Frest* – There is a Frost (Zalman Rosental, Kishinev, Besarabia, 1923)
205. *Bai Dem Shtetl Shteit A Shtibel* – Near the Town Stands a *Shtibel* (Zalman Rosental, Kishinev, Besarabia, 1924)
206. *Got Fun Av'ro'hom* – God of Abraham (Efraim Orbach, New York, 1940)
207. *Ich Bin A Yis'ro'el* – I Am A Jew (Efraim Orbach, New York, 1940)
208. *Hey Trai'ger* – Hey Porter (Y. Karni, Tel Aviv, 1949)
209. *Kie'ler Shti'ller O'vent Vint* – Quiet Evening Wind (Yaakov Fichman, Kishinev, Besarabia, 1925)
210. *Kab'tzo'ni'sher Ha'Mav'dil* – A Poor Man's *Hav'da'la*
211. *Schlof Mein Kind* – Sleep my child (Shalom Aleichem, Kishinev, Besarabia, 1923)
212. *Mir Ve'len Zein* – We Will Be (Yaakov Marinov, New York, 1938)
213. *Got Is Rhuh* – God Is Resting (H. Levik, Los Angeles, 1954)
214. *Af Bri* – A Prayer for Rain
215. *Ich Gib Dir Got* – I Give You God (Yehoash, Los Angeles, 1952)
216. *D'voi're'le* – a Chasidic love song about Devora (Zalman Shazar, Los Angeles)

This List of Compositions was compiled with the kind assistance of Noam Brown.

Other Leib Glantz Books

"Zeharim — In Memory of Leib Glantz"

[Hebrew and Yiddish]
Edited by Eliezer Steinman; prepared for publication by David Vinitzky.
Published by the Tel Aviv Institute of Jewish Liturgical Music, Tel Aviv, 1965.

Leib Glantz's Selected Works — "Rinat Hakodesh Series"

[English and Hebrew]
Edited by David Loeb; prepared for publication by Yehoshua Zohar.
Published by the Tel Aviv Institute of Jewish Liturgical Music in conjunction with the Israel
Music Institute (I.M.I.), Tel Aviv, Israel:

Volume 1: *Nu'sa'chei Te'fi'la* (Prayer modes for solo cantor).

Volume 2: *Te'fi'lot Leil Sha'bbat* (Friday Evening Service).

Volume 3: *Te'fi'lot Sha'bbat* (Sabbath Morning Service).

Volume 4: *Ha'llel Ve'Sha'losh Re'ga'lim* (Hallel and Three Festivals).

Volume 5: *Se'li'chot* (Penitential prayers).

Volume 6: *Ya'mim No'ra'im* (High Holidays).

Volume 7: *Shi'rim* (Songs).

S'lichot Service for Cantor, Chorus and Organ, by Leib Glantz

Edited by David Loeb.
Published by the Hallel V'Zimra Association, Montreal, Quebec, Canada, 1965.

Books can be ordered online at: www.TheManWhoSpokeToGod.com

Contents and Duration of the Two Compact Disks Accompanying This Book

CD 1: Composed & Sung by LEIB GLANTZ

Minutes:Seconds

1.	*She'ma Yis'ra'el*	(Hear O Israel)	4:05
2.	*Te'fi'lat Tal*	(Prayer for dew)	4:35
3.	*Kol A'do'nai*	(The voice of the Lord)	3:57
4.	*Bir'kat Ko'ha'nim*	(The Priestly Blessing)	4:06
5.	*Ein Ke'Er'ke'cha*	(There is no comparison to You)	3:54
6.	*Ki Hi'nei Ka'Cho'mer*	(As clay we are in the hands of the potter)	4:17
7.	*Sho'mer Yis'ra'el*	(Guardian of Israel)	4:37
8.	*Ez'ke'ra E'lo'kim*	(I remember, O God)	5:53
9.	*She'va Pe'a'mim "A'ta"*	(Seven times "Thou")	8:59
10.	*Ha'loch Ve'Ka'ra'ta*	(Go and proclaim to Jerusalem)	11:52
11.	*A'hav'ti*	(I love that the Lord hears my voice)	6:43
12.	*Be'Tzeit Yis'ra'el*	(When Israel exiled from Egypt)	6:22
13.	*Ma'oz Tzur*	(O mighty rock of my salvation)	3:25
		Total time of CD 1:	72:54

CD 2: Composed & Sung by LEIB GLANTZ

Minutes:Seconds

1.	*A'na Be'Cho'ach*	(We implore You)	7:31
2.	*U'Ve'Nu'Cho Yo'mar*	(And when the Ark rested)	7:06
3.	*Le'chu Ne'ra'ne'na*	(Come, let us sing to the Lord)	10:56
4.	*Eich Nif'tach Peh*	(How can we open our mouths?)	4:07
5.	*Be'Mo'tza'ei Me'nu'cha*	(As the day of rest departs)	2:35
6.	*Zo'cha'lim Ve'Ro'a'dim*	(Shuddering and trembling)	2:40
7.	*Yo'tzer A'ta*	(You created every living being)	1:12
8.	*Ma'rom*	(O most high!)	1:58
9.	*P'ne Na*	(O God, consider the suffering)	3:11
10.	*Re'tze A'ti'ra'tam*	(Accept their pleas)	3:39
11.	*Te'vi'ei'nu*	(Bring us to Your Holy Mountain)	6:01

12.	*She'ma Ko'lei'nu*	(Hear our voice)	0:48
13.	*Mach'ni'sei Ra'cha'mim*	(O Angels of mercy)	5:21
14.	*Kol Me'ka'desh*	(Whoever sanctifies the Sabbath)	3:13
15.	*D'ror Yik'ra*	(He will proclaim freedom)	3:20
16.	*D'voi're'le*	(Debora)	4:26
17.	*A'cha'rei Mo'ti*	(After my death)	4:28
		Total time of CD 2:	72:44

The two Leib Glantz compact disks accompanying this book were edited by Noam Brown and technically executed by Ronen Geva at the Eshel Studios in Tel Aviv, Israel.

Hebrew Transliteration and English Translation of the Song Texts of the Two Compact Disks Accompanying the Book

Compact Disk 1

1. She'ma Yis'ra'el

She'ma Yis'ra'el, A'do'nai E'lo'hei'nu, A'do'nai E'chad.
Hu E'lo'hei'nu, Hu A'vi'nu, Hu Mal'kei'nu, Hu Mo'shi'ei'nu,
Ve'Hu Yash'mi'ei'nu Be'Ra'cha'mav Shei'nit Le'Ei'nei Kol Chai,
Li'hi'yot La'chem Le'E'lo'him, A'ni A'do'nai E'lo'hei'chem.

Hear O Israel: the Lord is our God, the Lord is One.
He is our God; He is our Father; He is our King; He is our Savior;
and He will let us hear, in His compassion, for a second time,
in the presence of all the living,
to be a God to you — I am the Lord, your God.

2. Te'fi'lat Tal

Tal Tein Le'Ra'tzot Ar'tzach. Shi'tei'nu Ve'ra'cha Be'Di'tzach.
Rov Da'gan Ve'Ti'rosh Be'Haf'ri'tzach, Ko'meim Ir Ba Chef'tzach. Be'Tal.

Tal Bo Te'va'rech Ma'zon. Be'Mash'ma'nei'nu Al Ye'hi Ra'zon.
A'yu'ma A'sher Hi'sa'ta Ka'Tzon. A'na Ta'fek La Ra'tzon. Be'Tal.

Dew — grant it to favor Your land. Designate us for blessing in Your joy — with an abundance of grain and wine by Your bounty. Re-establish Jerusalem, the city in which You delight – through dew.
Through dew bless our food. In our bounty let there be no scarcity. To the nation that You led like sheep, please fulfill her desire – with dew.

3. Kol A'do'nai

Kol A'do'nai Cho'tzev La'ha'vot Esh.
Kol A'do'nai Ya'chil Mid'bar, Ya'chil A'do'nai Mid'bar Ka'deish.
Kol A'do'nai Ye'cho'lel A'ya'lot Va'Ye'che'sof Ye'a'rot, U'Ve'Hei'cha'lo Ku'lo O'mer Ka'vod.

A'do'nai La'Ma'bul Ya'shav, Va'Yei'shev A'do'nai Me'lech Le'O'lam.
A'do'nai Oz Le'A'mo Yi'ten, A'do'nai Ye'va'rech Et A'mo Va'Sha'lom.

The voice of the Lord strikes flames of fire.
The voice of the Lord causes .the desert to tremble; the Lord shakes the desert of Kadesh.
The voice of the Lord causes the does to calve, and strips the forests bare;
and in His Sanctuary all proclaim His glory.
The Lord sat enthroned at the Flood; the Lord will reign as King forever.
The Lord will give strength to His people; the Lord will bless His people with peace.

4. *Bir'kat Ko'ha'nim*

E'lo'hei'nu Ve'lo'hei A'vo'tei'nu,
Ba're'chei'nu Va'Bra'cha Ha'Me'shu'le'shet
Ba'To'ra Ha'Ke'tu'va Al Ye'dei Mo'she Av'de'cha,
Ha'A'mu'ra Mi'Pi A'ha'ron U'Va'nav,
Ko'ha'nim Am Ke'do'she'cha, Ka'a'mur:
Ye'va're'che'cha A'do'nai Ve'Yish'me're'cha;
Ya'er A'do'nai Pa'nav Ei'le'cha, Vi'chu'ne'ka;
Yi'sa A'do'nai Pa'nav Ei'le'cha, Ve'Ya'sem Le'cha Sha'lom.

Our God and God of our fathers,
bless us with the threefold blessing
written in the Torah by Moses Your servant,
and pronounced by Aaron and his sons
the *Ko'ha'nim* , Your consecrated people, as it is said:
The Lord blesses you and guards you.
The Lord makes His countenance shine upon you and be gracious to you.
The Lord turns His countenance toward you and grants you peace.

5. *Ein Ke'Er'ke'cha*

Ein Ke'Er'ke'cha, Ve'Ein Zu'la'te'cha, E'fes Bil'te'cha, U'Mi Do'meh Lach.
Ein Ke'Er'ke'cha, A'do'nai E'lo'hei'nu Ba'O'lam Ha'zeh,
Ve'Ein Zu'la'te'cha Mal'kei'nu Le'Cha'yei Ha'O'lam Ha'Ba.
E'fes Bil'te'cha Go'a'lei'nu Li'mot Ha'Ma'shi'ach,
Ve'Ein Do'meh Le'cha Mo'shi'ei'nu LiT'chi'yat Ha'Mei'tim.

There is no comparison to You, there is nothing except for You,
and there is nothing without You, for who is like You?
There is no comparison to You Lord, our God, in this world;
and there will be nothing except for You, our King, in the life of the world to come.

There will be nothing without You, our Redeemer in Messianic days;
and there will be none like You, our Savior, at the day of Resuscitation of the Dead.

6. *Ki Hi'nei Ka'Cho'mer*

Ki Hi'nei Ka'Cho'mer Be'Yad Ha'Yo'tzer.
Bir'tzo'to Mar'chiv U'Vir'tzo'to Me'ka'tzer.
Kein A'nach'nu Be'Yad'cha — Che'sed No'tzer.
La'Brit Ha'Beit Ve'Al Tei'fen La'Yei'tzer.

Ki He'nei Ka'E'ven Be'Yad Ha'Me'sa'tet.
Bir'tzo'to O'chez U'Vir'tzo'to Me'cha'tet.
Kein A'nach'nu Be'Yad'cha — Me'cha'yeh U'Me'mo'tet.
La'Brit Ha'Beit Ve'Al Tei'fen La'Yei'tzer.

As clay we are, as soft and yielding clay
That lies between the fingers of the potter.
At his will he moulds it thick or thin,
And forms its shape according to his fancy.
So are we in Thy hand — God of Love;
Thy Covenant recall and show Thy mercy.

As Stone are we — inert, resistless stone
That lies within the fingers of the mason.
At his will he keeps it firm and whole,
Or at his pleasure hews it into fragments.
So are we in Thy hand — God of life;
Thy Covenant recall and show Thy mercy.

7. *Sho'mer Yis'ra'el*

Sho'mer Yis'ra'el, Shmor She'ei'rit Yis'ra'el,
Ve'Al Yo'vad Yis'ra'el — Ha'Om'rim She'ma Yis'ra'el.

Sho'mer Goy E'chad, Shmor She'ei'rit Am E'chad,
Ve'Al Yo'vad Goy E'chad — Ha'Me'ya'cha'dim Shim'cha, A'do'nai E'lo'hei'nu A'do'nai E'chad.

Sho'mer Goy Ka'dosh, Shmor She'ei'rit Am Ka'dosh, Ve'Al Yo'vad Goy Ka'dosh — Ha'Me'shal'shim
Be'Shi'lush Ke'du'sha Le'Ka'dosh.

Mit'ra'tze Be'Ra'cha'mim U'Mit'pa'yes Be'Ta'cha'nu'nim,
Hit'ra'tze Ve'Hit'pa'yes Le'Dor A'ni Ki Ein O'zer.

A'vi'nu Mal'kei'nu, Cha'nei'nu Va'A'nei'nu, Ki Ein Ba'nu Ma'a'sim,
A'seh I'ma'nu Tze'da'ka Va'Che'sed Ve'Ho'shi'ei'nu.

Guardian of Israel, guard the remnant of the people of Israel.
Let not disaster overcome Thy people of Israel who daily proclaim: "Hear, O Israel!"

Guardian of the chosen people, guard the remnants of these people,
Let not disaster overcome these unique people who proclaim daily:
"The Lord is our God, the Lord is One!"

Guardian of Thy holy people — guard the remnants of this nation,
Let not disaster overcome these holy people who proclaim daily in their prayers
three-fold sanctifications to the Holy One.

You who are propitiated by pleas for mercy and conciliated by supplications,
be propitiated and conciliated to an afflicted generation, for there is no one else to help.

Our Father, our King, be gracious to us and answer us.
Even though we are without good deeds —
for the sake of Your great Name, be merciful with us and save us.

8. *Ez'ke'ra E'lo'him*

Ez'ke'ra E'lo'him Ve'E'he'ma'ya, Bir'o'ti Kol Ir Al Ti'la Be'nu'ya,
Ve'Ir Ha'E'lo'him Mush'pe'let Ad She'ol Tach'ti'ya!
U'Ve'chol Zot A'nu Le'Ya Ve'Ei'nei'nu Le'Ya.

Mi'dat Ha'Ra'cha'mim A'lei'nu Hit'gal'ge'li, Ve'Lif'nei Ko'neich Te'chi'na'tei'nu Ha'Pi'li.
U'Ve'Ad A'meich Ra'cha'mim Sha'a'li.
Ki Chol Lei'vav Da'vai Ve'Chol Rosh La'cho'li.

Ye'hi Ra'tzon Mil'fa'ne'cha Sho'mei'a Kol Bich'yot, She'Ta'sim Dim'o'tei'nu Be'Nod'cha Li'he'yot,
Ve'Ta'tzi'lei'nu Mi'Kol Ge'zei'rot Ka'shot Ve'Ach'za'ri'yot.
Ki Le'cha Le'vad Ei'nei'nu Te'lu'yot.

I remember, O God, and I moan when I witness every city built on its own site,
while Jerusalem, the city of God, is razed and cast down to the depth of the abyss.
Yet despite all this, our faith in God does not falter.

O Attribute of Mercy, be moved compassionately toward us.
Present supplication before our Maker, and plead for mercy on behalf of our people.
For our hearts are faint and our heads are weary.

May it be Your will, You who hearest our weeping, to store our tears in Thy heavenly urn.
Save us, O God, from cruel and harsh decrees. For towards Thee alone we cast our eyes.

9. *She'va Pe'a'mim "A'ta"*

A'ta Ni'glei'ta Be'A'nan Ke'vod'cha; Al Am Kod'she'cha Le'Da'ber I'mam.
Min Ha'Sha'ma'yim Hish'ma'a'tam Ko'le'cha Ve'Nig'lei'ta A'lei'hem Be'Ar'fa'lei To'har.
Gam Kol Ha'O'lam Ku'lo Chal Mi'Pa'ne'cha. U'Vri'yot Be'Rei'shit Char'du Mi'me'ka.

A'ta Ri'tzatz'ta Ra'shei Liv'ya'tan, Tit'ne'nu Ma'a'chal Le'Am Le'Tzi'yim.
Ve'Yo'du Sha'ma'yim Pil'a'cha A'do'nai. Af E'mu'nat'cha Bi'Ke'hal Ke'do'shim.

A'sher Be'Ya'do Ne'fesh Kol Chai, Ve'Ru'ach Kol Be'sar Ish.
Ha'Ne'sha'ma Lach Ve'Ha'guf Pa'a'lach. Chu'sa Al A'ma'lach.
Ha'Ne'sha'ma Lach Ve'Ha'guf She'lach.
A'ta'nu Al Shim'cha A'do'nai A'sei Le'Ma'an She'me'cha.
A'ta Ya'tzar'ta O'lam'cha Mi'Ke'dem, Ki'li'ta Me'lach'te'cha Ba'Yom Ha'She'vi'i,
Ve'Shim'cha Ha'Ga'dol Ve'Ha'Ka'dosh A'lei'nu Ka'ra'ta.

A'ta Ka'dosh, Ve'Shim'cha Ka'dosh, U'Ke'do'shim Be'Chol Yom Ye'ha'le'lu'cha Se'la,
Ki El Me'lech Ga'dol Ve'Ka'dosh A'ta: Ba'ruch A'ta A'do'nai, Ha'El Ha'Ka'dosh.

A'ta Zo'cheir Ma'a'sei O'lam U'Fo'ked Kol Ye'tzu'rei Ke'dem.
Le'Fa'ne'cha Nig'lu Kol Ta'a'lu'mot Va'Ha'mon Nis'ta'rot She'Mi'Be'rei'shit.
Va'A'kei'dat Yitz'chak Le'Zar'o Ha'Yom Be'Ra'cha'mim Tiz'kor:
Ba'ruch A'ta A'do'nai, Zo'cher Ha'Brit.

A'ta E'chad Ve'Shim'cha E'chad, U'mi Ke'Am'cha Yis'ra'el Goy E'chad Ba'A'retz;
Ve'Ya'nu'chu Vam Kol Yis'ra'el Me'Ka'de'shei She'me'cha:
Ba'ruch A'ta A'do'nai, Me'ka'desh Ha'Sha'bbat.

A'ta Har'ei'ta La'Da'at, Ki A'do'nai Hu Ha'E'lo'him, Ein Od Mil'va'do.

God, *You* revealed Yourself in a cloud of glory to *Your* holy people, and spoke to them.
From the heavens. *You* enabled them to hear *Your* voice, and *You* revealed yourself to them
in the purest clouds of heaven. The world trembled before *You* and all beings of creation
were in awe.

You crushed the heads of the leviathan, leaving it as prey for scavengers of the desert.
The heavens shall praise *Your* wonders, O Lord;
the assembly of the holy shall extol *Your* faithfulness.

Our souls are *Yours* and our bodies are *Your* creation.
Lord, have compassion upon *your* creation.
The soul is *Yours* and the body is *Yours*,
We sanctify Thy Name and we stand before *You* honoring *Your* Name.
You formed this great world from the very beginning; *You* completed *Your* awesome work by the Seventh Day, and proclaimed *Your* holy Name upon us.

You are holy and *Your* Name is holy, and holy beings praise *You* daily for all eternity, for *You*, O God, are the great and Holy King. Blessed are *You* Lord, our Holy God.

You remember the deeds of the world and recall all that was created in the ancient days. Before *You* are revealed hidden things and myriad secrets from the very beginning of creation.
With Mercy, O God, recall the binding of Isaac for the sake of his descendants:
Blessed are *You*, O Lord, He who remembers the covenant with his people.

You are One and *Your* Name is One; who other than Israel, *Your* nation, is *Your* flock on this earth.
May Israel, the sanctifiers of *Your* Name, enjoy resting on the Sabbath. Blessed are *You*, O Lord, who sanctifies the Holy Sabbath.

You have proven to all mankind that the Lord is God; there is none else beside Him.

10. *Ha'loch Ve'Ka'ra'ta*

Ve'Al Ye'dei A'va'de'cha Ha'Ne'vi'im Ka'tuv Lei'mor:
Ha'loch Ve'Ka'ra'ta Be'Oz'nei Ye'ru'sha'la'yim Lei'mor:
Ko A'mar A'do'nai: Za'char'ti Lach Che'sed Ne'u'ra'yich, A'ha'vat Ke'Lu'lo'ta'yich,
Lech'teich A'cha'rai Ba'Mid'bar, Be'E'retz Lo Ze'ru'ah.
Ve'Ne'e'mar: Ve'Za'char'ti A'ni Et Be'ri'ti O'tach Bi'mei Ne'u'ra'yich,
Va'Ha'ki'mo'ti Lach B'rit O'lam.
Ve'Ne'e'mar: Ha'Ven Ya'kir Li Ef'ra'yim, Im Ye'led Sha'a'shu'im,
Ki Mi'dei Da'bri Bo Za'chor Ez'ke're'nu Od. Al Kein Ha'mu Me'ai Lo,
Ra'chem A'ra'cha'me'nu, Ne'um A'do'nai.

And by the hands of Thy servants, the prophets, it is written:
Go and proclaim so that Jerusalem may hear:
Thus said the Lord: "I remember the devotion of your youth, the love of your bridal state, how you followed Me in the wilderness, in a land that was not sown."
And it is stated: "I will not forget My covenant with you in the days of your youth, and I will establish unto you an everlasting covenant."
And it is stated: "Is not Ephraim My beloved son, my precious, caressed child?

For whenever I speak against him, I still remember him with affection. Therefore My heart yearns for him; I will always have mercy and compassion for him," so says the Lord.

11. *A'hav'ti*

A'hav'ti, Ki Yish'ma A'do'nai Et Ko'li, Ta'cha'nu'nai
Ki Hi'ta Oz'no Li, U'Ve'Ya'mai Ek'ra.
A'fa'fu'ni Chev'lei Ma'vet, U'Me'tza'rei She'ol Me'tza'u'ni, Tza'ra Ve'Ya'gon Em'tza.
U'Ve'Sheim A'do'nai Ek'ra: A'na A'do'nai Mal'ta Naf'shi.
Cha'nun A'do'nai Ve'Tza'dik, Ve'E'lo'he'nu Me'Ra'chem.
Sho'mer Pe'ta'yim A'do'nai, Da'lo'ti Ve'Li Ye'ho'shi'a.
Shu'vi Naf'shi LiM'nu'chai'chi, Ki A'do'nai Ga'mal A'lai'chi.
Ki Chi'latz'ta Naf'shi Mi'Ma'vet, Et Ei'ni Min Dim'ah, Et Rag'li Mi'De'chi.
Et'ha'leich Lif'nei A'do'nai, Be'Ar'tzot Ha'Cha'yim.
He'E'man'ti Ki A'da'ber: A'ni A'ni'ti Me'od.
A'ni A'mar'ti Be'Chof'zi, Kol Ha'A'dam Ko'zev.

I love that the Lord hears my voice, my supplications.
He has always inclined His ear to hear me; therefore I will call upon Him as long as I live.
Pains of death encircled me; the agony of the grave seized me;
I was in distress and sorrow.
But I called upon the Name of the Lord: "Please, O Lord, save my life!"
Gracious is the Lord and righteous; our God is merciful.
The Lord protects the simple beings; when I was brought down low, He saved me.
Be again at rest, my soul, for the Lord has dealt kindly with me.
Thou hast delivered my soul from death, my eyes from tears and my feet from stumbling.
I shall walk before the Lord in the world of the living.
I have kept my faith in the Lord even as I cried out: "I am greatly afflicted."
I have faith even when I declare in haste: "All mankind are deceitful."

12. *Be'Tzeit Yis'ra'el*

Be'Tzeit Yis'ra'el Mi'Mi'tzra'yim, Beit Ya'akov Mei'Am Lo'ez.
Hai'ta Ye'hu'da Le'Kod'sho, Yis'ra'el Mam'she'lo'tav.
Ha'Yam Ra'ah Va'Ya'nos, Ha'Yar'den Yi'sov Le'A'chor.
He'Ha'rim Rak'du Che'Ei'lim, Ge'va'ot Kiv'nei Tzon.
Ma Le'cha Ha'Yam Ki Ta'nus, Ha'Yar'den Ti'sov Le'A'chor.
He'Ha'rim Tir'ke'du Che'Ei'lim, Ge'va'ot Kiv'nei Tzon.
Mi'lif'nei A'don Chu'li A'retz, Mi'lif'nei E'lo'ha Ya'a'kov.
Ha'Hof'chi Ha'Tzur A'gam Ma'yim, Cha'la'mish Le'Mai'no Ma'yim.

When Israel exiled from Egypt— the house of Jacob left the people of alien tongue,
Judah became God's sanctuary and Israel His dominions.

The sea beheld and fled; the Jordan's stream turned back.
The mountains skipped like rams and the hills like lambs.
What ails you, O sea, that thus you flee? O Jordan, that you turn backward?
O mountains, why do you skip like rams? O hills, like lambs?
Tremble, O earth, before the Lord's presence, the presence of the God of Jacob,
He who turns a rock into a pond of water and the flint into a flowing fountain.

13. *Ma'oz Tzur*

Ma'oz Tzur Ye'shu'a'ti, Le'cha Na'eh Le'Sha'bei'ach.
Ti'kon Beit Te'fi'la'ti, Ve'Sham To'da Ne'za'bei'ach.
Le'eit Ta'chin Mat'bei'ach, Mi'Tzar Ham'na'bei'ach.
Az Eg'mor Be'Shir Miz'mor, Cha'nu'kat Ha'Miz'bei'ach.

Ye'va'nim Nik'be'tzu A'lie, Azai Bi'mei Chash'ma'nim,
U'Far'tzu Cho'mot Mig'da'lie, Ve'Tim'uh Kol Ha'Shma'nim.
U'Mi'No'tar Kan'ka'nim, Na'a'sa Nes La'Sho'sha'nim.
B'nei Bi'na, Ye'mei Shmo'na, Kav'uh Shir U'Re'na'nim.

O mighty rock of my salvation, to praise Thee is a delight!
Restore our Holy House of prayer and there we will present thanksgiving-offerings.
When You prepare havoc for the foe that maligns us,
I shall then conclude, with song and psalm, the dedication of the Alter.

Greeks gathered to attack me in the days of the Hasmoneans.
They broke down the walls of my towers, and polluted all our sacred oils.
From the last of the remaining flasks, a miracle was performed for Israel.
Men of wisdom then decreed eight days for song and joyful psalms.

Compact Disk 2

1. *A'na Be'Cho'ach*

A'na, Be'Cho'ach Ge'du'lat Ye'min'cha Ta'tir Tze'ru'ra.
Ka'bel Ri'nat Am'cha, Sag'vei'nu, Ta'ha'rei'nu, No'ra.
Na, Gi'bor, Dor'shei Yi'chud'cha Ke'Va'vat Sham'rem.
Bar'chem, Ta'ha'rem, Ra'cha'mem Tzid'kat'cha, Ta'mid Gam'lem.
Cha'sin Ka'dosh, Be'rov Tuv'cha Na'hel A'da'te'cha.
Ya'chid Gei'eh, Le'Am'cha P'neh, Zoch'rei Ke'du'sha'te'cha.
Shav'a'tei'nu Ka'bel, U'She'ma Tza'a'ka'tei'nu, Yo'de'a Ta'a'lu'mot.

We implore You, by the great power of Your right hand, to set free the bound one.
Accept the prayers of Your people, strengthen us, purify us, O awesome One.
Almighty heroic God, those who foster Your Oneness, guard them like the pupil of an eye.
Bless them, purify them, have pity on them,
and may Your righteousness always lead your people to the truth.
Powerful Holy One, with Your abundant goodness — guide Your congregation.
Unique and exalted God — turn to Your nation, those who are mindful of Your holiness.
Accept our prayers and hear our cry, Thou who Knowest all mysteries.

2. *U've'nu'cho Yo'mar*

U'Ve'Nu'cho Yo'mar: Shu'va A'do'nai Ri've'vot Al'fei Yis'ra'el.
Ku'ma A'do'nai Lim'nu'cha'te'cha, A'ta Va'A'ron U'ze'cha.
Ko'ha'ne'cha Yil'be'shu Tze'dek, Va'Cha'si'de'cha Ye'ra'nei'nu.
Ba'a'vur Da'vid Av'de'cha, Al Ta'shev P'nei Me'shi'che'cha.
Ki Le'kach Tov Na'ta'ti La'chem, To'ra'ti Al Ta'a'zo'vu.
Eitz Cha'yim Hi La'Ma'cha'zi'kim Bah, Ve'Tom'che'ha Me'u'shar.
D'ra'che'ha Dar'chei No'am, Ve'Chol Ne'ti'vo'te'ha Sha'lom.
Ha'shi'vei'nu A'do'nai Ei'le'cha Ve'Na'shu'va; Cha'deish Ya'mei'nu Ke'Ke'dem.

And when the Ark rested Moses would say,
"Return, O Lord, to the myriads and thousands of Israel's families."
Arise, O Lord, unto Your resting place, You and Thy glorious Ark.
Let Your priests clothe themselves in righteousness,
and let Your devout followers sing with joy.
For the sake of David, Your servant, reject not Thy anointed.
"For I have given you good instruction, therefore do not forsake My Torah."
It is a tree of life for those who grasp it, and those who support it are fortunate.
Its ways are ways of pleasantness and all its paths are peace.
Cause us to return to You, O Lord, and we shall return; renew our days as of old.

3. *Le'chu Ne'ra'ne'na*

Le'chu Ne'ra'ne'na La'A'do'nai, Na'ri'a Le'Tzur Yish'ei'nu.
Ne'kad'ma Fa'nav Be'To'da, Bi'Z'mi'rot Na'ri'a Lo.
Tze'dek U'Mish'pat Me'chon Kis'e'cha, Che'sed Ve'E'met Ye'kad'mu Fa'ne'cha.
A'sher Yach'dav Nam'tik Sod, Be'Veit E'lo'him Ne'ha'lech Be'Ra'gesh.
A'sher Lo Ha'Yam Ve'Hu A'sa'hu, Ve'Ya'be'shet Ya'dav Ya'tza'ru.
A'sher Be'Ya'do Ne'fesh Kol Chai, Ve'Ru'ach Kol Be'sar Ish.
Ha'Ne'sha'ma Lach Ve'Ha'Guf Pa'a'lach, Chu'sa Al A'ma'lach.
Ha'Ne'sha'ma Lach Ve'Ha'Guf She'lach, A'do'nai, A'sei Le'ma'an She'me'cha.
A'ta'nu Al Shim'cha, A'do'nai, A'sei Le'ma'an She'me'cha.

Ba'a'vur Ke'vod Shim'cha, Ki El Cha'nun Ve'Ra'chum She'me'cha.
Le'ma'an Shim'cha A'do'nai, Ve'Sa'lach'ta La'A'vo'nei'nu Ki Rav Hu.

Come, let us sing to the Lord, and let us call out to the Rock of our salvation.
Let us greet Him with thanksgiving; with praiseful songs let us call out to Him.
Righteousness and justice are Your Throne's foundation;
kindness and truth precede Your countenance.
Together let us share a sweet secret, and in the House of God let us stride with emotion.
For His is the sea — for He made it, and His hands created land.
The soul of all life is in His hand, as well as the spirit of all human flesh.
The soul is Yours and the body is Your creation; have mercy upon Your labor.
The soul is Yours and the body is Yours; O Lord, have compassion upon your toil.
We come before You with reliance on Your Name, O Lord;
therefore, act to preserve Your Name's sake.
In honor of Your Name, our "Gracious and Merciful God,"
forgive our sins, even though they are abundant.

4. *Eich Nif'tach Peh?*

Eich Nif'tach Peh Le'fa'ne'cha, Dar Me'tu'chim?
Be'Ei'lu Fa'nim Nish'poch Si'chim.
Ha'lach'nu A'ch'rei Mas'ot Shav U'Ma'du'chim,
Ve'Hik'shi'nu O'ref Ve'Hei'Az'nu Me'tza'chim.

Ka'ma Yi'sar'ta'nu Al Ye'dei Tzi'rim U'Shlu'chim,
Lo Hik'shav'nu Le'Mo'rim Ve'lish'mo'ah La'Mo'chi'chim.

Me'Az Ve'Ad A'ta A'nu Ni'da'chim,
Ne'he'ra'gim, Nish'cha'tim Ve'Nit'ba'chim,
So'rad'nu Me'tei Me'at Bein Ko'tzim K'su'chim,
Ei'nei'nu Cha'lot Lim'tzo Re'va'chim.

Por'chei Am'cha A'sher Le'veil So'cha'chim,
Tze'fer Va'E'rev La'ma Matz'li'chim?
Ka'mim Le'mu'lach Ne'a'tzot So'cha'chim,
Re'tzu'tzim, Ba'meh A'tem Bot'chim.

Sho'chen Ad Ve'Ka'dosh, Tze'feh Be'El'bon A'nu'chim,
Tmu'chim A'le'cha U'Ve'cha Mit'a'chim,
Be'Nora'ot Ye'min'cha Ni'va'sha Lin'tza'chim,
Ki Al Ra'cha'me'cha Ha'Ra'bim A'nu Ve'tu'chim.

How can we dare open our mouths before You, God, the one who dwells in heaven?
In what manner can we pour forth our prayers?
For we have rejected Your just and righteous paths,
clinging to abominations and despicable deeds.
We, who have believed in vain delusions, we have been obstinate and insolent.

Our deeds have provoked Your burning wrath; our sacred shrine has become desolate.
Your prophets often admonished us! Yet we refused to heed to their warnings.
As a result, through the ages we have endured exile, suffered homelessness,
tyranny, slaying and slaughter.

We, Your people, have survived barely a few, scattered among piercing thorns.
Our eyes are dim and there is no relief in sight.

Those who oppress Your people, those who bow to idols -
why do they prosper both in morning and evening?
They rise up against You, defiantly asking us their blasphemous question:
"You broken backs! In whom do you trust?"

Holy and eternal God! Behold the shame of those who sigh,
those who depend on You.
May Your awesome might save us for eternity,
for upon Your abundant mercy we trust.

5. Be'Mo'za'ei Me'nu'cha

Be'Mo'tza'ei Me'nu'cha Ki'dam'nu'cha Te'chi'la,
Hat Oz'ne'cha Mi'Ma'rom, Yo'sheiv Te'hi'la,

Lish'mo'a El Ha'Ri'na Ve'El Ha'Te'fi'la.

As the day of rest departs, we approach You with earnest plea,
O You, dweller of the heavens above, bend down and listen to our hymn of praise.

Hear our songs and our prayers.

6. Zo'cha'lim Ve'Ro'a'dim

Zo'cha'lim Ve'Ro'a'dim Mi'Yom Bo'e'cha,
Cha'lim Ke'Mav'ki'ra Mei'Ev'rat Ma'sa'e'cha,
Ti'nu'fam Me'cheh Na Ve'Yo'du Pe'la'e'cha,

Lish'mo'a El Ha'Ri'na Ve'El Ha'Te'fi'la.

Shuddering and trembling before You on the day of Your arrival,
shaking before Your burden of wrath, like a woman bringing forth her firstborn,
O God, wipe away the filth of their sins, and they will praise Your great wonders.

Hear our songs and our prayers.

7. *Yo'tzer A'ta*

Yo'tzer A'ta Le'Chol Ye'tzir No'tzar,
Ko'nan'ta Me'Az Te'ref Le'chal'tzam Mi'Mei'tzar,
Le'cha'ne'nam Chi'nam Mei'O'tzar Ha'me'nu'tzar,

Lish'mo'a El Ha'Rina Ve'El Ha'Te'fi'la.

You created every living being.
You constantly rescued us from distress,
and pardoned us even though we were not worthy.

Hear our songs and our prayers.

8. *Ma'rom*

Ma'rom, Im Atz'mu Pish'ei Ke'ha'le'cha,
Na Sag'vem Mei'O'tzar Ha'Mu'chan Bi'zvu'le'cha,
A'de'cha La'chon Chi'nam, Ba'im Ei'le'cha,

Lish'mo'a El Ha'Ri'na Ve'El Ha'Te'fi'la.

O Most High! Even if Your people's wanton sins have grown so great,
please, kindly strengthen them with Your heaven's treasures.
To You they come to seek this undeserved gift,

Hear our songs and our prayers.

9. *P'ne Na*

P'ne Na El Ha'Tla'ot Ve'Al La'Cha'ta'ot.
Tza'dek Tzo'a'ke'cha Maf'li F'la'ot.
Ke'shov Na Chi'nu'nam, E'lo'him A'do'nai Tze'va'ot.

Lish'mo'a El Ha'Ri'na Ve'El Ha'Te'fi'la.

O God, consider the suffering, and not the sins.
Consider those who cry to You as righteous — O creator of wonders!
Please listen to their supplications, God, Lord and Master of Legions.

Hear our songs and our prayers.

10. *Re'tzei A'ti'ra'tam*

Re'tzei A'ti'ra'tam Be'Am'dam Ba'Lei'lot.
She'ei Na Ve'Ra'tzon Ke'Kor'ban Ka'lil Ve'O'lot.
Tar'eim Ni'se'cha O'seh Ge'do'lot,

Lish'mo'a El Ha'Ri'na Ve'El Ha'Te'fi'la.
El Me'lech Yo'shev Al Ki'sei Ra'cha'mim.

Accept their pleas and sacrifices as they stand before You throughout the night.
Grant them favor as they offer their sacrifices.
Display before them Your miracles — He who performs great deeds.

Hear our songs and our prayers.
Almighty King, who sits on the throne of mercy.

11. *Te'vi'ei'nu*

Te'vi'ei'nu El Har Kod'she'cha, Ve'Sam'chei'nu Be'Veit Te'fi'la'te'cha, Ke'mo She'Ka'tuv:
Va'Ha'vi'o'tim El Har Kod'shi, Ve'Si'mach'tim Be'Veit Te'fi'la'ti,
O'lo'tei'hem Ve'Ziv'chei'hem Le'Ra'tzon Al Miz'be'chi,
Ki Vei'ti Beit Te'fi'la Yi'ka'rei Le'Chol Ha'A'mim.

Bring us to Your Holy Mountain and exalt us in Your House of Prayer, as it is written:
"And I will bring them to My Holy Mountain, and I will exalt them in My House of Prayer;
their burnt-offerings and their slaughtered sacrifices will be welcome on My altar,
for My house will be called a House of Prayer for all the nations."

12. *She'ma Ko'lei'nu*

She'ma Ko'lei'nu, A'do'nai E'lo'hei'nu, Chus Ve'Ra'chem A'lei'nu,
Ve'Ka'bel Be'Ra'cha'mim U'Ve'Ra'tzon Et Te'fi'la'tei'nu.

Hear our voice, Lord our God, pity us and be merciful with us;
Accept our prayer with compassion and kindness.

13. *Mach'ni'sei Ra'cha'mim*

Mach'ni'sei Ra'cha'mim, Hach'ni'su Ra'cha'mei'nu Lif'nei Ba'al Ha'Ra'cha'mim.
Mash'mi'ei Te'fi'la, Hash'mi'u Te'fi'la'tei'nu Lif'nei Sho'mei'a Te'fi'la.
Mash'mi'ei Tze'a'ka, Hash'mi'u Tza'a'ka'tei'nu Lif'nei Sho'me'a Tze'a'ka.
Mach'ni'sei Dim'ah, Hach'ni'su Dim'o'tei'nu Lif'nei Me'lech Mit'ra'tze Vi'De'ma'ot.

Hish'tad'lu Ve'Har'bu Te'chi'na U'Va'ka'sha Lif'nei Me'lech El Ram Ve'Ni'sa.
Haz'ki'ru Le'Fa'nav, Hash'mi'u Le'Fa'nav, To'ra U'Ma'a'sim To'vim Shel Shoch'nei A'far.

Yiz'kor A'ha'va'tam Vi'cha'ye Zar'am, She'lo To'vad She'ei'rit Ya'a'kov.
Ki Tzon Ro'eh Ne'e'man Ha'ya Le'Cher'pa, Yis'ra'el Goy E'chad Le'Ma'shal Ve'Li'She'ni'na.

Ma'heir A'nei'nu E'lo'hei Yish'ei'nu, U'Fe'dei'nu Mi'kol Ge'zei'rot Ka'shot
Ve'Ho'shi'a Be'Ra'cha'me'cha Ha'Ra'bim, Me'shi'ach Tzid'ke'cha Ve'A'me'cha.

O angels of mercy; please usher in our pleas for mercy before the Master of Mercy.
O angels of prayer, please cause our prayers to be heard by He who listens to prayer.
O angels of outcry, please bring our passionate outcry to He who hears our cries.
O angels of tears, usher in our tears before the King who finds favor through tears.

Exert yourselves and multiply supplication and petition, before the King, the Almighty God. Remind Him, impress upon Him, of His Torah and of our good deeds — we who dwell in dust.

May He remember our love of Him and grant life to our offspring, so that the remnants of Jacob may not be lost. For the flock of Moses, Your the faithful shepherd, has become a disgrace; Israel, the chosen nation — has become a parable to be ridiculed.

Quickly answer us, the God of our salvation, and redeem us from any harsh decrees; and with Your abundant mercy may You save Your righteous anointed priests and Your nation.

14. *Kol Me'ka'desh*

Kol Me'ka'desh She'vi'i Ka'Ra'ui Lo, Kol Sho'mer Sha'bbat Ka'Dat Mei'Cha'le'lo,
Se'cha'ro Har'bei Me'od Al Pi Fo'a'lo, Ish Al Mach'nei'hu Ve'Ish Al Dig'lo.

O'ha'vei A'do'nai Ha'Me'cha'kim Le'Vin'yan A'ri'el, Be'Yom Ha'Sha'bbat Si'su Ve'Sim'chu,
Ki'Me'Kab'lei Ma'tan Nach'li'el, Gam Se'u Ye'dei'chem Ko'desh Ve'Im'ru La'El,
Ba'ruch A'do'nai A'sher Na'tan Me'nu'cha Le'A'mo Yis'ra'el.
A'zor La'Shov'tim Ba'She'vi'i Be'Cha'rish U'Va'Ka'tzir Le'O'la'mim,
Pos'im Bo Pe'si'a Ke'ta'na, So'a'dim Bo Le'Va'rech Sha'losh Pe'A'mim,

Tzid'ka'tam Taz'hir Ke'Or Shiv'at Ha'Ya'mim, A'do'nai E'lo'hei Yis'ra'el A'ha'vat Ha'A'mim,
A'do'nai E'lo'hei Yis'ra'el Te'shu'at O'la'mim.

Whoever sanctifies the Sabbath properly, and whoever safeguards the Sabbath from
desecration, his reward is exceedingly great in accordance with his deed. Every man is within
his own camp, every man under his own banner.

Lovers of the Lord, who long for the rebuilding of His Holy Temple — rejoice and be happy
on the Sabbath day. While receiving the gift of God's heritage, raise your hands and declare
before Him – "Blessed is the Lord Who granted the Sabbath rest for His people, Israel."

Forever support those who refrain from plowing and harvesting on the Sab
May their righteousness shine forth like the light of the Seven Days. The Lord, God of Israel
– our people's love! The Lord, God of Israel – our eternal savior!

15. *D'ror Yik'ra*

D'ror Yik'ra Le'Ven Im Bat,
Ve'Yin'tzor'chem Ke'mo Va'Vat,
Ne'im Shim'chem Ve'Lo Yush'bat,
She'vu Ve'Nu'chu Be'Yom Sha'bat.

De'rosh Na'vi Ve'U'la'mi,
Ve'Ot Ye'sha A'se I'mi,
Ne'ta So'rek Be'Toch Kar'mi,
She'ei Shav'at B'nei A'mi.

He will proclaim freedom for all men and women,
and protect them like the apple of His eye.
Honored will be your names, never to cease.
So rest and be content on the holy Sabbath day.

Seek my sanctuary and my home,
and show me a sign of salvation.
Plant a vine within my vineyard,
and listen to the laments of my people.

16. *D'voi're'le*

Ba-Bam… Ba-Bam…
Aye, Aye, Aye, Aye… D'voi're'le.
Ba-Bam… Ba-Bam…
Oy, D'voi're'le — Aye… Aye…

Sheyn Vie Zi'ben Vel'ten Iz Mein D'voi're'le!
Ba Mein Rebben's Me'la'veh Mal'ke, Shpeyt Ba'nacht,
Tief Far'tracht, Iz Ge'ze'sen Sheyn Vie Zi'ben Vel'ten, D'voi're'le, D'voi're'le,
Un fun Ye'ner Me'la'veh Mal'ke,
Got Mein Got, Nacht Noch Nacht, Hat Ba'loich'ten
Mein Ne'sho'me — D'voi're'le, D'voi're'le.
Oy'gen Vie Die Him'len Bloi Un Lo'ken Hel
Vie Mor'gen'Toi, Oy'gen Vos Der'ma'nen Oft
'Chob Ge'baynkt, Ge'vart, Ge'hoft, Oy — Bam Bam Bam Bam Bam Bam...
'Chob Dem Rebben Nisht Ge'folgt,
Hot Mich Got Ge'shtroft!
'Chob Dem Rebben Nisht Ge'folgt, Oy — Nisht Ge'folgt,
Hot Mich Got Ge'shtroft!
Bam...Bam...Aye....
Sheyn Vie Zi'ben Vel'ten Iz Mein D'voi're'le!

Ba-Bam... Ba-Bam...
Aye-Aye-Aye-Aye, D'voi're'le! Ba-Bam... Ba-Bam,
Beautiful like the seventh heaven!
At my rabbi's *Me'la've Mal'ka* celebration, late at night —
I dream of D'voi're'le — immersed in thought she sat there, my D'voi're'le.
Since that *Me'la'veh Mal'ka* —
oh my God, my dreams continue night after night.
Every night my heart is conquered by D'voi're'le.
God! Oh my God! Thinking of her brightens my soul. D'voi're'le! D'voi're'le!
Her eyes are blue like the sky! The locks of her hair are like morning dew.
Her beautiful eyes sing to me.
I yearn for her, I wait for her, and I pray.
Oy — Bam-Bam... Bam-Bam...
Oh my woes: I did not listen to my Rabbi, oy — my Rabbi's voice,
so God punished me.
Oh my woes: I did not listen to my Rabbi, oy — my Rabbi's voice,
so God punished me.
My D'voi're'le! Oh so beautiful — the light of the seventh heaven shines from my
D'voi're'le's face!

17. *A'cha'rei Moti*

A'cha'rei Moti Sif'du Ka'cha Li:
Ha'ya Ish – U'Re'u: Ei'ne'nu Od.
Ko'dem Zma'no Meit Ha'Ish Ha'Ze,
Ve'Shi'rat Cha'yav Be'Em'tza Nif'se'ka.
Ve'Tzar Me'od! Od Miz'mor E'chad Ha'yah Lo,

Ve'Hi'nei A'vad Ha'Miz'mor La'ad,
A'vad La'ad!

After my death, say this eulogy for me:
"There was a man who died before his time,
leaving his poetry, the song of his life, unfinished.
And what a shame! He had one more song to sing, and now it's gone,
That song is lost, lost forever."

Poem by Chaim Nachman Bialik

Glossary of Hebrew and Foreign Terms

A'do'nai Ma'lach — (Hebrew "the Lord has ruled"). The opening words of Psalm 93; also the name of the musical prayer mode (*Nu'sach*) to which it is chanted.

A'ha'va Ra'bbah — (Hebrew "Great Love"). The opening words of a benediction preceding the prayer *She'ma*; also the name of the musical prayer mode (*Nu'sach*) to which it is chanted.

A'kei'da — (Hebrew "the binding"). The sacrifice of Isaac, by his father, Abraham; thereafter the many prayers alluding to it.

A'mi'da — (Hebrew "stand"). The prayer of eighteen [actually nineteen] benedictions, which is recited while standing.

A'mud — (Hebrew "pole") also called *Bi'ma*, pulpit or podium — a pedestal in the center or in the front of the synagogue. The *To'rah* scrolls are placed on the *Bi'ma* when they are read. It is also used as a podium for leading prayer services by the cantor or the master of prayer (*Ba'al Te'fi'la*). Sometimes there is an additional lower lectern called *A'mud*.

A'ron Ha'Kodesh — the Ark in which the *To'rah* scrolls are kept in the synagogue.

Av — The eleventh month of the Jewish year, except in leap years when it becomes the twelfth month. The ninth day of *Av* [*Tish'ah Be' Av*] is the anniversary of the destruction of the Holy Temple.

A'vo'da — (Hebrew "service"). Generally, a divine worship or liturgy; in particular, the recitation of the service of the Temple on the Day of Atonement, *Yom Ki'ppur*, as described in its *Mu'saf* prayer service.

A'vo'da Za'ra — (Hebrew "strange worship"). The term for any form of idolatry or paganism.

A'vot — (Hebrew "fathers"). The first benediction of the *A'mi'da* prayers, recalling the patriarchs and God's recognition of their merits.

Ba'al K'ri'ah — (Hebrew "Master of Reading"). The lector of Scripture; an office often filled by the *Cha'zan* [cantor], or by a learned layman of the congregation.

Ba'al Te'fi'la — (Hebrew "Master of Prayer"). The designation of the elected (not appointed) honorary leader of the prayer service, mostly a non-professional.

Ba'ka'sha — (Hebrew "petition"). A type of penitential prayer, closely related to *Se'li'cha*.

Ba're'chu — also: *Bar'chu*. (Hebrew "praise Ye!"). The opening word of the call to worship, with which important prayer services begin.

Bar Mitz'va/Bat Mitz'va — the age of religious maturity when a boy or girl is responsible for fulfilling the *Mitz'vot* (commandments and privileges). This occurs for boys at age 13 and girls at age 12.

Beit Mid'rash — a Jewish house of study of religious themes.

Bir'kat Ha'Ma'zon — (Hebrew "benediction of food"). The grace blessing after meals.

Cha'nu'ka — (Hebrew "dedication"). The commemoration of the rededication of the Holy Temple in Jerusalem, after the Maccabean victory over the Greeks [end of the third century B.C.E.].

Chasidism — (from Hebrew *Cha'sid*, "pious"). A designation of Jewish sects, which occurred at least three times in history, each time with a different meaning: 1) during the second commonwealth; (2) in the Rhineland during the High Middle Ages; (3) in Eastern Europe, after the seventeenth and during the eighteenth century. This latest movement is still active. Originally it was conceived as a revolt against rabbinic legalism.

Cha'ti'ma — (Hebrew "seal"). The formal end of a prayer or its closing *Bra'cha* (blessing), which seals it.

Cha'zan — (Hebrew from Aramaic). The appointed and paid precentor of the synagogue. Originally an elevated sexton, the *Cha'zan* achieved the office of precentor or cantor during the seventh and eighth centuries, when he appeared as poet, singer, and arranger of *Pi'yu'tim* (liturgical poems, see: *Pi'yut*).

Cha'za'nut — cantorial. A type of vocal improvisation practiced by the *Cha'zan* (cantor). Its frequently highly ornamented style, tonality, and motif structure vary regionally.

Chutz'pah — (Hebrew "audacity, cheek, guts, nerve, boldness, temerity").

Daven/Davened/Davening — an exclusively Yiddish verb meaning "pray"; it is widely used by Ashkenazic Orthodox Jews. It has become Anglicized as "Davening."

Din — (Hebrew "law, verdict"). A law or ordinance without reference to its provenance or date.

Du'chan — (Hebrew "priestly privilege of blessing the congregation"). In particular, the practice of blessing the congregation of worshippers by the *Ko'ha'nim* (priests, descendants of the Aaronide dynasty).

D'vei'kut — (Hebrew "attachment to God.") Devoutness, devotion, coupled with sublime joy.

Ei'cha — (Hebrew "how!"). The first word of the Book of Lamentations, which serves as the Hebrew title for the book. The Lamentations are recited on the Ninth day of the Hebrew month of *Av*, to commemorate the anniversary of the destruction of the Holy Temple.

Fortissimo — (Italian). The part of a musical composition marked to be performed very loudly.

Ga'bai — (plural: *Ga'ba'im*). Officers in charge of the proper operation of the synagogue. They also conduct the *To'rah* reading, standing on either side of the *To'rah* reader.

Ga'lut — (Hebrew "dispersion"). The term for Israel's exile.

Ga'on — (Hebrew "leader"). Title of a person of central Rabbinic authority with strong legal powers; later, an honorary title similar to "Excellency."

Ge'ma'ra — (Hebrew-Aramaic "completion"). The sum total of Talmudic discussions on the text and contents of the six books of *Mish'na* and related matters.

Ge'shem — (Hebrew "rain"). The prayer for rain that is recited in solemn manner on the eighth day of the holiday of *Su'ccot*, when the rainy season usually begins in the Near East.

Ge'vu'rot — (Hebrew "powers, great actions"). The second benediction of the *A'mi'da*, which ascribes all powers to God.

Gust (Gusten) — used by Ashkenazic cantors in connection with the scales used in chant. Synonymous with *Shtey'ger* and prayer mode. It implies the general characteristic style of the chant. From the Latin word *Gustus*.

Haf'ta'ra — a portion from one of the books of the Prophets read each Sabbath to compliment the *To'rah* portion that was read.

Ha'gga'da — (Hebrew "narration, tale"). The generic term for any non-legalistic text of rabbinic literature. In particular it refers to the ritual narration of the Exodus rendered at the family home feast celebration on the eve of Passover [Hebrew *Se'dder*].

Ha'ka'fot — (Hebrew "circuits"). The ritual march of the worshippers carrying the scrolls of the *To'rah* around the synagogue altar on the festival of *Sim'chat To'rah* [the rejoicing of the *To'rah*].

Ha'la'cha — (Hebrew "course, way of going"). The collective term for all post-biblical laws and legal opinions as well as discussions pertaining to them.

Ha'llel — (Hebrew "praise"). The collective name of Psalms 113 through 118, which are chanted on many festive occasions throughout the year.

Has'ka'la — (from Hebrew *Se'chel*, "reason"). The period of Jewish enlightenment beginning with Moses Mendelssohn (1729-1786), and reaching, especially in Eastern Europe, to the end of the nineteenth century. It may be considered the beginning of the "modern age" for European Jewry.

Ha'Tik'va — (Hebrew "hope"). The Zionist movement's anthem with lyrics by Naftali Herz Imber (1856-1909). Since the establishment of the state of Israel, it has become Israel's national anthem.

Hav'da'la — (Hebrew "separation, distinction"). The highly symbolic ceremony at the end of the Sabbath, to distinguish it from the ordinary weekday.

High Holy Days — *Rosh Ha'Sha'na* (the Jewish New Year) and *Yom Ki'ppur* (the Day of Atonement). Frequently, also used to refer to the 10-day period between these two holidays (*A'se'ret Ye'mei Te'shu'va*).

Ho'da'ah — (Hebrew "recognition, thanks"). A general term for all thanksgiving prayers.

Ho'sha'na Ra'bbah — (Hebrew "Great Hoshana"). The name of the sixth day of the *Su'ccot* festival holiday, on which many of the *Ho'sha'not* ("save now") are chanted.

Ho'sha'not — (Hebrew plural of *Ho'sha'na*, "save now"). A collective term for those prayers of the *Su'ccot* festival that close with the refrain *Ho'sha'na*.

Ka'bba'la — See *"Zo'har."*

Ka'bba'lat Sha'bbat — (Hebrew "Welcome of the Sabbath"). The first part of the Friday evening liturgy, consisting of psalms and liturgical poems (*Pi'yu'tim*).

Ka'ddish — (Aramaic "sanctifying"). A very ancient prayer, dating back to early Christian times, perhaps antedating Christianity. It may best be described as the Great Doxology of Judaism, or Consecration. The liturgy contains five types, of which the best known are the mourner's *Ka'ddish*, recited during the year of mourning for one's close relative, and the half-*Ka'ddish*, which serves as an emphatic conclusion to each major section of the liturgy. Interestingly, none of these texts contains any reference to death.

Ka'va'na — (Hebrew "direction, orientation"). A general term for intensity and concentration in prayer.

Ka'vod — (Hebrew "honor, glory"). A term that has both secular and theological significance. In its theological use, the *Ke'vod A'do'nai* may be paraphrased as "glory of the Lord."

Ke'ddu'sha (or *Ke'du'sha*) — (Hebrew "sanctification"). The expanded preamble to the third benediction of the *A'mi'da* Prayers. It is based upon a poetic juxtaposition of Is. 6: 3 and Ez. 20: 25. There are five variants of the text of the *Ke'ddu'sha* in liturgical use.

Ki'ddush — (Hebrew "sanctification"). The ritual blessing of wine.

Ki'nah — (Hebrew "dirge"). The generic name for all laments and dirges for the dead. They play a large part in ritual, literature, and music of the Near East from ancient times.

Kosher — Food that is permissible to be eaten according to biblical and rabbinic standards; most notably, this precludes pork products, shellfish, and any combination of meat and milk products.

La'chan — (Arabic-Hebrew "type of melody"). The medieval designation of a melody type, not quite a mode, more typical than an individual melody. It comes nearest to a melody pattern.

Lu'lav — (Hebrew). The festive bouquet that is ritually used during the *Su'ccot* festival, consisting of palm branches, myrtle, willow, and a special citrus fruit called *Et'rog*.

Ma'a'riv — the evening prayer service.

Mach'zor — (Hebrew "cycle"). The prayer book containing the annual cycle of prayers for festivals, High Holy Days, and fast days. (Not for weekdays and Sabbath prayers, where a prayer book called *Si'ddur*, is used).

Maf'tir — (from Hebrew *Haf'ta'ra*, "dismissal"). The closing section of the *To'rah* lesson; also the name given to the lay reader who is called up for the reading of that section, and who then proceeds to read the Prophetic portion.

Ma'kam (*or.* **Ma'qam**) — (Arabic "place, standing place"). Any established pattern in Arabic poetry and music.

Mal'chu'yot, Zich'ro'not, Sho'fa'rot — (Hebrew "kingdoms, remembrances, *Sho'far* sounds"). The three central prayers of the *Rosh Ha'Sha'na* New Year liturgy, consisting of scriptural centos, referring to the topics alluded to in the titles: God's kingdom; God's promises and faithfulness to them; God as supreme judge on the Day of Judgment.

Mas'kil — (from Hebrew *Has'ka'la*). One who participated in the *Has'ka'la* movement (see above). A Jew educated in the secular disciplines, generally a rationalist and frequently non-observant.

Ma'so'ra — (Hebrew "tradition"). The intensive grammatical, phonetic, and textual arrangement of the Hebrew Bible; it

occupied many generations of Hebrew scholars from the fifth to the tenth centuries. The Masoretic text of the Bible is the generally accepted one.

Ma'tza — unleavened bread eaten on the eight days of the Passover holiday — a commemoration of the Exodus from Egypt. The biblical narrative relates that the Israelites left Egypt in such haste, they could not wait for their bread dough to rise. The resulting product was *Ma'tza* (Exodus 12:39). In commemoration of the Exodus, eating regular bread is forbidden on the Passover (*Pe'ssach*) holiday.

Me'sho'rer — (Hebrew "singer, poet"). The old designation for a vocal soloist, not necessarily of sacred music. Later it became the name of a paid chorister in the synagogue, or a member of a choral ensemble.

Mid'rash — (Hebrew). All post-biblical, rabbinical, and medieval explanations of the Bible, especially those of legendary or sententious exegesis.

Min'cha — (Hebrew "gift"). Originally the name of a sacrifice in the Temple, offered during the afternoon. In the synagogue, the title of the afternoon prayer service.

Min'hag — (Hebrew "custom"). A normative tradition in all its aspects (liturgy, pronunciation, customs, folklore, clothing, mores, etc.).

Mish'na — (Aramaic "second law"). The six sections of the oral tradition of Jewish Law, as compiled under the aegis of

Rabbi Yehuda the Prince (ca. C.E. 200). The *Mish'na* forms the nucleus of all further discussions and expounding of rabbinic literature (see "*Ge'ma'ra*," "*Tal'mud*").

Mi'Si'nai Nu'sach (or *Nu'sach Mi'Si'nai*) — ("Tunes from Mount Sinai"). The collective designation of some of the oldest and most solemn melodies of the Ashkenazic tradition. It consists of a group of fixed prayer melodies that have been associated with certain texts from time immemorial. These fixed melodies are not subject to improvisation, elaboration or any kind of change. They are always sung in their definite crystallized form. They include some of the most beloved and important prayers of the liturgy.

Mitz'va — (Hebrew "commandment, privilege"). From its literal meaning of commandment, to the later significance of an ethically commendable act, the word traveled a long path, characteristic of the development of Jewish ethics.

Mu'saf — the "additional" prayer service in the synagogue that follows the *Shach'rit* service on Sabbath and festival mornings, following the reading of the *To'rah*.

Ne'gi'na — Hebrew: melody. Also: *Ne'ggi'na*.

Ne'i'la — (Hebrew) literally "the locking of the gates." It is the closing prayer service on the holy Day of Atonement — *Yom Ki'ppur*. It is the final opportunity to beseech God for forgiveness.

Ni'ggun — Hebrew and Yiddish: melody; especially the wordless tunes of the Chasidim. Also: *Ni'gun*.

Nu'sach — a concept in Judaism that has two distinct meanings: 1) the style of a prayer service (*Nu'sach Ashkenaz*, *Nu'sach Sepharad*, etc.); 2) the melody of the prayer service according to when the service is being conducted. These are the ancient Jewish prayer modes, passed down from generation to generation.

Nu'sach Ash'ke'naz — is the style of service conducted by Jews originating from areas of Central and Eastern Europe.

Nu'sach Se'pha'rad — is the style of service conducted by Jews originating from Spain and Portugal, as well as the countries to which they moved after the expulsions from Spain and Portugal. In addition, some Central and Eastern European Jews, especially Chasidim, adopted some Sephardic customs emulating the practice of the Kabbalists, most of whom lived in the land of Israel.

Nus'Cha'ot — Plural of *Nu'sach* in Aramaic. In Hebrew the plural is *Nu'sa'chim*.

O'mer — (Hebrew). The "counting" of the 49 days between the holidays of Passover (*Pe'ssach*) and Pentecost (*Sha'vu'ot*).

Pe'ssach — the holiday of Passover, a festival commemorating the Exodus of the Jews from slavery in Pharaoh's Egypt in the days of Moses, as described in the Book of Exodus.

Pianissimo — (Italian). A part of a musical composition marked to be performed very softly.

Pi'yut — (Hebrew "poem"). A liturgical or religious poem, with meter and sometimes rhyme, inserted into the fixed liturgy.

Pu'rim — a holiday commemorating the deliverance of the Jews of Persia from their persecutors as told in the Book of Esther.

Py'tan — a composer of Jewish liturgical poems.

Ra'bbi — (Hebrew: "Rabbi"). A person appointed as a Jewish religious leader.

Re'bbe — (Yiddish). The title of a Chasidic rabbi.

Rosh Ha'Sha'na — (Hebrew "New Year"). The feast of the New Year holiday, which occurs in September or October, at the beginning of the Hebrew month of *Tish'rei* according to the Jewish calendar.

Se'dder — a festive feast held on Passover in Jewish homes during which the story of the Exodus from slavery in Egypt is retold and reenacted, reading and singing from the *Ha'gga'da*.

Se'der Ha'Te'fi'la — (Hebrew "order of the prayer"). The prescribed and traditional framework of the liturgy for any specific day of the Jewish year.

Se'fer — (Hebrew "book"). In the narrower sense, a handwritten scroll of the Pentateuch (*To'rah*).

Se'li'cha — (Hebrew "pardon"). A category of penitential prayers for God's forgiveness and mercy.

Se'li'chot — (Hebrew, plural of *Se'li'cha*). A penitential prayer service conducted at midnight, on the Saturday night before *Rosh Ha'Sha'na* (the Jewish New Year holiday).

Sephardic — Jews from Spain, France, North Africa, Arab, and Eastern countries, with specific religious traditions.

Sha'bbat — (or: *Sha'bat*) — the Jewish day of rest, which begins Friday at sundown and concludes Saturday after sundown after three stars can be clearly visible in the sky. During the Sabbath it is forbidden to perform any work.

Shach'rit — (Hebrew "dawn, morning"). The morning prayer, which is mandatory for the observant Jew.

Sha'lom U'Vra'cha — (Hebrew "peace and blessings"). *Sha'lom* also translates to the greetings "Hello" and "Goodbye."

Sha'losh Re'ga'lim — The Three pilgrimage festivals: *Pe'ssach* (Passover), *Sha'vu'ot* ("Pentecost"), and *Su'ccot* ("Tabernacles"). The Israelites living in ancient Israel and Judea would conduct a pilgrimage to Jerusalem three times a year, during these festivals, as commanded in the *To'rah*. In Jerusalem, they would participate in festivities and ritual worship in conjunction with the services of the *Ko'ha'nim* ("priests") at the Holy Temple. After the destruction of the Temple by the Romans in the first century, the actual pilgrimage is no longer obligatory upon Jews, and no longer takes place on a national scale.

Sha'mash — (Hebrew: literally "servant"). Refers either to the 9th candle which is used to light the other 8 candles on the *Cha'nu'ka* holiday, or to one who serves as the custodian of the synagogue, a "beadle."

Sha'vu'ot — (Hebrew "weeks"). The springtime festival commemorating the revelation of the *To'rah* at Mount Sinai. Its name derives from its date, exactly seven weeks after Passover — Pentecost. It is also the celebration of the first fruit (*Chag Ha'Bi'ku'rim*).

Shchi'na — the Divine Presence.

She'ma — (Hebrew "hear"). The first word of the Jewish profession of faith, *She'ma Yis'ra'el* — "Hear O Israel: The Lord is our God, the Lord is One" (Deut. 6: 5).

Shir — (Hebrew "song, poem"). It can mean both a poem and its chant. The scriptural *Shi'rim* are the Canticles such as the song of Moses at the Red Sea, the Song of Deborah or The Song of Songs (*Shir Ha'Shi'rim*).

Shli'ach Tzi'bur — (Hebrew "one who represents the congregation;" he who leads the worshippers in prayer.

Sho'far — a ram's horn blown especially on *Rosh Ha'Sha'na* (the New Year holiday) and at the concluding *Ne'i'la* prayer service of the Day of Atonement —*Yom Ki'ppur*. Blowing the *Sho'far* is a symbol of national independence and freedom.

Sho'mer Yis'ra'el — (Hebrew "guardian of Israel"). A liturgical poem (*Pi'yut*) that begins with these words.

Shtey'ger (or: **Steyger**) — (Yiddish). A loose and imprecise term in the professional language of cantors, indicating a mode of prayer or its intonation.

Si'ddur — (Hebrew "ordered matter"). The traditional prayer book for weekdays and Sabbaths in contrast to *Mach'zor*, the prayer book for festivals and High Holy Days.

Sim'chat To'rah — A festival celebrating the joy of the Law of Moses and the completion of the year's cycle and subsequent new beginning. It is observed on the 22nd or 23rd day of the Hebrew month of *Tish'rei*, at the end of the *Su'ccot* festival.

Skar'bo'va — a term used interchangeably with *Mi'Si'nai Nu'sach* — the Jewish prayer modes so called originating from Mount Sinai.

Sprechstimme and **Sprechgesang** — (German for "spoken-voice" and "spoken-song"). These are musical terms used to refer to a vocal technique that falls between singing and speaking. Though sometimes used interchangeably, *Sprechgesang* is a term more directly related to the operatic recitative manner of singing (in which pitches are sung, but the articulation is rapid and loose like speech), whereas *Sprechstimme* is closer to speech itself (not having emphasis on particular pitches).

Su'ccot — the autumn festival marking the harvest season and commemorating the wandering of the Israelites in the wilderness of the Sinai desert for 40 years following their Exodus from Egypt.

Ta'a'mei Ha'Mi'kra — (Hebrew "signs of Scripture"). The usual name of the Masoretic accents of Hebrew Scripture (cantillation of the bible). Also termed *Ta'a'mei Ha'Ne'gina.*

Ta'cha'nun — (Hebrew "for mercy"). The general term for all supplicatory prayers.

Tal — (Hebrew "dew"). The prayer for dew that is recited in solemn manner on Passover; thereafter, a short sentence is said in every service until *Su'ccot* (see also: *Ge'shem*).

Tal'mud — (Hebrew "study"). There are two forms: the Babylonian and the Palestinian (or Jerusalemite) texts. It consists of the *Mish'na,* the *Ge'ma'ra* referring to it, and various commentaries and super-commentaries, which are compiled in large folio sets in stereotyped fashion.

Te'fi'la — (Hebrew "prayer," plural: *Te'fi'lot*). The general term for the spoken, written, or chanted liturgical prayer. In a more particular sense, it refers to the *A'mi'da* prayers.

Te'fi'lot Ke'va — (Hebrew "fixed prayers"). The oldest obligatory prayers of Jewish worship. *Ka'ddish, Ke'ddu'sha, A'mi'da, She'ma, Ba're'chu,* and most of the

Shach'rit service belong to them, as opposed to the *Pi'yu'tim.*

To'rah — the law of God as revealed to Moses on Mount Sinai and recorded in the first five books of the Hebrew Scriptures (the Pentateuch).

Trope (**or** ***Trop***) — a system of graphic signs used in scriptural cantillation; each *Trope* expresses a ready-made motif; connecting these motifs creates a mode. The term, implying a musical style, was used by the Biblical and Talmudic commentator Rashi. Tropes are used to chant sacred books; there are trope systems for *To'rah, Haf'ta'ra, Ei'cha* (Lamentations) and the *Me'ggi'lot* (Scrolls).

Yar'mul'ka — Yiddish: a head covering worn out of respect for God; In Hebrew: *Ki'ppah* (skull-cap). Also: *Yar'mul'ke.*

Yahr'zeit — the anniversary of one's death.

Ye'shi'va — (Hebrew-Aramaic "session, academy"). A rabbinic academy, wherein the *Tal'mud* and later rabbinical sources are the main course of study.

Yish'ta'bach — (Hebrew "exalted!"). The opening word of an ancient prayer; thereafter, the name of the prayer mode (*Nu'sach*) in which the prayer is traditionally chanted.

Yom Ki'ppur — (Hebrew "Day of Atonement"). The holiest day of Judaism. A full day of fasting, yet also defined as "the Sabbath of Sabbaths," a day of collective repentance and prayer for Jews in the synagogue.

Yo'tzer — (Hebrew "creator"). A section of the daily morning *Shach'rit* prayer service.

Z'mi'rot — (from Hebrew *Ze'mer*, "song"). The traditional songs, chanted by the family in Jewish homes on Friday evenings, Sabbaths and holidays, before and after meals. Also: *Ze'mi'rot.*

Zo'har — (Hebrew "splendor"). The title of the fundamental book of the *Ka'bba'la.*

In its present form the *Zo'har* originated in Spain during the thirteenth century. The *Ka'bba'la* is the ancient Jewish tradition of mystical interpretation of the bible, first transmitted orally and using esoteric methods (including ciphers). It reached the height of its influence in the later middle ages and remains significant in Chasidism to this day.

Index of Names

General Index

About the Author

Jerry (Ezra) Glantz, the son of Miriam and Leib Glantz, was born in Hollywood, California in 1945. The Glantz family realized its Zionist dream by immigrating to the newly declared independent State of Israel in 1954, and settled in the city of Tel Aviv.

Jerry served as an officer in the IDF (Israel Defense Forces), and studied towards a B.A. in Political Science and Labor Economics, a Masters degree in Business Administration and a Doctorate in Political Science. He is currently a researcher and lecturer on Terrorism and Middle East affairs.

After serving as an executive in the Israeli Bank Hapoaalim, Glantz founded two economic entities: medical high tech (Israel), and agricultural high tech/farming (Bahamas).

Jerry Glantz was honored to represent the United States as an athlete in the 1976 Montreal Summer Olympic Games. He is also an accomplished aircraft pilot.

He is the proud father of Shani (movie actress and singer in L.A.) and Tomer (singer and song-writer in Israel).